SUPERVISION

2nd Edition

SUPER VISION

THE THEORY AND PRACTICE OF FIRST-LINE MANAGEMENT

KRIS COLE

Copyright © Pearson Education Australia 2001

First published 1998
Second edition 2001

Pearson Education Australia
Unit 4, Level 2
14 Aquatic Drive
Frenchs Forest NSW 2086

www.pearsoned.com.au

Senior Acquisitions Editor: Julie Catalano
Senior Project Editor: Nicole Le Grand
Cover and text design: R.T.J. Klinkhamer
Indexer: Russell Brooks
Typeset by Midland Typesetters, Maryborough
Printed in Malaysia

1 2 3 4 5 05 04 03 02 01

National Library of Australia
Cataloguing-in-Publication Data

Cole, Kris.
  Supervision: the theory and practice of first-line management.

  2nd ed.
  Bibliography
  Includes index
  ISBN 1 74009 292 9.

  1. Supervision of employees. I. Title

658.302

A division of Pearson Education Australia

CONTENTS

PART I

Workplace Practice ⋯⋯⋯⋯⋯ *1*

3 Leading by example: personal skills for supervisors   *78*

4 Organisation structures: understanding the changing organisation   *115*

PART II

Managing Operations • • • • • • *237*

PART III

Managing People •••••••••*577*

22 Leading work teams *662*

23 Providing work instructions and delegating duties *701*

24 Managing conflict and grievances and counselling poor performance   *724*

HOW TO USE THIS TEXTBOOK

Chapter Opening Vignettes set the chapter contents in a work context.

Overviews establish learning objectives and a framework for revision and exam preparation.

From Theory to Practice shows you how the theory in the chapter applies in real life.

The Big Picture provides a more strategic overview of the theory, so you can understand it in a wider context.

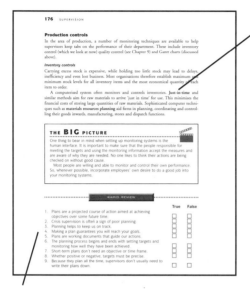

Key terms are highlighted and defined in the Glossary at the end of the text.

Apply your Knowledge exercises allow you to put into practice what you have learned.

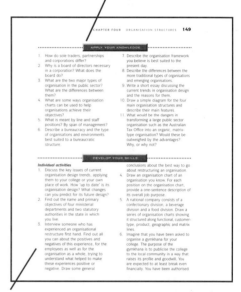

Rapid Review true and false questions help you check your progress. Answers are provided at the end of each chapter.

Boxes contain information that extends, explains or summarises information provided in the chapter.

Develop your Skills individual and group activities allow you to extend your skills and apply them to real life situations.

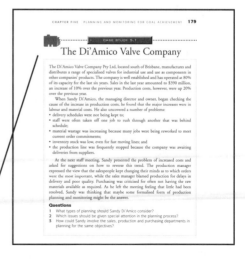

Case Studies encourage you to integrate what you have learned and apply the concepts discussed in the chapter.

ACKNOWLEDGMENTS

Ideas and material for this book came from many sources—from my personal supervisory and management experiences; from the experiences of practising supervisors, managers and specialists; from the stimulating discussions on management development programs in which I have been involved in the private, public and not-for-profit sectors, universities and TAFE colleges, and from the research and publications of numerous scholars.

I would like to thank particularly the hundreds of course participants I have worked with whose ideas and experience are included in this book. I would also like to express my sincere appreciation to David Frith of the South Australian Employers Chamber for his generous assistance with Chapter 7, dealing with health, safety and welfare.

Thanks also to Warren Mills, at the CR Consulting Group in Melbourne, who has contributed many ideas, insights and suggestions and to Bob Donaldson for clarifying my thinking on competency-based training.

Thanks also to Sue Dalziel and Yukinobu Naganawa of Hikarigaoka Girls High School, Okazaki, Japan, and Shitoshi Sugimoto of Nippon Express Company Ltd, of Nagoya, Japan, for their thoughtful research and information on the *Ohshimizu* products of Japan Railways East.

Special thanks go to Annie Macnab, Program Manager: Centre for Management Studies, Central TAFE in Western Australia, for her many comments and suggestions on how to make the book more practical and interesting for readers.

I would also like to thank the outstanding team of editors at Pearson Education Australia who have, once again, been terrific to work with.

Most of all, I would like to thank the readers of this book and commend you for your efforts to improve your skills and understanding of the theory and practice of first-line management.

PREFACE

A lot has changed in the world of management and in the world itself in the last few years. Supervisors are operating in a different environment and have different expectations placed on them by their organisations. The variety of supervisor's job titles points to these changes: first-line managers, team leaders, leading hands, department managers and assistant managers are just a few of these. Whatever we call them, their role is undoubtedly one of the most important in any organisation.

Supervising is a practical, hands-on job. To do it well, a combination of technical skills, people skills and conceptual skills are needed. These form the strong and stable framework for your day-to-day activities. Underlying these skills is a host of personal attributes such as integrity, trustworthiness and self-understanding. These give substance to the framework of skills.

Whether you are a practising or an aspiring supervisor, I hope this book will provide you with both the practical information and the theoretical grounding you need to do your job with excellence. Whatever industry or type of organisation you work in, I hope you will recognise the problems presented in this book and identify with the suggested ways of dealing with them.

The book is organised into three parts: workplace practice, managing operations and managing people. A clear table of contents and index will help you find the specific information you are looking for.

Each chapter begins with a vignette that sets the chapter contents in a work context. End-of-chapter rapid review questions, application questions and skills development questions and activities will guide you to manage, assess and extend your learning and understanding. Case studies at the end of each chapter will help you to put into practice what you have learned and test your competency.

An Instructor's Manual is available to guide discussions on the vignettes, questions and case studies. We have a website www.prenhall.com/cole_au.

If you're one of the many people who would like to see useful web site addresses given in the book—so would I! Unfortunately, these addresses change so quickly that many would be out of date by the time you looked them up. I think the best bet is to use a good search engine and search by topic. You'll be able to find good sites this way.

If anyone would like to contribute ideas or suggestions for the next edition, I would be delighted to hear from you. My email address is KrisCole@bax.com.au.

Kris Cole

Other books by Kris Cole

Crystal Clear Communication: Skills for Understanding and being Understood, Prentice Hall, Sydney, 1993 and 2000. Also available in German, Mandarin and Bahasa Indonesian. An Indian subcontinent edition will be available in 2001.

Office Administration and Supervision: A Text for the New Office Manager, Prentice Hall, Sydney, 1992, with Barbara Hamilton.

How to Succeed at a Job Interview, Gleneagles Publishing, Adelaide, 1991, with Don Cole. First published in 1982 by E.P. Publishing London.

Kris Cole's next book will be on time management.

PART I

WORKPLACE PRACTICE

Whether it's a Scout troop, a community theatre group, a rock band, an assembly line, a team of rocket scientists, a motorcycle gang or a local go-cart team, people who band together to achieve their individual and common goals need support and guidance. They need someone who is willing and confident enough to monitor and take overall responsibility for their activities and achievements. They need someone they can trust to 'do the right thing' and do it to the best of their ability. They need someone who can inspire them, empower them and set the right example.

Whether we call these people supervisors, superintendents, team leaders, section managers, leading hands, coordinators, area managers, directors, first-line managers, front-line managers, department heads, chiefs, bosses, sergeants or captains, their role is unique and one of the most important in any organisation.

They are at the interface between non-managers, or 'workers', on the one hand and more senior managers on the other. They are the only managers who have direct and daily contact with the workforce. Who else can influence the output, morale, service excellence and cost-effectiveness of a work group so directly?

The Australian Mission on Management Skills, established by the Honourable John Dawkins MP, and led by Alan M. Priestley from BHP, concluded that well trained, skilled and competent managers, *particularly supervisors*, are vital to Australia's economic future. Without them, we will not be able to compete in the increasingly complex and competitive international marketplace.

Clearly, the supervisor's role is

one of the most crucial in any organisation.

But before we can be of much help to an organisation or a group of people who have banded together to achieve results, we need to be able to manage *ourselves*.

In Part I, after examining the changing role of the 21st century supervisor, we look at the important foundation skills of communicating with others. We examine self-awareness and personal development and look at the personal skills that supervisors need, such as time management and stress management. This sets the stage for the next two parts of this book: *Managing Operations* and *Managing People*.

CHAPTER 1

THE SUPERVISOR'S CHANGING JOB AND WORKING ENVIRONMENT

A good supervisor

As Ben Fredricks left for work on Monday morning, his mind was busy with thoughts of his new job. As of today, Ben was a section leader! When Joe retired as leader of the Parks and Gardens Planning and Maintenance section, Ben was asked to take over. Of course, Ben was delighted. Supervising a section represented a big step up into the ranks of management.

But now he was not so sure. What was he supposed to *do*? The work itself was no problem—he'd done most of the jobs in his section over the years. He was well qualified technically ... But it was all the rest of it—whatever that was. What *was* it that Joe used to do when he sat in his office? Sure, he had to assign overtime and check on it and he had dealt with one or two discipline matters when they arose. He interviewed and inducted people who joined the section. And there were meetings with the other section leaders about next year's plans and what new equipment to buy and so on. But surely there was more to supervision than this ...

And how should he act with his new 'team'—his old workmates? Of course, they were still a team, but now he was no longer part of it. Or was he? He was certainly the person most responsible for the team's achievements and morale, and its contributions to the rest of the Parks and Gardens Department.

When all was said and done, was he, Ben wondered, the sort of person who would make a good section leader?

████████ OVERVIEW ████████

The roles and responsibilities of supervisors are changing dramatically and comprehensively. Greater skills and knowledge are being demanded of supervisors and the challenges and rewards of their jobs are myriad. In this chapter, you will discover the variety of roles and responsibilities that supervisors have.

- Can you describe the average Australian supervisor in terms of age, strengths and weaknesses, where they are employed, and how much training and education they have had?
- Do you know how and why their working environment is changing?
- Can you describe the roles and responsibilities of supervisors and how they fit into an organisation?
- Can you identify the three levels of management, the ten managerial roles and the five management functions all supervisors and managers carry out?
- Do you know the difference between supervising, managing and leading?
- Do you know the six groups to whom supervisors are responsible?
- Can you claim to be a 'competent supervisor' and can you develop a plan to improve your supervisory skills?

WHO ARE AUSTRALIA'S SUPERVISORS?

Are you a practising or aspiring supervisor? In this chapter, you will learn about the roles and responsibilities of supervisors and how their working environment is changing in dramatic ways.

The Australian Bureau of Statistics tells us that one in every ten employees is a manager. The National Industry Task Force on Leadership and Management Skills, chaired by David Karpin and known as the Karpin Committee, estimated that Australia has a total of 890 000 managers. About half of them are over 40 years of age. Just over half (about 511 000) are employed in the 80% of Australia's enterprises that have four or fewer employees.

Just under half of Australia's managers are front-line managers, or supervisors. These 400 000 managers are at the interface between more senior managers on the one hand and the rest of the workforce on the other.

Every year, about 30 000 people are appointed to their first management position. Most of them are promoted from being a member of a work team to supervising or leading it. Many of these people will remain at this first-line management level for the rest of their working lives. Other supervisors are graduates who are appointed to supervisory roles to gain 'shop-floor' or 'grass-roots' experience before moving further up the management ladder.

How well trained and skilled are our managers?

Despite the profound importance of managers to Australia's economic well-being, it seems that managers in our major overseas trading partners are better trained and qualified for management than our own managers. They are more likely to have qualifications beyond secondary level and more likely to have been trained in supervisory skills before their appointment. For example, Department of Employment, Education and Training figures in 1991 showed that only 20% of Australian managers held a first degree. In Germany the comparable figure was 63% and in Japan and the United States it was 85%. The Karpin Committee estimated that nearly half of Australia's first-line managers had no formal training for their role.

Once appointed to management, do our managers catch up on their training or update their skills? Again, it seems that Australian managers do not compare well with other countries. Australian managers spend on average seven days a year, or 3% of their time, on training and development activities. This is far behind the world's best practice. (Motorola, for example, has a goal that each employee, not just managers, receives 20 days training a year.)

As a result of its findings, the Karpin Committee was critical of the skill levels and performance of Australian managers relative to managers in OECD (Organisation for Economic Cooperation and Development) and many Asian countries. They strongly recommended that we provide better training and education for our managers and potential managers of all levels in order to secure our economic future and standard of living.

Training and education in what? We need to improve in the areas of entrepreneurship, global orientation, interpersonal skills, strategic skills and teamworking (including the ability to cooperate with, and use, the skills of a more diverse workforce). We also need to make further improvements to our customer service orientation and commitment to quality.

Barraclough and Co. compiled a report for the Karpin Committee called *Experienced Insights: Opinions of Australian Managers; Ideals, Strengths and Weaknesses*. Based on surveys of several hundred chief executives, human resource professionals, management consultants, executive search firms, academics, company directors and professional bodies, it identified the strengths and weaknesses of Australian managers (see Box 1.1 below).

A ROSE BY ANY OTHER NAME?

Not too many years ago, we called most first-line managers 'supervisors'. Now we often refer to them as team leaders, section heads, coordinators, first-line managers, front-line managers or, simply, managers.

BOX 1.1 STRENGTHS AND WEAKNESSES OF AUSTRALIAN MANAGERS

Strengths	*Weaknesses*
■ hard-working	■ short-term view
■ flexible and adaptable	■ lack of strategic perspective
■ innovative and inventive	■ inflexible
■ technically sound	■ complacent
■ egalitarian	■ poor at teamwork and empowerment
■ independent thinkers	■ unable to cope with individual differences
■ open, genuine and direct	■ poor interpersonal skills
■ honest and ethical	

Source: *Industry Task Force on Leadership and Management Skills*

This reflects their increased status and responsibilities. As organisations have restructured and downsized, many of the duties formerly carried out by middle managers now fall to the first-line manager, or supervisor. In turn, the work team now does many of the supervisor's former duties. Decision making and other forms of authority have been pushed further and further 'down the line' as employees at all levels take on more responsibility and a more active role in achieving results.

What kind of rose: linchpin, pig-in-the-middle or worker?

Whatever we call them, supervisors are the managers closest to the workers. They are the links, or linchpins, between an organisation's more senior managers and its employees. To many employees, they personify the organisation as a whole. They serve as a focal point for attitudes, values and models of how to behave towards customers, the organisation and the job itself. Because of their closeness to the workplace and the workforce, supervisors are often in the best position to translate management's vision and goals to employees and to explain workers' feelings to senior management. This makes supervisors key people in knitting together a group of people—management and workers—into a coordinated organisation that works effectively and harmoniously to achieve its objectives. Unfortunately, this can sometimes lead to a 'pig-in-the-middle' feeling because supervisors can easily see, and often identify with, both sides of an issue.

This closeness can also lead to loyalty problems. On the one hand, supervisors work very closely with non-management employees and, in many cases, were part of this group before their promotion to management. They may continue to identify with the workforce and more senior managers may mentally continue to place them there, too. This means that, on the organisation chart, supervisors may be 'managers' but in people's minds (sometimes even in their own minds) they are 'workers'. There is no doubt too that in some organisations, supervisors are 'glorified workers', expected to carry out the same tasks as the people they supervise—supervision is an add-on extra.

LEVELS OF MANAGEMENT

For the past 200 years there have been three **levels of management**: senior, middle and first-line, or supervisory, management. Although organisations are rapidly becoming flatter and the traditional pyramid shape may even be disappearing, we can still identify these three levels (see Figure 1.1).

Senior management is the highest level. These people are responsible for setting the strategic vision, policies and direction of an enterprise and developing long-term plans to guide the organisation, help it thrive and produce real value for its stakeholders. Many titles describe these jobs:

- executive and non-executive director
- managing director
- marketing manager
- human resources director
- general manager
- permanent head of a government department
- chief financial officer
- chief executive officer.

Middle management comprises all those levels between senior management and first-line management. Middle managers develop the tactics, specific policies and shorter-term

FIGURE 1.1   TRADITIONAL PYRAMID OF MANAGEMENT LEVELS

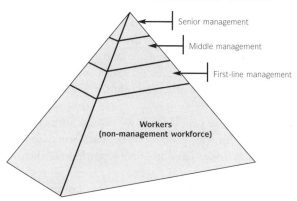

plans to achieve the organisation's overall goals and vision, and guide the organisation on a day-to-day basis. In the private sector, these people might have such titles as:

- sales manager
- chief accountant
- production manager
- chief engineer.

In the public sector, titles include:

- secretary, Department of X
- shire engineer
- assistant secretary
- procurement officer.

In the not-for-profit sector, titles might be:

- volunteer manager
- support group leader
- education coordinator
- information officer
- development officer
- office manager.

First-line management lies at the interface between the non-management workforce and the rest of management. Whatever their title—supervisors, superintendents, team leaders, section managers, leading hands, coordinators or area managers—these people deal with day-to-day production and service issues. They work directly with their non-management teams to ensure their products or services are produced to the required standard in the safest and most efficient way possible.

What will happen to these three levels of management as organisations restructure in radical ways to meet the demands of their marketplace? It is likely that they will take on less significance as the traditional 'pyramid' and hierarchical relationships of organisational life disappear and the new paradigms described in Figure 1.13 take hold (see also Chapter 4). However, as we will see, the need for first-line managers, or team leaders, is likely to grow.

SUPERVISING, MANAGING OR LEADING?

As the traditional pyramid crumbles, the distinctions between supervising, managing and leading are blurring. In the past, we tended to use the term 'manager' to refer to those who had other managers or supervisors reporting to them—middle or senior managers—while we tended to reserve the title 'supervisor' for first-line managers. Titles are changing. We may be seeing a trend towards more inclusive, less 'hierarchical' job titles.

If we think of a supervisor as a 'first-line manager', we could say that the *skills* required to supervise and to manage are the same. It is the *degree* to which supervisors need these skills and the *time frame* involved that differentiate managers at different levels. Supervisors, for example, work with shorter time frames of, say, a week or a month, while middle managers work with a time perspective of several months; senior managers often work with a time perspective of several years.

In a different sense, we *supervise* people while we *manage* a function (such as finance) or a resource (such as time). In this way, people can be managers without being supervisors: credit managers, for example, may have no one reporting to them and so would be managers but not supervisors.

In any event, people at any level have a *supervisory role* if others report directly to them. People at any level have a *managerial role* if they are responsible for achieving functional objectives or monitoring and allocating important resources within the organisation.

> **'A supervisor is a manager who helps others achieve results by establishing and communicating goals and securing or providing the necessary resources.'**

Similarly, the distinction between managers and leaders is increasingly irrelevant. Today, all managers, at every level, and indeed many employees, need leadership skills.

It has been said that leading is an attitude while managing is a skill. Leaders create the vision and set goals and guidelines. Managers follow a plan within the guidelines to achieve the goals while adhering to policies and procedures. Rob Meates, a teambuilding and leadership consultant in Victoria, puts it this way:

> **'Leaders lead into the unknown.
> Managers manage the known.'**

Box 1.2 summarises some of the main differences between leaders and managers. (We will discuss this further in Chapter 15.)

FIVE MANAGEMENT FUNCTIONS

We have traditionally grouped a manager's skills and activities into five functional areas: planning, organising, staffing, leading and monitoring (see Figure 1.2).

Planning

Planning involves establishing a goal and objectives and deciding how best to achieve them. What needs to be accomplished? By when? What needs to be done to make it happen? Who is best equipped to do it?

As the saying goes:

> **'If you fail to plan, you plan to fail.'**

Things don't happen by themselves: we need to plan them carefully. After all, a goal without an action plan is just a wish!

BOX 1.2   LEADING VERSUS MANAGING

Leaders
- create ideas and innovate
- encourage experimentation
- create change
- push out the boundaries
- challenge the status quo
- ask what and why
- establish and live values
- lead by example
- inspire
- involve
- participate
- encourage
- support
- set direction
- focus on people
- focus on the longer term
- do the right things
- use interpersonal skills

Managers
- control and administer
- give direction
- work to established procedures
- work within the boundaries
- protect the status quo
- ask how and when
- 'do as I say'
- rely on authority
- plan and coordinate
- solve problems
- delegate
- monitor
- adhere to direction
- focus on the task
- focus on the short term
- focus on the bottom line
- do things right
- rely on control and formal authority

FIGURE 1.2   THE SUPERVISOR'S MANAGERIAL FUNCTIONS

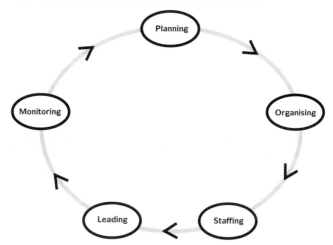

Today, planning also involves innovating. We need to make continual improvements, however small, if our enterprise or department is to prosper. No matter how well we do things, failing to make improvements is a recipe for disaster in today's rapidly changing environment.

Organising

People, materials, equipment, machines, time and money are all resources. They need to be arranged and coordinated so that the plans can be successfully carried out. Supervisors also need to organise themselves. If they can't do that, they have little hope of organising others.

Staffing

It is often said that people are an organisation's most valuable resource. They need to be *attracted* to the organisation, *recruited* to join it and *trained* to do their jobs effectively. They need to be treated well so the organisation *retains* them, because losing employees is expensive.

This function is destined to become increasingly important as labour becomes scarce, knowledge and expertise more valuable, and organisations organise themselves in different ways to meet the challenges of their ever-changing environment.

Leading

Effective leadership is concerned with supporting, guiding, influencing and inspiring others. Setting a good example, developing team spirit, involving and motivating people and building morale are a few of the important leadership skills. The leading function consumes a large part of most managers' time and, like the staffing function, it is becoming increasingly important.

Monitoring

'How are we doing?' is the monitoring question. Are we operating within budget? Are we meeting production and sales targets? Are our plans progressing as expected? 'Keeping tabs' on things by watching critical control points and sensitive spots alerts us to potential problems so we can take corrective action in plenty of time.

Some common key indicators of performance that supervisors monitor are:

- budgets
- time taken
- standard costs
- quality ratios
- staff turnover
- materials usage
- equipment usage
- machinery usage
- absenteeism
- safety measures.

SUPERVISORY ROLES

Managers wear a number of 'hats'. A Canadian researcher, Henry Mintzberg, called these hats **roles**. We act out the parts, or roles, that a given situation requires. Mintzberg believes his research shows that managers at all levels play roles that fall into three groups. Box 1.3 shows the ten managerial roles Mintzberg identified.

Three **interpersonal roles** arise from a manager's formal authority and involve leadership, communication and official supervisory duties. The interpersonal roles lead to three types of **informational roles** that serve to keep people informed on matters that affect them. These in turn lead to four **decisional roles** that call for managers to exercise judgment in dealing with problems, allocating resources and dealing with others.

These three groups of roles are a good way of describing and understanding how managers spend their time. The amount of emphasis given to each role depends, of course, on the type of organisation, the job duties being carried out and the level of the manager concerned.

BOX 1.3 MANAGERIAL ROLES

Interpersonal roles

Figurehead role	Acting in an official capacity, e.g. presenting awards, signing documents or time cards
Leader role	(We discuss this role in detail in Chapter 20)
Liaison role	Communicating with people both inside and outside the organisation

Informational roles

Monitor role	Collecting information so as to remain 'in the picture' and detect changes or problems
Disseminator role	Distributing information from both internal and external sources to management, employees and colleagues
Spokesperson role	Representing the organisation to external people and groups; representing employees to management and vice versa

Decisional roles

Entrepreneur role	Initiating changes and improvements, discovering problems, innovating solutions
Disturbance-handler role	Dealing with matters such as breaches of discipline, conflicts, grievances and the unexpected problems that can arise even with the most careful planning
Resource-allocator role	Deciding who shall do what, when and with which resources; scheduling time, materials, work and other resources
Negotiator role	Making agreements with groups or individuals, both inside and outside the organisation

THINK ABOUT IT!

How is supervising a department like a wheel?

‘ *When you get it moving right,*
it gathers its own momentum
and just needs managing.
But when it falls over,
it takes a lot of work and effort
to get it up and running. ’

Tracy Hobbs, Manager
Townsville, Queensland

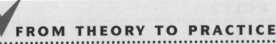

FROM THEORY TO PRACTICE

Imagine that you are a supervisor in a coffee shop. For each of the five managerial functions explained above, list five supervisory activities that you would regularly undertake.

WHAT DO SUPERVISORS DO?

The working life of most supervisors is hectic. Box 1.4 shows some of their many duties.

Supervisors' need a great deal of mental flexibility and physical stamina to get through their busy days.

Take a closer look at Box 1.4. Which activities are *physical*? Which are *mental*? Some *physical activities* involve 'practical' or non-supervisory work. Other physical activities involve communication: telling somebody something, writing, talking on the telephone, looking for possible problem areas, training employees, and so on.

Other equally important, but not so obvious, supervisory activities include those *mental activities* upon which the ultimate success of the physical activities depends: planning, problem solving, decision making, reading details of new job requirements, innovating, empowering others and keeping track of 'the big picture'.

BOX 1.4

A SUPERVISOR'S TYPICAL DAY

- conduct a safety check
- solve a technical problem
- greet staff as they arrive
- cover for absences
- distribute work/allocate tasks
- assign people to work groups
- prepare for a presentation
- read mail and reports
- motivate individuals and teams
- make decisions
- initiate improvements
- monitor and improve productivity and results
- interview a potential employee
- evaluate work done
- do 'practical' (non-supervisory) work

- supervise trainees
- order materials
- check stocks
- check or assure quality
- attend a team meeting
- carry out routine administration
- counsel a team member
- prepare rosters
- monitor and manage resources
- solve problems
- represent their team, inside and outside the organisation
- train and coach employees
- schedule work
- write letters and reports
- monitor output and expenses against budget

THE SUPERVISOR'S SKILL SET

At every level of management, some proficiency in each of the following skill groups is necessary:

- technical job-related skills
- interpersonal skills
- conceptual skills.

While the technical job-related skills differ from job to job, the interpersonal and conceptual skills are common to all managerial jobs. However, the mix of these skills varies from one management level to another, as Figure 1.3 shows.

FIGURE 1.3   SKILLS REQUIRED AT DIFFERENT LEVELS OF MANAGEMENT

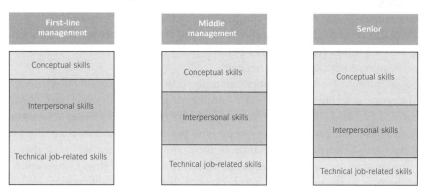

Technical job-related skills

Supervisors need to understand the nature of the jobs and processes, methods, procedures and administration systems used in their department and organisation. Manufacturing supervisors, for example, must understand the technical aspects and machine operations of their section's activities; they must also understand how to measure, record and report production in order to monitor it effectively.

To supervise well, you don't have to be the most skilled operator in your team. But you do need to have a sound understanding of the skills people need to carry out the jobs in your section and you need to be aware of how each job contributes to the other jobs in your section, to the section's overall output and to your organisation as a whole.

Interpersonal skills

Do you know anyone who lacks interpersonal skills? These are the people who open their mouth and 'put both feet in', people who rub others up the wrong way or who say just the wrong thing at the wrong time, or to the wrong person.

Whereas technical skills are concerned mainly with procedures and equipment, interpersonal skills help us work with, lead and motivate others, and communicate with people in an **empathic** and **assertive** way. Interpersonal skills are needed at all levels of management in order to work with others to attain the desired results.

These skills are founded on **self-awareness**. To work well with others, we must first understand ourselves: our own feelings, beliefs, values and attitudes, our perceptions of the world, our motives for getting things done. We need to understand and accept that everyone is different, with different skills and abilities, beliefs, values and desires. This helps us understand

and empathise with beliefs and viewpoints different from our own, which in turn helps us communicate effectively with others. (We examine this more closely in Chapter 14.)

As a result of its investigations, the Karpin Committee concluded that Australia's managers need to develop their interpersonal skills much more. In fact, the research carried out by Barraclough and Co. identified interpersonal skills as the most needed characteristic of the modern manager. (You will recall from Box 1.1 that this is an area where Australian managers are less than satisfactory.)

The core interpersonal skills are:

- *Clear communication.* The best idea is worthless unless others understand it. Supervisors spend more than 75% of their time communicating, so they need to do it well.
- *Assertiveness and empathy.* Supervisors work with and through other people. This requires the ability to see things from the other person's point of view as well as the skill to state your own requirements clearly and precisely.
- *Integrity and charisma.* Good supervisors can inspire others to work cooperatively to achieve results. Integrity is acting honestly and according to your ethical values and principles. Charisma is a personal magnetism that inspires loyalty and enthusiasm. Charisma and integrity are a powerful combination—people who possess both 'practise what they preach' or 'walk their talk'. They have the courage of their convictions; they 'say what they mean and mean what they say', avoiding duplicity, trickery and game playing. Others know they can trust them to do the right thing, and because of that, willingly follow their lead.
- *Respect for others.* It is difficult to imagine an effective supervisor who doesn't respect others and value their feelings, ideas, desires and contributions.
- *Ability to be a team player.* Modern supervisors must be able to work cooperatively and effectively with others both inside and outside the organisation. They must work well with their work teams, other supervisors and senior management. They must also cooperate with people from other departments in the organisation. Increasingly, they must work well with people from outside their organisation: the public, suppliers and customers.

These skills should be so much a part of us that we apply them continuously, as automatically as breathing. These are not attributes to be turned on and off and applied only when a need arises—they must be part of everything we say and do.

Conceptual skills

This ability to see the 'big picture' is becoming increasingly important as the world changes at an ever-quickening rate. Conceptual skills help us to understand the role an organisation plays in the social, economic and community life of a nation. They help us understand how each part of an organisation contributes to the success of the whole: how purchasing, manufacturing, sales and finance interrelate; how sound supervision is critical to the overall success of the organisation; how mutually rewarding relationships with supplier organisations is a requirement for success. Conceptual skills help us to stand back and see the forest as well as the individual trees.

Supervisors also need conceptual skills to:

- understand how a change in one section or system could affect other sections or systems;
- comprehend the ramifications of a plan or an idea;
- think things through and recognise possible implications and effects of decisions on others;

- identify the cause of a problem when things go wrong, so they don't just treat a 'symptom';
- get to the heart of a problem and take appropriate action;
- anticipate future problems and implement preventive action;
- understand the systems they work within; and
- coordinate the many activities they engage in.

Six of the top eight characteristics of the ideal manager identified by Barraclough and Co. in its research for the Karpin Committee fall into the conceptual skills category. These are listed in Box 1.5. (The remaining two characteristics require interpersonal skills.)

BOX 1.5 CHARACTERISTICS OF THE IDEAL MODERN MANAGER
....

- a strategic thinker
- visionary
- flexible and adaptable to change

- able to manage him or herself
- ethical
- able to solve complex problems and make decisions

Skills alone aren't enough

The way we use our skills depends on our mind-set and personal attributes. Over 250 experienced supervisors from a variety of industries all over Australia and New Zealand were asked to list what skills and attributes they believed contributed most to a supervisor's success. Box 1.6 summarises their response. You will notice that some skills and attributes overlap and that the line between some is blurred. These qualities and skills combine to make up an effective, competent supervisor.

FROM THEORY TO PRACTICE
....

Use the list in Box 1.6 as a checklist to assess how well you match the criteria needed to be a successful supervisor.

THE COMPETENT SUPERVISOR

Competencies are used by those who design training programs and by organisations to determine a person's level of skills for job placement, promotion and pay rate purposes. The Standards and Curriculum Council of the Board of the Australian National Training Authority (ANTA) endorsed a set of *generic management competency standards for front-line management* based on the Karpin Committee findings. They are shown in Box 1.7.

This is just one competency model of what it takes to be an effective supervisor. Because the role is changing rapidly, there are other models. Many large organisations are developing their own competencies or tailoring published competencies to meet their own needs.

Clearly, being a competent supervisor requires more than just physical skills. Conceptual skills and interpersonal skills are becoming increasingly important. Attributes and personal values are also part of a supervisor's skill set.

SKILLS AND ATTRIBUTES NEEDED BY SUPERVISORS

BOX 1.6

Skills

- empowers others ✓
- respects others ✓
- team player ✓
- leads by example ✓
- communicates clearly and assertively ✓
- reasons problems out ✓/✗
- delivers results ✓
- strong company knowledge ✓/✗
- persuasive ✓
- good organiser ✓/✗
- clear thinker ✓/✗
- strategic thinker ✓
- empathic ✓
- sets goals ✓/✗
- listens to others carefully ✓/✗
- manages time well ✓/✗
- leads others strongly ✓/✗
- sets limits ✓/✗
- solves problems thoughtfully ✓/✗
- plans in advance ✓/✗
- makes sensible decisions ✓/✗
- delegates effectively ✓/✗
- exhibits job-related technical skills ✓/✗
- coordinates the efforts of others ✓/✗
- uses resources carefully ✓
- motivates others to work well ✓
- confronts issues tactfully and diplomatically

(✓ + ✗ − 26/7/01)

Attributes

- genuine respect for others ✓
- task first, self second ✓/✗
- doesn't 'throw in the towel' when results are poor or when the pressure is on ✓
- self-confident ✓
- determined and persistent ✓
- clear sense of task ✓
- clear vision ✓/✗
- risk taker, no fear of failure ✓/✗
- fair ✓
- passionate and enthusiastic ✓
- inspires others ✓
- thorough approach ✓/✗
- self-disciplined ✓
- patient and understanding ✓
- practise what you preach
- efficiency-minded ✓
- sense of responsibility ✓
- willing and able to learn ✓
- takes responsibility for decisions ✓
- ethical, displays honesty and integrity ✓
- professional image ✓
- innovative ✓/✗
- 'people person', caring, approachable ✓
- consistent ✓/✗
- flexible ✓/✗
- strength of character ✓
- tolerant ✓/✗
- attracts competent employees ✓
- keeps confidences ✓
- trusting and trustworthy ✓
- accurately assesses people and situations ✓
- searches for 'better ways' ✓
- level-headed ✓
- 'self-starter' ✓
- loyal to team, organisation and customers ✓
- builds self-esteem in others ✓
- identifies and uses others' strengths ✓
- receptive and open-minded ✓

FROM THEORY TO PRACTICE

Using information from Boxes 1.6 and 1.7, take a few minutes to tick your competencies, skills and attributes that match those needed and highlight any you need to develop further.

MANAGEMENT COMPETENCY STANDARDS FOR FRONT-LINE MANAGEMENT, AUSTRALIAN NATIONAL TRAINING AUTHORITY (ANTA)

Theme	Unit	Element
Leading by example	Unit 1: Manage personal work priorities and professional development	1.1 Manage self 1.2 Set and meet own work priorities 1.3 Develop and maintain professional competence
	Unit 2: Provide leadership in the workplace	2.1 Model high standards of management performance 2.2 Enhance the organisation's image 2.3 Influence individuals and teams positively 2.4 Make informed decisions
Leading, coaching; facilitating and empowering others	Unit 3: Establish and manage effective workplace relationships	3.1 Gather, convey and receive information and ideas 3.2 Develop trust and confidence, facilitating and empowering others 3.3 Build and maintain networks and relationships 3.4 Manage difficulties to achieve positive outcomes
	Unit 4: Participate in, lead and facilitate work teams	4.1 Participate in team planning 4.2 Develop team commitment and cooperation 4.3 Manage and develop team performance 4.4 Participate in, and facilitate the work team/group
Creating best practice	Unit 5: Manage operations to achieve planned outcomes	5.1 Plan resource use to achieve profit/productivity targets 5.2 Acquire resources to achieve operational plan 5.3 Monitor operational performance 5.4 Monitor resource usage
	Unit 6: Manage workplace information	6.1 Identify and source information needs 6.2 Collect, analyse and report information 6.3 Use management information systems 6.4 Prepare business plans/budgets 6.5 Prepare resource proposals
	Unit 7: Manage quality customer service	7.1 Plan to meet internal and external customer requirements 7.2 Ensure delivery of quality products/services 7.3 Monitor, adjust and report customer service
	Unit 8: Develop and maintain a safe workplace and environment	8.1 Access and share legislation, codes and standards 8.2 Plan and implement safety requirements

Continued . . .

Theme	Unit	Element
		8.3 Monitor, adjust and report safety performance
		8.4 Investigate and report non-conformance
	Unit 9: Implement and monitor continuous improvement systems	9.1 Implement continuous improvement systems and processes
		9.2 Monitor, adjust and report performance
		9.3 Consolidate opportunities for further improvement
Creating an innovative culture	Unit 10: Facilitate and capitalise on change and innovation	10.1 Participate in planning the introduction of change
		10.2 Develop creative and flexible approaches and solutions
		10.3 Manage emerging challenges and opportunities
	Unit 11: Contribute to the development of a workplace learning environment	11.1 Create learning opportunities
		11.2 Facilitate and promote learning
		11.3 Monitor and improve learning effectiveness

Source: *Australian National Training Authority, Generic Management Competency Standards for Frontline Management, ANTA, 1996.*

BOX 1.8   **SELF-CHECK** ··

The competent supervisor can answer 'Yes' to the following questions:
- ❏ Can I handle the entire range of necessary tasks?
- ❏ Do I know enough about my product and internal and external customer service?
- ❏ Can I take effective action when things go wrong?
- ❏ Can I get along with others and 'fit in'?
- ❏ Can I express myself tactfully and clearly?
- ❏ Am I able to understand others' points of view even when I disagree?
- ❏ Do I 'walk my talk'?
- ❏ Can I motivate and inspire enthusiasm in others?
- ❏ Do others follow my example willingly, without coercion?
- ❏ Am I committed to my customers, both internal and external?
- ❏ Do I continually search for better ways to do things?
- ❏ Do I bring out the best in others and give them a chance to 'spread their wings'?
- ❏ Am I able to forge a strong team that works together to achieve results?
- ❏ Am I able to use the resources of my team or department effectively?
- ❏ Do I correctly identify and use people's strengths?
- ❏ Do I train and develop people patiently and willingly?
- ❏ Do I make an effective team member and make positive contributions to my own team of supervisors?

Continued . . .

❏ Do I respect all my colleagues, suppliers and customers as I expect them to respect me?
❏ Do I manage myself and my own time well?
❏ Do I develop and maintain a safe working environment?
❏ Do others listen to me and respect my opinions?
❏ Can I solve problems creatively?
❏ Can I easily retrieve, understand and manage information?
❏ Do I continually try to learn new things, stretch my skills, extend my knowledge base?
❏ Am I able to understand the 'big picture' and take it into account in my day-to-day activities?
❏ Do I have 'business acumen'—an understanding of how organisations work, how work is organised, how to manage quality, customer expectations, service, budgets, a sound grasp of legislative, ethical and environmental issues?

How do you measure up?

Is there such a thing as an 'ideal supervisor'? The traits and skills that make a person terrific in a job are probably situational—dependent on an organisation's culture, industry, operations, size, and so on. In other words, apart from core competencies, different organisations need different things from their leaders at different times.

Box 1.9 shows how the role of the supervisor has changed over the past 30 years and how it is likely to evolve.

BOX 1.9 THE EMERGING FRONT-LINE MANAGER PROFILE

1970 *The supervisor*	*1995* *The organiser*	*2010* *The leader/coach*
■ male	■ male, possibly female	■ male or female
■ supervises from position of authority	■ management expects supervision, group wants leadership	■ leader and coach
■ operates in a hierarchical organisation structure	■ middle management vastly reduced	■ operates in a flat organisational structure
■ values control, organisation, motivation by authority, technical expertise	■ values control, organisation, teamwork	■ team leader reports direct to senior management
■ low-pressure work environment	■ stressful environment due to organisational restructuring	■ values performance management, facilitative, participative leadership, empowerment
■ experienced in field	■ experienced in field	■ environment emphasises best practice, benchmarking, quality, customer service
■ trade qualification	■ trade qualification	■ most have TAFE level qualification or degree
■ little formal management training	■ 50% have formal management training but little organisational support for further learning	■ all have formal training for position and organisational support for further training and learning

Source: Adapted from *Karpin Report Task Force Research: Management Skills in Australian Industry Sub-Committee, 1995*

FROM THEORY TO PRACTICE

Talk to three people about their managers to identify what key competencies they possess. Look for behavioural evidence before concluding they possess these competencies. Ask: 'What do they say or do that shows they have this competency?' or 'How do you know they have this competency?'

THE SUPERVISOR'S CHANGING ENVIRONMENT

Every decade it seems, has its unique, defining characteristics:

1960s   Innovation.

1970s   Industrial strife and conflict.

1980s   Entrepreneurialism and conspicuous consumption.

1990s   Downsizing, de-layering and breaking of the psychological contract of steady employment in return for reasonable productivity.

2000s   Continued job insecurity, outsourcing and change, formation of the knowledge economy.

For the foreseeable future, change will be our constant companion. The ancient Chinese had a blessing:

'May you live in interesting times.'

This is a mixed blessing—while 'interesting times' can be positive, energising and uplifting, they are also complicated times of great change, great stress and great challenge. We live in interesting times.

Our working environment will continue to be unpredictable and turbulent. Box 1.10 summarises some of the forces shaping our future.

BOX **1.10** **CHANGES AFFECTING US**

- *Political* changes (e.g. we are becoming 'greener'), more regulated through government policy
- Changes in *society*, particularly lifestyles and work patterns
- Greater *competition*, both at home and abroad, and pressures to customise products and services
- Growing speed of *technological* innovations, particularly information technology and nanotechnology, leading to new products and new work methods, making some skills obsolete and creating the need for new areas of skill
- Changes in *consumer* spending and customer expectations
- Breakthroughs in *science* and *medicine*, particularly biotechnology and genetics
- Changes in the background, training and expectations of *employees*
- Increasing *globalisation* as the world becomes smaller, large corporations become transnational and markets are no longer bordered by national boundaries

THE **BIG** PICTURE
....
How can supervisors gain the commitment and loyalty of growing numbers
of casual, outsourced and part-time workers?

These changes are profound and create immense challenges for managers at all levels in
all sectors. As the private sector struggles with globalisation and a changing marketplace,
the public sector faces deregulation, budget cuts, public sector reform and privatisation.
The not-for-profit sector faces its own blend of challenges, too, particularly the competition
for money and skilled and motivated volunteers and paid employees.

Box 1.11 examines some of these changes in more detail and Box 1.12 highlights trends
that will affect supervisors.

BOX 1.11   THE SUPERVISOR'S CHANGING WORK ENVIRONMENT
....

Social trends

- The 'nuclear family', which emerged during the Industrial Revolution, is being
  joined by increasing numbers of other household types (e.g. it is estimated that, in
  the UK, one in three people will be living alone, married couples will be in the
  minority and one in five fathers will be househusbands by 2020).
- The population is ageing and life spans increasing; this may mean that labour
  becomes scarce due to a shortage of younger workers, as it already has in most
  OECD (Organisation for Economic Co-operation and Development) countries.
- The population, and therefore the workforce, is becoming more diverse and inclusive
  of women, immigrants and non Anglo-Saxon races; the typical worker may soon no
  longer be a white male. This means supervisors will need skills to nurture and prosper
  from a diverse workforce.

Emerging technologies

- Biotechnology and nanotechnology (ultra-small—e.g. motors the size of a pinhead),
  computers and telecommunications will change the way we use space, energy and
  materials and the ways we communicate with each other, store and retrieve and pass
  on knowledge. For example, the 'information superhighway' already allows us to
  access anything and anybody, anywhere, anytime.
- Technology combined with the rising costs of city property mean that SOHOs
  (small offices/home offices) and virtual offices will increase in popularity and workers
  will be more isolated from each other. This means that supervisors will need to create
  a vision and culture that will inspire people and help work teams keep up with
  changing times. They will increasingly manage individuals who work 'out of sight'
  and virtual work teams.

Continued . . .

Globalisation

■ Economic activity conducted on a global basis, where the world is the single economic unit, is accelerating and replacing internationalisation. This is made possible by advances in transportation and communications technology. In the near future, supply chains, product design, financing, risk management and support services will be global and global mergers will become common. This means supervisors will need ever-stronger conceptual skills and a clear overall understanding of how business and economies operate.

■ Freer trade between countries means no company is insulated from its best competitors, wherever they are. This means the drive towards ever-greater efficiency, productivity, quality and service will continue. Employment levels will continue to tighten as the best producer dictates employee numbers. This means the working environment will remain 'tough'.

Employment patterns

■ According to the Australian Bureau of Statistics 1996 Census, part-time employment is growing and full-time employment shrinking, as a proportion of the total workforce.

■ Research by the University of Sydney's Australian Centre for Industrial Relations Research and Training (ACIRRT) found that casual employment increased from 16% of the workforce in 1984 to almost 26% in 1996.

■ The number of contractor jobs and part-time jobs has also risen (ACIRRT).

■ We now have the highest proportion of temporary workers in any OECD country except Spain (ACIRRT).

■ The average working week increased from 37.8 hours in 1986 to 42.4 hours in 1994 for full-time employees (ACIRRT).

■ Enterprise bargaining has brought about new working arrangements such as 12-hour shifts, annualised hours and time off in lieu of overtime pay.

Organisation structures

■ Since the Industrial Revolution, companies have become progressively larger, driven by the quest for economies of scale. Recently, this trend has reversed. The cost of complexity is beginning to outweigh economies of scale and organisation structures are becoming simpler, with a greater focus on efficiency and autonomy. Other organisation structures are replacing the traditional pyramid.

THE **BIG** PICTURE

The Australian Workplace Industrial Relations Survey found that employees believe they are working harder, are under more stress and are more dissatisfied with the work/family balance. Only 37% said they felt that management at their workplace could be trusted. Supervising an insecure, overworked, stressed and distrustful workforce demands a variety of skills. How can we ensure our supervisors are up to the challenge?

**BOX 1.12   SOME PREDICTIONS FOR SUPERVISORS'
WORKING ENVIRONMENTS**
....

- Women will continue to launch more companies than men.
- Small business will continue to create most new jobs.
- Skills and knowledge will become outdated faster than ever.
- Specialisations will grow and narrow, making generalist managers and supervisors more necessary.
- Individuals will have more responsibility, resources and authority.
- Self-organising teams will come into their own, made up of individuals with complementary skills, knowledge and abilities.
- The number of virtual teams, where members work apart rather than in proximity, will grow.
- Layers of management will continue to shrink, made possible by email, video conferencing and other technology.
- Despite the Asian economic problems, Pacific Rim economic growth is expected to exceed that of the rest of the world.
- Technology will drive economic growth and continue to change our working world.
- Corporate ethics will emerge as a prime consideration of stakeholders, including employees and customers.
- Good corporate citizenship (enterprises taking an active part in improving the quality of life in the communities that they and their customers live and work in) will provide a competitive edge.

Figure 1.4 contrasts the 'good old days', characterised by predictability and protectionism, with today's operating environment, marked by uncertainty and fierce competition. These changes are making our organisations more vulnerable and difficult to guide. It is no wonder that many managers in all sectors and at every level feel beleaguered and besieged.

....

FIGURE 1.4   CHANGES AFFECTING ORGANISATIONS

The 'good old days'	The situation today
■ Protected domestic markets, through tariffs and import quotas	■ Open markets and severe competition
■ Regulated finance industry (e.g. characterised by 'cheap money' to business)	■ Deregulated finance industry and 'expensive money'
■ Fixed and predictable exchange rates	■ Floating and unpredictable exchange rates
■ Regulated labour market	■ Deregulated labour market
■ Europe and America tended to influence business methods and trade	■ Unpredictable and fluctuating share market
■ Liberal/National parties stood for capital and Labor Party stood for labour	■ Japan and Asia/Pacific influence business methods and trade
■ Economy based on agriculture, raw materials and manufacturing	■ Labor, Liberal and National parties all stand for capital and commerce
■ Bureaucratic, hierarchical organisation structures based on the old military model	■ Economy based on service and information
	■ Flatter and simpler organisational structures with fewer people at middle management levels

The challenge

Managers at all levels in all sectors will need to understand and manage these issues. First-line managers are becoming increasingly essential in instigating and managing change, introducing workplace improvements and ensuring that productivity and quality standards are met efficiently and effectively. They must:

• become better at anticipating, recognising and dealing with emerging trends and their implications;
• improve their ability to identify and respond to potential opportunities and threats from the environment, especially those from competing organisations;
• find ways to provide better service to their customers, both inside and outside the organisation;
• find ways of encouraging all members of an organisation to support fully the changes that will need to be made to ensure survival and prosperity;
• adopt an 'innovation focus' to keep up with opportunities and make continual improvements to the way results are achieved;
• learn to be flexible and comfortable with change;
• understand and use technology; and
• have a continuous learning and development orientation.

If we are to remain prosperous and retain our high standard of living, we must rise to these challenges. Yet the transition from the old to the new is difficult for many people whose world views, values, skills and attitudes have all been shaped in a very different environment. We need to adopt new 'mind-sets', or paradigms: ways of looking at the world. Box 1.13 summarises some of the old and new paradigms.

These new paradigms will affect all organisations and all employees and will have a significant impact on every supervisor's role. Issues such as *award restructuring, enterprise bargaining, industrial democracy, training, retraining* and *multiskilling,* and *health, safety* and *environmental issues* will continue to dominate management's thinking and activities in the

BOX **1.13** OLD AND NEW PARADIGMS

●●

Old paradigms	*New paradigms*
■ one-off learning	■ continuous, lifelong learning; learning organisations
■ authoritarian management practices	
■ chain of command	■ open management practices
■ 'scientific management': we can control people and find the 'one best way'	■ flexible organisations, particularly multifunctional teams
■ control	■ empowered teams manage themselves and their processes
■ coercion	
■ decision by command	■ commitment
■ cost control	■ cooperation
■ periodic improvements	■ decision by consensus
■ 'us' and 'them'	■ innovation
■ hierarchy	■ continuous improvements
	■ us together
	■ synergy

future. *Total quality management (TQM)*, *customer service excellence, benchmarking* and *re-engineering* will remain important in increasing our competitiveness. Concepts such as *empowerment, knowledge management* and *learning organisation* will take on deeper meaning and fresh importance in the supervisor's job.

THE **BIG** PICTURE

- How can we meet customer demands for ever-higher quality and service?
- How can we attract and retain the best people?
- How can we best compete successfully in a global marketplace?
- How can we make most effective use of emerging technologies?
- How can we meet or exceed our stakeholders' evolving expectations?
- How can we continually update and make best use of the skills of all our employees?
- How can we motivate and manage people who are located away from us?

THE MODERN SUPERVISOR

The changing work environment means that the skills, attributes and qualities required of the workforce at all levels will continually expand. Let's see what this means for the supervisor.

The old world: yesterday's circumstances, yesterday's supervisors

In yesterday's world there was little need for inspiration and leadership. It was not uncommon to appoint someone to a supervisory position as a reward based on length of service, or to promote a good performer or popular figure to the position of supervisor. As a result, 'yesterday's supervisors' often moved from the role of a worker one day to that of a supervisor the next with no preparation or training.

Not trained in how to supervise others, they often adopted the supervisory style of their predecessor or other managers. A general management style that we could describe as *autocratic*, *directing* and *controlling* passed down from one generation of managers to the next. All this is changing. Box 1.14 contrasts the skills and roles of yesterday's supervisor with a modern supervisor.

Tomorrow's supervisor

As we've seen, rapid and unpredictable change characterises today's work and social environments. What might have worked yesterday is unlikely to work in today's vastly different environment. We can no longer structure organisations and manage people as we did 'yesterday'. Tomorrow's managers, like tomorrow's organisations, will be distinctly different.

They will have broad management skills and styles, which they will continually adapt and develop. They will manage in inclusive ways and work cooperatively with people from many cultures, with a workforce composed of both sexes and from varying backgrounds.

YESTERDAY'S SUPERVISOR, TODAY'S TEAM LEADER

Yesterday's supervisor	Today's team leader
■ director	■ leader
■ controller	■ facilitator
■ examiner	■ coach
■ superior	■ mentor
■ overseer	■ coordinator
■ commander	■ helper
■ inspector	■ trainer
■ all-powerful	■ empowerer
■ order-giver	■ delegator
■ competitor	■ cooperator
■ administrator	■ enabler
■ manage through fear and compliance	■ manage through spirit and enthusiasm
■ controller	■ communicator

They will deal skilfully with a complex and rapidly changing environment. They will structure their organisations in a variety of flexible ways to compete effectively in an unpredictable global environment and marketplace.

Some of 'tomorrow's supervisors' are already here. Here is what they have to say:

'In this job, you have to remove the hurdles, the things that stop people from doing the good job they want to do, the things that frustrate them— the hassles! That's my job: to make the job of the team hassle-free!'

'I think it's important to emphasise the positive. To "catch people doing something right", as they say.'

'I work to build a team that works well together and helps each other out. I want them to respect each other, trust each other and innovate. And I want them to have fun while they do it!'

'If someone makes a mistake, I treat it as a learning experience. We sit down and figure out what went wrong so it won't happen again. Then we see if there's anything else we can learn from it. After all, no one intentionally makes a mistake, right?'

'I think of myself as a life-long learner; I call it the 3-L principle of life. It's really important we don't get caught up in a rut and that we continually look for better ways to do things. The Japanese call it kaizen ...'

'I work with my team. We do things together: solve problems, make decisions, get the job done. I oversee the process but basically the way I see it is: We're all in this together!'

THE 21ST CENTURY

Dramatic and rapid change is likely to persist well into the 21st century. We will continue to become a less industrialised society and more information and service based. Pressure on

THE **BIG** PICTURE
Unprecedented change? Was there ever a 'good old days'? The beginning of the 20th century heralded dramatic changes, too:
- the agrarian economy gave way to the industrial economy
- electricity transformed our lives
- railways brought our cities and the bush closer together
- the telephone revolutionised communication

the first-line manager to increase productivity and lead in a more participative, consultative way will persist. Technological advances will proceed in leaps and bounds. Work patterns will continue to change dramatically. Our economy will be volatile until it adjusts and gives way to a global economy. Competition, both at home and abroad, will carry on.

Long-term planning will become even more imperative. 'Either/or' thinking will give way to multiple options. In our political and organisational institutions, the trend of decentralisation is likely to continue. Flatter and simpler organisation structures mean that networking will replace traditional hierarchies as a means of getting things done. As the backgrounds, training, education and expectations of employees continue to change, people will expect more opportunities to participate in decisions that affect their working lives. We are likely to see increasing government deregulation, a far more diverse workforce at all levels, and promotion based on talent and performance as we move through the new century. Consumer spending and demands will continue to change. Sensitivity to environmental issues will increasingly become a focus.

Most of us will face one or more major career changes—not just job changes but entire career changes—before the end of our working lives. Technology will have increasingly greater impacts on our lives as computers and other aids become more available and necessary if we are to maintain or grow our competitive position in the world.

RESPONSIBILITIES TO STAKEHOLDERS

What is the primary duty of management? To deliver profits to shareholders? To reduce costs? To nurture an organisation so it will survive in the long term? To provide meaningful work? To make a contribution to society?

Our ideas are changing. Organisations are increasingly seen as having responsibilities to several groups of people. These **stakeholders** are shown in Figure 1.5.

Responsibility to owners

An organisation's first duty is generally considered to be to its proprietors. In the private sector, this is the shareholders, private individuals as well as institutional investors, who invest in an organisation to make money. We can regard taxpayers as 'owners' in the public sector because it is they who fund the operations through their taxes. In a not-for-profit organisation, we can think of those individuals and organisations who contribute funds to its operations as the 'owners'.

FIGURE 1.5 THE RESPONSIBLE MANAGER

These 'owners' want a fair return for their investment. In the private sector, this is profit. For public and not-for-profit organisations, a satisfactory service might be considered a fair return. 'Owners' also want to know their investment is being prudently managed.

Senior management determines the guiding principles and strategies that will provide owners with the best return on their investment. First-line managers are directly concerned with the most efficient production of the organisation's end product or service. Supervisors' responsibility to owners, then, is to operate their department in such a manner as to give the most satisfactory return on owners' investment.

Responsibility to employees

As society changes, people's expectations of work and the workplace itself changes. Organisations need employees to be more flexible in their work skills and job performance. Employees want more flexible and supportive working arrangements.

These changes mean that supervisors are playing an increasingly important role in ensuring that employees have clear and specific goals to work towards, are properly trained, are using their skills and abilities to the fullest and are given the organisational support they need to do their jobs well. Supervisors also have a responsibility to see that each employee is treated fairly and to safeguard their job satisfaction, health, safety and well-being.

Responsibility to customers and/or clients

A supervisor's basic responsibility to customers is to help the organisation produce a product or provide a service that customers or clients want, at a price they are willing to pay. Supervisors also have a responsibility to customers for the integrity and quality of their organisation's product or service. This responsibility entails a continual striving to improve products or services so that they continually represent better value for the customer and, in turn, enhance the organisation's reputation.

Responsibility to suppliers

Many organisations aim to forge genuine **trading partnerships** with their suppliers based on open and trusting relationships. They believe that strength comes from mutually beneficial relationships. As more organisations 'contract out' for services such as accounting, training, computing, maintenance, and so on, this holds true for both suppliers of materials and suppliers of services.

Supervisors are responsible for developing and maintaining cooperative relationships with people from supplier organisations.

Responsibility to the wider society and government

Business ethics and **corporate citizenship** refer to the fact that organisations also have responsibilities to their community beyond mere compliance with local, state and federal government legislation and regulation. Phrases like the *triple bottom line* are being heard more and more. This phrase incorporates an organisation's impact on:

1. society
2. the environment
3. the economy.

Currently, triple-bottom-line reporting is a voluntary form of disclosure. Many believe it is also an opportunity to deflect pressure from special interest groups, avoid costly and damaging public relations fiascos and establish a competitive advantage. A reputation for good corporate citizenship can be a genuine method of differentiating an organisation from its competitors and building a loyal customer base.

All managers have an important role to play in ensuring that their actions conform not only to the letter of the law but also to its spirit. In particular, this places a responsibility on supervisors to be aware of laws that affect people in the workplace—equal opportunity, health, safety and welfare, and environmental controls. Corporate citizenship also involves concerns such as human rights, family-friendly workplaces, environmental protection and community development.

Responsibility to the closer community

Think globally   To be successful, organisations must be globally focused, for the world holds both our marketplace and our competitors.

Act locally   Organisations must also be 'good neighbours', responsible and active members of their closer community.

Supervisors have a responsibility to help their organisation do both.

Philanthropy Australia says about one-quarter of donations comes from the corporate sector. Companies like Body Shop, Rio Tinto, and the AMP and RACV Foundations are well known for their charitable contributions. Westpac Bank is one of Australia's largest corporate donors: its Community 2000 program and other community and business sponsorships give away over $8 million a year. They view their contributions as giving back to the community where their employees and their customers live and where they make their money.

HOW CAN YOU LEARN TO SUCCEED AS A SUPERVISOR?

Learn to manage yourself. How well do you manage time? How well do you manage stress? Are you comfortable with change? Can you keep 'many irons in the fire'? How well do you understand your own motivations and 'operating style'? Which skills do you use well and which do you need to develop further?

Develop your communication skills. How well do you present face-to-face? To a group? In writing? How skilled are you in working with others to organise and monitor, solve problems, and make plans and decisions?

Develop your technical skills. Learn about the technology of your industry and talk to those in it to find out about its culture and patterns of work.

Experience will be a wonderful teacher if you are prepared to acknowledge and learn from your mistakes; as the saying goes:

'There are no mistakes, only feedback.'

Learn from others and make successful supervisors and managers your **role models**. How do they work with others and provide leadership? Hone your skills and knowledge through formal education, reading, attending training seminars, and listening to and learning from others.

Set specific and measurable goals for yourself with clear time-lines. If you know clearly where you're headed, you will get there more easily. Think about the skills you already have: technical skills, interpersonal skills and conceptual skills. Think about the useful qualities and characteristics you already possess. Look back through this chapter to identify other skills that you think will help you achieve your goals. Plan to develop and strengthen them. This is a lifetime journey with no finish line.

OPPORTUNITIES FOR SUPERVISORS

Supervision offers abundant opportunities to those prepared to accept the challenge. Every organisation is a potential source of employment and advancement. People who can manage themselves, lead others and achieve results are valuable to any organisation.

Simply wanting to become a supervisor won't make you one. Study, hard work, personal commitment, experience, and on- and off-the-job training must come first. Becoming a successful supervisor is a long but rewarding process.

Supervisors are special people. This book will help you to recognise and develop the skills you will need to be effective in this challenging and rewarding career.

RAPID REVIEW

	True	False
1. Supervisors don't need special skills or training other than how to do the work of their section.	☐	☑
2. Today's supervisor is just as likely to be called a team leader or department manager as a supervisor.	☑	☐
3. The role of the supervisor is becoming more important.	☑	☐
4. A supervisor's job is a varied and challenging one.	☑	☐
5. To be successful, a supervisor needs sound technical, conceptual and interpersonal skills.	☑	☐
6. Managerial roles are like 'hats' we put on according to the requirements of the situation we are in.	☑	☐
7. A manager's job can be said to revolve around four functions: planning, organising, leading and monitoring.	☑	☐
8. Senior managers plan within longer time frames than first-line managers and they need to use more conceptual skills.	☑	☐
9. Today's supervisor could be called autocratic, directing and controlling.	☐	☑

	True	False
10. Being a supervisor is a totally different job to being a manager.	☐	☑
11. Change from all directions is affecting the job of the supervisor.	☑	☐
12. The skills a supervisor needed 30 or 40 years ago are basically the same skills that a supervisor needs today.	☐	☑

APPLY YOUR KNOWLEDGE

1. Based on the information provided in this chapter and other research you are able to do, develop a profile of the typical Australian supervisor and describe this person's strengths and weaknesses.
2. The supervisor's position has sometimes been referred to as 'the meat in the sandwich'. Why would this be so?
3. Write a short essay explaining the technical, conceptual and interpersonal skills needed by supervisors, providing some examples of each.
4. Brainstorm a list of the main qualities and attributes of an 'ideal modern supervisor', explaining your reasons.
5. Explain the five management functions that have traditionally described a manager's role.
6. Prepare a diagram relating the activities a supervisor carries out in a typical day to the roles a manager undertakes and to the five managerial functions discussed in this chapter.
7. Prepare a diagram, visual or symbolic representation that distinguishes between senior, middle and first-line management in terms of their duties and job titles.
8. Describe and contrast the role of 'yesterday's supervisor' with 'tomorrow's supervisor'. Summarise the factors that have led to these changes. What are some of the main issues supervisors must deal with today that they didn't deal with 30 years ago?
9. Write a short essay or draw a sketch explaining the differences between leading, managing and supervising, as you understand them.
10. List and give examples of the stakeholders to whom supervisors are responsible.

DEVELOP YOUR SKILLS

Individual activities

1. Interview a practising supervisor in your college or organisation to find out what they do during a typical working day. List their activities under the headings of *interpersonal skills*, *technical skills* and *conceptual skills*. Which of the roles identified by Mintzberg do they carry out? Find out how they view their responsibilities to their organisation's owners, its customers or clients, employees, suppliers, the wider society and the closer community. Based on your discussion, list the qualities and attributes you believe your interviewee possesses as a supervisor. What is his or her job title?

2. 'Being a supervisor is hard work.' Do you agree? Why, or why not? Provide examples to illustrate your reasons.

3. 'Being a supervisor is common sense. I treat people the way I want to be treated.' To what extent is this 'the whole story'?

4. Should supervisors be a part of the teams they lead? Should there be a line between 'friend' and 'boss'? If so, where and how should it be drawn? Provide two or three examples to illustrate your position.

5. What special problems might exist when a person is promoted to supervise the team they were once part of?

6. In the chapter it was stated that a supervisor needs to have integrity. What does this mean? Think of a scenario that would indicate a supervisor lacks integrity. What would the ultimate results be? Think of a scenario where a supervisor displays integrity. How would integrity affect a person's ability to supervise effectively?

7. It was also stated in the chapter that good supervisors have 'charisma'. What does this mean? Who do you know who has charisma? List three things about this person that indicates to you he or she has charisma.

8. Relate the skills, qualities and characteristics needed to be a successful supervisor to your own situation. Use this information to benchmark your own skills and attributes. Identify five areas you intend to work on personally to improve your own supervisory abilities. Make sure these are clear and specific. When you have identified five areas, develop an overall strategy to follow over the next three or four months that will develop your skills and knowledge in the areas you have targeted. You may want to refer to Box 1.8.

9. Refer to the information in the chapter on what a supervisor does in a typical day. Relate these activities to the managerial roles identified by Mintzberg. Relate them to the five managerial functions. You might want to draw up a matrix or a checklist.

10. Relate the five managerial functions of planning, organising, staffing, leading and monitoring to the role of a homemaker. Relate them to the activities you carry out in your own life. Relate them to the activities of a senior manager and contrast them with the activities of a supervisor.

11. Obtain a copy of an organisation chart from an organisation you know about (e.g. your college, where a friend or relative works, or where you work). Identify each of the three levels of management on this chart. Save the chart to use again in Chapter 4.

12. What do you believe a supervisor should do if the interests of the shareholders seem to conflict with the interests of the employees? An example of this might occur when the most economical way to do a job is less safe than another way. Which stakeholder group should take precedence? Is there really a conflict in the case outlined here?

13. Can you recall the Olympic 'ticketing fiasco' that was reported in the media in Spring 1999? Write a short essay discussing this situation in relation to the responsibilities an organisation's management has to its various stakeholders.

14. How can the paradigm 'There are no mistakes, only feedback' be useful to you personally? Give some examples of situations in which it might be useful.

15. Do you recall your first few days as a supervisor? What were your feelings and thoughts? What were you most concerned about? What were you most looking forward to? Write a short essay describing this. If you have never supervised, what do you think your initial feelings, thoughts, concerns and hopes will be?

Group activities

1. Interview someone who has been responsible for the work of others (a supervisor) for five or more years. Find out as much as you can about their job; then report your conclusions back to your study group and compare them with others' conclusions. What is the most common job title? How do their duties and responsibilities compare?

   Some questions you might want to follow up are:
   - What is their job title?
   - Has it changed over the past few years?
   - What are their main responsibilities?
   - How has their job changed over the last few years?
   - What do they like best and least about their job?
   - What is the most challenging part of their job? The most rewarding?
   - What training have they received to do their job?
   - What training do they believe all supervisors should have in order to do their job well?
   - Do they feel as if they are part of the management team? Why, or why not?
   - Do they ever feel as if they're the 'meat in the sandwich'? Why, or why not?
   - What is the biggest single lesson they have learned as a supervisor?

2. In small groups, adapt Box 1.8 on the competent supervisor into questions to assess the competency of a full- or part-time student of management. Use this to determine your own competencies as a student!

3. Using Mintzberg's role descriptions as a basis, interview a first-line manager to find out as much as you can about what their job entails. Prepare a report for your class relating what this person does to Mintzberg's roles.

4. Box 1.7 shows ANTA's competency model of the first-line manager. In small groups, develop a one or two sentence example or description of each Theme and Unit. If you can, write these descriptions so they reflect a supervisory setting.

5. What technical, interpersonal and conceptual skills do you think a successful student of supervision needs? Discuss this in your study group and make a list that summarises your thoughts.

6. Compare your answer to question 4 of *Individual activities* with others in your class. What is the general consensus?

7. How would you describe an 'ideal supervisor' in your organisation? Compare this with other people's descriptions.

Marg's Big Chance

Daniel had been production supervisor of a hearing aid manufacturing facility for seven years. Under his supervision it had grown to become Australia's largest and most modern hearing aid manufacturing operation.

When the general manager left to pursue his career with another organisation, Daniel was invited to apply for the position. Something that would factor heavily in this promotion would be whether he had trained a suitable replacement to supervise production.

Marg Thiele was the obvious choice. In her four years as section leader of the assembly section, she had shown herself to be loyal, dependable and competent. She had a good way with people and the assemblers respected her knowledge, experience and enthusiasm.

Daniel would now need to discuss the possible opening with her. He wondered how he should describe the role of production supervisor and whether he would need to 'sell' Marg on its benefits—after all, it was a demanding and challenging role.

Questions

1   How should Daniel describe the role of supervising? What general approach should he take?
2   What management skills and abilities should he stress as being the most important? Why?
3   What do you think the company's reasoning was when it considered whether Daniel had trained a replacement for his own role?

Geoff's Retirement

It was time to enjoy the rewards of his long years of hard work. After 27 years as the hospital's catering superintendent, Geoff was about to retire.

As he contemplated his imminent departure, he looked back over his career. It had been a long and rewarding one, now that he had the benefit of hindsight. He had made many mistakes—especially in the early days—and he had learned a good many lessons the hard way. He'd seen a lot of changes, too, not only in how things were done, but also in the way people expected to be treated by management.

Many managers and many workers had come and gone in Geoff's time and he liked to think he had represented a force for stability in the hospital. His years of experience combined with a willingness to accept new ideas had helped take it through the bad times and into its current modern high-tech, 'customer focus' era. And, he reflected, he'd contributed quite a few of those good ideas himself.

His staff, colleagues and management respected him. He'd trained a replacement thoroughly and Judy was now ready to step into his shoes. He'd taught her everything he could about 'captaining a tight ship' where the crew worked hard and well together and had fun doing it.

As he mulled over the trials, tribulations and triumphs of supervising, Geoff realised it had been a significant source of learning and development for himself as a person. Not only had it taught him a host of management skills but, more importantly, it had taught him a lot about people—himself included.

Questions

1 If you had the opportunity, what three questions would you ask Geoff about how to be a good supervisor?
2 How would you assess Geoff's strengths as a supervisor?
3 What training would Geoff have had to provide in order to make Judy a successful supervisor?

Answers to Rapid Review questions

1. F   2. T   3. T   4. T   5. T   6. T   7. F   8. T   9. F   10. F   11. T   12. F

CHAPTER 2

THE COMMUNICATION FOUNDATION

Talk, talk, talk

Aldo studied the time log he had been keeping for the past week and was astonished to see that he spent about 80% of his working day 'communicating'. Communicating to his staff, his manager, other supervisors; communicating to people in other sections and departments of the organisation; communicating to people outside the organisation; communicating on the telephone, in group meetings, individual discussions and interviews; communicating in writing through memos, emails, reports, proposals ... the list was endless!

Next, he turned his attention to the checklists he had been keeping of complaints and rework from his section. It looked as though communication may well be at the bottom of many of those, too.

Faced with the difficulties caused by poor communication and the massive amount of time he spent each day simply getting messages across to people and understanding the messages of others, Aldo decided he would need to become better at this business of communication. But how?

Most managers spend 75%–90% of their time in one of the four communication modes (writing, reading, speaking, listening), so you would think they'd be good at it. Yet poor communication is at the bottom of most misunderstandings and problems, minor and major. In this chapter we look at the process of communication, face-to-face and in writing. You will see how important it is that you are clear about your purpose so that you can structure and present your information and communicate it clearly and persuasively. The better you communicate, the better you will supervise.

- What is the supervisor's role in effective communication?
- What is involved in giving good information?
- What is involved in gathering good information?
- What can supervisors do to improve communication?

- What can you do to become a better listener?
- How can you improve your body language and other non-verbal communication signals you send out?
- When should you communicate in writing?
- How can you write acceptably for business?

WITHOUT COMMUNICATION, NOTHING HAPPENS

As Box 2.1 shows, supervising revolves around communicating. Supervisors need to be able to *give good information*: explain the goals to be achieved, the work to be done, discuss who will do it, show employees how it should be done, and so on. The other side of the coin is *gathering good information*: skilful listening, questioning and observing to uncover peoples' feelings, thoughts, motivations, ideas and opinions.

Just as good communication can unite a group of employees and help them work as a team, it can also weld the various parts of an organisation together into an enterprising, efficient and effective whole:

- Effective communication between an organisation and its customers helps it to provide more useful products or services.
- Effective communication between sales and production departments helps production plan to meet anticipated requirements more efficiently and helps salespeople give more accurate information to customers.

BOX 2.1 CONSTANT COMMUNICATION

Written	Verbal	Electronic
Memos	Formal group meetings	Emails
Reports	Scheduled face-to-face meetings/ interviews	Internet information
Faxes	Impromptu face-to-face meetings	Electronic group conferences
Letters	Scheduled phone conversations	Virtual meetings, e.g.
Circulars	Impromptu phone conversations	videoconferences
Journals	Voice mail	
Proposals	Teleconferencing	

- Effective communication between finance, research and development, and marketing helps an organisation develop strategies to meet market demands.
- Effective communication between supervisors, employees and safety representatives helps an organisation to operate more safely and economically.

Communication is a vital and constant component of organisational life. Whether written, oral or symbolic, it serves to transmit information from one person (or group) to another person (or group). Box 2.2 shows some of the many ways we can communicate with others (and ourselves) at work.

BOX 2.2 TYPES OF COMMUNICATION

Interorganisational	Communication between organisations, e.g. customer/supplier negotiations or negotiations to acquire another company
Intraorganisational	Communication within an organisation, e.g. meetings or discussions between departments
Intergroup	Communication between groups within an organisation
Intragroup	Communication within a group
Interpersonal	Communication between individuals
Intrapersonal	We even talk to ourselves, e.g. to help us remember something or think something through

---

THE COMMUNICATION CLIMATE

Sadly, most employees tell us that poor communication causes more organisational problems than any other issue. It is the most quoted cause of organisational frustration and failure to perform.

What is the communication climate in your organisation or in some of the groups you belong to? In other words, what is the nature and content of upward, downward, lateral and external communication?

While everyone in an organisation communicates, management sets the tune for this climate. How well they establish open and clear communication with each other, employees and other stakeholders sets the stage for how fruitfully ideas and information are exchanged

---

THE **BIG** PICTURE

Paradoxically, a number of trends are making organisational communication more difficult and more important. The number of full-time employees is decreasing as many organisations downsize while the number of part-time and contract workers is increasing. Relationships with suppliers and customers are becoming more important and community expectations are increasingly reflecting a 'triple bottom line'. How can organisations improve the quality of their communications both internally and externally?

throughout the entire organisation and with external suppliers and customers. The effectiveness of the resulting communication affects the organisation's morale, productivity and, ultimately, its success.

First-line managers set the scene for the type of communication that will take place in their department and with other departments. This also directly influences quality, output and morale .

THE SUPERVISOR'S ROLE IN EFFECTIVE COMMUNICATION

As the link in the communication chain between their own and other departments in the organisation and between management and workers, supervisors need to be good communicators.

Particular communication responsibilities of supervisors include:
- ensuring that all members of their group understand their own, each other's and their department's objectives;
- ensuring that members of their group understand what the organisation stands for, where it is heading and how they contribute to this 'big picture';
- ensuring all members of their group understand their department's and the organisation's procedures and regulations;
- ensuring that all members of their team are able to carry out their duties;
- establishing a climate where employees feel free to ask questions, contribute ideas and challenge the status quo;
- explaining the organisation's changing requirements of its employees; and
- communicating the needs and requirements of their work team to senior management.

FROM THEORY TO PRACTICE

Answer each of the following questions and think of some recent examples that support your claim.
- Are you well informed?
- Do you put your brain into gear before opening your mouth by thinking about what you are going to say and how you can say it most effectively?
- Are you consistent, or do you say one thing today and something different tomorrow?
- Do you work to build the mutual trust and respect that are the foundation of open, honest communication?
- Are you clear in your communications, never leaving people wondering: 'What did s/he really mean by that?'

THE COMMUNICATION PROCESS

Have you communicated once you've told someone something? The answer is 'no'! As you have probably experienced, successful communication does not always take place when people talk. As Figure 2.1 shows, a message needs to be transmitted clearly and decoded

FIGURE 2.1   A TWO-WAY MODEL OF THE COMMUNICATION PROCESS

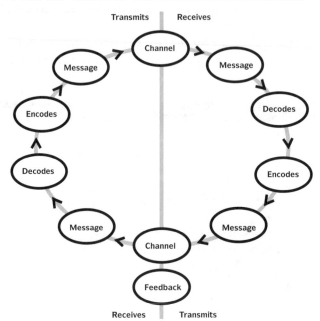

(interpreted) correctly. To be transmitted clearly, it needs to be encoded accurately; this includes words and other symbols and, if communication is face-to-face, body language. A multitude of barriers that are always present must be overcome in order to encode and decode a message correctly.

True communication involves the transfer of information and understanding from one person (or group) to another. It is successful only when the *receiver* understands it in the way the *sender* intended.

The sad truth is that what we believe we have said is not really important. What is important is the message that is received. If the message received is not the same as the message we sent, *unintended communication*, or *miscommunication*, has occurred. If it is the same, we have succeeded: *intended communication* has taken place.

Does this mean that we must agree with everything people say? Again, the answer is 'no'! We don't have to *agree* with the message—we just need to *understand* it.

Figure 2.2 shows the *process of communication*. The speaker sends a message to another person or group. The signal must pass through physical and environmental barriers such as noise or distance, which make it more difficult to receive. It must also penetrate barriers within the receiver who will sift, sort and often distort the message based on their understanding and interpretation of the signals, their own previous experience and their mind-set and existing beliefs. Will the communication succeed? It depends on how successfully both sender and receiver can overcome the external and internal barriers.

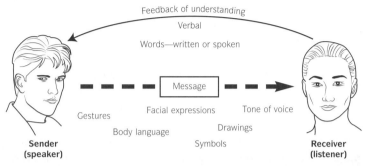

FIGURE 2.2   EFFECTIVE COMMUNICATION INVOLVES THE TRANSMISSION OF AN IDEA FROM A SENDER TO A RECEIVER WITHOUT A CHANGE OF MEANING

COMMUNICATION BARRIERS

Communication barriers disrupt the flow of information and waste time, money and goodwill. They cause output to fall, teamwork to break down and morale to drop. Box 2.3 shows the top ten communication barriers that supervisors face. Recognising and overcoming them will help you become a more effective communicator and a better supervisor.

BOX 2.3 SUPERVISORS' TOP TEN COMMUNICATION BARRIERS

1. Language

The words we choose, the way we structure a sentence and the way we say it can all be major obstacles to effective communication. Outsiders seldom understand *jargon* (specialised technical terms or phrases). *Slang* can also hinder communication if others do not know its meaning.

Some words are emotive, some neutral, some vague, others pompous. Many words have several meanings, while others are open to different interpretations or have different connotations. Think of the many possible meanings and responses to the words 'police', 'order' and 'nuclear'. The different emotions and images that are stirred by an individual's perception of such words will greatly affect the communication process. How many meanings of the word 'supervise' can you think of? (Roget's *Thesaurus* lists more than 13.)

'Killer phrases', or negative statements, often block communication. They dismiss an idea or suggestion without explaining why and often make the person who offered the idea feel put down. Expressions such as 'That will never work' or 'No way!' discourage people from coming up with ideas. Have you ever used any of the killer phrases shown in Box 2.4?

2. Perceptions, prejudice and stereotyping

People tend to hear what they expect to hear, see what they expect to see and think what they have always thought. We all tend to ignore things that don't fit into our

Continued . . .

pattern of expectations, or reshape them so that they do fit our mind-set. Do you think supervisors need the 'strength' to tell others what to do, that they should be obeyed without question? Or do you see their role as needing stamina and patience to talk through contentious issues and find solutions that satisfy all concerned? How you see the role of a supervisor will guide how you communicate as a supervisor, and to other supervisors.

Some supervisors think all workers are basically lazy and only come to work for the money; others believe that most people want to do a fair day's work for a fair day's pay. Such perceptions will cause supervisors to communicate differently with different employees.

People usually evaluate what they hear in relation to their own position, background, previous experiences and perceptions. If employees think of supervisors as the 'enemy' they will be predisposed to disagree with whatever they say. If they see supervisors as experts, they will listen closely and receptively to what they say.

Prejudging a person or a situation usually 'leaks' through in our communications. For example, deciding who or what is at fault for a spoiled production batch or a customer complaint before hearing all the facts, closes our minds and cuts off communication. We'll never hear what really happened.

If we think we know just what a person is going to think, do or say because we've 'met their type before', or because all people of that 'sort' are the same, we will communicate our attitudes and beliefs in subtle ways. Those concerned will begin to behave in the ways we expect and may even give up trying to communicate with us at all. People tend to rise or sink to meet others' expectations.

Stereotyping and prejudice can result in what we call the **Pygmalion effect** or the **halo/horns effect**. As the names imply, this effect can work towards positive as well as negative ends. If we treat people in a manner that implies we expect the best of them, we will often get it. On the other hand, if we indicate, even in the most subtle way, that we don't expect much from someone, that is probably what we will get too.

3. Self-image

Our **self-image** is how we see ourselves: professional or amateur, strong or weak, eloquent or inarticulate, friendly or shy, confident or anxious. Our self-image is reflected in what we say and do and colours our communications, whether as receivers or senders. A poor self-image is a significant barrier to effective communication and successful supervision.

4. Status

Status, or a person's position in terms of power or importance in an organisation, can also be a barrier to clear communication. It can restrict people from speaking freely to those 'up' or 'down' the 'ladder'. In the presence of a senior executive, for example, some employees may not feel able to express their thoughts, ideas or dissatisfactions openly and clearly.

Continued . . .

5. Incongruity

Sometimes a person's body language doesn't support their words. This causes a communication *incongruity*. When this occurs, most people believe a person's body language and their own eyes, over their ears and the other person's words. Can you imagine a supervisor saying: 'You did a great job there!' in a sarcastic tone of voice or while walking away and looking away from the person?

6. Individual factors

Sometimes we need to take physical abilities into account when communicating with others. For example, we may need to speak up or speak more clearly when communicating with a person who is hard of hearing, or we may need to make an effort to match the height level of a person confined to a wheelchair. Accommodations such as these can greatly reduce physical barriers and lay the foundations for good communication.

People in one age group often have different values and world views from those in other age groups. A 'generation gap' can make it difficult for people to understand each other's point of view, which increases the chances of miscommunication. Similar gaps can exist when people from different cultures and even backgrounds come together.

7. Environmental barriers

Noise, interruptions and distractions can get in the way of clear and complete communication. They steal our attention and can make communication all but impossible.

When the communicators are not face-to-face, misunderstanding can occur more easily. This is because we cannot see the expressions, gestures and other signals that help communicate the true meaning of a message. It also makes it more difficult to establish rapport, ask questions, check out meanings or express confusion.

8. Time and timing

In today's pared-down organisations, people often don't have the time to communicate thoroughly and ensure they've been understood. In their rush, they might give an incomplete, unclear or poorly thought-out message.

Poor timing can also cause a communication to fail. Should a supervisor explain a new procedure to an employee who is just about to rush home and begin annual leave?

9. Message complexity

Information that supervisors need to give can be very complex. Sometimes, the sheer volume of information causes overload.

10. Listening

The supervisor's lament is: Why don't people listen!! We examine how to encourage people to listen later in this chapter.

BOX **2.4** **KILLER PHRASES**

- It won't work.
- We haven't time.
- We're not ready for it yet.
- Good idea but our department is different.
- That's all right in theory, but can you put it into practice?
- We've tried it before.
- Too hard to administer.
- It's against our policy.
- Come on, let's be practical.
- We've never done it like that.
- It's not in the budget.
- The experienced people won't use it.

- Let's get back to reality.
- Let's form a committee.
- It's too academic.
- Who do you think you are?
- You haven't considered …
- It needs more thought.
- Don't be ridiculous.
- Let's not step on their toes.
- That's too modern/old-fashioned.
- Let's discuss it some other time.
- You don't understand enough about it.
- We're too small/big for that.
- You must be joking!

AVOIDING COMMUNICATION BREAKDOWNS

Effective supervisors are aware of the obstacles that threaten successful communication, and take steps to overcome them. Otherwise, these barriers would play havoc with their effectiveness and peace of mind.

Avoiding communication breakdowns takes common sense, practice and effort. Here are some guidelines for hurdling the barriers to clear communication. We all use them occasionally. The trouble is, most of us don't use them often enough.

Ask for feedback

As Figures 2.1 and 2.2 show, feedback turns communication into a two-way process, with both sender and receiver actively trying to reach mutual understanding. Although feedback is essential to good communication, it is not always possible to get feedback immediately (e.g. with written communications).

Because face-to-face communication permits immediate feedback, it is usually a more reliable way to transmit ideas and information. This is why a great deal of business communication is oral (although it is often followed up in writing for confirmation or for future reference). Talking directly with a person allows us to ask questions to clear up any misunderstandings. When we're giving information, observing non-verbal feedback can give clues to how well the other person has understood us. When we're gathering information, it can help us clarify what someone is *really* saying.

Whether your message is oral or written, *encourage questions and comments* so that you can see and hear whether your message has been received and understood as you want it to be. *Use your eyes.* They are an important tool in good communication. Look for non-verbal signs of agreement, disagreement, surprise, hesitation, confusion or lack of understanding. Listen to tone of voice—this will often indicate the receiver's degree of agreement or commitment and will further reinforce the message.

Make time for feedback to give the receiver a chance to ask questions to clarify and build on or add to your ideas. When we establish an atmosphere that encourages two-way communication, people feel able to disagree and present alternatives. Since unspoken

FROM THEORY TO PRACTICE

How to encourage feedback

- The way you ask for feedback is important. If you say 'Do you understand?' the receiver is likely to say 'Yes' to avoid the embarrassment of looking stupid. That's why it is better to ask *what* a person understands. Use an **open question** (one that cannot be answered merely with a 'yes' or 'no') to encourage a full response. Then you can hear for yourself whether your message has been understood in the way you intended.
- If someone hasn't understood fully, make sure you don't make them feel embarrassed.
- Rephrase your message—saying something in a different way often helps get your message through. Try giving an example, building on existing knowledge or giving a demonstration.
- If this doesn't work, ask what in particular you need to clear up. See it as your responsibility to communicate clearly, not the other's responsibility to understand.

concerns and oppositions only grow and cultivate resentment, it is better to discuss them early on and reach an understanding. Employees will respect you more for encouraging and allowing two-way communication and feedback.

> 'If people do not understand you, fall down before them and beg their forgiveness, for in truth, you are to blame.'
>
> Dostoyevsky (1821–81)
> Russian novelist

Offer feedback

Offering feedback is an important supervisory skill. People need, and deserve, to know how they are doing and that their efforts are noticed and appreciated. Feedback is a great way to do this. Is their performance up to scratch? Is it excellent or merely acceptable? How could it be improved? Is the department as a whole meeting objectives? We discuss how to offer feedback in greater detail in Part III.

Consider your words

Long, complicated sentences and unfamiliar words confuse people. Speak and write to be understood, not to impress. Use 'plain English' to avoid the jargon barrier. Mentally review 'the six C's of communication' shown in Box 2.5 to help you choose the most suitable words. Simple, clear language goes a long way to achieving understanding.

Repeat, repeat, repeat

Repeating a message several times using different words, different expressions or different examples can help get your message through. Choose the number and type of repetitions to suit the other person's experience and background and the nature and complexity of the message.

<table>
<tr><td colspan="2">BOX **2.5** **THE SIX C's OF COMMUNICATION**</td></tr>
<tr>
<td>
■ Is it **C**lear?
■ Is it **C**omplete?
■ Is it **C**oncise?
</td>
<td>
■ Is it **C**oncrete?
■ Is it **C**orrect?
■ Is it **C**ourteous?
</td>
</tr>
</table>

You can repeat your message in subtle, but very effective ways. For example, you can use more than one channel of communication, such as confirming a telephone call with a memo or note.

Use empathy

Empathy means being able to see a situation as the other person sees it. To empathise with another, ask yourself: 'What must it be like for this person?' Trying to see things from the other's point of view makes us better communicators. What are their feelings, opinions, desires, concerns and attitudes?

Native Americans have an expression that explains empathy:

'**To truly understand another, we must walk a mile in their moccasins.
And before we can walk in another's moccasins,
we must first take off our own.**'

Empathising is not the same as agreeing or sympathising. To put yourself 'in another's shoes' means understanding how they feel. You don't have to agree with them in order to do this.

Empathy helps us understand the possible effects that our communication could have. Whether you are speaking to an employee for making too many personal phone calls or simply giving a reminder when tea break finishes, the way you express yourself and show your concern will have an effect on the way your message is received and understood.

To see how well you have understood the concept of empathy, think about how you would define these three words:

- Apathy: _non-feeling, lacking interest or understanding for another._
- Empathy: _To put yourself in anothers shoes - to see things from there point of view._
- Sympathy: _Sympathise - understand there problem and feel for there situation - Compassion._

Consider timing

Sometimes communications fail simply because of poor timing. You can overcome badly timed communications by asking for (or working out for yourself) specific times when your message would be most welcome or effective. Consider the consequences of poor timing and select the best time.

When you're in a hurry, consider also the consequences of a message not being received and acted on properly. You'll probably find it will be worth taking the extra few moments to communicate fully.

Be positive

Use *igniter phrases* instead of *killer phrases* (see Box 2.4). Which would you rather hear?

☺ *That won't work.*	☺ *That could work if …*
☺ *That isn't quite right.*	☺ *You're making great progress!*
☺ *Just put it over there for now.*	☺ *You're finished? That's great! Thanks very much!*
☺ *Where'd you get that idea?*	☺ *That's an interesting idea—let's try it!*

Select the location

When possible, talk somewhere that will encourage open communication. Talking over problems in a quiet area, free from noise and distractions, is much easier than trying to discuss difficulties in a noisy office or in the hustle and bustle of a busy factory. Talking in the cafeteria or going for a short walk through the factory might make communication flow more easily. You may not always be able to choose the best spot to talk, but try to choose a suitable location whenever possible.

Think it through first

Have you ever opened your mouth only to insert a foot? The more important or complex a communication is, the more we should think it through in advance.

Listen

Listening is another way to reduce communication barriers. Listening plus empathy helps avoid misunderstandings, arguments, delays and mistakes.

LISTENING: CRUCIAL TO GOOD COMMUNICATION

'Nature has given to man one tongue, but two ears,
that we may hear from others twice as much as we speak.'

Epictetus the Greek (AD 60–120)

Most of us spend about 30% of our days talking and 37% to 45% listening. We probably do more listening than just about any other human activity except breathing. But how well do we really listen?

Listening properly is hard work. It is all too easy to 'switch off' or listen only with 'half an ear' when we have other things on our mind. Do you ever not listen properly for any of the following reasons?

- You're not really interested in what the other person is saying.
- You 'turn off' because you don't like the speaker or the message.
- You assume in advance that what someone has to say is uninteresting or unimportant, or that you know what they are going to say.
- You ignore what someone is saying because it is in conflict with what you already 'know' or believe.
- You filter what you're hearing to select only the bits you want to hear.
- Distractions stop you from giving your full attention to the speaker.
- You think you have something more important to say and listen only for a point where you can break in.
- Your concentration wanders and you lose the thread of the message.

- You are waiting politely for a break in the flow of talk so that you can speak.
- You are mentally rehearsing what you will say as soon as the other person draws breath.
- You are waiting alertly for flaws in the other's argument that you can pounce on.
- You are mentally criticising the speaker's delivery instead of hearing their real message.
- You become angered or upset when you disagree with something someone says.
- You overreact to certain words or phrases.
- You focus only on trying to get your own point of view across.
- You'd rather be speaking than listening because it feels more 'in control' of the communication.
- You listen only for facts and not the feelings behind the facts.
- You pretend to be attentive while thinking about something else.
- You're busy daydreaming or clock-watching.

When you 'listen' like this, you're not going to receive the real message, however important it may be. Since people can usually sense when we are not giving them our full attention, poor listening creates its own barriers to full and clear communication.

Perseverance and willpower will overcome many of these listening traps. Following the 'how to listen effectively' diagram in Figure 2.3 will also help improve your listening skills.

'True listening is one of the greatest compliments we can pay a person.'

FIGURE 2.3   HOW TO LISTEN EFFECTIVELY

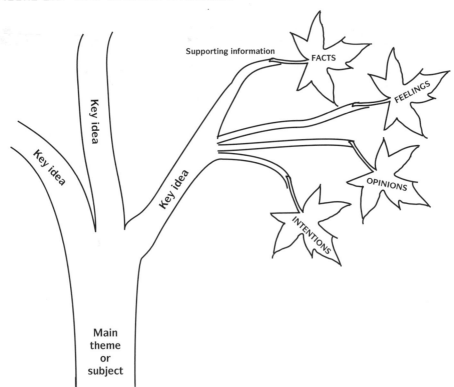

True listening is about trying to understand how other people see things and what the real meaning of their message is. It is hard work. If you don't believe that, consider this: when we listen hard, with concentration, with our eyes and hearts as well as our ears, our bodies undergo certain specific physiological changes. Our blood pressure, body temperature and pulse rate all increase. These are the same physiological changes that would occur if we were to step outside and dig a ditch or run a marathon.

Listening well is a skill that needs determination and practice. When we are really listening, our non-verbal behaviour will show the speaker that we are truly paying attention.

Do you need to improve your listening skills? Follow the tips in the *From theory to practice* section below.

FROM THEORY TO PRACTICE

Tips for better listening
- *Listen to the* words *a person is saying as well as* how *those words are being said*. This is listening with your heart and your eyes as well as with your ears.
- *Give the speaker your undivided attention*. This helps the speaker give you full information.
- *Beware of personal biases*. Even if you don't like a person's general approach or the subject being discussed, don't let this stop you from hearing what is being said. Listen to understand the message without letting biases or preferences, whether negative or positive, distort the real meaning.
- *Ignore mental distractions*. Thoughts wandering to a forthcoming meeting or concerns about an unresolved problem can block your ability to listen. Banish all extraneous thoughts; listen to fully understand the speaker's point of view and see things through their eyes. If papers on your desk are distracting you, put them to one side.
- *Ignore environmental distractions*. A noisy printer or photocopier, a ringing telephone or another conversation being held within earshot can easily steal your attention and break your concentration. If such distractions do interrupt, pull your thoughts back on track and ask questions. Have phone calls held, diverted or picked up by voice mail. The person doing the talking felt it was important enough to talk to you in the first place, so respond with your full attention.
- *Use your free mental time*. Because we can think three to four times faster than people speak, we can use our 'free mental time' to concentrate, evaluate and watch the body language of the speaker. Don't waste this opportunity. Think over what is being said carefully, rather than daydreaming or allowing your thoughts to wander.
- *Be alert to any implied meanings*. Getting the facts alone is not enough. An employee may tell you she is thinking of resigning to take a better job, yet after discussion you learn that the job she is considering is at a similar level of responsibility, with only slightly higher pay. The real difference seems to

Continued . . .

be that the new job will offer her more scope to try out new ideas. Listening 'between the lines' may lead you to conclude that she would stay with you if you could offer more creative opportunities. Only by truly listening will you be able to hear the 'real' message.

- *Don't interrupt or change the subject.* Just as interrupting people is discourteous, changing the subject is also impolite if someone is talking about something that is important to them. Remember:

> **'It is just as rude to step on someone's thoughts as it is to step on their toes!'**

- *Summarise often.* This will achieve four things. It will help you to keep your attention focused on what is being said. It will help you make sure you have understood the message in the way the sender intended it. It will give the speaker a chance to correct or clarify any points that need it. And it will show the speaker that you are listening, providing an incentive to continue communicating with you, then and at other times too.

- *Show you are listening.* You can do this non-verbally by nodding in appropriate places, by using eye contact or by repeating key words or phrases the speaker has used. This actually helps the speaker to continue—nobody likes talking to brick walls. Sitting on the edge of the chair and leaning slightly forward can keep you from becoming so comfortable that you begin to daydream.

- *Look at the speaker.* Don't let your eyes wander around the room, or look at the floor or out of the window. When your eyes wander, your mind will too. Watch people's eyes and other body language to pick up more about the meaning they are placing on their words.

- *Ask questions to clarify.* If you are unclear or unsure about what someone is trying to convey, help them communicate more clearly by asking questions. Most people want to make themselves clear and will appreciate your efforts to understand.

- *Clear up any unclear or ambiguous words.* There are four occasions when you might want to ask questions to help the speaker be more specific. The first is with vague words. For example, if someone says to you 'I want a better job', you might think to yourself: ' "Better" is an imprecise word; I wonder what "better" means to this person?' You could ask something like: 'What would make a job better for you?' or 'How would a job need to be different from your current job for it to be better?' The answer would give you an insight into what the speaker is looking for in a job.

Second, people sometimes use words that can be understood in different ways by different people. If this is the case, ask a question to clarify which meaning they intend.

Third, someone may use hazy generalisations or make comparisons. Generalisations such as 'Everyone knows ...' (who is 'everyone'?) or 'They all say ...' (who are 'they'?) are too vague to communicate much. Ask a question to find out what they mean.

Continued . . .

Finally, vague comparisons can be unhelpful and meaningless and sometimes we need more precise information: 'This is the best job I've ever had!' (What is 'best' about it? 'Better' than what other jobs?) Or 'That's the biggest botch-up I've ever seen!' (What precisely is wrong with it? If you are supposed to fix it, you'll need a clear idea of what is wrong.)

To listen well, you need a genuine desire to build empathy and understanding. It may be hard, and it certainly requires effort and practice, but the results are well worth it.

Poor listeners and proficient listeners

We can overcome most of the bad habits that poor listeners share by beginning—today—a concerted campaign against them. With practice and determination, we can also develop many good habits that effective listeners share.

Why not start now? Look at the characteristics of poor and effective listeners in Boxes 2.6 and 2.7 and circle two or three bad habits you intend to stop. Then circle two or three habits you intend to adopt to improve your listening skills.

BOX 2.6 THE BAD HABITS OF POOR LISTENERS

- Interrupting.
- Jumping to conclusions.
- Finishing others' sentences for them.
- Frequently (and often abruptly) changing the subject.
- Inattentive body language (tapping pencil, looking impatient).
- Not responding to what others have said.

- Failing to ask questions.
- Failing to give feedback.
- Failing to check out their understanding.
- Being easily distracted.
- Allowing communication barriers (discussed earlier) to interfere with good communication.
- Fidgeting.

BOX 2.7 THE GOOD HABITS OF EFFECTIVE LISTENERS

- Looking at the speaker in order to observe body language and pick up subtle nuances of speech.
- Asking questions.
- Summarising frequently, repeating in their own words what the speaker has said. This checks understanding and gives feedback that they are listening.
- Giving speakers time to articulate their thoughts.

- Remaining poised, calm and emotionally controlled.
- Responding with nods and 'uh-hums'.
- Looking alert and interested.
- Letting people finish what they are saying before giving their opinion.
- Checking their understanding by repeating the other's point of view before disagreeing.

Listening that helps, listening that hinders

Of the four types of listening, two are helpful and two are unhelpful. *Passive listening* and *interference listening* are unhelpful while *acknowledgment listening* and *active listening* are helpful.

Passive listening

We usually engage in passive listening when we are part of a large audience or watching television. We gaze at the speaker (or television set) but give no non-verbal signals or other forms of feedback to indicate that we have heard or understood.

This is fine in a theatre or while watching television, but it can be very disconcerting in one-to-one or small-group situations. Because of the damage **passive listening** can do to communication, it's best avoided.

Interference listening

We all have thoughts, feelings, ideas and opinions running through our minds as someone speaks. If we voice them, verbally or non-verbally, directly or indirectly, misunderstandings, misconceptions, frustration, irritation and communication breakdown are the likely results. This is because there is little empathy present in **interference listening**.

Look at the examples of interference listening in Box 2.8. No wonder it is often considered aggressive and disrespectful.

Acknowledgment listening

With **acknowledgment listening**, we make what we call *minimal encouragers*—eye contact, leaning slightly forward, nodding the head and making soft 'uh-huh' sounds to show we're following the speaker. This encourages the speaker to continue without disrupting their flow. It isn't surprising that acknowledgment listening gathers twice as much information as passive listening.

Its main drawback is that it provides little feedback to the speaker about whether your understanding is accurate.

> **'No one ever listened himself out of a job.'**
> Calvin Coolidge (1872–1933)
> US President

Active listening

Active listening involves responding to the speaker by restating the gist of what the other person has said, without agreeing or disagreeing with it, and without adding your own thoughts, feelings, experiences or ideas. Does that sound like a guaranteed way to stop a conversation in its tracks? Exactly the opposite! It's good for when you want to:

- concentrate on another person's meaning without judging, sending signals or using other types of interference listening;
- show acceptance of the speaker;
- show the speaker you are trying to understand;
- encourage the speaker to continue;
- help the speaker to further explore their feelings and thoughts;
- understand what a person is really saying and 'read between the lines';

BOX 2.8   TYPES OF INTERFERENCE LISTENING

Judging

■ Criticising, making and conveying negative evaluations, especially of a person	'You're just being silly.'
■ Blaming	'You're wrong.' 'It's your fault.'
■ Name calling, ridiculing, shaming	'That's a dumb idea.' 'That's ridiculous.' 'Tell me another one.'
■ Diagnosing, playing amateur psychologist	'Your problem is …' 'You're lazy/can't cope with the pressure/have a problem with authority figures …' 'You're just saying that because …'
■ Praising or criticising evaluatively	'You're a good/bad worker/person.' 'With that attitude, you'll go far.'

Sending signals

■ Excessive/inappropriate questioning: asking a string of rapid-fire questions early on in a conversation or when it is inappropriate to do so	'What are the facts?' 'What happened then?' 'What did he say?' 'What happened next?' 'What did you do?'
■ Advising, offering unasked-for advice	'Let me tell you what you should do …' 'Have you tried …'
■ Ordering	'You must …' 'You stop …'
■ Threatening, warning	'You'd better …' 'If you …'
■ Moralising, preaching	'You should …' 'You ought …'

Avoiding the other's concerns

■ Reassuring	'Think about the positive side.'
■ Consoling	'Look at it this way …'
■ Sympathising	'No need to worry.' 'Experience tells me …'
■ Diverting, distracting	'Let's deal with it later.'
■ Changing the subject	'By the way, did you …'
■ Logical argument: Trying, through the use of logic, to convince the other that their worries, concerns, point of view, are not valid and yours are. Can also be used to 'browbeat' or 'railroad'	'If you'll only think it through, you'll see …' 'Common sense suggests …'
■ Responding in clichés	'Every cloud has a silver lining.' 'Things are always darkest before the dawn.'

- provide feedback about whether, or how fully, you have understood;
- prevent or minimise misunderstanding, miscommunication and unintended communication;
- defuse emotion by showing the other person that you have heard them; and
- understand and empathise even when you don't agree with the speaker.

Clearly, active listening opens up the communication process so it flows more easily. It is a useful and sophisticated listening skill and it is well worth putting in the training and practice required to master it.

Guidelines for active listening

Listen carefully and mentally summarise the speaker's point of view. Then repeat it back, usually in the form of a statement (not a question). You can repeat a key word or phrase the other person has said, although it is probably better to rephrase it, keeping the meaning the same. If you haven't got it exactly right, the speaker can easily correct you.

Box 2.9 gives some examples and Box 2.10 summarises how to do this. As Box 2.9 shows, there are two areas you can focus on when giving an active listening response:

1. the *feelings*, or emotional content (either stated or implied), of what the speaker has said; or
2. the *meaning* (subject matter) of what they have said.

The last point in Box 2.10 can be difficult because it's easy for interference listening to creep in, especially when we disagree with what the other person has said. However,

---

BOX **2.9** **ACTIVE LISTENING RESPONSES: FEELINGS AND MEANINGS**

Sender	Receiver	
'I'm so fed up I could scream! I'll never get through all this in time.'	'You're feeling really snowed under.' (*feelings*)	or 'You're got a lot on your plate and it seems like you'll never get it finished.' (*meaning*)
'Don't you people have anything better to do than pick on us?!'	'It sounds like you think we're being unfair to you.' (*feelings*)	or 'You'd prefer to do it the usual way.' (*meaning*)
'That way is no good— I'll do it my way!'	'You sound annoyed that I'm making a suggestion about a different way of doing things.' (*feelings*)	or 'You're worried a different approach might not work?' (*meaning*)
'Work, work, work and never a word of thanks. They treat us like cattle around here!'	'You're feeling discouraged because no one seems to recognise all the hard work you put in.' (*feelings and meaning*)	
'I'm loving my job; it's worked out better than I ever hoped it would.'	'You must be feeling really pleased with the way things have turned out.' (*feelings*)	or 'You're really glad you made the move.' (*meaning*)

GUIDELINES FOR ACTIVE LISTENING

BOX
2.10

1. Reflect the speaker's feelings or meanings in your own words.
2. Soften with phrases like:
   'You feel …'   'You think …'
   'It seems to you …'   'You sound as though …'
   'You look …'   'It must be …'
   'If I were you, I'd feel like …'
3. Use statements, not questions.
4. Allow thoughtful silences and wait out pauses.
5. When several feelings are expressed, focus on the last one.
6. Only express what's there—don't start guessing, adding to or subtracting from the speaker's statements.
7. Use neutral words when rephrasing or summarising the speaker.

remaining neutral is important—even a good active listening response can thwart communication solely through a judgmental tone of voice or by non-verbally expressing agreement, disagreement, astonishment or outrage.

When to use active listening

You don't need to listen actively all the time. Use this skill together with acknowledgment listening, summarising, asking questions to clarify and other effective two-way communication techniques. Use active listening especially when:
- you are not quite sure what somebody really means but don't want to ask outright;
- you want to make sure you have understood correctly;
- you are about to disagree;
- you can hear emotion in the speaker's voice;
- someone is talking about their feelings and emotions;
- someone is talking about a personal matter or problem; or
- you want to reassure the speaker that you are listening open-mindedly and non-judgmentally.

These are just the times when interference listening is most often and most wrongly used!

How to listen with discernment

Listening for the main theme, as shown in Figure 2.3, will help you concentrate and listen better. Making mental or written notes, using words, symbols or pictures, is also helpful. This forces you to summarise what the speaker is saying, which keeps your mind 'on track' and helps you remember the main points in the message.

Because most of us take in information best through our eyes (83%–87% of everything that gets into our brain enters through the eyes; only about 11% goes in through our ears), writing down key ideas makes sense.

> **'Q: Why do you always walk around
> with a pad and pencil, Uncle Albert?
> A:** So I can see what I'm thinking.'
>
> Albert Einstein (1879–1955)
> Physicist

Don't take down all the details—this will stop you from listening! Instead, jot down the key ideas, words and phrases, just enough to remind you of the speaker's main points.

NON-VERBAL COMMUNICATION

When you think of communication, does spoken, or **verbal**, **communication** spring to mind first?

Words are some of the many symbols we use to transmit ideas to others. As we've seen, they can be big barriers to communication—slang, jargon, different meanings that can be attached to the same word—all mean that successful communication must depend on more than words alone.

Words are important, yet, as Box 2.11 shows, there is definitely more to communication! *How* we say something is usually more important than the words themselves. Our tone of voice, gestures, movements, the way we stand, facial expression—all add to (or detract from) our words. In fact, non-verbal communication is so important that if it does not agree with the verbal part of a message, people will believe the body language over the words. That's why supervisors need to take particular care that their verbal and non-verbal communications are *congruent*.

Whether we intend to or not, we communicate through *facial expressions, tone of voice* and other forms of **non-verbal communication** and *body language*. Even the clothes we wear send messages to others. *Symbolic communication* can be through spoken or written words, through drawings and gestures (e.g. thumbs up for 'great') or through our clothing, objects on our desk, and other symbols. People receive an enormous amount of communication, often subconsciously, through non-verbal signals: a wink, a nod, a smile, a tear, a gesture, a yawn, heavy breathing, a blush, silence.

Successful communication also depends on intangible things such as whether we like, trust and respect the communicator. We examine this further in Chapter 14. For now, let's look at three types of non-verbal communication that are particularly important to supervisors: symbolic communication, body language and personal space.

BOX 2.11   HOW IMPORTANT ARE WORDS?

In fact, we achieve only a small portion of our communication through the spoken or written word. In a conversation between two people, for example, only 7% of the message is likely to come from the actual words that are spoken. The remaining 93% of the message that is received and understood comes from body language (55%) and tone of voice (38%).

Symbolic communication

Symbolic communications such as the size of someone's office and the type of furnishings in it are status symbols in some organisations. The clothing people wear is often a sign of rank or of the kind of work they perform. Clothing and personal grooming can signal the way we expect others to treat us. For example, does the managing director of your company or the head of your department wear more formal clothing to work than other employees? What does the way you dress, the jewellery you wear, the car you drive, the items on your desk say about you?

Body language

Body language holds many messages. Our *posture* tells others how confident we are and signals our status in relation to our companions and our 'ownership' of our surroundings. The *speed, pitch, tone* and *volume of our voice* subtly communicate the importance of our message, our degree of commitment to it and our self-confidence.

Here are some tips to help you make sure your body language supports your communication:

- Sit or stand facing the other person or at right angles and, as far as possible, on the same level.
- Keep an open body posture (most people interpret crossed arms or legs as closed and defensive).
- Centre your attention on the other person.
- Avoid fiddling, fidgeting and other nervous mannerisms.
- Lean slightly forward to show interest and attention.
- Make good eye contact—not too much, which is overpowering, and not too little, which indicates lack of attention or self-confidence.

Monitor the other person's body language, too, particularly any changes that could indicate agreement, disagreement or another emotion. Do people step back from you, which could mean you are invading their personal space? Are they listening to you attentively or fidgeting so much that you may decide it would be better to continue the conversation at a more convenient time?

Personal space

We are all inside an invisible 'space bubble'. If someone enters it, we become very uncomfortable. With close friends and family, this personal space zone shrinks to as small as 15–46 centimetres; at work most of us prefer others to keep to a distance of 'arm's length'. With people we do not know well, or dislike, our 'bubble' expands even further.

We can observe differences in personal space zones between country and city dwellers: country dwellers usually prefer bigger space zones than city dwellers. People from different cultures also have characteristic personal space zones: the personal space zones of Arabs and Southern Europeans, for instance, tend to be smaller than those of people born and raised in Australia and New Zealand.

Supervisors need to be aware of this. If you invade the personal space of people you work with, they will feel ill at ease. They may not be aware of the reason, but they will feel uncomfortable around you. This will make it difficult for them to concentrate and communicate with you. Getting too close to people can make you seem 'pushy', while leaving too much distance can make you appear 'stand-offish'. 'Keep your distance' to the correct zone if you want people to feel comfortable around you.

WHEN TO PUT IT IN WRITING

There comes a time in every supervisor's job when spoken words aren't suitable. It may be a report to your manager on why your department's overtime costs exceeded budget; it may be a letter to a customer explaining how your product is suited to their needs; or it may be a note to an employee confirming your discussion that unless certain improvements are made in their job performance, termination of employment will result.

Shortcomings of written communications

Despite their usefulness, written communications have some drawbacks. Before opting to put something in writing, make sure that it is really necessary to do so and take measures to overcome the problems listed here.

1. They are usually one-way and there is no opportunity for immediate feedback. How can you be sure whether the person receiving your note or memo has understood the message in the way you intended it?
2. A letter or memo may be delayed or lost.
3. There is no guarantee when it will be read or even if it will be read.
4. Written documents are not as personal as a face-to-face, or even a telephone, conversation.
5. They may be difficult to read and open to misinterpretation.
6. They can be costly to prepare in terms of time and money.

Who are the poor writers?

Have you met any of the poor writers shown in Box 2.12?

FROM THEORY TO PRACTICE

Put it in writing if:
- you want a record for future reference. This is particularly important with complex material or when new systems or procedures are being introduced. People can study what you have written, take it in at their own pace and refer to it later. Not only is it permanent but, because most of us remember more through our eyes than through our ears, putting it in writing makes a more lasting impression.
- you want your message to be authoritative. People are more ready to believe the written word.
- you want to deliver a precise, carefully thought-out message. You can write, edit and rewrite your words until they say just what you want them to say, clearly and accurately. You can include graphs, maps, diagrams and other pictorial aids to help get your message across.
- there are problems of distance. Letters and memos may be less costly than face-to-face meetings.
- you need to convey the same information to large numbers of people and ensure that everyone receives the same message.
- you want to reinforce or confirm an earlier verbal message.

BOX 2.12 POOR WRITERS

- *Curt Cathy* mistakes brevity and terseness for conciseness. She needs to add warmth, friendliness and courtesy to her letters.
- *Rambling Ronnie* switches from one thought to another as he writes, just as they occur to him. He needs to structure his information into a logical flow; only planning will achieve this.
- *Pompous Paula* writes in clichés and platitudes and is concerned with her own importance. She needs to unbend a bit and focus on what she wants to communicate instead of on herself.
- *Arrogant Arthur* often brushes aside complaints, makes demands rather than requests, and generally writes in a way that shows he thinks he is better than the person he is writing to. He needs to use more empathy and courtesy.
- *Right Rhonda* is more concerned with proving herself right and the reader wrong. Instead of handing out blame, she should look for a solution acceptable to both herself and her reader.
- *Exact Emma* is always correct, but so insistent on precision that only a statistician can understand what she has written! She should realise that sometimes facts and figures need explanation if misunderstandings are to be avoided, and that it isn't always necessary to include *every* detail.
- *Fearful Fred* is frightened of making a direct statement in case he's held accountable. He should be more clear and positive and willing to speak for himself.
- *Punctilious Paul* is similar to Exact Emma but, where Emma is cold, Paul is boring and lulls his readers to sleep. He needs to draft his letters with a particular reader in mind.
- *Technical Ted* writes well—to other technicians who understand his jargon. The rest of us are left behind unless he remembers to explain technical terms or use terms familiar to us.
- *Excusing Ellie* always comes up with excuses about why something was late, wrong or not as good as it should have been, instead of offering an apology and a solution to correct the situation. She needs to focus on the future and what will be done, not on the past and apportioning blame.

Officiousness, poor organisation, muddled flow of thoughts, too much or too little detail—these are common writing traps. But the two most common traps are *verbosity* and *poor writing style*.

- *Verbose Victor* equates bulk with importance. He needs to pare down his overly wordy writing by cutting out unnecessary words and phrases.
- *Flowery Flora* writes in an unnatural, unnecessarily formal, flowery style. She needs to write more as she speaks and refer to the 'six C's' discussed earlier.

Whatever your reason for putting it on paper, you can write effectively if you follow the guidelines given below. These help you write in a clear, readable business style.

THE **BIG** PICTURE

Time is tight in most organisations. This makes it increasingly important that people write in clear, plain English.

Be clear about what you want to say

Before writing anything—a letter, report, memo or notice—be sure you understand clearly what you hope to achieve. Is it to inform? Persuade? Entertain? If your purpose is fuzzy, your writing will be fuzzy, too.

Organise your thoughts

If you know what you want to say, it's easy to organise your thoughts. One way is to answer these questions: Who? What? How? When? Where? Why? and Next steps? For example, suppose you want to write to your manager or head of department about the need for a departmental picnic. Your outline for writing might be:

- *Who*? The employees in the accounting department and their families.
- *What*? A family picnic and sports day.
- *How*? Each family brings its own food and drinks for a barbecue. Activities will include football, tennis and cricket.
- *When*? Any time in January but near Australia Day would be best.
- *Where*? Where barbecue facilities, picnic tables, tennis and recreation areas are available. One suitable location would be Belair Park.
- *Why*? To promote team spirit and a sense of belonging among the employees in the department.
- *Next steps.* You volunteer to canvass the employees to determine degree of interest, set a date and venue and book the venue by the end of the month.

Another way to ensure your ideas follow each other logically is to start from the beginning. If you are writing about a building, begin with your thoughts about the foundations and proceed to build on each thought until you get to the roof. Cover each particular subject (e.g. the foundations, the floors, the walls) in separate paragraphs. This gives your writing a logical progression and makes it easier to read and understand. Box 2.13 shows some other ways to organise your thoughts.

BOX 2.13 WAYS TO ORGANISE AND STRUCTURE YOUR THOUGHTS

- **Time:** e.g. past → present → future
- **Space:** e.g. geographical, or from a central point outwards
- **Causal:** e.g. the facts and their results, or the problem and its causes
- **Process:** e.g. from the raw material to the finished product
- **Principle:** e.g. from the theory to the practice
- **Problem:** e.g. from the problem to the solution

Which is the most suitable?

Group your ideas

Each sentence should contain one idea. Each paragraph should contain a group of related ideas.

Like a good story, your written communications should have a beginning, a middle and an end. The beginning introduces the subject; the middle contains the information you wish to convey; and the end summarises what you have said and points towards what should happen next.

Keep it short and simple

Good writing is concise. We shouldn't use unnecessary words in a sentence any more than we would use unnecessary parts in an engine. Say what you want to say in as few words as possible, then stop.

This is not to say that you should only write in short sentences or avoid details or explanations. It means you should use enough words to communicate your message while avoiding extra sentences and words that don't add anything. Make every word count.

Good writing is simple and direct. Conciseness adds punch and force. Box 2.14 lists some excessively wordy, flowery and trite expressions and shows how to simplify them. Figure 2.4 illustrates how you can prune unnecessary words.

BOX 2.14 UNNECESSARY AND FLOWERY WORDS AND TRITE PHRASES

Wordy	Better
■ in view of the fact that	■ because
■ in the event that	■ if
■ consensus of opinion	■ consensus
■ during the month of April	■ during April
■ for the reason that	■ because, since
■ prior to	■ before
■ subsequent to	■ after
■ pursuant to your request	■ as you asked
■ during which time	■ while
■ until such time	■ until
■ are of the opinion	■ believe
■ in order that	■ so
■ in addition to	■ also
■ at the present time	■ now
■ a large number of	■ many
■ with reference to	■ about
■ in the majority of instances	■ mostly
■ in the neighbourhood of	■ about
■ according to our records	■ we find
■ on a regular basis	■ regularly
■ in the absence of	■ without
■ in excess of	■ over
■ is sorry for	■ regrets
■ has no confidence in	■ doubts
■ is in accord with	■ concurs, agrees
■ in the near future	■ soon

FIGURE 2.4 PRUNING UNNECESSARY WORDS

~~as of~~ now   my ~~personal~~ opinion
~~at a price of~~ $60.00   each ~~and every one~~ of us
enclosed ~~herewith~~   first ~~and foremost~~
we can supply them in ~~the following colours:~~   I am ~~in the process of~~ preparing
  blue, red, green ...   during ~~the course of~~
one of the main factors is~~, of course, the~~   ~~take into~~ consideration
  ~~question of~~ quality   ~~give a description~~ describe
we seldom ~~ever~~ make this mistake   ~~reached an agreement~~ agreed
it is blue ~~in colour~~

Use short words

If you need a long word, use it. Otherwise, go for familiar, precise words. Box 2.15 shows
how to turn some long words into short words for greater impact and readability. Only use
a long word if:

- it is more familiar to the reader than a short word—for example, 'sponsorship' is more
  familiar to most people than 'aegis';
- it is unique and can't be replaced by a short word—for example, inventory, appreciation,
  communicate;
- it would add richness or special meaning or is more exact than a short word—for
  example, 'courier' is more precise than 'send';
- it is economical, replacing a lot of small words—for example, 'destination' is more
  economical than 'the place to which someone is going'.

BOX 2.15 **LOSE THE LONG WORD—USE THE SHORT WORD**

Long	Short	Long	Short
Participate	Share	Approximately	About
Abundance	Lot	Utilise	Use
Difficult	Hard	Commencement	Beginning
Initiate	Start	Frequently	Often
Remunerate	Pay	Terminate	End
Endeavour	Try	Assistance	Help
Residence	Home	Consequence	Result
Anticipate	Expect	Initiate	Begin
Administer	Give	Aggregate	Total
Alternative	Choice	Demonstrate	Show
Fundamental	Basic	Indication	Sign
Majority	Most	Regulation	Rule
Reiterate	Repeat	Requirement	Need
Similar	Alike	Subsequent	Later
Accomplish	Do	Apportion	Assign
Application	Use	Primarily	Mostly
Manufacture	Make	Incorporate	Include
Terminate	End	Abbreviate	Shorten
Visualise	See	Ultimate	Final

> 'I never write metropolis
> when I can get paid the same sum for city.'
>
> Mark Twain (1835–1910)
> Author and humourist

Write naturally

When you write, use words you typically use in speaking—words that come to you easily. Don't try to sound like something you're not or be unnecessarily formal. If you would normally say 'We took the long way 'round', don't write 'We arrived via a circuitous route.' Ornate, elaborate, overblown words and phrases can be off-putting and cloud your meaning.

It is easier and more effective to write using your own speaking style. When you sit down to write, speak your thoughts mentally (or even aloud) as you put them on paper. This should help you to write more freely and make your writing more alive, more interesting and easier to understand.

Don't be glib

Overly casual writing lacks sincerity and promotes mistrust. Which approach would you consider more seriously: 'Do I have an idea for you! If you're interested in making our department more productive, read on.' Or: 'I have developed a plan which I believe could increase our department's productivity by up to 8%. I have outlined this plan below and would appreciate an opportunity to discuss it with you next week.'

Be positive and precise

Instead of saying: 'John is not very often at his machine on time', leave out the negative and include specific information. Say: 'John is usually 5–15 minutes late in getting to his machine.' Don't write: 'This door should never be left open', but rather 'Always close this door.' Most of us don't like being told what is not or what we should not do. We want to know what *is* and what we *should* do. Avoiding negative statements and words will improve your writing style and help people remember your message more accurately.

Write actively, not passively

'*The moon was jumped over by the cow*' is a passive sentence. As you can see, it lacks punch and clarity. '*The cow jumped over the moon*' is active and strong. Active writing is generally a better style. Place the *actor* (in this example, the cow) in front of the *action* (jumped) to make the flow of the sentence clear and powerful.

Occasionally, for reasons of tact, you may decide to write in the passive voice. For example, it is more diplomatic to say: '*We believe there was an error in your last invoice,*' than '*You invoiced us incorrectly.*'

Write for your reader

Bear your readers' needs and interests in mind and use words and terms they will readily understand, interpret and visualise. Avoid technical terms when writing to someone with a non-technical background. If you are providing information about fertiliser to farmers, write about the amount they should apply to each hectare and by how much it will increase the yield and their profits; don't talk about 'marginal analysis' or 'nutritional content per microgram'. These concepts may be more important to a scientist than a farmer.

Use white space to be reader-friendly

People will groan when they pick up a document or letter filled with long paragraphs, tiny margins and small print. Make your document reader-friendly:

- break up the text with headings;
- use a font size of 12 points or larger;
- leave at least 5 cm margins; and
- use as much white space as possible.

People are more likely to read your documents if they are well set-out and have 'eye appeal'.

Check spelling and grammar

You can always use a dictionary or spell-check function on the word processor to check the spelling of an unfamiliar word, or you can use another word that you know how to spell. Some words seem to be continually misspelt—Box 2.16 lists some of them. (Remember that there is sometimes more than one acceptable spelling for a word, for example, 'judgement' and judgment' are both acceptable.) Box 2.17 lists pairs of words that are often misused.

Grammar is sometimes more difficult to take care of, although most word processing programs have a grammar checking function that can be useful. You can always ask someone (a friend, a secretary) to look over your writing for errors. Everyone needs this— even great authors have editors check their writing for grammar and spelling. Follow their example and ask for help.

These tips for good writing are summarised in Box 2.18, the six steps to good writing.

BOX 2.16 COMMONLY MISSPELT WORDS

conscientious	questionnaire	embarrass	psychology
occurrence	necessary	conscious	federal
prejudiced	comparative	government	benefited
acquaintance	omitted	exaggerate	accurate
environment	apparent	parliament	definitely

BOX 2.17 PAIRS OF WORDS OFTEN MISUSED

accept	except	imply	*infer
too	two/to	personal	personnel
formerly	formally	principal	principle
affect	effect	practise	practice
adapt	adopt	stationary	stationery
moral	morale	there	their

THE SIX STEPS TO GOOD WRITING

Step 1   *Be clear about your purpose.* Why are you writing this? What do you want your reader to know? To do? How do you want your reader to feel?

Step 2   *Plan what you will say.* Jot down the key points you want to make. Then put them in a logical sequence. Then gather any facts you will include.

Step 3   *Draft your document.* Have a specific reader in mind and write to that person. Why should they read it? Use the WIFM factor to help you: What's In it For Me? Ask this question from the reader's point of view. Be yourself: use normal language, not flowery and not overly formal. Aim for a readable, natural flow of ideas.

Step 4   *Edit it.* Read through your document to ensure that it is clear and says what you want it to say. Change any obscure words to familiar words, long words to short words, complex sentences into shorter, simpler ones. Prune unnecessary words and get rid of any trite phrases.

Step 5   *Type or word process the final draft.*

Step 6   *Check it carefully.* If time allows, it often helps to leave it for a day or two before the final check. Don't just glance over it but really check it through. Does it make sense? Are words spelled correctly and is grammar correct? Does the information flow smoothly? Are there logical transitions between major points? How does the layout look? Are margins big enough? Is there enough space between paragraphs? Erasures, overtyping and poor-quality print in written documents will cause them to lose their 'eye appeal' and look unprofessional.

Setting out documents

Business letters

If you are writing on a blank sheet of paper, use the format shown in Figure 2.5. If you use company stationery or 'letterhead', omit your return address because this will be printed on the letterhead.

Memos, fax sheets and reports

Follow the format your organisation uses. Many organisations have memo and facsimile pads or stationery with printed headings, and word processing programs have standard templates you can use.

Memo headings normally show the information given in Figure 2.6. If you don't have pre-printed memo stationery, insert this information at the top of your memos.

Facsimile messages are usually headed with the information shown in Figure 2.7 or these details are set out on a standard fax cover sheet.

Report formats vary from organisation to organisation. You might want to insert a title page and table of contents (such as that used in the front of this book) for long formal reports. You can omit these, however, in shorter, more informal reports. Box 2.19 shows a

FIGURE 2.5 PARTS OF A BUSINESS LETTER

222 Kent Street	
PERTH WA 6002	*(your address)*
10 January 2001	*(date)*
Mr John Jones	
Sales Manager	
XYZ Pty Ltd	
SYDNEY NSW 2002	*(receiver's name and address)*
Dear Mr Jones	*(salutation)*
RE: PURCHASE ORDER 0517	*(heading)*
Please send me . . .	
	(body of letter)
Yours sincerely,	*(complimentary close)*
John J. Smith	
(position title)	

FIGURE 2.6 HEADING FORMAT FOR A MEMO

Date: _____

To: _____

From: _____

Subject: _____

Copies to: _____

FIGURE 2.7 FAX COVER SHEET FORMAT

To: _____ (company name)

Attention: _____ (person to receive the fax)

Fax No: _____ (their fax number)

From: _____ (your name)

Fax No: _____ (your fax number)

Date: _____

Subject: _____

No. of pages _____ (total number of pages of the fax, including cover sheet)

BOX 2.19   TYPICAL LAYOUT OF A FORMAL REPORT
....

1. Title page
2. Table of contents
3. Summary
4. Introduction/terms of reference/ objectives
5. Conclusions
6. Recommendations
7. Findings
8. The formal close (signature/s, date)
9. Appendices
10. Acknowledgments
11. References
12. Endnotes
13. Bibliography

---

typical layout of a formal report. You may not need to use all the sections shown; your own judgment and knowledge of the contents of the report and its recipients will help you decide which sections you need. Follow the protocol of your organisation using a sample report as a guide if you need to.

You could also attach a *letter of transmittal* using the format shown in Figure 2.5. The body of the letter explains what you are attaching (a copy of the report), why you wrote the report (who requested you to do it), when you wrote it, etc. Use the Who? What? How? When? Where? Why? Next steps? approach previously discussed.

Many managers like an *executive summary*. This quickly indicates what your report is all about, saving your reader the need to wade through all the details. The summary contains your main findings and the actions you recommend. It is normally placed as the first section of the report.

It is usual practice to put your conclusions and recommendations before the supporting details that back them up. When you do this, your reader can have in mind what you concluded while reading the findings and facts upon which you based your conclusions.

Set out your report attractively, with plenty of white space and in a clear, readable font. Try to break long reports into sections, similar to the way in which this book is divided into parts and chapters. Consider using paragraph and section headings that summarise the contents for the readers. You may wish to number each section consecutively (Section 1, Section 2, etc.) and number the paragraphs within sections (1.1, 1.2, 1.3, 2.1, 2.2, etc.) to make it easier for people to refer to specific contents when discussing or responding to your report. Be sure to follow the writing guidelines discussed earlier in this chapter.

Email

Email can be transmitted within a company over its internal network, or intranet, or externally, usually over the Internet.

If you're connected at work, you might be receiving over 100 emails a day! An inexpensive, rapid and handy tool, the Internet also has the potential to be a huge time-waster. Here is some 'netiquette' to bear in mind to ensure your emails add value and will be read.

- *One screen.* Try to keep your emails to one screen in length so people don't need to scroll down.

- *One subject.* Keep to one subject per email. If you need to write to someone on several subjects, think about sending them as separate emails—this makes it easier for the receiver to file them. Include a clear subject title so your receiver can assess whether to open your email now or later.
- *Focus.* Who are you sending this to? Why? What do they need? What do you want them to do? People are busy, so get to your point quickly, preferably in the first paragraph.
- *Send all.* Avoid hitting the 'send all' button at all costs. Not everyone is interested in the same thing. Think: *Do they need it? Will they be interested in it? Does it affect them? Would I send this as a memo?*
- *Action.* You might use the 'To' box for recipients from whom action is needed and the 'CC' box for information only.
- *Attachments.* Don't send 'cute' attachments on business emails. They take time to download and are often not appreciated by busy people. If you need to send an attachment, inform the recipient in the body of your email what it's about and why you're sending it. That way they can make an informed decision about whether to open it.
- *Replying.* People expect an instant reply with emails, so try to respond within 48 hours. If you can't respond in full, reply briefly saying when you plan to do so.
- *Resending.* Should you repeat the sender's message in your reply? Do so if having their original message attached will help the sender. Beware of creating lengthy chains of messages.
- *Forwarding.* If you are forwarding something to several people, think about using the blind copy button so that a long list of recipients doesn't appear on everyone's screen.
- *Salutation and close.* You can begin with 'Dear' followed by the person's name, or use just the person's name. Close with 'Thanks', or 'Regards', and your own name.
- *Tone.* Keeping emails brief and to-the-point doesn't mean making them blunt or curt. Remember 'please' and 'thank you' and other courtesies. Write in a conversational tone. Avoid third person words like 'employees', 'management', 'they'. Personalise wherever you can: *you, your, our, we, I, my, us.* If you make a request, give a reason to avoid sounding too direct. If you can, put a 'you' or 'your' in the first few lines, or include a benefit to the reader or the reason for your request.
- *Capitals.* Avoid using all capital letters as this is read as SHOUTING!
- *Clarity.* Follow the *Crystal Clear* email rules shown in Box 2.20.
- *Keep cool.* Don't write in anger! Compose the email if you want to, but save it rather than send it.
- *Spelling.* Don't forget to proofread and use the spell-check function before you hit the send button. Email is so instantaneous, it's easy to let our writing standards lapse. Why mar your credibility or professionalism?
- *Humour.* Avoid it. Email lacks the supporting visual and vocal clues that help people interpret it correctly.
- *Emoticons.* These are 'cute' little symbols made from punctuation marks (e.g. :-) for a 'smiley face') and are probably best avoided for business use.
- *Proliferation.* Emails may seem disposable, but they're not. In fact, they're one of the hardest forms of electronic communication to erase. The instant you send an email you have created four copies (one on your PC, one on the receiver's PC, one on your server,

CRYSTAL CLEAR EMAILS

- Put important information, directions and requests for action in the first three lines.
- Keep your sentences short—less than 20 words.
- Keep paragraphs to less than ten lines.
- Double space between paragraphs.
- Use bullet lists and numbered lists.
- Use lots of headings in bold (or caps if your system doesn't allow bold) to separate sections of longer messages.
- Highlight key points in bold.
- Leave some white space for 'breathing room'.

Source: Adapted from K. Cole, *Crystal Clear Communication*, 2nd edn, Prentice Hall, Sydney, 2000

and one on your receiver's server). Automatic backups create more. A year after sending an email, there could be 50 or more copies. So watch what you say.

- *Liability.* Don't say anything on an email that you wouldn't want printed in a newspaper or that would embarrass your organisation. Emails are easy to retrieve and their contents have been used in legal proceedings. An employer can be held liable for the content of emails, even if the contents go against their stated policy.

'Better safe than sorry.'

- *Security.* Think of emails as an open forum. Your employer has a right to read your emails if you're using its PC and Internet access. Many audit electronic mail randomly to ensure nothing is being sent that would embarrass them or harm their business or image. This isn't spying—it's prudent management.
- *The human touch.* Don't let emails become substitutes for face-to-face or telephone conversations. Guard against emailing the person down the corridor or in the next office. Supervisors who lose the 'human touch' find it difficult to get things done.

Evaluating your writing

After you've written your report, memo or letter, read it over with the questions in Box 2.21 in mind.

THE **BIG** PICTURE

Email messages written quickly and carelessly have shown up in lawsuits. Organisations need to encourage employees to think about what they say. Guidelines are probably needed to protect the organisation's image as well as for legal considerations.

BOX 2.21   **EVALUATION CHECKLIST**

_____ Was it necessary to write this?

_____ Is my communication timely?

_____ Does it contain all the facts? Are they correct?

_____ Is my main message concise, clear and direct?

_____ Is my message logically organised and easy to read?

_____ Did I use terms and language my readers will understand?

* _____ Did I use any big words where short, simple ones could do the job better?

_____ Did I state my points positively?

_____ Did I put related topics and ideas together?

_____ Is my writing natural and professional without being glib? Does it reflect me?

* _____ Did I use ten words when four would do the job better?

_____ Did I use correct spelling and grammar?

* _____ Did I explain anything I didn't need to?

_____ Did I avoid 'cute' and pretentious words?

_____ Did I avoid slang and dialect unless I needed them for clarity?

_____ Can my message be easily understood by the readers?

_____ Does the layout help easy reading and reference?

_____ Is my tone friendly and courteous?

_____ Did I write actively, not passively?

If you can tick each of the above except the three with an asterisk (*), then your written communication should be an excellent one.

RAPID REVIEW

		True	False
1.	Supervisors need to be good communicators if they are to carry out their responsibilities effectively.		☐
2.	Barriers to effective communication will always exist and therefore need to be recognised and dealt with.		☐
3.	Effective communication means that you must agree with what the other person is saying or that they must agree with what you are saying.	☐	

	True	False
4. While feedback is important, it isn't necessary if you have explained yourself clearly enough.	☐	☑
5. Empathy means agreeing with what the other person has said.	☐	☑
6. Active listening should be used all the time.	☐	☑
7. If you have stated your point of view clearly, you will have communicated successfully.	☐	☑
8. Poor listening habits include interrupting, letting your mind wander, thinking about how you will reply and fidgeting; these bad habits will reduce your effectiveness as a communicator.	☑	☐
9. Passive listening is polite because it means you don't speak, interrupt or distract the speaker with nodding or 'ah-has'.	☐	☑
10. Body language accounts for the largest part of any face-to face message.	☑	☐
11. Invading someone's personal space will make them feel uncomfortable and cause problems in the communication process.	☑	☐
12. Only about 7% of our verbal communication is likely to be achieved through actual words.	☑	☐
13. If a speaker's body language and their words are incongruent most people will believe the body language.	☑	☐
14. Open and effective communication is vital to any organisation.	☑	☐
15. Supervisors don't need to be particularly skilled at communicating because they can just tell people what to do.	☐	☑
16. A letter or memo can provide a useful record for future reference.	☑	☐
17. Unfortunately, there is no guarantee that written communications will ever be read or understood.	☑	☐
18. A good layout makes a document more inviting to read and easier to understand than one with little white space, few headings and long paragraphs.	☑	☐
19. It's best to put all the information down on paper and allow the reader to organise it in their own mind, in the way that suits them best.	☑	☒
20. Because emails are so quick, we don't need to give much thought to their layout or composition.	☐	☑
21. Letters, reports and memos with long sentences and lots of big words usually indicate a well written, carefully thought-out and authoritative document.	☐	☑

··················· **APPLY YOUR KNOWLEDGE** ···················

1. Discuss the relationship between effective communication and effective supervision.

2. How would you define effective communication? Use your definition to explain how the communication process works.

3. What causes communication to break down? List ten barriers that have affected you and explain some steps you could have taken to overcome each of them.

4. Give an example of a time when a pattern of expectation, or mind-set,

caused you to ignore a communication that didn't 'fit in'.

5. What is meant by 'hearing' with your heart and eyes as well as your ears?

6. Using short examples, explain each of the four types of listening and their effect on the communication process.

7. Explain the advantages of active listening and give examples from your own experience when it should be used.

8. 'If God wanted us to talk twice as much as listen, we'd have all been given four mouths.' Discuss, and include reasons why people in our culture are often poor listeners.

9. We all 'read' non-verbal communication instinctively. The difficulty is being conscious of what we are 'reading' and why. Discuss.

10. From the information given in this chapter and your own experience, identify some of your own poor writing habits and explain what you can do to overcome them.

11. Summarise the most important things to remember when writing reports, letters and memos.

12. An 18th-century book on how to write letters stated that we should write all our correspondence using the everyday language we use to speak. Nearly 300 years later, we are still writing in 18th-century language! Discuss.

13. If you have answered any of the questions in this section in the form of an essay, edit your writing to make it more clearer and easier to read by following the guidelines outlined in this chapter.

DEVELOP YOUR SKILLS

Individual activities

1. Study the characteristics of effective and ineffective listeners. Select five bad listening habits you believe you have. List at least five things you can start doing now to overcome them.

2. Find a group of people talking together that you can observe quietly from a short distance away. Ignore what they are saying. Instead, observe their body language. Who seems to be the leader of the group? Who likes who? Does anyone feel uncomfortable or left out? Is anyone impatient or bored? Is anyone angry? Are they good friends or just acquaintances? Give reasons for each answer.

3. List and analyse three communication barriers you have experienced recently and explain the steps you could have taken, or could still take, to reduce or remove them.

4. Relate interpersonal communication to intraorganisational communication and explain how each contributes to personal and organisational effectiveness.

5. Write the steps for preparing and laying out a report.

6. Investigate the grammar options on the word processing system you use, particularly the readability indices. Find out what each of them measures and what a 'readable' score is.

7. Write a report following the format outlined in this chapter, and the steps you prepared in activity 5 above, discussing the weaknesses of written communications and giving some examples to support your answer. Your report should also explain what can be done to overcome these problems and when written communications should be used.

8. For the next three days, keep a log of all your communications. Write down the nature of the communication (telephone, face-to-face, reading, writing, email, etc.) and the purpose of the communication (to reach a decision, pass the time, solve a problem, seek information, give information, etc.). At the end of the three days, tally up your communications. What does this tally tell you? Compare your results and conclusions with others in your class.

Group activities

1. Divide into pairs and hold a conversation with the objective of finding out all you can about what your partner enjoys most in life right now. Listen using passive listening responses. What happens to the speaker? To the receiver?

   Now switch roles so that the speaker becomes the listener, and this time use interference listening responses. What happens to the speaker? To the receiver?

2. Divide into pairs again and hold a conversation with the objective of finding out all you can about either (a) what your partner enjoys most or (b) a problem or difficulty your partner has recently faced. Use active listening responses and attentive body language to help you discover this information.

   Afterwards, check your understanding by summarising your partner's thoughts and feelings; ask for feedback on how accurately you have understood. Then make some notes together summarising what helped you to achieve understanding and anything that hindered you.

   Then switch roles and repeat the activity.

3. Among the people you know, identify someone you believe is an effective communicator. Spend some time with them and try to identify any special behaviours, actions or skills that they use to communicate well. List these, and discuss your findings in class.

4. In small groups, make two lists, one of the key skills you believe are needed in sending information and one of the skills needed in receiving information. Then make two more lists, one of the responsibilities of senders, the other of the responsibilities of receivers.

5. Consider three people you feel you have empathy with. Write three qualities of each person that you believe help to create feelings of empathy between you. Discuss these in your study group and compile a list of factors that help people develop empathy.

6. Divide into pairs and take turns saying these ten words: 'I really enjoy my work and I love my boss.' See how many meanings you can give this sentence by just changing your voice and the way you emphasise different words.

7. Brainstorm in groups of five or six for three minutes to list as many words as you can that begin with the letter 'C' which describe effective communication. How many did you come up with? Compare your answers with other groups in your class.

8. In small groups, go through some recent reports or essays you have submitted and edit them to make them more readable.

The Christmas Party

The annual Christmas party for the Baker Wire Company was held last year in early December. As usual, it was an all-family affair, with partners and children of employees invited. At the end of the party, Father Christmas appeared with bags of goodies for the children, presents for the partners and bonus cheques for the employees.

Mr Goodman, the owner and manager, traditionally said a few words on the occasion. Then, after a polite round of applause, the wishing of 'Merry Christmas' and a handshake with Mr Goodman, everyone usually went home. This year was no exception. Everything went as usual until Mr Goodman rose and made the following remarks:

'Fellow employees and friends: this year is the 30th anniversary of the founding of the Baker Wire Company. Some years were good; some were trying. But, in all, they have been good years for most of us.

'This has been a difficult year financially. Sales and profits have eroded and expenses and costs have pushed steadily upwards. All this has had a dampening effect on profits and as a consequence we are not in as strong a position as we have been in the past. The only hope I can see for a continued strong growth and a financially sound business is for us to cut expenses. This means we will have to reduce labour costs—along with any other expenses we can control.

'I know that many of you are restless. Some of your children are hard to manage at this hour and you want to be on your way, but I did want this opportunity to say a few words to you. This business is our entire life. We all have to nurture it, like we do our children, if we want to see it develop and grow.

'I know that most of you have heard on the grapevine that business has been increasing at a decreasing rate and that profits and bonuses will suffer this year. Part of this rumour is true.

'I am very concerned about those who will remain with me through the future years. I want to see your children develop into strong and loyal young people. I want to see them married and establishing homes of their own.

'New ideas call for new wage and productivity agreements and I hope that in the coming months we can generate better ones in the true spirit of enterprise bargaining.

'Finally, let me wish you all a Merry Christmas. In summary, this has been a memorable year and I am happy to give each employee a bonus remembrance.'

With that, Mr Goodman called out names and employees came forward to get their cheques.

Employees found that their bonus had been significantly increased over last year's. When the party broke up, some families started towards the door. A good many, however, gathered in small groups, talking. 'What did the old man mean?', 'Will some of us be fired?' were the types of questions they were asking.

Questions

1   Mr Goodman intended to reassure his employees that their jobs were safe and the company was sound, provided that some necessary changes were made. What evidence is there for this statement in Mr Goodman's speech?
2   Mr Goodman was forewarning his employees about the hard times and redundancies to come. What evidence is there for this statement in Mr Goodman's speech?
3   What do you think Mr Goodman had in mind for his message? Why do you think this?
4   Assuming Mr Goodman had this message in mind, rewrite it to make it clearer.

CASE STUDY 2.2

Simon Speaks

Simon was recently appointed to the position of area manager for a chain of eye care stores. Each store, depending on its size, had one or more qualified optometrists and two or more trained optometric assistants who worked with clients to select flattering spectacle frames, show them how to use and care for contact lenses, carry out minor repairs to spectacles, and so on. They also did most of the administrative work in the stores such as booking client appointments and handling billing.

When Simon took on the role, he was told his primary objective was to ensure the staff in each store worked as a team, with their main focus on customer service and profitability. Simon took up his position enthusiastically.

He visited each store, calling the staff together, introducing himself and giving a 'pep talk' on the importance of teamwork and customer service. 'We're in the new age of customer service and really adding value for our customers,' he said. 'You can look on your jobs as filling in time between 9 am and 5 pm or you can see yourself as part of a great team, helping to improve the quality of our customer's lives.' Simon always closed his talk with the example of a football team working together to score goals and how each member of the team, playing their assigned position, was important to the success of the whole team.

Then Simon met with each staff member individually. He asked everyone what they liked and disliked about their jobs, whether they felt everyone in the store was 'pulling their weight', whether staffing levels were right or were they employing too many people, whether any systems could be tightened up to reduce costs. He asked everyone if they could speed up their service to customers by agreeing an average length of time to spend with each one, so they could serve more customers in a day. He also took the opportunity to inform the optometric assistants that they would need to be more vigilant in following up overdue accounts. 'I intend to introduce a seven-day account period in order to help our cash flow,' he explained. 'At the end of the day, we have a business to run and our shareholders expect us to make a good profit. We all need to do our bit in this and I expect you to do yours.'

Simon concluded each interview with the statement: 'I'd like you to feel free to tell me anything you can about the way this store is *really* running. I'm all ears.'

Once he completed the visits to each of his stores, Simon based himself in his office and wasn't seen again in the stores. He began a concerted campaign to reduce costs, sending memos instructing staff to make sure customers paid their bills within seven days and telephoning stores when the amount of outstanding accounts reached a certain level. He sent a memo to optometrists requesting that they limit their use of the fax machine in order to cut costs (they often faxed each other articles from their professional trade journal of advances in eye care and customer service techniques which they had found useful). He instigated a survey to find out the length of time each optometric assistant spent with each customer. He issued a report on what staff should be doing to improve the quality of their customer service.

Rumours began circulating about Simon. 'He's all talk,' people were saying. 'He says one thing and means another.' 'He talks teamwork but he really wants to cut back on staff.' 'He talks big about customer service, but we don't see him practising what he preaches!'

Questions
1   Did the questions Simon asked the staff in their interviews reflect his stated commitment to teamwork and customer service? Why, or why not?
2   Was Simon's 'pep talk' reflected in his subsequent dealings with employees?
3   What problems do you see in Simon's communications with the store staff?
4   People sometimes say one thing and do another. How does this show up in their communications with others?

CASE STUDY 2.3

Sandra's Solution:
Putting It In writing!

'Sandra, would you mind coming in here for a moment? I want to talk about the standard operating procedures. I'm concerned because I don't think they're being followed correctly.'

'Sure, Linda. What is it you're worried about?'

'Well, I have four items here that were completed today. They clearly show the SOPs weren't adhered to. I'm worried not only from a quality point of view but also from the safety aspect. I'd hate to see anyone get hurt.'

'Yes, I know what you're getting at. Short cuts are being taken. The problem is, sometimes it doesn't matter and sometimes it does. The staff don't seem to be taking that into account.'

'Mmm. Yes, well, the SOPs have been very carefully worked out and I really expect everyone to follow all of them all of the time. What do you think we can do about this?'

'Well, as it happens, we had a meeting and thrashed it all out only last week. Or at least, I thought we'd thrashed it out. I don't want to call another meeting because we're running to tight deadlines over the next few weeks. How would it be if I drafted up a memo reminding everyone to follow procedures?'

'That's one option. Do you think it would work?'

'Well, no, I guess not. If the meeting didn't work, I don't suppose a memo would do much.' Pause. 'Maybe the problem is the procedures are just too complicated for people to get straight. Now that I think about it, that did come up at the meeting. Hmm. What if I rewrote the SOPs in key point form so they could be referred to and followed at a glance? We could post them by the work stations then. That might just do the trick.'

'Thanks, Sandra. That sounds like a good idea. How long do you think it would take you?'

'Oh, not long. I know most of them off by heart anyway and I'll just refer to the manual to make sure I don't leave anything out. I think if I get stuck into it, I could have them ready by tomorrow.'

'Great! Why don't you write them up and I'll see you tomorrow at coffee to see how you're getting on. I'll take a look at them before you post them, if you like.'

'Yes, okay, great. See you tomorrow.'

Questions

1   Was Sandra correct in thinking the memo wouldn't work? Why, or why not?
2   How will having key point SOPs to refer to help the situation?
3   If Linda's boss asked her for a short report summarising the problems with following standard operating procedures, how could it be structured? Prepare an outline showing the main sections.
4   Analyse the conversation between Linda and Sandra and list the elements that made it effective.

Answers to Rapid Review questions

1. T 2. T 3. F 4. F 5. F 6. F 7. F 8. T 9. F 10. T 11. T 12. T 13. T
14. T 15. F 16. T 17. T 18. T 19. F 20. F 21. F

CHAPTER 3

LEADING BY EXAMPLE: PERSONAL SKILLS FOR SUPERVISORS

Sam's dilemma

Sam was at a career crossroads. Should he accept the sideways move that he had been offered? It would certainly widen his experience in the organisation, but did it in some way imply a 'slap on the wrist'? Maybe he wasn't involved enough in corporate politics and was now paying the price. Maybe his 'image' wasn't right. Maybe he hadn't nurtured the 'right people' or developed a strong enough network of supporters. Or maybe it really *would* be a good long-term career move.

What direction should his career take? What could he do to become a more effective supervisor and, also important, what could he do to be *seen* to be an effective supervisor? What personal skills did he need to strengthen?

Change jobs or not: what should he do? When all was said and done, it boiled down to what he wanted out of life, anyway. Just what was that?

OVERVIEW

How do you know whether you have what it takes to be a good supervisor? In this chapter you will discover the personal skills supervisors need. You will learn how to develop them and manage yourself and your job.

- Do you know how to set sensible goals that will motivate you and help you succeed?
- Do you know how to find, and benefit from, a mentor?
- Can you survive the quagmire of organisational politics?
- Do you know why you should build strong networks and how to build them?
- Can you manage your personal image for maximum success?
- Can you analyse an organisation's culture and know what to do to fit into it well?

- Can you assess a person's power and influence and build your own personal power?
- Do you blame others when things go wrong or are you mature enough to take responsibility?
- Do you know how to build an effective working relationship with your boss and get your ideas implemented?
- Are you comfortable making presentations to small groups and can you make them well?
- Do you manage your time effectively or do you work hard, achieve little and pay the price in stress?

AM I UP TO IT?

Would it surprise you to learn that many managers feel like 'frauds'? That is, deep down, they wonder if they are up to their job. Are they qualified? Are they the sort of person others respect? Will people follow their lead? Are they quick-witted enough to make important decisions? Have they enough conceptual skills for a strategic overview? Are they really as skilled and talented as others seem to think they are?

Developing your personal skills in managing yourself and your job can go a long way towards reducing the self-doubts that most managers have. After all, before we can manage others, we must first be able to manage ourselves! We cannot realistically expect to be responsible for leading others before we accept responsibility for ourselves.

SETTING PERSONAL GOALS

In 1953 the graduates of Yale University were asked if they had written down clear, specific goals and if they had a plan for achieving them. Only 3% had taken the time to do this. Twenty years later, a follow-up study showed that same 3% were worth more (in terms of dollars) than the other 97% put together. Not only were they financially better off, but they also seemed to be better off in more difficult-to-measure areas such as their happiness and joy from life. A similar study was repeated with the 1972 graduates of the Harvard Business School MBA program. The follow-up study in 1992 had nearly identical results. These studies show the power of goal setting.

It's been said that:

'If we don't know where we're going, any road will get us somewhere.'

To achieve our goals, we must know clearly what they are.

People who are successful, by any criteria, have clear goals and action plans. They usually write them down and review and update them every year.

Values

To have a sound life plan, you need to know what your values are. Values are deeply and strongly held beliefs and principles. They are so much a part of us that they are often buried beneath our conscious awareness. Our **value system** covers such things as what we believe is right and wrong, good and bad, should and shouldn't be. It provides an 'inner compass' that guides our actions and decisions.

What do you hold dear? What do you want from life? What is important to you? To find out your own values, turn to Box 3.1. Circle the values you believe are most important. Then select the ten most important values from those you've circled. These are the top ten values by which you live your life. They describe what you hold to be true, important and worthwhile. They silently guide your behaviour, your communications and the choices you make about the way you live your life and manage your career.

How to write a life plan

Most of us are happy to plan, and indeed expect to plan, most things—a holiday, a day's outing, even a trip to the supermarket. Yet few of us, less than 3%, it appears, plan the most important event of all—our own lives! Take some time out to develop your own life plan— it will set you on the road to achieving your life goals.

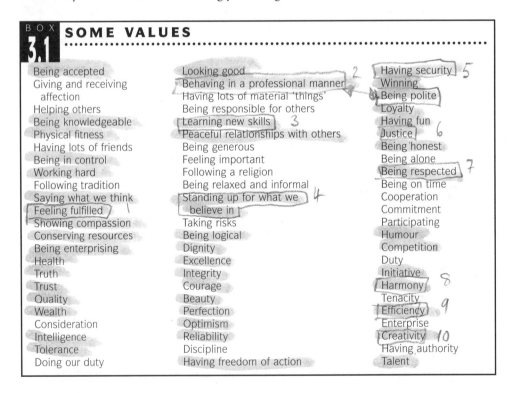

BOX 3.1 SOME VALUES

Being accepted	Looking good	Having security
Giving and receiving affection	Behaving in a professional manner	Winning
	Having lots of material 'things'	Being polite
Helping others	Being responsible for others	Loyalty
Being knowledgeable	Learning new skills	Having fun
Physical fitness	Peaceful relationships with others	Justice
Having lots of friends	Being generous	Being honest
Being in control	Feeling important	Being alone
Working hard	Following a religion	Being respected
Following tradition	Being relaxed and informal	Being on time
Saying what we think	Standing up for what we believe in	Cooperation
Feeling fulfilled		Commitment
Showing compassion	Taking risks	Participating
Conserving resources	Being logical	Humour
Being enterprising	Dignity	Competition
Health	Excellence	Duty
Truth	Integrity	Initiative
Trust	Courage	Harmony
Quality	Beauty	Tenacity
Wealth	Perfection	Efficiency
Consideration	Optimism	Enterprise
Intelligence	Reliability	Creativity
Tolerance	Discipline	Having authority
Doing our duty	Having freedom of action	Talent

FIGURE 3.1   DEVELOPING A LIFE PLAN

Role	Key person from this role	What they would say at your 75th birthday party	Key themes
Partner			
Parent			
Son or daughter			
Employee			
Student			
Committee member			
Sibling			
Supervisor			
Volunteer worker			
Colleague			
Club member			
Friend			
Other key roles			

Think about your various life roles: partner, parent, supervisor, student, and so on (see Figure 3.1). Think about your major life areas: your career, your mental and physical health, your personal life, and so on (see Figure 3.2). What are you aiming at in each of these areas? What sort of person do you wish to be in each of them? How do you want to relate with others? What contributions do you want to make?

Spend some time alone with a pencil and notepad thinking around these questions. Some people like to imagine the 'significant others' in their life making a speech at their 75th birthday party. What would they say? (See Figure 3.1.) Others like to sit quietly and write down all the words and phrases that describe them, or that they would like to describe them (see Box 3.2). Others make mind maps. Everyone needs to find their own 'best way' to do this. Do what feels right for you. However you prefer to do it, spend time on this because this plan will give your life overall direction and guidance. It will give power to your leadership.

Now look back over your thoughts. What are the common themes? Set some specific goals in each of the main areas of your life (see Figure 3.2.). Set yourself some *longer-term goals*, goals to work towards over, say, the next two or three years. Then divide these into *short-term objectives* that you can realistically expect to achieve in, say, the next six to 12 months. If these still seem 'far away', chunk them down again into *targets* with a shorter

FIGURE 3.2   SETTING LIFE GOALS

Major life area	Goals (3 year goals)	Objectives (6–12 month goals)	Targets	Measures or milestones	Action steps
Career					
Health					
Personal life					
Family life					
Social life					
Community life					
Spiritual life					

BOX 3.2 DEVELOPING A PERSONAL VISION AND LIFE PLAN
....

Step 1   List all the words you can think of that describe you when you are *at your best*. Include words that you would *like* to describe yourself with and words that you would like your friends, family and colleagues to use about you. Aim for about 75 words. Here are some to get you started:

Dedicated	Responsible	Persistent	Reliable
Leader	Unique	Persuasive	Trustworthy
Fair	Sincere	Honest	Hard-working
Enthusiastic	Calm	Balanced	Thoughtful
Empathic	Funny	Caring	Forceful
Considerate	Assertive	Thorough	Dynamic
Loving	Inventive	Creative	Fun-loving

Step 2   Select the ten or so most important or significant words and use these to develop one or two sentences that describe you and your beliefs. This is your personal vision.

Step 3   Now decide *how* you can become more like your vision. For example, if part of your vision is to be a caring person, ask yourself: 'What do I need to do to be more caring?' Brainstorm a list of specific things you could do.

Step 4   Use this list to develop a specific action plan. What will you do? When will you do it? Who will you do it with? Where will you do it?

---

time frame. Keep asking: 'What will I need to do to achieve this?' until you arrive at a clear goal which you can 'see' yourself achieving.

Next ask yourself: 'How will I know I've succeeded in this?' Write down three or four specific *measures*, or *milestones*, by which you can assess your progress towards each goal. Then list the first two or three steps you will need to take to achieve each target. Remember:

'A goal without an action plan is just a wish.'

Develop your own personal vision and life plan using or adapting the methods shown in Box 3.2 or Figure 3.2. Then do a 'reality test'. Box 3.3 suggests questions to help you consider how committed you are to your personal life plan and goals.

PLANNING YOUR CAREER

Once you know your life goals, you are in a good position to plan your career. Careers do not often consist of promotion following on promotion until you become the chief executive.

What sort of work activities do you enjoy and which do you dislike? Your career plan should begin with a thorough analysis of your skills, abilities and restrictions. The career audit shown in Figure 3.3 will help you here.

Your career plan may include a promotion or two (or even three). It may include one or more sideways moves in order to gain experience in a range of jobs and tasks, or to increase

BOX 3.3 **ACHIEVING YOUR LIFE PLAN**

For each key theme in your life plan and for each of your goals and objectives, ask yourself:

- How well am I achieving this now?
- Is my goal challenging enough?
- Is it clear?
- Have I defined the action steps clearly?
- What do I need to do to move closer to my goal? Do I need further formal education, or to read more, for example?

- Are the people around me supporting me in reaching my goals?
- Do I consciously 'live' my vision, even when it's difficult?
- Am I willing to pay the price (time and effort) to succeed?

FIGURE 3.3   CAREER AUDIT

Talents/aptitudes/flairs

What are you good at? For example, a knack for working with machines or numbers, for detailed work or for fixing things?

Problem solving, Sourcing, planning, communicating, diplomacy. dealing with people.

Abilities

What skills and knowledge have you acquired? For instance, working with facts and figures, thinking up ideas, analysing problems, dealing with people, researching information. (Don't restrict yourself to skills learned at work—think about your hobbies too!)

dealing with people, art, methods, analysing - collecting info. Co-ordinating many tasks/projects.

Activities enjoyed most

What work activities do you most enjoy? For example, helping others? Tasks offering structure? Freedom? Flexibility? A sense of achievement? Solving problems?

Solving problems, helping others, structure yet flexibility too. Achievements. Involvement - projects, variety

Restrictions

What restrictions exist concerning the job you would take? For example, can you only work days? Are you able to work weekends? To travel away from home? To put in long hours?

lack of experience/knowledge - formal (.Age) - reporting, business practices - In depth.

Options

What types of job does all this suggest you should consider further?

Project mgt, troubleshooter, mediator type roll, Teaching ?

job interest. It may need a 'downward' move to pick up a skill that is important to you, taking a job with different working hours or responsibilities to give you more personal time, working on special projects, standing in for someone on leave, contributing to committees, or moving into an entirely different field. You may decide to stay in your current role if it provides you with the level of interest and challenge you want, or to develop your current job by adding to your current duties and perhaps passing others on that no longer motivate you.

Don't assume your organisation is looking after your career for you. Once you have decided the direction your career will take, list the options open to you, remembering that there are many ways to accomplish a goal. Then think about the additional skills, knowledge and experience you will need to gain to achieve your career goals. Finally, establish some career milestones, with target dates, to aim for. Keep up to date in your field and keep adding new skills. Join professional associations to extend your networks. Take charge of your career.

MENTORS

Wouldn't it be nice to have a knowledgeable and experienced person 'show you the ropes', teach you, encourage you, help you learn from your mistakes, advise you on career options and fill you in on office politics? People who do this are called **mentors**. They are usually older, more experienced people higher up in the organisation who take an interest in you and your career. Although they are often in the same organisation, they are not necessarily your direct manager or even from your department. Wherever they are, however, they are people who can provide help, advice and support as you travel along your career path.

Some organisations believe the process of mentoring is so important that they have formalised it. As part of the career planning and performance review process, employees complete personal development plans and state their development goals. Then they either select a mentor or one is assigned to them. These mentors because of their experience, expertise and background, can help employees achieve their goals. In some organisations, the mentor and mentee, or protégé, meet informally or semi-formally once a month to discuss progress, difficulties, future plans, and so on. In other organisations, the frequency and type of meeting is left up to the people concerned. Many organisations find that this formal mentoring process is a reliable way to help employees develop their skills and build networks throughout the organisation.

Most often, though, mentoring is an informal, voluntary process. Mentors usually choose the people they will help, so if you notice a more senior manager spending time with you and offering advice, listen carefully!

Would you benefit from a mentor but don't have one? You could be proactive and make the first approach. Look for someone who:

- is well respected;
- has the life and work experience necessary to help you deal with issues of concern to you and the skills you want to improve;
- is a good listener—you don't want them to solve problems for you but help you uncover your own solutions;
- is candid—so you'll get both the positive and constructive feedback you need; and
- will keep your conversations confidential.

THE **BIG** PICTURE

In *The Odyssey*, Homer tells us about Odysseus, who was leaving for the siege of Troy in 1194 BC. He wanted to make sure his son, Telemachus, would be well looked after, so he asked a friend to care for the boy and teach him, advise him, and be his friend. The name of Telemachus's guide was Mentor.

When you ask someone to be your mentor, make it clear what help you think you'll need, and put time limits on it. Don't rush up and say, 'Will you be my mentor?'

ORGANISATIONAL POLITICS

Wherever people come together, politics will occur as individuals jostle for their place in the pecking order, for influence and for respect. Organisational politics affect all members of the management team, including supervisors; they often affect non-management employees, too.

Should you become involved in politics? Politics are a reality in any organisation. It is pointless to discuss the rights and wrongs of politics although, certainly, people spend a great deal of energy politicking that they could undoubtedly use more productively. You may find it useful to think of politics as a game to be played in order to gain the influence you need to make the best contribution you can to your organisation.

'Playing' organisation politics is about managing your image in a positive way, fitting in with, and contributing to, the organisation's culture, recognising who has formal and informal power and influence, and networking with them. It is about managing your boss, getting your ideas implemented, and such things as finding out who to 'stay away from' and whose opinions you should listen to most carefully.

Organisation politics probably need to be played to some degree by managers at every level. Those who overplay politics, though, usually lose out eventually. An ability to play politics, without the underlying management and technical skills, abilities and values to support it, is not enough in most modern organisations.

FROM THEORY TO PRACTICE

Who is getting promoted in your organisation? Whose ideas are implemented? Who is offered the interesting assignments? What skills and traits do they have in common? Observe the people one or two levels above you—what do they have in common?

The answers to these questions will be different in an organisation that is expanding to one that is downsizing. An organisation's culture, industry, size and environment determine the competencies, skills and attribute sets that are most valued.

NETWORKING

⋮... A recent study by Luthans, Hodgetts and Rosenkrantz of over 450 managers found that the managers who were promoted fastest spent 48% of their time **networking**; managers who were ranked as 'average' spent only 19% of their time networking.

Networking is not just about seeing and being seen, or petty politicking. It is about learning what information is important to people, how they like things presented, what they're thinking about, what information they need from others, and how and when it should be presented. Developing this kind of understanding helps you get things done and make things happen.

A network is an informal web of relationships inside and outside your organisation that you can call on for help, information, advice and support; you can extend the same to others in your network. It is a way of expanding your sphere of influence and increasing your sources of information. The more people you know and come together with, the more information you will have access to, and the more 'behind-the-scenes' influence you will gradually come to hold.

Interacting formally and informally with people inside and outside your organisation is part of networking. Being active in service clubs, social clubs, industry groups and other special-interest groups related to your work and interests is an important means of networking. Attending seminars and conferences and generally getting out and about and putting yourself, your industry and your organisation forward in a good light is also part of networking.

YOUR IMAGE

⋮... Cynics say image is everything. Realists recognise the importance of image in organisational life and take steps to ensure that others see them in the best possible light. Here are six ways to present a positive image:

- *Create winning teams.* Recruit high-calibre people, train them well and support their efforts. Generate enthusiasm, enhance employees' self-esteem, and set and achieve high performance standards.
- *Develop a reputation as reliable and competent.* Deliver the goods, complete projects successfully, understand your industry and your organisation, manage people well and 'talk sense'.
- *Communicate openly, honestly and tactfully.* An important part of a professional image is establishing a reputation for reliable and straightforward communications balanced with consideration for others.
- *Make sure you are associated with success.* Give credit where credit is due and, without 'blowing your own trumpet', ensure that others know about your achievements. Have plans to improve things and discuss your plans with others. Take time to make your team's successes known and talked about throughout the organisation and avoid empty publicity that you cannot back up with solid achievement.
- *Build networks.* Try to be in the right place at the right time and build relationships with influential people. Demonstrate, by word and deed, your loyalty and commitment to your job, your department, your organisation and your customers.
- *Look and act the part.* Make sure your attitude is generally positive. Dress in the manner considered appropriate in your organisation, or for the job to which you aspire. Make sure

your personal style blends well with your organisation's culture so it is clear to others that you belong in your job.

BUILDING TRUST

According to leadership scholar Warren Bennis,

'Trust is the lubrication that makes it possible for organisations to work.'

Trust is fragile. It takes time to build and only seconds to destroy. Once lost, it can be difficult to earn back. Supervisors need to be especially sensitive to the need to gain and keep the trust of their work teams and colleagues and the management of their organisation. Here are six keys to building trust:
- Be considerate and empathic.
- Remember the little things.
- Keep commitments.
- Clarify expectations.
- Be loyal.
- Be sincere.

ORGANISATION CULTURE

The culture of an organisation is the collection of behaviours and attitudes by which it operates. It is made up of people's beliefs, values, ways of working and assumptions and translates into **norms**, the unwritten code of behaviour, or the 'rules' of 'how we do things around here'. These norms have a strong influence on the way every organisation operates, on its morale and on its effectiveness. Some of the many ways you can gauge an organisation's culture are shown in the *From theory to practice* box on page 88.

The answers to these questions describe the culture of your organisation. This is important for two reasons:
1. You need to observe the unwritten organisational codes in order to be seen to 'fit in' and to operate effectively within your organisation's culture.
2. As a leader, you need to know what the norms of your work teams are and ensure that they support, not undermine, the organisation's mission and goals.

Subcultures

No organisation is a homogeneous mass of individuals who all look alike, think alike and act alike. Within an organisation's overall culture, subgroups form, made up of departments, work groups and cliques. Each of these subgroups has its own **subculture**, or operating code: its own common language, dress, rituals, 'hangouts' and performance expectations.

Get to know what subgroups exist in your organisation, what functions they perform, which are the most and least influential, knowledgeable, and so on. Who are their informal leaders? Who is in the 'inner circle' and who is excluded from it? Observe and find out what makes one group different from another so that you can overcome any barriers you might find when trying to deal with members of different subcultures. The more you know about the various subcultures of your organisation, the more effectively you will be able to work with them.

Corporate culture generally filters down from senior management; we interpret what we should do from what they do (not what they say). This applies to work-team subcultures,

FROM THEORY TO PRACTICE

List some words that describe your work team and the way people work together and individually. Now answer these questions:

- What behaviours are rewarded and respected? What behaviours are 'punished' or disapproved of?
- How do people treat external customers? Internal customers? Each other?
- How would you describe the management and supervisory style?
- What are people's attitudes towards their job and the organisation?
- What is the work ethic—for example, is it a 'She'll be right!' or a 'Get it right!' approach to work? How hard do people work?
- What priorities do they select?
- How much fun do people have while they're working?
- Do they socialise at all? What do people do at breaks and for lunch?
- How much attention to detail do they pay (or not pay)?
- How would you describe people's work areas? Cosy, friendly, business-like, clear desks, messy desks, etc.?
- What are the attitudes and practices regarding health, safety and the environment?
- What time do people arrive at and leave work?
- How formally or informally do they dress?
- What style of language do they use?
- Where, how and by whom are decisions made?
- Is there a relaxed or a more formal (or even a tense) atmosphere?

too: people take their cues from the team leader. The actions of the supervisors and senior managers either reinforce or undermine the written rules, goals and mission of the organisation. In this way, corporate culture and subcultures can help an organisation move forward or hold it back.

FROM THEORY TO PRACTICE

Leaders at all levels can help build a strong corporate culture.

- Make it clear to people what you stand for.
- Pay attention to details.
- Generate pride in the organisation and how individuals contribute to it.
- Be positive.
- Make your department's goals and vision clear to everyone and repeat them often.
- Walk your talk.

If you don't help create a positive culture, be prepared to pay the price of a negative one.

> ## THE **BIG** PICTURE
> ···
> Management needs to establish a culture that supports its vision and
> goals. Does it want innovation or entrepreneurialism? If so, it will have to reward
> risk takers and 'wave makers'.

POWER AND INFLUENCE

:··· In the next chapter we look at organisation structure and organisation charts. This is the
formal organisation. Important as it is to the way an enterprise functions, it is only part
of the picture. The other part is the **informal organisation**, or power and influence
hierarchy.

Power gives us some authority over the behaviour of others. Formal power can 'get us
what we want'.

Influence is another matter. The chief executive's secretary may have little formal power
but tremendous influence (or informal power). Others in the organisation, often at middle
and junior level, may have influence because of their expertise in certain key areas or their
close contact with those in power.

Are you politically astute enough to know who holds influence and power in your
organisation and include them in your networks? To find out who actually has power and
influence, you need to read between the lines of your formal organisation chart. Who
generates ideas? Who can convince others when no one else can? Whose opinion counts?
Who are the informal, unofficial leaders? What are the important networks and cliques?
Who socialises with whom? Who recruited whom? Who trained whom?

Power rarely lies with just one person; more often it rests with a group of people who
respect each other and share similar ideas, values and experiences, and a similar vision for
their organisation.

Where will your power and influence as a supervisor come from? There are six sources.
Three are based on formal authority or *position power*, three on influence, or *personal power*.

Position power

Position power is based on someone's formal authority in the organisation. *Legitimate power*
refers to a person's right to issue orders and instructions and someone else's duty to carry
them out. When we feel we 'should' do something because 'the boss says so', we are
responding to legitimate power.

Reward power is based on someone's ability to distribute something of value: pay
increases, promotion, positive performance appraisals, overtime, interesting work assignments. When we do something in the hope of getting something in return, we are responding to reward power.

Coercive power is based on fear. It rests on someone's ability to discipline. If we do
something in order to avoid an unpleasant outcome—for example, criticism, withholding
of overtime or termination of employment—we are responding to coercive power.

Position power is based on the formal authority a person holds and the resources they are officially able to control. In the past, supervisors relied heavily on this formal power, but this reliance has diminished in recent years.

The 19th-century French novelist, Honoré de Balzac, observed:

'Power is not revealed by striking hard or often, but by striking true.'

He was, perhaps, commenting on the difference between position power and personal power.

Personal power

Personal power describes a person's informal influence. *Expert power* comes from people's special skills and knowledge, usually gained through study and experience, and their 'track record'. Expertise attracts both admiration and respect. Much of a supervisor's authority derives from job knowledge. When we do something because we assume our manager knows best, expert power is influencing us. Supervisors should ideally have some expertise in the technology and work of their group. Knowledge of the organisation as a whole and how it operates is also part of job knowledge. Knowing what needs to be done and where, when, why and how it should be done will earn you a great deal of personal respect. Expert power is built through training and the wisdom of experience.

Referent power is sometimes known as charismatic power. It is based on the goodwill, liking and respect that someone has earned. It is that special something in the personality that attracts followers. Part of it comes from the ability to build cooperative and supportive working relationships. Supervisors who take the time and trouble to develop sound relationships with others increase their power base. Rapport, a good working relationship, mutual respect, friendship and admiration all play a part. When we do something because we want to be supportive or cooperative towards a manager we like, that manager's referent power is influencing us.

Integrity is another aspect of referent power. Acting consistently to a clear set of standards and personal guidelines that fit in with and support the organisation's standards, and not deviating from them, is very powerful and attractive to others.

Information power comes from the interesting information and knowledge a person has and can share with others. This might include explaining the reasons behind a decision, providing training, or passing on inside information about 'behind the scenes' goings-on in the organisation. When we do something because we can now understand the reasons for it due to our manager's clear explanation or good training, information power is influencing us.

Influence is the more important and reliable power base of today's supervisor. It rests on personal qualities, attributes and knowledge that people respect them for possessing. Qualities such as self-respect and respect for others, integrity, honesty, trustworthiness and strength of personal vision and values are particularly important in building personal power. (See also Chapter 19 for a discussion on authority and power.)

Building your personal power

The changes that are occurring in our organisations and in society are increasing the importance of personal power. This means that supervisors need to know practical ways of building their own personal power. Sixty successful first-line and middle managers from a variety of industries all over Australia and New Zealand were asked how they built their own personal power. Box 3.4 summarises their responses.

BOX 3.4   BUILDING PERSONAL POWER

- Ask rather than tell.
- Show respect for your staff: treat each of them as a VIP.
- Walk your talk—practise what you preach.
- Be informed and share your information with your staff.
- Be approachable.
- Be 'fair dinkum'—know that loyalty is a two-way street.
- Be honest and sincere in your feedback.
- Make it happen!
- Acknowledge good effort and praise good work.
- Build and be part of high-performing teams.
- Acknowledge and assist the achievement of both personal and team goals.

- Demonstrate trust in your staff.
- Delegate increasingly larger responsibilities.
- Show empathy with your staff's personal problems.
- Hire good people.
- Give adequate training.
- Remember the social side of work— have some fun!
- Keep equipment up to scratch.
- Make sure staff uniforms look good, so that we feel good.
- Maintain adequate staffing levels.
- Know your staff's strengths and weaknesses, likes and dislikes.
- Respect yourself and others.

FROM THEORY TO PRACTICE

You have planned on a promotion within a year. How will personal image, networking, organisational politics, power and organisational culture work for you or against you? What can you do to minimise negative influences in any of these areas?

Blame or responsibility?

Imagine a supervisor who goes around blaming others, circumstances or the environment for his misfortunes and problems. Or when things don't go according to plan, or someone makes a mistake, she rants and raves but does nothing to get things back on track or show the employee what to do next time? Such a supervisor would have very little personal power and probably wouldn't last long in the role.

Taking responsibility increases people's personal power as well as their overall effectiveness.

'Don't just see problems. Solve them.'

BOX 3.5   SELF-CHECK

- ❑ Do you accept responsibility for making things happen?
- ❑ When things go wrong, do you see what you can do to put them right?
- ❑ Do you treat mistakes—your own or others—as learning opportunities?
- ❑ Is your focus on the future?
- ❑ Is your orientation proactive?

MANAGING YOUR BOSS

Do you tend to think your boss is the person responsible for establishing and maintaining a good working relationship with you? Think again—managing your relationship with your boss is part of your job, too. The responsibility goes both ways.

While managing your relationship with your own manager can take time and energy, it can increase your effectiveness in your job and save a lot of problems in the long run. You will need a good understanding of your manager as well as of yourself, particularly regarding strengths, weaknesses, work style and foremost concerns.

What is in your boss's 'world'? What issues and concerns are uppermost in his mind? What are her organisational and personal goals? What pressures are on him from his own boss and colleagues? Does she prefer to receive information through memos, formal meetings or informal discussions? Does he like to know all the details or just the end result? Is she task-focused or more people-oriented? Knowing these things will help you fit in with your manager's working style and support your manager better. If you don't know the answers to these questions, you are flying blind and misunderstandings are inevitable.

Seek information about your boss's goals, problems and pressures. Use your empathy and pay attention to behavioural clues. Question your manager to find out what is expected of you; find ways to let your manager know what your own needs and expectations are. If your boss doesn't accept one of your recommendations or ideas, try to look at the situation from your boss's point of view.

See yourself as your boss's partner in achieving results and meeting priorities. Just as you are dependent on your manager for help, guidance, resources and information, your manager depends on you for help and cooperation. Accept your boss's decisions and ideas and work to make them succeed.

Do what you're asked to do. If you disagree, explain why and offer an alternative.

Don't expect your boss to be perfect—no one is. If you're unhappy with your boss's style of managing you, suggest ways you could work better together. Don't focus on personal shortcomings but on specific behaviours. Describe them in objective, not judgmental or critical, terms. Say what you *do* want, not what you *don't* want and focus on the future and what you'd like to happen. (See also Chapter 24.)

FROM THEORY TO PRACTICE

Here are five questions to ask your boss:
1. What are my key result areas and main goals?
2. What operating guidelines do you want me to work within?
3. How will we measure my performance?
4. How do you prefer to receive progress reports and general information?
5. How can I help you do your job better?

Maybe you already know the answers to these questions. What does that tell you about your boss and the organisation you work for?

Do you feel uncomfortable telling others about your achievements? Here are some ideas to project a positive image to your manager without becoming boring or developing a reputation as a braggart.

• Schedule a meeting every few weeks to update your manager on your work, what you've accomplished, what problems you have resolved or are working on, and generally how things are going. Be objective and factual to avoid bragging.

• Report any big problems early on before they grow, and take the facts with you (see Chapter 11).

• Aim to come up with one good idea a month to present to your manager. It doesn't have to be anything major. How can you serve customers better, smooth out the workflow, create a motivating atmosphere? If one a month seems too many or too few, adjust your target.

• Prepare a summary to share with others about what you learned on a seminar or workshop you attended. Put what you've learned into practice and let your manager know how well it worked.

• Listen to any tips your manager passes on about how you can do your job better and put them into practice.

GETTING YOUR IDEAS IMPLEMENTED

It goes without saying that your ideas need to be well thought out, practical and cost-effective! But that isn't the end of the story. You can do a number of things to help get them implemented.

First, test them on a few people. This will help you gauge likely responses, concerns and questions, and allow you to prepare more thoroughly for your final presentation. You might also be able to incorporate others' ideas into your proposal, allowing them to feel some ownership of it and respond more positively to it. Get your manager's input, too.

Build support. In what order should you approach people when getting their support? Who should you speak to face-to-face and who would prefer a memo? How do others in the organisation go about getting their ideas accepted? Who will support you and who should you get onside before formally putting forward your recommendations? Running your ideas by several people first provides a 'comfort level' with a proposal from having heard it before.

Who is likely to oppose your ideas? Prepare for opposition, too—sometimes we are so positive about our own ideas that we don't see potential opposition. In your previews with others, ask: 'If someone were to object to this idea, what do you think the objection might be?'

When it's time to present your ideas, do so effectively:

✓ Write down your ideas clearly and persuasively and set them out well.

✓ Take into account the recipient's preferred mode of dealing with information (see Chapter 19). For example, does the person whose approval you need prefer to consider the overall picture or to know all the details?

✓ Focus on what is important to the decision makers (bottom line, effect on morale, public image) to encourage a positive response.

✓ Take into account how your ideas will be evaluated and who the decision makers will consult. A direct, formal approach to your immediate manager may not always be the best strategy. Perhaps it would be better to float the idea informally, over a coffee, say, with your manager or with someone else who has power and influence.

FROM THEORY TO PRACTICE

Strategies for ideas implementation

- Give your good ideas time to mature in your own mind. Without rushing off every time you have a brainwave, float them early in their development with a few people whose opinions you trust.
- Find one or two colleagues you can use as regular sounding boards to assess the viability of your ideas and gather suggestions on how you could improve them.
- Be flexible enough to amend your ideas as new information or different opinions come to hand.
- Think through any obvious pitfalls and arguments against your ideas. Forewarned is forearmed.

EFFECTIVE PRESENTATIONS

Most supervisors are called upon to make presentations. While they will vary in their degree of formality, preparing and making presentations is an important skill that most supervisors need.

Unfortunately, making a presentation rates high on most people's list of fears. Why? Nerves! Nerves are caused by lack of knowledge, lack of preparation and lack of confidence. We can overcome all three by knowing our material thoroughly, by preparing carefully and by practising.

Preparing a presentation

Step 1   *Write your objectives.* What is the main purpose of your presentation? Have a definite goal in mind and keep it clearly visible as you prepare it.

Step 2   *Analyse your audience.* Who will you be making the presentation to? Why will they be attending it? What is their background knowledge of the subject? What do you want them to think, do or feel as a result of it? What will it take to persuade them?

Step 3   *Decide what to say.* Brainstorm the points you could make and the supporting evidence you could use. Jot down your ideas as they occur to you. There's no need to write in full sentences, just key ideas.

Step 4   *Select your material.* Bearing in mind your audience, objectives and the time available for your presentation, look over your ideas. Cross out any that aren't necessary.

Step 5   *Organise your material.* Put the ideas you do want to use into a logical sequence. Make sure it flows well, with one point leading easily into the next. (See Chapter 2 for some ideas on structuring material.) Remember, you're still working in key

FROM THEORY TO PRACTICE

Tips for making presentations

- Take a few deep breaths before you begin to relax and deliver some oxygen to your brain.
- Project your voice strongly and clearly so that it can be heard, and articulate the words clearly. People don't want to strain their ears to hear you.
- Strive for a conversational tone of voice which expresses enthusiasm and commitment to your topic. A low-level, monotone or lifeless voice is guaranteed to put even the kindest audience to sleep.
- Avoid filler words and non-words—'uhm', 'ah', 'ya know', and so on.
- Use gestures to emphasise key points. Be natural and relaxed, neither stiff as a soldier at attention nor a fidgeting bundle of nerves.
- You may want to move around a little bit (it helps to release tension) but avoid rocking, shuffling or pacing back and forth. Like fidgeting, this only distracts your audience.
- Make eye contact with as many people as you can. Let your eyes meet with the eyes of audience members for at least five seconds, or a complete thought. This makes you look confident, establishes rapport, gets you some feedback and personalises your information.
- Refer to your notes when you need them but, at all costs, avoid reading out your presentation word for word.
- Know the audience is on your side.
- Relax and be yourself!

words in this step. Think about any visual aids, handouts or other aids you could use that will help people to grasp your ideas.

Step 6 *Write the talk.* Some people prefer to write their presentation out in full, using complete sentences. Once they are more practised at making presentations, though, most prefer to stick with a key point outline using only words or phrases. This ensures they won't bore their audience by reading their presentation word for word.

Once you have written the main *body* of your presentation, develop a short *introduction* that will make the audience want to 'sit up and listen'. What would grab their attention? Is there a startling fact or piece of information you could begin with? Or a short story that would lead nicely into your topic? Your introduction should capture the audience's attention and interest, and establish your objectives. Finally, write a short *conclusion* summarising your main points and pointing to next steps. Don't forget to thank people for their attention.

Step 7 *Practise.* The more times you run through your presentation, the more confidence you will gain and the better it will be. Practise out loud, standing up (if you'll be delivering it standing up). Time it to make sure it's the correct length.

Your goal is not to memorise, but to know clearly what you are going to say so that you will only have to glance at your notes occasionally. Consider using index cards with key words or phrases on them.

Making a presentation

Here is where all your hard work pays off. Don't worry about your nervousness—everyone gets slightly nervous. Think of your presentation as an expanded conversation with a few friends. Focus on your audience and on making sure they understand your message. This will help take your focus off you and your nerves.

MANAGING YOUR TIME

'Time is a non-renewable resource, equally available to us all to squander or to spend wisely.'

Time is a concept by which we structure and calibrate our lives. It exists only in our minds. It is an abstraction that some people seem able to do more with than others! One of a supervisor's most challenging tasks is to make the best use of the time available. After all:

'If you can't manage your own time, what *can* you manage?'

Poor time management leads to harassment and stress. You can easily spot poor time managers: they are the ones who rush around, often trying to do several things at once, but actually achieve very little by the end of the day. Having fallen into the 'activity trap', they go home and, when asked 'What did you do today?' can't really say. They are the ones who worry—usually about all the things they have left undone. They are the ones whose jobs control them, not the other way around. They may work hard, but they don't get things done. Working hard and being effective are two entirely different things. Results, not activity, are what count.

The key to effective time management

Most supervisors find their days are so busy it is impossible to do everything. Effective supervisors have learned to make decisions about what they will do *now*, what they will do *later*, what they will *delegate*, and what they will only do *if time permits*. To do this, they need to understand their overall *job goals* and **key result areas**—those areas of responsibility which, if effectively attended to, ensure their own and their department's overall success.

Knowing these, they can prioritise their tasks and concentrate on the activities that will contribute *directly* to their overall job goals. It helps them to distinguish between important and unimportant, vital and superfluous.

Important or just urgent?

Many poor time managers become caught in the trap of dealing with urgent matters and end up lurching from one crisis to another. In fact, they often create their own crises by not attending to important matters before they become urgent! A clear overview of their job would help them distinguish what's *urgent* from what's *important*.

Important tasks are usually those directed at longer-term contributions to job goals and *key result areas* (see Chapter 8). These are the essential matters we need to attend to. Urgent

FIGURE 3.4 URGENT VERSUS IMPORTANT

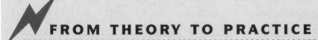

High

Importance

| Attend to yourself or delegate | Attend to these matters yourself |
| Postpone or delegate | Attend to if time or delegate |

Low   **Urgency**   High

tasks often have a short-term flavour and are not necessarily important. We can often delegate them or do them later. Figure 3.4 explains how to deal with urgent and important matters.

Knowing what is important in your job allows you to be *proactive*. You can consciously choose to do the most important things. Poor supervisors and poor time managers, on the other hand, are often *reactive*. They attend to whatever crops up, whatever is at the top of their in-tray, whatever makes the loudest or strongest attempt to gain their attention. Supervisors who are reactive are not in control—they are being controlled by outside events and often end up 'spinning their wheels' as a result.

FROM THEORY TO PRACTICE

To be a good time manager, focus on what you want to achieve and proactively make time to do things that will move you towards your goals.

The 80:20 principle

A late 19th-century Italian mathematical economist and sociologist named Vilfredo Pareto developed the 80:20 principle. Sometimes called the **Pareto principle**, it states that a small proportion of people/effort/time (20%) accounts for a large proportion of the results (80%). For example, 20% of salespeople in a sales team account for 80% of sales; 20% of customers yield 80% of the profits; 20% of the employees cause 80% of the problems.

In time management terms, the principle means, for example, that 20% of our efforts yield 80% of our good results; 20% of our interruptions account for 80% of our wasted time, and so on. This is illustrated in Figure 3.5.

FIGURE 3.5 THE PARETO PRINCIPLE

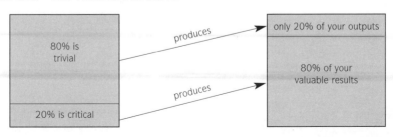

| 80% is trivial | produces → | only 20% of your outputs |
| 20% is critical | produces → | 80% of your valuable results |

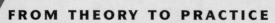

FROM THEORY TO PRACTICE

What are your critical '20 per centers'? What are the four or five things you do that are crucial (or if you don't do them, there will be a price to pay)? If you find this difficult to answer, it may be because you don't have a clear job description or clear life and job goals. You may not know what you're supposed to do. Better find out!

Time logs

Try keeping a time log for one week based on the format shown in Figure 3.6. You might be surprised at how you spend your time! Time logs often show that we waste a lot of time and spend frightening amounts of it on unnecessary and low-priority, unimportant activities. They can also show that we are not doing some of the things we should be doing.

Analysing your time log can be very enlightening. Ask yourself these questions:

- Did the activity contribute to a key result area? In other words, was it *important*?
- Was it *urgent*? If so, did I do it *reactively* (because something or someone else caused me to do it)? Or did I do it *proactively* (because I set out to do it)? Doing too many urgent tasks indicates a '*crisis management*' style.
- Was the task *not important* and *not urgent*? If so, why did I do it?
- If it was *urgent but not important*, could I have delegated it?
- Did I do many *non-urgent but important* tasks? This is a sign of good time management.
- Did I do a lot of *urgent, important* tasks? Why did I leave them to the last minute? Could I have completed them more effectively if I had done them earlier? Does this indicate I work in crisis management mode?
- What is the overall balance between *urgent* and *important* tasks? While individual jobs vary, doing too many urgent tasks can be stressful and a sign of poor time management.

Don't let urgent, unimportant matters get in the way of important tasks.

FIGURE 3.6   TIME LOG FORMAT

Time	What I was doing	Analysis	
		Urgent	*Important*
8.30			
8.45			
9.00			
9.15			
9.30			
9.45			
10.00			
10.15			
10.30			
10.45			

'When the disposal of time is surrendered to the chance of incidents, chaos will reign.'

Victor Hugo (1802–85)
Dramatist and novelist

Time management tips

Being effective means *doing the right things*; being efficient means *doing things right*. Supervisors who manage their time skilfully are both efficient and effective. Clearly, it is a waste of time to do the wrong or unnecessary things efficiently. Establishing your main job goals and key result areas will help you to use your time effectively. It will help you to set priorities on all the things you need to do so that you can make sure you do the most important things. Only then does it make sense to learn techniques to use your time efficiently as well. This is where time management tips come in.

A sample of techniques for better time management that many supervisors have found useful is given in Box 3.6.

BOX 3.6 TIME MANAGEMENT TIPS

- *Set smart goals and deadlines.* Successful people set stretching but realistic goals. Good time managers set themselves similar deadlines so that work doesn't expand to fill the time available.
- *Try not to do work yourself that you could safely delegate.* This allows you to concentrate on the most important aspects of your job and up-skills your staff as a bonus.
- *Try the Swiss cheese approach* for large, important matters and projects that require a lot of time and effort: break them down into smaller tasks and make a start on them. Even though you can't finish the project in one go, you will probably find that, after your series of smaller 'attacks', all you need is one final 'assault' to pull everything together. This technique is useful because supervisors often don't have large blocks of time available to devote to time-consuming but important matters.
- *Keep a daily or weekly 'to do' list, showing priorities.* You may not always be able to complete everything on it, but the sense of order and peace of mind that a list helps to create will more than compensate for the time it takes to write it. You will also have a sense of accomplishment as you cross items off the list as you complete them. Many supervisors make their last task of the day writing up their 'to do' list for the next day. This helps them to start work fresh each day, knowing precisely what they want to accomplish.
- *Keep a clear desk or work area.* After all, your desk is not intended as storage space! If your desk is clear, you won't have several things vying for your attention and breaking your concentration. This means that you will need a sensible filing system and a place for everything—and be willing to put things away when you are not using them. The few minutes you spend doing this will make it quicker and easier to retrieve that memo or file than searching for it on a messy desk. Only your 'to do' list, your telephone, computer, and the job you are currently working on should be on your desk.

Continued . . .

- Wherever possible, *group like activities together*. For example, try to complete several phone calls in a block of time, write memos and letters in another block of time and read your incoming mail in a third block of time. This helps give a flow to your work and means you won't have to stop and mentally readjust as you would if you hopped from one type of activity to another.
- *Learn to say 'no' (nicely) to avoid management monkeys*. Henry Mintzberg of McGill University says that too many of us have too many 'monkeys': tasks passed on to us by our own staff. Has one of your employees ever presented you with a problem relating to their own job? If you said 'Leave it with me and I'll see what I can do' when you could have said 'That's a tricky problem. What do you plan to do about it?', you have accepted a 'monkey'!

  'Monkeys' can be a great waste of time and would be better, and more properly, done by the person who 'owns' the monkey. If you suffer from management monkeys, try the above approach.
- *Don't kid yourself with 'busy work'*. Many tasks are marginally worth doing but are neither important nor urgent. We do them because we enjoy doing them or because they provide a convenient excuse for putting off other, more important or more difficult work. They might provide a false feeling of activity and accomplishment, but they stop us from doing tasks of far greater benefit.
- *Make the best use of your prime time*. Everyone has their own unique 'energy cycle'— periods when they are full of bounce and energy, periods when they are a bit flat and periods in between. Learn to use your prime times of highest energy for activities requiring careful thought and effort. Try to avoid interruptions during your prime time.
- *Discourage visitors!* Don't have too many seats in your office—it will only encourage visitors. And try not to sit facing the door; this encourages people to drop in, too.
- *Manage your in-tray and emails*. Set aside one or two periods during the day for looking through your in-tray and checking your emails rather than dealing with each one as it arrives. To avoid temptation, you may want to move your in-tray away from your desk and switch off from the Internet or intranet. When you do deal with them, don't sort through them but deal with each one in turn. Take some action on it: deal with it; delegate it; file it to bring forward at an appropriate date; throw it away; or delete it (you can always get another copy later if you find you need it).
- *Don't procrastinate!* If something needs to be done, do it. Putting it off won't make it go away or make it any easier. Let 'Do it now!' be your motto.
- *Carry an ideas notebook*. Many supervisors find that a small, pocket-sized notebook is ideal for jotting down ideas and things they want to remember as they occur to them. This 'takes a load off their brains' and stops them feeling overburdened, trying to remember everything.
- Regularly ask yourself: *What's the best use of my time right now?* When several things are demanding your attention at the same time, this simple question can be a great help in establishing priorities.

FROM THEORY TO PRACTICE

Select three time management techniques that you believe could help you use your time better. Begin a campaign to build them into your routine over the next three weeks. Then assess how effective they were.

DO SUPERVISORS GET STRESSED?

Everyone gets stressed! Without stress we would die. As the saying goes:

> 'Without stress, we'd never find the get up and go
> to get up and go! '

Stress is a natural occurrence and a daily event, from the low-key choice of what clothes to wear to the high-key stress of starting a new job.

> 'To be alive is to be under stress.'
>
> Dr Lawrence Hinkle
> Cornell University Medical School

It is when we cannot control a stressful situation or our response to it that it becomes a problem.

The problem with stress

There are two types of stress: **eustress**, or the good kind of stress that makes us feel motivated and alive, and **distress**, which worries us and undermines our ability to cope, both physically and mentally. According to the Australian Chamber of Commerce and Industry, distress ranks in the top ten categories of workplace injury, in both self-reports and compensation claims.

Eustress and distress are different for everyone. What is challenging eustress for one person may be threatening distress for another and irrelevant to a third—just another thing to deal with and take in their stride.

Eustress helps organisations and individuals by providing a drive to succeed. Distress, on the other hand, drains us. It can raise absenteeism, accidents, industrial disputes and labour turnover. It can lower the quality and quantity of work, creativity and job satisfaction. It can make us physically ill. The problem with stress, then, is distress. We should recognise and deal with it before these costly effects occur.

Causes of distress

Whenever the constraints, demands and pressures placed on us by ourselves, our society, our home or work lives outweigh our ability to respond to them, become too much to cope with, or threaten to become too much, we experience distress. Both *external events,* such as other people's behaviour, time pressure or social situations, and *internal events* such as our own feelings, behaviour or thoughts, can trigger distress.

We might, for instance, feel constrained from doing something we want to do, or feel pressured to do something we feel unable to do. Equally, distress can result from a *lack* of demand, when our capabilities are underused. Repetitive, monotonous work, for example, is a source of distress for many people.

Sources of distress are called **stressors**. Box 3.7 shows some common stressors grouped into a number of areas.

Stress-prone people

The ability to face life's demands varies greatly between people. Different genes, life experiences, backgrounds and capabilities combine to make our *demand: capacity ratios* very diverse.

Evidence indicates that there is such a thing as a stress-prone person, called a Type A person. *Type A* people talk, move and even eat quickly, are very competitive, are always in a hurry, impatient (they hate to wait in queues, for example) and anger easily. They try to do several things at once and often have few interests outside work. They even have more car accidents.

Type B people are relaxed and easygoing in their pursuit of their life and daily goals. They are casual about appointments and seldom feel rushed, even when under pressure. They have a variety of interests, yet do one thing at a time. While Type As often bottle up their stress and try to cope with it alone, Type Bs tend to talk it out with others.

BOX **3.7** **STRESSORS**

Home life
- Holidays
- Beginning/ending an important relationship
- Change in number/type of social activities
- Death of spouse, family member, close friend
- Major change in family arrangements
- In-law difficulties
- Gaining a new family member
- Personal injury or illness
- Pregnancy
- Major change in living conditions (e.g. moving home, remodelling)

As an individual
- Ageing
- Feeling unattractive
- Outstanding personal achievement
- Sense of inadequacy
- Change in eating habits
- Revision of personal habits (e.g. dress, manners)
- Change in residence

In your job
- Pressure
- Conflict with boss/colleagues
- Promotion (or lack of promotion)
- New job
- Not enough skills to do the work
- Boredom
- Job termination or retirement
- Organisation readjustment (e.g. merger, restructure)
- Major change in working hours/ conditions

Your finances
- Inability to pay bills
- Making a major purchase
- Taking out a mortgage/loan

In your environment
- Traffic
- Noise
- Pollution
- Crowding
- Fear of nuclear war
- Rising prices

Many psychologists see Type A and Type B behaviour at opposite ends of a continuum. A few people are completely Type A or Type B but most fall somewhere between the two extremes.

Type As and Type Bs perceive their environment differently. The way we perceive our environment will, in part, determine the degree of distress we experience. For example, we have all seen drivers in a traffic jam, clenching the steering wheel with white-knuckled fists, eyes bulging, shouting at other drivers, fuming at traffic lights … . For these Type A drivers, the traffic jam is a distressing experience and will cause a variety of short-term physiological responses. If they are frequently caught up in traffic jams and respond like this, we would also expect to see some longer-term physiological responses.

Type B drivers are more philosophical in heavy traffic. They use the time to clean their fingernails, listen to music, make plans for the coming day or muse over the day's happenings. In many ways, then, stress is a matter of our perception of a situation.

Stressful situations are often more complex than a traffic jam, but the same principles apply: on the one hand, we have a *stressor*—a traffic jam; on the other, we have our perceptions of it—'It's going to make me late' (stress!) or 'Traffic should flow smoothly' (stress!) versus 'Heavy traffic again today' (no stress). The way we see a situation and the messages we give ourselves about it will determine how distressing it is for us. This, combined with our skills at coping with life's situations and at relaxing, largely determines our stress level.

Other short-term factors, such as fatigue and how much we have 'on our plate', also affect our ability to deal with a stressor. In addition, we sometimes find demands on us motivating and inspirational when at other times they become the 'back-breaking straw'. At some point, 'gearing up' for an activity or event may stop being *eustress*, which energises us, and become *distress*, which wears us down.

So we don't all react to stress in the same way, nor do individuals always react in the same way to a particular stressor. Some handle stress poorly compared with others, while some actively seek stress. The question is not how to avoid stress, but how best to cope with it to avoid its harmful consequences.

How stressed are you?

Look at the stress-ometer in Figure 3.7 (on page 104). This lists some common sources of stress that supervisors face. Indicate how each measures up for you on the stress-ometer by placing a mark on each line, in the appropriate direction, at the point you think most applies to yourself. The further out you place each mark, the more distressful or eustressful the item is for you.

Now look at the results. What do they show you about your present work demands, home life and lifestyle, and your health habits?

What happens when we become stressed?

Whatever its source, stress produces very real physical, emotional and behavioural responses. It doesn't really matter whether an event is eustress or distress: going on holiday can be just as stressful as having an argument with the boss.

Each stressful event affects our body by demanding an immediate readjustment or adaptation of our natural defence mechanisms. Both the *intensity* and *number* of stressful

FIGURE 3.7   STRESS-OMETER

10	Distress	0	Eustress	10

_____ Place of employment undergoing major changes _____

_____ Technological changes affecting your work _____

_____ Marriage/primary relationship _____

_____ Job dissatisfaction/satisfaction _____

_____ Significant job changes _____

_____ Friends and social life _____

_____ Self-esteem _____

_____ Time _____

_____ Physical appearance _____

_____ Joys (or lack of them) _____

_____ A different team member _____

_____ Feeling of discontent/content _____

_____ Feeling dissatisfied/satisfied _____

_____ Feeling in charge of your life _____

_____ Problems in getting along with your boss _____

events are important. Stress accumulates. If we don't take steps to reduce its negative effects our overall stress level will rise, putting our physical and mental well-being at risk.

As stress accumulates, a variety of *physical responses* usually occur. For instance, the artery walls constrict, which increases blood pressure, heart rate and muscle tension (these are the ancient 'fight/flight' responses). The observable signs of this include sweating, flushing, teeth grinding and fist clenching. Less observable signs include nausea, loss of appetite and disorientation. Because they take place at a subconscious level, our body's reactions can be difficult to relate directly to a stressor.

Dr Hans Serle first identified **burnout** in the 1920s. He called it 'the syndrome of just being sick'. It is a common end result of the physical responses to an accumulation of stress.

If people fail to recognise these symptoms and deal with the stressors in their lives, they may experience longer-term physical stress-related disorders. These include elevated blood pressure, headaches and migraines, ulcers, heart attacks, kidney disorders, some cancers, some skin allergies and a generally lowered resistance to disease.

FROM THEORY TO PRACTICE

What parts of your body tense up when you are under stress? Tension is a common physical sign of stress. Other physical symptoms include skin eruptions, headaches, an upset stomach, sweaty palms, increased heart rate, loss of sex drive, jaw clenching, uneven or rapid breathing, diarrhoea and a generally lowered resistance to infections such as colds and influenza.

If stress builds up, people respond *emotionally* with such symptoms as depression, apathy, tension, resignation, anxiety, negativism, mood swings, a sense of helplessness, dissatisfaction, low self-esteem, rigidity of views and uncertainty about whom to trust. Various types of psychological disturbances may occur in the longer term if the stress is not managed.

Behaviourally, people become short-tempered, irritable and easily upset over trifles. They may procrastinate or have difficulty in concentrating, organising themselves or making decisions. They may develop a loss of appetite or a sudden change in habits, for example, in smoking or the use of drugs or alcohol. They may experience troubled sleeping patterns, sensitivity, forgetfulness and difficulty in dealing with new situations. They may notice a gain or loss of weight or other change in appearance, or become easily fatigued. Again, if the stress is not dealt with, these responses become more severe.

MANAGING STRESS

There are four steps to managing stress:

1. *Learn to recognise your own physical, emotional and behavioural responses to stress.* These will alert you to the presence of a stressor you may be unaware of. If you know about your own body's stress signals, you will be able to recognise and deal with a stressor more quickly.

2. *Identify the events, or stressors, that are causing the stress.* Box 3.8 shows some common causes of stress in the workplace. As you look through them, tick any that apply to you. The more items you tick, the more your job may be a source of stress to you and the more important it becomes to take action to manage your stress levels. As you look through the sources of stress in Box 3.8, note that these stressors can affect all

---

BOX 3.8   SOURCES OF STRESS IN THE WORKPLACE

- Technological change
- Organisational restructuring
- Being trapped in a work situation where there is little opportunity for control over your job
- A lack of input in decisions which affect your job
- Unclear goals and objectives
- Inconsistent or insufficient recognition of effort
- Little opportunity to learn from the job
- Little opportunity to learn new skills
- Little opportunity for job challenge
- Time pressures and other deadlines
- Partner's attitude towards your work
- Top management not understanding work-related problems
- Under-use of skills
- Wide variation in work pressures (too much one day, too little the next)

- Monotonous, repetitive work
- Supervision that undermines self-esteem and personal dignity
- Work not acknowledged as making a meaningful contribution—'busy work'
- Unpleasant or dangerous physical work environment
- Social isolation in the workplace
- Poor relations with colleagues or supervisor
- Inadequate resources to do the job
- Uncertain security of employment
- Role conflict or ambiguity
- Organisational politics
- Firing or disciplining an employee
- Overtime
- Working with budgets or new technology
- Feeling rushed or working long hours

supervisors, managers and employees and that supervisors can be a source of stress to employees through their supervisory styles.

3. *Take steps to reduce or eliminate stressful situations, or deal with them differently.* Since prevention is always better than cure, it may be possible to modify some environmental factors. If you cannot do this, try changing the way you view them. Change your self-talk (see Box 3.9).

4. If you still experience distress, *act to reduce the stressor's negative effects.* Try some form of *stress management* (meditation, yoga, relaxation training, exercise, self-talk). Your family doctor can put you in touch with specially trained people who work in the area of stress management. Many colleges and universities run evening classes in stress management techniques. Some 'New Age' bookshops can put you in contact with people who work in the stress management area.

Turning to alcohol, drugs, food, cigarettes or other short-term coping mechanisms may provide some temporary relief, but in the long run they are worse than doing nothing; they merely cover up the distress and fail to deal with its source or your responses to it. Medication is another approach but this, too, is a short-term 'holding' strategy. It provides a pause in which you can learn longer-term, safer stress-management techniques. Box 3.10 has some immediate suggestions for relieving stress.

> **'The thing I fear most about stress is not that it kills,**
> **but that it prevents one from savouring life.'**
>
> Dr Hans Serle

Helping your staff overcome stress

Researchers have explored the relationship between job content and stress in white- and blue-collar settings in both public and private sectors. They have found that stress is not restricted to managers and supervisors; it is also a problem on the shop floor, in the office and dealing with the public. The potential cost of distress to employees, organisations and society is significant, so supervisors need to be alert to the possible stress signals of their employees.

BOX 3.9 EXAMPLES OF SELF-TALK TO REDUCE STRESS

- *Preparing for a stressful event*
  'What needs to be done?'
  'I can develop a plan to handle it.'
  'OK, I'll think this through calmly and logically.'

- *Coping with the feeling of being overwhelmed*
  'I will concentrate on what I have to do right now.'
  'I'll pause for a minute and relax.'
  'What's the most important thing to do first?'

- *Confronting and handling a stressor*
  'I can do it.'
  'Keep calm and take a slow breath.'
  'I can meet this challenge.'
  'Relax.'
  'I'm in control.'

- *Reinforcing self-talk*
  'Well done!'
  'I did it.'
  'I wasn't 100% successful this time but I'm getting better.'
  'Next time I can do it.'

FROM THEORY TO PRACTICE

Coping with stress

- Know yourself and make sure your work allows you to use your strengths and concentrate on your talents.
- Set goals. Know where you are headed and what your objectives are.
- Review your work and personal priorities regularly and delegate wherever possible.
- If you are not succeeding with one approach, don't try harder—think of a better way.
- Say 'I could' or 'I want to' instead of 'I should' or 'I have to'.
- Give yourself time to yourself.
- Compete with yourself, not others.
- Accept that you cannot do everything. Apply principles of time management.
- List your outside activities and interests and plan them into your diary. Don't be a 'workaholic'.
- Determine your optimum weight and maintain it with health-giving foods.
- Exercise regularly. Regular physical exercise is one of the best and healthiest ways to reduce tension in your life.
- Decide your minimum sleep requirement and ensure that you get it.
- Ask yourself whether you are having fun. If the answer over a long period is 'no', try to work out why.
- Identify things that are causing you to feel stress. At work, you may need to alter your job or work habits. At home, stress arises from the conflict of unsolved problems; discuss them openly with your partner and work out solutions together.
- Examine your self-talk and the way you think about stressors. Perhaps you can look at the situation differently and give yourself more positive messages.

BOX
3.10

SIX STEPS TO RELIEVE STRESS

1. *Talk it out.* When something worries you, don't bottle it up.
2. *Escape for a while.* When things go wrong, take a break. Distance can add objectivity and clear thinking.
3. *Work off your anger.* Do something constructive with your pent-up energy.
4. *Do something for others.* If you feel yourself worrying about yourself all the time, try doing something for someone else.
5. *Take one thing at a time.* Take a few of your most important or urgent tasks and get to work on them, one at a time.
6. *Don't try to be 'Superman'.* No one can be perfect in everything.

Source: *US National Mental Health Association*

Stress in the workplace seems to be worsening because of *job overload* due to restructuring which requires fewer people to do more with less. In 1995 the Department of Industrial Relations surveyed 19 000 Australians and found a dramatic rise in stress levels. Fifty-seven per cent of employees surveyed said their job stress was up while only 4% said it was down; the other 39% reported no change in their stress levels. Clearly, a growing number of employees are unhappy and dissatisfied at work.

Poor job design can cause *job underload* or *job overload*. A repetitive job, having too little to do and/or a lack of control over your work or pace of work can be just as distressing as having too much to do and too many pressures. Poor supervision (e.g. under- or over-supervision, or conflict with the supervisor), dissension in the work team, and unclear or conflicting goals and objectives are common causes of stress at work.

It affects quality of life at home: stressed people are not only less effective and productive at work, but also grumpy and hard to live with. The flow-on effects include frayed tempers, harassment and bullying.

Box 3.11 offers some tips on how to help reduce the stress load of team members.

BOX 3.11 HOW TO HELP PEOPLE PERFORM EFFECTIVELY

- Provide work that allows some personal choice in the way it is carried out and the sequence in which it is done.
- Encourage participation in decisions that affect the job holder.
- Set clear goals and targets and provide adequate feedback on performance.
- Induct new recruits thoroughly.
- Provide training as an ongoing, updating process.
- Provide consistent rewards for output.
- Review performance gaps at the time of occurrence.
- Provide opportunities for employees to try new duties and different tasks.
- Design jobs to have even work pressures.
- Encourage group working procedures and friendly work relations.
- Provide secure and fair personnel practices.
- Ensure that the work environment is free of hazards.
- Incorporate some downtime into people's schedules, especially those at the front line dealing with customers or the public.
- Reduce customer contact hours through rostering.
- Train staff about stress to help them identify the sources of stress for them and learn how to manage it.
- Make sure people take their breaks—tea breaks, lunch breaks, holidays.

RAPID REVIEW

	True	False
1. Since a lot of our values are subconscious, we needn't worry about them.	☐	☐
2. Having a 'real career' depends on the ability to get one promotion after another.	☐	☐
3. Organisational politics can waste a lot of people's time and energy which could be spent more productively.	☐	☐
4. Appropriate networking can help people be more effective in their jobs and careers.	☐	☐

	True	False
5. People need to manage their 'image', or how others perceive them, if they want to get ahead.	☐	☐
6. An organisation's culture is made up of its unstated, informal codes of behaviour.	☐	☐
7. Supervisors can use power for either positive or negative ends.	☐	☐
8. Position power is becoming more important in today's business environment.	☐	☐
9. Successful supervisors focus on how to do something, not on what's stopping them.	☐	☐
10. The responsibility for the manager–employee relationship falls squarely on the boss's shoulders.	☐	☐
11. Careful preparation and practice of a presentation, and focusing on your listeners' understanding of your message rather than on yourself, are two things you can do to calm your nerves when making a presentation.	☐	☐
12. You can't manage your time effectively unless you know clearly what your job goals and key result areas are.	☐	☐
13. We should always work on the most urgent matters first.	☐	☐
14. We should prioritise all the things we need to do so that we can work first on the most important matters, those contributing to our goals and key result areas.	☐	☐
15. You should arrange to do the most difficult and important tasks, and those requiring the most effort and concentration, during your prime times or periods of peak energy.	☐	☐
16. Stress is a fact of life. It's how we deal with it that counts.	☐	☐

APPLY YOUR KNOWLEDGE

1. We are advised to network but we are also told to discourage visitors in order to make better use of our time. Where is the happy medium?

2. How does a supervisor's image influence the way their section performs? How might supervisors develop an image that attracts the support of employees and management?

3. What people *do* is more telling than what they *say*. Similarly, an organisation's culture is more indicative of its future prosperity and effectiveness than its official mission statements and brochures. Discuss.

4. Over the last 20 years, personal power has become more important than position power. Why would this be so?

5. Write a short essay summarising what you see as the key issues in organisation politics, power and influence.

6. Consider the statement 'Power corrupts and absolute power corrupts absolutely.' What does this mean in relation to organisation power? What are some of the ways in which organisations ensure that no one has absolute power?

7. Develop a step-by-step action plan showing the steps you might take to

get an idea implemented at work or in your college. Begin with the first time you thought of the idea and go through to its final approval.

8. Develop a flow chart for preparing a presentation.

9. What happens in the long term if people do not recognise and deal with their stress? Explain how this occurs.

10. 'Being able to manage stress is more important to supervisors than being able to avoid it.' Discuss this statement as it applies to the modern supervisor.

11. What suggestions can you offer someone suffering from the negative effects of stress?

DEVELOP YOUR SKILLS

Individual activities

1. Develop a five-year career plan following the guidelines given at the beginning of this chapter.

2. Find someone you know who is either a mentor or has been mentored. How would they describe the relationship? How did mentoring or being mentored come about for them? What do they see as the benefits of mentoring? Are there any disadvantages? Is all lost if someone doesn't find a mentor? Prepare a five-minute presentation for your class.

3. Interview a first-line or middle manager and find out about the politics and culture of their organisation. Prepare a five-minute presentation for your class.

4. Describe the organisation culture of your place of work or your college. Are there any differences between it and the subculture of your own workplace or college department?

5. Relate managing your relationship with your boss to managing your relationship with your teacher.

6. Select a topic from this chapter or any other chapter in this book you have studied so far and prepare a five-minute presentation to give to the class on what you believe to be the most important points about your topic. Try to select a topic that you can illustrate with one or two examples from your own experience.

7. List your three main goals and five to seven key result areas, either for your job or as a student. Keep a time log for two days (based on the log shown in Figure 3.6) either during working hours or during college and study time. Analyse it in the way described in this chapter.

8. From the time management tips section of this chapter, select a time management technique that you, have not used before. Use it conscientiously for a period of three weeks and report back to the class on its effectiveness.

9. What are your stressors? What are your personal stress symptoms and responses? Based on the information provided in this chapter, develop a realistic and workable plan to manage the stress in your life.

Group activities

1. The teacher will ask each of you to select a slip of paper with a classmate's name from 'the hat'. The paper will also show one of a range of dates of future class meetings when you will be doing some groupwork. On this date, you are to 'mentor' the person whose name you have drawn from the hat. Don't tell them you're mentoring them, just do it. Do whatever you can to include them in the conversation and class discussion, seek their opinions, help them develop their thinking, build their self-confidence, and so on. When everyone has had their turn mentoring and being mentored, discuss what happened, how you felt as a mentor and mentee, what the effects of mentoring were. Why is mentoring such a popular and useful organisational tool for building people's skills and developing their talents?

2. Imagine this scene: you enter someone's work area and see a tidy desk with only a telephone, PC and a file of papers on it. You enter another work area and see a plant on the window ledge, some plaques and diplomas hanging on the wall, and a family photo on the desk. What do you think the objects people choose to have around them in an office might say about them?

3. Form into groups of three with people you feel comfortable with. Offer feedback on each other's image. Confine your feedback to objective and non-evaluative statements. Some areas you might want to ask for feedback on are: How 'professional' do I seem to you? Does my attitude come across as proactive, positive and 'can do' or as reactive, negative and 'blaming'? What could I do to seem more proactive, positive and 'can do'? Do I seem confident without blowing my own trumpet? When offering feedback, be prepared to cite examples to illustrate your points.

4. In groups of three or four, develop a strategy to establish and maintain the trust and support of your immediate manager(s). (If you are not working, devise a strategy to establish and maintain the trust and support of your immediate family or the people you live with.) What are your objectives? What specific behaviours will you need to adopt? What specific action steps will you need to take?

5. Pair up. Discuss how to use the diagram in Figure 3.6 on page 98 to help set priorities and manage time better. Together, fill in what would be some typical tasks in each of the four quadrants for supervisors and for students.

6. Select and investigate a stress management technique. Prepare a short presentation on it for the class that includes evidence of how it helps to manage or reduce stress.

Exciting Times?

Murray was watching the CEO's video address to employees around the Pacific Rim. 'We are facing challenging and exciting times,' the CEO was saying, '… challenging because our industry is in one of its periodic slumps and many innovative improvements to our business will be required.

'Exciting because the company is developing a new computerised stock and invoicing system for use throughout the region. And exciting because the new "flatter" organisation structure, designed to speed up response to changes in the marketplace, has recently been implemented,' the CEO continued.

'*This* will take a bit of getting used to!' Murray thought.

'We all need to work smarter, not harder,' the CEO was saying. 'We all need to focus on clear goals. We all need to take stock of the way we do our jobs and find ways to do them better.' Then he quoted loosely from *Alice in Wonderland*: 'In today's environment, if we're just standing still, we're going backward!'

Murray knew what that meant: their competition was constantly seeking ways to improve and, if they didn't too, they'd be left behind. And he knew about working smarter, not harder: on the company time management course he'd recently attended, the trainer had said they all worked *hard* (and didn't he know it) and now they needed ways to be more effective. Well, he was game to give that a try!

Murray's mind wandered to the key result areas and targets he had developed for himself on the course. He had discussed them with his manager and, with a few minor adjustments, they agreed on them. Now that he knew what he was supposed to be doing, he could see he had been wasting a lot of his efforts and energy on low-priority areas. The time log he kept prior to the course confirmed it.

He would put some of the time he saved from working smarter to good use learning the new computer system the CEO mentioned. It wouldn't be easy, but he figured he'd learn it, as he'd learned other things.

Murray had also realised, from his exercise in establishing goals, that he wanted to be promoted to a bigger department with more responsibilities. The trainer had also touched on career management. She spoke about organisational politics, networking, power and influence and image. He found it all a bit intimidating. Surely, if he improved the way he did his job, management would notice and give him the promotion he wanted? But, he gathered, it didn't always work quite that simply. Unfortunately. 'But where to begin?' he mused.

'Yes, these are exciting times,' the CEO was saying. 'I want you all to succeed in your jobs and take our business on to bigger and better things. I want you to be proud of yourselves and the excellent service we provide our customers. I want you to constantly search for better ways of doing things, to work smarter, not harder.

'Thank you for your attention. I look forward to a challenging and exciting year with you all.'

'Yes,' Murray thought, 'it will be both of those!'

Questions

1 Has Murray approached 'working smarter' sensibly? What further tips could you offer him?

2 What steps could Murray take to manage his career so that he gets the bigger department he wants?

3 What skills do you think Murray should concentrate on acquiring?

4 What stresses would you expect the employees to suffer as a result of the newly implemented organisation structure and the forthcoming computerised stock and invoicing system? What could supervisors do to make these changes easier for employees?

CASE STUDY 3.2

On The Move

Now that senior management had shown its faith in her abilities by promoting Jocelyn to supervise the front of house staff at the theatre, she was determined to be the best supervisor that she could. She knew her mentor from the personnel department, Sue, must have had a lot to do with her promotion. Sue had recruited her to the theatre complex three years ago and seemed to have taken a personal interest in her since.

She was always friendly, never failing to take a few minutes to chat to Jocelyn about the goings-on in the theatre, plans for upcoming events, personnel moves between the departments, and so on. Several times she had requested that Jocelyn be put on working committees looking into various aspects of client service and productivity. This had given Jocelyn a broad understanding of the workings of the theatre and exposed her to people from every department at all levels. Sue had even arranged for her to undertake a few project assignments in different areas of the theatre, as well as be on the very high-profile Enterprise Bargaining working group.

Jocelyn made the most of these opportunities, learning everything she could and contributing as fully as she felt able. She tried to 'dress the part' when she was on these special committees and teams; in fact, she took her cues from the way Sue dressed. She was friendly and cheerful with everyone and made a conscious effort to keep up her contacts with people once the committees disbanded.

In this way, Jocelyn gradually became known throughout the theatre complex as a dedicated, hard-working, cheerful and effective employee. Her supervisor appreciated her efforts too. She always presented information to him the way he liked it, came up with good ideas and suggestions and seemed to motivate the rest of the team. So when it came time for him to move on from supervising the front of house, he was happy to endorse Sue's recommendation that Jocelyn step into his shoes.

Questions

1   Analyse Sue's influence as Jocelyn's mentor.
2   Discuss Jocelyn's skills at networking and image-building.
3   Explain the sources of power and influence Jocelyn seemed to be using most and discuss how she acquired these.

Answers to Rapid Review questions

1. F   2. F   3. T   4. T   5. T   6. T   7. T   8. F   9. T   10. F   11. T   12. T   13. F
14. T   15. T   16. T

CHAPTER 4

ORGANISATION STRUCTURES: UNDERSTANDING THE CHANGING ORGANISATION

Finding their way around

Employee relations officer Martha Boyle sat at her desk pondering how best to induct this year's work experience students to the Electricity Corporation. She began brainstorming a list of all the things she would need to tell them. Then she organised it into a logical sequence.

When they reported to her on their first day, she would explain how the Corporation had been set up by an Act of Parliament and recently privatised as part of government policy. She would outline its charter and provide them with a booklet on the Corporation's mission and strategic objectives, and its key policies on customer service, equal employment, health, safety and welfare, and the environment.

Then she would explain how the Corporation was structured and how this had changed dramatically over recent years. She would give them the current organisation chart and explain how the various functions related to each other. This would be a good way to give the students an idea of the work flow of the Corporation and start them thinking about areas they might want to focus on to develop their skills.

She would explain the variety of employment options with the Corporation, ranging from full-time core employees to part-time, casual and temporary employees, to self-employed and employed-by-others contractors for various lengths of time depending on the project they were assigned to. People could work from home sometimes or always, from mobile offices and from temporary site offices. They could take time off for parental leave, study leave and sabbatical leave. Many employees had several other jobs too, some doing work quite different to the work they performed for the Corporation, others doing very similar work. She would explain, that in some parts of the organisation, the 'office' had become an informal place of information exchange and formal and informal meetings between people whose base of work was elsewhere.

Martha thought she would take them through a few examples of how employees' careers had taken very different paths within the Corporation. These students would certainly have a lot of decisions to make and a wealth of options open to them in their working lives, and it wouldn't hurt them to start thinking them over now.

OVERVIEW

How much do you know about the internal workings of organisations? The way an enterprise organises itself affects how easily it achieves its objectives and how enjoyable it is to work in. In this chapter, you will discover how important an organisation's structure is and how it affects the way it operates.

- When should organisations change the way they are structured?
- How should you go about designing an organisation strucuture?
- How do today's organisation structures differ from those of ten or 15 years ago?
- What distinguishes the public, private and not-for-profit sectors and how are corporations set up and run?
- What is the difference between line and staff positions, and why are 'unity of command' and 'span of management' important?
- What are the four basic frameworks of organisations and what other types are emerging in today's global and knowledge economy?
- What are learning organisations, holistic organisations and virtual organisations?
- How does re-engineering, or core process redesign, change an organisation?
- How does an organisation's structure affect its culture?
- Will downsizing, restructuring and outsourcing ever end and will everyone eventually become teleworkers, temporary workers, contract workers or casual workers?
- How do all of the changes organisations are experiencing affect supervisors?

DESIGNING ORGANISATIONS

An **organisation structure** is the framework that links an enterprise's people and functions. It is created from a process called **organisation design**. The right structure will help it achieve its vision and goals for the least cost and effort. The wrong one will get in the way.

As the examples in Box 4.1 show, organisation structures need to suit the purpose of the organisation and the wishes of its **stakeholders**.

Before we can structure an organisation, we must first know clearly what we are trying to accomplish and understand the critical issues we face. Then we can design an organisation to achieve what we want done.

THE THREE SECTORS

Before examining how organisations can structure themselves, let's look at each of the three main sectors: the private, the public and the not-for-profit.

The private sector

Sole traders

A **sole trader** is the single owner of a business. This person usually manages the business, although sometimes a paid professional manager is employed. Sole trader businesses tend to be small because of the difficulty of raising large amounts of capital for expansion.

DIFFERENT NEEDS, DIFFERENT STRUCTURES
....

If you were organising some people to build a viewing stand for a pageant you wouldn't appoint a board of directors, a general manager, a sales manager, a procurements officer, a training manager, and so on. Such a large, formal organisation would be too cumbersome and slow to get the stand built quickly and efficiently. A more informal, self-managing organisation would probably do the job better: you might hire a couple of joiners, explain the type of stand you want and discuss where to get the materials. This would probably be a temporary organisation that would end as soon as the stand was built; and the structure would not need to be elaborate. Flexibility and good communication would be critical and these would be helped by a simple organisation structure.

Contrast this organisation with the one that would be needed to operate a bank. In a bank, you would want permanence and growth, safety for depositors, compliance with banking laws and regulations, and profitability. Procedural integrity would be critical. With different objectives, your organisation structure would be different. You would need a board of directors to guide the bank strategically, a CEO to guide its operations, a banking operations manager to ensure its activities were carried out smoothly, and many other positions formally knitted together to help you achieve your objectives both daily and in the long term.

Partnerships

In a **partnership**, two or more people own the business. Partnerships are very useful when a sole trader is not able to cope single-handedly with the amount of work available, when more money is required for expansion of the business and/or when the original sole trader does not have all the skills required to manage the business successfully. The partners usually share the day-to-day management of the business.

Sole traders and partners own all the profits of the business and have unlimited liability. That is, in the event of the firm becoming insolvent, they are totally responsible for paying all its liabilities (debts). Unless a partnership agreement states otherwise, the law assumes the partners will split the profits and contribute equally to the payment of business debts.

Corporations

A **corporation** exists independently of its owners (the shareholders) and the people it employs. A corporation is an 'artificial person' (hence the expression 'the body corporate'). This means that the corporation continues even while its managers and workers come and go.

There are two kinds of corporations: proprietary companies and public companies. Unlike sole traderships and partnerships, both can issue shares to raise capital for the operation of the business.

A **proprietary company** (**private** in Queensland) is registered under the provisions of the various Companies Acts. It can have no more than 50 owners (excluding employee shareholders). The right to transfer shares is restricted, and a proprietary company cannot invite the general public to subscribe in its shares. The company must have the words 'Proprietary Limited' or their abbreviations (Pty Ltd) as part of its name.

A **public company** must have a minimum of three directors and there is no limit on the maximum number of shareholders. They must have the word 'Limited' or its abbreviation as part of its name. The companies listed on the stock exchange are public companies.

The liability of shareholders in relation to either type of corporation's debts is limited to the unpaid amount (if any) of their respective shares.

Corporations are required by law to have a **board of directors** to represent the shareholders. The Board's role is to establish strategies and policies and to monitor and guide the operations of the enterprise. Box 4.2 gives an example of how a board guides a company. With the guidelines established, it becomes the management team's responsibility to see that the goals are achieved and the strategies and policies followed.

Board members

An *inside board*, or *executive board*, is one whose directors also work in the company. An *external* or *non-executive board* is made up of directors not employed by the company.

The advantages of an inside board are that its members know the company, its markets, operations and problems intimately. Yet this can sometimes mean they are 'too close to the woods to see the trees', whereas external directors can sometimes see matters more

---

BOX 4.2   BEST SHIRTS LIMITED

The board of Best Shirts wanted the company to be the largest and best known Australian shirt manufacturing business. Together with their senior management team they decided that, to achieve this, they needed several brand names of shirts in every price range of the domestic (Australian) and Asia Pacific markets. Their strategy was to make Australian-designed shirts in several factories close to their regional markets.

The board then established policies in a number of areas including personnel, manufacturing, finance, and community and customer relations. For example, it set a personnel policy that all promotions would be based solely on merit and that the company would try to promote from within wherever possible. The board also set general objectives for the senior management team to achieve, including a 15% return on investment each year.

At its monthly meetings, the board reviewed key measures of the company's performance, reviewed senior management's major plans to continually improve the business, and generally ensured the company was meeting its obligations to its stakeholders.

Recently, the management team proposed building an additional plant in South-East Asia. They believed this would improve the company's competitive position and increase its market share because the proposed location was closer to raw material supplies and had access to more economical transport for the finished product to its target market. The board considered and approved the proposal, agreeing that it would enhance the company's trading position and position it well for continued growth towards achieving its vision.

objectively. They can also bring fresh, outside points of view and a range of experience and perspectives to bear on problems and policies.

Most Australian companies aim for the benefits of both executive and non-executive boards by appointing **mixed boards** made up of both insiders (executive directors) and outsiders (non-executive directors).

In the aftermath of the 'excesses of the 1980s', **corporate governance** has emerged as an important issue both in Australia and overseas. This refers to the way organisations are governed and controlled. Some guiding principles of good corporate governance are shown in Box 4.3.

Corporate officers

Who are the corporate officers and what do they do? Box 4.4 shows some typical job titles of the senior level of managers, and brief explanations of the duties associated with these positions.

 BOX 4.3   CORPORATE GOVERNANCE

It is expected that boards and executives will use due care and diligence to:
- Approve, scrutinise and monitor strategies, plans, budgets, performance and key decisions
- Appoint and evaluate senior management and auditors
- Scrutinise and monitor risks and controls
- Oversee external communications—for example, with shareholders
- Ensure legal and regulatory compliance
- Act independently and objectively, without domination by one individual or faction
- Take professional advice

Effective governance provides reasonable assurance to stakeholders that the organisation is achieving its goals in an acceptable way.

 BOX 4.4   SENIOR CORPORATE OFFICERS

General manager (GM) or *chief executive officer* (CEO)
The most senior manager in the company. Responsible for operating the business profitably and according to the guidelines established by the board. Because this is a wide-ranging job, the board normally gives the CEO broad authority.

Company secretary
Passes on the decisions and requirements of the board to the company's senior managers. Attends all board meetings, keeps minutes of the meetings, maintains the corporate books, issues and transfers stocks and handles the board's correspondence. This position requires formal study and qualifications.

Continued . . .

Finance manager, chief financial officer (CFO) or *financial controller*
Manages the financial activities of the company. Organises and uses the corporation's financial resources to finance its operations by collecting money owed to the business (debts), obtaining credit or borrowing money, maintaining an acceptable level of cash flow and operating funds, and so on. Usually a qualified accountant; reports to the general manager. In large companies, *credit managers, cashiers, accountants, bookkeepers, internal auditors* and others reporting to the finance manager help with this function. In smaller organisations, one person, either the owner (in very small firms) or a sole accountant (in slightly larger ones) may carry out all these tasks.

Management information services manager (MIS manager)
Has responsibility for all computers within the organisation. May be assisted by an *operations manager* (who runs the day-to-day operations of the computer systems), a *development manager* (responsible for writing and developing computer programs to meet the present and future needs of the organisation), a *technical manager* (the 'all-rounder' or technical 'guru' who handles all specialist tasks) and, more recently, a *communications manager* (responsible for all the computer and telephone communication networks the organisation operates).

Personnel or *human resources manager*
Secures, trains and maintains an adequate workforce for the whole company in both the short and long term. Maintains records on important measures such as staff turnover and safety, and oversees performance appraisal procedures, remuneration and superannuation, succession planning, the career development and training of employees, and other employee relations matters. In large organisations may be assisted by *personnel* or *HR officers, recruitment officers, payroll supervisors, superannuation managers, training managers* and others.

Purchasing and supply manager or *materials manager*
Procures the necessary raw materials, parts, tools and other supplies from outside suppliers. May report to the *plant* or *production manager*, but the position is now recognised as being of such importance that, in many organisations, the materials manager reports directly to the general manager.

Plant or *factory manager*
Has overall responsibility for manufacturing operations. May be assisted by a *production planning manager* (plans the work to be done, determining when and where it should be done and issuing the necessary manufacturing orders and specifications), *industrial engineer* (develops safe and efficient ways to manufacture goods and perform work with less effort), *safety officer* (works to increase the health, safety and welfare of employees) and others.

Sales manager
Coordinates the activities of the business's sales force and is responsible for reaching budgeted sales levels.

Continued . . .

Marketing manager
Coordinates the activities of the sales and marketing departments. Responsible for planning the marketing activities to help the sales department achieve its goals and for developing long-term plans for products (or services) and market development including designing and overseeing the corporate 'image', market research, product development, packaging, pricing, promotions, distribution channels and advertising campaigns. Because the functions are so closely related, the sales manager reports to the marketing manager in many companies.

The public sector

Directly or indirectly, the public sector governs the country, protects it, educates its people and provides public and community services according to the policies and requirements of the elected government.

Australia has a multi-tiered form of government. The Commonwealth government in Canberra governs the country as a whole, taking responsibility for such areas as defence, health, foreign policy, social services, taxation and many other areas relating to the national interest. The state governments manage the affairs of individual states. Within each state there are local and city councils, as well as a range of statutory semi-autonomous bodies.

The structure of the various forms of **public sector** organisations is determined, in the first instance, by the Australian Constitution—the book of rules by which the country is governed. In the case of statutory bodies, Federal or State Parliament agrees on a 'charter' that sets out how these organisations should be structured, although it leaves the fine detail to the appointed senior managers.

Let's examine the public sector organisations of the Commonwealth of Australia. These are reasonably typical of most state organisations, too.

Government departments

The activities of government are divided into functions, each with its own department: for example, Defence, Finance, Attorney General's, Health and Family Services, Taxation. A chief executive officer, known as the permanent head of department, heads them. Permanent heads usually remain in their positions no matter which political party or combination of parties is in power. They are responsible for structuring and managing their organisation so that it achieves the government's objectives.

Each department also has a *secretary* who is the government's contact with the department. Because many government departments are large, each departmental secretary often has a number of *deputy secretaries*, each responsible for managing and administering different functions. In very large departments, each deputy secretary might have a *first assistant secretary* responsible for specific areas who, in turn, may have a number of *assistant secretaries* reporting to them, responsible for divisions within the first assistant secretary's responsibility.

Statutory authorities

Sometimes referred to as a **quango** (quasi-autonomous government organisation), a statutory authority is a government agency established by a statute, or Act of Parliament. While most are subject to some form of ministerial control, the degree of control depends on the amount of freedom, or autonomy, which the establishing government judged necessary for its effective functioning. In the main, statutory authorities tend to have more independence than government departments. The structure of most falls somewhere between that of government departments and large private sector organisations.

There are many examples of statutory authorities in Australia, some Federal, others state. We have seen a trend in recent years to run these organisations more along the lines of private sector companies; in some cases, such as Qantas, the Commonwealth Bank, some state water and electricity authorities and Telstra, they have been 'privatised' (made public companies) or semi-privatised. When this happens, the state or federal government is often a major shareholder in the newly privatised organisation.

Public sector reform

In 1998 a new, simplified, principles-based Public Service Bill replaced the old *Public Service Act* of 1922. It replaced the highly centralised, prescribed and regulated activities of public servants, which had resulted in costs being at least twice as expensive as best practice, with a more modern and responsive service.

Department heads now have the freedom to develop and implement their own arrangements for appointment, advancement, transfer, performance management and discipline rather than following highly prescribed standard terms and conditions across the service. As a result, many government bodies are moving to an **enterprise bargaining** system with individual contracts replacing awards. Many are developing corporate vision and mission statements, setting goals and managing performance in ways similar to the private sector. It is hoped the continued reforms of the APS will allow it to respond more effectively to the increased expectations of its clients and provide better value for money as a result.

The not-for-profit sector

The scouts, the Alzheimer's Association, the Salvation Army, the RSPCA—these organisations form a significant part of our economy and, in many cases, are taking the lead in both management style and organisation design. Although they have no 'bottom line' to measure their effectiveness directly, **not-for-profit organisations** are concerned with money—they have to be! They must continually raise funds in a competitive marketplace if they are to succeed in their mission. However, money is not the objective, as it is in private enterprise, but the means to the end: fulfilling their mission.

These organisations must perform if they are to survive. They must work out clear strategies for their organisations, and organise and manage themselves well. This requires an up-to-date and relevant organisation design and excellent leadership and performance management. The leaders of these organisations, perhaps more than any other type of organisation, must know how to empower workers and use their skills and drive to the full. After all, many of the workers are volunteers who can easily leave if they feel they are not contributing in a meaningful way.

In most not-for-profit organisations we will find a controlling body, usually called a board of directors, which establishes overall direction and strategy. Board members are often volunteers, too.

Organisations in each of these sectors can structure themselves in any of the ways described below. Functional organisations, customer-type organisations, geographic location-based organisations, linking-pin organisations, matrix organisations and even product-type organisations can all be suitable.

ORGANISATION CHARTS

Organisation charts diagram the structure of an organisation. They show how people are grouped into *functions* and show *reporting lines* (who reports to whom), the **span of management** (how many people report to a manager) and the *lines of authority and responsibility*. They show how the activities of an enterprise and the various groups that make it up are held together and coordinated into a working whole. Organisation charts reflect the formal structure of the organisation.

They can highlight a number of potential problems. Problems of *duplication of effort*, **unity of command** (where an employee reports to two or more bosses) and *span of management* (where a person is supervising too many or too few employees) usually show up clearly, so a more effective structure can be designed.

An up-to-date organisation chart of a department helps employees understand their responsibilities by showing how their department is structured and how it relates to the rest of the organisation. Of course, charting the framework of an organisation doesn't in itself ensure that it will be well structured. However, organisations that keep up-to-date charts are usually well structured, possibly because the charts keep people aware of the structure and provide an opportunity to make changes if they seem to be needed.

Drawing an organisation chart

Software programs are available that do most of the charting automatically. If you need to construct an organisation chart by hand, the rules for drawing a 'top down' chart are shown in Box 4.5.

 BOX 4.5 **DRAWING AN ORGANISATION CHART**

1. Arrange functions and departments horizontally.
2. Show job holders vertically according to their grade or position in the organisation.
3. Use rectangles of equal sizes to indicate job positions.
4. Place all rectangles for positions on the same authority level on the same horizontal level (space allowing).
5. Enter straight vertical lines to show the flow of authority at the top and exit them at the bottom centre (lines of authority do not run through a rectangle). Use heavy black lines to emphasise the flow of line authority between any two positions and broken horizontal or vertical lines to show the sources of advice and service.
6. If the chart centres on a position or department, the rectangle representing this position or department can be the largest one on the chart. The rectangles above and below the key figure should then be a smaller size.
7. On any individual chart, show at least one level above and two levels below the primary position or level being charted.

If you want to draw a sideways or upside-down chart, alter the axes for the functions and positions accordingly. For example, a traditional *'top down'* design shows the most senior people at the top of the chart. A *'sideways'* chart shows functions vertically and individual jobs horizontally. The senior people are at one side with successive levels moving to the right or left (instead of appearing below the senior levels as in a traditional chart). Figure 4.1, illustrating the organisation design of a manufacturing company, shows such a 'sideways'

FIGURE 4.1   A SIDEWAYS ORGANISATION CHART FOR A MANUFACTURING COMPANY WITH A FUNCTIONAL STRUCUTURE

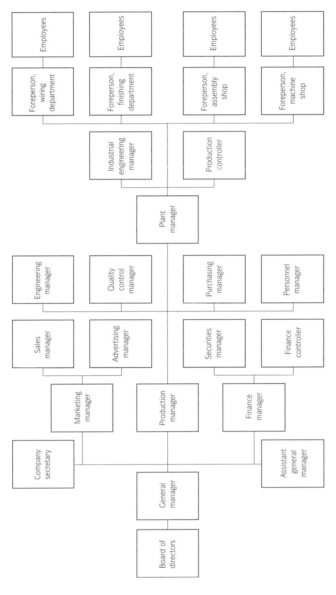

chart. Another option is the *'upside down'* format, where senior management appears at the bottom of the chart, symbolically 'supporting' the rest of the workforce above them (see Figure 4.2).

FOUR PRINCIPLES

Line and staff positions

People in **line positions** produce goods or services. In manufacturing firms, they make the product; in hospitals, they deliver health care; in service organisations, they serve the customers.

People in **staff positions** serve or advise people in line positions. Accountants, personnel and training people, most office workers, cleaners, industrial engineers and safety officers are usually in staff positions. People in line positions don't normally report to those in staff positions, although we often see a dotted line between them to indicate the staff employee as a source of advice to the line employee.

Does it seem as if line positions are more important to an organisation? That staff positions would be outsourced and line positions retained as 'core'? Think of Nike and the PC industry (see page 131). Sometimes the staff, not line, positions are more critical to a business!

Unity of command

Convention has it that an employee should report to only one person. This is called **unity of command.** It is based on the thinking that having more than one boss could create a situation of potential conflict and confusion.

As you may have guessed from the military-style language, this principle flourished in the days of hierarchy and bureaucracy. Today, however, organisations need to be flexible and responsive to their environment, and this principle may be eroding. Temporary teams, for example, often form to undertake special projects and then disband, contractors

FIGURE 4.2   AN UPSIDE-DOWN ORGANISATION CHART BY CUSTOMER TYPE

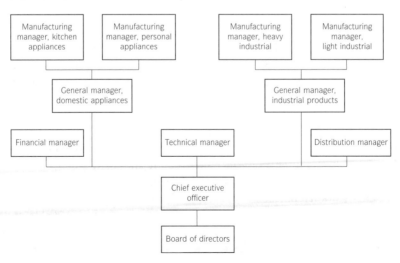

or part-time workers are often brought in to work in one or more areas, employees are often temporarily seconded to other areas. The matrix organisation, by design, has people reporting to two or more supervisors.

Span of management

The **span of management** is the number of people a person can effectively supervise. It's important to get this right because supervising too many people can lead to under-supervision and supervising too few people can lead to oversupervision.

The number of people we can effectively supervise depends on several things. Are they scattered or together? Do they do the same job or different jobs? Do they work inter-dependently or independently? How skilled is the supervisor? How exacting are the quality standards? How complex are the jobs?

Group size

Evolutionary psychologists have found that people feel most comfortable and work best in groups of less than 150 members. This does not refer to the immediate work group, but the wider group: a factory, a head office, a regional operations centre.

ORGANISATION TYPES

Before we can decide how best to arrange the people and functions of an organisation, we should know what type of organisation we want. Internally, we need to consider the organisation's vision and objectives and the type of culture that would best achieve them. The organisation's size and the types of jobs and employees play a part. To some extent, the organisation design that will work best also depends on the preferences of senior managers.

We need to consider external forces, too, particularly the operating environment. Some environments call for decentralised organisations, others for centralised organisations. Some suggest a mechanistic form, others an organic form. Some circumstances invite a 'tall' organisation structure, others a 'flat' structure.

Let us consider the various types, or frameworks for organisation design, and the situations they suit best.

Bureaucracies

Developed by the Romans more than 2000 years ago, this is perhaps the most familiar organisation type to many people. While we often think of **bureaucracies** as slow moving and rule-obsessed, they don't have to be. In fact, many organisations organised along bureaucratic lines are efficient and effective, and this in part explains why this structure has survived.

We tend to think of large organisations as bureaucracies, particularly public enterprises and the public service itself. Large private sector organisations, not-for-profit organisations and unions have also favoured a bureaucratic structure and many still do.

In fact, bureaucracies were once considered the ideal form of organisation structure. The features of the traditional bureaucracy are shown in Box 4.6.

Bureaucracies are best suited to large organisations operating in stable and predict-able external environments. This no longer describes the environment in which most modern organisations currently operate. **Industrial democracy** (also known as **worker**

THE CLASSIC BUREAUCRACY

BOX 4.6

- A rigid hierarchical structure
- Well defined lines of authority
- A set of rational rules and regulations
- Specialised tasks

- An impersonal climate
- Managers who are professional officers rather than owners

participation), which gives non-management workers more say in decisions affecting their work, and **public sector reform** are two attempts to make bureaucracies more responsive to their environment and customers and more satisfying to those who work within them.

Many present-day bureaucracies, therefore, no longer have all the features of the classic model of bureaucracy listed above. In an attempt to ensure consistency and fairness in the way they operate, today's bureaucracies have retained formal lines of communication, responsibility and authority, and formal rules for promotion, but operate within a very much more 'open' (i.e. communicative, or 'transparent') climate.

Figure 4.3 shows a typical bureaucratic organisation structure.

Linking-pin organisations

'Linking-pin' organisations highlight the overlapping nature of jobs and the interdependence of people in various job roles. As shown in Figure 4.4, the leader of one team is also a member of a more senior team.

Do you want to encourage a continual flow of information and ideas? Show how everyone links together when you draw your organisation chart.

Central and decentralised designs

Where is decision-making authority located? Many organisations in today's dynamic business environment, where rapid and continuous change requires prompt decisions, have found it effective to place the authority for decision making as close as possible to 'the action'. These organisations are **decentralised**. They are usually *'flat'*, with fewer levels of management than their centralised counterparts. 'Flat' organisations give people at each level greater responsibility and, usually, more decision-making authority.

When all decisions must be referred to a higher authority for implementation, the structure is **centralised** and is usually 'taller' (i.e. with more levels of management). The more managerial positions there are between the operator level and senior management, the taller and more hierarchical the organisation structure is.

One isn't 'bad' and the other 'good'. Each works in the right circumstances. What is important: innovation or uniformity? Rapid responses to a volatile market, or reliability and consistency in a stable environment? Flexibility and creativity, or controls, checks and balances? Are the markets being served diverse or uniform? If the former, go for a less formal, decentralised organisation structure; if the latter, a taller, centralised bureaucratic structure would probably be better.

Mechanistic and organic organisations

It can be useful to think of organisations as **mechanistic** or **organic**. Box 4.7 shows the distinctions between them.

FIGURE 4.3 ORGANISATION FOR THE EDUCATION DEPARTMENT OF A STATE GOVERNMENT

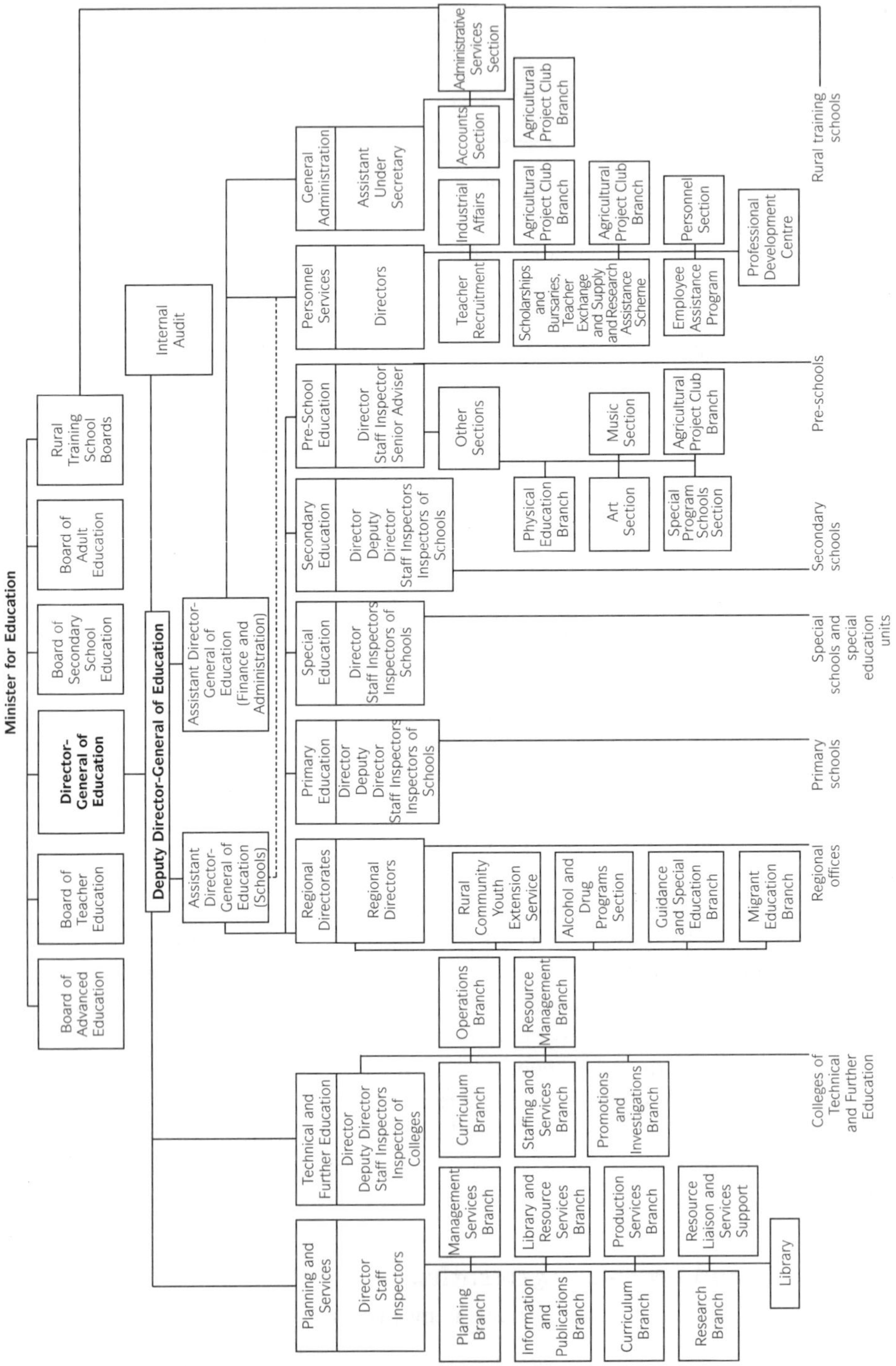

FIGURE 4.4   LINKING-PIN ORGANISATION HIGHLIGHTS THE FLOW OF INFORMATION
AND IDEAS

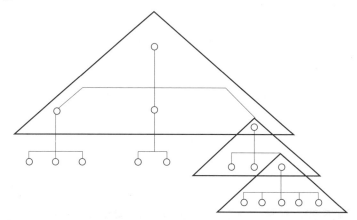

MECHANISTIC AND ORGANIC ORGANISATIONS

Mechanistic organisations
- Jobs are highly specialised and standardised (e.g. assembly lines).
- Authority is concentrated in a small management group at the top of the organisation.
- Communication is mostly downwards, by orders and directions.
- Conflict is resolved by the supervisor or manager.
- Organisation members identify more with the organisation as a whole.
- Prestige is based on position in the hierarchy.

Organic organisations
- There is less standardisation of jobs and greater flexibility in them (e.g. research and development teams).
- Authority is concentrated across the organisation, in people with the relevant skills and knowledge.
- Communication takes the form of advice, discussion and mutual consent.
- Conflict is resolved through the interaction of the people concerned.
- Organisation members identify more with their work team than with the organisation as a whole.
- Prestige results from individual competence.

Does the environment tend towards stability and predictability? A mechanistic or bureaucratic model might be more appropriate. Or is the environment more dynamic, changing and uncertain? If so, an organic structure might be needed. There seems to be a trend towards more flexible, organic organisation structures in Australia.

Matrix organisation

Do you recall the principle of *unity of command*? Despite this principle, a **matrix organisation** purposely has people reporting to more than one supervisor. Many organisations are experimenting with this as a way of spreading scarce professional skills across an organisation and encouraging rapid decision making, transfer of knowledge and experience, and maximum flexibility and creativity.

A **multifunctional team**, for example, is responsible for delivering an entire product or service, from design to marketing, manufacturing, delivery and after-sales service. They usually include people from all functions of the organisation: marketing, manufacturing, engineering, quality assurance, finance and human resources. Their members often report to the team or project supervisor as well as to their own functional supervisors.

A matrix-type organisation might appear as shown in Figure 4.5. This shows a temporary project team type of matrix organisation. Workers in each of the projects are under the authority of two people—the functional manager (vertically) and the project manager (horizontally). Figure 4.6 shows the food company from Figure 4.11 organised as a matrix organisation.

As you can see from these two figures, matrix organisations can split people's loyalties. Industrial psychologists have learned that most people prefer to identify with one group at a time, which may explain why matrix organisations don't seem to have worked as well as logic suggests they should.

EMERGING ORGANISATION TYPES

:... The command and control hierarchy suited the industrial era. What will suit the new business era of knowledge?

FIGURE 4.5   MATRIX ORGANISATION STRUCTURE

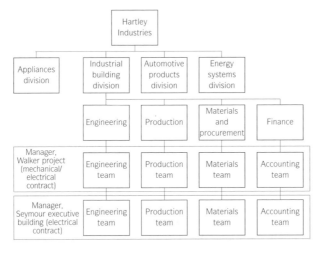

FIGURE 4.6   A MATRIX ORGANISATION

THE BIG PICTURE

Think of Nike—its employees only design shoes and market them. Everything else is outsourced.

Think of the PC industry—everything is outsourced except marketing.

The skill is not running the business but optimising the value chain of partners.

Is this the organisation of the future?

Organisations have undergone more radical restructuring since 1985 than at any other time since the modern corporation evolved in the 1920s. Different frameworks are evolving as labour-intensive manufacturing gives way to service organisations such as tourism, gardening and personal services, and information- and knowledge-based enterprises. Specialised niche support organisations from industrial cleaning to information technology management are burgeoning as large organisations contract out many of their non-core functions.

Different kinds of organisations need to be designed differently. The pyramid is crumbling. What is replacing it?

Charles Handy has given us two interesting images that describe emerging organisation types: the shamrock and the donut, and Arie de Geus a third: the learning organisation.

The shamrock

The shamrock symbolises the three main groups of workers we will find in most organisations: core workers, contractors and flexible workers. The *core workers* perform the critical jobs of the organisation, those that the enterprise cannot afford to contract out. They will eventually make up less than one quarter of all its 'employees'. These indispensable executives, highly qualified professionals, technical specialists and managers will work long and hard hours and will be well remunerated in return.

Contractors will eventually be responsible for up to 80% of the value that is added to a product or service. They will perform important clerical, marketing, training, accounting and other types of specialist work to support the core workers. The temporary, part-time and casual workers the organisation needs to work on one-off projects or to fill in during busy times comprise the *flexible* workforce.

THE BIG PICTURE

These three groups of workers will each have different expectations of the organisation and different levels of commitment to it. They will need to be paid and organised differently to full-time employees. They must be managed and supervised differently too, and be made to feel part of the total organisation.

Whether they are core workers, part-timers, temps or contractors, people won't be 'workers' or 'managers' as much as individuals, professionals, specialists, leaders, executives or service providers.

THE BIG PICTURE

Most organisation growth will be based on the shamrock model—growth through outsourcing, or the donut model—growth through breaking operations into lots of small profit centres. Many would say organisation growth can only occur within the larger framework of becoming a learning organisation.

Donuts

Donut organisations are not so much decentralised organisations as groups of semi-independent, largely autonomous business divisions or companies. They are held together by a small team of hard-working, professional managers at a head office, which acts as a coordinating core. This core sets strategic direction and operating criteria, and provides specialist advice for satellite groups of companies.

The learning organisation

The term **learning organisation** describes an organisational culture as much as an organisational type. Based on knowledge gaining and sharing, learning organisations are fast becoming a modern organisational imperative. Box 4.8 shows the three types of knowledge this style of organisation is based on and suggests some ways to measure each.

We look more at learning organisations and how to build them in Chapter 13.

Holistic organisations

Are organisations 'shrines to shareholders' or can they be more humane? Is it possible to bring soul and spirit into the workplace in the face of huge bottom-line pressures?

There is a growing movement, particularly in the United States, that believes work can have a deeper significance to us all, be more fulfilling and add meaning to our lives. They believe a more organic, humanistic workplace with 'soul' that honours employees as individuals will be the vehicle that drives productivity and increases shareholder value. They want to enlarge the focus from results only to results plus employee well-being. Organisations, they say, are both economic and human systems and to survive, they must balance both.

This can be done through building **holistic organisations**. This is a 'whole' approach that takes the entire system, not just its economic aspects, into account. Downsizing and cost cutting, for example, need to be part of a wider, longer-term cultural change which encourages happy, healthy, committed and productive employees who are, after all, an organisation's most valuable asset and most significant competitive edge.

THE BIG PICTURE

The rate of change is such that yesterday's organisation structures are today's waste paper. Organisations are rapidly becoming less about physical structures and infrastructures and more about networked affiliates united by a common purpose and culture.

| BOX 4.8 | THE UNSEEN ORGANISATION STRUCTURE |

Karl-Erik Sveiby, of Sweden, classifies knowledge, or intellectual capital, into three categories:

Some possible measures of value

1. **Structural capital:** patents, trademarks, copyrights, databases, software, customer files, systems and networks, the organisation structure—what's left when the employees go home. This could also be called an organisation's knowledge database. We need to learn how to make it accessible to all employees. (Shell does this in part through videoconferencing; Andersen Consulting has a Knowledge Exchange; PriceWaterhouse has Knowledge View.)

   Are all systems helping? Are any hindering?

   Suggestions made versus suggestions implemented

   Time to market (how long to develop new products and services)

   Estimated cost to replace databases

2. **Relationship capital:** the value of established relationships with customers and suppliers. We need to learn to manage these relationships with excellence so they turn into profits, repeat business, cross-selling, referrals and ideas-sharing. (When Boeing designed its 777 jet, suppliers, customers and users [e.g. frequent fliers and aircrew] all had input; the result was almost universal acclaim.)

   Customer retention rate

   Customer satisfaction measures

   Value of brand

3. **Human capital:** the skills, knowledge and productivity of an organisation's employees, individually and collectively, which enables them to provide solutions to customers. We need to know how to make the most of human capital.

   Turnover rate among top performers

   Innovation (e.g. 3M has a goal that at least 25% of annual sales come from products less than four years old)

   Employee attitudes towards their job and company

Virtual organisations

Can you imagine an organisation where people who work in teams have never met face-to-face? Where communication is electronic and meetings are held by videoconference or

FROM THEORY TO PRACTICE

On a scale of one to ten, how would you rate your organisation on each of the following elements of a holistic culture?
- Flexible hours
- Workplace agreements and practices that honour personal needs
- Focus on results, not time taken
- Open-book management (sharing information about the enterprise)
- Equity participation (rewards based on the financial performance of the organisation and individual performance)
- Managers with people skills and emotional intelligence
- Nurturing creativity
- Environmental responsibility

online chats? Many organisations are already blending virtual with 'real' and this may be just the tip of the iceberg as organisations become more global.

By their very nature, **virtual organisations** are decentralised and organic. They offer the opportunity to change traditional structures and ways of operating. It is now possible to run a large global business from a spare bedroom, to have key employees living in different cities or countries and to operate around the clock.

Process organisations

As we see in Chapter 9, some organisations are using a process called **re-engineering** or **core process redesign** to change the way they are organised. Instead of organising vertically, based on functions, products, customers or regions, process organisations are organised across core processes. Each core process, from beginning to end, is the responsibility of a senior executive who has sufficient influence to obtain required resources to make the process flow smoothly.

While a traditional organisation structured around functions, products, customers or regions is likely to know its precise manufacturing costs, product sales, and so on, it

THE **BIG** PICTURE

Here are some questions managers are grappling with as workplaces become more 'virtual'.
- Do we need to recruit people with special qualities to enable them to work away from an office successfully?
- What sort of training and experience will people need before they can work effectively in a virtual environment?
- How can we best resolve conflict in a virtual environment?
- How can we build trust and loyalty in a virtual team?
- How do we manage the performance of people we don't see face-to-face every day?

generally doesn't know how often it fills orders correctly or how long it takes to get a new product to market profitably. Process organisations do. They measure their success on process goals rather than on a unit's efficiency, emphasising entire processes rather than discrete tasks, and teamwork and customers rather than hierarchy.

Process organisations who get it 'right' are reaping big benefits in terms of productivity, profitability, and customer and employee satisfaction. They include Texas Instruments' calculator business, Owens Corning and IBM (see also Chapter 9).

ORGANISATION STRUCTURES

Let's look at some specific organisation structures. These are the structures that organisation charts depict. Each is suitable in all three sectors. As you read through them, try to relate them to the frameworks discussed above.

Functional

In a **functional structure**, relationships are arranged so that one person is responsible for each function: finance, production, distribution, and so on. It might look like that shown in Figure 4.1 (page 124). Functional managers report to the general manager and are responsible for their particular function. For example, the finance manager is responsible for all activities directly related to finance throughout the whole organisation.

This works reasonably well in a smaller organisation but, as organisations grow and become more complex, functional structures tend to become bureaucratic which creates problems of accountability and slows decision making.

Customer type

We often see customer-type structures in large organisations that have a range of products or services going to different customers, especially if different manufacturing or processing techniques are used. In these organisations, a separate division looks after each **customer type**. For example, a firm making both small electric appliances for domestic use and electric motors and generators for industrial use would probably be organised into divisions according to customer type, with each division having its own manufacturing, marketing and sales functions.

Figure 4.2 (page 125) illustrates such a company. Here, head office retains control of essential staff functions. Figure 4.7 (page 136) shows a common alternative. Here each division has responsibility for its own finance, production and distribution.

Product

In this type of organisation structure, there is one division or department for each major product or service group. Figure 4.8 shows an organisation divided into three main product groups:
1. frozen products
2. fresh products
3. tinned products

This can work well if the organisation is not widely spread out geographically and not large. If this is the case, most organisations opt to organise along geographic lines.

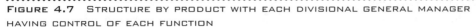

FIGURE 4.7 STRUCTURE BY PRODUCT WITH EACH DIVISIONAL GENERAL MANAGER HAVING CONTROL OF EACH FUNCTION

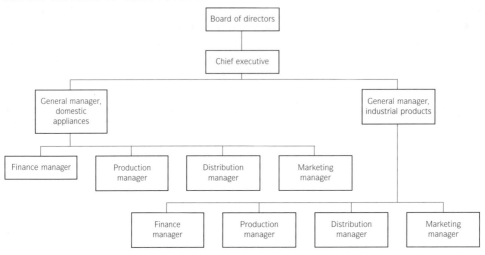

FIGURE 4.8 A PRODUCT GROUP ORGANISATION

	VIC-TAS	NSW	QLD	WA	SA-NT
Manager, Frozen products					→
Manager, Fresh products					→
Manager, Tinned products					→

Geographic location

This type of organisation is quite popular in Australia, where it is not uncommon to have manufacturing plants in one or more states and neighbouring countries, and sales branches in all major cities in the region. Figure 4.9 shows a much larger company with the same product lines as in Figure 4.8 organised along geographic lines.

FIGURE 4.9 A GEOGRAPHIC ORGANISATION

	Manager, South-East Asia	Manager, Greater China	Manager, Pacific Rim	Manager, Eastern Europe
Frozen products				
Fresh products				
Tinned products	↓	↓	↓	↓

WHICH ORGANISATION STRUCTURE IS BEST?

There is no such thing as the one right organisation structure, at least not in the current times of turbulent change. Many types of organisations, very different from one another, exist, each designed for a special task, culture and marketplace.

The best structure is the one that allows the organisation to make the best use of its internal resources, particularly people, and helps them to achieve the organisation's objectives in its current environment.

The key point to remember is that the environment is changing rapidly, radically and in unpredictable ways. To meet the changing conditions, we need to modify organisation structures far more frequently than in the past. We are likely to see flatter, more organic, organisation structures emerge in many organisations over the next few years. They will probably be more flexible and informal structures with non-traditional work patterns (see below).

THE INFORMAL ORGANISATION: HOW STRUCTURE AFFECTS CULTURE

As we saw in Chapter 3, every organisation has two systems in operation: the formal and the informal. The officially recognised lines of authority, communication, control and responsibility, which reflect the organisation structure, comprise the *formal system*. This is the system we have been discussing, the system we see illustrated in organisation charts.

The second is the *informal system*, the unofficial and invisible yet very real way the enterprise operates. An organisation's culture needs to support its structure. If it doesn't, its official organisation chart will bear no relationship to the way it actually operates. More dangerously, if the unofficial organisation contradicts the official organisation, it will quickly undermine it. People will know something is wrong but they may not know what.

This means that, whatever structure is selected, it can't work properly if people don't want it to. People individually and the culture as a whole need to be aligned and in harmony with the structure and the organisation's purpose. As we've seen in earlier chapters, first-line managers are critical to getting these elements 'right'.

In turn, organisation structure can influence the informal organisation by allowing or blocking access to people, functions and channels of communication. Where people are located, lines of communication and authority, how centralised decision making is, and team size and composition all affect the way people relate to each other and the general culture of the organisation.

FROM THEORY TO PRACTICE

How is your organisation structured?
- Is the structure clearly defined and well understood?
- Does the structure promote clear, simple communication between work units?

CURRENT TRENDS IN ORGANISATION DESIGN

For most of the last 200 years, most organisations operated in environments that evolved slowly and were reasonably predictable. As a result, organisation structures seldom changed. They were structured so that supervisors gathered information and passed it up to management who would decide what to do about it and pass their decisions down to supervisors who, in turn, informed the workforce.

As Figure 4.10 shows, a supervisor's main function in these organisations was to ensure the orders of senior management were carried out and operations and employees were kept stable and 'under control'. Yesterday's managers at all levels worked to reach predetermined outcomes along predetermined paths.

Just as the Industrial Revolution changed the nature of work and the attitudes and habits of workers, the Information Revolution is changing the face of business, economic and social life, transforming everything it touches.

Organisations no longer operate in a marketplace that resembles, even remotely, the environment of 40 years ago. In only one generation, the environment has changed drastically and, with it, ways of managing and structuring organisations. Organisations are being forced to redesign and 'reinvent' themselves in order to keep up with the changes, lower their costs, increase their efficiency and competitiveness, and satisfy their customers more effectively.

Here's what Tony Priestly, of BP Chemicals says:

> **'Anyone who thinks the present level of chaos is going to stabilise just does not understand the world we live in.'**

How best to restructure to meet these changing circumstances is not immediately obvious and many organisations are struggling with this challenge. Although there has already been substantial change, there is certainly more to come.

FIGURE 4.10 INFORMATION FLOW IN YESTERDAY'S ORGANISATIONS

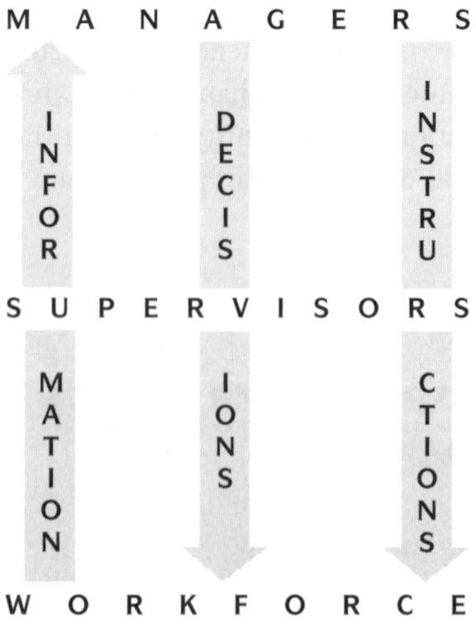

A DIFFERENT LANGUAGE FOR ORGANISATIONS

Old words
- Structures
- Systems
- Inputs and outputs
- Control
- Directing
- Maintaining
- Chain of command
- Authority
- Hierarchies

- Solid
- Stable
- Structured training and development

New words
- Cultures
- Networks
- Synergies
- Outsourcing
- Leadership
- Flexibility
- Participation, empowerment
- Multiple partnering
- Temporary project teams, self-managed work teams, virtual teams
- New working arrangements
- Adapting
- Individual responsibility for learning

THE **BIG** PICTURE

Four key questions
1. From our customer's perspective, what is our essential activity?
2. Which core functions must we retain to maintain the value of our essential activity?
3. How can we outsource the other activities?
4. How can we develop these outsourcers into robust partnerships and manage the partnering relationship?

We're already talking about organisations differently, as Box 4.9 shows. The 'old words' reflect a mechanistic organisation where all functions were performed in-house. The new words reflect an organic organisation with a range of partners and a range of employee types.

Restructuring and downsizing

The most noticeable and far-reaching change that has occurred in all sectors is **downsizing**. In all OECD (Organisation for Economic Cooperation and Development) countries, most large companies have reduced the number of people they employ on at least one occasion. Australia has done its share of downsizing, too, cutting back numbers employed by one-third to one-half. In fact, Australia has downsized more than any other OECD country.

Downsizing has flattened the traditional organisation pyramid considerably. The layers of management have been reduced from an average of seven (and often more) to an average of four (or less). Middle management has suffered the bulk of job cuts. As middle management jobs disappear, first-line management has taken on more of their roles and responsibilities.

Downsizing and **restructuring** usually go hand in hand. Some organisations downsize first, cutting jobs in an effort to improve their profitability (wages and salaries are one of the largest expenses of most enterprises). Job cuts are often followed by some form of restructuring to make the best use of those left behind.

Sometimes the organisation restructures first, filling the jobs with existing employees; any employees finding themselves without a position become redundant. This type of restructuring is usually more far-reaching and dramatic than the restructuring that results from downsizing first.

Outsourcing

Outsourcing is usually cheaper than employing a permanent full-time worker or workers because it avoids many of the costs of employment such as superannuation, insurance and office space. Many organisations have decided to contract out non-core services and sell off non-core activities. Divisions and departments shrink as non-essential work is sub-contracted to growing numbers of people in the 'flexible workforce'. This has given rise to a 'lean and mean' organisation with opportunities to become less bureaucratic and formal. Decision making and responsibility can be pushed downward, lines of communication opened up and information can move more freely around the organisation.

Sadly, both international and Australian research shows that the new flatter organisation structures have a negative impact on people and morale. Poor leadership, lack of career development, inappropriate rewards, increased workloads, and stress and confusion are other serious and unwanted side effects of restructuring.

THE **BIG** PICTURE

Organisations will need to learn to manage the process of restructuring more sensitively and professionally in order to avoid costly negative 'fallout'. They must find ways to manage, with grace and dignity, the departure of employees for whom there is no work; the way this situation is managed sends clear messages to those left behind and to the community. They must find ways to motivate those left behind. They must also find ways to motivate and remunerate the different types of workers they are employing and find ways to make them all, including subcontractors and part-timers, feel 'part of the team' and operate according to the organisation's values and mission.

Opportunities and problems arising from downsizing and outsourcing

The outsourcing resulting from downsizing has created huge opportunities for small business start-ups and growth, and for individuals to become self-employed.

Not surprisingly, restructuring can also cause problems: for those left behind, for those left without jobs and for the organisations themselves. These are summarised in Box 4.10.

THE **BIG** PICTURE

Who will look after the interests of the self-employed? Will we see a version of the medieval guilds emerge?

BOX 4.10	**PROBLEMS ARISING FROM DOWNSIZING**

For people whose jobs are redundant	Many people's sense of identity comes from their work; finding themselves without meaningful employment can cause deep emotional wounds. On a practical level, people who have been made redundant as a result of downsizing face the challenge of marketing their skills and experience to other organisations and paying their bills in the meantime.
For those left behind	Those 'spared the axe' can feel a sense of guilt. The 'survivor syndrome' can result in confusion, fear, apathy, depression and other mental and emotional problems. Survivors also feel the pressure of bigger workloads and more responsibility. As organisations search for ways to help them, systems and processes change. Old skills lose their value and new and different skills are required. New work teams form, others disband. There is a lot of change to get used to.
For the organisations	Short-term productivity increases and cost reductions can be offset by longer-term productivity loss, poor morale and workplace injuries. 'Corporate anorexia' can make it nearly impossible for people to do their jobs well—ironically, they have too much to do to spend the time required to do things right. Long working hours (usually unpaid overtime) can cause problems in people's personal lives, work-related stress and eventual burnout. Organisations can lose the goodwill and trust of those employees it has retained.

With all the difficulties associated with downsizing and restructuring, job insecurity, mistrust and cynicism have replaced employee loyalty in many organisations. And not for the first time in history:

'We trained hard ... but it seemed that every time we were beginning to form up into teams we would be reorganised ... I was to learn later in life that we tend to meet any new situation by reorganising; and a wonderful method it can be for creating the illusion of progress while producing confusion, inefficiency and demoralisation.'

General Gaius Petronius (1st century AD)*

Organisational change, particularly downsizing, restructuring and outsourcing, are coming far too quickly for many people to feel comfortable with. As we see in Chapter 12, most people find change upsetting, particularly the unpredictable, uncontrollable, discontinuous, multidirectional sort of change that is creating the uncertainties being experienced in organisations right now.

---

* Legend has it that, for his bluntness, the unfortunate General was charged with treason and forced to kill himself.

People issues and resistance to change may become more difficult obstacles as restructuring increases in frequency. Better training, more open communication and speed seem to be three important keys to successfully redesigning an organisation.

Restructuring itself is changing

The pressures for change are relentless and the real restructuring has only just begun. We can expect organisations to restructure continuously, at least over the next ten years. Answers to the problems discussed above must be found or organisations will pay the price in both human and economic terms.

Changing an organisation's structure cannot be a repair kit for a failing enterprise or a one-off adjustment. It can no longer be 'slash and burn' and mere cost cutting through a drastically reduced head count. Restructuring must purposefully move companies forward to deal with ever-changing challenges and opportunities. Only a clear strategic intent will transform an enterprise into one able to thrive in a dynamic environment.

Even successful organisations will need to restructure—just because an enterprise is doing well doesn't mean it can 'rest on its laurels'. Complacency and inertia are dangerous— witness IBM's clinging to mainframes while the market moved towards PCs, or Toyota retaining its conservative sedan styles while the market moved to sporty 4WDs. Just because an organisation structure is working today, it doesn't mean it will work tomorrow.

FROM THEORY TO PRACTICE

How to restructure

Research conducted by Professor Carlos Cordon and others at IMD, Lausanne, points to five critical issues:

1. See restructuring as a proactive break with the status quo, not as changing deckchairs on the *Titanic*. Start with a clean sheet of paper and see your enterprise through fresh eyes.
2. Be crystal clear about why and how restructuring will take place and precisely what its results will be.
3. Form a diverse group from all areas and functions of the organisation to drive the change, and provide the training and resources they will need to do the job properly.
4. Keep the pace swift, not sluggish. Restructuring should not 'drag out'. The faster the restructure, the more likely it is to deliver the expected results, and the longer the 'breathing space' between restructures.
5. Monitor critical milestones and adjust course as necessary.

TELEWORKING—THE NEW WAY OF WORKING

Two key and interrelated features of the changing work patterns are emerging. We've already mentioned that work that is not integral to the organisation is being contracted out. Work is also moving to the people, back into their homes (ironically, where it was prior to the Industrial Revolution). Figures from the Asia Pacific Telework Association tell us that, in

1998, about 4% of workers in Australia were '**teleworkers**'. This figure is now about 15% and will be over 25% by 2010.

Driving the new ways of working are factors such as the increasing cost of city office space, increasing traffic congestion during commuter rush hours and the increasing costs of commuting created by 'urban sprawl'. Advances in communications technology (email, videoconferencing, real time online chats, etc.) are allowing the new work patterns to emerge.

Box 4.11 shows how non-traditional work settings allow non-traditional workplace practices.

NON-TRADITIONAL WORK SETTINGS, NON-TRADITIONAL WORK PRACTICES

The Chief of Staff of the US Army, General Dennis J. Reimer, telecommutes routinely and communicates by email with 350 officers around the world. He also uses a web-based network called America's Army Online, which includes an intranet chat room. The general can raise issues with officers and receive advice and opinions quickly, often within hours. The furthest afield officer is kept 'in the loop' and can communicate with the general as easily as officers in the next office at the Pentagon.

General Reimer believes telecommuting helps both his productivity and his communication. Technology allows him to keep in touch and build collaborative teamwork across the organisation and around the globe. As an added bonus, he and his employer save on travel costs and time.

SOHOs and mobile offices

SOHO describes the small office, home office phenomenon. SOHO people are contractors doing jobs previously done by full-time permanent employees, employees working from home all or part of the time; or self-employed people working from home either full-time or part-time. In the United States, one-third of workers works from home; by 2002, that figure is expected to rise to one-half.

Home-based working is such a major growth area of employment that the Home-based Business Association has been established in Australia. Nor is home-work necessarily menial: one-fifth of homeworkers are in the top 10% income bracket.

Other teleworkers work from a mobile office such as a vehicle.

THE **BIG** PICTURE

Most surveys indicate that by 2010, 25% of Australian and 40% of US workers will be working from home. The National Institute of Labour studies disagrees. Humans are social animals who crave contact in an office. Who is right? We'll see!

Hotelling and hotdesking

Office 'hotelling' is another phenomenon where employees book an office for a particular day or days and arrive to find it furnished with their own personal memorabilia—family photos, favourite reference books, etc. 'Hotdesking' is similar but less 'personal': employees book desks and/or office space by the hour, day or week and bring their own accoutrements with them. This saves on costs because one desk can serve up to six employees. Enterprises that want to encourage their people to telecommute without cutting all ties find these two options economical and workable.

Satellite offices

Satellite offices, or 'telecottages', are fully equipped offices run by public or private sector organisations for their own teleworkers, or run by community or private groups for independent workers to lease.

A network of telecottages can be located close to where workers live or close to the customers, and in suburbs and regions where rent is considerably cheaper than expensive city centre locations. Employers benefit from lowered accommodation costs and a broadened pool of potential employees; employees benefit from easier commuting.

One size doesn't fit all. Most organisations will probably benefit from a mixture of alternative telecommuting solutions: shift workers sharing offices or hotdesking, hotelling for travelling or mobile workers, satellite offices for some employees and contractors, SOHOs for others.

The benefits of teleworking

Telecommuting can increase productivity, lower costs and make employees happy.

People can work when, where and how it suits them. Home-based workers often report higher energy levels, improved motivation and greater work satisfaction. In the United States, 87% of teleworkers believed they were significantly more productive and effective under the new working arrangements.

Overseas studies have reported a 20% increase in productivity when workers move their place of work from the organisation's premises to their own home for lower costs. Productivity increases result from time previously spent travelling being spent working, avoiding the usual office interruptions, and so on.

Typical cost savings include reduced workers' compensation claims (about one-third of claims result from incidents travelling to and from work), reduced absenteeism (people are more likely to work at home if they or their children are ill) and savings on office accommodation and related costs.

IBM, for example, reported cost savings of more than $US100 million annually in its North American sales and distribution unit when it moved to telecommuting; AT&T improved its cash flow by 30% by eliminating unneeded offices and consolidating others, and reducing related overhead costs. Studies in Australia show an average 15% improvement in productivity, dramatic increases in quality of work, process improvements and greater innovation from home-based working.

It isn't all roses, though. Box 4.12 summarises both sides of the telecommuting equation.

Box 4.13 shows how some companies have successfully introduced new ways of working.

BOX 4.12 ADVANTAGES AND DISADVANTAGES OF TELECOMMUTING

Benefits

- *Cost reduction:* fewer offices to maintain means lower costs of real estate and overheads.
- *Increased productivity:* workers in alternative workplaces tend to be more productive, spend less time on intra-office distractions and politics, and spend more time working and with customers.
- *People benefits:* many employees like working from home, working to suit themselves and appreciate the additional independence and flexibility. People can work where and when it suits them, be close to their families, eliminate the time expense and stress of commuting. They are free to set up their work spaces to suit their own tastes and work habits. This can give organisations an edge in attracting and retaining talented, motivated employees.
- *Qualitative improvements* in hard-to-measure aspects such as customer and employee satisfaction.
- *Better communications:* far-flung employees need not be out of sight, out of mind, but can have as rapid and as equal a say as office-based workers. This is very empowering. Electronic methods can speed communication, discussion and information sharing without the pitfalls of lengthy and costly meetings.

Disadvantages

- *Adaptation difficulties:* some people find it difficult to adapt to working from home. They find it lonely, miss the structure of regular office routines and the buzz of people around them. They may lack the space at home to devote to an office.
- *Management issues:* managers, too, need to learn new skills and methods of working, relating with and supervising telecommuters.
- *Support:* it can be difficult to design a structure and build a culture that supports telecommuting.
- *Initial set-up costs:* providing the technology, connecting telephone and fax lines, is not cheap if large numbers of employees are involved. Some employers provide an allowance to furnish the home office, which adds to the expense.
- *Practical hurdles:* remuneration, for example, can be tricky. What if a virtual team is built, with members working in SOHOs in Hong Kong, Sydney, Orange and Singapore? Each of these cities has different costs of living and people living there are on different salary scales. Yet they're each doing the same job! Technology can be tricky, too. Computer software and hardware must be standardised, people trained, etc. Full technical support must be provided. Perks can be problematic, too. What if your main office offers a gym or subsidised canteen—how will you compensate home-based or satellite workers?

INTRODUCTING NEW WAYS OF WORKING

IBM believes much of the success of its initiative was because it was a bottom-up effort. Senior management provided direction and goal, but the planning was carried out and implemented at lower levels, by the people who would be affected.

Merrill Lynch runs a telecommuting lab in its main office where work stations are set up and prospective telecommuters spend two weeks in the simulated home office, communicating with their managers, customers and colleagues solely by phone and email. If they don't like it, they find out before it's too late.

AT&T runs a survival training course: how to reserve work space, how to route the phone and pager, how to access the database. They teach alternative working arrangement 'norms' including time management, dressing for work, leaving specific messages on voice mail, how to make it clear to others at home that you're 'going to work', how to switch off from work, and how to actually leave your office when you're tempted to stay, how to have a balanced life and not feel guilty for jogging in the afternoon because you make up the time later.

Temporary, contract and casual workers

Workers of the future won't be described as full-time or part-time employees. They might be part-time workers with several jobs, casual workers with one or more jobs, temporary workers, contractors, or any combination of these. They may be employees, self-employed or even both. Charles Handy coined the term *portfolio workers* to describe people who have several part-time jobs or contracts which together make up full-time work. There will be no typical worker, at least in the first part of the 21st century!

KEY TRENDS AND THEIR IMPLICATIONS FOR SUPERVISORS

The changes taking place in all sectors have enormous implications for organisation design specialists and supervisors alike. To be an effective supervisor in the 21st century, you will need a different set of skills from those needed in the last century.

As structures become less hierarchical and more flexible, you will need to be a leader who motivates and helps people to learn, grow and develop their talents, to help the organisation achieve its vision (see Chapters 20, 21 and 24). You will need sound business and decision-making skills and be able to accept increased levels of responsibility and accountability (see Chapters 1 and 11).

As organisation designers increasingly structure enterprises around information skills and knowledge, not specialist skills, you will need to know how to open communication channels and help people network their knowledge and information (see Chapters 2, 13 and 15). You will need to be able to develop and lead both real and virtual teams (see Chapter 22).

As organisations contract out all but their core business, you will need skills to oversee projects handled by non-employees, functions performed by non-employees and services provided by non-employees. You will need to develop skills to make them feel 'part of the team' and buy into the vision and objectives of the organisation.

As organisations enter the global economy, you will need skills to participate in and supervise virtual teams and virtual employees. You will need solid conceptual and interpersonal skills to deal effectively with people from different countries and regions (see Chapters 18 and 19).

As technology continues to advance, you will need to embrace continuous learning and learn to manage the knowledge worker and people you only see occasionally (see Chapter 13). You will need to focus on results, not time spent as the number of technical and professional jobs increases (see Chapter 8).

As consumers become more discerning, you will need to search continually for new ways to enhance levels of customer service and provide ever more satisfaction to your customers (see Chapter 10).

As society continues to change, you will need to learn to manage an increasingly diverse group of workers and focus on people as individuals, not as numbers (see Chapter 18).

As the triple bottom line takes hold, you will need conceptual skills and process management skills to ensure that rules, regulations and laws are complied with in their spirit as well as their letter (see Chapters 1 and 17).

As the number of general management jobs declines, the need for specialist managers who are also highly skilled at managing people will increase markedly. Despite the trend to reduce staff numbers, the total number of management, professional and technical jobs will probably increase as the economy grows and cluster in the functional and technical areas. This means that you can expect job opportunities for supervisors and team leaders to increase while jobs for middle managers shrink.

In career terms, your promotion path will probably shorten and you cannot expect a career of one promotion following another. Most people will reach their career ceiling earlier and the ceiling will be lower. If your paradigm is back with the traditional organisation structure, you might find this disappointing. If you accept and work with the new paradigm, you can satisfy your needs for job satisfaction, growth and continual learning through sideways moves and taking on new and exciting projects.

····················· RAPID REVIEW ·······················

	True	False
1. The purpose of organisation design is to structure an organisation to achieve its goals efficiently and effectively.	☐	☐
2. Only private sector organisations need a board of directors.	☐	☐
3. Not-for-profit organisations are not concerned with money.	☐	☐
4. An organisation chart is a diagram showing how the various people and functions in an organisation officially fit together.	☐	☐
5. An organisation chart reflects both the formal and informal structure of an organisation.	☐	☐

	True	False
6. Although staff people perform critical functions, in most cases they are not considered 'core' personnel.	☐	☐
7. Supervising too many people can lead to oversupervision.	☐	☐
8. The principle of unity of command is applied as strongly today as it ever was.	☐	☐
9. Both internal and external factors influence the way we design an organisation.	☐	☐
10. The organisation pyramid is alive and well.	☐	☐
11. Decentralised organisations have flat structures enabling them to empower their people and respond quickly to market needs.	☐	☐
12. Centralised mechanistic organisations make it difficult to respond to rapidly changing circumstances.	☐	☐
13. Organisations are becoming flatter as the pyramid gives way to more flexible organisation forms.	☐	☐
14. The term 'shamrock' refers to the three types of employees who work in modern organisations: core workers, flexible workers and contract workers.	☐	☐
15. Because knowledge and information is critical to organisational effectiveness, many organisations are trying to become 'learning organisations' that acquire, disseminate and use knowledge freely among employees.	☐	☐
16. The importance of people's loyalty to organisations is encouraging some enterprises to become more 'holistic'.	☐	☐
17. Any organisation can be a virtual or partially virtual organisation if it has the technology.	☐	☐
18. The four main organisational structures are: functional, customer type, product and geographic location. These can combine with any framework: bureaucratic, linking-pin, organic, etc.	☐	☐
19. There is always one best organisation structure for any given situation.	☐	☐
20. Although we have recently seen a dramatic increase in how frequently organisations redesign and restructure themselves, that will now slow down.	☐	☐
21. Middle management has been most affected in terms of job loss in the recent redesign and downsizing of organisations.	☐	☐
22. Today's worker may be virtual or 'real', home-based or office-based, part-time or full-time, self-employed or employed by someone else.	☐	☐
23. The need for first-line managers is likely to grow in the years ahead.	☐	☐
24. 'Hotelling' means you work from an office based at a central city hotel.	☐	☐
25. Because of the changes affecting organisation design and structure, supervisors of the 21st century will need very different skills from supervisors of the 20th century.	☐	☐

APPLY YOUR KNOWLEDGE

1. How do sole traders, partnerships and corporations differ?
2. Why is a board of directors necessary in a corporation? What does the board do?
3. What are the two major types of organisation in the public sector? What are the differences between them?
4. What are some ways organisation charts can be used to help organisations achieve their objectives?
5. What is meant by line and staff positions? By span of management?
6. Describe a bureaucracy and the type of organisations and environments best suited to a bureaucratic structure.
7. Describe the organisation framework you believe is best suited to the present day.
8. Describe the differences between the more traditional types of organisations and emerging organisations.
9. Write a short essay discussing the current trends in organisation design and the reasons for them.
10. Draw a simple diagram for the four main organisation structures and describe their main features.
11. What would be the dangers in transforming a large public sector organisation such as the Australian Tax Office into an organic, matrix-type organisation? Would these be outweighed by the advantages? Why, or why not?

DEVELOP YOUR SKILLS

Individual activities

1. Discuss the key issues of current organisation design trends, applying them to your college or your own place of work. How 'up to date' is its organisation design? What changes can you predict for its future design?
2. Find out the name and primary objectives of four ministerial departments and two statutory authorities in the state in which you live.
3. Interview someone who has experienced an organisational restructure first hand. Find out all you can about the positives and negatives of this experience, for the employees as well as for the organisation as a whole, trying to understand what helped to make these experiences positive or negative. Draw some general conclusions about the best way to go about restructuring an organisation.
4. Draw an organisation chart of an organisation you know. For each position on the organisation chart, provide a one-sentence description of its overall job purpose.
5. A national company consists of a confectionary division, a beverage division and a food division. Draw a series of organisation charts showing it structured along functional, customer-type, product, geographic and matrix lines.
6. Imagine that you have been asked to organise a gymkhana for your college. The purpose of the gymkhana is to publicise the college to the local community in a way that raises its profile and goodwill. You are expected to at least break even financially. You have been authorised

to establish a committee to help you and have been allocated a small budget (although you will have to supplement it with additional fund-raising yourselves). What sort of organisation structure will best achieve your objectives? Design this organisation and draw it, following the rules explained in this chapter.

Group activities

1. In small groups, contrast the advantages and disadvantages of bureaucracies and organic organisations.
2. In groups of five or six, discuss the organisation types that best suit a volatile marketplace, skilled and committed employees, and an industry requiring creativity and flexibility. Then come up with a metaphor, a symbol or a drawing that represents this organisation structure.
3. In small groups, review the changing conditions (covered in this chapter) that organisation design must cater for. Then brainstorm the ways in which these changes could affect you as supervisors in the years to come.
4. Form teams of five or six to undertake a simple problem-solving activity. Structure half the teams hierarchically, with a 'supervisor' reporting to a 'general manager'. The general manager will make the decisions and the supervisor will pass these on to the rest of the 'workers' in the group to carry out. Structure the remaining teams flexibly, allowing team members to decide how best to solve the problem. When the problems have been solved, compare how the two types of structure affected task achievement, communication and the 'culture' of the teams.
5. In groups of three, and without consulting the organisation chart of your college, try to draw it following the guidelines given in this chapter. Then compare it with the official organisation chart your teacher will provide. Do they differ? What are the reasons for any differences?
6. Form the class into two teams. One team will take the position: *Holistic organisations are naive and unrealistic in the face of huge bottom-line pressures*. The other half will take the position: *Unless organisations become more humane and holistic, they will not attract and inspire the people they need if they are to thrive*. Develop your thoughts in your teams

CASE STUDY 4.1

Harris Hardwood

In 1981 Sam Harris was an entrepreneur with a vision: to manufacture and sell top quality Australian turned hardwood handles for all types of hand tools and implements. To achieve his dream, he established Harris Hardwood Handles, first as a sole tradership, later as a proprietary limited company. Thanks largely to the quality of his work and the care with which he selected timber, his business grew and prospered to what it is today. The current organisation is illustrated in Figure 4.11.

Sam was a strong-willed individual. He personally directed and supervised the efforts of all his employees. He gave orders directly to his sales representatives as well as to the plant workers.

His 'second-in-command' was Tom Jenkins, his plant supervisor. Tom had been with the company since it began. The workers really liked Tom. He was a capable worker himself and was to a large extent responsible for the success of the firm. He had a 'way' with people that made them like and respect him; he was the one who most often coordinated the overall efforts of the plant personnel.

Sales were under the direct supervision of Sam's only son, John Harris, now 27 years old. After receiving a degree in chemistry, John had begun a career with one of the larger chemical companies. Two years ago his father had insisted that he return home to work in the family concern and, somewhat reluctantly, he did.

Although John did a respectable job, it was apparent to most of the employees that he had neither the drive of his father nor the personality of Tom Jenkins. The accountant–office manager and the plant mechanic were both satisfactory in their respective areas, although neither seemed to possess the characteristics necessary for further advancement.

On 18 April 2000, Sam Harris died suddenly and his son sold the business to the Bayside Timber Mill. At the request of the new owners, the operation and name of Harris Hardwood Handles were to remain the same until they could undertake some form of reorganisation.

The Bayside Timber Mill is owned by Australian Fine Timber Limited. Its managing director, Tim Sykes, has a free hand within operating guidelines set by head office. Three kilometres from the Harris plant, Bayside is a bustling concern. Figure 4.12 illustrates the current organisation structure of the Bayside Mill.

....

FIGURE 4.11   ORGANISATION CHART OF HARRIS HARDWOOD HANDLES

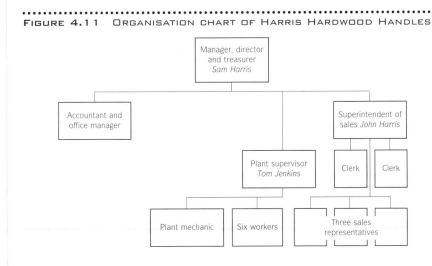

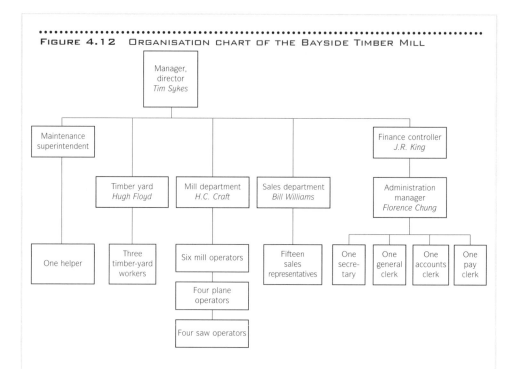

FIGURE 4.12   ORGANISATION CHART OF THE BAYSIDE TIMBER MILL

Tim Sykes has an outgoing personality and is generally regarded as a 'natural-born' salesperson. Although 52 years old, he often travels the sales territory with his sales team and invariably sales increase substantially when he makes the rounds with them. The financial controller, J.R. King, is highly regarded as a trustworthy and talented accountant and, unofficially, is considered to be Tim's 'second in charge'.

Also reporting to Tim are Florence Chung and Bill Williams. Florence controls all aspects of administration, including secretarial services, payroll and billing. She is a conscientious and dedicated employee, and Tim often wonders how she manages to ensure everything is done in such an organised fashion.

Sales are under the direction of 29-year-old Bill Williams, who is quite competent as a representative but has experienced some trouble in keeping his team satisfied with, and enthusiastic about, their work.

Hugh Floyd, in charge of the timber yard, is a practical person who does a good job keeping the company supplied with timber of the right kind and quality. He devotes his major attention to purchasing, sometimes to the detriment of the general running of the timber yard itself. H.C. Craft, head of the mill department, is recognised by all employees for his ability in mill and timber work. Although nearing retirement, H.C. not only runs his department efficiently, but he often finds time to help Hugh Floyd in his timber yard operations.

Upon acquiring Harris Hardwood Handles, Australian Fine Timber Limited faced the problem of how to consolidate and organise the two operations effectively, not just for the immediate future but also for the next several years.

Questions

1 Prepare an organisation structure combining the two companies. Explain your reasons for selecting the framework and the particular structure you use. State the overall objective you want the organisation structure to contribute to. Assume that John Harris will leave the company as soon as he can. If you believe an existing employee cannot fill a needed position, label that position 'vacant'.

2 What problems will you expect the two merged organisations to face as they 'get to know each other'?

3 In the early days at least, what influence would you expect the informal organisation to have on the way the two groups of employees work together?

CASE STUDY 4.2

Lancy's Laboratories

Paul Lancy started his dental laboratory in 1971 as a sole trader, making dentures, dental implants and crowns. Due to the high quality of his work, his laboratory grew quickly and in 1973, after he qualified, his brother joined him as a partner. On the advice of his accountant, Lancy's Laboratories became a proprietary limited company in 1974. By then, they had six technicians and an administrative assistant working in the lab.

When Paul and his brother began focusing intensively on customer service during the 1980s, the lab's business mushroomed and another six technicians were hired. They also began doing facial reconstructive implants for the cranio-facial unit at City Hospital.

The company began an apprenticeship scheme in 1989 to ensure a continual flow of qualified technicians to allow continued expansion of the business. In the early 1990s, Paul took up the cry of partnering and developed strong mutually beneficial links with his suppliers, which further strengthened the business. He also forged links with laboratories overseas and developed a network of specialist manufacturers of dental and facial prostheses. For example, the lab could email a three-dimensional image of a jaw to a company in Sweden who would design and make a near-perfect implant and deliver it to Lancy's for finishing, all within five working days.

The lab had always been a relaxed and enjoyable place to work and, in the late 1990s, Paul modernised it and upgraded its physical working atmosphere. Last Monday, one of his most experienced and valued technicians, John Booth, approached Paul saying that his mother had been taken seriously ill and would need continual home care for several months at least. Could he take leave for this, or would he need to resign?

This started Paul thinking. Although it was highly specialised, John could do quite a lot of his job from home if he took some of his equipment with him. In fact, since everyone had most of their own equipment, perhaps others would be interested in this. Some of the more technically advanced techniques using specialised equipment would still need to be done in the lab, of course, but, clearly, this didn't apply to everything. What about the office support people? Perhaps some of them might appreciate the opportunity to work from home one or two days a week. Thanks to a telephone switching system, he already had a home-based contact person available 24 hours a day for the benefit of his overseas partner labs and this was working out really well. What other new working arrangement might add value to his business, customers and trading partners?

Questions

1 What are the options open to Paul as he considers possible new working arrangements?
2 How would you expect a revised organisation structure to influence morale and efficiency in the lab? How might it affect relationships with partner labs, suppliers and customers?
3 What are the potential benefits and disadvantages to incorporating new working arrangements? On balance, what would you advise Paul to do?

Answers to Rapid Review questions

1. T   2. F   3. F   4. T   5. F   6. F   7. F   8. F   9. T   10. F   11. T   12. T   13. T   14. T.   15. T   16. T   17. T   18. T   19. F   20. F   21. T   22. T   23. T   24. F   25. T

CHAPTER 5

PLANNING AND MONITORING FOR GOAL ACHIEVEMENT

Computers as an aid to monitoring

Morris was surveying the fruits of his labour. As the production supervisor, he had been part of a temporary project team set up to help design a major upgrade to the company's computerised production planning and control system. He had been particularly keen to ensure the weekly summary printout would be both informative and easy to read.

As well as showing a detailed summary of the previous week's production runs, it would now show which machines were producing at acceptable quality and speed levels, which way they were heading in terms of quality and speed trends, which operators were meeting their targets, where bottlenecks were occurring, even exactly where raw material quality was not up to scratch—all in graph form. This would make it much easier to read than the previous printouts and he would be able to spot potential problem areas even more quickly.

Gone were the days of pouring over and interpreting pages of figures. With this improved monitoring information, Morris could spot at a glance just about everything he needed to know to make sure production plans were achieved and operations ran smoothly. Life would be even easier now with better and quicker feedback on his department's performance.

OVERVIEW

Supervisors who don't plan well are usually surrounded by chaos, missed delivery dates, schedules falling behind, idle machines and people running around like the proverbial 'chooks with their heads cut off'. In this chapter, you will discover how to avoid that.

- Do you know how to develop sound plans and monitor them?
- Do you know what distinguishes a good plan from a poor plan?
- Can you identify the types of plans that guide an organisation and explain what they should be based on? Can you explain how they differ from the plans a supervisor makes?

- Do you know the difference between a vision, a mission, a goal, a target and an objective?
- Can you apply the six steps to planning and explain why they are necessary?
- Do you know the seven types of plans that supervisors need to be familiar with?
- Do you know how and why to protect your plans and how to monitor how well they are working?

IF YOU FAIL TO PLAN

We often plan without realising it. Can you imagine arranging to meet a group of friends for a picnic without first agreeing who will bring what food, who will bring the barbecue, chairs and rugs, where you'll go and precisely when and where you'll all meet up? Or not having an alternative plan in mind in case of rain?

For the much more complex job of running an entire organisation, department or section, we need to have goals, targets and time frames clearly established and plans written down. As the saying goes:

'If you fail to plan—you are planning to fail.'

Planning is an important function performed by managers at every level of an organisation. Whether they are simple plans like holiday rosters or training timetables, or complex plans like production plans or business plans, or whether they involve just one department or an entire organisation, planning is necessary for both day-to-day effectiveness and long-term strategic success.

Plans are projected courses of action aimed at achieving objectives. They aim to coordinate action so that goals can be reached in the most efficient and effective way.

Just having a plan, of course, doesn't guarantee success. However, without planning, the probability that you will achieve your goals other than by accident is remote. Wishing doesn't make things happen—planning and action make things happen. Knowing precisely what you need to do and how you intend to do it will greatly increase your chances of success. Plans are the rudders that guide us towards our objectives.

... You plan to fail

'Those who plan can make things happen; those who don't plan have things happen to them.'

Have you ever heard the expression: *The right hand doesn't know what the left hand is doing?* It's usually applied to someone who is a poor planner.

Many supervisors grumble that they would love to plan if only they had the time. They are usually the ones who are too busy putting out 'bushfires' to develop an overall plan of 'fire prevention'. Other supervisors say there are so many physical demands on their time that they don't have time to sit down and plan. However, both these excuses actually point to the need for planning. Time spent in planning pays off, because it prevents emergencies and crises and keeps things running smoothly.

Whereas much of a supervisor's work is physical in nature, planning is mental work. Some supervisors put planning into the 'too hard' category and avoid it. Some don't plan because they have never thought about it or don't have any idea how they should go about it. This may be an excuse for today, but not for tomorrow. If they don't learn, their jobs will be that much more difficult. The unexpected will keep happening at the most inopportune times.

The message is clear: successful supervisors are the ones who plan their work and work to their plan. Fortunately, everyone can learn to plan and once non-planners begin planning they find it becomes 'second nature'. They get into the habit of thinking things through and formulating plans because they know that a well thought-out plan will save time and prevent hassles. They learn to make time, often early in the morning or late in the day, to review their department's objectives, update plans, monitor actual results against plans, look over upcoming work and plan for the future.

THE BENEFITS OF PLANNING

.... As the Australian Army is fond of saying:

'Prior planning prevents poor performance.'

Planning provides the groundwork for the future and gives us a way to track performance and assess achievements. It helps eliminate duplication of effort and expense. It helps use people's efforts effectively, coordinate employees and their jobs, minimise disruptions and meet schedules more easily.

Good plans help us identify and focus our efforts on important issues. They give our efforts purpose and direction. They help us reach our goals by telling us what needs to be done and in what order. When they are communicated well, everyone knows why something is being done, what is to be done, who is to do it, where it is to be done, when it is to be done and how it is to be done.

When people know this, they feel that things are under control and they are able to perform better. When we know what we're doing, we can take steps to ensure that needed tools, people, information and materials are available to meet requirements. We won't get caught short.

Thinking things through in plenty of time frees us from crisis management—responding quickly and under pressure. Planning can also help reduce uncertainty and help us anticipate and prepare for change. Planning the work and following the plan gives us better control over costs. Knowing what everyone should be doing and what materials and equipment should be used will contribute to smoother operations. Because of its importance, planning needs to be part of every supervisor's regular routine.

As someone once said:

'Planning pays off. It wasn't raining when Noah built the Ark.'

Given the importance of planning, we'll look first at strategic business planning and then at how supervisors plan for their departments.

VALUES, VISION AND MISSION: THE CORPORATE DNA

To be successful, every enterprise needs a clear set of values, a vision and a mission. General Electric, Disney, Sony and Hewlett Packard are four examples of how values-driven businesses consistently outperform their competitors. Many supervisors have found that their teams benefit from a vision and mission, too.

As we saw in Chapter 3, **values** describe what a person or an organisation believes is important. An organisation's values are its internal principals that guide its actions and the behaviour of its employees. Here are some extracts from the Ulster Bank Group's values:

- Fair and honest
- Added value for our customers
- Going the 'extra mile'
- Innovation and creativity
- Leadership by example
- Shared purpose and individual responsibility
- Performance and achievement

They link into its vision, which is:

'Through the relentless pursuit of excellence, we will be the preferred financial services group on the island of Ireland.'

A **vision** provides a clear picture of what everyone is striving to achieve. It unifies employees, describes *what we do* and defines an enterprise's (or team's) fundamental purpose. The vision provides a starting point for moving forward and the means of both assessing progress and responding to change. It gives a sense of purpose. Visions need to challenge, stretch and inspire people so they know their effort is worthwhile.

FROM THEORY TO PRACTICE

Do you recall Johnson & Johnson's Tylenol crisis? A number of mysterious deaths in Chicago in the early 1980s were linked to the painkiller Extra-strength Tylenol. It seemed that some capsules had been laced with cyanide.

J&J's values were set out in a document called *The Credo*. It clearly put saving lives before profits and steered the company successfully through the crisis. They told consumers not to use the product, ceased production, stopped advertising and recalled over $US100 million worth of Tylenol capsules from the shelves.

Their prompt and honest action ensured that damage to the business was short-term and, despite the incident, Tylenol is still one of their most successful products.

A **mission** describes *how we do it*, or how the vision will be achieved. It is more specific. The mission reflects senior management's standards in such areas as customer service, employee relations, product or service quality and reliability, and profitability.

Box 5.1 shows how values, vision and mission link together for AMP.

Visions and missions should focus, motivate and inspire employees, and define the organisation to its customers and suppliers. They set the broad, long-term direction, purpose and goals for the organisation and provide guidelines for day-to-day decision making.

 BOX 5.1 AMP'S VALUES, VISION, MISSION AND GOALS

Values
We are customer focused.
We are market oriented.
We are committed to people.
We achieve through teamwork.
We are results driven.
We act with integrity.
We take responsibility for ourselves.

Vision
AMP helps people achieve their dreams and provides peace of mind.

Mission
We will be the best at providing valued solutions, superb service and excellent results.

Goals
For employees: The employer of choice, we recognise, reward and develop our employees; a great place to work.
For shareholders: Excellent financial results, outperforming the market and our sector.
For advisers: Valued products, superb support services and high rewards for high performance.
For customers: Financial solutions to meet their needs, including high quality advice and service.

THE BIG PICTURE

Three key strategic questions:
1. What business should we be in?
2. What are we best capable of?
3. Is there a good fit between our desired business and our capabilities?

Together, the values, vision and mission achieve five things:
1. They help the organisation to understand its place in the changing marketplace and employees to focus on what's important.
2. They provide a framework for the business plan (see below).
3. They guide day-to-day activities and act as a reference point for decision making.
4. They send a clear message to stakeholders about who the organisation is, what it will achieve and, in broad terms, how it will achieve it.
5. They enhance an organisation's reputation and help it attract like-minded employees.

They need to be clear, concise and memorable. Everyone in the organisation needs to be able to understand what they mean, not only for the organisation as a whole but for them personally. Here is the vision statement of Chrysler Corporation of America:

'To produce cars and trucks that people will want to buy, will enjoy driving and will want to buy again.'

Here is the vision statement of Virgin Atlantic Airways:

'As the UK's second long-haul carrier, to build an intercontinental network concentrating on those routes with a substantial established market and clear indication of growth potential, by offering the highest possible service at the lowest possible cost.'

Which statement is clearer to you? Which would you find easier to explain to employees if you were their supervisor? Which do you think is more inspiring?

Here's is Disney's vision statement:

'To make people happy.'

Its mission statement goes on to explain how Disney will do this.

Once written, vision and mission statements can change. Fifteen years ago, Microsoft's vision was:

'A computer on every desk and in every home.'

Its vision now encompasses the Internet and related technologies.

Whose job is it?

Do you think strategy is a senior management prerogative? Traditionalists like Michael Porter of Harvard Business School do, but others, such as McGill University's Henry Mintzberg and author Gary Hammel, believe everyone should, and does, participate. The

---

THE **BIG** PICTURE

Devising a snappy vision and clear mission is only the beginning.
Organisations that frame them and leave them hanging on a wall but do nothing to 'live the dream' only breed cynicism. Values, vision and mission need to be a daily part of people's working lives.

e-technology consulting company, EDS, for example, involves thousands of employees in developing its strategy. Intel's middle managers pushed the company toward micro-processors when its senior executives were still focused on memory-chips.

According to Mintzberg, even if senior managers set strategy, middle managers decide which ideas to push, which to let languish. Salespeople decide what to sell, to whom and how. Individual employees decide whether and how much they will support the vision and strategies in their day-to-day behaviours. Some strategies are modified, others abandoned. Says Mintzberg:

'A single action can be taken, feedback can be received, and the process can continue until the organisation converges on the pattern that becomes its strategy.'

Compare this organic view of strategy with the organic view of organisations discussed in Chapter 4.

GOALS, OBJECTIVES AND TARGETS: THE TEAM DNA

A **goal** describes what we want to achieve overall. Think of a goal as the light at the end of the tunnel. This means that goals are usually destinations we are aiming for longer term. At the broad organisational level, this is the vision and mission of the organisation. Like the vision and mission, goals guide us in our decisions and actions. This is why smart supervisors have clear team and departmental goals. Here's how it works:

If one of your departmental goals is to *provide a safe, healthy and satisfying work environment* and you need to make a decision about who to assign to a new task, you would make this decision bearing that goal in mind: *Who would be able to do the job safely? What further training, if any, might they need? Who would derive the most job satisfaction from the assignment?* This is how goals guide our choices. They also help us to respond to change more easily because they give us a clear picture of where we want to be in the long term. Box 5.2 contrasts organisational mission statements and departmental goals. Departmental goals need to support organisational goals.

An **objective** is shorter-term than a goal, which means it can be more specific. Objectives provide clear measuring posts as we proceed towards our goals. The best objectives are measurable and time-framed. The examples below show how departmental goals (or an organisation's mission) might be broken down into objectives.

Goal	Objectives
• To encourage and reward employee contributions and participation.	• To nominate at least one employee from my department for the biannual Customer Service Hero award and to win this award at least once every two years.
• To build the most reliable and environmentally sound vehicle batteries in New Zealand.	• To have a pass rate at final test stage of, or better than, 99.5% by June 2003.
• To be the largest retailer of passenger tyres in Australia.	• To have 25% market share as measured by our total sales and to have 3% more stores than our nearest competitor by February 2005.

SOME ORGANISATIONAL AND DEPARTMENTAL MISSION STATEMENTS

An organisation's mission gives us something concrete to aim for:

- to provide timely, caring and helpful advice and support to the families and carers of Alzheimer's sufferers;
- to build the most reliable and environmentally sound vehicle batteries in New Zealand;
- to be the largest retailer of passenger tyres in Australia;
- to provide the fastest, friendliest and most reliable customer service in our industry.

A department's goals also give team members something to aim for:

- to provide a safe, healthy and satisfying work environment for employees;
- to encourage and reward employee contributions and participation;
- to establish and maintain supportive and responsive relationships with all internal customers;
- to maintain gross profit contribution levels at, or exceeding, 26%.

Targets are normally even shorter-term and more specific than goals. For example, you might have a target of updating team members every three months on the Customer Service Hero award and ask team members to nominate their Service Hero every month so the final nominations can be selected from this group; you might also decide to have your own departmental monthly Service Hero award, with the award being two cinema tickets or similar. You might divide an objective of a battery pass rate at final test stage of, or greater than, 99.5% by June 2003 into performance targets of shorter time intervals specifying a gradual, measurable increase in pass rates. You might set a target of opening three new stores in each state per annum over the next three years to achieve the objective of having 3% more stores than the nearest competitor by February 2005. Box 5.3 shows some common terms for targets.

TERMS FOR TARGETS

- *Percentages* (95% on-time deliveries; attendance rates increased by 3% over the next three months)
- *Time* (all complaints to be investigated within three working days; turnaround time from the word-processing centre to be two working days or less for documents of less than 20 pages)
- *Absolute prohibitions* (safety footwear to be worn at all times; no smoking on the premises at any time)
- *Frequency of occurrence* (stocks to be checked monthly; weight samples to be taken hourly)
- *Averages* (an average of 15 documents per day per operator to be completed and distributed)

These targets are *specific, measurable* and *trackable*. Targets should also be *achievable* and *relevant* to the mission and goals of the organisation and department.

Figure 5.1 shows the relationship between goals, objectives and targets. Keep 'chunking down', or refining, your goals until you arrive at objectives and targets you can work with and that you feel are meaningful, believable and specific enough to provide a sense of direction.

FIGURE 5.1   GOALS, OBJECTIVES AND TARGETS

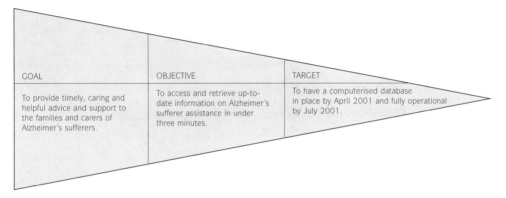

GOAL	OBJECTIVE	TARGET
To provide timely, caring and helpful advice and support to the families and carers of Alzheimer's sufferers.	To access and retrieve up-to-date information on Alzheimer's sufferer assistance in under three minutes.	To have a computerised database in place by April 2001 and fully operational by July 2001.

THE SIX STEPS TO PLANNING

Figure 5.2 shows the six-step planning process. You can see it is an ongoing process, with the achievement of one plan often leading to starting on another one. As we see in Chapter 9, an iterative process like this helps us plan for continuous improvement.

As you read through the six steps, think how they would apply to developing a business plan to achieve an organisation's vision and mission, and how they would apply to developing a departmental plan to achieve the department's goals and objectives.

1. *Establish a realistic goal and targets.* What specifically are you trying to achieve? As far as possible, make this a quantifiable, time-framed goal. What will indicate you are succeeding? Specific measures of performance to aim for—targets—makes achieving your goals easier. It makes monitoring (step 6) easier, too.

   *To achieve _____(goal)_____ by _(date)_*

2. *List all the things that will need to happen* in order to achieve your goal. Try brainstorming (see Chapter 11) or use the five Ws and one H 'triggers' (What? Who? Where? When? Why? How?) to determine what needs to be done, who will do it and all the other details.

3. *Sequence the activities* in the order in which they should occur. Network diagrams and flow charts are useful tools in this step because they provide a visual representation of your plan. Assign target dates and, if applicable, individual responsibility to each activity.

4. *Communicate your plan* to those who will be involved in it or affected by it. If everyone is aware of your objectives and how you hope to achieve them, they will be able to help you. Involving others increases your chances of success.

FIGURE 5.2 THE PLANNING PROCESS

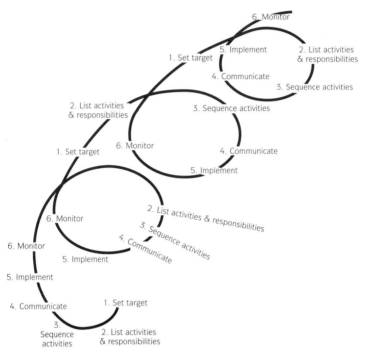

5. *Implement your plan.* Once you are happy that it is complete and that you have communicated it well, put your plan into action. You might think about conducting a force field analysis (see Chapter 11) prior to implementation.

6. *Check your progress* against the plan to make sure your original targets and time frames are being achieved. Monitoring is your insurance. Your aim is to find out in plenty of time if things are going off the rails so that you can take effective corrective action. Because it is such an important part of every supervisor's role, we examine monitoring later in this chapter.

FROM THEORY TO PRACTICE

Express your goals, objectives and targets in positive outcomes (what you *do* want, not what you *don't* want). For example, 'a 99.5% pass rate' not 'a 0.5% failure rate'.

Aim at clear, concise action plans that are flexible and that others will easily understand. Flexibility allows you to alter your plans if changes occur or if something goes wrong. It does not mean being imprecise, however. The more detailed you make your plans, the easier it will be to deal with anything that does change or go wrong.

Supervisory planning calls for precision about what is to be done (target), when it is to be done (today, tomorrow, next Friday), where it will be done (at the workplace, in the stockroom), how it will be done (steps to be taken) and who will do it (list people by name). Figure 5.3 shows a simple planning format that you can adapt to suit your needs. Use the five Ws and one H 'triggers' to ensure you have thought your plan through fully.

It's a good idea to put your plans in writing. However informal the plan may be, most of us are not able to keep everything in our heads. We need to jot things down on paper so that we can study them, spot flaws and make changes. Written plans are also easier to communicate to others, and are there for future reference.

It is a good sign to see a plan that is a bit dog-eared and scribbled-upon, because this is evidence that it is being used, revised and referred to—that it is a working document, not one that just takes up space in the filing cabinet or on the bulletin board.

FIGURE 5.3   A BASIC PLANNING FORMAT

What is to be done (target)?	*When* is it to be done (target date)?	*Where* will it be done?	*How* will it be done (the tasks involved, stages/ key-points)?	*Who* will do it?

TYPES OF PLANS

•... Let's look at some of the types of plans supervisors normally work with.

Short-term and long-term plans

To achieve the organisation's vision and mission, senior managers make *strategic* or *business plans*, which outline the general strategies to be followed. These are *long-term plans* that generally look ahead three to five years, although time frames vary depending on how dynamic and volatile the organisation's environment is.

First-line managers plan for their own department. They may be longer-term plans aimed at achieving departmental goals and objectives, or shorter-term *operational plans* detailing the daily, weekly or monthly operations of their department. These plans cover periods of up to one year and show precisely how the organisation's longer-term plans and objectives will be achieved.

As plans become more short-term, they generally become more specific. While the six-step planning process remains the same, long-term plans are developed by taking a 'helicopter' overview and looking further ahead and farther afield. Operational plans usually need a helicopter view, too, but from less high up.

Business plans

All enterprises, small, medium and large, need to develop and follow a business plan, normally established by the board of directors and senior managers. The business-planning process charts the course for the organisation's future, typically looking ahead three to five years. The aim is to discover superior ways of adding value for stakeholders and provide overall direction for activities and focus for the energies of the organisation.

The four essential questions to answer in order to make a business plan are:

1. *Who are we?* (What are our values and vision?)
   Many organisations are involving all employees in answering this question. This ensures that people throughout the organisation understand and support the organisation's values and vision.
2. *Where are we now?* (What are our strengths, weaknesses, opportunities and threats?)
   Key points that capture the current position include the number of employees, annual turnover, core market segments, chief business activities, customers and competitors. (See *SWOT analysis* on page 167.)
3. *Where do we want to be?* (What are our longer-term mission and goals?)
   Measurable objectives are set for where the organisation intends to be, for example, desired turnover, staff levels, customer profile, potential markets.
4. *How will we get there?* (What strategies will we use? What actions do we need to take?)
   Key strategies that will enable the enterprise to reach its goals might include staff training, marketing plans, funding growth, new product or service development. The actions needed become the business plan.

Comparing where the organisation is now (the answer to question 2) and where it wants to be (question 3) is called a **gap analysis** (see Figure 5.4). From this, the business plan is developed, detailing how to 'bridge the gap', or move from the current situation to the desired situation. The plan becomes the basis for business decisions to ensure that actions, processes and expenditure will close the gap between 'where we are now' and 'where we want to be'.

THE **BIG** PICTURE

Three ways to create more value for stakeholders:

1. *Operating methods:* designing more reliable, more efficient, cheaper or quicker ways of doing things through, for example, process re-engineering, time savings, benchmarking, total quality management, empowerment or continuous improvement.
2. *Future scanning:* defining factors critical to future success, for example, competitive strategy, scenario analysis, identifying a range of potential outcomes to base strategy on, trends analysis.
3. *Behaviour and culture:* ensuring the attitudes and behaviours of employees support the organisation's vision, for example by developing a learning culture, training and development, participative leadership.

FIGURE 5.4   GAP ANALYSIS

SWOT analysis

SWOT analysis

Business plans are generally based on an analysis of the enterprise's internal strengths (S) and weaknesses (W), and the threats (T) and opportunities (O) in its external environment (*SWOT analysis*). This means taking a long hard look at such factors as:

- Who are our customers and what do they really want?
- How strong are our relationships with them?
- What is the growth potential, profitability and quality of our products and/or services?
- How do our employees currently measure up for the future in terms of skills, flexibility and potential?
- How sound are our plant, equipment and operating systems, particularly their age and suitability for the future, and how do they compare with the competition's?
- How stable is the financing of our organisation, how secure is our cash flow, how are our assets distributed, how are our relationships with creditors and debtors?
- What does the external environment, particularly technological, political and consumer trends, hold in store for us?
- What is likely to happen in our marketplace, particularly changes and trends in government regulation, trends in technology and consumer patterns, opportunities for expansion and threats from new or existing competitors?

From the SWOT analysis, the five to seven critical issues facing the company can be identified and dealt with.

Business plans usually contain a series of measurable, challenging, clear and compelling goals covering the various activities of the enterprise. For example:

- *Sales:* Achieve $1 billion annual sales worth $60 million profits by the end of the 2003 financial year.
- *Operations:* Open six factories in three countries by 30 June 2001; implement a self-financing equipment upgrading plan by 1 July 2000.
- *Safety:* Have an injury-free factory by 1 July 2002.
- *Administration:* Standardise the financial reporting and accounting systems across all sites by 30 April 2001.
- *Employees:* Achieve an employee turnover rate of less than 5% by 30 June 2001.
- *Quality:* Complete ISO 9000 quality certification on 70% of sites by 30 June 2002.

Clear plans like this mean that individual departmental plans can be established, each directed at helping to achieve the overall business plan.

THE BIG PICTURE

Five resource areas of the enterprise need to support the vision and business plans, if they are to be achieved:

1. The *structures*: includes the physical layout, organisation design, finance and budgeting.
2. The *staff*: includes the recruitment and selection processes, succession capabilities, attitudes and motivation.
3. The *skills*: includes training for the future as well as the present in technical and interpersonal skills, leadership, and strategic and conceptual thinking.
4. The *systems*: includes training systems, administration and information systems, customer service and delivery, sales, productivity, wastage, cost control and other operating systems and processes.
5. The *culture and values*: 'the way things are done'; includes problem solving and communication methods, leadership style, trust, responsibility and accountability.

Figure 5.5 shows the business-planning process in its wider context. You can see that, if any one area is resisting the selected strategy, it can do enormous damage.

Operational plans

Work schedules, departmental training plans, and health and safety improvement plans are some typical operational plans with which supervisors are involved. They generally look ahead one week to one year and so are shorter-term than the overall business plans they support.

Operational plans provide specific details of what is to be done to achieve the established overall goals of the business plan and the department's own more specific objectives (see Box 5.4). They have their own precise objectives, which supervisors are normally involved in setting. Many supervisors involve their team in developing the actual operating plans to meet the objectives. In some organisations, specialist staff may work with supervisors to help formulate these operational plans.

Specific plans and project plans

These are plans needed for once-only activities or special occurrences. They can be very complex and preparing them can be highly specialised. Computer programs, techniques such as PERT (program evaluation review technique) and other types of network diagrams and flow charts are often used to schedule the specific steps, highlight any critical sequences and monitor progress.

Specially formed temporary project teams are often charged with preparing and monitoring these specific plans and the process can be so complex that external consultants and contractors are brought in to assist. These temporary project teams need to use all the skills of team decision making and problem solving discussed in Chapter 11.

FIGURE 5.5   THE PLANNING OVERVIEW

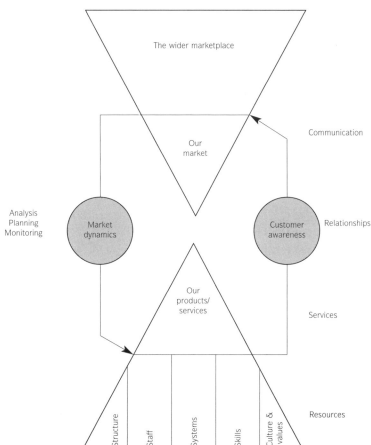

Standing plans

Standing plans represent procedures that must be adhered to for a specific situation. They are the programmed decisions referred to in Chapter 11. They are established in accordance with overall organisation policies and strategies. Evacuation procedures in the case of fire, or the process to follow in issuing a formal reprimand to an employee, are examples of standing plans.

PROTECT YOUR PLANS

'Anything that can go wrong will go wrong.'

Murphy's Law

'Murphy was an optimist.'

O'Toole's Law

As most of us have experienced, plans sometimes go off the rails. A strike at a supplier's plant might mean a delay in receiving needed raw materials; an 'act of God', such as a flood or

FROM MISSION TO BUSINESS PLAN TO OPERATIONAL PLAN

Part of a mission statement might be *to be a sought-after place of employment*. The business plan might set three goals to make this happen:
1. world-class health and safety systems within two years;
2. best-in-the-industry leadership at all levels within 18 months; and
3. top-quartile remuneration within five years.

These goals would flow on to the various departments in the enterprise and be translated into shorter-term departmental objectives. A production department, for example, might set the following goals:
• improve safe working practices in a department to reach an accident-free target of 100 days by the end of the financial year; and
• reduce reportable accidents to three per annum by May 2002.

The training department might set an objectives to:
• provide team-building and leadership training to all managers during this calendar year.

fire, may cause a setback. Absenteeism, resignation of key staff, or simply underestimating how long tasks will take to complete can wreak havoc with plans. The unexpected always seems to happen.

We might never know if we don't monitor our plans. Keeping a watchful eye on progress against plans lets you adjust quickly to changing conditions while continuing to move in the right direction. It's easy to take swift remedial action when a plan shows what should have been done, who should have done it, how it should have been done, and when and where it should have been done. This makes it easy to spot where things are going wrong and fix them—provided you monitor your plan!

Have you heard of the joiner's rule?

> ‘Measure twice.
> Cut once.’

Even a carefully monitored plan does not guarantee that you will achieve your goals. We need to take steps to protect them from the outset. Here are some guidelines to follow before putting your plan into place:
1. When you have completed your plan, ask yourself: ‘What could go wrong?’ Brainstorm all the things that could happen to turn your well thought-out plan into a disaster.
2. Study your list and cross out anything that is well outside the range of reason.
3. Now decide what you can do about those that are left (see Box 5.5).

As the old saying goes:

> ‘Forewarned is forearmed.’

BOX 5.5   PROTECTIVE PLANS

Adaptive plan: Some things you might have to live with. How can you live with it more comfortably or minimise its effects?

Preventive plan: You might be able to ensure other things don't occur by devising a plan to stop them from happening.

Contingency plan: Specify the actions to take if 'it' does happen.

THE GANTT CHART

The **Gantt chart**, developed by Henry L. Gantt in the early 1900s, is a useful planning tool. It was first widely used by supervisors during World War I to aid in planning and controlling operations in war materials plants.

On a piece of paper you can easily construct a Gantt chart like the one in Figure 5.6, which shows a plan for painting a house. Each activity is listed at the left side of the chart (vertically). Time is shown horizontally (in hours, days, etc.). Note that the plan calls for the scraping and sanding to be completed by midday Tuesday. As work starts and progresses you fill in the *actual* line below the appropriate *planned* activity. The actual time required to scrape and sand was all day Monday and Tuesday.

To make a Gantt chart you need to:
- plan and list step by step what needs to be done (the activities or tasks);
- show when each task should start and when it should finish;
- determine when the overall project should be completed; and
- as time passes, add your 'actual' lines to keep track of how your plan is progressing and to see whether you are ahead of or behind schedule.

In this way, Gantt charts serve both as a planning and a monitoring tool. They are also useful for indicating where two or more activities can occur at the same time. For example, from the Gantt chart in Figure 5.6 we can see that some of the priming can be carried out while some of the scraping is still being done, and the trimming can begin while the painting is being finished.

FIGURE 5.6   GANTT CHART FOR PAINTING A HOUSE

Activity	Time				
	Monday	Tuesday	Wednesday	Thursday	Friday
Scrape and sand bad spots	----------	-----			
Prime bare spots		---			
Paint house			------	---	---
Trim house				-----	---

------- Planned   .... Actual

MONITORING, THE PARTNER OF PLANNING

Planning and monitoring are partners: planning establishes what we will do, while monitoring helps us determine if, and how well, we are doing it. *Monitoring is the process of measuring and comparing actual results or work in progress with planned performance.* What percentage of production is meeting quality specifications? How many units are being assembled per hour? How long are technicians spending on service calls? What is our monthly sales value? How many customers have we served today? How many orders were filled on time? How many patients did we treat this week? These are all results we can monitor and compare with the expected or planned figures to discover how well we're doing.

Monitoring keeps us aware of what is going on. It may reveal the need to modify plans, to use the available resources differently, to alter the way we give directions, to reschedule activities, or even to change the monitoring methods themselves. A good monitoring system helps us know how we are performing in relation to our targets and what changes, if any, are needed to keep performance at a satisfactory level.

Through timely and effective monitoring, supervisors can find out whether their work and the work of their department are on target and their plans being achieved. It provides an early warning so that any necessary corrective action can be taken in plenty of time. It also highlights potential problem situations and thus reduces the need for 'management by crisis'. Monitoring, then, helps us to keep on top of things—the activities of people, equipment and other key factors—so that performance meets established goals.

FOUR STEPS TO MONITORING

Step 1: Establish areas where monitoring is needed

What is most important to your operations: production, cutting costs, improving quality, increasing sales, delivering on time, improving customer satisfaction, lowering employee turnover, reducing stock levels? Where are the danger points? What would cause the most damage if it went wrong?

Step 2: Establish specific measures to monitor

> 'What gets measured gets done.'
> W. Edwards Deming

Establish what is really important and monitor that: measure what counts most; keep tabs on critical points; monitor key objectives and targets. Take measures that give you a lot of information easily and quickly.

In the customer service area, for example, you might ask yourself what factors are most important in satisfying your customers: time? cost? quality? product reliability? Measure whatever your customers care about most.

Measure what supports the organisation's vision and mission—it's no good saying you value teamwork and then measuring only individual contributions, for example.

Process versus results measures

Traditional measurement systems measure results. They are historical measures and will show you whether something has gone wrong. They are the scorecards of sales results, market share reports, profit results, cost of production reports, mystery shopper surveys, financial reports and many human resources monitoring systems.

They are called **lag indicators**. They measure results after the process is completed, when it's too late to correct the problem. They don't tell you how you came by the results or what you should do differently. You are then faced with taking retrospective corrective action if the results are unsatisfactory. This is always more difficult than taking timely corrective action.

'No one ever won Wimbledon by keeping their eye on the scoreboard.'

Most systems-generated monitoring has, until recently, focused on lag indicators. State-of-the-art monitoring systems, however, give us as many lead indicators as possible.

Lead indicators are the 'ball'. They are the most effective monitoring measures because they provide an early warning when things are not going as expected. They measure what *is* happening as the process occurs. While lag indicators tell us only whether we *have achieved* targets, lead indicators show us whether we *are achieving* them. If results are unsatisfactory, we can take corrective action quickly, before more serious problems arise. Lead indicators also highlight when things are going particularly well so that we can work out why in order to repeat those conditions.

'You win by keeping your eye on the ball.'

Lead indicators can also point to the type of corrective action that should be taken or the area in which it should be taken. They are the ones to measure and monitor if you are able.

To decide what lead indicators to measure, identify the critical tasks needed to complete the process satisfactorily. Then design measures that track the progress of those critical tasks.

Step 3: Compare what is happening with what should be happening

Once you know your precise goals and objectives and how to measure their achievement, monitoring becomes a simple matter of comparing what *is* happening with what *should be* happening and (sometimes not so simply) taking corrective action. Some amount of variation will always occur. Your task is to decide what variations are important enough to warrant moving onto step 4, and taking action.

Step 4: Take action as necessary

If you find actual performance is not meeting desired performance, you will need to take some sort of action. Five types of action are discussed in Box 5.6.

DON'T OVER-MONITOR!

Identify and monitor only those activities that have the greatest bearing on output in terms of quantity, quality, time, cost or safety. Measure these at specific points where variations from plans would indicate that performance was falling below expectations, or in danger of doing so.

Don't monitor too many things or you'll spend all day studying reports! As a general rule, if you are regularly monitoring more than 15 measures, go back to the drawing board and simplify. Box 5.7 summarises the characteristics of an effective monitoring process.

BOX
5.6

FIVE TYPES OF CORRECTIVE ACTION

1. *Interim action.* This buys you time to find the cause of the substandard perform-ance and correct it. However, like the Dutch boy with his finger in the dyke, it is merely a stop-gap action.
2. *Adaptive action.* Occasionally, we will have set our sights unrealistically high during the planning phase, or something important has changed. For any number of valid reasons, we may not be able to live up to the performance standards set. This is when we must take adaptive action to enable us to live with the inevitable.
3. *Corrective action.* Corrective action eliminates the cause of the substandard performance. It gets performance back on the rails.
4. *Preventive action.* This is action that removes the cause of a potential performance shortfall. It is here that monitoring can make its most valuable contribution. Early warning of a problem gives us the opportunity to take preventive action so that the problem is avoided.
5. *Contingency action.* Sometimes monitoring may show a negative trend or only hint that performance might be dropping below expectations. In this case, we would take contingency action, or make some stand-by arrangements to remedy a difficulty that may (or may not) occur.

BOX
5.7

THE CHARACTERISTICS OF AN EFFECTIVE MONITORING PROCESS

Accuracy	The information is accurate and reveals the facts needed for appropriate action.
Timeliness	Information is available in sufficient time for corrective or other action to be implemented.
Economy	The benefits of gathering the information are greater than the costs of gathering it.
Ease of understanding	The information is understood by those it affects and those who will take action on it.
Meets needs	It meets the needs of the individuals and the organisation.

COMMON MONITORING TOOLS

Supervisors deal with a variety of monitoring tools in their day-to-day work. They design many of them themselves. These are usually quick and simple. Other more complex and detailed monitoring systems are usually generated by the system itself for the information of management at all levels. Some of the more common of these systems-generated monitoring measures are explained below.

FROM THEORY TO PRACTICE

How to ensure that your monitoring system is effective:

- When deciding what to monitor, bear in mind the overall goals, objectives and targets of your department and organisation.
- If you can, involve the people whose performance will be measured in establishing monitoring systems and procedures. Teamwork and results benefit when a work team designs its own monitoring systems.
- Make sure that the monitoring information can be collected or produced and used relatively quickly and easily. It must be worth the time and effort to collect and document it, and worth the time and effort to analyse it or make use of it in some other way.
- Try to incorporate management by exception, where you will be advised as soon as a critical activity deviates from the expected.
- Track lead indicators that will help you and your team gauge progress.
- Ensure that monitoring feedback is timely as well as accurate so that you will be aware quickly of any deviations from standard. The data need only be accurate enough to provide sufficient information to enable you to identify problems and take appropriate action.
- Make sure it is clear who is responsible for taking any corrective or other action that may be required.
- Coordinate what is being monitored to avoid duplication.
- When your monitoring system shows that things are going according to plan, don't forget to provide 'pats on the back'!

Financial controls

Budgets

Budgets are a common financial planning and control device. Sales budget, purchasing budget, training budget, advertising budget are all common types of budgets supervisors deal with, either trying to *reach* budget (e.g. sales budget) or stay *within* budget (e.g. advertising budget).

Balance sheets, profit and loss accounts and funds statements

These also monitor the financial performance of an enterprise. They help determine trends and possible reasons for them and can be used to monitor a firm's financial strength.

The *balance sheet* describes the financial situation of a company on a specified date. It is like a 'stocktake' of the company's affairs expressed in dollars and cents. The balance sheet shows what the business owns and what it owes.

The *profit and loss account* compares the income from all sources with the expenses incurred to determine the net profit (or loss) the business made during the accounting period.

The *funds statement* shows the source and application of funds—where money has come from and where it has gone to during the accounting period.

Utilisation
Delivery attainment
Inventory
Housekeeping

Production controls

In the area of production, a number of monitoring techniques are available to help supervisors keep tabs on the performance of their department. These include inventory control (which we look at now) quality control (see Chapter 9) and Gantt charts (discussed above).

Inventory controls

Carrying excess stock is expensive, while holding too little stock may lead to delays, inefficiency and even lost business. Most organisations therefore establish maximum and minimum stock levels for all inventory items and the most economical quantity of each item to order.

A computerised system often monitors and controls inventories. **Just-in-time** and similar methods aim for raw materials to arrive 'just in time' for use. This minimises the financial costs of storing large quantities of raw materials. Sophisticated computer techniques such as **materials resources planning** aid firms in planning, coordinating and controlling their goods inwards, manufacturing, stores and dispatch functions.

THE **BIG** PICTURE

One thing to bear in mind when setting up monitoring systems is the human interface. It is important to make sure that the people responsible for meeting the targets and using the monitoring information accept the measures and are aware of why they are needed. No one likes to think their actions are being checked on without good cause.

Most people are willing and able to monitor and control their own performance. So, whenever possible, incorporate employees' own desire to do a good job into your monitoring systems.

RAPID REVIEW

		True	False
1.	Plans are a projected course of action aimed at achieving objectives over some future time.	☐	☐
2.	Crisis supervision is often a sign of poor planning.	☐	☐
3.	Planning helps to keep us on track.	☐	☐
4.	Making a plan guarantees you will reach your goals.	☐	☐
5.	Plans are working documents that guide our actions.	☐	☐
6.	The planning process begins and ends with setting targets and monitoring how well they have been achieved.	☐	☐
7.	Short-term plans don't need an objective or time frame.	☐	☐
8.	Whether positive or negative, targets must be precise.	☐	☐
9.	Because they plan all the time, supervisors don't usually need to write their plans down.	☐	☐

	True	False
10. Supervisors are not affected by business plans because they operate at a different level.	☐	☐
11. Operational plans support business plans and detail how their overall objectives will be achieved.	☐	☐
12. Once written, plans should be strictly adhered to.	☐	☐
13. A Gantt chart can be used to monitor a plan.	☐	☐
14. Once plans are in place, they usually look after themselves.	☐	☐
15. Lead indicators point to the future while lag indicators point to the past.	☐	☐
16. You should monitor as much as possible since you never know where problems could crop up.	☐	☐

APPLY YOUR KNOWLEDGE

1. In what way is planning like a ship's rudder? Use the analogy of a rudderless ship to explain the effects of a supervisor failing to plan.

2. List several reasons why a supervisor might not plan. In your opinion, which, if any, of these reasons is valid?

3. Several supervisors were having a chat about their jobs. The topic of planning came up. One supervisor said he never planned and that he believed it was a waste of time for first-line supervisors to go through the motions of planning so that their department would look good on paper. Anyway, he didn't have time to sit down to plan—he had 'real work' to do. The supervisor then turned to you and said, 'Don't you agree with me?' What would you expect of the performance of this supervisor's section? Discuss the benefits to a supervisor and employees of effective planning. How would you go about explaining the value of planning to this supervisor?

4. Use a real-life example to describe the six steps to planning. Explain why each step is important. Why might it be said that planning is a continuous process?

5. Discuss the differences between business plans, standing plans and operational plans.

6. Why do plans sometimes fail? What actions can we take to safeguard the success of our plans?

7. List and illustrate by example five types of action that can be taken to rectify a plan that is not working or to correct substandard performance.

8. Why is monitoring an essential partner to planning? How does it help supervisors?

9. Outline the four steps to monitoring, giving an example of each.

10. Explain the difference between lead indicators and lag indicators.

11. Explain the characteristics of an effective monitoring system.

12. Do you know anyone who got married recently? Ask them how they organised their wedding and reception. Take notes on what they say, and then relate what they did to the six steps in planning. How did they know whether everything was going to be 'all right on the day'? Did they make any contingency or preventive plans or did they just 'hope for the best'?

Individual activities

1. Describe a time when you made the time and effort to develop a plan. Was it helpful? Relate the plan you made to the six steps of the planning process described in the chapter. What conclusions can you draw about making plans?

2. Write yourself a personal vision and mission statement covering the next five years. Discuss how this will help guide your actions and make important decisions. You can use one of the models from this chapter, or refer to Chapter 3 if you like.

3. Johnson & Johnson had its Tylenol crisis; Herron Pharmaceuticals had its paracetamol crisis; SmithKline Beecham had its Panadol crisis. Research and compare how each of these companies handled their crisis and how this reflected their corporate vision and mission.

4. Draw up a Gantt chart for revising for your next major exams. Use this as both a planning and a monitoring tool.

5. Interview a supervisor and find out what monitoring tools he or she and the work team use. Ask to be shown some of these tools and find out how they help. Write a short essay explaining how these tools help them and in what ways they conform to the characteristics of an effective monitoring system.

Group activities

1. You and three friends are planning to drive across the Nullarbor this winter. You will be using a reliable 4WD vehicle. In small groups, prepare a detailed plan for the preparations you will need to make for your trip.

2. Draw up a Gantt chart for the preparations for your trip across the Nullarbor.

3. Now protect your plan, following the guidelines outlined in this chapter.

4. Obtain and study the values, vision and mission statements and the business plan of your college or place of employment. What does the vision tell you about the organisation as a place to work? What does it tell you about its role in the community? The way it operates? What it believes in? What its business is and how it will achieve its vision? Would these documents aid in day-to-day decision making? Are they inspiring and memorable? Are they clear and concise? Could they guide the actions of employees?

    Undertake a brief gap analysis. How far do you believe the organisation is now from where it wants to be? Is it moving in the right direction? Judging from its business plan, how does it plan to close the gap?

5. Develop a simple monitoring system to keep you on track in your studies following the guidelines given in this chapter.

6. Find examples of three system-generated monitoring tools in your organisation or college and explain to the rest of the class how they are used.

The Di'Amico Valve Company

The Di'Amico Valve Company Pty Ltd, located south of Brisbane, manufactures and distributes a range of specialised valves for industrial use and use as components in other companies' products. The company is well established and has operated at 80% of its capacity for the last six years. Sales in the last year amounted to $390 million, an increase of 10% over the previous year. Production costs, however, were up 20% over the previous year.

When Sandy Di'Amico, the managing director and owner, began checking the cause of the increase in production costs, he found that the major increases were in labour and material costs. He also uncovered a number of problems:
- delivery schedules were not being kept to;
- staff were often taken off one job to rush through another that was behind schedule;
- material wastage was increasing because many jobs were being reworked to meet current order commitments;
- inventory stock was low, even for fast moving lines; and
- the production line was frequently stopped because the company was awaiting deliveries from suppliers.

At the next staff meeting, Sandy presented the problem of increased costs and asked for suggestions on how to reverse this trend. The production manager expressed the view that the salespeople kept changing their minds as to which orders were the most important, while the sales manager blamed production for delays in delivery and poor quality. Purchasing was criticised for often not having the raw materials available as required. As he left the meeting feeling that little had been resolved, Sandy was thinking that maybe some formalised form of production planning and monitoring might be the answer.

Questions

1   What types of planning should Sandy Di'Amico consider?
2   Which issues should be given special attention in the planning process?
3   How could Sandy involve the sales, production and purchasing departments in planning for the same objectives?

Joan Simon Discovers The Need To Monitor

Joan Simon had just been promoted to the position of sales supervisor in charge of eight sales representatives, two key account managers and three merchandisers.

As a key account manager prior to her promotion, all she had needed to look after was herself—making sure she serviced her clients properly, that goods were delivered, that they sold well and that her clients received the sales and merchandising support she deemed necessary. A simple spreadsheet system plus diligent use of her diary had always sufficed.

But now that she was sales supervisor, she had a whole team of others to look after as well as all the sales in the territory, product promotions, expenditures, business development and the like. The first thing she had to do, she decided, was set up some monitoring systems—systems that would quickly and easily give her the inform- ation she needed to manage her area. How her predecessor had managed, she didn't know—he must have kept track of everything in his head.

Joan began asking around. Her secretary suggested she set up a computerised log for each representative and key account manager, showing their sales to date against their budgeted sales. That way she would know who was meeting targets and who might need a bit of help or 'jollying along', as she put it. Her secretary also suggested a similar log for each customer, showing not only their purchases but also their credit situation. That would help in her cash-flow budgeting.

Joan's manager suggested that she apply management by exception principles with each of her staff and incorporate it into the distribution department's weekly summaries to her.

Questions

1 What should Joan's first steps be in establishing an effective monitoring method?
2 What monitoring systems do you think would be most appropriate to Joan's needs. Why?
3 What are the dangers of Joan following her predecessor in not setting up and following through with any monitoring systems?

Answers to Rapid Review questions

1. T   2. T   3. T   4. F   5. T   6. T   7. F   8. T   9. F   10. F   11. T   12. F   13. T
14. F   15. T   16. F

CHAPTER 6

LEADING AND ATTENDING MEETINGS

The stand-in

Grace's boss has asked her to chair the quarterly superintendents' meeting in four weeks' time. He has delegated everything to her—choice of venue, the time and duration of the meeting, choice of agenda—the whole works.

Where should she begin? What should she do first? What should she say when the day of the meeting finally arrives? How should she keep order? This was a major event in the superintendents' calendar and an opportunity for her to show how well she could organise and manage an event. She wanted to make sure she got everything just right.

When he handed her the assignment, Grace's manager gave her a few words of advice. 'Grace,' he said, 'do your preparation for the meeting well in advance. If you have everything planned and thought out, things will fall into place.'

'Preparation?' thought Grace. 'What should I prepare first? How should I prepare? What should I prepare!?'

Meetings are an important part of life in most organisations and supervisors need to understand how they work. In this chapter, you will ifnd out how to participate in meetings, how to lead them and how to stop them going off the rails.

- Do you know why meetings are such an integral part of organisational life?
- Do you know when a meeting should be called and when it should not be?
- Do you know which of the ten types of meeting best suits which purpose?
- How should you decide who to invite to a meeting?
- What are you responsible for if you are asked to lead a meeting? How can you avoid the common mistakes meeting leaders make?

- Do you know which roles and behaviours help and which hinder a meeting's progress?
- What is special about virtual meetings?
- Do you have the skills you need to be an effective meeting leader?
- Can you deal with disruptive meeting participants?
- Do you know how to participate effectively in a meeting?
- What is formal meeting protocol?

WHY HOLD MEETINGS?

We are social beings. Since we first walked this earth, people have come together in small groups to plan, make decisions, learn from each other, support each other and have fun. Meetings are part of our culture. We have even developed technology to allow us to hold meetings between people in different cities, states or countries. **Teleconferences** (meetings with simultaneous telephone line connections allowing a group of people to hear and speak to each other), **videoconferences** (the same, plus participants can also see each other) and **online chats** (real-time conversations held on screen via the Internet) are becoming commonplace. Never has it been easier for people to meet.

Yet many supervisors claim that they meet too much. They complain that too many meetings achieve little, waste time and run on without a purpose. It is also true that meetings can give an illusion of progress where, in truth, none exists.

However, despite all the complaints about meetings, there is no readily available substitute for them. When properly planned and run, they can make a significant contribution to an organisation's effectiveness. They can be a good way to give people information on a more personal basis than, say, an official notice or a memo. They can gather information, opinions and ideas and achieve consensus. They can provide a forum for identifying and solving problems and allow full and open discussion on particular points.

In addition to these **task functions**, meetings serve other, more subtle **maintenance functions** in organisations. They can define the team and make people feel part of it: those who attend a work group meeting are part of the team, while those who do not attend are not a part. In this way, meetings can help to make a group more cohesive and can help build our attachment to it. People can easily look around and clearly see the group of which they are part. In fact, the only time many work groups exist as a group and work together as a team is during a meeting.

When they are well led and everyone contributes, they can create a pool of shared knowledge and experience: a meeting provides an opportunity for a group to revise, refresh and add to its shared understandings and knowledge. This can help a group grow and develop and increase the speed and efficiency of communication between members.

Meetings can clarify the collective aims of the team: they help group members to understand the aims of the group as a whole and where their own work fits in. They can create commitment to decisions and objectives, especially if consensus methods are used. In this way, meetings can help people do their jobs better.

Meetings clearly show who the official team leader is—often a meeting is the only time when the supervisor is clearly seen as the leader of the group, rather than as a person doing a job or the person to whom the others report individually.

Meetings, then, serve useful functions in both task and team maintenance areas (see below and Chapter 22 for a discussion on task and maintenance functions). They are not only a means of sharing and working with information, but they also get people working together and build a sense of belonging, shared responsibility, shared goals and team spirit.

Supervisors need, however, to guard against the potential weaknesses of meetings in order to attain their potential benefits. These are summarised in Box 6.1.

> 'Meetings are indispensable when you don't want to do anything.'
> John Kenneth Galbraith
> Economist

BOX 6.1   MEETINGS FAIL WHEN ...

- They have unclear objectives or a loose agenda.
- They take up time and produce nothing, frustrating people and resulting in opportunity lost on other work that *does* achieve results.
- One or two dominating people use them as a 'soapbox' and prevent others from airing their views.
- Good ideas get lost because they go unsaid or they're ignored.
- They start late and finish late.
- They create bickering, resentment and power struggles.
- They waste time on irrelevant side-issues, hobby-horses, going over old ground, etc.
- They delay decisions and avoid action.
- Their cost in terms of money and time is not outweighed by results.

- People seek the lowest common denominator, or 'easy way out', in reaching agreement.
- Political alliances or status differences inhibit open discussion and information exchange.
- Poor records are kept resulting in loss of ideas, information and action plans.
- Poor or rash decisions are reached (e.g. people compromise their feelings and opinions, they bow to group pressure or they fail to take individual responsibility in meetings).
- They are called too frequently and unnecessarily.
- The wrong people are invited.
- They are used to pretend a team is being involved in a decision or plan when they're only there to 'rubber stamp' it.

TYPES OF MEETINGS

:... Meetings can serve a variety of purposes. Before calling one, know why you're calling it.

Information-giving meetings

Call an information-giving meeting if you need to give information to a group of people. Use slides, overhead transparencies or videos to reinforce your verbal message. Allow some discussion and questions, but keep the focus on providing information to the meeting members.

Information-giving meetings are useful when the information to be shared:

* is complex or controversial;
* has major implications for the meeting members;
* needs to be heard from a particular person;
* there is symbolic value in giving the information personally;
* some discussion or information exchange is required; or
* clarification or comments are necessary to help people make sense of the information.

Before calling this type of meeting, be sure you cannot get the information across more cheaply and effectively in other ways, such as one-to-one, over the telephone, or in writing by memo or email.

Team-briefing meetings

This is a commonly used method of cascading information through an organisation. It is a particular type of information-giving meeting used to keep employees up to date on matters of importance. Team leaders are briefed by their own managers and, in turn, brief their team members following a standardised format. We look at how to prepare and deliver team briefings in detail in Chapter 22.

Information-seeking or information-exchange meetings

Do you want to gather opinions, facts and other information or give people the opportunity to discuss and exchange ideas? Use this type of meeting to ask questions and hear opinions. Aim to achieve a full and open discussion with all members participating.

The new ideas meeting

When you want to generate ideas or develop new concepts or ways of doing things, call a new ideas meeting. Ask questions such as: 'What are our options?' and 'How could we ...?' Aim for the full participation of all meeting participants.

Brainstorming sessions are the best known type of new ideas meeting. As you know, brainstorming helps people to generate ideas. The technique starts members thinking and communicating. Ideas are explored, refined and developed. Out of all the ideas offered may emerge an innovation in the form of a new product, process or concept that is the creation of the entire group—with each person contributing ideas to make up the whole. (See also Chapter 11.)

Information-seeking and new ideas meetings combine the knowledge, skills, ideas and experience of several people at once. Hold them when something new, such as a way to cut costs or introduce a new procedure, needs to be developed. With everyone contributing, creative solutions are more easily conceived.

Problem-solving and decision-making meetings

Call this type of meeting when you need to consider, analyse, discuss and agree on solutions, and either recommend a decision or make one. (See also Chapter 11.) Aim for a free and lively discussion that builds on the diverse talents, backgrounds and experiences of meeting members.

In problem-solving meetings, you are looking for solutions and innovations. What seem at first to be 'wild' ideas often turn out to be excellent ideas after a little polishing and refining. Problem-solving meetings typically go through four phases:

1. Exploring the problem: the problem is defined and analysed and objectives for its resolution set (steps 1, 2 and 3 of the problem-solving and decision-making process discussed in Chapter 11);
2. Searching for solutions (step 4);
3. Evaluating alternatives and selecting the most suitable one(s) (step 5); and
4. Developing the action plan and follow-up procedures (steps 6 and 7).

This process may take place over a series of meetings if the problem is complex.

Introducing-change meetings

These meetings are similar to information-giving meetings. Use a meeting to introduce change when you want to explain it fully, help your team to understand the reasons for it and gain their support. Current examples of introducing-change meetings are meetings held to introduce an organisation restructure or to introduce enterprise bargaining to an organisation.

Since change is disturbing to most people, it is important to explain the change fully and clearly and allow time for questions, discussion and dissent. If there is a great deal of dissent, it is tempting (but a mistake) to close the meeting with a 'Well, that's the way it is!' Explore any and all concerns fully; it is unrealistic to expect quick acceptance of change and you must be prepared and able to discuss the issues involved and allow people time to air their thoughts and opinions. We explore how to introduce and lead change in Chapter 12.

Planning meetings

When you want people to help plan something, perhaps in order to increase their support or to draw on their expertise, call a planning meeting. Members can either decide or offer suggestions on what will be done, who will do it and where, and when and how it will be done. Guide them to distribute responsibilities and tasks, set priorities and decide or suggest action steps. Ideally, begin with a desired outcome or goal to be accomplished and aim to end with a clear action plan to achieve it.

Quality meetings

Quality circles and team quality meetings are common forms of meetings that combine many of the types of meeting discussed above. Their objective is to identify problems, make improvements to work systems and provide better service to internal and external customers. (Quality circles are discussed more fully in Chapter 9.)

WHEN TO HOLD MEETINGS

Sometimes five minutes spent with six people individually is more effective and productive than a half-hour meeting with them all together. How can you decide whether a meeting will be worth the time and trouble? Call a meeting when:
- there is no better or less expensive way to get the job done (telephone, fax, memo, word of mouth, email);
- you need to present information to a group of people quickly and you don't want to write it;
- you need to gain commitment;
- you want to motivate people and create energy about an idea;
- you need other people to help solve problems or implement solutions or decisions; or
- you need to generate discussion or ideas.

The question is not whether to have meetings—we will. The question is, how can we make the best of them? Skip the meeting if:
- there is nothing specific to discuss;
- you've already made up your mind;
- you don't need others' input;
- involving others would only complicate matters;
- it's just a substitute for real work or a stalling device;
- it's only to rubber-stamp a decision; or
- it's a power trip.

TASK AND MAINTENANCE ROLES OF MEETING LEADERS

Meetings are most successful when leaders attend to both **task** and **maintenance issues** (see also Chapter 22). Here are some ways leaders can meet the task needs of a meeting.
- Make the outcomes or objectives of the meeting crystal clear.
- Follow the agenda.
- Keep the discussion to the topic at hand.
- Make sure all members understand the issues and why they are being discussed.
- Clarify any points members make that are not clear.
- Help members build on each other's experience and knowledge.
- Summarise often.
- Gather facts and opinions, ensuring that opinions are clearly labelled as opinions and not masqueraded as facts.

These actions will all help to prevent misunderstanding and confusion, and help the group achieve the objectives of the meeting.

Less obvious are the team maintenance contributions that leaders need to make if a meeting is to progress satisfactorily. These include:
- establishing a friendly and supportive climate where contributions can be freely given;
- acknowledging members for their contributions;
- relieving tension (or allowing it to be relieved) with a little humour; and
- valuing and respecting members (even disruptive members) as people.

Team maintenance skills help to set the tone for a meeting. They show other meeting members what behaviours are valued and appreciated.

'In meetings, I try to be sure that everybody has an opportunity to speak. I'll ask questions so that people who haven't spoken will have the opportunity to say something. When it gets to the point where we seem to have reached a consensus I might say: "Well let me try and sum up and see if this is where we are." Sometimes somebody doesn't agree and then we have to talk a bit longer. Then I'll try to sum up again. But a successful meeting depends on how much everybody participates, not on how long it goes on.'

John de Butts
Former chair of American telecommunications giant AT&T

Observing group processes

Have you ever noticed that the 'atmosphere' is different in certain meetings? Some meetings are relaxed and informal while still being 'business-like'; others are stiff and awkward; some are filled with undercurrents and game playing.

Leaders should observe the ways in which the group 'works' during the meeting. These are called **group processes**. What style of communication is used? Aggressive? Assertive? Passive? What tone of voice do people use? What sort of questions are asked and how are they asked? Is the language formal and stilted or friendly and informal? What is the body language of the meeting participants? Answers to these questions can give you important information about how well the group is working, how involved members are and how committed they are to achieving the meeting objective.

What are the communication patterns—who talks to whom, for how long and how often? Who supports who? Are cliques or factions developing? This indicates internal tension in the group and decreases the likelihood that the group will be able to work optimally.

Who do people look at when they talk? This can show you who the informal leader is, the person who wields the most influence among the group. Who interrupts who? This can show you who wields the least influence in the group; yet this does not make their contributions or opinions any less valid and you should remain aware of your responsibility to ensure everyone has a say.

THE **BIG** PICTURE

Four important meeting roles:

Gatekeeper	Makes sure everyone has an opportunity to speak.
Coordinator	Summarises progress and leads to next step.
Compromiser	Helps people who disagree to build on their viewpoints and reach agreement.
Clown	Relieves tension through humour.

What group norms are apparent? For example, do people turn up on time or late? Prepared or unprepared? Do people hold side conversations during the meeting or does everyone attend fully to whoever holds the floor? The group norms can give you an insight into the workings of the group.

If you feel the norms and group processes are harming meeting productivity, you will need to address this. One way is to ask the group to develop some ground rules for how it wants to operate in the meeting. Figure 6.1 shows an example of the ground rules one team agreed. Each team should develop and agree its own ground rules.

COMMON MISTAKES IN LEADING MEETINGS

'A meeting is an event where minutes are kept and hours lost.'

Inadequate leadership will ruin any meeting. Here are the top ten common mistakes meeting leaders make and how to avoid them:

1. *Failure to prepare.* Not thinking through your objectives, not working out the issues that will need to be addressed and not gathering the information you will need are big mistakes, but common ones, especially for busy supervisors. The more you think a meeting through and prepare for it, the better it will go. As we saw in Chapter 5, prior planning prevents poor performance.

2. *Failure to inform others in plenty of time.* Meeting members need to prepare too, even if it is only to study the agenda and do a bit of thinking about it beforehand. Give people the agenda early enough to allow them to prepare for the meeting. Two or three days is usually enough and not so long that people misplace it or forget about it.

3. *Poor sequencing of agenda.* Don't fall into this trap. Follow the guidelines for preparing an agenda discussed below.

FIGURE 6.1 MEETING GROUND RULES

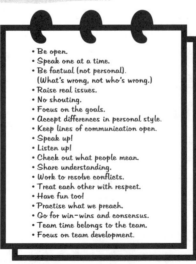

- Be open.
- Speak one at a time.
- Be factual (not personal).
  (What's wrong, not who's wrong.)
- Raise real issues.
- No shouting.
- Focus on the goals.
- Accept differences in personal style.
- Keep lines of communication open.
- Speak up!
- Listen up!
- Check out what people mean.
- Share understanding.
- Work to resolve conflicts.
- Treat each other with respect.
- Have fun too!
- Practise what we preach.
- Go for win-wins and consensus.
- Team time belongs to the team.
- Focus on team development.

4. *Allowing the group to wander from the point and failing to finish on time.* Allowing digressions and rambling shop talk is sure to kill any meeting. Keep discussions on track and to the point and don't let the meeting drag out!

5. *Failure to record decisions and agreements.* Make sure you keep a note of all action items and decisions reached. Follow them up.

6. *Arriving late and starting late.* Supervisors are busy people but, if the meeting leader is late, what kind of example is that setting for the rest of the members? Next time, they are likely to turn up late, too. Similarly, delaying starting a meeting until everyone is present sets a bad precedent. Start on time.

7. *Launching straight into the agenda without attending to maintenance issues* is a common mistake. Open the meeting on a pleasant note; welcome people and thank them for coming. Say a few words about what you hope the meeting will achieve and, if you have them, draw members' attention to their meeting guidelines.

8. *Inhibiting free discussion* by asking leading questions, offering suggestions, or defending rather than exploring. Meeting leaders are only human and can easily fall into the trap of fixed opinions or ideas. When this happens, they are apt to cut off anyone who disagrees with them. Instead, use a different point of view as an opportunity to explore an issue more deeply.

9. *Dominating.* Some leaders seem to believe that chairing a meeting gives them a licence to do all the talking themselves and force their own ideas on everyone else. They need to develop skills in discussion leading and consensus leadership. The opposite mistake is being too *laissez-faire* and focusing more on making the meeting 'enjoyable' than on the goals of the meeting. Keep maintenance and task issues balanced and keep the main purpose of your meeting in mind.

10. *Rushing.* Some leaders speed through the meeting and don't provide time for the group to develop its own solution or approach. Make sure everyone has a chance to air their thoughts, hear everyone else's and develop a joint approach.

HOW TO PLAN A MEETING

Planning and conducting meetings is becoming an increasingly important supervisory role.

'Any meeting worth holding is worth planning.'

Running a meeting and leading discussions requires one set of competencies and planning a meeting another set. Planning skills include establishing objectives, selecting participants, selecting a time and place and planning and distributing the agenda.

Establish objectives

Every effective meeting works towards established objectives. Before you do anything, think it through. Ask yourself: 'What is this meeting intended to achieve?'; 'How will I know whether it is a success or a failure?'; 'What do I want the "atmosphere" of the meeting to be like?' Make sure you have very clear and specific objectives in mind or, better still, written down. Here are some other questions to think through beforehand:

• What decisions will we need to make at the meeting?
• What topics, information and issues will we need to cover?

- What issues are likely to come up?
- What things need to happen before the meeting can take place?
- How will I convey my objectives to the meeting members?
- Is a meeting really necessary or is there some less expensive and less time-consuming method of reaching my objectives?

Who should attend?

Next, select participants. Sometimes you will automatically include your whole department. At other times, you will invite only those who are key to the agenda: those who are affected by the outcome of the meeting, or those who can best contribute to it—people with relevant knowledge, skills or experience, who will support you, whose commitment is needed, or who have resources that you need (e.g. time, budget, other people, influence).

To avoid inhibiting some members, try to select participants who are about equal in rank. If it is necessary for people from different levels or interest groups in the organisation to attend, try to obtain a rough balance of status and power among them. Think about including specialists from different areas of the organisation in order to get good representation and a balanced group.

> 'Meetings ... are rather like cocktail parties.
> You don't want to go but you're cross not to be asked.'
>
> Jilly Cooper
> Author

Try to keep the numbers reasonable. Four to seven is ideal and a tolerable number is ten, while the outside limit is 12. Any more than this and the meeting will be difficult to control. It will be harder to get each member contributing fully and difficult to hold everyone's attention. Large numbers also mean the meeting is likely to last longer.

If you can't get the numbers down, try holding two smaller, separate meetings. Another idea is to form subgroups that will discuss the issues in advance. Each group can then send a representative to the main meeting. If all else fails, perhaps you can structure the agenda so that some members join at half time while others leave.

The two-thirds rule

The two-thirds rule is a good rule of thumb to follow: *each person attending a meeting must be directly concerned with two out of three, or two-thirds, of the agenda items.* This will stop you from wasting people's time.

Not everyone needs to attend the entire meeting. Invite people in for specific sections of an agenda to avoid wasting their time.

Where and when to hold a meeting

Now, set the time and place of the meeting. Of all the factors contributing to the success of a meeting, one of the most important is where you hold it. Your choice of location will have a subtle but significant impact on the meeting and send out messages about its importance, style, and so on. So where will you hold it? A neutral conference room? More formally in your office? Informally around a coffee table? The appropriate setting depends on your objectives for the meeting, so choose the location accordingly.

Look for comfortable seating, temperature and ventilation, relative quiet and freedom from distractions. You might hold a brief, informal meeting in your own department, or in the main work area or office. However, if difficult problems are to be tackled and the meeting may be long (more than 20 minutes), opt for a conference room or a quiet, well lit, temperature-controlled room arranged so that all members can see and hear each other.

Think about seating

Do you want to encourage cross-talk and idea sharing? Arrange seating in a hollow square or U-shape. Do you want the focus to be on the meeting leader? Use a semi-circle. Is it an information-giving meeting? Seat people in chairs in rows, 'classroom style'. Are you behind schedule? Don't sit—stand up and meet!

What time of day is best?

Select a time during working hours that is convenient for everyone. Although they work in some organisations, meetings held outside working hours are seldom effective because employees reason that the subject matter cannot be too important if the meeting isn't held in working hours. They may also resent having their personal time taken up for what is essentially company business, even if the outcome does affect them.

What time of day is best? Early in the day, people are fresher and possibly have fewer problems on their minds. They may also be more eager to get on with the meeting so they can fulfil their other commitments. Later in the afternoon, a meeting may take on a more leisurely tone. If you fear a meeting will go on too long, start it an hour before lunch or going-home time. Schedule items that need to be kept brief for ten minutes before the meeting is to close.

How long should meetings last?

To avoid people becoming restless, try to keep meetings to less than an hour. If a meeting must go on longer than one hour, schedule short breaks every 50–60 minutes.

Planning the agenda

Some meetings are called to achieve only one thing—for example, to give information or to reach a decision. Others have several objectives and cover several items. Your next task, therefore, might be to plan and distribute the agenda. You should already have a fairly good idea about what you will need to cover and this is the time to put it in writing. Even small, informal meetings benefit from agendas because they focus the meeting and provide a sense

FROM THEORY TO PRACTICE

Ask yourself these five questions when planning a meeting:
1. What do I want the meeting to accomplish?
2. How can we best accomplish it? Is a meeting the best way or is there a better way?
3. Who should attend?
4. When is the best time to hold the meeting?
5. Where is the best place to hold it?

of direction. Because they indicate the meeting's purpose and highlight what is relevant to the discussion, agendas also clarify and speed up meetings.

When writing your agenda, *keep it results-oriented*. Use verbs to begin each item: Decide ... Plan for ... Generate ideas about ... Discuss ... Get opinions on ... and so on. Emphasise your intended outcome.

The order of the items is important, too. Try to sequence them logically, so that they build on each other. You could also sequence them from the easiest to the most difficult or controversial, or the most to the least urgent. Since people tend to be more lively and creative during the early part of a meeting, you could put items that will require a lot of mental work first. You could schedule items of great interest to everyone for the lull in the meeting that seems to come 15–20 minutes after its start. You could put the most important item number two on the agenda to allow people to warm up. Put routine matters and FYI items (For Your Information) towards the end. Be aware of the choice and make it consciously. Try to end a meeting with an item that will give members a sense of unity and/or with an item that will achieve something positive.

Here are some guidelines to follow:
• Make the agenda specific—not vague.
• Don't try to cover too much—keep the number of items within reasonable limits.
• Avoid topics best handled by individuals or subgroups.
• Separate information exchange and problem analysis from problem solving.
• Specify start and finish times.
• Circulate the agenda and supply any relevant background information before the meeting—but keep it brief!
• Consider the approach you will take as meeting leader, the opening remarks you will make and how you will introduce each topic on the agenda.
• Gather any materials (visual aids, handouts, etc.) that you will need.

HOW TO LEAD A MEETING

Meeting-leading skills are important for supervisors. The way you open and close a meeting, lead focused discussions and keep the energies of the meeting directed at the desired outcomes are key factors in its success.

Opening a meeting

Be the first there so you can *greet meeting members as they arrive*. This sets the scene and establishes a friendly and open atmosphere. Making people feel comfortable from the start is an important maintenance function. It opens discussions and promotes cooperation.

Start the meeting on time. If you start late, you penalise those who were on time and reward the latecomers.

Begin by indicating precisely what you expect the meeting to accomplish. Clearly state your objectives for the meeting at the beginning to ensure a shared understanding of its purpose and topics. This will help people focus their attention on the meeting's objectives.

Preview and confirm the agenda. This will give everyone a chance to ask questions and generally orient themselves to the content of the meeting. It will also signal the importance of the agenda and your objectives and will encourage meeting members not to drift away from them.

Leading discussions

You have probably called a meeting because you need something from the other participants—relevant information, ideas, agreement to a decision or commitment to a change in procedures. Your success in achieving these goals will depend not so much on what you know about the topics to be discussed, but on how well you can invite free and open participation.

To lead a discussion well, you need to *know where you're headed*. Keep the objectives of the meeting clearly in mind and maintain the focus on them. This will help you ensure that meeting members don't wander from the issues that need to be discussed.

Listen carefully. Ensure that ground already covered is not dealt with again, and that discussions don't drag on. Make sure there is no futile, ineffective or irrelevant discussion; for example, it is always unproductive to discuss mistakes of the past that can't be changed.

If you are listening carefully, you will hear the main points and be able to *summarise* them, enabling the group to move on. You won't end the discussion before all points have been covered or before agreement is reached, but you will close discussions when it is clear that:

• consensus has been reached;
• more facts are required before further progress can be made;
• the meeting needs the views of people not present;
• meeting members need more time to think or discuss something with colleagues not present;
• events are changing rapidly and are likely to alter the basis of discussion quite soon;
• there is not enough time to discuss the issues fully; and
• two or three members can settle the topic being discussed outside the meeting without taking up the time of everyone present.

Allow group members to explore all sides of the issues fully. Don't let debate lead to confusion—keep clarifying and summarising.

Ask people to discuss what they know, not what they don't know. Don't ask for input on matters people know nothing about, have no expertise in, or have no solid data or

⚡ FROM THEORY TO PRACTICE

When a group strays off track or gets stuck, ask:
■ Where do we go from here?
■ What's the solution?
■ What are our options?
■ What are our objectives?
■ Which way do we want to proceed?

Or:

■ Back up and redefine the problem.
■ Summarise progress.
■ Take a short break.

information about. They might be willing to help you out with their uninformed opinions, but you may then find yourself having to ignore those opinions.

Hold your own ideas until last. This will help to avoid **groupthink** and rubber-stamping and encourage a more open response, since your team may not want to openly disagree with you or challenge your opinions.

When moving on to a new item, explain its purpose and objectives.

When a decision is reached, be clear about what it is and how it will be implemented.

Closing a meeting

Clarify what will happen next; that is, who is responsible for doing what and by when. Double-check that all decisions and actions to be taken have been recorded and confirm that these will be distributed to all meeting members. If appropriate, *fix the time and place of the next meeting.*

Finally, *thank the members of the group for their participation and spend a few minutes talking about how well the meeting went.* Always try to end a meeting on a positive note with a sense of accomplishment. One way to do this is to summarise a major achievement of the meeting. Do not omit this important maintenance issue.

After the meeting

Make a brief written summary of the major points discussed and conclusions reached. This will be a useful memory aid, even if it is only a handwritten note in your diary. Alternatively, you may wish to write up a concise set of minutes and distribute them to the meeting participants. Show decisions reached, tasks assigned and timelines for any action or follow-up. This is a good idea if a lot of material was discussed, if the points made need to be referred back to or if an action plan was drawn up.

Show each agenda item with a brief summary of the discussion, conclusions reached, action agreed and the person(s) responsible for taking the action. Also, show the time the meeting ended and the date, time and place of the next meeting. Don't forget to follow through on actions to be taken.

The minutes of quality circle meetings are often posted on a special noticeboard, so that other teams can follow the progress of the circle.

FROM THEORY TO PRACTICE

Five ways to encourage participation:
1. Ask each person for their thoughts, one at at time.
2. If the topic is non-confrontational and doing so won't set up a win–lose climate, ask for a show of hands.
3. Ask an open-ended question.
4. Put your question or issue in writing. Give all members a copy and ask them to quickly jot down their response. Collect them and read them to the goup.
5. Ask quiet members by name: 'Pat, we haven't heard from you on this— what are you thinking?'

LEADING A TELEPHONE OR VIDEOCONFERENCE

These can save a lot of time and expense if they're run well. Before you begin, clarify people's roles. Who will operate the camera if it's a videoconference? Who will call the others in case the connection breaks? Who will introduce the others and keep discussions on track?

Send out the agenda and any background information about a week in advance. Stress the importance of preparation; to keep the meeting flowing, participants will need to be ready to ask and answer questions.

Begin as usual by outlining why the meeting is being held, how long it will last and exactly what needs to be accomplished during the meeting. Unless you're sure all participants know each other, introduce each one and provide a bit of background information so everyone knows how the other members can contribute.

Here are guidelines to follow whether you're leading or participating in the meeting.

- In a telephone conference when you can't see everyone, it's easy to forget who is actually 'present'. Draw your own 'map' to keep fully tuned in: write the names of those present on a piece of paper and put it in front of you. If it helps, draw it out as you would if people were sitting around a conference table.
- Never interrupt a speaker.
- Don't shift and move about in your chair or tap pencils, shuffle feet, etc. The microphone will pick it up as distracting background noise.
- Don't hold a side conversation.

Extras for videoconferences:

- Stay away from wearing white (which is 'too hot' for the camera), red (which 'bleeds') or stripes (which look wavy on camera).
- Don't lean into the camera, towards listeners in a videoconference; it will look too aggressive. Stay 7 to 10 feet away from the camera.
- Keep reasonably still and refrain from hand gestures to avoid creating distractions. Use slower and smaller movements than you would in a face-to-face meeting.

SKILLS FOR MEETING LEADERS

You will need a number of skills to lead a meeting effectively. Four of the most important skill sets are:

1. Attaining the objectives of the meeting by guiding and maintaining a focused discussion that stays on track and follows the agenda.
2. Leading a balanced discussion by ensuring that all sides of an issue get equal 'air time', and that all members have a say and are listened to by tactfully curbing the talkative and encouraging the quiet to speak.
3. Avoiding manipulating the group to get your own way and steam-rollering your wishes through.
4. Managing your body language. Meeting members keep their eyes on the leader, so be aware of your posture (erect, positive) and your facial expressions (lively, interested, encouraging).

Are you willing to take a back seat when leading a meeting? To quietly guide the discussion through the agenda, summarise key points and invite quieter members to speak? Except in

TIPS FOR MEETING LEADERS

Before the meeting
Clarify your objectives for the meeting: to gather ideas, to seek possible solutions to a problem, etc.
Write the agenda.
Minimise the number of items on it.
Minimise the number of people attending (follow the two-thirds rule).
Send out the agenda in advance so that people can prepare.

During the meeting
Start on time.
Have a finish time to concentrate people's minds.

Make sure members are comfortable (but not too comfortable!).
Think about omitting the tea and biscuits.
Focus the energy of the group on its task.
Ensure the group's agreed meeting guidelines are followed.
Encourage participation.
Help the group reach solutions everyone can live with.

After the meeting
Write and distribute action minutes that indicate *who* is to do *what* by *when*.

COMPETENCIES OF MEETING LEADERS

Type of meeting	Leadership competencies needed
Information-giving meeting	Credibility, confidence, knowledge of subjects to be discussed.
Information-seeking or information-exchange meeting	Ability to encourage people to provide information and express their ideas; ability to lead open discussions and create a climate of sharing and support; ability to give group members the confidence to speak up and make all members feel they have made a significant contribution to the discussion.
New ideas meeting	Ability to promote an atmosphere that encourages a free and easy discussion of the topic; to remain neutral and objective; to draw out ideas, encourage participation and promote a full discussion of any concepts that the group may evolve.
Problem-solving and decision-making meeting	Ability to draw out a full and frank analysis of the problem; to move discussion back on track when it wanders, without offending the speakers; to encourage participants to express their thoughts and opinions; to talk only enough to keep the discussion to the point; to summarise the sentiments of the group, striving constantly to secure maximum and evenly spread participation; to follow the problem-solving steps presented in Chapter 11 to structure and guide the meeting to a successful conclusion.
Introducing-change meeting	Ability to have and show empathy, listen actively and communicate clearly why the change is necessary and the results you expect; discussion-leading and conflict-management skills.
Planning meetings	Planning and discussion-leading skills; the ability to help members work efficiently and effectively through the planning process, help them analyse the strengths and weaknesses of their plans and formulate appropriate preventive or contingency actions; clear and logical thinking and strong conceptual skills.
Quality meetings	In addition to the competencies outlined above, leaders also need to be able to use the various statistical problem identification and analysis tools discussed in Chapters 9 and 11.

information-giving meetings, you will usually be most effective when you do the least talking. Limit your contributions to one sentence or one question at a time. Don't pull rank, but think of yourself as the meeting's servant rather than its master. Strive to assist the group to achieve the meeting's goals effectively; gently interpret, clarify and move the discussion forward. In decision-making meetings, help the group reach a consensus that everyone understands and accepts. Box 6.2 summarises some tips for meeting leaders.

Other aspects of the leader's role and the competencies required will vary depending on the type of meeting. Some of the main skills needed by meeting leaders are listed in Box 6.3.

KEEPING CONTROL

Experience, self-confidence and a clear agenda are the best tools for keeping control. Carefully observe other good meeting leaders to see what tips you can pick up from them. You will probably notice that they use more direct control than they would normally exert when strong and potentially disruptive feelings are present, when the group is moving towards a decision or when time pressure is significant.

Short of formal parliamentary procedures, two of the more common and less intrusive techniques for keeping control that you will see being used are making a short summary after each contribution and using a flip chart to summarise. (This is handy for writing up the minutes afterwards, too.) Non-verbally, a glance at the clock, a raised eyebrow or a subtle stare can sometimes do the trick.

Don't use control techniques to dampen down differences of opinion and strong feelings—this would only be likely to strengthen them and increase tension. Disagreements are natural and often become stronger if they are not aired openly.

DISRUPTIVE PARTICIPANTS

What do you do about members who are compulsive talkers, tend to argue over every point, digress, carry on private conversations or won't say anything? All these meeting members present problems for a leader.

The dominator
Some people just talk too much! It seems they use every meeting to shout, bully and monopolise the discussion. They waste the meeting's time and destroy its sense of purpose. If you know these types in advance, try seating them to your extreme left (or right if you are left-handed); this makes it easier to avoid seeing their attempts to get the floor. If they do get the floor, let them have a reasonable amount of time, then interrupt by saying, 'You've got some good points there. Now let's hear what others think.'

The non-contributor
Some people are timid and become self-conscious when required to speak before a group. Don't embarrass them by asking a difficult, direct question. Instead, invite them to respond to questions you know they can answer. Thank them for their contributions to help them overcome their hesitation. Your task is to encourage them to speak so that the rest of the group can hear their worthwhile contributions.

The friendly chatterbox
When one member starts whispering or giggling in a side conversation, the meeting is disrupted. You can ignore it for a while but not to the point where the chatterbox irritates everyone else. You might stop speaking and wait for them to be quiet. If this doesn't work, you could say to the talkers, 'If you
Continued . . .

have something to say, please speak up so that everyone can have the benefit of your comments.' As a last resort, you could really put them on the spot by asking them to summarise the last few proposals and evaluate their feasibility—they will probably have difficulty recalling them. But be aware that such tactics could cause a loss of goodwill towards you, not only from the chatterbox but also other meeting members.

The critic
Some people seem to criticise everything, no matter what it is—good ideas, a point of view, helpful suggestions. They always see the down-side but seldom offer anything positive in return. They just say 'No, that won't work' without explaining why or offering an alternative. This saps the meeting's energy, goodwill and creativity. Don't allow it.

You may need to state explicitly the brainstorming rules (see Chapter 11) and gently remind critics of them each time they criticise unnecessarily. Or ask them what they do like about a suggestion, or to explain how they think it could be improved. This may help to refocus the critic on the positive.

Try treating a critic's caustic comments and criticism as though they were normal and routine. If possible, rephrase and restate them so that they appear to be conforming with the group and ask for a response from other members: 'Terry feels that this approach would be a waste of time. What do the rest of you think?' Consider not having the critics at your next meeting, but bear in mind that with a bit of 'retraining' they may have a useful role as devil's advocate.

The digresser
The irrelevancies that tend to crop up in meetings can try the skill and tact of even the best meeting leader. Questions and comments that lead the group astray are sometimes referred to as 'red herrings'. They sidetrack the meeting and retard its progress. Your job as leader is to keep meeting members focused on the objectives. There are several useful techniques.

You can say: 'This is an interesting observation. How does it fit into our problem?' This may cause the group to see the digression and return them to the topic under discussion. Or, if possible, gradually tie in the remote comments with the problem at hand. If this doesn't work, try summarising what has been said so far. This should serve to reorient members and focus their attention on the main discussion. You might have to point out that 'this discussion is interesting, but I suggest that we postpone it until next month's meeting when we will discuss that topic'. If none of this works, you might simply have to rule the discussion out of order and move on with the agenda.

The day-dreamer
There's often one person in a meeting who appears to be deep in thought or in a world of their own. They often respond well to the same treatment as the non-contributor.

The hesitator
Sometimes people have a good point to contribute but just can't seem to get the words out or string them together as well as others do. These people need patience and support if their worthwhile contributions are to see the light of day. Encourage them to speak if you think they have something to say. Try summarising their thoughts when they've finished and thank them for their contribution.

The show-off
Show-offs like to be clever. They deter others from listening to just about anything they have to say, which is a pity because sometimes they have good ideas. Quickly and briefly summarise each of the show-off's contributions and make sure to thank them whenever they do make a good point—often, all that show-offs want is acknowledgment for their cleverness. This might stop them showing off without blocking their good ideas.

The unprepared
It seems that every organisation has its own 'forgetful' people who continually turn up to meetings unprepared and without the information that the rest of the meeting needs to get on with the agenda. Remind these people to prepare before the meeting and let them know you don't intend to make a habit of doing their remembering for them.

The broken record
Have you ever known someone who keeps repeating the same point over and over, even when the subject has moved on? Gently remind them that their views have already been noted.

As a general approach to a disruptive group member, try calmly, assertively and politely confronting the member, either privately or in the meeting, with an 'I' message. Name the behaviour you don't like, and say why you don't like it and what you would like instead. For example, you might say to the friendly chatterbox: 'Chris, when you talk while someone else is addressing the meeting, I get quite distracted. I'd really like to have just one person speaking at a time.' You will be surprised how well this works!

Another good technique, especially in groups of more than six, is to nominate three or four people at a time, selecting the speakers who need to be restrained first. 'John, you first, then Jane, then Jacob, and after that we'll hear from Jenny.' This puts pressure on the earlier speakers to be succinct, since the people after them are waiting their turn. If they hog the floor anyway, remind them of the queue still waiting their turn.

FROM THEORY TO PRACTICE

To evaluate your meeting, ask yourself the following questions:

- Was the meeting necessary?
- Was everyone clear why they were there?
- Did I prepare and send out a notice or agenda in advance, giving the date, time and place?
- Did I select an appropriate meeting room with the necessary equipment (overhead projector, flip chart, etc.)?
- Did the group genuinely participate or merely rubber-stamp my wishes?
- Was the meeting short enough to keep the group's attention?
- Did contributions come evenly from all members?
- Did we cover all aspects of the topic?
- Did we discuss the problem thoroughly before suggesting solutions?
- Did we reach a consensus?
- Did participants hear each other out without interrupting?
- Did I manage conflict openly and constructively, in a win–win spirit?
- Did we follow the agenda as intended?
- Did I encourage members to keep their comments to the point?
- Did I direct discussions to keep them on track?
- Did I avoid assuming that silence meant agreement?
- Did I invite only those people who needed to be there?
- Did I close the meeting on time and end on a positive note?
- Did we develop a workable action plan?
- Did I listen actively?
- Did I keep an open mind and remain neutral?
- Did I summarise frequently?
- Did I handle difficult meeting members effectively, without destroying any positive contributions they were willing to make?
- Were action points noted and minutes recorded and distributed to the participants?

If you can honestly answer 'yes' to most of the above, pat yourself on the back—you have run a good meeting.

ATTENDING MEETINGS

If you are not leading a meeting but will be a member, you still have some work to do.

- Before the meeting, think about the items on the agenda and do any research that would help you make a valuable contribution.
- Arrive on time—tardiness is disrespectful to others.
- Bring any necessary information and paperwork, with copies for others if this would be helpful.
- Participate, don't just take up space. Follow what's going on.
- Be positive in your attitude towards the meeting leader and other members.
- Manage your body language. Don't fidget, gaze out of the window, roll your eyes, constantly check your watch, tap your feet, drum with your pen … This can disrupt a meeting, break people's flow of thought and talk, and make you very unpopular.
- Use only your share of the speaking time.
- Organise your thoughts before speaking, in your head or on paper. This saves everyone's time and projects a positive professional impression.
- Make your comments clear and loud enough to be heard.
- Stick to the point and keep your contributions relevant to the subject under discussion. Don't digress, ramble or side-track. Omit personal stories unless they make a point, and skip 'inside jokes'.
- When speaking, address the entire meeting (or the chair in a more formal meeting) not just one other meeting member. Make eye contact with everyone.
- Don't play 'devil's advocate' for the sake of it.
- Don't dump data. Have supporting evidence by all means but don't bore people with it. Make your point succinctly; if people have questions, pull out some of your detailed information.
- Keep your own special interests in check.
- Avoid one-on-one discussions and conversations.
- Keep the floor by saying: 'I have three points I'd like to make on this issue. First, …' Keep numbering as you go so that people will know you haven't finished when you pause to draw breath. If you let people interrupt you, they will. Keep your points brief, though!
- Don't translate: 'I think what Bill is trying to say is …' If someone translates for you incorrectly, correct them: 'Actually, Bill, that isn't quite what I meant. What I meant was …'
- If you disagree, speak up but don't be disagreeable. Disagree in a helpful way. Show you've heard and understood by paraphrasing in neutral language; then express your reservations, concern or confusion in a way that shows you are open to hearing the answer. If you disagree with an idea or proposal, have an alternative to offer. Don't set a pattern of always disagreeing or seeing the negative side. Offer solutions and encouragement too.
- If you're asked to contribute and you don't have anything to say, it's perfectly acceptable to say: 'I can't add anything to what's been said' or 'I don't know anything about that and I don't want to confuse the issue'.
- Develop your listening skills.

- Encourage good ideas suggested by others.
- Follow through on any promises you make or actions you agree to take.
- Do not accept tasks that do not properly belong to you or your work group.

FORMAL AND INFORMAL MEETINGS

Meetings can vary greatly in their degree of formality. Some meetings can be very informal, and may seem more like a discussion group or conversation among colleagues. The atmosphere in such meetings is usually quite relaxed and casual. Don't let this fool you—some very significant matters are discussed and important decisions made in informal meetings.

Most work-team meetings and other meetings that supervisors attend are run informally. This is particularly so with smaller groups and people who meet together regularly.

At the other extreme are formal meetings which follow certain set, and often written, procedures. The larger the number of people attending, the more the meeting needs formal rules to keep people focused and speaking one at a time. Committees brought temporarily together for special purposes and comprised of people who don't know each other often use formal procedures. So do professional bodies and institutions, city councils and boards of directors. Official meetings between employer and employee representatives often follow formal meeting procedures, too.

The officials and protocol of formal meetings

People are elected or appointed to carry out certain important duties on behalf of the meeting. The *chairperson* leads the meeting, ensures that the rules (constitution) of the meeting are followed, maintains a sense of order and direction, opens and closes the meeting, introduces each topic on the agenda, calls on members to speak and calls for votes. Members of a formal meeting make remarks only when invited to do so by the chairperson and these remarks are usually made 'through the chair'—that is, they are directed at the chairperson.

Good chairpeople give each participant the opportunity to speak and ensure that no one dominates or in any other way disrupts the meeting. They are impartial and objective in dealing with all sides of the topics under discussion. They circulate agendas before the meeting and see that any members who are necessary to the meeting will be there.

The *secretary* is responsible for preparing and distributing the minutes of each meeting, carrying out any correspondence or other written communication as instructed by the meeting, arranging a suitable venue for the meeting, arranging any necessary background information or paperwork for members to refer to, and for preparing and distributing the agenda before each meeting as directed by the chairperson.

Formal meetings follow parliamentary protocol procedures. They have rules, or a *constitution*, that guide how the meeting will be conducted and how many members must be present before the meeting can take place; this is called a *quorum*. The secretary officially lists *attendance* (i.e. who attended the meeting) and also *apologies* received (advance notification from any members not able to attend the meeting). *Absences* are often officially recorded too (people who didn't turn up and omitted to put in an apology).

These last three items normally appear in the *minutes* of the meeting. The first item on the *agenda* of most formal meetings is for the chairperson to call for the minutes of the previous meeting to be *approved*. This means the members agree that they are an accurate reflection of the previous meeting. The chairperson then signs the minutes, which are placed in a special minutes file for storage and future reference.

Before the group can discuss or vote on a matter, a meeting member must *propose* it as a *motion*. Another member must then *second* it. This ensures that two persons (at least) agree that the matter is worth discussing. In very formal meetings, the chairperson will ensure that people speaking for the motion and speaking against it alternate.

A meeting member can propose an *amendment* to the wording of a motion before it is voted on. Another meeting member would need to second the amendment. After the discussion and before the group votes on a motion, the original proposer is often given *the right of reply* to say a few final words about the motion.

When a *vote* is taken, people vote *for* or *against* the motion or they may *abstain* from voting. Voting can be by ballot, verbally, or by a show of hands. If a majority of meeting participants vote in favour of a motion, it is *carried* and becomes a *resolution*. The secretary records this, as well as the key points of discussion (who said what) in the minutes.

Roles in informal meetings

In less formal meetings, the supervisor or senior person often 'takes the chair'. A popular alternative is to rotate the chair among meeting members. This gives them valuable experience.

The chairperson often acts as *recorder*, or secretary, too, jotting down important points raised by meeting members (minutes). Again, this role can be usefully rotated among meeting members. Traditionally, the recorder kept individual notes for later posting or distribution. A workable variation is for the recorder to take the notes on a flip chart, whiteboard that has a photocopying facility or a laptop projected onto a screen or the wall. This way, meeting members can see what is being recorded. No one has to worry that their point has been missed (they can see it hasn't). Visible minutes also help to focus meeting members on the topic at hand.

A very useful role that is becoming popular in informal meetings is that of *meeting facilitator*. This is a different role from the chairperson role. While the chairperson is formally in charge of the meeting, the facilitator's job is to lead the *process* of the meeting and ensure everyone has a say, staying away from *content* (i.e. they would not normally contribute any ideas themselves). For example, in a brainstorming session, the facilitator would ensure that everyone was contributing and no one criticising. The meeting facilitator would also point out if meeting members were not following their agreed guidelines. Again, the role of facilitator can be usefully rotated among group members.

AGENDAS AND MINUTES

:... Whether a meeting is formal or informal, agendas and minutes are a good idea. As we've discussed, **agendas** list the topics to be covered during a meeting and what is to be achieved. They help to keep people focused and let them know what is coming up. When distributed prior to the meeting, they help people prepare for it. Agendas also show when and where the meeting will be held and sometimes indicate the estimated time that will be spent on each topic.

Agendas specify what *will happen* at a meeting. They look towards the future. In establishing the outline and time schedule, however, they should not be so rigid that they cannot be adjusted. Some topics can take longer to discuss than anticipated and others may arise that were not foreseen.

The chairperson is responsible for preparing the agenda. Chairpeople sometimes invite members to submit agenda items for the next meeting. They should check that the items submitted are appropriate to that particular meeting. With sensitive or ambiguous topics, the chair should clarify with the person who suggested the agenda item just what they wish to discuss before agreeing to place it on the agenda. To increase the efficiency and effectiveness of the meeting, the agenda should be distributed to members before each meeting, giving them enough time to prepare for it.

Minutes are a record of what has been said and agreed during a meeting. They are historical, specifying what *did happen* at the meeting. They should indicate the time, date and place of the meeting and accurately reflect its tone and any main themes. As mentioned above, minutes also show who was in attendance and list the apologies received; they name any presiding officials and indicate when and where the next meeting will be held, if this is known.

RAPID REVIEW

		True	False
1.	Meetings can give the illusion of progress.	☑	☐
2.	Meetings can also serve a number of useful purposes.	☑	☐
3.	Meetings should only be called when a supervisor is having difficulty reaching a decision alone.	☐	☑
4.	More than ever before, today's supervisors need to be skilled in leading and participating in meetings and discussions.	☑	☐
5.	All types of meetings rely on participation and achieving consensus among meeting members.	☑	☐
6.	The way that meeting leaders carry out their responsibilities will set the tone for the meeting and is an important factor in achieving a successful outcome.	☑	☐
7.	Depending on the type of meeting, supervisors need different competencies to lead them, although they need to have both task and maintenance competencies in all meetings.	☑	☐
8.	Quietly observing the group processes during a meeting can give a lot of clues about how well the team is working together and how effectively the meeting is being led.	☑	☐
9.	Once the objectives of the meeting are explained clearly to the group, the meeting will usually run itself.	☐	☑
10.	It is preferable to prepare an agenda and minutes for all meetings, however informal.	☑	☐
11.	Meeting leaders need to be better at talking than listening.	☐	☑
12.	Participating in meetings is easy because you have no responsibilities.	☐	☑

APPLY YOUR KNOWLEDGE

1. Explain how participating in a meeting can make a person feel part of a team or group and increase its cohesiveness.
2. Give a short description of each of the seven main types of meetings.
3. When should supervisors hold a meeting? When are meetings inappropriate?
4. Thinking about both the task and maintenance needs of a meeting, discuss the steps supervisors can take to ensure their work group reaches consensus.
5. List and explain seven things you can do in order to lead a productive meeting.
6. Discuss the task and maintenance issues a meeting leader needs to be sensitive to.
7. List some specific things you can do to become a better participant of the next meeting you attend.

DEVELOP YOUR SKILLS

Individual activities

1. What are the major weaknesses of meetings you have attended? Considering what you have learned from your own experience and from this chapter, what do you believe meeting leaders could do to overcome these weaknesses?
2. What types of meeting have you participated in? Consider meetings with your family, friends, fellow students and clubs and organisations to which you may belong, as well as work meetings. Write a short paragraph describing four of them. Discuss the skills needed by the leader and the participants in each. In retrospect, what could either the meeting leader or the participants have done to make each of these meetings more effective?
3. Describe task and maintenance needs that were present in the last formal or informal meeting you attended and how the person who chaired the meeting met (or failed to meet) these needs.
4. At the next meeting or study group you attend, list the helpful and unhelpful behaviours of the meeting leader. Do the same for meeting participants.
5. At the next meeting or study group you attend, sit quietly and observe group processes. Make a note of them and use them to write a short critique summarising the task and maintenance issues in the meeting.
6. Relate the role of a meeting leader to the role of a classroom teacher.
7. Attend a formal meeting at your college or local council and observe the protocol followed. Prepare a short report on it.

Group activities

1. The next time you attend a meeting or a study group, observe the proceedings and compile two lists: one of member behaviours that seemed to help the meeting and one of member behaviours that seemed to hinder it. Share your list with others in your class and agree on a combined list.
2. Refer to activity number 6 of *Develop your skills, Individual activities* in

Chapter 4. Prepare an agenda for your first committee meeting.

3. Now outline your plan for leading this meeting, following the guidelines given in this chapter.

4. Plan and lead a 20 minute class meeting on a topic you are studying. Decide in advance what type of meeting it will be. After the meeting finishes, evaluate how well you planned and ran it. Ask others for their feedback, too. What can you do better next time?

5. When you participate in a class meeting led by one of your classmates in question 4 above, analyse your own effectiveness as a meeting member. List two or three things you can do to improve your effectiveness.

6. Hold a class meeting on a topic suitable for reaching a consensus decision. Appoint a leader to lead this meeting, following the guidelines set out in this chapter for achieving consensus.

7. Imagine you are participating in a meeting. Brainstorm all the things that could disrupt the meeting, for example, a friend continually whispering to you, or someone interrupting you when you're trying to speak. Then discuss each meeting disruptor and decide one or two actions you could take to turn the situation around.

CASE STUDY 6.1

Gathering Good Ideas

You are the supervisor of a department with 26 employees divided into three work groups, each with a team leader. As Australia Day approaches and the general workload eases up a bit, you thought it might be a good idea for your department to show its appreciation to its internal and external suppliers and customers in a fun way. You don't want this to involve great expense but you do want to do something a bit different that will really have an impact. You decide to canvass your staff to see what ideas they can come up with.

Questions

1   What type of meeting or meetings would you hold for this purpose and how would you organise it (or them)?

2   Would you ask all employees to one big meeting, or would you hold two or three small meetings? What would your cut-off point be in terms of numbers?

3   What would you say to open the meeting? How would you proceed from there?

CASE STUDY 6.2

Electric Components Company

As his first assignment with the Electric Components Company, Frank Romanowski was placed in charge of the company's central store. The company is a large nationally known business engaged in the design, manufacture and sale of many types of electronic products. Amplifiers, recorders, speakers and transmitters are just a few of its products. Commonly used parts in these products are stocked and issued to factory substores from one centralised store. Over 10 000 different parts are stocked, including various sizes and types of screws, nuts, bolts, panels and circuit boards.

As a recent graduate, Frank was eager to 'make good' and he introduced several improvements. One of his problem areas was maintaining a sufficient stock of 72 different sizes and lengths of screws and nuts. He wondered about the necessity for the various sizes and decided to see what could be done to reduce the number.

On checking product specifications, he found that the design engineers had specified for each product that a screw must extend beyond the nut exactly two threads. This, he discovered, accounted in part for the large variety of screw lengths he was required to stock. Further, he found that each design engineer chose whatever diameter screw they felt appropriate for the product. This accounted in part for the variety in the diameter of the screws. In general, the number of threads per millimetre was fairly standardised.

After talking to several of the design and product engineers, Frank believed that the variety of stocked screws could be reduced. Accordingly, he prepared a report for management showing the excess dollars tied up in allegedly needless varieties of screws. The plant manager was impressed with the report and decided that a meeting should be called to discuss the subject further. Frank was asked to chair the meeting.

Questions

1. Around what theme should Frank organise the meeting?
2. Who should attend it?
3. Draft a possible agenda for the meeting. What, if any, background information will need to accompany the agenda when it is sent out?
4. Should this meeting be formal or informal? Why?
5. Can Frank do anything prior to the meeting to help ensure that his ideas are accepted?

Answers to Rapid Review questions

1. T   2. T   3. F   4. T   5. F   6. T   7. T   8. T   9. F   10. T   11. F   12. F

CHAPTER 7

HEALTH, SAFETY AND WELFARE

'We just haven't got the time ...'

John Adams, the maintenance supervisor, and Kathy Stambanis, a worker representative on the safety committee, are having a rather heated discussion. John is explaining why he doesn't take what Kathy and the committee consider to be a 'better attitude' towards safety matters.

'Kathy, that's all very well,' he says, 'but if I did every little thing the letter of the law demanded, we'd never get any work done around here. And it's just too expensive to do everything you want us to do. I do what I can, you know that, but I just can't stop every time some small thing needs a guard or this or that—we have to get the job done. Be reasonable, Kathy.'

'Come off it, John, we're not asking you to do the impossible. We're worried about some of the things we've seen people in your department doing and we want you to look into it. We don't want any nasty accidents or anyone getting hurt.'

'What are you talking about, Kathy? My people can look after themselves.'

'For instance, John, what about when Bill climbs up to get at the pipe fittings over the tanks? That's a very high ladder he's using and there's never anyone at the bottom holding it for him. What if someone bumped into the ladder and he fell off—he could break his neck!'

'Oh, for heaven's sake, Kath—now you want two people doing what one can do!'

'If that's what it takes, yes. An accepted safe work practice is for ladders to be "footed" by another person at all times. Or you could secure it at the top. As long as he's protected. It needn't take up much time at all—or extra people, for that matter. And another thing—Alf is constantly running the dicing machine without the guard on it.'

'Well, of course he is—how else can he see if he's fixed it properly?'

'John, you know as well as I do that he should put the guard back on before starting up the machine. It's too dangerous otherwise. And another thing—your people aren't wearing some of their safety gear when they come into my section. It sets a bad example. All we're asking, John, is that you take a little more care in seeing that your people are following the safety procedures. It doesn't look good when they just ignore them as if they were special. Safety procedures apply to us all. Here, I've listed these points for you so that you and your work team can think about what you will do to put matters right.'

.... OVERVIEW ....

Given the emotional, physical and monetary costs of poor health, safety and welfare at work, supervisors need to be aware of how the legislation helps them to reduce risks and accidents and make the workplace safer, healthier and more productive. In this chapter you will learn about health, safety and welfare from a 'big picture' point of view and from a supervisor's day-to-day perspective.

- Are your responsibilities as a supervisor different to the organisation's responsibilities under the legislation? What are employees' responsibilities?
- What are safety committees and who are safety representatives? Are they different from safety officers?
- What is the difference between a hazard and a risk? How can you identify them? What should you do if you become aware of a hazard or risk?
- Can you explain the three steps supervisors can take to make the workplace safer?

- What can you do to supervise for safety?
- What causes an accident? Are some employees accident-prone?
- What should you do if there is an accident at your work site?
- Do you know how to write safety instructions?
- What is the difference between a safe working environment and a healthy working environment?
- How do workers' rehabilitation and compensation work?

ACCIDENTS HURT

One in 12, or over 650 000 people in Australia suffer a work-related illness or injury every year. As a result, at least 170 000 people are absent from work for five or more days.

Over 2700 Australians are killed each year as a result of work-related accidents and incidents—that is, more than seven people killed every work day. Five hundred of these deaths occur as a direct result of traumatic workplace accidents, mostly through crushing, falls and electrocution. An estimated 2200 deaths are a result of industrial diseases, particularly cancers caused by chemicals and other long-term occupational diseases such as asbestosis. These figures do not include stress-related deaths.

Occupational accidents, injuries and diseases are expensive. The total cost of an accident, for example, is difficult to measure precisely, but will include such things as:
- medical costs;
- workers' compensation costs (insurance premiums paid by employers and the associated administrative costs);
- damage to buildings, equipment, machinery;
- delays and interruptions to products and services;
- the effect on staff morale;
- other staff costs such as recruitment, training, overtime and working time lost by sympathetic onlookers;
- the time spent investigating an accident; and
- damage to public and industrial relations.

These costs are in the order of $20 billion per year. Employers bear approximately 40% of this cost, those injured bear 30% and the general community bears 30%.

Safety professionals tell us that the total cost of an occupational accident or disease to an organisation is, on average, six times the dollar value of the workers' compensation claim. It can be up to 50 times greater. Figure 7.1 shows the 'iceberg effect' of some of these hidden costs.

Apart from these financial costs, there are also humanitarian costs. Pain and suffering, loss of enjoyment, permanent disability or death, loss of earnings, the psychological effects of an accident and its consequences, and disruption to a victim's private life are only some of these.

There are also costs to the community, which must, for example, provide hospitals in which to treat injuries and support facilities for permanently injured workers.

There is a further cost to society. Not only could we wipe up to $20 billion off our national debt through improved health, safety and welfare practices, but we could increase the number of productive working days in Australia. According to government figures,

FIGURE 7.1   THE ICEBERG EFFECT OF THE FINANCIAL COSTS OF ACCIDENTS AND INJURIES IN THE WORKPLACE: DIRECT AND INDIRECT COSTS

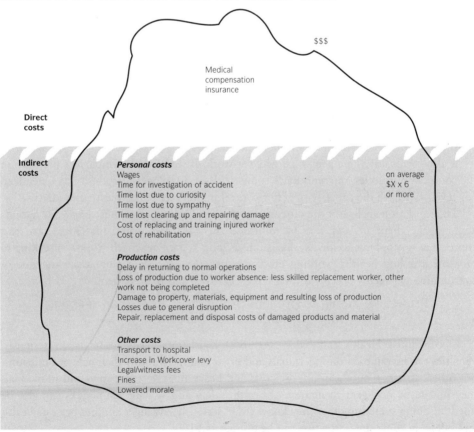

about 20 to 23 million working days are lost annually due to workplace injuries. This is over five times the working days lost through industrial disputes and is a significant loss in terms of exports and industrial earnings. As Figure 7.2 shows, the costs of poor health and safety in the workplace are like a pebble dropping into a still pool of water—the repercussions can go on and on.

FIGURE 7.2 THE RIPPLE EFFECT OF INJURY

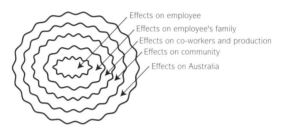

Effects on employee
Effects on employee's family
Effects on co-workers and production
Effects on community
Effects on Australia

THE LEGISLATIVE FRAMEWORK

In New Zealand, a variety of legislation exists to ensure health and safety in the workplace. In Australia, the legislation is state- and territory-based. Although the details vary slightly between states and territories, and between the two countries, the pieces of legislation share common themes and intentions. Figure 7.3 shows the types of Acts and regulations in the health, safety and welfare area.

The legislation covers all persons at any workplace, including state and local government premises, private offices, workshops and factories—that is, all places where people work. Employers must protect the health, safety and welfare of their employees and other people on their premises, including visitors, self-employed people, voluntary workers and subcontractors, from risks arising from the work activities.

It also covers anywhere people go while at work. If we leave the employer's premises in the course of our duties, our workplace comes with us. Employers' responsibility extends to wherever they have the capacity to act or control matters related to health and safety.

The legislation spells out the outcome: stopping accidents. You must find your hazards and manage them *in your way* to minimise the risk. Two companies may have two approaches to stopping accidents; this is fine as long as each approach works. In seeking to promote safe and healthy working environments, the legislation emphasises the role of consultation between workers, or their representatives, and management.

> 'Proactive: acting to prevent problems, rather than reacting once problems have occurred.'

Occupational Health and Safety (OH&S) legislation needs to be taken seriously. Penalties can be imposed on individuals and organisations who, by their acts or omissions, put others at risk. Courts can impose costs and heavy fines on companies and individuals they find to be negligent in matters of health, safety and welfare. Employees can also be fined for doing something that they know could seriously endanger another person's health and safety; in some states, the fine can be as high as $1000.

FIGURE 7.3   HEALTH AND SAFETY LEGISLATION IN AUSTRALIA

Acts
Set principles and philosophy

Regulations
Pick up particular issues of the Acts

Codes of practice
Give practical guidelines for putting the regulations into effect

Australian standards
Provide details

As an example of employer liability, in South Australia penalties for offences can reach $220 000 and/or five years' imprisonment. Fines may be imposed for *each person* put at risk. For example, if one worker is injured or killed but six people have been exposed to the same risk, the person responsible for exposing them to the risk (often this is the supervisor) will be fined not just once for the person who was injured or killed, but six times, to cover each person who could have been injured or killed.

Other states impose fines per incident. Every state is different. In some states, corporate fines can be as high as $500 000 per incident. Personal fines for supervisors found negligent are generally between $1000 and $10 000, but could exceed these figures. Jail sentences can also be imposed. People in Victoria have been charged with manslaughter for negligence under the *Occupational Health and Safety Act*.

Prosecutions can be expensive and time-consuming. In deciding whether an organisation or person has been negligent or failed to meet their duty of care, the courts consider several factors:
• Was the accident *foreseeable*?
• Was it *preventable*?
• Was it *reasonable* to provide methods to prevent it?
• Was there *causality*, or a direct link between the negligence and the injury?

If the answer is yes, you and/or your organisation are legally accountable and penalties will be imposed. Penalties will also be imposed if an organisation or person has breached a health and safety regulation.

As with any legislation, health, safety and welfare legislation will only make our workplaces as safe as we want them to be. Supervisors are important in setting a good example in upholding not only the law but also the spirit of the law.

> 'OH&S management system: the arrangements for managing occupational health and safety including accident investigation procedures and general work procedures.'

EMPLOYER RESPONSIBILITY

Safety begins at the top. Health and safety legislation aims to ensure that employers in all sectors provide safe and healthy work environments for their employees. It places ultimate responsiblility on the employer for the health, safety and welfare of employees and others on its premises.

As Figure 7.4 shows, employers' responsibilities for providing safe systems of work come under five interconnected areas.

> 'Duty of care: the legal obligation of employers to ensure that their business, so far as is practicable, does not harm employees or the general public.'

Management commitment

Senior management must understand the principles and philosophy of managing the organisation with full regard to health, safety and welfare matters. The chief executive officer or other senior person must be fully conversant with the relevant legislation and ensure the organisation takes all possible steps to comply with it. Senior management must also ensure that health and safety measures are adhered to, assess their effectiveness and ensure that information about any accidents that occur is properly recorded. They should give safety matters the same degree of attention as functional areas such as production, finance and supply.

Departmental managers should act in the same way with regard to their departments as the chief executive acts on behalf of the entire organisation. In addition, they should become more directly involved in the detailed activities of the health and safety program.

FIGURE 7.4   EMPLOYERS' RESPONSIBILITIES FOR PROVIDING SAFE SYSTEMS OF WORK

This includes ensuring that procedures and systems of work are planned, dangerous machines guarded, processes and work flow organised safely and efficiently, and systems of education and training with regard to safety and health requirements set up and carried out.

Employers must also provide a sufficient number of workers to do the job safely; people must not be expected to work beyond the bounds of reasonable human effort.

Policies and procedures

Senior management must develop written health, safety and welfare policies, programs and procedures, make them available, and monitor their effectiveness. Health and safety policies are not just documents to hang on a wall. They must contain considerable detail, describing the organisation's arrangements for health, safety and welfare, specifying how accidents will be prevented and investigated, the type of safety training and education it will provide, and the safety reporting and recording procedures it will follow. They should also address any specific hazards in the organisation, set improvement targets in key health and safety areas, and specify the resources available to put the policy into practice and the mechanisms that will review its effectiveness.

Through the policies and procedures it puts in place, employers must protect employees and others on its premises, including members of the public, from such things as electricity, fire, explosions, falling objects, radiation, noise and exposure to harmful substances such as lead and asbestos. They must ensure that the buildings and land, and the equipment, operations and processes carried out at the workplace are safe for everyone.

Consultation

Consultation between employers and employees is a positive approach to health and safety in the workplace. Employers and employees should develop agreed procedures for consultation. For it to be effective, employees and their representatives should have access to relevant information, including information on hazards or potential hazards, work conditions, work organisation, and plant, equipment and materials used in the workplace.

Genuine consultation means that everyone has equal access to the same information and they are given sufficient time and opportunity to consider it. If one party makes a decision and limits discussion to the timing and method of implementation, while refusing to discuss the decision itself, this is not genuine consultation. Box 7.1 indicates when consultation should take place.

Consultation is an ongoing process and should begin as soon as possible when workplace changes are being contemplated or introduced. This means you can take employees' experience and expertise into account when it can most effectively be used. Consultation

---

BOX **7.1** **WHEN TO CONSULT**

- When planning to change work or work processes
- When deciding how to implement regulations
- When identifying hazards
- When assessing their risk
- When deciding how best to control risk
- When implementing risk-control measures
- When reviewing the effectiveness of control

can take place directly with employees, with health and safety representatives (for local issues) or with health and safety committees (for organisational and strategic issues).

Consultation provides all employees with an opportunity to have a say in matters that affect their health, safety and welfare. It allows the organisation to access the detailed knowledge that employees have of the risks related to the work they perform. This is valuable not only in identifying and assessing risks but in working out what control measures would be most effective and economical.

Training

Employers must provide adequate safety training and instruction to ensure that employees understand and follow safe and correct procedures at all times. Training needs to be ongoing and consistent to be effective.

Hazard management

'Hazard: anything with the potential to harm life, health or property.'

Employers must make the workplace safe and free from risks to health. To do this, they should first identify risks and hazards, and then manage them according to the preferred order of control, or prevention hierarchy, shown in Box 7.2.

THE SUPERVISOR'S RESPONSIBILITIES

Are you a practising supervisor? Then you should consider yourself your employer's representative in health, safety and welfare matters. It is you who sets the safety climate, enforces safety procedures and answers for the safe work practices of your work area. Employees will get their impressions of the meaning of 'safety' from what you say and, more importantly, what you do. Safe working practices are only as good as you insist they be. You are the key person in any health and safety program.

BOX 7.2 PREVENTION HIERARCHY

1. **Eliminate**: remove the hazard. For example, change the job so people don't have to lift any more. If you can't do that,
2. **Substitute**: use a safer alternative. For example, find a safer chemical that will do the job. If you can't do that,
3. **Change to a safer working practice**: change how the job is done. For example, provide lifting hoists or trolleys. If you can't do that,
4. **Use engineering controls**: design the problem out. For example, put a guard on a moving part of a machine. If you can't do that,
5. **Organise training**: provide or upgrade employees' skills. For example, teach people how to do the job more safely. If you can't do that,
6. **Use personal protective equipment**: this is the last line of defence. For example, hard hats, hair protection, ear plugs.

You have significant responsibility and accountability on a daily basis for successfully implementing your organisation's health, safety and welfare policy and programs. Here is a checklist of things you should be doing:

Do you:

- Provide leadership and direction to employees to help them contribute towards the organisation's health and safety objectives?
- Ensure that your work team consistently follows correct and safe working habits, methods and procedures?
- Ensure that your work team consistently uses proper tools, equipment and safety aids?
- *Always* set a good example in health, safety and related matters?
- Develop an atmosphere in your department that is generally conducive to employee health and safety?
- Stay alert to discover and correct any unsafe methods and practices (including 'horseplay')?
- Never allow any deviations from, or relaxation in, the prescribed safety standards?
- Promote safety continually?
- Make sure, through training and supervision, that each of your employees has not only the desire to work safely but also the knowledge and equipment to do so?
- Plan production operations with safety as well as efficiency as their central theme?
- Establish a known warning or disciplinary system for failure to observe safety requirements?
- Consult employees to find out what problems and hazards they experience and how they think these can be rectified?
- Periodically analyse work procedures to ensure they are as safe as possible?
- Carry out regular hazard identification, assessment and control inspections?
- Prioritise, minimise and control any hazards identified?
- Make regular use of demonstrations, meetings, informal talks and any other ways in which you can convey safety information and positive safety attitudes?
- Provide ongoing help and safety training and instructions?
- Ensure that preventative maintenance is carried out and good housekeeping standards are maintained?
- Educate employees on what is and is not a safe practice?
- Make sure employees know the safety rules and their responsibilities for carrying them out?
- Allow adequate time for the job and minimise haste and speed which lead to mistakes, fatigue and clouded judgment?
- Make sure employees know the organisation's safety arrangements and communication system, accident, incident and injury procedures, and fire emergency procedures?
- Make sure employees are aware of any specific hazards and how to deal with them?
- Investigate any accidents and near misses and complete accident and injury reports?
- Monitor your department's accident, injury and near-miss statistics to identify any patterns, trends, danger periods, etc. so that action can be taken?
- Develop good working relationships with safety officers, safety representatives and safety committee members?
- Inspect any new items purchased for possible hazards?

EMPLOYEES' RESPONSIBILITIES

'Duty of care: the duty of employees to ensure their acts or failures to act do not harm themselves or others around them.'

Employees have a legal duty to cooperate with their employer in ensuring the health and safety of their workplace. This involves taking reasonable care to protect themselves and others around them: employees must not, through their acts or omissions, endanger themselves, their co-workers or members of the public. This means, for example, that employees must ensure they are not affected by alcohol or other drugs while at work, that they should follow safety procedures, use the equipment provided for health and safety purposes, and obey reasonable instructions in relation to health and safety.

Who R our Safety 'officer' – is it the Safety Reps?... Do they know?

THE ROLE OF SAFETY OFFICERS, SAFETY COMMITTEES AND SAFETY REPRESENTATIVES

Health and safety officers

Many organisations employ a trained safety officer or industrial engineer to help, advise and oversee health, safety and welfare matters. They usually report to a senior person in the organisation who can exert considerable influence to help them achieve health and safety goals. Although their role is a staff one (see Chapter 4), if safety officers discover an imminent and serious danger during a routine hazard inspection, they usually have the authority to stop work until the danger is rectified.

Safety officers are thoroughly familiar with health and safety legislation, regulations and codes of practice, methods of investigating and preventing accidents, the best ways to guard machines and other means of protecting the organisation's workforce. You can go to them for guidance and advice on anything to do with the health and safety of your work team or work area. They will help you plan for safety, while you will see that the plans are carried out.

Safety officers frequently become involved in the formulation of their organisation's health and safety policy and accident prevention program. Other duties include:
- reporting to and advising management on all safety matters;
- advising and guiding line staff;
- investigating accidents and incidents;
- keeping and monitoring accident and incident records and statistics;
- supervising safety training;
- examining plant, equipment, processes and working methods;
- conducting *safety audits* (examining the systems in place for managing occupational health, safety and welfare) and *hazard identification surveys* (examining workplaces to identify specific and potential hazards);
- serving on the safety committee as technical adviser;
- preparing safety instructions and advising on safe working practices;
- organising the circulation of safety information; and
- conducting fire and other emergency protection activities through drills and exercises.

Health and safety committees

The legislation of some states requires the establishment of health and safety committees. These are composed of elected employee representatives and nominated members of the management team, including supervisors. They can be an effective way of involving people from all levels and areas of the organisation in health and safety matters and encouraging them to work cooperatively towards common safety goals.

While a safety officer is a safety expert, a safety committee is made up of people concerned about health and safety and who are knowledgeable and well trained, but not expert, in safety matters. Their focus is on strategic health, safety and welfare issues that relate to the organisation as a whole, considering policy matters that have an organisation-wide impact. They tend not to become involved in departmental or work area issues.

Health and safety committees have six main functions:
1. To encourage effective *cooperation* between management and employees in initiating, developing, carrying out and monitoring measures designed to ensure the health, safety and welfare of employees.

2. To assist in *resolving* health, safety and welfare issues that arise in the workplace.
3. To assist in the formulation, review and distribution (in appropriate languages) of health, safety and welfare *policies, practices* and *procedures*.
4. To consult on any *proposed changes* to health, safety and welfare policies or changes to workplace practices and procedures which may affect health, safety or welfare.
5. To review developments in *rehabilitating* employees who suffer work-related injuries.
6. To assist in the *return to work* of employees who have suffered from work-related injuries and the employment of workers who suffer from any form of disability.

Additional functions might include those shown in Box 7.3.

The number of health and safety committees should be kept to the minimum required to provide the necessary coverage of the workplace and work performed. There is no ideal number of committee members. The aim is to ensure that membership represents a cross-section of employees. Many organisations rotate committee membership every one or two years so that as many people as possible serve on them.

A number of things contribute to the effectiveness of safety committees:

- Regular committee meetings. Many organisations have found that once a month is suitable.
- Carefully prepared agendas for every meeting to ensure that discussions don't ramble or become confused.
- Thorough training in health and safety matters for committee members.
- Selecting members based on a genuine interest in health and safety matters.
- Encouraging a climate of openness and trust so that members feel free to express their opinions.
- The full support of senior management: having a management representative acting as chairperson, providing a comfortable, well furnished meeting room and secretarial assistance, and allowing members time off work to attend meetings and safety training seminars are ways that management can support health and safety committees.
- Providing the safety committee with any necessary information such as accident statistics so that they can base their recommendations on a full knowledge of the situation.

BOX 7.3

HEALTH AND SAFETY COMMITTEES: ADDITIONAL FUNCTIONS

- Reviewing the availability of resources for health, safety and welfare.
- Establishing a priority list of health and safety issues to be addressed.
- Developing and monitoring an injury-reporting system.
- Developing a purchasing policy for new plant, equipment or substances that addresses health, safety and welfare issues.

- Developing procedures to ensure compliance with new and existing regulations and approved codes of practice.
- Developing and monitoring methods for conducting regular safety inspections of the workplace.

Health and safety representatives

Legislation in some states provides for work groups to elect a health and safety representative to look after their interests on health, safety and welfare matters. Health and safety representatives usually focus on departmental or work area health and safety matters. They assist, for example, in investigating accidents and near misses, carry out hazard inspections, and may accompany government safety inspectors on inspections of their workplace.

Health and safety representatives are key players in consultation at workplace level. They should be your first point of contact in consulting with employees on health and safety issues. Employees can raise any major concerns they have over health and safety issues through these representatives who would bring them to the attention of the supervisor or appropriate manager. For minor issues, employees should consult directly with their supervisor.

Safety representatives are valuable allies for supervisors. Think of them as an extra pair of hands, ears and eyes to help you identify and control hazards. Consult them on any changes to the workplace that might affect the health, safety or welfare of the employees they represent.

HAZARD AND RISKS

'Risk: a measure of the likelihood and severity of potential injury or illness resulting from a hazard.'

There is a difference between a hazard and a risk. A **hazard** is something that, by its very nature, is likely to cause an accident or injury. A **risk** is the likelihood that it will do so. For instance, it is hazardous to cross a road—a passing vehicle might hit you. Before crossing a road, we should assess the risk of being hit. The risk would be higher at peak hour, in the dark, the more slowly we cross and/or the faster the traffic moves. The greater we assess the risk to be, the more necessary it is to take steps to minimise it. In order to minimise the risk to ourselves, we might only cross the road with the traffic lights, look carefully in both directions before crossing, wear light-coloured clothing after dark and cross at a brisk pace.

MAKING A SAFER WORKPLACE

Your main occupational health and safety obligation lies in identifying and controlling hazards. You should not only be aware of the hazards in your department but also of their

---

THE BIG PICTURE

Changes in the workforce resulting from structural changes in the workplace over the last 20 years (see Chapters 1 and 4) have resulted in fewer people employed in manufacturing and more in service industries. This is altering the pattern of injuries; for example, manual handling injuries are decreasing.

As new work patterns and types of jobs are becoming more commonplace, evidence is indicating that the newer categories of workers (part-time, teleworkers, contractors, etc.) are experiencing higher levels of workplace injury and accidents than core and full-time employees.

relative risks. Eliminate the hazards or, if you can't do that, minimise the risks they present.

Follow these three steps for making a safer workplace: (1) identify hazards, (2) assess their risks and (3) control them.

Step 1: Identify hazards

To identify hazards, study the accident, injury and incident statistics of your department. Look for patterns such as:

- *What types of accidents*, injuries and incidents occur most often? Is it mostly falls, back injuries, or cuts and abrasions, for example?
- *Where* do most occur? Does one location stand out among all the others for a higher rate of accidents, injuries or near misses?
- *When* do accidents, injuries or near misses occur? Is there a particular time of day—for example, the beginning or end of a shift—during which they tend to happen?
- *Who* is involved? Is it mostly new employees, old hands, people under training or some other identifiable group who seem to be most at risk?
- *What types of machinery*, processes or equipment are involved?
- *Which hazards*, if they did result in an accident or injury, would be most serious? How likely is each hazard to occur?

Answers to questions such as these can tell you a great deal about where to begin your accident prevention program. Use your own experience and consult with other employees and safety practitioners to identify hazards and assess their risk.

Have a look at the rules and regulations and your systems and procedures of work. Do these adequately take into consideration the health, safety and welfare of the workforce? If not, amend them. Conduct a job safety analysis and rewrite the safety instructions if necessary.

Box 7.4 summarises further tips to hazard identification.

Where are most hazards found?

We can find hazards anywhere, particularly:

- wherever people handle material, especially heavy or awkward-to-handle items, and where forklift trucks, cranes and hoists are involved. Manual lifting is a hazard and a common source of injury, especially to the back;
- around machinery, especially machines run by operators and those with unguarded or poorly guarded moving parts (e.g. pulleys, flywheels, belts, chains, gears);
- wherever people walk: on stairs, ladders, aisles and scaffolds;
- wherever people use hand tools: a variety of hand and eye injuries result from the improper use, poor maintenance or poor design of hand tools, particularly when personal protective equipment is not used; and
- wherever people use hazardous substances and chemicals.

Give special attention to the hazards in your work area. Once you know what they are, you can set priorities and concentrate your attention on those hazards with the highest risk.

Step 2: Assess risks

We know that smoking is a health hazard. The number of cigarettes a day people smoke and their family health history are measures of the risks of smoking to an individual. All hazards

BOX 7.4 IDENTIFYING WORKPLACE HAZARDS

- Investigate an accident, injury or incident ('near miss' event) immediately. Pinpoint the factors that contributed to it. Find out why policies, procedures and practices failed so that recurrence can be prevented.
- Conduct regular, well organised safety inspections or surveys of work areas and work practices to identify hazards. It is a good idea to use an inspection checklist to guide you.
- Objectively and regularly analyse procedures and systems of work to identify hazards you may have overlooked before.
- Examine the accident, injury and incident statistics for your department to identify hazardous tasks, equipment or processes.

- Pinpoint the most hazardous jobs and set priorities for correcting them.
- Respond to employees' concerns and questions on health and safety, whether they make them directly to you or through the health and safety representative. Act on the issues raised and provide prompt feedback on them. This will encourage employees to report hazards and become more safety conscious.
- Inspect new items for hazards (e.g. tools, chemicals, machines).
- Consult employees. This is one of the easiest and most effective ways to identify workplace hazards. Employees are usually well aware of what can go wrong and why.

have a degree of risk attached to them. It makes sense to concentrate on those hazards with the highest risk first.

Assess the risks of each hazard you identify. Consider these three factors:

1. *Severity.* How potentially *serious* would an accident caused by this hazard be? We would deal differently with the risk of a small cut and the risk of death.
2. *Frequency.* How *often* is a person exposed to the hazard? We would deal differently with a frequent, say daily or weekly, exposure than with an infrequent, say once a year, exposure.
3. *Probability.* How *likely* is it that an accident will result from the hazard? The higher the probability, the more urgency there is in eliminating or minimising the risk.

Based on your assessment, determine priorities for dealing with hazards, beginning with those with the highest risk.

Step 3: Control risks

As summarised in Box 7.2, there is a six-tiered prevention hierarchy to follow to control risks. The best is to *eliminate the hazard*. The last line of defence is *personal protection*. We call this the last line of defence because it is usually the least effective. Personal protective devices include hard hats, hair protection (hairnets), earplugs, earmuffs, hoods and shields, safety goggles and glasses, self-contained air-breathing apparatus and filter respirators, gloves, safety shoes and boots, aprons and overalls. The main drawback of personal safety devices is that they don't eliminate, reduce (provide a safer alternative or safer working practice) or segregate (through engineering) the hazard. Safety equipment is only a thin line of defence between the employee and the unsafe condition. This is why you should make every effort to eliminate, minimise or segregate the hazard that necessitates the use of such equipment.

The other drawback to personal safety devices is that they can be unsightly, restrictive or cumbersome to use. Employees often prefer not to use them, despite the dangers of not doing so. Nevertheless, it is your responsibility to ensure that employees use them if they are needed. People can become so familiar with a job that they become careless in their use of safety equipment, which further increases the risk of an accident. When it comes to safety, there is no excuse for lenient supervision.

Think of these possible actions to control risks as a series of preferred steps. As shown in Figure 7.5, first, try to eliminate the hazard. If this is not possible, reduce it by substitution

FIGURE 7.5   THE HIERARCHY OF RISK CONTROL

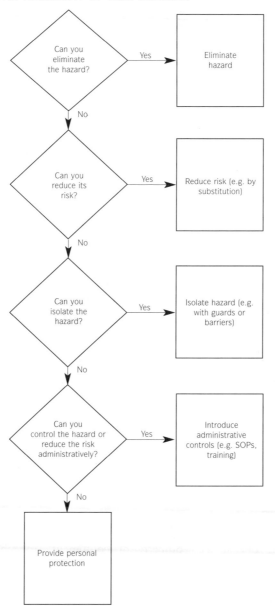

or isolation. If you can't do this, introduce administrative controls. Your last resort is personal protection.

Box 7.5 summarises the main steps you can take to control risks.

BOX 7.5

CONTROLLING RISKS

- Select and implement appropriate control measures in consultation with employees, engineers and health and safety specialists.
- Carry out preventive maintenance and corrective actions to maintain control of hazards.
- Develop safe working procedures for hazardous jobs and update them regularly.

- Ensure personal protective equipment is appropriate, maintained and used correctly.
- Provide job instruction, information and ongoing training so that employees always perform work safely.
- Supervise employees to ensure they always follow safe working procedures.

THE IMPORTANCE OF SAFETY

How would you feel if one of the people you were responsible for was seriously injured or killed? How would you like to be the one to take the bad news to the family? No supervisor wants this.

For this reason, legislation puts a definite moral obligation on employers to protect their employees. Whenever a personal injury occurs in your department, you could be held responsible, and even fined or jailed, if an investigation shows that the accident was foreseeable and could reasonably have been prevented.

In both offices and factories, there is a clear relationship between effective safety practices and efficient working practices. Preventing accidents reduces operating and production costs. Apart from the obvious costs, accidents also have hidden or indirect costs, such as lowered morale and lost time. Whether costs are direct or hidden, they all affect the cost and profit position of your department.

Accidents destroy efficiency, interfere with production and make your job harder. It is not just major accidents that cause trouble; a series of minor accidents can keep a workplace in a state of inefficiency and uncertainty. Accidents are symptoms that something is wrong in a department; a high accident rate is a sign of a lack of control over people, materials and processes that spells inefficient operations.

Suppose an employee is injured in an accident. Work is likely to be held up. Machinery or equipment may be damaged. Colleagues will be affected: there will be people rushing to assist and sympathetic onlookers, which means lost production. You will be called away from whatever you are doing, for minutes or maybe for hours. You may need to reorganise staff and production and find, and possibly train, a replacement worker to continue the job being done by the injured worker. You will probably need to make arrangements for the replacement or repair of damaged property or equipment. You must spend time investigating the cause of the accident and preparing an accident report.

Accidents cause delays and lower morale. A good safety record helps an organisation attract and retain good staff.

SUPERVISING FOR SAFETY

Safety doesn't happen by itself. You have to promote it constantly and consistently. How should you begin? First, set a good example yourself. The more safety-conscious you are, the more safety-conscious your work team is likely to be.

Focus on identifying and managing hazards to ensure a safe workplace. Consult employees for their ideas on how to improve health and safety. Their suggestions are likely to be good ones, since they are involved (often more than their supervisors) in the day-to-day operation of the machines and work processes.

Departmental hazard inspections are an indispensable part of hazard control and accident prevention. Work with employees, safety representatives and committee members to develop a checklist. Figure 7.6 shows how you could set out a safety inspection report, and Box 7.6 lists points to watch out for when conducting a hazard inspection. You can easily turn this into an inspection checklist.

'Inspection: an examination of a workplace and work activities to identify any hazards present and to check the effectiveness of existing controls.'

Use positive and constructive feedback to motivate employees to work safely. Carefully supervise each new employee to make sure your selection has been correct. Watch especially for any signs of unsafe work practices and correct them early, before they become a hard-to-break habit.

Participate in emergency drills for first aid, fire and evacuation. Provide sufficient training and information on safety rules, regulations, work systems and procedures. If people know what the safe method of working is and how important it is to work safely, there is a greater chance they will follow the safety procedures.

FIGURE 7.6   SAFETY INSPECTION REPORT

Date of inspection..
Department/section...
Inspector(s)..

Hazard found	Location	Person notified	Action taken	Date	Initials

POINTS TO LOOK FOR IN SAFETY INSPECTIONS AND HAZARD AUDITS

BOX 7.6

Tidiness and cleanliness
- Rubbish lying around
- Overflowing rubbish containers
- Debris from work not regularly cleaned up
- Loose paper, wood or packaging
- Inadequately cleaned washroom facilities
- Fire exits and fire-fighting equipment blocked by rubbish or clutter

Physical environment
- Aisles and working areas cluttered
- Inadequate distance between workers or machines
- Low ceilings or door jambs
- Uneven surfaces
- Unguarded lift shafts

Staircases, gangways and platforms
- Stairs loose or uneven
- No anti-slip treads
- Handrails loose or non-existent
- Platforms too narrow, no anti-slip surface
- No proper ladders to platforms
- Loose rungs or holding bolts
- No 'fall-back' protection on high ladders

Lighting
- Lighting inappropriate to task
- Wrong colour tint for work involved
- Poorly located
- Flickering fluorescent lights
- Shadow or glare
- Natural lighting not being fully utilised, dirty windows
- Electric light fittings dirty

Floors
- Oily or greasy
- Wet and slippery
- No provision for hosing down
- Inadequate drainage
- Non-slip finish?
- Sloping ramps with no handrails, or slippery surface

Dust and fumes
- Protection against dust and fumes?
- Extraction or ventilation systems?
- Warning notices?

Ventilation and air-conditioning
- Adequacy of natural ventilation: can windows be opened easily?
- Does air-conditioning work?

Storage areas
- Easy access?

- Racks and bins fixed solidly?
- Safe access to high shelves?
- Proper labelling of all contents?
- Warning signs for dangerous goods?

Electrical
- Frayed cords, exposed conductors
- Broken plugs
- Broken or cracked switch-boxes
- Unmarked, uncoloured push buttons and switches
- Metallic appliances properly earthed?

Piping (gas, water, high pressure, etc.)
- All pipes colour coded or labelled?
- Leaks or drips
- Dents
- Obvious corrosion
- Properly supported?
- Insulated or protected where necessary?

Boilers, heaters, vats, pressure vessels, etc.
- Properly certificated?
- Obvious mechanical deficiencies
- Flammable materials stored separately?

Asbestos
- Loose or flaking insulation on pipes, etc.

Machine guarding
- Dangerous or moving parts accessible
- Shaft ends, pulleys, vee belts, crushing points, gears, etc. covered?
- Warning signs?

Fire extinguishers
- Action in case of fire: clear and visible notices?
- All extinguishers currently tested and tagged as OK?
- Extinguishers properly fixed?
- Easily accessible, areas not blocked?
- Position properly signed?
- Proper type for hazard?
- Direct phone dial-out after hours?

Flammable materials and dangerous goods
- Storage certificated under *Dangerous Goods Act*?
- Quantities not exceeded?
- Provision to prevent spillage?
- All containers labelled correctly and clearly?
- Warning signs, hazardous accident procedures displayed?

Continued . . .

Chemical storage
- Safe storage (i.e. freedom from heat and moisture)?
- Proper separation?
- Ease of access?
- Material safety data sheets (MSDS)?
- Decontamination materials as required?
- First aid materials?

Emergency exits
- Clearly signed?
- Unobstructed?

First aid
- Adequate number of kits and contents?
- Clear identification?
- Easily accessible: not locked, or locked away?
- Rest area with cot, basin and hot and cold water?

Work posture
- Correct manual handling technique?
- Obvious poor posture and work heights, either standing or sitting
- Seats, stools, work benches obviously not suited to worker
- Over-reaching required

Tanks, pits and trenches
- Free of noxious liquids and fumes?
- Adequate free-flowing or forced ventilation?
- Safety ropes and ladders?
- Cave-in protection?
- Workmate 'standing by outside' procedure?
- Warning signs?

Finally, constantly follow up to see that safety procedures and safe work practices are being followed. As discussed in Chapter 5, it is not enough just to make a plan—you must also follow up to see that it is working effectively.

HOW GOOD HOUSEKEEPING HELPS

Housekeeping—the standard of cleanliness and tidiness of a workplace, is a reliable indicator of how well supervised and how safe the workplace is. Many workplace accidents and injuries result from poor housekeeping—fires start in piles of rubbish or oily clothing, for example. Cluttered aisles, stairs and work areas invite accidents and are also fire hazards.

Good housekeeping means keeping the workplace clean, tidy and well lit. This includes floors, machines, passageways, windows, lights and reflectors. Anything else to do with the work environment, such as clean air, temperature and noise, can also be considered a target for housekeeping. Creating and maintaining a clean, safe working environment is a good way to boost morale as well as reduce accidents.

WHAT CAUSES AN ACCIDENT?

Accidents don't happen by themselves. They are not 'acts of God' or bad luck. All accidents are caused. At the root of every accident is a failure in a system of work, a machine or a piece of equipment.

FROM THEORY TO PRACTICE

Supervisors who suspect that an employee is under the influence of drugs or alcohol and do not take steps to protect them could be prosecuted. Do you know the signs of a problem and where to turn for help?

This is why you should treat all accidents and near misses seriously and investigate them, whether or not injury results. When you have determined the chain of events that led to the accident or near miss, take steps to eliminate or minimise the hazards, acts or omissions that contributed to it. The most common contributing factors to accidents are:

- faulty planning of work processes;
- faulty work practices;
- poor housekeeping;
- poor machinery and equipment maintenance;
- inadequate training;
- inadequate supervision;
- personal factors such as stress, error or inappropriate behaviour; and
- miscellaneous conditions such as weather (e.g. excessive heat) or time of day (e.g. at the end of a shift).

Systems failure or *poorly designed work systems* lie at the bottom of 80%–90% of accidents. This includes technical, mechanical or other physical causes, such as defective parts, unguarded machinery or worn-out hand tools. Supervisors and employees should regularly monitor the condition of such items to identify defects and take prompt corrective action. Continually monitor systems, methods and procedures of work, and seek ideas for improving them through consultation.

Human error is a major factor in only 10%–20% of accidents; after all, people do not injure themselves intentionally. Where human error has occurred, there should, in most cases, be no attachment of blame. An error is merely an act that is inappropriate. Human error includes unsafe or inappropriate behaviour by an employee such as absent-mindedness, tiredness, forgetfulness or ignorance of risk. These can usually be traced back to inadequate training and/or supervision.

If an accident occurs in your department, learn from it. Collect accident and incident information and present it in a useable way.

Are some employees accident-prone?

Some people do have more accidents than others and are sometimes labelled 'accident-prone'. This does nothing to improve employee health, safety and welfare. A person's poor safety performance is usually a symptom of a system failure which we can take steps to correct. Box 7.7 summarises what might place so-called 'accident-prone' employees at risk and what might contribute to their level of risk.

As you can see, these problems are not the employee's fault. Good supervisors place employees in jobs that suit them, and train and supervise them correctly. They ensure that employees know and follow safe and efficient working methods, that carelessness is not common or seen as acceptable practice and that they use plant and equipment properly. Good supervisors manage hazards appropriately.

An employee who does not respond to training and correction is more liable to injury than the average worker. You should place such employees in jobs where their efforts can be effectively and safely used. Placing them under hazardous conditions is a menace to themselves and to others. It is also in contravention of the health and safety legislation. If an employee continually disregards safe working procedures, you should take disciplinary action.

BOX 7.7

LEVEL OF EMPLOYEE RISK AND POSSIBLE CAUSES

Cause of accident	*Contributing factors*
■ Poor sight, poor hearing or lack of stamina	Poor job placement
■ Dislike for the job or of the supervisor	Poor job placement; poor supervision
■ A level of intelligence too low for the job they are required to do	Poor job placement; poor training or supervision
■ Insufficient manual skills to perform the job the way it should be done	Poor job placement; poor training; poor supervision
■ Poor use of plant and equipment	Poor training; poor supervision
■ Existence of hazards	Unsafe work systems; poor supervision
■ Carelessness	Poor training; poor supervision
■ Failure to follow safe work practices	Poor training; poor supervision
■ Stress, fatigue	Poor supervision; poor work systems allowing for long or double shifts

---

Stress is an interesting factor: there is a growing body of evidence showing that people under stress have increased vulnerability to injury. Lack of sleep, worry about personal matters, grief, extremes of temperature, poorly placed machinery controls or poorly angled chairs, boredom, frustration, noise, poor lighting, monotony and poor supervision can all cause employees stress.

Blaming accidents on employees is clearly no answer.

WHAT TO DO IF AN ACCIDENT OCCURS

The supervisor concerned and others involved in health and safety matters, such as the safety officer or health and safety representative, should report and investigate every accident and incident as soon as possible after they occur. Reconstruct the chain of events leading up

---

THE **BIG** PICTURE

According to the Australian Workplace Industrial Relations Survey, 1995, stress is the second most common cause of injury or illness in Australia (after dislocations, sprains and strains) and the major form of injury for professionals, managers and white-collar workers.

With its varied and often hidden symptoms (depression, cynicism, loss of concentration, excessive distrust, memory loss, mood change, headaches, tiredness, etc.) it can be difficult to spot in the workplace. One obvious indicator is increased absenteeism. Getting to know your staff will make it easier to identify and spot the stress symptoms.

Employers have a duty to provide a safe and healthy work environment and conditions that cause stress not only lower productivity but may also breach an employer's duty of care.

to it. Which can you do something about? Which can you ensure never happen again? When deciding which factors are the primary causes of accidents or near misses, make sure you select those you really can do something about.

It is important to investigate near misses (incidents that do not result in injury or damage to property) as well as accidents. There are nearly always several 'near misses' leading up to an accident involving injury. We need to catch them before this happens (see Figure 7.7).

The object of the investigation is:
• to find the facts, particularly which system failure led to the accident;
• to analyse all the circumstances involved; and
• to select remedies to eliminate or reduce the hazard, or, if this is not possible, to reduce and manage the risk it presents.

Accident investigations include interviewing any witness to the accident and the person involved in order to determine the factors that contributed to it. Carry out these interviews in a friendly, informal atmosphere; they are not cross-examinations. Your aim is to identify why policies and procedures failed so that action can be taken to prevent another accident.

Investigations should take place where the accident occurred. Leave everything exactly as it was when the accident happened, especially in the case of serious injury. If necessary, take steps to prevent further injury to persons or damage to equipment. In most cases, serious injury will need to be reported to the relevant government body for possible investigation by a factory inspector. An internal report should also be filed.

FIGURE 7.7 TYPES OF ACCIDENTS

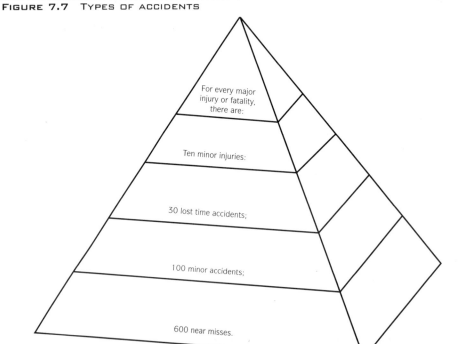

For every major injury or fatality, there are:

Ten minor injuries:

30 lost time accidents;

100 minor accidents;

600 near misses.

FROM THEORY TO PRACTICE

Use the critical incident technique to catch near misses and prevent them from becoming serious injuries:

1. Ask employees to recall how many incidents with potential for serious injury they have been aware of over a certain period, say six months. (All statements will be kept confidential.) These are often not reported due to peer pressure, embarrassment at admitting a mistake, not wanting to spoil a good safety record, fear of punishment, the significance may not be realised, complacency, etc.

2. Use the information you gather to develop specifically targeted programs to manage the hazards uncovered.

After an accident, it is important to debrief staff about what occurred and what is happening to the injured person. Explain what workplace arrangements and adjustments are being made, and what corrective action is being taken to ensure a similar accident does not occur.

In the case of minor accidents, the injured person should report to the first aid centre, where they will receive treatment and be provided with a report form. They take this form to the supervisor who should complete it after discussing the accident with the victim and conducting any necessary investigations. The form normally then goes to the safety officer or other nominated person who may decide to investigate further, or simply record and file it for statistical purposes.

Employees should report all near misses to the supervisor. It is a good idea to have a special form for this for the supervisor to complete and give to the safety officer or other nominated person.

WRITING SAFETY INSTRUCTIONS

Issuing written safety instructions for such procedures as handling hazardous materials, operating machines or caring for tools is an important safety measure. Never use them as the only means of reducing hazards but as a useful supplement to safe working methods.

If you are responsible for writing safety instructions, follow these three steps:

1. *Break the job down* into its component parts. Follow the **job breakdown** method shown in Chapter 16, using the stage and key point headings.
2. *Carry out a safety analysis,* determining the possible hazards and safety requirements of each stage.
3. *List the ways of carrying out the job safely and any precautions,* which should be shown as key points on your job breakdown.

You will need to actually perform the job—as many times as is necessary to ensure that you don't overlook anything. You might find that opening or closing a guard is awkward and could cause back strain. You might discover that moving something from one place to another is done at an inconvenient height or breaks an otherwise smooth sequence of movements. Or you might find that a word-processing keyboard is positioned in such a way as to cause eyestrain or occupational overuse syndrome. Don't forget to examine any drawings, tools, work permits and other factors associated with the job when you conduct a job safety analysis.

Specify in your safety analysis any special skills or qualifications a job-holder would need. For example, you might find that an employee needs special training or certain manual skills or dexterity, or special coordination, to perform a job safely. Incorporate these requirements into the personnel specification, discussed in Chapter 15; a poorly selected or unsuitably placed employee is more likely to be injured than one whose capacities match the job requirements.

If a job is particularly hazardous, you could list any necessary safety precautions separately. Figure 7.8 shows a typical form for preparing safety instructions. Alternatively, you could use the standard form outlined in Chapter 16 and mark any special safety instructions or precautions under key points in red, or draw special attention to them in some other way.

As you can see, preparing safety instructions is neither difficult nor time-consuming. The real challenge lies in keeping them up to date and ensuring that people follow them at all times. One way to do this is to involve the people who must follow the instructions in writing them. You can do this through the safety committee or some other less formal method of consultation.

EMPLOYEE WELFARE

Health and safety legislation places considerable emphasis on occupational health and welfare. Employers must not only provide a safe working environment; they must also ensure that it is, as far as possible, also a healthy one. This includes providing a working

FIGURE 7.8   SAFETY INSTRUCTION SHEET

| Job. . . . . | | | |
| Prepared by . . . . Approved . . . . Date. . . . . | | | |
Stage	Key point	Hazards	Safety precautions

environment that is free from stress. Stress may result from lack of privacy, or noise that disrupts concentration, in addition to the many other causes mentioned in the section on accident proneness. Workplaces should also be well lit and ventilated, and as attractive as is practical.

Providing amenities and facilities not directly related to safety is also part of employee welfare. This includes, for example, ensuring that there are enough toilets, drinking water, hot water facilities and space for eating meals.

One of the main spin-offs of employee health and welfare has been the issue of smoking in the workplace and the effects of passive smoking. Most Australian employers have declared their offices and plants 'smoke-free zones' so as not to place employees' long-term health and welfare at risk. New Zealand passed the *Smoke Free Environment Act* in 1990, requiring every employer, in consultation with employees, to prepare a written policy on smoking in the workplace. Employees who do not smoke, or who do not wish to smoke at work, must, as far as is reasonably practical, be protected from smoke in their workplace.

WORKERS' REHABILITATION AND COMPENSATION

Employers are required to insure their workers against occupational injury. The intent is no-fault compensation and the rehabilitation of injured workers. The aim is to get people back into the workforce as quickly as possible after suffering an industrial injury. If this is not possible, lump-sum compensation payments can be made; however, because the emphasis is on rehabilitation, these payments tend to be made only for death or disablement.

Insurance premiums are calculated according to two factors: the industry category of the employer and the individual employer's safety record. The more dangerous the industry, the higher the premiums. The better the organisation's safety record, the lower its premiums.

Workers' rehabilitation and compensation is designed to cover income lost as the result of an industrial accident or disease, the associated medical expenses and retraining costs if the injured person must establish a new career as a result of the accident.

WHERE TO GO FOR MORE INFORMATION

Various state and Commonwealth government publications deal with issues of safety, covering areas such as accident prevention, designing for safety, fire safety, noise and hearing conservation and office design.

You can obtain copies of the relevant Acts through your state government printer, which also produces a variety of other explanatory booklets on safety matters. The Australian Standards Association prepares many standards in the area of safety, including AS1885, which deals with work injury statistics. The National Occupational Health and Safety

THE **BIG** PICTURE

Violence in the workplace, either assault or threats, is an emerging concern. It can pose a physical or a psychological hazard. Employers are responsible for managing this hazard, too.

Commission, the National Safety Council, employer associations, unions and state Occupational Health and Safety Agencies are other excellent sources of information.

	True	False
1. If employees took more care, there would be fewer accidents.	☐	☐
2. Poor safety habits cause accidents, death, lower efficiency and higher costs.	☐	☐
3. A variety of legislation including Acts, regulations and codes of practice aims at ensuring workplace health, safety and welfare. It emphasises the role of consultation and hazard management in preventing accidents and provides penalties for failure to act within the law.	☐	☐
4. Employers, supervisors and employees all have responsibilities under the legislation.	☐	☐
5. Organisations only need to have employee consultation mechanisms if they feel it is necessary.	☐	☐
6. All supervisors should stress the importance of accident prevention.	☐	☐
7. Accident-prone employees should be fired for their own safety.	☐	☐
8. Accidents can occur anywhere, although they tend to be concentrated wherever people walk, lift or handle material, or where there are tools or machinery.	☐	☐
9. Poor housekeeping contributes to many accidents.	☐	☐
10. An accident needs to be investigated only if it results in an injury.	☐	☐
11. Near misses don't need to be reported to supervisors if no one was hurt or nothing was damaged.	☐	☐
12. We should concentrate first on eliminating or reducing hazards with a high risk of occurrence.	☐	☐
13. Because it's often easiest to provide, supervisors should issue personal protection whenever a hazard is identified.	☐	☐
14. Safety instructions should specify the safe and correct procedure to use when carrying out a job and list any special hazards or risks, as well as any special qualifications the job-holder should have.	☐	☐
15. We are all held responsible for not doing anything that could harm others or ourselves.	☐	☐
16. Organisations with poor safety records pay through higher insurance premiums.	☐	☐

APPLY YOUR KNOWLEDGE

1. Why is safety an important consideration in every supervisor's job?
2. In what ways does safety 'pay'?
3. Compare and contrast the health, safety and welfare responsibilities of the senior management team and supervisors.
4. What is the function of safety committees and who should serve on them?
5. Contrast the role of the health and safety officer with the health and safety representative.
6. Give an example to illustrate the difference between a hazard and a risk. Describe how you would assess the risk in the example you give.
7. How can supervisors go about finding out the main cause of accidents in their area? Explain what supervisors should do once they have identified a hazard or group of hazards in their work area.
8. Why are personal protection devices the last alternative in safety programs?
9. What are some specific things supervisors can do to manage hazards and prevent accidents?
10. Are some people accident-prone? What should supervisors do about people who seem to have more accidents than others?
11. Describe the procedure for investigating accidents.
12. How can the work environment affect people's health and welfare?

DEVELOP YOUR SKILLS

Individual activities

1. Interview someone who has experienced, or been associated with, a workplace accident. Find out how the accident affected them, their family and their employer. What factors led to the accident? What steps were taken to prevent such an accident happening again? Prepare a report to share with your class.
2. Interview a safety officer, safety committee member or safety representative. What are their duties in relation to health, safety and welfare matters? What support does their organisation provide them in carrying out their duties? What are their main challenges?
3. Gather some health, safety and welfare policies from organisations in your area. Analyse them to find their main objectives and how they plan to achieve them. The public relations or human resources departments of organisations can provide you with this information.
4. Join a supervisor, safety officer or safety committee in a hazard inspection. Learn as much as you can about the potential hazards in the organisation and how they can be spotted. How is the inspection documented and acted on?
5. Interview a supervisor to find out the steps their organisation takes to prevent accidents and how they see their own role in accident prevention.
6. Write a safety instruction for changing a bicycle tyre or lighting a campfire.
7. Obtain information on your state's workers' compensation and rehabilitation program and requirements, and prepare a short report summarising your findings.

Group activities

1. Form into study groups to gather information on federal and state legislation, including Acts, regulations, codes of practice and standards, assigning one area to each person. Summarise your findings and compare them with other study groups in your class.

2. Using the prevention hierarchy in Box 7.2 and the hierarchy of risk control in Figure 7.5, form into small groups and develop plans to deal with the following hazards:
   - climbing a ladder to change a light bulb located in a wall fixture 4 metres from the floor;
   - preparing a metal cleansing solution using caustic chemical ingredients;
   - stacking shelves with products requiring repetitive lifting and bending;
   - driving a vehicle whose brakes fail to work intermittently;
   - moving items of work, some of which have sharp edges that could cut your hands;
   - storing turpentine and other flammable solvents in a shed;
   - accepting delivery and storing away heavy and awkward packages containing flour and other kitchen supplies in a restaurant;
   - using a bread slicer that operates without the guard.

3. In small groups, discuss the respective positions of Kathy and John in the vignette at the beginning of this chapter. What can Kathy do to encourage John to cooperate?

CASE STUDY 7.1

Dangerous Videos

Glenda Marina supervises several video rental outlets in the metropolitan area. Each outlet has a small core of permanent staff and several casual part-time staff who come in as required. In general, the employees of the outlets are friendly, responsible and work well together. She personally trains each one in their duties and pays special attention to ensuring they understand and apply the safety procedures included as part of the standard operating procedures.

While safety isn't a major issue, it nevertheless remains in the back of Glenda's mind as something to be aware of. She doesn't want anyone getting hurt since, apart from the personal consequences, she has her staffing levels finely tuned and really can't afford people to be off work due to injuries.

Glenda's accident, near miss and injury statistics are similar to other groups of stores in the chain. The company benchmarks LTIFR (lost time injury frequency rate) figures for each group of stores, using Pareto charts. The main cause of injury is back injury due to incorrect lifting; this is most likely to occur when boxes of newly released videos arrive and the staff off-load them into the back room before sorting and coding them and placing them on the shelves. The second biggest cause of injury is strain resulting from staff stocking the highest and lowest shelves. The third main cause of injury results from falls due to overbalancing when putting up display material such as posters.

Glenda's group of employees normally benchmark in the best 50% of stores in the chain, and, as the figures are reasonably low anyway, she is content.

Until last quarter's figures came out, that is. These showed a marked increase in falls in all but one of the stores she was responsible for. The resulting lost time due to injuries had also weakened her labour utilisation performance figures for the period. Her own personal efficiency, she felt, had decreased, too, because dealing with the injuries diverted her attention from other important matters. Clearly, she needs to manage this outbreak of accidents before it becomes an epidemic.

Questions

1 How seriously do you believe the company takes health and safety? What is your evidence?
2 Outline what Glenda's next steps should be.
3 If Glenda decides that the cause of the increase in injuries is employees not following safety procedures, especially when putting up display materials, how could she ensure that employees followed safety procedures? What contingency plans would you advise regarding employees who do not follow safety procedures after being made aware of their importance?
4 Since Glenda supervises several stores and cannot be everywhere at once, how could she go about monitoring employees' observance of safety procedures?

CASE STUDY 7.2

Brown (Estate Of) Versus Ace Building Contractors

Ace Building Contractors are a small, owner-operated building company that works mostly on building and remodelling private homes in its township. A few permanent and part-time employees work in the office and are responsible for billing and materials ordering. A few casual labourers are also employed as needed. Ace subcontracts specific projects to self-employed tradespeople such as bricklayers, painters, electricians, plumbers and carpenters. Because it is reasonably efficient in the way it manages and supervises its building projects, and because it tries to employ only 'tried and tested' tradespeople, Ace has a sound reputation in the community for good quality work at reasonable prices.

Last spring, it sent a crew to erect the frame for a new home in Warraringa. A building inspector paid an on-site visit and found a ladder in a bad state of repair. It had a broken rung and a lean that could easily (and often did) lead to the ladder slipping sideways. The site supervisor immediately cut off the rung and directed Al Browne to throw the ladder on the rubbish heap for later removal.

One month later, Browne and a co-worker were weatherboarding the house using a ladder. The co-worker was holding the base while Browne was up the ladder nailing the boards. Browne ran out of nails and sent his co-worker to get more. Meanwhile, he re-climbed the ladder to check some previous work. As he was doing this, the ladder fell sideways, bringing Browne down onto the cement driveway. Browne was fatally injured.

Subsequent investigation revealed that Browne was not wearing a hardhat or safety boots. The supervisor stated that he had 'nagged Browne for ages' about wearing safety gear but had recently given up. It was also discovered that the ladder used that day was the one found by the inspector to be unsafe. The only repair was a jammed wooden rung used to replace the one that had been cut off.

Browne's co-worker stated that there was no other ladder available on the site and they were keen to get the job completed to meet their contractual obligations with the homeowner.

Questions

1   What could the site supervisor have done to prevent the accident?
2   What could Ace Building Contractors have done to prevent the accident?
3   Is Ace liable for prosecution?
4   Is the supervisor liable for prosecution?

Answers to Rapid Review questions

1. F   2. T   3. T   4. T   5. F   6. T   7. F   8. T   9. T 10. F   11. F   12. T   13. F
14. T   15. T   16. T

PART II

MANAGING OPERATIONS

In Part I we examined workplace practice. We studied the changing role of the supervisor and looked at the core skills of verbal, non-verbal and written communication. We examined personal development from a supervisor's perspective and looked at the personal skills that supervisors need to be successful. We saw how organisation structures are changing in dramatic ways and suggested that they will continue to change. We also examined how to plan and monitor for goal achievement, how to lead and attend meetings and how to develop and maintain a healthy and safe working environment.

In Part II we turn to the specific skills you will need to manage operations. These fall into the areas of building performance and productivity, total quality management, managing innovation, introducing and facilitating change,

managing customer service, solving problems and making decisions, and contributing to a workplace learning environment.

You can learn these aspects of supervision but you must also apply them. You may know in theory, for example, the seven steps needed to solve a problem, but you must follow them if they are to be of any use to you.

Applying any new skill can be difficult and even frustrating at first. But practice makes progress. Look at it this way: if an expert showed you how to hold a tennis racket or a golf club in a way that would make your strokes more effective, the new way would at first feel awkward to you. Perhaps the first few times you tried the new grip, it might not work as well as the old way because you would not be used to it. But if you persevered you would eventually find that the new grip did indeed improve your game. The same principle applies to the skills covered here. Try them out, work with them until you become familiar with them, and you will find that you become a more effective supervisor.

CHAPTER 8

BUILDING PERFORMANCE AND PRODUCTIVITY

Paulene's predicament

Paulene was in a quandary. Since taking on the job of supervising the administration function of a large car dealership 18 months ago, things had hummed along nicely. Between them, she and her small staff of three people were able to juggle the work of accounts payable and receivable, correspondence, customer liaison, bookkeeping, and so on, quite nicely.

Then Debra announced she was pregnant and might not be returning after maternity leave, but would like to keep her options open. Management decided not to replace her, which meant that, for at least six months and perhaps more, administration would be 25% understaffed. What could they do to make sure the work was still completed properly and on time without overstretching those who were left?

What a predicament! Although Paulene didn't run what she would call a 'super-tight ship', she didn't think there was 25% slack in their working days! She decided to convene a staff meeting to look at the jobs that needed to be done and see if they could streamline the systems of doing them. Perhaps some tasks were unnecessary and others could be done more easily. She thought they should have a look at the way the jobs were designed, too. She wondered if she would be able to make a case for purchasing some timesaving accounting software?

Effective supervisors know how to help people perform at their peak. They see supervising as an *enabling* function, one that makes it possible for people to do the best job they are capable of. In this chapter, you will discover how to identify and remove barriers to poor performance and also how to help people find ways to do the good job that most of them want to do.

- Do you know the five essential elements, or keys, to quality productivity and performance and how to use them to build better results?
- Do you know how to make sure people know what to do? Can you help people identify their Key Result Areas and write SMARTT targets for people to achieve?
- Can you apply the hot stove principle to ensure ground rules are followed?
- Do you know how to make sure people know how to and want to do their jobs well?
- Do you know how job design and job placement affect a person's motivation and ability to do their job well?
- Can you explain why a person may not do their job well even if they know what to do and how to do it?
- Do you know how leadership affects productivity? Can you explain the six things effective leaders do to build performance and productivity?

HELPING PEOPLE ACHIEVE: FIVE KEYS TO BUILDING PERFORMANCE AND PRODUCTIVITY

To build performance and productivity and help people perform at their peak, supervisors need to know how to remove barriers to poor performance and how to help people find ways to do the good job that most of them want to do. This means they need to make sure:

1. people know *what to* do;
2. they *want to* do it;
3. they know *how to* do it;
4. they have a *chance to* do it; and
5. they have effective *leadership* and guidance.

Together, these make up the five essential elements, or keys, to quality productivity and performance. In this chapter, we see how you can use them to build better results in your department.

Think of these five elements—*what to, want to, how to, chance to* and *led to*—as the five 'keys' to unlocking quality performance, productivity and goal achievement. Supervisors need to manage them. They don't happen by chance. If you manage each of them well, you will unlock people's ability to perform well, increasing their productivity and job satisfaction, and enhancing their ability to achieve goals and satisfy customers.

KEY 1: WHAT TO

People need to know clearly and specifically what is expected of them. This is called *role clarity*. Clear roles and responsibilities give people something to focus on and strive towards; without them, they're working in the dark. They encourage people to monitor their own performance which in turn encourages individual accountability for performance and results.

As Figure 8.1 shows, there are three aspects of the *what to* key: the framework made up of *job purpose, key result areas* and clear *targets*; non-task goals; and the *hot stove principle*.

● ●

FIGURE 8.1   THE THREE ASPECTS OF THE WHAT TO KEY

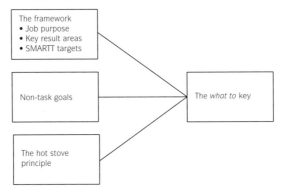

The framework: job purpose, key result areas and targets

Some supervisors make the mistake of giving employees a series of tasks to do without explaining why the tasks are important or placing them in the context of the wider work and objectives of the department and organisation. Tasks in isolation can easily overwhelm people and seem meaningless, destroying motivation.

The way to prevent this is to give tasks a framework. Grouping them into key result areas (KRAs) aimed at achieving an overall job purpose provides such a framework.

Job purpose

A clear **job purpose** puts a person's role and responsibilities into context. It acts as a personal job vision or mission statement. Box 8.1 shows some typical job purpose statements.

Job purpose statements like those shown in Box 8.1 are motivating and provide overall guidance in how people should do their jobs. They show what is important and why the job exists. You may have heard the saying

'If a job is worth doing, it's worth doing well.'

With time at a premium in most organisations, perhaps we should think of it this way instead:

'ONLY a job worth doing is worth doing well.'

A job purpose statement makes sure job-holders know why their jobs are worth doing and what to focus their efforts on.

Key result areas

Key result areas (KRAs) describe the main areas of accountability and responsibility of a job. For example, an assembly line supervisor might have the following KRAs:
- output: quality, quantity, cost, timeliness
- machine utilisation

- staffing
- leadership
- health and safety
- industrial relations
- continuous improvement

A retail store supervisor might have the following KRAs:
- housekeeping
- stock
- customer relations
- leadership
- continuous improvement
- sales budgets
- administration

Notice that each KRA is written using one to five words and contains no verbs. This is because they name *areas* of accountability. Most jobs have five to nine key result areas. There is no 'pecking order'—each KRA is as important as every other KRA. If someone fails to achieve results in any one key area, the entire job suffers.

To achieve results in each KRA, we need to *do* things—tasks. Carrying out a series of tasks correctly achieves results in a key result area. This is how KRAs put tasks into context. Each task we do should be contributing in some way to achieving results in a KRA. If it isn't—why are we doing it? (See also Chapter 3.)

BOX 8.1 JOB PURPOSE

Training officer	To design and deliver training products that develop and extend the skills of employees in my organisation, so that they and the organisation succeed and prosper.
Retail store supervisor	To achieve or exceed sales and other targets in a way that delights my customers, my staff and myself.
Retail sales assistant	To present myself and the store professionally and advise and interact with customers in a way that will make them want to return repeatedly to purchase from us.
Assembly line supervisor	To help my team produce quality product within time and cost budgets so that the organisation's reputation is enhanced in the marketplace both as a quality producer and a quality employer.
Assembly line operator	To work with the team to produce the best possible product within the company's cost and other requirements so that I feel proud of my contribution and customers are glad they bought from us.

Targets

Once we know a job's overall purpose and key areas of responsibility, it's time to set **targets**. These indicate how well we're achieving what we've set out to do. They help us monitor performance—our own and employees'.

Each key result area should have two (or sometimes three) targets, often called **key performance indicators (KPIs)**, **measures of performance (MOPs)** or measures of success (MOSs), which can be used to track performance. (Tasks should have targets, too. We'll revisit this in Chapter 16.)

Choose targets that measure the most important or critical aspects of the KRA and in some way contribute to the overall goals of the department. Make sure each target is SMARTT:

Specific and concise
Measurable
Achievable
Related to the overall department and enterprise goals
Time-framed
Trackable, or easily monitored.

For example, a poor target would be to 'reduce defects in your work to a minimum'. This target is not clear, specific or time-framed. Neither the employee nor the supervisor would ever know whether it had been reached. For example, consider the following:

• An employee had ten parts rejected because of cosmetic flaws.
• Twelve parts were rejected because they would not function properly.
• The total number of rejects was reduced from 80 to 50.

In which case did the employee reach the target? There is no way of knowing the answer because the target is not specific or measurable. It doesn't tell you what a 'minimum' number of defects is and by when this minimum number should be reached.

If, instead, the objective is for the employee to 'increase the number of parts passed for finish quality to 99% and the number of functional units produced to 92% of daily output by the end of the current quarter', then you would know whether the performance target had been reached. Targets like these are also easily tracked, or monitored, which means that corrective action can be taken quickly.

People don't want to wait for their supervisor to tell them whether they are doing a good job; they want to monitor their performance themselves. 'Trackable' targets offer a measuring stick that lets job-holders judge for themselves how well they are doing. The more frequently they can measure their performance, the more their motivation and productivity are likely to increase, provided the targets are achievable (yet challenging).

If a task is too easy, people won't put much effort into it, yet if it is too hard and employees don't believe they can do it, they won't put in much effort either. Targets should also contribute to overall organisational, departmental or job goals.

Ideally, targets should be established jointly with the employee. Together, you identify, agree on and write down what must be accomplished, by when and to what standards. Make sure they relate only to those parts of a job that are actually under the employee's control.

Targets tend to fall into five main areas:
1. cost
2. quality
3. quantity
4. time
5. safety

Box 8.2 outlines the 'language' of targets. Use these categories to help you write targets with your team members. Remember to use positive terms—focus on what you *do* want, not what you *don't* want.

Not all job duties fit easily into the categories shown in Figure 8.2. Such concepts as 'leadership' or 'dependability' are difficult to specify and measure. For areas like these, you will need to use your imagination and knowledge of the job and its requirements to determine targets. If, for example, one of the areas in which you are appraising a leading hand is leadership, you may choose to monitor such factors as how well a successor is developed, how well and how quickly new employees are inducted into the department and trained or how well they work as a team. For dependability, you may look at whether a person gets the facts before leaping in with both feet, whether reports and paperwork are accurate and punctual or whether outstanding items are followed up and completed.

The framework of job purpose, key result areas and SMARTT targets helps to build performance and productivity because people know precisely what they need to achieve, when they need to achieve it by, and why it's important. They can monitor their own performance and will be motivated to find ways to continually improve it if the other keys are in place.

BOX **8.2** **TERMS FOR TARGETS**

Term	Example
Percentages	x% pass rate; y% downtime, 90% of customers greeted within 12 seconds.
Frequency of occurrence	Stocks to be checked every three months; mail to be sorted twice daily.
Averages	x per week, per day, per hour; x documents to be prepared daily; y items to be completed hourly, 80% of telephone queries to be answered successfully by first point of contact.
Time limits	All accidents or near misses to be investigated within three working days; all calls to be answered within four rings.
Absolute obligations	All linespeople to wear approved safety gear when climbing telephone poles; all site personnel and visitors to wear hard hats and safety boots at all times; all assembly line workers to wear safety masks inside the designated area.

Non-task goals

Many jobs depend on non-task goals, too, if they are to be performed effectively. Examples of non-task goals are:

- Be cooperative, friendly and helpful to colleagues and customers.
- Try to finish one task before moving on to another.
- Make our customers glad they are dealing with us.
- Look for better ways of doing things.

These are often left as unstated group norms which employees must infer, or 'pick up' for themselves. It's better to make them explicit, though, so you can be sure people understand them and work towards achieving them.

The hot stove principle

The third and final aspect of the *what to* key is the **hot stove principle**. These are 'bottom-line' rules and regulations that apply to everyone. They often involve safety, standard operating procedures, housekeeping standards, working with others and customer service.

Just as we can see from a distance whether a stove is hot and will burn us if we touch it, everyone should know your bottom-line rules *in advance* and know that they will be 'burned' if they break or bend them. Just as when we touch a hot stove we are burned straight away, the consequence of breaking or bending a bottom-line rule should be *immediate:* if someone breaks a 'hot stove' rule, discuss it with them straight away (and in private) to make sure it doesn't happen again. A hot stove is *impartial:* everyone who touches it is burned. Don't play 'favourites'—bottom-line rules apply to everyone. Hot stoves are *consistent:* people are always burned if they touch one. The hot stove rules in your department need to apply to everyone, all the time. (See Figure 8.2.)

FIGURE 8.2 THE HOT STOVE PRINCIPLE OF BOTTOM-LINE RULES

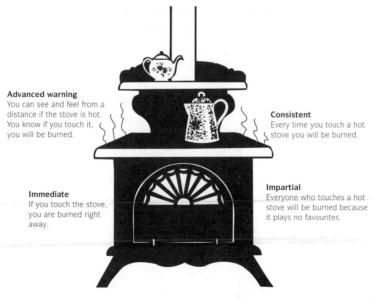

Advanced warning
You can see and feel from a distance if the stove is hot. You know if you touch it, you will be burned.

Consistent
Every time you touch a hot stove you will be burned.

Immediate
If you touch the stove, you are burned right away.

Impartial
Everyone who touches a hot stove will be burned because it plays no favourites.

FROM THEORY TO PRACTICE

Immediate	John, I see you aren't wearing your hairnet.
Advance warning/	You know you need to wear it when you're working with
Consistent	food and I've pointed it out to you before.
Impartial	Everyone needs to wear a hairnet—it's a legal requirement. Please put it on now.
Advance warning	The next time I see you working with food without a hairnet, I will be forced to begin a formal discipline procedure. I don't want that to happen.

If you manage these three aspects of the *what to* key well, people will know clearly what you expect of them. This is the first key to unlocking quality performance, productivity and goal achievement.

KEY 2: WANT TO

The second key is the *want to* key. People will do a job only as well as they want to do it. As the saying goes:

> 'People can work hard when they have to;
> but they work harder when they really want to.'

The *want to* key also has three aspects: job design, job placement and motivation (see Figure 8.3).

Job design

Job design is the way a job is structured in terms of its specific duties, responsibilities and tasks. It can be an important source of job satisfaction and can influence both the quality and quantity of work done.

FIGURE 8.3 THE THREE ASPECTS OF THE WANT TO KEY

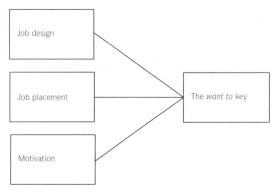

The design of a particular job is often established over time, sometimes haphazardly and often informally. Supervisors should periodically examine the contents of each job in their department or section to ensure they make the best use of people and resources.

The basic principles of job design are that each job should:
- have a clear set of objectives;
- allow the job-holder to have as much control over their job as technology allows;
- allow the job-holder to complete a whole job or piece of work wherever possible;
- contribute significantly to the organisation; and
- cover a variety of subject matter, pace and method of work, experience and training, not be made up of a series of mundane, repetitive tasks.

Henry Mintzberg from McGill University once said:

> **'If you want people to do a good job,
> give them a good job to do.'**

A 'good job' often involves the three Es: enlargement, enrichment and empowerment.

The three Es: enlargement, enrichment, empowerment

Job enlargement means expanding a job *horizontally*: the job-holder takes on more duties at the same level of responsibility. **Cross-skilling** and **multiskilling** are forms of job enlargement.

Job enrichment means expanding a job *vertically*, increasing the depth of the employee's responsibilities. If the additional duties are at a higher level of responsibility, multiskilling can result in job enrichment.

Empowerment is an expanded form of job enrichment. Empowered employees or teams take on many responsibilities previously carried out by supervisors or middle managers.

Job enlargement, enrichment and empowerment usually require training to expand the job-holder's skills. Particularly with empowerment, training must include the areas of interpersonal skills and such skills as problem solving and decision making, and leading and participating in meetings.

The increased responsibility and job interest that result from enlarging, enriching and empowering jobs can improve job design and increase motivation and therefore job performance and productivity. Organisational flexibility and responsiveness is often increased, too, which can in turn strengthen an organisation's customer and supplier relationships. Empowerment often has the additional benefit of enabling the organisation to restructure its internal relationships and ways of working to make it more efficient and competitive. (See also Chapter 13 for a further discussion on empowerment and Chapter 14 for a discussion on job redesign.)

Job placement

Have you heard the saying:

> **'Square pegs for square holes;
> round pegs for round holes.'**

Correct job placement is the second important part of the *want to* key.

Work needs to suit people's *temperaments* and *work style preferences.* If we are temperamentally suited to the type of work we are doing and enjoy doing it, we will derive satisfaction from it and want to do it well.

For example, some people enjoy detailed work while others prefer to take a 'broad brush' approach. Some people are happy working on their own while others want to be part of a friendly, cooperative team. Some people like a chance to move about while others prefer to stay in one place. Some people need a lot of variety in their work while others prefer a routine or predictable work environment. (See also Chapters 15, 19 and 22.) Placing people in jobs that suit their work preferences and temperament means they will enjoy them and derive satisfaction from doing them well. This releases their ability to perform well and be productive.

'Horses for courses.'

What do the jobs in your workplace call for in the way of work preferences and temperament? There will probably always be aspects of everyone's job that they'd rather not have to do. Smart supervisors try to minimise this as much as possible and build tasks that job-holders will enjoy into their jobs. Matching people to the jobs they do is a proven way to build performance and productivity.

Motivation

We examine motivation in detail in Chapter 21. For now, let us say that motivation comes from within and encourages people to 'do their best'. Without motivated employees, performance and productivity will be low.

To be motivated, people need satisfactory pay and working conditions—physical motivators, or what Herzberg called the '**hygiene factors**'. These are important. If they meet people's needs, they will turn up to work. But if these are the only rewards they get, they will only do the 'bare minimum', enough to get by. We won't build better performance and productivity with 'hygiene factors'.

To unlock performance and productivity, we need to provide psychological rewards, or 'motivators'. Things like knowing that you are doing something worthwhile and reaching your goals (which links back into the *what to* key), feeling appreciated and proud of the contribution you are making, using your talents and developing your potential, and being treated with respect will encourage people to give their best efforts. Supervisors have a great deal of control in meeting employees' psychological needs.

The *want to* key helps you motivate employees and match their attributes and abilities with job requirements.

KEY 3: HOW TO

If people know *what to* do and *want to* do it, can we set them to work? Not unless they also know *how to* do the job.

Training and experience

This key is about competency: people need to be properly trained in how to do the job *and* given the time to build their skills and confidence. As we see in Chapter 16, this means patiently and clearly showing people the correct and safe way to do a job, step by step, then giving them time to build their skills and confidence through experience.

Explaining purpose and importance

This is also a good time to explain the job purpose and why each task is important and to discuss non-task goals and bottom-line rules. Training provides supervisors with a tailor-made opportunity to let staff know that what they do makes a difference, an important element in establishing positive attitudes, motivation and the desire to perform well.

Creating a learning environment

As Figure 8.4 shows, there is a fourth aspect to the *how to* key: building an enterprise through learning. Unless people's skills are developed, maintained and extended, the organisation cannot develop and prosper. Training and continual learning is our investment in the future of the enterprise.

The *how to* key helps supervisors build their department's performance and productivity and the enterprise as a whole through training and contributing to a workplace learning environment. (See also Chapter 13.)

FIGURE 8.4   THE FOUR ASPECTS OF THE HOW TO KEY

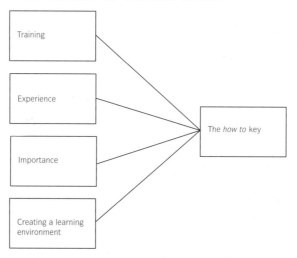

| Training |
| Experience |
| Importance |
| Creating a learning environment |

The *how to* key

KEY 4: CHANCE TO

If a person knows *what to* do and *how to* do it, and *wants to* do it well, why do we sometimes get poor performance and low productivity? This is where the *chance to* key comes in. This key aims to ensure that work methods, systems and procedures and other mechanisms in the job environment contribute to and assist productivity. Often, they do the opposite— they get in the way of people doing a good job.

There are five aspects to the *chance to* key: tools and equipment, work systems and procedures, time and information, team support, and what is called 'acts of God' and personal problems (see Figure 8.5).

Tools and equipment

Poor, faulty, badly designed and maintained, or inadequate tools and equipment are a more common cause of poor performance than we might think. Supervisors should ensure the

FIGURE 8.5   THE FIVE ASPECTS OF THE CHANCE TO KEY

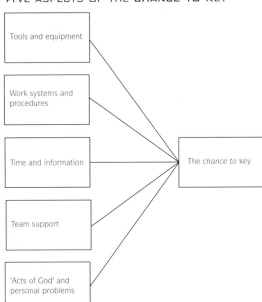

tools and equipment in their department are well designed, properly maintained and suited to the job at hand.

Work systems and procedures

Cumbersome work systems and procedures not only discourage people from doing a good job, but they can actually prevent them from doing a good job. Because they usually develop over time as additions and changes are made *ad hoc* and informally, unwieldy work methods mushroom unnoticed. This is an all-too-common cause of less-than-optimal performance and productivity.

Supervisors and their work teams should examine how they do things. Are there any unnecessary steps or backtracking? Where are the 'hiccups and hassles' in work systems and procedures that make employees' lives difficult? How can systems and procedures be streamlined? How can we redesign any awkward steps or procedures so they can be carried out smoothly and easily? Each step should flow logically and easily into the next. (In the next chapter, we look at how to use flow charts and other techniques to help you analyse and improve work systems and procedures.)

Making sure all the work systems and procedures help employees do a good job, not hinder their efforts, will make a big contribution to building performance and productivity.

Time and information

Most organisations these days are running 'lean and mean'. While reduced staffing levels can reduce overheads, it can also mean that sometimes people just don't have the time to do a job properly or to pass on information fully.

How much time is wasted in your department by doing a job a second or third time because someone didn't have enough time or information to do it right the first time? Studies in Australia have shown that this can be as high as 33% of a working week. Imagine saving 13 hours per person per week by eliminating rework!

Get people into the habit of doing things 'right first time' and passing on needed information. Make sure they have the right job aids, feedback on performance and the time and information they need to do their job well.

Team support

People working together can achieve far more than people working on their own. If team members don't understand what everyone is trying to achieve, if they don't share common goals and purposes, if they don't support and value each other's efforts, work becomes unnecessarily difficult. This is another major barrier to work performance, productivity and goal achievement. We examine how to build and lead high-performing work teams in Chapter 22.

If supervisors don't manage these four aspects of the work environment well, it is not surprising that employees lose their willingness to put in the effort required to do their jobs well. The barriers to productivity and goal achievement will 'grind them down' and sap their motivation to perform. Make sure your team members have the *chance to* do their jobs well.

'Acts of God' and personal problems

The **85:15 rule** tells us that, provided people know clearly what is expected of them and are trained to do it well, 85% of the causes of poor performance and low productivity can be found in the work environment—the four aspects of the *chance to* key examined above. 'Acts of God' and personal factors will account for only 15% of poor performance.

'Acts of God' are things we can't do anything about. If your factory or office floods or loses its electricity, it will be difficult to get production or invoices out on time. Personal factors include the occasional 'bad hair' day, domestic problems that are so pressing it is difficult to concentrate properly on work or severe personal problems such as alcohol or drug abuse.

It makes sense to concentrate your efforts at improving productivity and performance where they are most likely to pay off—in the work environment—doesn't it?

KEY 5: LED TO

Sound leadership that sets clear goals and a good example provides the final touch to building performance and productivity. Even if all the other keys are in place, poor leadership can spoil it all.

Supervisors need to practise what they preach, lead by example, coach, empower and help employees to do their jobs well. We looked at some aspects of this in Chapter 1, and we look further into the extensive and challenging topic of leadership in Chapters 19, 20 and 22. Here we review the six characteristics of successful leaders, which help them to build performance and productivity (see Figure 8.6).

Self-esteem

Successful supervisors have high self-esteem. In other words, they value and respect themselves. This leads to the self-confidence they need to supervise others well and manage operations properly.

FIGURE 8.6 THE SIX ASPECTS OF THE LED TO KEY

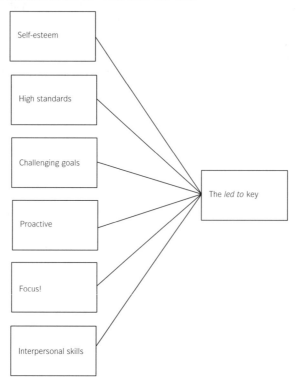

The secure sense of self that comes from high self-esteem allows them to consistently build the self-esteem of those around them. Since only people with high self-esteem can perform their jobs with excellence, building self-esteem in others also builds performance and productivity.

High standards

Supervisors who know how to build performance and productivity also know the importance of setting high standards and expecting the best—of themselves and others. After all:

> 'Mediocrity is a choice.
> So is excellence.'

Challenging goals

People with high standards and high expectations set challenging (yet achievable) goals. In aiming high, people are often able to achieve more than by aiming low. As the Italian proverb points out:

> 'By asking for the impossible, we obtain the best possible.'

Proactive

Supervisors with a record for building performance and productivity are invariably proactive. They take responsibility for making things happen. They don't sit back and wait, blame others or find excuses for not achieving goals or meeting high standards. (See also Chapter 3.)

Focus!

To meet the high standards and achieve the challenging goals they set for themselves and others, a steady focus is needed. Supervisors who build productivity and performance 'keep their eyes on the ball'. They keep their goals clearly in mind and find ways to achieve them, despite the obstacles.

Interpersonal skills

Building performance and productivity also takes a high degree of interpersonal skill. Communicating and working effectively with others enables supervisors to have the influence they need to encourage and guide people to lift their performance and productivity.

THE PDCA CYCLE

The **PDCA cycle**, or Plan–Do–Check–Act cycle, is an essential tool for building performance and productivity. Sometimes called the Deming Wheel, the cycle was actually developed by Walter Shewhart, a contemporary of Edwards Deming and a fellow total quality management proponent (see Chapter 9). Its purpose is to ensure that improvements are made in a consistent way and that, once made, they are retained.

Step 1—Plan	Planning is the first step in the cycle. You identify a problem or concern, obtain factual information about it and set a target to improve it.
Step 2—Do	Next, you analyse the information, form tentative conclusions, develop a plan to achieve your improvement target and test it out in a trial run.
Step 3—Check	Then, check your results. Has the plan worked? Does it need to be refined?
Step 4—Act	Now, take action to incorporate the change(s) into the standard operating procedure. This might involve training, altering the design of a machine, moving the location of equipment or changing supplier specifications. Standardise the changes, build them in to the process, communicate them and document the changes.

The PDCA cycle helps you to identify areas for improvement, plan and implement improvements and ensure they work and become part of the standard way of doing things. (See Figure 8.7. You will learn how to use the tools referred to in this figure in the next chapter.)

FIGURE 8.7 THE PDCA CYCLE

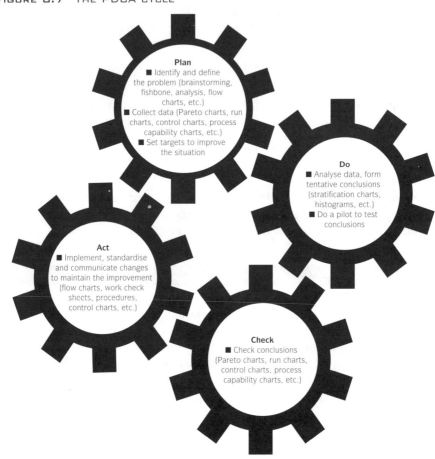

Plan
- Identify and define the problem (brainstorming, fishbone, analysis, flow charts, etc.)
- Collect data (Pareto charts, run charts, control charts, process capability charts, etc.)
- Set targets to improve the situation

Do
- Analyse data, form tentative conclusions (stratification charts, histograms, ect.)
- Do a pilot to test conclusions

Act
- Implement, standardise and communicate changes to maintain the improvement (flow charts, work check sheets, procedures, control charts, etc.)

Check
- Check conclusions (Pareto charts, run charts, control charts, process capability charts, etc.)

RAPID REVIEW

	True	False
1. Unless there is role clarity, if a person performs well it will be mostly by chance.	☐	☐
2. Clear targets that allow people to monitor their own performance are motivating and help build productivity.	☐	☐
3. Job-holders need a vision or mission statement for their own jobs.	☐	☐
4. The 'hot stove principle' should apply only to new and inexperienced workers.	☐	☐
5. 'Bottom-line' rules involve matters such as safety, standard operating procedures, housekeeping standards, working with others and customer service.	☐	☐
6. Unless people want to do a good job, they won't.	☐	☐

	True	False
7. A good job design can motivate a person and encourage good performance while a poorly designed job can demotivate a person and lead to poor performance.	☐	☐
8. Supervisors should place people in whatever jobs the operations require them in; if you cater to people's personal likes and dislikes, the boring jobs will never get done.	☐	☐
9. Chances are, if employees aren't doing their jobs properly after a supervisor has shown them what to do, it's because they're just not interested in the job.	☐	☐
10. Supervisors need to make sure tools and equipment are well designed, well maintained and suitable for the job.	☐	☐
11. Dumb systems and procedures demotivate people and sap their desire and ability to be fully productive.	☐	☐
12. If supervisors don't lead by example, employees are likely to lose their will to produce quality work.	☐	☐
13. Setting high standards and challenging goals increases performance, provided the goals aren't impossible to attain.	☐	☐
14. The PDCA cycle helps supervisors and their teams identify things to improve, study them, make improvements and make the improvements part of the standard systems.	☐	☐

APPLY YOUR KNOWLEDGE

1. Discuss the supervisor's role in helping people attain total quality performance, productivity and goal achievement.

2. Explain each of the five essential elements, or the five keys, to productivity, giving an example of each from your own experience.

3. Use the five keys to explain how to build performance and productivity. Explain what would happen if one of these keys were not managed properly. Select one 'deficient' key to use to illustrate your point.

4. Using examples from a current or past job, develop a job purpose statement and key result areas. For each key result area, write one or two SMARTT KPIs that would help you track your performance. Then write some non-task goals. Were or are there any bottom-line rules? If so, what are they?

5. Referring to a job you are familiar with, or the job from question 4 above, analyse how well it is designed by applying the job design principles in this chapter.

6. Discuss how supervisors can apply the 'hot stove principle' to ensure that people in their work team follow bottom-line rules correctly and consistently. Provide some examples of rules in your home, college or workplace to which the 'hot stove principle' could be applied.

7. If people are not placed in jobs that suit their skills and preferences, they are unlikely to do a good job. Discuss how thoughtful job placement can build performance and productivity.

8. If you have already studied Chapter 21, relate the five keys (of productivity) to Vroom's expectancy theory of motivation discussed in Chapter 21.

9. If you have read Chapters 1 and 6, explain why we may expect to see more job enlargement, enrichment and empowerment and why supervisors may need to become familiar with the principles of job design and job redesign and the five keys to unlocking productivity and performance.
10. Referring to question 5 above, analyse how well the *chance to* key is or was operating and what, if anything, could be done to improve it.
11. If people don't do a job properly, they probably need to be disciplined. Discuss.
12. Think of the best supervisor you know. In what ways did the characteristics of supervisors who build performance and productivity apply to them?

·   DEVELOP YOUR SKILLS   ·

Individual activities

1. Describe the role of a student in your college by listing the key result areas involved.
2. Based on the key result areas you listed in the above activity, write some targets and non-task goals that apply to your role as a student. Ensure the targets meet the SMARTT criteria described in this chapter.
3. Write one SMARTT target, or KPI, for each of Carole's KRAs in Case Study 8.1 opposite.
4. List three non-task goals for each of the following jobs: cashier in a petrol station, office clerk, receptionist at the local council, assistant in a video shop, computer help-line adviser.

5. Illustrate by an example from your own experience why it is important that people know that the tasks they do make an important contribution to their department and organisation.
6. Interview a job-holder to find out as much as you can about their job as it relates to the five keys. What conclusions can you draw about how effectively this person's supervisor builds performance and productivity?
7. Have you ever been in a situation where you didn't achieve as much as you had hoped to? Analyse the reasons for this using the five keys.
8. Explain how the characteristics of effective leaders would also help you as a student.

Group activities

1. In small groups, refine the following 'fuzzy' targets to make them SMARTT:
   - improve quality of output in an engine parts factory
   - be friendly to customers at a retail sales check-out
   - answer the telephone properly in a busy office
   - lower your reject rate on an assembly line
   - do your job in an economical way (secretary)
   - make more widgets in a widget factory
   - serve customers more quickly at a Tax office help desk
   - do the job safely (gardener)
   - don't exceed the speed limit (taxi driver)
   - prepare the report as quickly as you can (clerical assistant)
   - reduce customer complaints at a Tax office help desk
   - get the best grades you can (student)

2. In small groups, apply the hot stove principle to the following situation: an employee comes into work 30 minutes late from lunch and it is obvious she has been drinking.

3. In groups of five or six, develop a list of tasks you enjoy doing and a list of tasks you dislike. Which ones do you do best? Why? Relate this to the *want to* key to productivity.

4. In small groups, develop a list of the temperaments and work-style preferences best suited to the following jobs:
   (a) waiter/waitress in a busy café
   (b) librarian
   (c) horse trainer
   (d) truck driver
   (e) children's swimming teacher
   (f) nurse
   (g) electronics assembly operator
   (h) hotel receptionist

5. In small groups, give examples from your own experience illustrating the following common causes of poor performance from the *chance to* key:
   - tools and equipment
   - team support
   - systems
   - time and information
   - job design
   Be prepared to explain these to the rest of the class.

6. In small groups, develop a plan for Paulene, in the opening vignette. What should she cover in the first meeting? How can she enlist her team's cooperation? What should be her general approach to the situation?

CASE STUDY 8.1

What's The Problem Here?

Carole had just been recruited as operations manager of a valet car parking service at a provincial airport. Until she joined, Ted Mezaros, the owner of the petrol station which ran the valet service, supervised the operations in addition to managing the petrol station itself. Carole's key result areas were:

✓ staff supervision and training
✓ daily operations
✓ customer service
✓ administration and banking
✓ identifying and making improvements to internal systems.

As part of familiarising herself with the business, Carole spent most of her first week at the customer reception counter observing the way the business was run. The systems seemed to work fairly smoothly and efficiently. However, Carole was disturbed by the way one of the reception assistants, Valda, interacted with customers.

Time and time again, she saw Valda ask the customers their name, registration number, make of car and flight details in what she considered to be a gruff and unfriendly manner. Valda failed to make eye contact, greet the customers, smile at them, wish them a pleasant journey or make any of, what Carole called, the 'small pleasantries'. During a lull towards the end of Valda's shift, Carole asked her to explain how she saw her job. This is what she said: 'I just do what Ted told me. I fill out the paperwork as quickly as I can because people are in a hurry to catch their flights, and as accurately as I can, so we have the right car ready for the right person at the right time when they return for it.'

Questions

1   What errors do you think Ted made in explaining Valda's job to her? How would you have explained it?
2   Prepare a job purpose statement for Valda's job. How will this make a difference to the way Valda does her job?
3   Who was at fault in the way Valda dealt with customers—Valda herself, or Ted? What do you think Carole should do now to improve the situation?

CASE STUDY 8.2

New Equipment At The Dry Cleaners

Just about everyone knew Margaret, who had worked for many years at the dry cleaners in a country town. She knew all her customers by name and always had a cheerful greeting and a few comments about local events as she organised their cleaning for them. Margaret was known to be smiling, cheerful, friendly and super-efficient. It would not be an exaggeration to say that she was responsible for much of the business enjoyed by the dry cleaners.

One day, a new cash register was delivered. 'This is a wonderful piece of equipment,' said the representative who brought it in. 'You'll be able to record everything you need to know with it, as well as make change! Here, let me show you.'

With that, he proceeded to give Margaret a two-hour lesson on how to use the new cash register. Access to the machine began with entering the customer's telephone number. Then the garment type, colour and fabric were coded in using a special key pad on the left-hand side of the machine. This was quite complicated, given the variety of possibilities. The machine automatically priced each garment as it was entered. Drop-off time was recorded automatically and the desired pick-up day and time (morning or afternoon) was to be entered by the operator, as were any special instructions. These were coded in using a different key pad at the right-hand side of the machine. The usual amount tendered/change owing function was also part of the machine, located on the central key pad.

Poor Margaret. After two hours of training, her head was spinning. After two weeks of fumbling with the new cash register, she was no closer to mastering it. She no longer had time to chat to her customers, as she was busy working out what to do on the machine and fixing mistakes. (Unfortunately, there was no quick and easy way to delete incorrect entries.) The new process took a lot longer than the old one which meant customers were kept waiting and tempers frayed. Margaret was embarrassed at her inefficiency—it was a nightmare. After six weeks, Margaret decided to retire.

Over the next six months, a succession of six new employees were hired, trained, struggled and quit. Business was falling off as long-time loyal customers took their dry cleaning to another outlet up the road.

Questions

1   Use the five keys to analyse what is going wrong at the dry cleaners.
2   Based on your analysis, what do you recommend the owners of the dry cleaning business should do to rectify the situation?

CASE STUDY 8.3

Eddie's Exhausts

Eddie's Exhausts is a national chain of auto exhaust specialists. Their motto is, 'Travel quieter and cleaner with Eddie's Exhausts'. Recently the chain had been experiencing a downturn in business which management believed reflected a general air of caution in the economy. In an effort to improve profits, they had allowed natural attrition to reduce the staffing levels in each of the stores in their chain. They were now running at about 60% of their usual staff numbers.

In an effort to attract more customers, management began a campaign of Superior Customer Service, based on improved levels of housekeeping, staff presentation (uniforms, etc.), upgraded customer waiting rooms and improved telephone technique. Store staff were now required to answer the telephone in three rings, saying: 'Welcome to Eddie's Exhausts. We'll help you travel quieter and cleaner. This is (staff member's name) speaking, how can I help you?'

Store staff were pleased with the company's upgrading of customer waiting areas and their uniforms and were more than willing to meet the improved housekeeping requirements. Because they were well aware that a great deal of their business was won over the telephone, they knew how important telephone technique was and already made every effort to be as professional as possible over the telephone.

The difficulty was, with reduced staffing levels in the stores, there was seldom any staff in the showroom area, where the phones were located behind the customer service counter. In the past, there had usually been someone behind the counter ready to deal with walk-in customers and tending to paperwork and housekeeping. Now, nearly everyone was out in the fitting bay, fitting exhausts.

In most stores, the fitting bay is located next to the customer reception area. When fitting exhausts, staff use 'dollies' to wheel themselves under a vehicle, or hoist the car into the air over a recessed working area, depending on how the store is equipped. Either way, access and egress is rather awkward.

It came to management's attention that few of the stores were actually answering the telephone in three rings and with the required greeting. They hired a casual 'mystery shopper' to telephone each of the stores randomly and note down which stores were answering correctly and which were not. They provided this list to the area managers in each state.

Most of the area managers responded by telephoning the stores they were responsible for which did not meet required telephone standards and telling them to 'get it right' from now on. The trouble was, things haven't improved. The general manager is furious as he considers telephone technique to be of primary importance in attracting customers.

Questions

1 Using the information provided in this chapter as a guide, what do you believe the main problem is with the telephone answering technique of store staff?
2 What do you recommend management does to address this problem?
3 Do you believe the area managers could have handled the problem better? What could they have done differently or in addition to the actions they took?

Answers to Rapid Review questions

1. T   2. T   3. T   4. F   5. T   6. T   7. T   8. F   9. F   10. T   11. T   12. T   13. T   14. T

CHAPTER 9

PROMOTING TOTAL QUALITY, INNOVATION AND CONTINUOUS IMPROVEMENT

The Quality Improvement Team

Jane gathered up her papers and prepared to meet her work team of four travel consultants and a trainee administration assistant in the boardroom. They were about to continue with their series of weekly Quality Improvement Team meetings. She was pleased with the way they were responding to their latest challenge: learning and applying total quality management (TQM) tools and techniques to identify and resolve problems and improve their work systems. Their aim was for things to flow more smoothly and to find ways to serve their customers even better.

In the first two meetings, they developed a list of 'team rules' for the way they would work together. Things like 'turn up on time', 'let everyone have their say', 'share your ideas even if they sound crazy!' were on the list that the team reviewed briefly at the beginning of each meeting to remind themselves of its contents. They also brainstormed a list of 'job hassles' and used the nominal group technique to prioritise them into the order they would work on them.

In their third meeting, the team used the fishbone technique to analyse the problem they selected to work on first: delays in ticket issuing. This showed them that there was a lot more to it than first met the eye! In the fourth meeting, the team finished 'fishboning' their problem and began to flow chart the ticketing process—first the way it was currently done, then the ideal way to do it.

Their fifth meeting was due to start in ten minutes and it wouldn't do to be late! They would continue flow charting the ticketing system and have a look at the check-sheets that two of the consultants had begun keeping since the last meeting to help analyse the nature of delays.

Jane and her team were making good progress and a real team spirit and energy was developing. Although they were still analysing the problem, Jane felt that they would be ready with a new, improved ticketing system in a couple of months' time. Whatever it was, she knew it would make everyone's life easier and enable them to offer a faster and more reliable service to their customers. She also knew that the business would benefit enormously from the improved teamwork that was already evident as a result of the quality improvement meetings.

OVERVIEW

'Close enough' is no longer good enough. Supervisors must be able to instil a culture that promotes quality, innovation and continuous improvement. In this chapter, you will find out how to do this.

- Can you explain how the quality movement has developed over the years and how modern enterprises assure, measure and monitor quality?
- Do you know why variation is the enemy of quality?
- How do quality circles operate?
- What is TQM? What are its six pivotal Ps and its five main platforms?
- What are Australian and international quality standards?

- How do organisations become quality-certified?
- What is the difference between continuous improvement and re-engineering?
- How does best practice benchmarking help organisations improve their quality?
- Can you explain and use the main TQM tools and techniques?

THE QUALITY IMPERATIVE

Traditional methods of improving an organisation—reducing labour and overhead costs—are no longer sufficient to ensure an organisation prospers. Quality has entered the equation. High quality is now imperative. Without quality, an organisation probably can't even be in 'the economic game'.

What is quality? Here is Joseph Juran's definition:

'Quality is whatever the customer says it is.'

Here is another definition:

'A quality product or service is one that meets or exceeds customer expectations.'

Monitoring quality—the old way

Traditional methods of quality control relied on inspectors, specially designated quality control personnel, to carry out quality control checks. Various techniques ranging from visual observations to complex testing and measurement were used to catch defects in work in progress and at final inspection (see Box 9.1). Unless a 100% monitoring system was used, which was very costly, it was virtually impossible to spot them all. The result was that poor quality products could, and often did, reach the customer.

Monitoring quality this way was time-consuming and expensive. It often resulted in lowered morale if employees felt that supervisors were 'checking up on them'. Paradoxically, traditional quality control approaches sometimes resulted in lowered quality standards because employees considered quality to be 'someone else's' concern.

Monitoring quality—the modern way

Building quality into the production or service provision process itself works better. Today, we focus on the *systems* or procedures used to deliver the service or produce the product.

BOX 9.1   A BRIEF HISTORY OF QUALITY

Inspection	Quality control	Quality assurance	Total quality management
Focus on the product	Focus on the product	Focus on building quality into the process	Brings together the best elements of these approaches and adds systematic tools and techniques to be used by everyone to continuously improve quality
Focus on detecting problems	Focus on controlling problems	Focus on preventing problems	
Tests every item	Tests samples	Monitors constantly	
Done at the end of a process	Done at stages through the process	Occurs during every stage of the process	
Relies on specially trained inspectors	Relies on trained production staff and QC inspectors	Relies on everyone	

Quality is built into them—that is, they are designed in such a way that defects are virtually impossible. If errors do occur, they are quickly spotted and fixed.

Focusing on preventing defects through better systems rather than trying to spot mistakes after they are made changes the way we monitor quality. Today, most quality control procedures are associated with statistical analyses and random or continual checking on performance. The aim is to spot problems as they occur and take corrective action as early as possible to ensure that the goods and services always meet the required quality standards. Whenever **variation** in key performance measures approaches or falls outside predetermined acceptable levels, action is taken to fix the process. This might mean recalibrating a machine, for example, or resetting tools.

Employees keep records to spot patterns of variation for immediate rectification and later analysis. Figure 9.1 shows a control chart with measurements taken and recorded hourly. As long as the readings remain inside the upper and lower control points, the quality of the product is acceptable. If the readings stray outside these points, the process is considered 'out of control' and action must be taken to bring the process back 'into control'.

While quality control systems do not automatically ensure perfect quality, they can help to identify and correct causes of below-standard performance. They can also prevent substandard products from being used further in the production process or being dispatched to customers. The focus total quality management (TQM) places on getting the systems right aims to stop substandard goods or services before they occur.

THE **BIG** PICTURE

Rule of thumb	A problem that costs $1 to fix in advance will cost $20 to fix during a process and $50 to fix afterwards.
Conclusion	TQM saves money.

FIGURE 9.1 CONTROL CHART

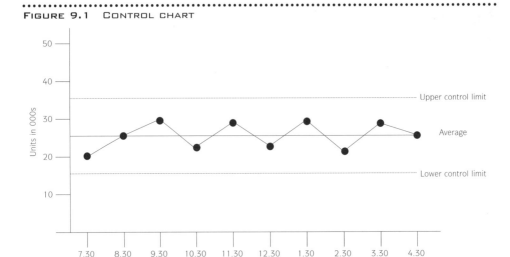

Today we see work systems and processes—not workers—as the major cause of poor quality. We know that such things as inadequate tools and materials, poor or inappropriate training, and production processes beyond the control of the employees are major causes of poor productivity and inconsistent quality and reliability (see Chapter 8).

Although people don't cause poor quality, involving them in improving it is one of the keys to total quality. All employees, not just specialists, are involved in quality improvement through the use of systematic, problem-analysis tools for monitoring quality standards, identifying and correcting poor quality and identifying opportunities and planning for continuous improvements.

The concept of total quality shows us that involving people in monitoring and improving their own quality of output achieves better outcomes than we have come to expect from the more traditional quality control approaches.

QUALITY CIRCLES

Quality circles are part of the approach to involving people and are an important aspect of the total quality movement. Employees form small groups that meet regularly, usually once a week for an hour, to identify and discuss quality problems and opportunities, and devise and implement appropriate solutions and strategies. The issues that quality circles address include such issues as quality, rate of output, smoothness of operations or work flow, obtaining materials, customer service and materials storage.

Quality circles are a special way of allowing groups to participate in problem solving and decision making in areas that affect them directly. (See also Chapters 6 and 22.) Their leader is usually trained in analytic, group problem-solving and decision-making tools and techniques and trains the group to use them. This is normally the supervisor or team leader of the work group concerned.

Using the tools and techniques discussed below, quality circles proceed through a clear-cut, systematic process to identify, prioritise and resolve problems they face at work. At the end of this process, the circle presents a report to management summarising the problem the circle has been working on, why it chose that problem, how it was analysed, what they found, and the circle's recommended actions. Common outcomes of a series of quality circle meetings are shown in Box 9.2.

BOX 9.2 TYPICAL RESULTS OF QUALITY CIRCLES

- reduced errors
- enhanced quality
- more effective teamwork
- greater job involvement and employee motivation
- enhanced problem-solving capabilities

- problem prevention
- improved communication
- enhanced working relationships
- personal development for the members
- greater safety awareness
- improved worker–management relationships

TOTAL QUALITY MANAGEMENT

Because of the importance of quality and reliability to today's consumers, we must continually improve our performance in these areas. **Total quality management (TQM)** has been the main vehicle for achieving this. It gives people the *tools* and *statistical techniques* to address the key challenges of:

✓ how to achieve higher quality;
✓ how to save money through lower inventory;
✓ how to develop and maintain flexible and well organised processes; and
✓ how to make most effective use of people and information.

Originating in manufacturing areas, total quality concepts have spread to all areas, including office, retailing and other non-manufacturing areas such as tourism, legal and accounting firms, airlines, car rental companies, hotels, credit card companies and universities. An all-embracing philosophy of total employee involvement, *TQM is a commitment to excellence in which everyone focuses on continuous improvement, quality, teamwork and total customer satisfaction.* It is an operational framework that emphasises six fundamental factors (see Box 9.3).

◤ FROM THEORY TO PRACTICE

Nichols Foods in England manufactures and packages foodstuff products for the vending and catering industries. Every employee in the factory has had two days' training in TQM tools and techniques and the whole plant stops work for an hour a week for quality circle work.

In the past three years, there has been a 50% reduction in changeover times, an 80% improvement in efficiency and a 50% cut in the number of customer complaints. Labour costs have reduced by one-third and profitability has more than doubled.

THE SIX PIVOTAL Ps

1. People
2. Processes
3. Performance

4. Planning
5. Productivity
6. Perfection

TQM is essential practice for most of today's successful organisations. Here are the three main results of a successful total quality management program:
1. continuous improvements to systems and processes;
2. 'de-hassling' people's jobs; and
3. providing total quality to the customer.

THE **BIG** PICTURE

Although TQM techniques originated in the United States, total quality management is often associated with Japan. The late Dr W. Edwards Deming, a leader in the total quality movement, was responsible for taking many TQM techniques and approaches to Japan after World War II. Box 9.4 summarises Dr Deming's message and Box 9.5 gives a synopsis of his famous 14 key points.

There is no doubt that this approach significantly helped Japan to achieve its 'economic miracle'. In less than 40 years, Japan moved from a non-industrialised society with a low standard of living to one of the most economically developed and powerful nations on earth.

Why TQM fails

Do the following principles sound sensible to you?
- examining and streamlining systems of production and service provision;
- forming teams and involving people at all levels in the organisation to identify and solve problems and make continuous improvements to work systems;
- using solid statistical information to examine problems and measure performance; and
- being customer-focused and customer-driven.

Most people would agree that these are good ideas. Yet studies in Australia and overseas have shown that up to 60%–80% of TQM initiatives have failed. Why?

DR DEMING'S MESSAGE ON TOTAL QUALITY

- Find out about your customers and what they want.
- Study and improve your products and services until they cannot be beaten.
- Involve everyone throughout the organisation, at all levels and in all disciplines.

BOX 9.5 DR DEMING'S 14 KEY POINTS ON TQM
···

1. Create a constancy of purpose towards improving products and services. Plan for the future.
2. Adopt a philosophy that makes delays, mistakes, defective materials and defective interactions between people unacceptable.
3. Build quality into the way you do things to eliminate the need for final checks and last minute 'fixes'.
4. Measure quality and price together; for example, don't award contracts based purely on the price tag.
5. Find problems and eliminate them by improving the system (redesign it, improve in-coming materials, maintenance, equipment, training, supervision).
6. Implement the best methods of on-the-job training.
7. Enhance supervision to help improve quality and productivity.
8. Drive out fear so that everyone in the organisation can work effectively.
9. Break down barriers between job functions and departments.
10. Eliminate numerical goals and slogans asking for improvement without explaining how.
11. Eliminate work standards that prescribe numerical quotas; focus on quality instead.
12. Remove barriers that stand between people and their right to pride in their work.
13. Implement a vigorous program of education and training.
14. Create a management structure that will push, every day, on the above 13 points.

Where TQM has failed to produce the desired results, it has largely been because it was introduced as a 'quick fix' with no genuine management understanding, support or commitment. The six main reasons for TQM not living up to expectations are:
1. Seeking quality certification merely as a marketing tool or because an organisation's customers require certification.
2. TQM programs becoming overly bureaucratic.
3. Continued reliance on inspection and checking procedures rather than building quality into the processes themselves.
4. A general lack of management interest and support, resulting in loss of momentum and lack of follow-through.
5. TQM programs 'added on' separately to the normal activities of the business.
6. Quality driven by a designated quality manager, not seen as part of everyone's job.

Why TQM succeeds

There are five main success factors associated with TQM when it is working well:
1. Management at all levels being serious about TQM and supporting it.
2. An organisation culture that focuses on quality.
3. Starting off on a small scale and gaining visible results before widening the introduction to the rest of the organisation.

4. Training people in TQM tools and techniques.
5. Providing organisational supports to allow TQM to work properly and become part of the culture (e.g. time and authority).

The potential benefits of successfully implementing TQM are enormous and well worth the effort.

AUSTRALIAN AND INTERNATIONAL QUALITY STANDARDS

Quality management is an internationally certifiable process. International standards (ISO9000 to 9004) and the Australian standards that mirror them (AS39000 to 39004) guide us to establish, administer, maintain and improve our organisation's competitiveness through our ability to provide a quality product or service. They focus on the quality systems we put in place to assure quality and provide recognised and recommended formats for quality systems to follow.

ISO9000 to 9004 and the equivalent AS39000 to 39004 series are five related standards. The ISO9001 series, for example, relates to manufacturing while standards in the ISO9002 series relate to primary producers. These standards are an internationally recognised model for ensuring that the supplier takes steps to assure quality during the many stages necessary in supplying a product or service.

They require an organisation to define, establish, explain and guide the way it designs, develops, produces, installs and services its products and services. It must document these procedures explicitly, setting out in writing precisely how it will achieve the specified quality throughout its entire manufacturing process (including design, inspection, measurement and testing) or its service provision process.

Organisations must also document other procedures, including, for example, procedures for maintaining machinery, training workers, purchasing and dealing with customer complaints. They must also keep quality records that monitor and report the organisation's quality performance. Other documents required include a quality policy that defines the organisation's approach to quality, an organisation quality manual, work instructions that explain how each service or manufacturing process is to be performed, position descriptions and improvement quality plans that explain how the organisation plans to improve its quality. These documents and records provide proof that an organisation has quality systems in place and that it follows them to guarantee quality and meet customer requirements as specified by the customer.

THE **BIG** PICTURE

Over 60 countries adhere to these international quality standards and most governments and major organisations around the world will only do business with organisations that have been certified as conforming to them. These organisations require their suppliers to be certified as the first step in assuring the quality of the products or services they supply.

Quality systems

A **quality system** is the way an organisation formally controls the processes or activities that directly influence the quality of the goods and services it produces. If we can predict with certainty the quality of the service or product we produce, our system is '*in control*'. An '*out-of-control*' system is haphazard: it sometimes produces good quality and sometimes doesn't. Measuring quality and setting up in-control systems capable of reliably and predictably delivering quality is a prime objective of TQM.

While we can think of TQM as a culture, or mind-set, that drives quality in an organisation, we can think of quality systems as the structure that enables us to produce quality products and services dependably. They are the procedures and processes we put in place to manage and ensure quality. Each organisation develops its own specific quality systems that reflect the nature and size of its operations. The focus is not on the traditional quality checking *at the end* of a process, but on how we build quality *into* each work process and system in the organisation.

Quality systems help an organisation increase quality, lower operating costs, reduce inventory and waste, improve systems design, improve the way it gathers and uses information and increase its flexibility.

Certification

Would you like to be sure that when you purchase something it will work properly? That its component parts are reliable? That the product will do what it's supposed to do easily? Certification offers this assurance. Customers can be sure that if their supplier is certified, it has a functioning quality system in operation capable of consistently producing a product or service that meets their requirements.

The process of becoming certified is exacting. However, organisations undertaking it benefit from a thorough 'spring cleaning' and a rethinking of the way they do things, with a resulting lift in their quality levels.

THE **BIG** PICTURE

The cost involved in certification is significant but may be the price required to stay in business since many organisations require their suppliers to be quality certified. The costs include fees to the accrediting organisation and countless hours of internal staff time to develop, install and document the systems. Surveys in Australia have shown that the average cost of implementing and gaining certification was $55 000 for small organisations and more than $200 000 for large organisations.

To counterbalance these costs, quality assurance (QA) certified companies gain better market access both domestically and overseas, improved customer satisfaction, improved quality and business performance, raised employee morale, and cost savings through reductions in materials handling, operating expenses, absenteeism and injuries. Some studies have estimated that the benefits of reducing costs through quality can amount to about 10% of sales.

The first step in attaining certification is to define and document the quality system to be followed. This entails analysing the processes and activities that the organisation carries out and improving them to eliminate the likelihood of errors and non-conformances (any product or service that fails to meet the agreed quality standard) by reducing variations in the systems and eliminating waste in materials and efforts. An organisation cannot be awarded quality certification if its systems are not in control and properly documented.

Documentation of quality systems is essential and is a demanding and time-consuming process. Internationally, 70% of organisations fail their first quality audit, 47% because of inadequate document control. Box 9.6 shows the most common problems relating to documentation, and Box 9.7 the three levels of documentation required.

COMMON PROBLEMS IN QUALITY DOCUMENTATION

- Lack of a consistent, standard approach to documenting policies and procedures:
  — multiple writing styles and tones
  — inconsistent levels of detail
- Inaccurate documentation
- Inaccessible documentation

- Poorly written and complex procedures:
  — inconsistent procedures for managing quality
  — poorly sequenced procedures
- Procedures not up to date

BOX 9.7

THREE LEVELS OF QUALITY DOCUMENTATION

Level A   A quality manual that states the policies and objectives of the organisation relating to quality

Level B   Operating procedures that cover individual departments and the tasks carried out

Level C   Work instructions that detail specifically how each task should be carried out in producing the product or service

---

An accredited independent third party known as an *auditor* must verify that these documents and their application conform to the model quality system described in the prescribed Australian or international standards. To attain certification, an organisation must first document its quality systems and then show the auditor that it carries them out. This includes providing all staff with necessary information and training in how jobs should be performed. The initial certification process usually takes 12 to 18 months. Once certification is awarded, regular 'check' audits or surveillance audits follow every six months, and a full and thorough audit is carried out every three years.

THE **BIG** PICTURE

Some companies are saying that certification hasn't really improved their business. Other companies are keeping their quality systems but giving up their certified status. They're finding it too costly to maintain for too few benefits. Good systems and, in particular, *traceability* (if a problem occurs you can trace back to find its source and fix it properly so it won't happen again) are what is required, they say, and a company doesn't need certification to have these. Are we seeing the beginning of the end of certification?

KEY ELEMENTS OF TQM

Box 9.8 summarises the five main platforms of TQM. Let's look at each of these in turn.

BOX 9.8   THE FIVE PLATFORMS OF TQM

1. Customer focus
   a) external customers
   b) internal customers
   c) trading partnerships
2. Work systems and processes

3. Continuous improvement
   a) process re-engineering
   b) benchmarking
4. People working together
5. Systematic analytical tools and techniques

Customer focus

Central to TQM is a strong customer focus. Three things in particular are important: finding out what external customers want and providing or exceeding it; working with internal customers to achieve continuous improvement and better results; and forming mutually beneficial relationships with customers.

Whether the customers are internal or external, TQM seeks to find answers to such questions as *Who are our customers?* and *What do they want from us?*

Since customers are our reason for existing and the people who will determine our continued existence, these questions are central to every organisation. If we don't satisfy our customers, we have no reason to exist. Another organisation with greater skill in identifying its customers and their needs, and meeting them reliably and in ways they want, will take our place.

External customers

We often think of **customers** as the people who purchase and use our products or services. They may be individual customers, such as the shopper who purchases a box of cornflakes. They may be the organisations we supply—for example, the supermarket chain that purchases the cornflakes in bulk or in pallets of two dozen pre-packaged boxes. Both of these customers are **external customers**.

Because we depend on them, it is essential to identify precisely who they are and exactly what they want from us. This will make us a **customer-driven organisation**. Becoming a customer-driven organisation often requires a change in approach from the more traditional

FROM THEORY TO PRACTICE

Swiss-owned Giroflex UK, a manufacturer of top quality office seating, uses simple flows and simple systems to make a relatively complex product. 'We're very close to mass customisation,' says Peter Hurley, the operations director. 'Every product is highly configurable and there are literally millions of possible permutations.'

Simple systems make sure the customers get exactly what they want, when they want it, at the price they want.

product-driven organisation which says, in effect, 'This is what we can produce. Do you want it or not?'

'We make cornflakes and we sell them in 500 gram retail packs supplied in pallets of 24 packs. Too bad if you want to buy 100 gram boxes; we don't make them.'

Product-driven organisation

'Did you say you'd like to buy our cornflakes in 100 gram retail packs? Let me find out how soon we can adjust our manufacturing process to accommodate you.'

Customer-driven organisation

Customer-driven organisations listen to their customers. They are also different from the **cost-driven organisation** which focuses primarily on reducing the costs involved in producing a product or service. 'Beat our competitors on cost' is their motto.

'Sorry, we can't do 100 gram packs. It would be too expensive to install the machinery.'

Cost-driven organisation

Which organisation would you rather do business with?

Identifying their customers, listening to them and meeting or exceeding their needs and wants is a primary objective of customer-driven organisations.

Internal customers

External customers 'pay the rent' but we shouldn't forget our **internal customers**. In many organisations, the various departments seem to operate in a vacuum. The left hand doesn't know what the right hand is doing.

- 'What! You needed this *urgently*? No one told me!'
- 'The salespeople keep sending in orders requiring uneconomic production runs. We just save them up until there's enough to make a run worthwhile.'
- 'How can I meet my deadlines if people don't give me the right information?!'

Marketing seems to fight with production. Production blames purchasing and supply for its problems. Sales battles with distribution. Departments operating in isolation, or 'silos',

FROM THEORY TO PRACTICE

Good links between the factory floor and administration services matched with simple, strong systems were a major factor in Caradon Trend, the UK electronics manufacturer, winning a highly commended place as British Institute of Management's 1999 *Best Electronics and Electrical Factory*. The colour of the paper in the sales office fax machines, for example, is changed daily to highlight any unanswered faxes. The dispatch and shipping teams, after-sales repair and warranty service teams are located in the same office as the sales team.

disrupt work, divert our energy and efforts away from the real problems, and do nothing to satisfy customers.

The TQM approach is different. Departments don't battle with each other but are suppliers and customers of each other. Production is a customer of purchasing; administration is a supplier to marketing, and so on. In this way, we can see the entire organisation as a **customer–supplier chain**. All departments, and everyone in the departments, work together to satisfy the customer.

TQM opens up the communication channels and develops a team environment where each division and department works together. Building bridges between design and manufacturing, administration, finance, purchasing and marketing and integrating them into one interdependent whole, each playing an important part and adding value, is an important aim of TQM.

'A chain is only as strong as its weakest link.'

Where are the weakest links in your organisation? How can you strengthen them?

Trading partnerships and external suppliers

TQM stresses the importance of working *with* our organisation's customers and suppliers in a cooperative relationship so that everyone wins. This approach is often referred to as a **trading partnership** where supplier organisations and the customer organisations collaborate to grow their businesses together.

This requires a changed mind-set from the more traditional 'adversarial' relationship that used to exist between supplier and customer organisations. This often did long-term damage to the goodwill that needs to exist between customers and suppliers and could, and often did, result in damaging both businesses. What good does it do an organisation, for example, to beat down a supplier's price so low that it goes out of business? That only creates the problem of finding a new supplier who can meet our needs, and the trials and tribulations that 'getting it right' with the new supplier entails.

In Chapter 10, we look more at customer service.

Work systems and processes

Traditionally, two ways to improve an organisation have been recognised: *capital investment*, which is expensive and one-off; and *cost reduction*, which works initially, but then what? TQM offers a viable third way to improve an organisation: improve its *systems*.

A major focus of TQM is developing quality systems and procedures that will reliably and efficiently meet customer requirements. It aims to simplify and streamline them to avoid unnecessary activities and duplication of effort and enable people to 'get it right first time'. If something goes wrong, we look to the system to see why it happened. The goal is to fix the system, not lay blame.

In improving our systems, we can focus on four areas:

1. *Our suppliers.* We must make sure that the inputs to our organisation in terms of raw materials, information, etc. meet our needs reliably and consistently.
2. *Throughout each process in the organisation.* Where do things go wrong? Where are the bottlenecks? Where is effort wasted? Where are materials wasted? How can this be prevented?
3. *Just before handover or delivery.*
4. *Post-sale or -service support and follow-up.* Are our customers happy three months later? How could we have made them happier?

This 'fix the systems' view helps us determine the best ways of doing things in all areas of the organisation. It helps us design systems that reduce the chance of error and reduce variation so that systems reliably and consistently produce at the quality levels required. It allows us to reduce or eliminate those activities that are not 'adding value' but are needlessly taking up time, effort and 'space'.

Managing and improving work systems eliminates duplication and unnecessary work. It helps develop and establish standards against which to monitor performance. The outcome is gains in quality performance, productivity and goal achievement.

FROM THEORY TO PRACTICE

Some questions to improve systems
Does this step:
- add value to the product or the customer?
- improve quality?
- improve service?
- improve productivity?
- improve communication?
- cut costs?
- increase employee motivation or morale?
- encourage innovation?
- speed decision making?

More questions to ask about each step in a process
- What would happen (*really*) if it didn't get done?
- Is someone else doing it? (duplication of effort)
- When did it start being done? Why? (It may have made sense once, but ...)
- Could someone else (inside or outside the company) do it better? More easily? Faster?

FROM THEORY TO PRACTICE

'The best way to improve the quality of an operation is to eliminate ... it,' says John Tonkiss, operations manager of Lucas Automotive Electronics, winner of the British Institute of Management's 1999 *Best Electronics and Electrical Industry Award*. The Birmingham, England, plant produces electronic control units such as cruise control, power steering and alarm systems for 16 car manufacturers including Ford, Nissan, Volvo and Honda. It has synthesised best practice in two industries: electronics and automotive component manufacture.

It has outsourced complexity in its supply chain operation. All suppliers deliver to an off-site warehouse managed and owned by a third-party contractor who delivers kits of components twice daily and takes away finished products for delivery to customers.

Training is first class and reinforced by carefully thought-out operations procedures which strive to eliminate variation.

Continuous improvement

Have you heard the saying, 'If it ain't broke, don't fix it'?

The TQM approach is different. Rather than 'leave well enough alone', its goal is **continuous improvement**. How can we make things a little bit better? How can we 'tweak' them, refine them, polish them? TQM says:

> **'It's better to do 100 things 1% better
> than one thing 100% better.'**

This results in *little step improvements* rather than *big step improvements*. Doing 100 things 1% better gives us little step improvements. A big step improvement, such as a major investment in a computer system or new machinery for production, is important but costly. Organisations can only afford occasional big step improvements. Little step improvements, on the other hand, are less costly and add up to improved productivity and performance in the long run.

The Japanese word for continuous incremental improvement is *kaizen*. The *kaizen* approach is:

> **'Let's keep examining everything we do and see how we can do better.'**

Do you think small improvements won't make that much of a difference? Actually, they make a huge difference. And in today's marketplace, they're essential.

> **'It takes all the running you can do
> just to stay in the same place.'**
>
> Lewis Carroll, *Alice in Wonderland*

We need to improve systems and procedures continually if we are to 'stay in the race'. In today's environment, 'if we're not getting better, we're getting worse'. If we don't improve

FROM THEORY TO PRACTICE

The Cheshire, England, factory of Henkel Consumer Adhesives, a German-owned chemical company, aims for responsiveness to its 1100 demanding retail customers through TQM techniques. Its 'can-do' improvement program has made major improvements to lead times and operations and its Total Productive Maintenance program has preserved older equipment at peak efficiencies.

continually, our competitors will eventually overtake us, no matter how good we are right now. The two key questions for continuous improvement are:
1. How can we do this better?
2. How else can we do this?

Process re-engineering

In some organisations **re-engineering** became synonymous with mindless retrenchments and the resultant ill-will and lowered morale among employees at all levels. If managed properly, however, re-engineering, or **core process redesign**, can offer a way to make big step improvements in the way we produce and offer our products and services. It involves first identifying the organisation's customers and what they want, then working backwards, using technology and systematic analytic methods, to radically redesign processes and operating procedures to achieve dramatic improvements in productivity and serve the customers more efficiently. It centres the organisation's activities on meeting the customers' needs.

FROM THEORY TO PRACTICE

After re-engineering the process of developing, building and launching new products, Texas Instruments' calculator business reduced the time it takes to launch a new product by up to 50%, reduced break-even points by up to 80% and became a market leader. Its return on investment more than quadrupled.

After implementing a re-engineering project and placing responsibility for processes with senior corporate executives, IBM achieved its goal of standardising its processes around the world to meet its customers' needs, a 75% reduction in the average time-to-market for new products, a significant increase in on-time deliveries and customer satisfaction and more than $12 billion in cost savings.

Owens Corning core process redesign placed cross-functional process teams under the leadership of process owners, resulting in a 50% increase in inventory turns, a 20% reduction in administrative costs and millions of dollars in logistical savings through vastly improved resource planning methods.

Re-engineering helps us see an enterprise not as a discrete entity but as part of a web of relationships and information systems.

Re-engineering is more than the *kaizen* incremental 'little step' improvements approach of streamlining a process or system to do it more quickly or more efficiently. It involves radically rethinking an organisation's processes, systems and procedures from top to bottom. It aims at great leaps forward in all measures of operating efficiency.

For example, ABB Distribution in Liverpool, New South Wales, an electric switchgear manufacturer, re-engineered its order–delivery chain for outdoor products. This reduced the cycle time from order to delivery from 27 days to seven days and cut inventory by two-thirds. Big step improvements indeed!

The end result of process re-engineering is usually:
- reduced specialisation
- reduced functionalism (silos)
- reduced non-value adding activities
- reduced overhead costs
- increased responsiveness
- increased productivity.

THE **BIG** PICTURE

Unfortunately 70% of re-engineering efforts fail to achieve impressive improvements. Why? Some organisations fail to start from the fundamentals: examining the business strategic plan and how to help each arm of the organisation to work towards achieving it. Others fail to begin by examining the markets and customers and then redesigning the organisation to meet their needs and wants. Some see re-engineering as a convenient way to reduce the workforce, close a factory or shut down a department; this isn't re-engineering but a tool to achieve predetermined objectives.

Despite the failures, re-engineering is almost a must for many organisations because of the potential gains that can result. Especially for companies that lag far behind their competitors, only great leaps forward can save them.

Benchmarking

How do we know how we're doing? **Benchmarking** offers us a reliable and consistent way to measure our performance, productivity, quality and innovation.

We establish meaningful key measures such as timeliness, inventory carried, accident-free days, number of errors or defects per 100 operations or units produced. These become our benchmarks to measure and monitor our performance.

We can use these benchmark measures in three ways. First, we can monitor our own department's quality, progress and improvements over time. We have objective measures of when to 'pat ourselves on the back'. This feedback is very motivating and helps encourage continuous improvements. If a quality benchmark measure suddenly drops, it can alert us to a problem in the system that we can study and rectify. In this way, benchmarking helps supervisors to monitor, maintain and improve quality levels.

FROM THEORY TO PRACTICE

In 1992 automotive component manufacturer Britax Wingard underwent a Nissan benchmarking study. It found that it didn't have a single operation that scored higher than 50% of world-class best practice. Two managers attended Toyota University in Japan to learn how to put things right.

Over the next seven years, the factory consistently applied TQM techniques. In 1999 it won the British Institute of Management's *Factory of the Year* award.

Second, we can compare our quality with other departments in our own organisation. An organisation with factories in Beijing, Kuala Lumpur, Melbourne and Bombay might benchmark key productivity and performance measures in each location and compare them with the others. If Melbourne has the most accident-free days, their work safety methods can be studied and copied by the other factories. If the Beijing factory has the highest number of orders delivered on time, the other factories can study and adopt its delivery methods.

Third, benchmarking allows us to compare our own organisation's performance in key measures of quality and efficiency with the performance of other organisations in our own or in different industries. This **best practice benchmarking** allows us to compare our own performance with the world leaders' performance in a particular area.

A finance department, for example, might set benchmarks for a number of key indicators of financial management such as average length of time taken to invoice a customer, errors per invoice, number of days for outstanding debts and interest earned on capital. They might find that a company in a different industry has been able to reduce outstanding debts to 15 days, and meet with that company to learn how they did it. Organisations can learn a lot from each other and benchmarking makes this possible.

THE **BIG** PICTURE

Total quality, benchmarking, process re-engineering, teams … Are these fads? No.

A competitor uses one of these techniques and gains a competitive advantage. So the rest use it too. The playing field is level again, and the bar is raised. So we need a new process to gain further competitive advantage. Failing to use it will be a disadvantage; using it will level the playing field.

Is quality a competitive advantage? It was once but no more. It's mandatory. Having quality won't ensure success but if you don't have it, you're sure to fail.

The penalties for not keeping up with the new ways of creating competitive advantage can be severe.

People working together

> 'When spider webs unite, they can tie up a lion.'
>
> Ethiopian proverb

To achieve ongoing improvements to processes, products, services and the organisation itself people must work together. This requires an attitude that places quality, teamwork and continuous improvement at the very centre of the organisation's culture.

> 'Quality is the way we do business.'

To achieve this, a culture based on shared values and vision, commitment to goals, an empowered, creative workforce of people willing to learn, change, develop and grow who operate in a team environment, and a supportive open management style is essential.

The quality culture must embrace the entire processing and service–delivery chain. All areas of the organisation need to work together through supportive internal customer–supplier relationships. There should be no demarcation between R&D, testing, finishing, design and administration. Everyone in the chain must take responsibility for their own actions and for working with others to achieve quality standards and continuous improvements. No one ever thinks that it is only management that can improve things in a total quality organisation.

Here are some words that describe total quality organisations:

- participative
- teamwork
- involvement
- commitment
- vision
- flexible
- responsive
- cooperative
- satisfying
- supportive
- skilled
- innovative.

Do these words describe your organisation too?

Box 9.9 shows a TQM best practice culture checklist based on surveys of Australian companies that have successfully implemented TQM and have been awarded certification.

People don't change their attitudes and become quality-conscious overnight. They need training in both the qualitative people skills of teamwork and participating in meetings, and

FROM THEORY TO PRACTICE

Simple practical improvements helped Reckitt & Colman's Hull, England, factory to win the British Institute of Management's 1999 *Best Process Factory* award. This suggestion from one employee prevents contamination to bottles, cuts down on packaging and shortens the loading time of empty bottles: ask the supplier to deliver empty Dettol bottles upside down. Simple, but worthwhile.

Small improvements like these add up. The Hull factory learned to make Dettol so cheaply it could be shipped to Australia more cheaply than we could manufacture it here. Sadly, the Australian factory was out-benchmarked and out-TQM'ed, and was closed.

FROM THEORY TO PRACTICE

TQM self-check questions
- What do I produce?
- Do I add value?
- Who receives what I produce?
- If I didn't do my job, who would be affected?
- Who depends on me?
- What improvements have I made lately to the way I do my work?

BOX **9.9** **BEST PRACTICE QUALITY CULTURE CHECKLIST**

Customer focus
❏ Do we define quality in terms of customer expectations and perceptions?
❏ Do we clearly understand our customers' expectations?
❏ Do we strive to meet and exceed those expectations?
❏ Do we have a service-level agreement with our key customers that formalises expectations and reviews procedures?

Planning
❏ Do we have a well tested strategic and quality plan that identifies our quality vision?
❏ Do our employees know and support our quality plan?
❏ Is our quality plan supported in day-to-day actions?
❏ Do we set quantifiable targets for improvements?

Process improvement
❏ Have we documented and standardised our key business processes and evaluated them against customer expectations?
❏ Do we continually improve these processes?

Supplier relationships
❏ Do we select our suppliers based on best value for money and their commitment to continuous improvement?
❏ Do we have well developed working relationships with our key suppliers?
❏ Do we have partnership arrangements with key suppliers that set out our expectations, performance standards and procedures, and problem-solving processes?

Involvement and commitment
❏ Do our managers and employees know they are each responsible and accountable for quality?

Continued . . .

❏ Are they trained in TQM tools and techniques, including team building?
❏ Do they have 'total quality attitudes' and behaviours?

Communication
❏ Do we measure our results and communicate them to all employees?
❏ Do we benchmark with other organisations?
❏ Do people share information and contribute ideas?

Leadership
❏ Is management fully committed to implementing total quality?
❏ Do they take a strong and visible role in leading change?
❏ Are they role models for total quality attitudes, actions and behaviours?

---

in quantitative techniques to identify, analyse and solve problems. Common topics in the first category of training include team building, participative practices, coaching and customer relations training, while topics in the second category of training include statistical and analytic problem-analysis techniques and statistical process control. We need to educate and motivate employees at all levels to focus on customer needs. They need to know how to work in a team environment and combine these skills with quality management disciplines. Only then can a true total quality culture emerge.

> 'In order to control your destiny, you must realise that you will stay ahead competitively only if you acknowledge that no advantage and no success is ever permanent. The winners are those who keep moving.'
>
> John Browne, CEO of BP
> Quoted in *Harvard Business Review*, Sept./Oct. 1997

Systematic analytical tools and techniques

Real information and data, not guesswork, hunches, trial and error, good luck or serendipity, is the only way to reliably promote total quality, innovation and continuous improvement and serve our customers better. TQM tools give us objective and systematic ways to identify and resolve problems, streamline systems and process and build quality into them. Box 9.10 shows how we can use the main TQM tools.

In Chapter 11 we look at four of these techniques for improving productivity and quality: the *nominal group technique, brainstorming, cause-and-effect diagrams* and *force field analysis*. The section below reviews the other TQM tools used to investigate and improve systems and procedures. These are an indispensable part of any total quality, innovation and continuous improvement effort.

Although individuals can apply these techniques, they are best used in a team environment. Moreover, the teams and individuals involved in doing a job know it best and are more likely to implement solutions that they have been involved in determining.

Supervisors are frequently involved in quality improvement and problem-solving teams using these techniques. They often lead these teams and are frequently responsible for teaching team members how to apply the techniques. They are also responsible for

BOX 9.10   HOW TO USE TQM TOOLS

- Tools to help identify the problem and decide which one to address first/next:
  - check sheets
  - circling
  - pie charts and flow charts
  - control charts
  - brainstorming
  - nominal group technique.
- Tools to help identify and analyse the problem:
  - Pareto charts
  - is/is not comparison
  - run charts

- stratification charts
- checkerboard analysis
- cause-and-effect diagrams.
- Tools to help analyse and resolve the problem:
  - histograms
  - scatter diagrams
  - control charts
  - process capability charts.
- Tools to help implement a solution:
  - the PDCA cycle
  - force field analysis.

developing the team's group dynamics and helping it to reach a stage where the members work together effectively.

Check sheets

Check sheets help you gather data based on sample observations so that you can detect and isolate patterns of non-conformances and variation. In other words, *check sheets highlight where things are going wrong.* They are a good starting point for problem solving and managing quality because they help you identify problems and find out which occur most often, and build a picture of them. They are a simple way to answer the question: 'How often are certain events happening?' and begin the process of translating opinions into facts.

Figure 9.2 shows that problem A occurred seven times, problem B occurred 13 times and problem C occurred six times. It seems that we should focus our attention on problem B, particularly as the number of times the problem occurred each week is consistent. If one week stood out from the others as having far more or fewer problems occurring, we would want to examine what happened during that week to see what we could learn from it.

To make a check sheet, follow these steps:

1. Agree on, and define precisely, the events you will monitor so that everyone is looking for the same thing.

FROM THEORY TO PRACTICE

In 1994 Italian-British owned Alenia Marconi Systems in Portsmouth, England, was in danger of being closed along with many of its sister factories throughout Europe. Management won a reprieve and the factory adopted TQM techniques, carefully trained its workforce and set about ruthlessly eliminating waste. Productivity soared 25% in two years; delivery performances were raised to world-class standards; rework levels were cut from 11% to 3% and work-in-progress slashed by 30%.

In 1999 the factory won the British Institute of Management's 1999 *Most Improved Factory* award.

FIGURE 9.2   CHECK SHEET

Problem	Week			Total
	1	2	3	
A	II	III	II	7
B	IIII	IIII	IIII	13
C	II	I	III	6
Total	8	9	9	26

2. Decide the time period over which you will collect data; this might be several hours or several weeks. Make sure you will collect enough data over a long enough period of time to be as representative as possible, but not so much data that collecting it becomes an end in itself. Make sure that your observations and samples will be *homogeneous*—that is, from the same machine, person, etc. If this is not the case, you should first *stratify* or group the samples (see stratification charts, below) and sample each one individually.
3. Design a form that is clear and easy to use, labelling each column clearly and making sure there is enough space to record your observations.
4. Collect the data. Ensure that people have time to collect it.
5. Examine your data. What does it tell you? What points need to be followed up? What further information do you need?

Circling

If you want to tighten up a very broad or complex issue, write it up on a flip chart and then circle the key words, as shown in Figure 9.3.

Each time you clarify, you sharpen your problem definition. If there is an 'and' in the definition, make sure you're not trying to solve two problems at once (as in this example). Split them and solve each separately.

FIGURE 9.3   THE CIRCLING TECHNIQUE TO SPECIFY BROAD OR COMPLEX ISSUES

How to (solve) (customer) (complaints) and (warranty claims.)

Solve = reduce?
        eliminate entirely?
        prevent?
Which customers?
What kinds of complaints?
What kinds of warranty claims?

Pie charts

As Figure 9.4 shows, **pie charts** are circular graphs where the entire circle represents 100% (not 360 degrees) of the data. The circle, or pie, is divided into percentage slices that clearly

FIGURE 9.4   PIE CHART: TIME USAGE OF SALES REPRESENTATIVES

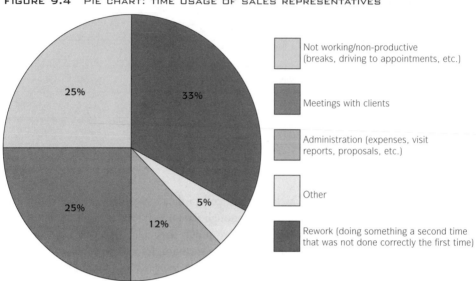

show the relative sizes (frequencies, amounts, etc.) of the data being studied. This helps you to describe a problem in a similar way to a Pareto chart, and it can also show you where to begin your problem-solving efforts. Be sure to mark the subject matter clearly, showing the percentages within the slices and what each slice represents.

Flow charts

A **flow chart** is a pictorial representation showing all the steps of a process or activity. It can help you decide which problem to address first or next, analyse a process to find out where value is (or is not) added, find out where duplication or hassles exist and where potential sources of trouble might occur. It can help you 'see' each step in a process and how it relates to the other steps, and it can highlight deviations from the ideal path a process should follow. Flow charts can also be useful training tools.

You can make a flow chart of any process, from manufacturing to administration to customer service, to show the flow of materials, or the steps involved in making a sale, servicing a product, serving a customer or producing an invoice.

To develop a flow chart, follow these steps:
1. Gather together the people who work in the system or process being charted.
2. Discuss and agree what steps the process *actually* entails and, using the symbols shown in Figure 9.5, diagram the process as it is *currently* followed.
3. Agree how the process should *ideally* occur if everything is working right, and diagram this.
4. Compare the two charts to find out where you can improve the process.

Make sure everyone is clear about the process that is being flow charted, including where it begins and ends. Make sure every feedback loop in the chart has an escape. There is

FIGURE 9.5   FLOW CHART

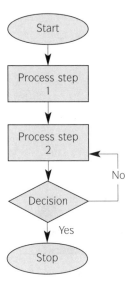

usually only one output arrow out of a process box; if you need more, this indicates that a decision diamond might be needed.

Pareto charts

Pareto charts are a good way to display the relative importance of all the problems or events you are examining. They are vertical bar charts that show the events or problems in descending order of quantity. In this way, they can direct your attention and efforts to the truly important problems and help you choose a starting point for problem solving.

In the example of defects found shown in Figure 9.6, we would want to investigate the causes of raw materials run-outs to try to stop this occurring. Then we would want to find the causes and sources of faulty raw materials and discuss this with our suppliers; we may even consider changing to a more reliable supplier. Next, we would want to investigate the types and causes of machine breakdowns and see what we could do to stop or reduce them.

Pareto charts can also help you to identify and describe a problem or its basic cause, plan to resolve it and monitor your success.

You can compile Pareto charts from check sheets or other forms of data collection. To construct a Pareto chart, follow these steps:

1. Select the problems to compare and rank by nominal group technique or using existing data (e.g. check sheets).
2. Select the unit of measurement (cost, frequency, percentage, etc.) and the time period to be studied (hours, days, weeks).
3. Gather the data.
4. Plot the data by listing the units of measurement vertically and each category (problem or event) from left to right horizontally in decreasing order. Mark the measurement and categories clearly. Combine the categories with the fewest items into one category called 'other', which goes at the extreme right as the last bar.

· ·
FIGURE 9.6   PARETO CHART: DEFECTS FOUND AT IN-PROCESS INSPECTION

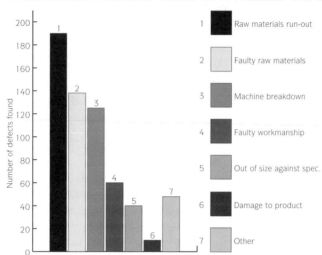

5. Draw a vertical bar above each category with the height representing the unit of measurement in that classification.
6. Study the Pareto chart to see what you can learn from it.

Pareto charts can provide surprising insights. For example, the two charts in Figure 9.7 illustrate the importance of examining a problem from different perspectives: resolving the most frequently occurring problems first might not be the most cost-effective way to proceed.

Figure 9.8 shows that we sometimes need to use our imagination when measuring problems and information. Showing defects by type and by machine doesn't give us very much information, but showing defects by shift really gives us something to investigate.

· ·
FIGURE 9.7   USING PARETO CHARTS TO IDENTIFY THE MOST IMPORTANT PROBLEMS THROUGH DIFFERENT MEASUREMENTS

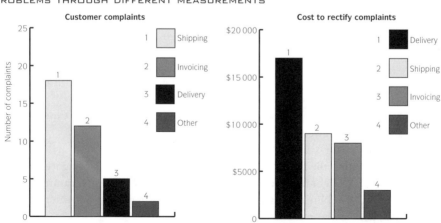

FIGURE 9.8   USING PARETO CHARTS TO ANALYSE INFORMATION IN DIFFERENT WAYS

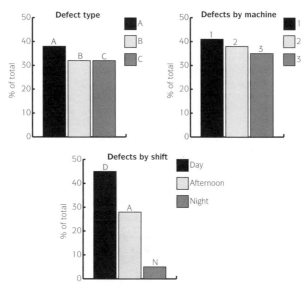

Figure 9.9 demonstrates how you can use Pareto charts to measure the impact of changes, with before and after comparisons. In the example shown, the number of complaints drops markedly after the introduction of a revised process flow.

Pareto charts can also help you to break down a problem (see Figure 9.10). This can help to isolate the causes of problems from their symptoms.

FIGURE 9.9   USING PARETO CHARTS TO MEASURE THE IMPACT OF CHANGE

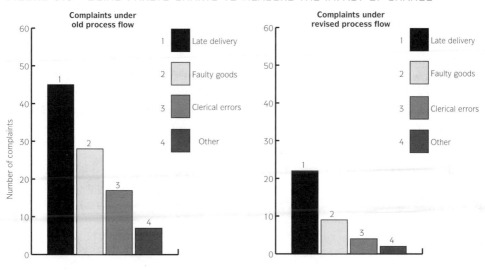

FIGURE 9.10   USING PARETO CHARTS TO BREAK DOWN A PROBLEM

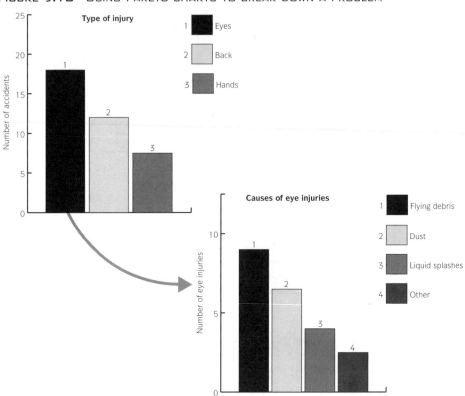

Use your common sense when constructing and analysing Pareto charts. For example, it may pay to resolve a recurring complaint from a major customer before resolving numerous other complaints from small customers.

Is/is not comparison

In one column, write down what you do know about the problem and, in the second column, write what you know is *not* part of the problem. Use the Where? When? How much or how bad? How often? Who? What? triggers (see Box 9.11).

Once you have written down everything you know about the problem, compare the *Is* with the *Is not* column, looking for differences and changes. These should give you points to follow up which could lead you to identify the source of the problem.

Run charts

Run charts are a simple way to show trends in processes such as machine downtime, yields, scrap, clerical errors, productivity or customer complaints. Seeing how things vary over time (are they getting worse, staying the same, or improving?) can help you either to identify and describe a problem or monitor a process.

Run charts are simple to construct and interpret. To make a run chart, plot what you are measuring as points on the graph and then connect the points. Make sure that you plot the

---

BOX 9.11

IS/IS NOT COMPARISON: ABSENTEEISM AMONG OFFICE STAFF

	Is	*Is not*	*Point to follow up*
Where?	general office	accounts public relations sales & marketing	Working conditions, hours of work, supervision: What is different about the general office?
When?	most days	no obvious patterns, e.g. Fridays or Mondays	Complete a check sheet to identify any hidden patterns.
Who?	mostly newer staff	not longer-serving staff	Make a histogram of age groups to check this. Check ages and profiles for 'job fit'. Check training and induction given to new recruits. Check their jobs for job interest: are they different from jobs of longer-serving staff?
How often?	about 17% on any given day		Benchmark with local organisations to see how bad this problem is.
How bad?	problem may be increasing	not getting better or staying the same	Check this year's absenteeism rates against previous years.
What?	mostly one-day absences	seldom longer than two days	

---

measurements in the order that you made them, since you are tracking them over time (see Figure 9.11).

Any wide variations deserve attention because they might highlight a problem in a process. Run charts can also highlight shifts in the average results. For example, when monitoring a system, an equal number of points should fall above and below the average. When this does not happen, it indicates that either an unusual 'event' or change has occurred in the system, or that the average has changed. If the shift is favourable, you should

---

FIGURE 9.11   RUN CHART

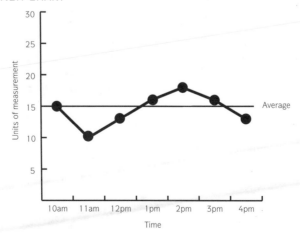

study it to find out why, so that you can make the change a permanent part of the system. If it is unfavourable, find out why it has occurred and eliminate the possibility of it happening again. You should also examine any steady increase or decrease in a trend since this would not be expected to occur randomly and would also indicate an important change that needs to be investigated.

Stratification charts

Stratification is a useful technique for analysing data to find improvement opportunities. It helps to sort out confusing data that actually mask the facts. This might happen, for example, when the recorded data are *non-homogeneous* (from many sources but treated as one number). Stratification can break these down into more meaningful categories or classifications to help you describe a problem, and focus on and monitor corrective action.

The run chart in Figure 9.12 shows, for example, that the number of minor injuries in a factory has been steadily increasing over the last 12 months. However, this is the total of all minor accidents. We don't know what type of accidents (scratches, cuts, bumps, burns) they are, where they are occurring (which department, which machines, which processes), when they are occurring (which shift, day of the week) or any other potentially important information.

FROM THEORY TO PRACTICE

Basing your decisions on data removes the danger of following someone else's opinion without question; reduces the chance of heated arguments and conflict; and enables you to be confident in your decisions. Here are some tips on charting:

- Remember that the point of charts and graphs is not to collect and display just any information. The point is to collect and display *meaningful* information—data you can use to analyse and improve your service or manufacturing processes.
- Base the data you use on random, representative samples taken from homogeneous groups. Gather it consistently (in the same way each time) to ensure the data is not biased.
- Show the name of the person or team who compiled it, the date the data was collected, the time span covered (time of day, shift, etc.), where the data was collected, who by and how (by instruments, observation, etc.) on every chart and diagram. Someone may need to refer to them in the future, so be quite meticulous in the way you label your charts.
- Keep it simple. Use the simplest appropriate tool or technique possible and don't overcomplicate your graphs.
- Use your common sense when interpreting graphs and charts.
- Don't make decisions based on just one piece of evidence. Gather some supporting information for your peace of mind and to ensure you have got it right.
- Get help from experts whenever you need it. That's what they're there for.

FIGURE 9.12   STRATIFICATION CHART

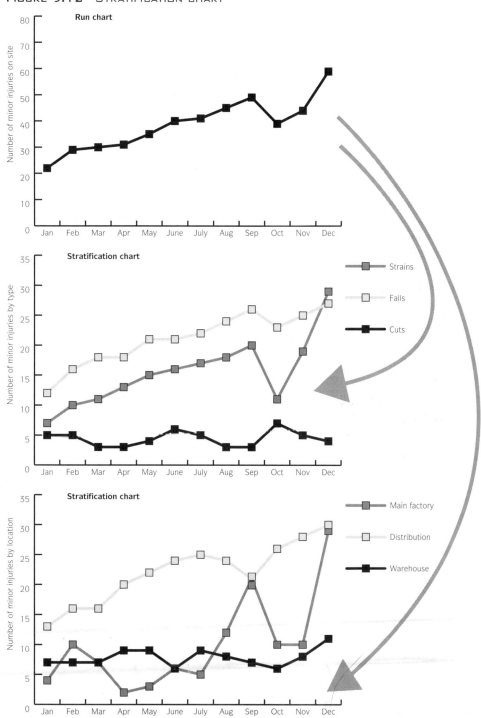

Stratification charts can show this information, making it easier to isolate the real problem and act to resolve it. The first stratification chart in the example shows that we should investigate the cause of falls first and try to reduce them, and then move our attention to strains. The second stratification chart shows that distribution seems to be a particularly bad area for minor injuries and we should focus our attention there, at least initially. It also indicates that the main factory had far higher than average minor injuries in September and December, which we should investigate.

Checkerboard analysis

As shown in Figure 9.13, a **checkerboard analysis** uses a matrix to analyse a problem. Elements of one key aspect of the problem go down one side and elements of another aspect across the top. Focus your attention on where they intersect. This example is from a chain of wholesale shops that serve mainly trade account customers but also sell to the general public. Problems have been experienced with delayed invoices sent from head office, particularly to non-account (general public) customers. The preparation of these invoices is based on information sent in by the shops. From the information shown in Figure 9.13, we would probably focus our attention on the form itself and the number of interruptions occurring in the shops as the forms are being filled out. How could the form be improved? What could be done to reduce the errors caused by interruptions in the shops? This might lead us to consider changing the system of information gathering itself. We would probably also want to clarify why the shops are providing insufficient information and the cause of the processing difficulties at head office.

Histograms

Histograms are bar charts that display the distribution of data by graphing the number of units in each category you are studying. As we have already seen with Pareto charts, it is useful to display bar graphs showing the frequency with which certain events occur. This is

FIGURE 9.13   CHECKERBOARD ANALYSIS

Problems at source \ Problems within accounts	Insufficient information	Inaccurate information	Details incorrect	Processing difficulties at head office	Accounts staff not clear about procedure	Total
Form for collecting information confusing and repetitive	✖	✖	✖		✖	4
Staff too 'hurried' to collect details correctly and/or fully	✖	✖	✖			3
Too many interruptions	✖	✖	✖	✖		4
Correct pricing information unavailable	✖			✖	✖	3
Forms not passed on to accounts quickly enough				✖		1
Forms not batched correctly at source				✖		1
Total	4	3	3	4	2	

Problem: How to speed up the invoicing process to non-account customers called *frequency distribution*. While Pareto charts display characteristics of a product or service, called *attribute data* (defects, errors, complaints, etc.), histograms display the distribution of *measurement data* (temperature, dimensions, etc.). This can reveal the amount of variation in a process, help you discover and describe a problem and monitor its solution.

Figure 9.14 shows a typical histogram. It shows the greatest number of units in the centre with a roughly equal number of units on either side. A *normal distribution curve*, or bell shape, is statistically what we could expect from any process, because every process will vary over time. Repeated samples of any process that is under control will follow this pattern.

If a histogram does not show this pattern, you need to investigate. Figure 9.15 shows an out-of-control process where the data are 'piled up' at points to the left of centre. A distribution like this is referred to as *skewed*.

When examining histograms, look at the shape of the distribution for surprises—for example, a distribution that you would expect to be 'normal' (a centred curve) but is skewed. Are most measurements skewed on the 'high side' or the 'low side'? Look for whether the 'spread' of the curve (*variability*) falls within specifications; if it does not, how far outside the specifications is it? Analyse the process further to find out what you can do to bring it into specifications.

To construct a histogram, follow these steps:

1. Gather your data (*data set*) and count the number of *data points* in your data set.
2. Determine the *range (R)* value for the entire data set. This is the smallest subtracted from the largest data point.
3. Divide the range value into a certain number of *classes (K)*, or bars on the chart, using the data in Table 9.1.
4. Determine the *class width (H)* using the formula below:

$$H = \frac{R}{K}$$

FIGURE 9.14   A HISTOGRAM OF A PROCESS THAT IS IN CONTROL

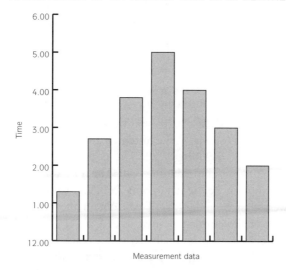

Measurement data

FIGURE 9.15   HISTOGRAM OF A PROCESS THAT IS NOT IN CONTROL

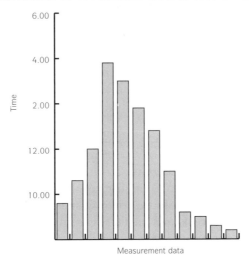

TABLE 9.1   CALCULATING THE NUMBER OF CLASSES REQUIRED, BASED ON THE NUMBER OF DATA POINTS

Number of data points	Number of classes
Under 50	5 to 7
51 to 100	6 to 10
101 to 250	7 to 12
Over 250	10 to 20

5. Decide where each bar on the histogram will begin and end by determining the *class boundary*, or *end points*. Take the smallest measurement in the data set and use that number (or round it down to an appropriate lower number) as the lower end point for your first class boundary. Then add the class width to your lower end point and this number becomes your next lower class boundary, as shown in the example below:

Smallest measurement in the data set = 7 = lower end point

class width = 0.20

7 + 0.20 = 7.20 = next lower end point

7.20 + 0.20 = next lower end point

Therefore, the first class (or bar on the histogram) would be 7 and would include all data points up to but not including 7.20. The next class would begin at 7.20 and include data points up to but not including 7.40. The third class would begin with data points at 7.40 and stop just before data point 7.60, and so on. Keep adding the class width to the lowest class boundary until you obtain the correct number of classes containing the range of all your data points.

This process makes each class mutually exclusive—each data point will fit into one and only one class (or bar)—and gives you an accurate histogram.

6. Construct a *frequency table* based on the number of classes, class width and class boundary, calculated above. This is actually a histogram in tabular form.
7. Construct a histogram based on the frequency table, as shown in Figure 9.16.
8. Use the histogram to diagnose variations and problems in a system. In the example shown in Figure 9.16, the data centres on 7.8 to 7.99, which is close to a normal curve. If the specification for the temperature were 5.5 to 8.5 with a target of 7, the histogram would show that the process is running high and producing too much unacceptable product. If, on the other hand, the temperature specification was 7 to 9 with a target of 8, our process would be in control.

When studying histograms, remember that some processes are naturally skewed; not all follow a natural, bell-shaped curve. If a class suddenly stops at one point without a previous decline in number, check your data for accuracy; someone may have made a mistake. If the histogram shows two high points, check whether two or more sources provided the data. If so, go back and get homogeneous data.

FIGURE 9.16   CONSTRUCTING A HISTOGRAM FROM A FREQUENCY TABLE

Frequency table

Class	Class boundaries	Mid-point	Frequency (number of data points falling into this class)	Total
1	7.00–7.19	7.1	I	
2	7.20–7.39	7.3	卌 IIII	
3	7.40–7.59	7.5	卌 卌 卌 II	
4	7.60–7.79	7.7	卌 卌 卌 卌 卌 II	
5	7.80–7.99	7.9	卌 卌 卌 卌 卌 卌 I	
6	8.00–8.19	8.1	卌 卌 卌 卌 I	
7	8.20–8.39	8.3	卌 卌 II	
8	8.40–8.59	8.5	III	
9	8.60–8.79	8.7	IIII	
10	8.80–8.99	8.9		

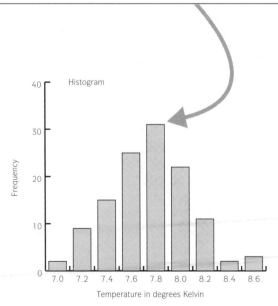

Scatter diagrams

Does overtime affect quality? Does training improve results? Does placing an advertisement on the right-hand side of a page affects sales? Does reducing the temperature in a process affect a product's quality? To know for sure, construct a **scatter diagram**. This will reveal any relationships between one variable and another, and possible cause-and-effect relationships. Scatter diagrams can't prove whether one variable causes another, but they will clarify whether a relationship exists and how strong it is. In this way, scatter diagrams help you determine the basic cause(s) of a problem.

The horizontal axis measures one variable and the vertical axis the second variable. Figure 9.17 is a typical scatter diagram showing a positive relationship or *correlation* between two variables. Notice that the plotted points form a clustered pattern. The direction and tightness of the *cluster* indicates the strength of the relationship between the two variables. The tighter the cluster and the more it resembles a straight line, the stronger the relationship between the two variables. Figure 9.18 shows other scatter diagrams and how they would be interpreted.

To make a scatter diagram, follow these steps:

1. Collect 50 to 100 paired samples of data that you think may be related and construct a data sheet as shown below.

Person	Weight kg	Height cm
1	73	178
2	82	155
3	100	191
.		
.		
.		
50	48	155

2. Draw the horizontal and vertical axes of the scatter diagram with the values increasing as you move up on the vertical axis and to the right on the horizontal axis. Put the variable being investigated as the possible 'cause' on the horizontal axis and the effect variable on the vertical axis.

FIGURE 9.17 SCATTER DIAGRAM—STRONG POSITIVE CORRELATION

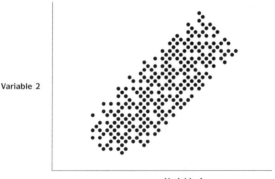

Variable 2

Variable 1

An increase in variable 2 may depend on an increase in variable 1. If we can control variable 1 we may be able to control variable 2.

FIGURE 9.18   SCATTER DIAGRAMS AND THEIR INTERPRETATIONS

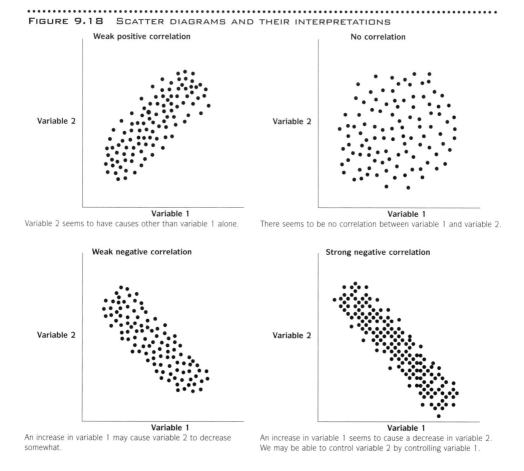

Weak positive correlation

Variable 2

Variable 1

Variable 2 seems to have causes other than variable 1 alone.

No correlation

Variable 2

Variable 1

There seems to be no correlation between variable 1 and variable 2.

Weak negative correlation

Variable 2

Variable 1

An increase in variable 1 may cause variable 2 to decrease somewhat.

Strong negative correlation

Variable 2

Variable 1

An increase in variable 1 seems to cause a decrease in variable 2. We may be able to control variable 2 by controlling variable 1.

3. Study the scatter diagram to see what you can learn from it.

Remember that negative relationships are as important as positive relationships, and that scatter diagrams only show relationships—they do not prove cause and effect.

Control charts

A **control chart** is a type of run chart that shows the upper and lower statistically acceptable limits of results drawn on either side of the average (see Figure 9.19). Note that these are statistically acceptable limits that may or may not be the same as customer requirements or specifications. They may be tighter than the customer requires (are you putting too much effort into this process?) or they may be looser than the customer wants (you'd better fix the process or risk losing a customer!).

All processes and systems have natural variation, but too much variation results in unreliable quality and increased costs. Control charts will show you how much variation exists in a process, whether this variation is random or follows a pattern, and whether or not the process is in statistical control. Thus, they will indicate whether a problem exists and help you implement and monitor solutions. For example, control charts will show you:

FIGURE 9.19   CONTROL CHART

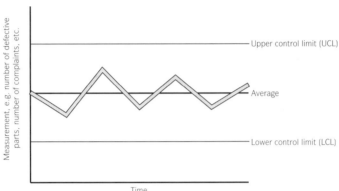

- how machine A's productivity and quality compares with machine B's;
- the running speeds, temperature, pressures and other factors in a process;
- how long it takes to complete a process (e.g. answering a customer query, resolving a customer complaint, sending out an invoice, making a sale); and
- when/how often delays are occurring.

To calculate the upper and lower control limits, the process is run without interference, samples are taken and averages calculated. This requires the use of complex statistical formulae and is usually done by specialists. Don't confuse the upper and lower limits of a control chart with specification limits. The former tells you what a process can do consistently and the latter tells you what you or the customer think you need.

Once the control limits are established, you can plot the sample averages onto a control chart and find out whether any of the points fall outside the control limits or form unlikely patterns. If either of these is the case, your process is statistically 'out of control' and you need to examine and fix it. Find out what event or events caused a result to be outside the control limits (remember the 85:15 rule from Chapter 8) and fix it so that it won't happen again. If the averages fall within the control limits, your process is in control. Although there will always be some variation in any system, you can probably improve your system (in this case, make it more reliable and predictable) by bringing the control limits closer to the average.

Figure 9.20 gives some indications of processes that are 'out of control', and suggests questions you could ask.

You can also use control charts as a monitoring tool by taking samples at regular intervals and plotting them on the control chart. This ensures that the process doesn't change in important ways and remains reliable. It will also highlight any non-conformances, or variations outside the control limits, that need investigation.

Process capability charts

A system may be 'in control', but that doesn't mean it meets your needs; it only means it is consistent (it may be consistently bad). This is where **process capability charts** come in.

FIGURE 9.20   OUT-OF-CONTROL SYSTEMS

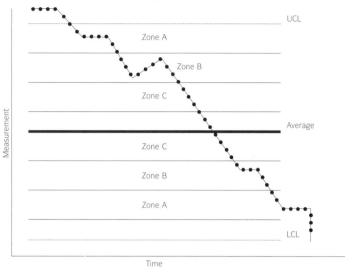

A process is 'out of control' if:

1. one or more points fall outside the control limits;
2. two out of three successive points occur on the same side of the centre line in Zone A;
3. four out of five successive points occur on the same side of the centre line in or outside Zone B;
4. nine successive points occur on one side of the average line;
5. there are six consecutive points increasing or decreasing;
6. there are 14 points in a row alternating up and down; or
7. there are 15 points in a row within Zone C.

Questions to ask with an out-of-control process

- Are the methods used changing?
- Did the samples come from different methods, machines, shifts or operators?
- What has changed in the process or the environment (e.g. maintenance procedures, training, overtime levels, raw materials)?
- Could the environment be affecting the process (temperature, humidity, etc.)?
- Could the equipment need maintenance?
- Have different measuring instruments been used that may not have the same degree of accuracy?
- Is everyone trained in how to carry out the process?
- Are the raw materials, information or other process inputs different?

They will show you whether a process, given its natural variation (as established by control charts) is capable of meeting the specifications. You can also use process capability charts to monitor a system and make sure your improvements are working. Capable systems meet the customer requirements every time because they are in control and the controls match the specifications.

As Figure 9.21 shows, capability charts show graphically whether or not your system is meeting requirements by showing the distribution of your process in relation to its specification limits.

A process capability index is calculated from the upper and lower specification limits, the measured natural variation in the process and the standard deviation in the process.

FIGURE 9.21   PROCESS CAPABILITY CHARTS

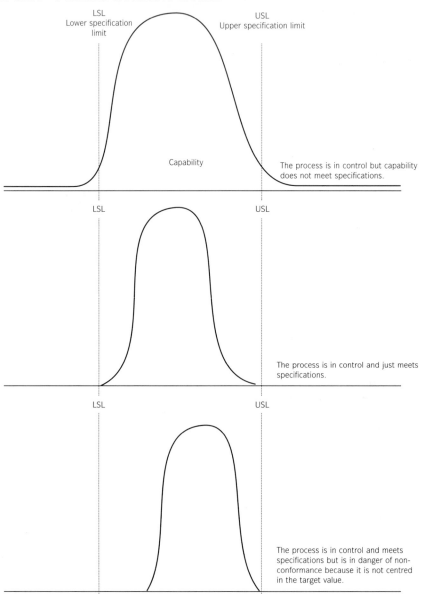

If the process variation exceeds the specification, too many defects are being made or services are not being provided satisfactorily. Even if the process variation is within specification, defects could still occur if the process is not centred on the specified target.

RAPID REVIEW

	True	False
1. Supervisors don't have to know all the answers, but they do need to be able to help their work team identify and fix problems.	☐	☐
2. A quality culture values customers, quality, cooperation and continuous improvement.	☐	☐
3. Total quality management is a Japanese technique.	☐	☐
4. TQM focuses on customers, teamwork and systems to ensure that organisation flourish.	☐	☐
5. TQM is a good 'quick fix' for organisations in trouble.	☐	☐
6. Unless an organisation needs quality certification as a marketing tool, there is no point in attaining it.	☐	☐
7. To attain quality certification, an organisation must put systems in place to assure product and service quality, document these systems and satisfy an auditor that it follows them consistently.	☐	☐
8. We need to make sure we know who our internal customers are and satisfy them.	☐	☐
9. Any sensible organisation will try to beat its suppliers down on price and award contracts solely on price.	☐	☐
10. The most successful organisations today are cost-focused.	☐	☐
11. 'If a system is working, don't tinker with it' is a sound TQM motto.	☐	☐
12. *Kaizen* is a Japanese word for total quality.	☐	☐
13. Process re-engineering helps organisations achieve a series of small, continuous improvements.	☐	☐
14. Benchmarking helps us measure and monitor our effectiveness in key areas.	☐	☐
15. A total quality culture is characterised by employees reporting flaws in production or problems with systems to management, which then fixes them.	☐	☐
16. A wide variety of tools can help us identify, prioritise and analyse problems, and implement and monitor solutions in order to improve systems and meet customer specifications more effectively.	☐	☐

APPLY YOUR KNOWLEDGE

1. In today's environment, if we're not getting better we're getting worse. Discuss.
2. Discuss how monitoring quality has changed over the years.
3. Is total quality management an essential philosophy and approach for today's organisations to follow or is it simply another 'flavour of the month'? Explain.
4. Discuss the factors involved in the success and failure of TQM programs.
5. Explain what quality systems do and the benefits of having them. Where do quality systems fit into the certification process?
6. Explain the five platforms of TQM and discuss how they help build performance and productivity and contribute to innovation and continuous improvement.
7. 'If you're not serving the customer, you'd better be serving someone who is.' Discuss.

8. How does establishing cooperative relationships with external suppliers benefit an organisation?

9. If you have read Chapter 8, explain the 85:15 rule and relate it to TQM's focus on systems and processes.

10. 'People are an essential element of TQM.' Discuss.

11. Describe the elements of a total quality culture.

12. Compare and contrast *kaizen* with process re-engineering. Why do many attempts at re-engineering fail to deliver the expected results?

13. Describe the systematic analytical techniques that can be used to identify and analyse problems.

14. Describe the systematic analytical techniques that can be used to identify cumbersome systems and procedures and streamline them.

······················· DEVELOP YOUR SKILLS ·······················

Individual activities

1. Design two simple quality systems for washing a car inside and out. Make the first system an old-fashioned one, to inspect for quality after the car is washed; make the second one a modern system to assure quality is built into the job. Which system would you rather have your car washed under?

2. Interview a representative of an organisation that has achieved quality certification to find out what it entailed. On balance, has certification helped them improve their operations and satisfy their customers better? Why, or why not?

3. Diagram an internal customer–supplier chain for your own workplace or college.

4. Interview a supervisor or manager you know to find out about the internal customer–supplier chain in their organisation. From your discussions, develop an assessment of whether the organisation tends to work more in 'silos' or as a true customer–supplier chain. Be prepared to explain your conclusions.

5. Find out how an organisation in your area uses benchmarking to monitor and improve its operations.

6. Describe a total quality culture and compare it with the culture of your own workplace or college.

7. How does the total quality control approach to building in and monitoring quality differ from, or resemble, the current approach your organisation (or an organisation you are familiar with) takes to quality control?

8. Gather the heights and weights of 15 people you know. Construct these as a histogram. Prepare a scatter diagram to find out the relationship between height and weight for these 15 people.

9. Time your drive to college or work for the next two weeks and plot the times on a run chart. What can you learn from it? What does the chart tell you about natural variation?

10. Analyse Case Study 5.1 using TQM's five platforms and make recommendations to improve the company's competitive position.

11. Referring to the vignette in Chapter 8 on page 239, what specific tools do you recommend Paulene and her team use to streamline the workflow?

Group activities

1. In groups of three, imagine you have just formed a quality circle to investigate why your chequeing account frequently shows a negative balance and rectify the situation. Plan out your first half dozen meetings, stating your goals for each. Include the tools and techniques you would use at each stage.

2. In groups of five or six, look through the synopsis of Dr Deming's 14 points (Box 9.5) and explain how each of them could be applied in a manufacturing environment, a retailing environment, a customer service environment (e.g. a hotel, casino, hospital or restaurant) and an office environment.

3. In small groups, prepare a flow chart for making a cup of coffee. Before you begin, decide the location of the coffee making facilities you will be charting—that is, in someone's home, at the café bar in the canteen?

4. Form into quality circles or quality improvement teams of five or six and apply the techniques shown in this chapter and in Chapter 11 to your concerns as students. Brainstorm and prioritise your problem areas and concerns. Select one that is within your control as students to analyse and resolve.

5. Work through the following scenario in small groups. Imagine you are a glass manufacturer. A customer wants glass panels made that are 1 × 1.5 m in size and no less than 3 mm thick, no more than 4 mm thick. Your current processing can cut the glass panels to the desired size but the thickness varies between 2.5 mm and 4.3 mm. What would a cost-driven organisation say? A product-driven organisation? A customer-driven organisation? Imagine you are a customer-driven organisation. Develop a range of possible approaches to satisfy the customer.

6. In small groups, imagine you are a bank manager who is concerned at the number of customers who are leaving your branch to move to a competitor down the road. When asked, most of them say the staff at the branch they are moving to are 'friendlier'. Develop a total quality approach to fix this problem. Make sure you include the five platforms and six Ps of total quality.

CASE STUDY 9.1

The Export Order

The Walden Ceramics Company has just accepted a large export order for its main product line—glazed earthenware planters. Because it means a 40% increase in sales and output the company will need to put on a second shift. They will also need to develop a way to assure product quality and delivery because penalties have been built into the export agreement for both substandard quality and late delivery.

The HR manager Kathryn Jarvis will develop a plan to recruit, induct and train the second shift. Malcolm Lewis, the production superintendent, has been asked to formulate a plan to assure product quality and delivery. This should include the entire process, from raw material ordering through to production scheduling, manufacture, glazing and final packing and dispatch.

Malcolm has recently been learning about total quality concepts at a management course he has been attending. The principles impressed him and he thought he would apply them as a way to involve employees in ensuring quality throughout the entire process. His first step would be to convene a cross-functional team of people made up from purchasing and supply, production scheduling, production, QA, engineering, administration and dispatch.

Questions

1 Develop an agenda for the team's first few meetings showing how they should approach the task of assuring a quality product and their goals for these meetings.
2 Would some form of benchmarking be appropriate? What measures of effectiveness might the company decide to benchmark? How might the company show these measures in a visual format?

CASE STUDY 9.2

Keeping The Customers Satisfied

Shelly Sanders had just been promoted to supervise the home furnishings department of the large department store where she worked. At the time of her promotion, the store manager made it clear to her that she was expected to turn around the poor showing of the department, particularly in sales, which were below budget.

Reasoning that a poor reputation in the marketplace might contribute to poor sales, one of the first things Shelly did was analyse the department's customer suggestions and complaints records. She wanted to gain a clear understanding of the current position of the department before deciding how to improve it. She used a check sheet to break down complaints and suggestions by frequency and type. Then she transferred the data onto a Pareto chart and found that the most common cause of customer complaints was problems with the delivery of furniture they had ordered.

Upon investigation she found that, when furniture was ordered, the manufacturer quoted a lead-time, which her staff passed on to their customers. Often, the manufacturer was late in delivery. In turn, manufacturers often blamed their suppliers for late delivery of raw materials.

However, because the store had no tracking system, the first the staff in the furnishings department heard of a problem was when a customer rang to complain that their order was overdue and to ask when delivery would be. The staff then had to find the order manually, check with the supplier to find out the new delivery date and then ring the customer back. This was time-consuming and created a lot of ill will between customers and the store.

Shelly realised she wouldn't be able to fix this problem on her own. She gathered her team together to brainstorm all the problems they experienced. Then they prioritised them and planned to resolve each of them in turn. They decided to assign some problems to 'working parties' so that they could work on more than one problem at a time. The staff seemed quite keen to get the ball rolling and see some results.

As it happened, the problem that the team agreed to work on first was the customer delivery problem.

Questions

1   Outline what the quality improvement team's next steps are likely to be as they work on the problem of customer delivery.
2   Will they need to involve their suppliers at any stage? If so, how could they do this?
3   Should Shelly have involved the staff from the beginning? Why or why not? What could she do to ensure their motivation remains high?

Answers to Rapid Review questions

1. T   2. T   3. F   4. T   5. F   6. F   7. T   8. T   9. F   10. F   11. F   12. F   13. F
14. T   15. F   16. T

CHAPTER 10

MANAGING FOR CUSTOMER SERVICE

A lesson on service levels

Con's motto is, 'You grow it, I'll mow it.' With his array of specialised tractors of various sizes and blades, there isn't much in the way of slashing he can't do. His business has grown entirely by word of mouth and Con's aim is, 'Once a customer, always a customer.' He goes out of his way to delight them with extra touches and total reliability.

He has two types of customers: industrial customers who contract him for big jobs; for example, the electricity company hires him to slash firebreaks under the power lines. 'It doesn't have to be pretty—just cut.' His other customer base is the domestic semi-rural property owners who want several acres at a time slashed. 'Now that *does* have to be pretty. These people don't just want a firebreak, they want a *nice* firebreak. I always spend extra time with the whipper-snipper and blower making their places look real nice.'

By 1999 Con's business had grown to the point where he needed to take on help. He hired people who were licensed to drive both the tractors and the heavy goods trucks he transported them on. He was careful to select people with a strong work ethic who enjoyed outdoor work and took pride in looking back on a job well done.

John was his star recruit. 'When he started though, boy, did he cost me money. His first week with me, he spent an entire day hand weeding between the electricity pylons where the machines wouldn't go! I had to explain to him the difference between what our industrial customers consider to be a "good job" and what our domestic customers want. No point spending time—and time is money—on things the customers don't care about. Well, we've got that sorted out now. I'm glad to say! John is going great guns and I plan to give him his own crew to supervise next season.'

The customer rules. In this chapter, you will find out what to do to make sure customer service is a primary focus of yourself, your department and your employees.

- What is the difference between an internal customer and an external customer? Is one more important than the other?
- How would you describe a customer-driven organisation? What three opportunities to take care of their customers do they make good use of and what are the five ways they do this?
- How good is your organisation's customer service? How customer-focused are you and your staff?
- Does a strong customer focus pay off?
- Can you contrast 'smile training' with trading partnerships and the integrated value chain?
- Can you recognise and describe the four levels of customer service?

- Can you avoid the four common mistakes made when measuring customer service levels?
- Can you explain the difference between customer satisfaction and customer loyalty?
- Do you know what a customer's four main psychological needs are and what to do to meet them?
- Can you explain a product or service in a way that will mean something to a customer?
- Can you explain what to do if a customer tells you about a problem they have experienced?
- Can you use a telephone as a customer service tool?

THE CUSTOMER SERVICE RIDDLE: WHAT IS ...

...... intangible and ephemeral ...

We can't 'touch' it as we can other products, and it has no shelf life; it is only as good as what is being delivered *right now.*

... can't be undone ...

If something goes wrong, we can't take it back like a substandard product. We can only try and make up for it.

... subjective ...

It is only as good as the individual customer perceives it to be.

... defines the whole but is delivered by one ...

Although it is part of an organisation's identity and its product, it is not given by organisations but by individuals.

Are your staff aware of the effect their behaviour has on your business? Could they state clearly what the customer service levels of their organisation are and how important it is to meet them? *Customer service* is one of the most direct tools we have for building loyalty, attracting repeat business, generating word-of-mouth (free) business and boosting profits. It might be full of paradoxes, but customer service can make or break your organisation.

Organisations may set standards but it is up to each individual service provider, every day, to meet them. Supervisors need to make sure the culture, systems, tools and equipment, time, information and other factors we looked at in Chapter 8 not only *allow* but also *encourage* front-line staff to provide quality customer service throughout the organisation.

Sensational service providers are professional. They are thoughtful. They go the extra distance. They look after their customers in ways the customers appreciate. They take pride in their work. We tend to think well of sensational service providers and badly of unprofessional, poor service providers.

WHAT IS ... A MOVING TARGET?

Quality customer service is no longer an add-on; it's expected. Once it was a 'nice thing to do'; now it's an essential thing to do. And what was once seen as 'good' service is now perceived by many as the 'bare minimum'. Our definition of 'good service' is constantly changing. The bar is continually being raised. Organisations that don't provide continually higher levels of customer service will wither.

'Customer service *is* the business!'

It may be a moving target, but today's customers typically make decisions on who they will and won't deal with based on the quality of service they receive.

Three hundred customers who were also service providers were asked to recall poor and excellent customer service experiences across a range of industries. Boxes 10.1 and 10.2 give a sample of what they said.

It's mostly the little things that alienate customers and cost an organisation goodwill. It's tempting to think they stem from individuals failing to take responsibility for making things happen and for treating the customer courteously, isn't it? But as we learned in Chapters 8 and 9, the real problem is poor systems, poor training, poor job design and placement, and poor supervision which allow or even encourage that to happen and which make it easy for mistakes to be made.

FROM THEORY TO PRACTICE

Kath was posted to Japan for two years. One of the first things she bought there was an answering machine for her apartment. A pleasant sales assistant from the department store helped her select the machine and explained how she should set it up.

A few days later, the sales assistant telephoned Kath to make sure she had been able to install it all right. 'I don't know, I think so; I haven't been out since I bought it, so haven't tested it. I've had the most terrible cold ...'

Later that afternoon, the sales assistant appeared on Kath's doorstep with cornflakes, milk, apples, chocolates and flowers. 'I thought since you haven't been out, you might need some food and I brought some flowers to cheer you up.'

Guess where Kath shopped for the rest of her two years in Japan?

BOX 10.1 ELEMENTS OF HORRIBLE CUSTOMER SERVICE

- Insufficient information provided
- Don't comply with requests or comply insufficiently
- Keep having to ask for the same thing
- Difficult to speak to a responsible person who can help
- Seldom return phone calls
- Attitude and treatment arrogant and ignorant—I'm made to feel like a nuisance
- Telephone transfer shuffle
- Lack of recognition as a regular customer
- Being called 'love'

- Put on hold (and being taken off hold when listening to the news or a good song!)
- Jargon and acronyms
- Lack of product knowledge so given bad advice
- Being rushed
- Go through whole process or explanation only to hear: 'I can't do it' or 'I can't help you'
- Order filled wrong twice
- Not keeping promises

BOX 10.2 ELEMENTS OF SENSATIONAL CUSTOMER SERVICE

- Mistakes fixed immediately—no questions asked, over and above what was required
- Attentive—looking at me, etc.
- Says back words I've said—shows listening
- Helpful and empathic

- Independent advice given in a professional manner
- Know what they're on about
- Readily available products
- Friendly atmosphere, relaxed, enjoyable—good first impression

Fortunately, it isn't any more difficult to please customers than to annoy them.

What were their biggest headaches as service providers? Their responses are shown in Box 10.3.

Do you notice anything about the list of customer service headaches in Box 10.3? If you have already studied Chapters 8 and 9, perhaps you noticed how poor systems and procedures led to a lot of difficulties with customers. Supervisors who make sure the five keys to performance and productivity are in place and adhere to total quality management principles (see Chapters 8 and 9) eliminate these customer service headaches.

INTERNAL CUSTOMERS, EXTERNAL CUSTOMERS

Retailers and hoteliers have customers. Who else has customers? Does a mail clerk have customers? How about an orderly in a hospital? A garbage collector? A volunteer for the

BOX 10.3 BIGGEST CUSTOMER SERVICE HEADACHES

- Customers don't understand what we can and can't do
- Getting customers to follow processes and procedures
- Head office restrictions
- Lack of stock

- Customers expecting 'a lot!'
- Expectations of 'cheap'
- Helping people interpret the product
- They want it tomorrow
- Management changing its mind

Salvation Army? Does an HR or IT department have customers? How about a finance department or a purchasing department?

Everyone has customers. Whatever sector they work in, whether they work directly with customers or behind the scenes, every employee has customers and every department has customers. Joseph Juran, a leader in the Total Quality Management (TQM) movement put it this way:

> **'If you're not serving a customer directly,
> you'd better be serving someone who is.'**

As we saw in Chapter 9, there are two kinds of customers. **External customers** are the people who buy or use our products or services. **Internal customers** are our colleagues, working in the same organisation as employees or contractors to provide goods and services to our external customers. They are part of the customer–supplier chain that makes and supplies the goods and services of an organisation.

If we are not able to identify and meet our customers' expectations, we will not be able to do quality work and provide quality service.

> **'We are always challenging ourselves. Are we making what customers want and working on the products and technologies they'll want in future? Are we organised most effectively to achieve our goals?'**
>
> Bill Gates
> Microsoft

FROM THEORY TO PRACTICE

Here are some questions supervisors and their staff should ask each other. Everyone should have the same answers or customer service will be patchy at best.

- Why does our department exist?
- What do we do? Why?
- Who are our customers?
- Who else benefits from our efforts? Who else uses the services or products we provide?
- Who are our most important customers? Why? How do we know this?
- What do they want from us? How do we know?
- What do our customers care about most? How do we know?
- How well are we satisfying them now in what they care about?
- How does the way we operate make it difficult to do business with us?
- Are we doing anything for our customers they'd rather we didn't or that they find irrelevant or unnecessary?
- Are we making their life easier?
- Are we making it harder in any way?
- What opportunities do we have to delight our customers?
- What are the best companies doing to delight their customers?

Whether customers are internal or external, supervisors need to find ways to identify their needs and help employees meet them.

WHAT ARE YOUR CUSTOMERS WORTH?

Some customers are very profitable, some are moderately profitable, some are marginal and some cost us money. The lifetime value of existing and future customers is known as **lifetime customer value** or LCV. Calculating the sum of the value of the current and future customers of a business is considered to be an increasingly valid way to assess its value. Many people believe that LCV is the only possible way to value many new Internet and e-commerce businesses. It is also a key success measure in many of these high-growth sectors as well as in more traditional industries.

Here is a simple way to calculate LCV:

> 'Take the average purchase value of the average
> customer per week (or month).
> Multiply this by 48 (or 11) to allow for holidays.
> Multiply this by the number of years you normally retain a customer.
> The answer gives you their lifetime value.'

LCV is important because it costs money to win a customer. It is said, for example, that it costs 1000 direct mailings to win one new customer and on average, the cost of winning new customers is five times greater than the cost of retaining existing customers. Since repeat business is free, repeat customers are 'money in the bank'.

> 'See your customers as appreciating assets and appreciate those assets.'

We can increase the lifetime value of a customer in four ways:
1. retain their business longer;
2. sell them more of what they're already buying from us;
3. extend the range of goods and services they buy from us; and
4. sell them more expensive items than they are currently buying.

> 'Think in terms of a customer's lifetime value. Everyone likes to
> feel you value their business and are interested in looking after
> them for a lifetime.'

THE **BIG** PICTURE

Why bother keeping a grocery store customer happy? Because over a ten-year period, a customer will spend on average $75 000 with a grocery store. Here's how that figure is calculated: the average customer spends $150 a week at a grocery store. Given 50 weeks a year (allowing two weeks holiday away from home) that's $7500 per year; over ten years, that adds up to $75 000.

> ## THE **BIG** PICTURE
> The lessons of LCV: don't waste time and money pursuing and keeping unprofitable customers. Focus on the market segments and customers that can generate a good return on investment and treat them so well they won't even consider going elsewhere.

CUSTOMER-DRIVEN ORGANISATIONS

In Chapter 9 we discussed the differences between **customer-driven organisations** and product-driven and cost-driven organisations. Customer-driven organisations know who their customers are and what they want. They develop work systems that are capable of unfailingly meeting customer needs and wants. They have customer-friendly systems and policies and use them to build strong relationships as part of the extended value chain (see below). Processes, people and management are all focused on the customers and on providing what they want.

Box 10.4 contrasts some traditional measures of a company's performance with more customer-focused measures. The way we look at an enterprise is changing as organisational paradigms change (see Chapters 1 and 4).

'Take care of the customers and the profits will take care of themselves.'

Soichiro Honda
Founder of Honda Motor Corporation

BOX 10.4   HOW DO WE SEE SUCCESS?

Success:	The traditional way	The customer-focused way
Value determined by:	Balance sheet	Profitability of customer relationships
Success measured by:	Market share	Value of lifetime customers
Keys to success:	Mass marketing and production	Mass personalisation and customisation
Driving force:	Production: we sell what we make	Customers: we provide customers with what they want
Business improvements:	Through investment in plant and equipment	Through investment in customer knowledge and relationships

---

FROM THEORY TO PRACTICE

Are your systems customer-friendly or customer-hostile? To decide, ask yourself whether they benefit the customer or the organisation.

Opportunities to 'take care of your customers' can occur:
- before you provide the product or service;
- while you are providing it; and
- after you have provided it.

Each of these three points contains five opportunities to delight customers and make sure we retain them.

1. Meet or exceed customer needs in our product or service.
2. Develop and maintain trust.
3. Offer clear and open communication.
4. Show that we understand our customers.
5. Show we can help our customers achieve their goals.

Box 10.5 suggests questions you can ask to find out how well you're serving your customers in five areas. They can apply before, during or after delivery. Each organisation will set targets and measure different aspects of these five factors because their customers will be looking for different things.

Is being customer-driven worth the effort? Box 10.6 shows a compilation of research conducted by Harvard Business School, the International Customer Service Association in Chicago, Illinois and PIMS (Profit Impact of Marketing Strategy).

BOX 10.5   HOW ARE WE DOING?

Focused	Is the service focused? Do staff focus on what the customer wants and needs and on meeting those needs? Or do they focus on what they can easily offer?
Fast	Is the service fast? To many customers, time is a precious commodity. Unless your staff are sure that customers have the time and desire for a lengthy interaction, train your staff to be efficient, prompt and swift without being brusque or rushing the customer.
Friendly	No customer wants to deal with a person who would clearly rather be somewhere else. Make sure your staff know the visual and vocal elements of friendly service.
Future-oriented	When a problem arises, do your staff focus on the past and why it went wrong, or on the future and what they will do to put things right? Customers prefer the latter.
Flexible	Do your staff have the authority to tailor their offering to suit customers' needs or must they blindly follow a prescribed system? Customer service will be superior if we allow staff flexibility in the way they offer it.

FROM THEORY TO PRACTICE

Here are some questions to ask to see how customer-focused you and your staff are:

1. Do our behaviour, our equipment and our premises inspire confidence in our organisation?
2. Do our customers believe we can meet their needs properly?
3. Are we willing to help customers courteously and promptly? Do our customers see us as courteous and prompt?
4. Are we known for delivering what we promise?
5. Do we give our customers the attention they deserve?
6. Do we tell our customers about our products and services using words they can understand?
7. Do we listen to what our customers tell us?

BOX
10.6

CUSTOMER SERVICE MATHS

- A 5% increase in customer retention equals between 25% and 80% increase in profits.
- Companies with a reputation for great service are able to charge up to 9% more for the goods and services they offer and grow twice as fast on average.

- Increasing your customer retention rate by 2% has the same effect on profits as cutting costs 10%.
- Organisations that emphasise customer service see 12 times the return on sales as those that put a lower priority on service.

BUILDING RELATIONSHIPS AND PARTNERSHIPS

The drive towards customer focus started in the 1980s. What began as 'smile training' and 'answer the phone in four rings' has become much more sophisticated.

In Chapter 9 we looked at getting the internal supply chain efficiencies right. Even this is not enough. Today, total quality companies manage the entire value chain, or **integrated value chain**, starting with their suppliers and finishing with their customers. As we saw in Chapter 9, with suppliers this means forging trading partnerships. With external customers, it opens up a whole new way of doing business.

Customers will increasingly demand to deal directly with suppliers, cutting out the go-between companies and retailers. Developing and servicing these new relationships will be challenging and rewarding to those companies who get it right first.

For many companies now, and increasingly in the future, the first point of contact with a customer will be the organisation's web site. A well designed site will let customers tailor products to suit their needs precisely. It will make it easy for them to find, configure and order products and services. (See, for example, *Cisco.com*, *Dell.com* and *travel.com.au*.)

How do we build lasting relationships with our customers? By getting our service levels right.

FOUR LEVELS OF CUSTOMER SERVICE

Supervisors need to make sure employees see relationships with customers not as 'one-off' encounters but as long-term relationships. It helps to analyse the service level you are offering using a four-level hierarchy: (1) meets basic needs, (2) meets expected needs, (3) meets desires, (4) offers sensational service. If you know where you are now, you can take steps to improve it.

Basic

'It goes without saying that a café will have a chair for me to sit on.'

This is the absolute minimum acceptable standard. It includes things we take so much for granted that we don't really notice them unless they're not present. We won't do business with an organisation that doesn't even meet our basic needs.

Expected

'I expect that chair to be clean.'

This is what we expect. We will do business grudgingly with organisations that meet only expectations. If competition arrives—look out!

Desired

'I'd also like the chair to be comfortable.'

This is what we'd like. When our desired needs are met, we're happy to do business with the organisation. They'll probably have our regular business, even our loyalty, provided an organisation offering something better doesn't come along.

Sensational

'Someone holds the chair for me as I sit down, brings the food to me and treats me like royalty.'

Sensational service delights customers. It might be an 'out of the blue' real and unexpected pleasure. Or it might be consistently superior service that is enough to make us notice and talk about it to others. Service like this wins loyal customers for life and generates word-of-mouth business.

'Sensational customer service makes every customer feel important and valued.'

It can sometimes be difficult to think outside our service paradigms to provide sensational service. What petrol station would think of offering a cut flower to each of its female customers on Valentine's Day, for example? Yet that's just what one petrol station north of Adelaide did and, several years later, people are still talking about it! Box 10.7 relates the four service levels to a delicatessen. What else would constitute sensational service in a deli for you?

FROM THEORY TO PRACTICE

Bernie the Printer had always provided service to a very desirable level. His prices were good, his designs and layouts professional, his quality excellent and timeliness acceptable. Gary had used him ever since setting up his business 12 years ago. He was happy with him and had even recommended him to a few people.

For his part, Gary was good steady business. Not a huge client by any means, in fact quite small, but he was regular, his jobs were easy and he settled his invoices promptly.

In March, Gary placed a repeat order for 500 business cards. 'Details all the same?' asked Bernie. 'Yep, nothing's changed. Same as before.'

Three weeks later, a terrible thought struck Gary. He'd just changed mobile phones and had a new number. The old number would be printed on the business cards. He rang Bernie immediately.

'Have you done my cards yet?'

'Yes, just finished them, as a matter of fact. They'll be dry by tomorrow.'

Gary explained why he'd rung and finished by saying, 'Well, it's all my fault and there's nothing we can do about it now. I'll collect the cards tomorrow and I'll just cross out the old number and write the new one in.'

Bernie took a note of Gary's new mobile number to change his records for the next order.

The next day when he went to collect his cards, Gary noticed that the new number had been printed on. 'What's this?!' he asked.

'Ah, well,' said Bernie, 'you're a good customer. I couldn't have you crossing out your mobile number and making your cards look tacky. The printing machine was still set up, so I ran you through another set of cards. No charge.'

Another customer for life.

FOUR LEVELS OF SERVICE IN A DELICATESSEN

BOX 10.7

Basic	clean, basic food supplies (bread, milk, etc.), well lit, someone serving, fridge works
Expected	smells clean, looks tidy, good personal presentation of staff, fresh stock, prompt and friendly greeting
Desired	gourmet pastries, varied stock, home-baked-style fresh food, friendly conversation from server, personal touch, nice tables and chairs to sit and eat, magazines provided, regular customers recognised, 'Thanks for your business'
Sensational	point out specials, free tastings, occasional free lollies for kids, ready-to-heat-and-eat home-baked meals, the smell of food being baked, home delivery service, personalised service

If we continually attempt to delight our customers by improving our service levels, we will be achieving *kaizen* or continuous improvement in our customer service and ensuring the future of our organisation (see Chapter 9).

BENCHMARKING

If customer service is to be more than pleasantries and smiles, we need to do four things:
1. Find out what it is our customers really need and want.
2. Specify and communicate precisely how we will meet their needs and wants.
3. Align the internal systems and culture so they support the desired behaviours and service levels.
4. Measure the level of service each customer actually receives.

Oops!

The staff of a large international airline was asked to identify the ten main needs of their customers. Their answers were compared with a survey asking customers what they needed. The staff got six out of the ten top customer needs wrong.

What does that tell us? It tells us two important things. First, it's easy to make assumptions, to see what we want or expect to see. We may think we know what our customers want, but we'll never know for sure unless we ask them. Second, we might waste resources 'satisfying' customer needs that aren't important and alienate customers by ignoring needs that are important.

Once we know what our customers want, we can set clear targets. In Chapter 8 we learned to make targets specific and measurable.

> **'If you can't measure it, you can't manage it.**
> **And you can't perform it.'**

Box 10.8 shows the four most common mistakes to avoid when benchmarking your customer service.

BOX 10.8 FOUR COMMON MISTAKES IN BENCHMARKING CUSTOMER SERVICE

1. *One-off studies.* It can be dangerous to generalise from surveys that measure quality at one point in time. They should be continuous or periodic.
2. *Measuring the wrong things.* Measure key service attributes, things that customers care about. These are the things that will differentiate us from our competitors.
3. *Ignoring the competition.* The competitors are out there, always trying to win over our customers. Find out how your customers, and theirs, perceive both you and the competition.
4. *Not updating measures.* Yesterday's sensational service is today's expected service. Keep what you're measuring current.

FROM THEORY TO PRACTICE

IBM Global Business tracks three types of metrics (measures): (1) 'hygiene' attributes—attributes of service quality everyone delivers; (2) attributes that IBM performs as well as their competitors; and (3) 'attractors'—attributes from which IBM creates more customer value than their competitors.

Mazda Australia measures customer service quality all year round on a Customer Service Index (CSI) and reports to dealers and employees quarterly. They benchmark and rank dealers of similar size across Australia to make the findings more meaningful.

THE **BIG** PICTURE

Spot the trends: Listen and act on what your customers are *saying*. But don't forget what they're *doing*. Spotting and responding to trends can give you an edge in the marketplace. To do this, get out and about with your customers; see what they're doing and how they're using your products or services. Talking directly to your customers can show you what is important to them, what they're thinking, where they're heading.

The ones that got away ...

Don't confuse satisfaction with loyalty. Satisfied customers will still move to the opposition: as the four levels of customer service show, even when we're meeting desired levels, we're still in danger of losing our customers. This means we should also be measuring defectors to learn why they left.

MOMENTS OF TRUTH

Jan Carlzon took Scandinavian Airline Systems from a loss of nearly $20 million to a profit of $54 million in 12 months. The cornerstone of this recovery was making the most of 50 000 **moments of truth** every day.

A moment of truth (MOT) is any contact a customer has with an organisation. MOTs can occur without any contact between a customer and an employee (e.g. over an automated telephone system or a web site) or they can involve direct contact, either on the telephone or face-to-face. These critical contact moments tell us about the quality of service an enterprise provides and builds an organisation's reputation in the marketplace.

Are the MOTs in your organisation at the basic level or are they sensational? Do they say *we care about our customers*? Often, it's the little things that count. Box 10.9 contrasts some phrases that inflame customers and create a poor impression, and even a hostile environment, with phrases that soothe and smooth customer relationships and create a pleasant and cooperative environment. Which are heard more around your organisation?

BOX 10.9 CUSTOMER SERVICE PHRASES TO LOSE AND TO USE

Phrases that inflame	*Phrases that soothe*
That should be no problem	I'm confident
If nothing gets in the way	If everything goes as planned
No worries	It's a pleasure or Happy to help
Why can't you ...?	How about ...?
You'll have to ...	What I'll need is ...
I can't have it for you until next Friday	I can have it for you next Friday
You don't understand.	Let me run through that for you again
I can't help you. You'll have to speak to ...	The best way I can help you is ...
No, because ...	Yes, as soon as ...
It can't be done because ...	We could do that if ...
What's the problem?	How can I help you?
I can't do it until next week.	I can do it next week.

THE **BIG** PICTURE

When employees are talking to customers, they aren't just speaking for themselves—they are representing your entire organisation. Train employees to treat every contact they have with customers as an opportunity to grow customer loyalty, win new customers and make more sales. Ensure that the internal mechanisms employees need to do this are in place—systems, procedures, training, tools and equipment, organisation culture; these are the things that really make or break good service.

FROM THEORY TO PRACTICE

Here's how to make the most of every customer contact: map your *customer service cycle*. Similar to a process or systems map that details the way work flows through a department, a service map identifies each step a customer takes to accomplish his or her objective with our organisation successfully.

Once you and your team have created the map, look at each individual step to find opportunities to exceed customers' expectations and make your organisation stand out from the competition.

For example, Disney's overarching vision is to provide 'magical memories'. At the Disney Yacht Club and Beach Club resorts, cross-functional teams of front-line 'cast members' (as service providers are called) service-mapped the arrival process. They identified the points of contact that guests experienced to check in: valet, front desk, guest services, bell services and housekeeping. They devised ways to make the entire process seamless and hassle-free and created a process known as the 'awesome arrival'—an integrated system that is swift, personalised and provides sensational service.

MEETING CUSTOMERS' PSYCHOLOGICAL NEEDS

... One of the reasons moments of truth are so important is that, however fleeting, they firmly establish how highly the organisation values its customers. This goes far deeper than logic; it gets to the heart of 'Who am I as a customer?'. The impression is strong and lasting because it involves emotions.

Customers have four main psychological needs. They need to feel:

1. *Welcome.* Are you glad to see me or am I a nuisance? Do you care enough about me to 'pass the time of day' with a bit of small talk or do you make me feel like an 'outsider'? Do you care enough about me to offer a fast loading and easy-to-navigate web site? Or to offer clean and well lit premises that I can enter easily and receive what I want promptly? What's my first impression of this place or this company?

2. *Important.* Is my business appreciated and am I a valued customer? Or do you not care about me or my business? Do you respect me and my needs? Do you care enough about me to draw my attention to a good buy or a new item or advise me on products if I need it? Will you customise for me so that I get exactly what I want? What do you do that makes me feel special?

3. *Understood.* Do you really understand what I want and need or are you just here to collect the money? How interested are you in providing me with exactly what I need? Are you listening to me? Are you willing to be flexible?

4. *Comfortable.* Do I feel physically as well as psychologically comfortable? How 'homey' and enjoyable does it feel to do business with you? How confident do you make me feel that you will take care of me properly and meet my needs?

As you can see, these needs are linked to each other—satisfying one often automatically helps to satisfy another. Make sure your staff understand that customers have these psychological needs and they know how to meet them.

More than two-thirds of customers who stop doing business with a company do so because of perceived indifference towards them. Their psychological needs haven't been met.

FROM THEORY TO PRACTICE

Pam could easily stop at any of five petrol stations between her home and work. More out of habit than anything, she usually stopped at the one at the main cross-roads on the way home. One day, she realised she needed petrol and had gone by her usual station. She stopped near the top of the hill, at the station closest to her home.

She filled her tank and went in to pay. 'What a nice bracelet!' said the cashier as they waited for her credit card to process. 'Thanks,' said Pam and they chatted a little about where she got it.

Pam's been buying her petrol there ever since.

FEATURES AND BENEFITS

When we're addressing a customer's product or service requirements, we can explain about the *features* of what we're offering, or we can explain how what we're offering will *benefit* the customer. Which should we stress? The general principle known as

'Not the sausage but the sizzle'

tells us to explain our product or service in terms of how it benefits the customer. It makes sure we talk to customers about what they are most interested in hearing.

For example, if someone is buying a camera to take bushwalking, it would make more sense to explain that it's light to carry around all day (not that it weighs 350 grams) and that it automatically adjusts for light (not that it has an automatic F-stop).

Box 10.10 shows the differences between features and benefits, using a broom as an example. To find the benefit of a feature, keep asking *So what?* until you have found the core reason that a particular feature is useful to a customer.

As you can see, some features have several benefits. Which should you mention to a customer? Listen as they talk about what is important to them and note the terms they use to describe their needs and wants. This will help you to focus on what is most important to the customer, select which benefits to mention and then explain them in terms the customer will readily understand.

BOX 10.10   FEATURES AND BENEFITS OF A BROOM

Features	Benefits
■ made of natural materials	■ environmentally friendly
	■ easy to obtain
	■ attractive in most locations
■ solid, sturdy construction	■ will last for years
	■ is robust enough for heavy jobs
■ long, solid wooden handle	■ easy to hold and use
	■ attractive and long-lasting
	■ strong
■ weighs less than 1 kilogram	■ light weight
	■ easy to carry
■ sweeps most surfaces	■ reliable and fast cleaning tool
■ low price	■ economical; anyone can afford it
■ easily available	■ easy to replace if you do wear it out
■ narrow silhouette	■ easy to store out of sight in most cupboards
■ long bristles	■ gets into most crevices and deep cracks
■ hard-wearing bristles	■ long-lasting

FROM THEORY TO PRACTICE

Does everyone in your organisation know both the features of their products and services and the benefits they offer their customers? Can they state the benefits in terms that will mean something to the customer?

SEE COMPLAINTS AS OPPORTUNITIES

Does your heart sink when you hear of a customer complaint? If it does, learn to see them as opportunities. There are five reasons for this:

1. Most of our customers don't bother to complain. In fact, most of us never hear from 96% of our unhappy customers. We should be grateful to the 4% that take the trouble to alert us to a problem.

2. When someone complains, it's seldom about an isolated occurrence. Rather, it's usually about something that is symptomatic of the way we do things. Complaints are actually valuable feedback about the way our organisation operates.

3. Customers who complain are usually our best and most loyal customers. In fact, complainers are more likely than non-complainers to do business with us again, even if we don't satisfactorily resolve the problem. Customers who don't care about our organisation or their relationship with it, those who don't expect to be doing business with us again, won't bother to complain. Why should they?

4. If we resolve a complaint well, we'll end up with an even more loyal and satisfied customer. In fact, between 54% and 70% will do business with us again if we handle the complaint well; 95% will do business with us again if we also handle the complaint quickly.

    Handling a complaint 'well' does not necessarily mean the customer gets their way. It does mean that the *process* of dealing with the complaint must satisfy the customer. There is a big difference.

5. When someone complains, they are giving us the benefit of the doubt and a chance to satisfy them. The alternative is that they will tell at least nine other people about their dissatisfaction with us. Those nine people will spread the bad news to about 20 other people. (One in five, or 20%, of people who have had a problem with an organisation tell more than 20 other people about it!) If we satisfactorily resolve a complaint, the customer will tell an average of five people about it.

THE **BIG** PICTURE

Effective complaint handling builds customer loyalty, gives you free market research information about customer opinions and problems, and allows the organisation to capitalise on a 'make or break' situation—to keep or lose a customer.

Handle complaints with respect and understanding

Since unhappy customers spread bad news more quickly than happy customers, it's in our interests to deal with complaints properly. It is not the end result that constitutes 'properly' but the *way* the problem is dealt with. Make sure you and your staff follow the four-stage process below if you want your customers to spread good news about you.

1. Hear the customer out

- Listen carefully, non-defensively and without interrupting.
- Keep calm.
- Don't argue.
- Use minimal encouragers—'Yes, I see', 'Sure'—to draw out the full story.

2. Honour what the customer says

- Thank the customer for telling you.
- If their facts are wrong, will correcting them serve any purpose? Often, the facts are beside the point. Arguing back and forth about what happened won't serve any purpose or undo what's happened. Even if you can't agree, at least acknowledge emotions and take some helpful action.
- Don't explain, blame, deny or excuse.
- Ask questions if you need to so you can fully understand the problem.
- Confirm your understanding by repeating both the facts and the customer's feelings (annoyed, inconvenienced, disappointed, etc.).
- Apologise if appropriate. This doesn't mean admitting guilt but showing empathy and understanding: 'I'm sorry this has happened. I'd like to resolve this for you.' Someone commiserating means someone cares.

> 'Customers don't care why it wasn't done but what will be done.'

3. Find a way to put things right

- Take responsibility for action. Do something to make it better.
- Focus on a solution.
- Find out what the customer wants, or offer a solution (depending on the issue and what you are able to do).
- Don't talk about what you *can't* do but what you *can* do and *when*.
- Avoid negative language. Say, 'There's something ...' not, 'There's nothing ...' Soften 'no' with 'I wish' or 'I hope' to show empathy not apathy.
- Decide what action you need to take.
- Agree on a course of action.

> 'Don't make excuses—make good.'
>
> Frank Hubbard

4. Act

- Act immediately.
- Follow through.

Keep records

Document complaints and problems for later study and analysis. Why did the problem occur in the first place? Fix the problem at its source so it can't happen again (see Chapters 8 and 9).

THE **BIG** PICTURE

The Customer Service Institute surveyed the complaints culture and service recovery in organisations across Australia. It seems we're more prepared to complain than many people think:

- 66% of Australians say they complain all or most of the time if they are unhappy with service.
- If we don't complain it's because of lack of time (61%), 'too much trouble' (55%) or 'Why bother? The organisation won't do anything anyway' (32%).
- 15% of complainers prefer to complain by letter. 97% of them expect an acknowledgment and 88% expect their complaint to be dealt with within two weeks.
- About one-third of people who complain in person expect their complaint to be resolved on the spot and 72% expect same-day resolution.
- The telephone is our preferred method of complaining and 57% of telephone complainers expect a same-day response. Nearly everyone (97%) expects their telephone complaint to be dealt with within a week.

How does your organisation measure up?

Even with a mind-set that sees complaints as opportunities, dealing with them can be stressful and difficult. Here are three things to do, and make sure your staff do, when dealing with complaints:

- Manage your own emotions.
- Manage the customer's emotions.
- Manage the issue.

Manage your own emotions

Although it may come across this way, remember:

'A complaint is not a personal insult.'

Complaints are seldom directed at a service provider personally, even if the customer's way of wording it makes it sound as if it is. Something has gone wrong and the customer wants it put right. So don't take the compaint personally.

THE **BIG** PICTURE

The Customer Service Institute's survey also found that:

- 66% of organisations still make it 'difficult' to complain.
- Nearly one-third of organisations don't capture important complaint information; they don't even know how many customers they are losing, or why they are losing them.

Is your organisation better than this?

In difficult situations, most people's natural tendency is to shallow-breathe. Quick, shallow breathing causes panic, confusion and fuzzy thinking. It drains oxygen from the brain and switches on the adrenalin reflex, which puts us into **fight–flight** adversarial mode. Out of breath means out of control—definitely not a way to earn points with unhappy customers.

If you feel yourself tensing up, relax and breathe deeply. This increases the flow of oxygen to the brain and heart, calms your nerves and helps you think clearly.

In Chapter 19 we learn the importance of **self-talk**, the silent messages we give ourselves. When faced with a customer complaint, support yourself with empowering, helpful self-talk: 'I can handle this; I'll do my best to help this customer; We'll get to the bottom of this and sort it out.'

> '**No one can make you feel inferior without your consent.**'
>
> Eleanor Roosevelt

And no one can make you feel *angry* without your consent. Professional service providers guide the conversation by modelling the behaviour they want from the customer. If we remain calm, polite and helpful, the customer probably will, too. Remember the **boomerang principle**: we get back what we send out—so be kind, not curt, to customers with a problem.

> '**Our greatest freedom is the freedom to choose our attitude.**'
>
> Victor Frankl

Manage the customer's emotions

How do you feel if someone isn't listening to you, brushing aside your concerns or ignoring your needs? The more customers feel service providers are doing this to them, the further to the right on the unhappy customer emotions scale they are likely to move (see Figure 10.1). The further right a customer moves on the emotions scale, the more likely they are to become upset and even angry and abusive.

FROM THEORY TO PRACTICE

John Powell, in *Why Am I Afraid To Tell You Who I Am?*, retells the late US syndicated columnist Sydney Harris's story about accompanying his friend to a news-stand. The friend greeted the newsman very courteously but in return received gruff and rude service. Accepting the newspaper shoved in his direction, the friend of Harris smiled and politely wished the newsman a nice weekend. As the two friends walked down the street, the columnist asked:
'Does he always treat you so discourteously?'
'Yes, unfortunately he does,' was the reply.
'And are you always so polite and friendly to him?'
'Yes, I am.'
'Why are you so nice to him when he is so unfriendly to you?'
'Because I don't want him to decide how I'm going to act.'
Don't let your customers decide how you're going to act either.

FIGURE 10.1 THE COMPLAINING CUSTOMER'S SCALE OF EMOTIONS

Service providers with poor interpersonal skills make customers feel they are pushing against them, instead of working with them. Not surprisingly, this upsets customers and encourages their emotions to escalate. It creates a difficult situation for both the service provider and the customer and loses goodwill for the entire organisation.

High self-esteem stops service providers from taking complaints personally. Strong interpersonal skills help them identify the customer's basic psychological needs, and meet them. Empathy helps them see the situation from the customer's point of view, which in turn helps them take the customer's concerns and needs seriously.

Communication skills help them ask questions to uncover the real problem and the customer's needs, and show the customer they've heard and understood the problem. Restating both the facts and the customer's feelings removes the need for customers to become upset or abusive.

Excellent service providers respect the customer's values and experience without jumping to conclusions, prejudging or evaluating (see Chapter 2). They look for the common ground and work *with* the customer to resolve the problem (see Chapter 24). They know that they and the customer are on the same side.

Manage the issue

This is precisely the way to manage the issue—to show the customer that we're on *their* side in wanting to sort out the problem. This means taking the 'we' approach, seeing the situation as a problem to be resolved, not a customer to be fixed. This results in a cooperative approach where the focus is on the future.

We need a 'helicopter' or 'big picture' view of what is going on. We know the organisation's situation, we've heard the customer's thoughts; now is the time to focus on the facts and on what we can do to try to put things right in the customer's eyes. Supervisors need to make sure their staff know the company line, what's possible, what's do-able.

WHAT IS ... PERSON-TO-PERSON BUT NOT FACE-TO-FACE?

Telephone customer service is one of the fastest growing industries in Australia. We have over 40 000 customer service operators who answer telephone queries or complaints, or sell or confirm orders. Most work for banks and finance companies, insurance companies, airlines and other enterprises with a wide customer interface. These professional telephone customer service providers aren't the only ones who need to know how to manage the phone as an important communications and customer relations tool—we all do.

The telephone is an important *moment of truth*. How is it answered? So softly you can hardly hear the person at the other end? So quickly you can't make out what they're saying?

Are people cut off instead of transferred, sent into a Twilight Zone of *Hold please*, a black hole of never-ending transfers or a nightmare of recorded messages? Do people in your organisation ever provide incorrect or misleading information? Are they ever rude?

Our telephone manner can contribute to good or to poor communication, relationships and customer service. It can save time or waste it, intimidate or assist. It is an important 'public relations' tool. How you handle yourself on the phone speaks volumes about you as a person. It leaves a lasting impression on people outside the organisation, about both you and your organisation. Professional or slap-dash, in control or flustered—the impression you give is up to you. The quality of your voice, the words and phrases you use and your general manner all come across loud and clear on the telephone.

You can use the telephone instead of a face-to-face meeting to save both time and money. You can be more personal with a phone call than with a memo or letter and more flexible because you can respond to questions and important information immediately. And the feedback you receive, although not as much as with face-to-face communication, is certainly greater than is possible through written communication.

Box 10.11 shows some ways to make sure the telephone works for you.

PLACING CALLS

Organise yourself. What is the purpose of your call? What information will you need to have to hand? What information do you need from the other person? Jot down the main points you want to cover. Don't be caught out having to say lamely: 'Now, let's see, there was something else I wanted to say to you … What was it?'

State your name and organisation and the purpose of your call. This serves as an introduction and helps the receiver to 'tune in' to the topic at hand.

BOX 10.11   AVOID TELEPHONE TRAGEDIES

- Speak clearly.
- Slow down.
- Identify yourself and your department or organisation when answering incoming calls.
- Identify yourself and the reason for your call, check you're speaking to the right person and ask if they have time to speak with you now when placing outgoing calls.
- Say it sweetly. Tone of voice accounts for between 70% and 86% of the message customers receive over the phone.
- Check that the person is available before forwarding a call and pass on the information you've gained so the caller doesn't have to go through it all again.
- If you need to place someone on hold, explain why and how long you expect this will take. Offer to ring them back if they'd prefer, specifying a time frame.
- Use the other person's name. If you don't know the person and their name is complicated, ask them to spell it out for you as well, so that you don't mispronounce it.
- Establish a comfortable rapport. Try to match the pitch, energy, pace and volume of your voice to the other party's. Use terms they will understand.
- Keep a special pad by the phone to record a general summary of all your calls, incoming and outgoing, and their date. This is an invaluable memory aid for future reference.
- Advise the switchboard and appropriate others if you are going out or will not be available for calls. Indicate, if possible, when you expect to return or when you will be available.
- End all calls on a positive note and, if appropriate, thank the other person for their time and help.
- Replace the receiver gently.

Ensure you are speaking to the right person. If that person is not available, find out the best time to reach them or ask that your call be returned. You should also ask if the other party has time to speak to you now—you won't get very far with someone who has their mind on other matters!

If you have several outgoing calls to make, try to place them one after the other. This follows a general principle of good time management: grouping like activities together.

Dealing with answering machines

Wait for your turn to speak, usually after the sound of a beep. Speak clearly and slowly. State your name (spell it if necessary), your organisation or department and the purpose of your call. Leave a number where your call can be returned and, if appropriate, when you will be available. The important point is to keep the message brief while stating clearly who you are, what the call is about and how you can be reached. Organising your thoughts before placing the call will help you avoid rambling into the machine and sounding unprofessional.

RECEIVING CALLS

The Australian Telecommunications Industry Ombudsman tells us that people become impatient after a 15-second wait and annoyed after 30 seconds. Answering the phone quickly conveys efficiency and indicates that you regard callers and their time as important.

'A smile is an inexpensive way to improve your looks almost instantly.'

Customers may not see your looks over the telephone, but they can hear your smile. Answer the telephone warmly, stating your name. This saves time, avoids confusion and makes the caller feel welcome. State your department, too. For example: 'Hello, Marketing Services Department, Sandy Smith speaking.'

Answer the phone clearly and take your time. Don't make the mistake of rushing and garbling all your words together.

If you need to gather further information, don't leave the caller dangling while you get it. Their time is valuable, too, so if you are likely to take more than a minute or so, explain the information isn't at your desk and you'll need to get it; offer to ring them back and tell them when this will be. Keep your promise. 'I can find that out from dispatch for you. This will take a few minutes. Would you like to hold or can I ring you back within 15 minutes?'

Give the caller your full attention. If you are in the middle of something more important, don't try to split your attention between this and the caller; either put what you are doing aside or offer to phone back.

Listen to what the caller is saying; ask questions to make sure you understand. Acknowledge that you are listening with the occasional 'Ah-huh' or short comment ('Yes, I see').

Check your understanding. If the caller is requesting information or asking you to do something, be clear about what it is. If you are being given information, repeat it back to make sure you have heard correctly. Apart from saving time in the long run, this will also increase the caller's confidence in you.

Take responsibility for satisfying the caller's needs. If you are not the best person to speak to, explain who is and transfer them. If that person isn't available, take a full message and pass it on. The onus is on you, not callers, to make sure their needs are met.

Putting callers on hold

Make sure it is convenient to put callers on hold. If they are likely to be on hold for more than a minute, explain this and ask if they would prefer you to ring them back. *Never put interstate or overseas calls on hold.*

Transferring calls

Repeat the caller's name and the details you have been given to the person you are transferring the call to. This will save the caller the frustration of having to repeat their message all over again.

Taking messages

Write down the name of the caller, asking them to spell it for you if necessary. If the name is complicated or difficult to pronounce, write it phonetically, too. Take brief details and explain what will happen next. Don't ask the caller to ring back.

Handling difficult calls

Do your people know how to respond to a confused or angry person or someone with a complaint or who is pressed for time? Market research analysts ACA Research studied workplace stress in 433 customer service call operators in 126 large Australian companies. They found their turnover was caused mostly by stress—usually from angry or irrational customers. The estimated cost of this turnover to the industry is $50 billion, or $10 000 per employee.

Know and follow the four steps outlined on page 323. Losing your temper won't change the attitude of the caller or make the communication go more smoothly. Apply the **boomerang principle** (politeness is usually contagious) and your ABCs—Always Be Courteous.

Let the caller have their say. Listen carefully and avoid interrupting, even if the caller says something inaccurate. Hear the whole story, showing interest and empathy. Use the techniques of active listening, asking questions to clarify and summarising.

Let the caller know that you have understood and state clearly and in positive terms what you will do to help. For example, say, 'I'll get back to you with the answer early next week' rather than 'I won't be able to find anything out about this until next week.'

Telephone rage

It sometimes seems that as society becomes more complex and people busier, the resulting stress is vented in a phenomenon known as 'rage'. Telephone rage is apparently becoming more common, encouraged perhaps by the impersonal nature of some telephone 'transactions' and the fact that it's easy for the 'rager' to remain anonymous.

Some organisations instruct their customer service telephone personnel to give an abusive customer three warnings before inviting the customer to call back later and disconnecting the call. Perhaps a better option is to offer to telephone the customer back or to transfer the caller to a supervisor or team leader.

'The telephone never gives me a minute's peace!'

Although the telephone is an important part of many supervisors' jobs, it can also be frustrating. Just as you settle down to analyse some figures, draft a letter, set targets with an employee or just take a minute to catch your breath, the phone rings.

Don't let the phone rule your day. If you receive calls continually throughout the day, consider organising a *'quiet interlude'* for yourself, a time when you are not available for calls. Switch on your voice mail or ask someone to take your calls so that you can return them at a more convenient time. Your quiet time should be at the same time each day, probably when the phone is generally the most 'quiet' anyway. Make this your thinking, planning and monitoring time. Let others in your department know so they can support your efforts to gain some peace and quiet.

YOUR TELEPHONE VOICE

We don't have body language to help us communicate when we're on the telephone, so we must make the best use of our voice. The actual words we use convey 30% or less of our meaning; our voice expresses more than 70% of our message. Our voice is a reflection of our mood and our personality. It can convey boredom, impatience, annoyance, confusion, hostility or lack of confidence. Equally, it can convey friendliness, courtesy, a desire to help, competence and professionalism.

Speak naturally, but be aware that it is often necessary to *articulate* your words more clearly over the phone. Take care that the *pitch* of your voice is not too high, too low or likely to be grating. Check that your speed, or pace, is not too rapid. Try to match the *energy level* and *volume* of your voice to those of the person you are speaking to; this will help to build rapport. Avoid using terms or jargon unfamiliar to the other party.

If your attitude is friendly, helpful, positive, patient and courteous, your voice is likely to follow suit. A desire to communicate in a way that the other will understand will help you to choose the most suitable words.

Which words to use?

The words you choose form the content of your message. In Box 10.9 we looked at phrases that inflame and phrases that soothe. Box 10.12 contrasts some grudging or unhelpful

NEGATIVE AND POSITIVE SENTENCES

Negative effect	Positive effect
You've come through to the wrong department.	Let me transfer you to someone who will be able to help you.
Ed's not in. You'll have to phone back later.	Unfortunately, Ed isn't in at the moment. Can I take a message and ask him to ring you later today?
I don't usually deal with complaints …	I'm happy to help!
No worries, mate!	I'll make sure Anne gets your message as soon as she returns.
You'll need to send me that information.	Would you please send that information to me so that I can deal with it quickly?
Could you hold for a few minutes while I try and find that file?	It might take me a couple of minutes to locate your file. Can I phone you back in about five minutes?

sentences that give a negative impression with more positive responses. Which would *you* rather hear?

Try to make all your sentences positive, helpful ones for maximum favourable impact.

·   RAPID REVIEW   ·

		True	False
1.	Although you can't touch it, store it or take it back, customer service is a very real reflection of how much an enterprise values its customers.	☐	☐
2.	For individual service providers to do their jobs well, they need the support of their supervisors, work systems and procedures and the other keys that unlock good performance discussed in Chapter 8.	☐	☐
3.	The expected threshold of what constitutes good customer service is continually rising.	☐	☐
4.	When it comes to customer service, it's often the little things that count most.	☐	☐
5.	If someone works in a back room and doesn't deal with customers or the public, it's fair to say they don't actually have any customers.	☐	☐
6.	Because internal customers don't pay the organisation any money, satisfying them isn't nearly as important as satisfying external customers.	☐	☐
7.	Increasing the lifetime value of a customer is an inexpensive way to secure the future of an enterprise; there are four ways we can do this.	☐	☐
8.	Customer-driven organisations focus on customer relationships, LCV, personalisation and customisation.	☐	☐
9.	Customer service may be important but you can't charge any more for it.	☐	☐
10.	An organisation can survive quite well providing the level of service customers desire but, if a better service provider comes along, the organisation may well lose its customers to it.	☐	☐
11.	Since we are familiar with our customers and what they want from us, all we need to do is measure how well we provide it; we really only need to do this once as a precautionary measure.	☐	☐
12.	Satisfied customers aren't necessarily loyal customers.	☐	☐
13.	An organisation would be mad to think it can manage every possible interaction it has with a customer.	☐	☐
14.	At the end of the day, buying a quality product at a reasonable price is really all most customers are interested in.	☐	☐
15.	Customers aren't generally interested in the technical ins and outs of a product or service; they just want to know what it will do for them.	☐	☐

	True	False
16. Since an organisation will always receive complaints, it doesn't pay to get too worked up about them.	☐	☐
17. If a customer has made a mistake about something when they're complaining, it's best to get that straightened out right away before going any further.	☐	☐
18. If a customer is shouting or rude, the service provider should respond in kind.	☐	☐
19. Before placing a call you should organise your thoughts, gather any information you need and jot down the main points you want to cover.	☐	☐
20. When answering the telephone, especially when you are in a hurry, it is not necessary to state your name or department.	☐	☐
21. Asking for and offering feedback to check understanding is important when placing or receiving telephone calls.	☐	☐
22. 'Quiet periods' can help supervisors avoid being slaves to their telephones.	☐	☐
23. It's a good idea to keep a special pad by your telephone to record a summary of all incoming and outgoing calls.	☐	☐

APPLY YOUR KNOWLEDGE

1. Discuss the reasons that customer service is important to an organisation. Is it more important to organisations in the private sector than in the not-for-profit and public sectors?

2. Look at the list of customer service headaches in Box 10.3. How valid are they? If you have completed Chapters 8 and 9, discuss what could be done to remove these headaches.

3. What do we mean by *sensational* customer service? Why is it important? Give an example to illustrate your answer.

4. US research shows that customers appreciate good service so much, they'll pay more for the same product in return for superior service. Do you think this is true of Australians? Why, or why not?

5. British research into the 'American "Have a nice day" culture' showed that yes, even in the UK, people like this, even though they suspect it isn't genuine. Even though the service provider isn't necessarily smiling because they're glad to see the customer but because they're told to, people want it anyway. Does that apply to Australia too?

6. Calculate the lifetime value of the average customer of your organisation. If you were supervising the service providers, how would you help them to increase the value of the average customer?

7. Contrast what *desired* and *sensational* customer service might involve in a fast food outlet and an expensive restaurant. What accounts for the differences?

8. Select either a not-for-profit organisation or an organisation in the public sector and discuss what the four levels of customer service might involve for them. How would they know for sure? How would they know what level of service they were providing?

9. How can an organisation manage customer interactions proactively and professionally to promote cordial relations and customer satisfaction?

10. Refer to the *From theory to practice* box on page 320 about where Pam buys her petrol. Analyse the psychological need or needs that the cashier met which influenced Pam to continue buying her petrol at this service station.

11. Explain what customer service providers can do to adopt a cooperative, rather than an adversarial, approach to dealing with customers.

12. Relate the telephone to the idea of *moments of truth* for an organisation. List some of the things supervisors can do to ensure they and their team make the best use of their telephone, and describe how they can stop the telephone from disrupting their day.

13. Write some guidelines to follow when placing and receiving calls, when taking messages and when dealing with 'difficult' callers. Include how the voice should be used.

·   DEVELOP YOUR SKILLS   ·

Individual activities

1. Think about a sensational service experience you have had, one where you were very impressed by the level of service you were offered. First, list the specific behaviours of the service provider; then describe the way they offered the service. Save your lists to use again in Chapter 15.

2. Think of an occasion when you made a telephone call to an organisation you didn't know much about. What general impression did you gain from the way your call was handled? Relate this to how supervisors' telephone techniques reflect both their own personality and abilities, and the capability and professionalism of their organisation.

3. The next time you make a business telephone call, analyse how well the telephone was answered and your call dealt with. Prepare a short memo outlining your findings and making recommendations on how the person or people you spoke to could improve their telephone technique.

4. Write two standard operating procedures (SOPs), one for receiving incoming calls and one for making outgoing calls.

5. You are about to place a call to a potential supplier organisation to request details about the range of in-house catering services they offer to companies conducting conferences and meetings. Following your SOP from activity 4 above, make some notes on what information you would like to find out and any information you might need to find before you place the call.

6. Think of the most difficult telephone conversation you have had at work in the last month. Jot down some notes about it: What was the reason for the call? What did you do well? What could you have done better? What will you do differently next time? What would you advise others as a result?

7. Referring to the vignette on page 306, do you believe Con has the 'right' attitude towards customer service? Why or why not? Use specific examples to support your position.

Group activities

1. This chapter commented on the fact that 'the bar is continually being raised' for customer service. In other words, what constituted desired or sensational service once is often considered expected or even basic today. As a class, generate some examples of this, using the four service levels (basic, expected, desired, sensational).

2. As a class, brainstorm a list of words or phrases that describe sensational customer service.

3. In small groups, develop a list of what would be included in the four levels of customer service for a petrol station. Compare your answers with other groups. Which group had the most unusual yet feasible ideas for sensational service? How difficult was it to 'think outside the box' to develop ideas for sensational customer service?

4. List some positive and negative *moments of truth* you have experienced. What distinguishes positive from negative MOTs?

5. In groups, discuss some pleasant and unpleasant experiences you have had as customers and analyse them, using the four levels of customer service. Which of your psychological needs as customers were and were not met? How? How did these pleasant and unpleasant experiences affect your relationship or future dealings with the organisations concerned?

6. One large Australian organisation has found that the concept of internal customers has developed adversarial relations rather than cooperative ones! A 'You're my customer so you have to do as I say!' attitude has grown and spread. To counteract this, they're encouraging people to think of the company as a family instead: 'Look after your family.' Do you think this would be a common problem? What sort of organisation culture would give rise to something like this? How likely to work is this organisation's attempt to counteract the problem? Prepare a short presentation to present to the class.

7. In small groups, study the list in Box 10.10 showing the features and benefits of a broom. What distinguishes a feature from a benefit? Now make up a list of features and benefits of either a quality system (e.g. a system that ensures quality customer service, or a quality production system) or a bicycle.

8. In groups of three, assign the roles of Caller, Receiver and Observer/Coach. Sitting with your backs together (so that you can't see each other), role-play the telephone call described in individual activity 5 above. The Observer should analyse the conversation for effectiveness and overall impressions presented by both Caller and Receiver: Were they professional, courteous, informative, helpful, etc.? Did their voice convey professionalism, interest and enthusiasm? Did they use positive rather than negative words and statements? The Observer/Coach should present their analysis and improvement recommendations to the Caller and Receiver at the end of the role play.

9. In groups of three, prepare a brief case study of a complaint a supervisor might have to deal with over the telephone. Assign the roles described above and, sitting with your backs to each other, role-play this call. The Observer/Coach should provide feedback to the person in the supervisor role on how well they handled the call and include feedback

on how well the supervisor applied the four steps of dealing with customer complaints.

10. Make a customer service map of a service cycle you are familiar with.

Identify points where service could be improved, redesigning the flow if necessary. (See the *From theory to practice* box on page 319.)

CASE STUDY 10.1

The Meal

Two couples went out for a meal to celebrate Sally's promotion to customer service supervisor at her firm, and Ben's completion of his course of study in first-line management at a local college. Because this was a special night, they chose a restaurant with a good reputation for quality service and food.

Upon arrival, they were seated by a pleasant waiter at a nice table and told the drinks waiter would be along soon. After about ten minutes, they were asked what they would like to drink, and after a further 20 minutes, the drinks arrived and with them the menus.

They eventually hailed a waiter and asked if they could order dinner. 'Yes, yes, I'll be right with you.' A few minutes later, a rather rushed-looking, flustered waitress took their order.

As this was a double celebration, the two couples were in no real hurry. However, after about 40 minutes, they began to wonder if they were ever going to see any food. They tried to catch the waitress' eye but couldn't. However, five minutes later, their first courses arrived. The food, as expected, was excellent.

The dishes were cleared and they commented how much they had enjoyed their food to the waitress. Twenty minutes later, the main courses arrived. Again the food was good, but the waiting was beginning to take its toll on the two couples. Because of the length of time they'd been there, they decided to skip dessert and coffee and ask for the bill.

The owner of the restaurant brought the bill over and asked how they had enjoyed the meal. Sally, believing that he really wanted to know, and knowing that he would never be able to improve his service without feedback from customers, spoke on the group's behalf. 'We really enjoyed the food,' she said, 'but we found the long waits for pre-dinner drinks and our two courses excessive. In fact, it rather spoiled our enjoyment of the meal.'

'But the food was all right?' asked the owner.

Questions

1   What does the owner seem to be focusing on in terms of customer service? Is this really what he should be focusing on?

2 What customer service elements do you consider important in a quality restaurant? Map the customer service cycle and list the measures of service you would benchmark.

3 List the *moments of truth* in an up-market restaurant. How can it meet its customers' psychological needs?

CASE STUDY 10.2

The Local Newsagent

In Laura's community there was only one newsagent. It stocked a large range of goods; it was well laid out and clean. Laura ran a small business from her home and found herself popping into the newsagent's at least once a week. Her purchases ranged from $3 to $15 most weeks.

Despite the fact that she was in there so frequently, the owner never appeared to recognise her. She was always business-like and efficient, however, and always gave the correct change. Laura didn't particularly enjoy going there, but there was no other newsagent conveniently close to home.

One day, another newsagent opened, at the other end of the main row of shops. It was equally convenient for Laura to go there, so she called in the next time she needed stationery supplies. The woman greeted her and introduced herself as Chris, asking whether she could help Laura find anything in particular. 'No thanks, I'll just have a look around first,' Laura replied.

She concluded that, although the shop wasn't quite as well stocked as the other one, it would easily supply her needs. She bought what she wanted and thanked Chris, who promptly said, 'Thanks, see you next time!' From then on, Laura purchased her stationery needs from the second newsagency. She enjoys going in there and having a quick chat with Chris while she browses and picks up supplies. Laura's average expenditure is in the range of $7 to $22.

Questions

1 What would you estimate is the LCV of Laura's business at each of the stores? How would you account for any difference?

2 How would you analyse the level of service provided by the two newsagents using the four levels of customer service?

3 What opportunities are there in a newsagency to provide sensational *moments of truth*?

4 How would you advise the first newsagent to proceed if she is to retain her customer base? In your answer, include a discussion on meeting the psychological needs of customers.

CASE STUDY 10.3

The Image Wrecker

Ring, ring.
> 'Yes?'
> 'Oh, hello, is that the computer centre?'
> 'You got it!'
> 'Oh. Well, I'm looking for Rowene Lipski. Is she there, please?'
> 'No, she's gone out.'
> 'Well, umm, do you know when I could get hold of her? It's rather important.'
> 'No, she didn't say where she was going.'
> 'I see. Well, would you mind taking a message?'
> Sigh. 'No, just hang on while I look for a pencil … okay, go ahead.'

Questions

1   Analyse this call, explaining what the person who answered did incorrectly and the possible effects of the errors.
2   Rewrite the conversation so that it is more courteous and business-like.

Answers to Rapid Review questions

1. T   2. T   3. T   4. T   5. F   6. F   7. T   8. T   9. F   10. T   11. F   12. T   13. F
14. F   15. T   16. F   17. F   18. F   19. T   20. F   21. T   22. T   23. T

CHAPTER 11

SOLVING PROBLEMS AND MAKING DECISIONS

Decisions! Decisions!

Khalid Bibi, the superintendent of the local council's Sports and Recreation Centre, was just returning from the weekly management meeting when he met the chief aerobics instructor. She said her team of part-time instructors were becoming more vociferous in their complaints about ventilation in the gymnasium and they would need to get the problem sorted out quickly. Then Mattie Smith, one of the best receptionists he had ever worked with, caught up with him to say she had been offered another job with an increase in pay and she wanted to speak to him about opportunities at the council.

When he got back to his desk, he found himself faced with a number of additional issues. A memo from Allan Ashmore, the CEO of the Centre, asked for his thoughts about whether, and how, to implement a proposed customer service program. There was a note from his partner requesting that he phone home immediately, and another from the maintenance contractor warning that problems seemed to be developing with the pool filtration system. The monthly Centre costs analysis showed an increasing trend in chemical and cleaning costs and, to top it all off, there was a candidate for a job opening in the cleaning staff waiting to be interviewed.

Everything always seems to happen at once, thought Khalid, as he considered which problems to tackle first.

Supervisors are constantly solving problems and making decisions. How well they do this is a significant component of their effectiveness. This chapter shows you how to apply sensible, systematic processes to build your confidence and skills in this area.

- Can you avoid the common traps in decision making and problem solving?
- Do you know which decisions deserve a lot of time and which don't? How about which decisions to make now, which to make later and which to delegate?
- Can you identify a potential problem and state it clearly?
- Can you explain the three distinct mental processes involved in solving problems and making decisions?

- Can you apply the seven steps to solving a problem?
- Are you creative enough and do you know how to boost your creativity?
- Do you know when and how to involve others in solving problems and making decisions?
- Can you recognise and avoid group-think?
- Do you know what to do when you've made a poor decision?

THE CHALLENGE

:...
'The problem is not that there are problems.
The problem is expecting otherwise and
thinking that having problems is a problem.'

Theodore Rubin

The best time to solve a problem is in its early stages. Good supervisors are aware that trouble is brewing and do something about it long before it becomes a crisis. In fact, it could be said that effective supervisors spend a lot of their time looking for problems to solve! They know where problems could arise and are sensitive to early warning signs. They deal with problems in a systematic, objective way before the problems are magnified or do too much damage.

They also accept that some problems cannot be *solved* in the sense that there is not always a perfect solution that will satisfy everyone fully. Some problems can only be *resolved* in the best way possible, taking all things into account. The more complex the problem and the situation, the more this is so. Just because there is no perfect solution, however, does not mean that any solution will do. Supervisor's develop and select solutions that meet carefully thought-out objectives.

Supervisors also make a lot of decisions and help others reach decisions. They decide in a timely and confident manner within their own and their organisation's ethical guidelines. Good supervisors think through the implications of a decision on other parts of the organisation and on its customers and explain the reasons behind the decisions they take to their staff and colleagues. They involve the team in solving problems and making decisions whenever they can. This generates more and better options, and trains and develops employees.

As decision-making authority is pushed down the flattened organisational hierarchy, as work teams become more involved under a leader's guidance, and as customer demands, technology and market conditions continually change, the need for reliable problem-solving and decision-making abilities is growing. The situation demands mental effort and clear thinking, courage, patience, self-discipline, skill and experience.

'Anyone can hold the helm when the sea is calm.'
Publius Syrus (1st century BC)

Before we examine the steps to follow, let's review the common mistakes.

TRAPS TO AVOID

'Most people spend more time and energy going around problems
than in trying to solve them.'
Henry Ford (1863–1947)
Founder, Ford Motor Company

Do you know anyone who is *too hasty* or *too slow* at reaching decisions and solving problems? Quick decisions and problems solved with a snap of the fingers frequently fail to consider people's feelings or the facts, while hesitation and endless 'research' causes unnecessary bottlenecks and delays, frustrates others and results in lost opportunities. Perhaps you have met the *conflict avoiders* who hesitate to upset anyone, the *worry warts* who agonise over every decision, no matter how small, or the *escapists* who cannot face a problem head-on but shuffle their feet, shuffle papers, facts and figures, and try to fool themselves and others that they are 'working on it'?

Fortunately, these traps can be overcome through training and through experience in using the seven steps outlined below. The six traps that we discuss next are more treacherous—the right-hand column has hints on how to avoid them. They arise not because we haven't followed the seven steps but because our brain sabotages our decisions. They involve the unconscious routines, or *heuristics*, that our brains go through when dealing with complexity.

It's easy to give too much weight to what we see or hear *first*, whether it's information, evidence, opinions, estimates or ideas. Stereotypes and prejudice, and previous similar experiences, can also act as anchors, even in the face of strong counter-evidence.

To avoid this trap, beware first impressions and information. View problems from different perspectives and don't automatically stick with whatever occurs to you first. Be open-minded and seek a variety of information and opinions. Beware of anchoring your team members with your own opinions

FROM THEORY TO PRACTICE

Seek information from several sources.
Don't overestimate the value of other people's opinions.
Don't underestimate the value of other people's opinions, either. Ignoring advice can be just as bad as accepting it without question.
Don't undervalue your own opinions or instincts, either.

Anchoring

It often seems easier to continue with things as they are, to maintain the *status quo*. The conventional wisdom of 'Leave well enough alone' or 'Let sleeping dogs lie' warns us not to do anything radical or different. Also, the less action we take, the less responsibility we feel and the less criticism we are open to. Doing nothing seems temptingly 'safe'.

Maintaining the *status quo* may be a good choice but don't do it just because it's easy and comfortable. Keep your objectives clearly in mind: does the *status quo* serve them well or would another alternative serve them better? Ask yourself: 'Would I select the *status quo* if it were just another alternative?'

Sticking with the status quo

Have you ever made a mistake and stuck with it, rather than cut your losses and change course?

Set aside your previous choice if it isn't working. What's done is done. Don't base future actions on a misguided attempt to recover your investment in time or money, or turn a poor decision into a good one. Prolonging a mistake only compounds its error. See the situation with new eyes. Ask for objective opinions, especially from people who were not involved in the original decision.

Not cutting your losses

'When you find yourself in a hole, the best thing you can do is stop digging.'
Warren Buffet

Seeing what you want to see

The brain seeks evidence that confirms and supports our point of view or preferred decision and avoids information that contradicts it. This affects where we go to collect evidence as well as how we interpret it, and causes us to put too much weight on supporting information and too little on opposing information.

Don't decide *what* you want to do and then figure out *why* you want to do it. Don't undermine the facts with expectations or biases. Don't accept confirming evidence without question. Admit that you may be inclined to think a certain way and open your mind to other ways. Consciously treat all the evidence and information objectively, both the pros and cons. Find someone to play devil's advocate and argue against your preferred decision. When asking others' opinions, don't ask leading questions.

Framing

The way we frame, or state, a problem or decision is important. It can guide us down one path or another, towards the *status quo* or away from it. It can highlight sunk costs or lead towards confirming evidence. Two types of frames in particular can distort decision making: gains *versus* losses, and different reference points. With the first, people will avoid risks when a decision is framed in terms of gains and will seek risks when a problem is posed in terms of avoiding losses. With the second, some wordings will put matters into perspective, others will emphasise, or make it look like, a no-win situation.

Frame decisions and problems in different ways. Don't automatically accept the way a problem is presented to you. Look for distortions caused by frames. Pose problems in neutral ways that combine gains and losses and reflect different reference points. Ask yourself how your thinking would change if your frame changed.

Estimating and forecasting

When we have regular feedback on the accuracy of our estimates (e.g. volume, time, distance or weight) we estimate fairly accurately. With uncertain events, however, forecasting is more difficult. Our jobs often require it, but seldom provide enough feedback on our accuracy to develop our estimating skills. The more uncertain, unusual or unfamiliar the subject of our estimate, the more risky estimating becomes. It's easy to become overconfident or overcautious, or rely too much on past events or dramatic events that have left a strong impression.

Be disciplined in making forecasts and judging probabilities. Consider the extremes. Examine all your assumptions. Try not to be guided by impressions, and use accurate facts and figures when you can.

These traps lurk in every stage of the problem-solving, decision-making process, especially with high-risk decisions when we are most prone to tricks of the mind. Each of these six heuristics can work in isolation or in combination with others. Forewarned is forearmed.

PROGRAMMED AND NON-PROGRAMMED DECISIONS

Some situations recur so often that organisations establish policies, standard procedures and rules and regulations for dealing with them. We call them **programmed decisions**. They provide a consistent solution that makes dealing with routine matters faster and easier. Anything that recurs regularly and has one best solution or course of action is suitable for a programmed decision.

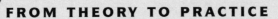

FROM THEORY TO PRACTICE

Computers can make and process many programmed decisions without any intervention by people. Take, for example, automated inventory control and purchasing. Once the minimum and maximum levels of stock to be carried have been determined and the optimal order size decided, a computer keeps track of the use of each item of inventory and automatically prepares and transmits orders when levels drop below a specified point.

Standard letters are another example of a programmed decision. The only decision to be made is which standard letter to use.

FIGURE 11.1   PROGRAMMED AND NON-PROGRAMMED DECISIONS

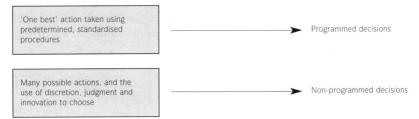

With today's rapid rate of change, the importance of making **non-programmed decisions** in an unpredictable environment is increasing. Non-programmed decisions are those that crop up less regularly and for which there are many possible satisfactory solutions (see Figure 11.1). How should we distribute work in the department? How should we divide computer time between users? How can we provide better services to our customers? These are the sorts of problems which need the seven-step problem-solving and decision-making model described below.

Decide now or later?

In Chapter 4 we learned to decide whether to do a task now, later or not at all by analysing its importance and urgency. We can do the same with problems and decisions. Give those that are important and urgent a high priority. Also give a high priority to those that are important but not urgent because, if you don't, they will become urgent and then you'll need to work on them under pressure. Delegate those that are just urgent but not important, or do them if you have time. You probably don't need to waste your efforts on those that are neither important nor urgent.

WHERE TO BEGIN?

There are several techniques to help you and your work team identify problems and potential problems and state them clearly. We looked at five in Chapter 9 and we examine three in this chapter.

- flow charts
- check sheets

- Pareto charts
- run charts
- stratification charts
- nominal group technique
- brainstorming
- cause-and-effect, or Ishikawa, diagrams

Nominal group technique

'The squeaky wheel gets the grease.'

Have you ever noticed that it is often the person with the loudest voice in the group, the most articulate person, or the most senior person, who gets their way? Others lose heart and interest because they feel their point of view will never be 'heard'.

The **nominal group technique** is a way of making sure this doesn't happen. It gives everyone in the group an equal say in deciding which problems to work on and in what order. This increases interest and commitment. The nominal group technique also clearly shows the wishes of the group.

The procedure is as follows:

1 Brainstorm (see page 352) problems that need to be resolved. A list of problems that a work group might brainstorm is shown in the left-hand column in Box 11.1.

2 Specify each problem clearly so that everyone has the same understanding of it. Examples are shown in the right-hand column of Box 11.1.

Make sure each problem is listed only once; guard against listing the same problem more than once using different words. For example, the following might all be different descriptions, or results, of the same core problem, different aspects of it, or different symptoms resulting from the same problem.

- lack of storage space
- some team members not fully trained
- in all procedures
- safety procedures not always followed

- people not putting tools away
- poor housekeeping
- lack of time.

3 Assign a letter to each problem (see Box 11.2).

4 Each team member then votes on which problem they believe is most important. In Box 11.2 there are five problems. Each member assigns a 5 to the problem they believe is most important, a 4 to the next most important problem, and so on, ending with a 1 next

---

BOX 11.1 — STATING PROBLEMS CLEARLY

Examples of problems	*Problems stated clearly*
■ Storage space	■ Lack of storage space
■ Tools	■ People not putting tools away
■ Safety procedures	■ Safety procedures not always followed
■ Housekeeping	■ Poor housekeeping due to lack of time and unclear priorities
■ Customer complaints	■ Increasing customer complaints

to the least important problem. One team member's vote is shown in Box 11.3.

If you are discussing a large number of problems, follow the 'half plus one' rule. Instead of ranking each problem, rank only half plus one of the problems listed. For example, if 22 problems are listed, 12 would be ranked. Each member would assign a 12 to the problem they believed most important, an 11 to the next most important problem, and so on.

5 Tally the ratings. For example, the results from a team of five voting on the ranking of problems to decide which to work on first might look like the ratings shown in Box 11.4. Problem C, safety procedures not always followed, has the highest score. This team thinks this is the most important problem to work on first. Problem B, people not putting tools away, will be worked on next, and so on.

Now that we know where to begin, we can launch the problem-solving process.

HOW TO SOLVE A PROBLEM AND MAKE A DECISION

What thorny problems have you solved recently? What sensible decisions have you made? Although we are not always conscious of the method we use, most of us follow quite similar steps in the problem-solving and decision-making process.

Figure 11.2 shows the sequence of these steps. You will see that the seven steps go through three distinct mental processes: analysing, imagining and evaluating.

BOX 11.2 PROBLEMS LABELLED

A. Lack of storage space
B. People not putting tools away
C. Safety procedures not always followed

D. Poor housekeeping due to lack of time and unclear priorities
E. Increasing customer complaints

BOX 11.3 ONE TEAM MEMBER'S RATING

Which problem is most important?

A. 1
B. 4
C. 5
D. 3
E. 2

BOX 11.4 TEAM RATING

Tally the ratings

A.   *1 3 2 2 3* = 11
B.   *4 5 3 3 2* = 17
C.   *5 4 4 4 5* = 22
D.   *3 1 1 5 4* = 14
E.   *2 2 5 1 1* = 11

 FROM THEORY TO PRACTICE

Another version of the nominal group technique is to brainstorm ideas to a flip chart and, when finished, give everyone coloured dots to put beside the ideas they like.

FIGURE 11.2 THE PROBLEM-SOLVING AND DECISION-MAKING PROCESS

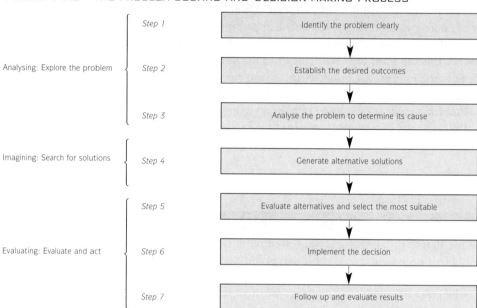

Analysing requires patience and clear and logical thinking, often spiced with a bit of 'intuitive insight'. *Imagining* requires creativity, the ability to let go of preconceived ideas, assumptions and long-standing beliefs and the mental energy to look beyond the obvious. *Evaluating* requires clear and logical thinking backed by the skills needed to implement the decision.

One: Explore the problem

Step 1: Identify the problem clearly

'A problem well stated is a problem half solved.'
Charles F. Kettering (1876–1958)
US engineer and inventor

You may have noticed that equipment seems to be breaking down more than usual, someone may have commented that 'our equipment is less reliable than it used to be' or your work team may have brainstormed a list of problems and decided to work on equipment breakdowns first. However, 'too many equipment breakdowns' doesn't describe the problem precisely enough to work on.

Box 11.5 lists three vague problems and suggests some questions that would help specify and clarify them. After asking and answering a number of questions, your problem statement for 'too many equipment breakdowns' might become: 'For the past three quarters, 60% of portable equipment over two years old used in the vans and in home offices have been failing before their service warranty expires; in previous quarters, the failure rate was 40%.' A clear problem statement like this gives you something to work with.

Don't move on to step 2 until you have clearly specified the problem you intend to solve.

QUESTIONS TO SPECIFY AND CLARIFY THE PROBLEM

General problem	Questions to ask
'Too many equipment breakdowns'	How many breakdowns? Which equipment? What is the nature of the breakdowns? When do they occur? What is happening when they occur? Who is involved? How regularly has the equipment been serviced? Has anything changed?
'Too many accidents'	What is the specific nature of the accidents? Where are they located?

FROM THEORY TO PRACTICE

- *Decide whether the decision is a big or a small one.* If you have a big decision to make, follow the seven-step procedure outlined below fully. If you have a small decision to make or a small problem to solve, don't spend hours agonising over it. This would steal your attention from more important matters.
- *For programmed decisions, rely on established company policy and practices.*
- *Don't put off making a decision or solving a problem until it becomes a crisis.* Get on with it! Stand back and consider the situation. Ask yourself when the decision has to be made. Then use the time available to make the best decision. If you do have a crisis, remember that you are the leader and your employees are looking to you for clear thinking and calm direction.
- *Remember to focus on solutions, not problems.* If all you can see is the problem, you'll never find a way around it. Pause, decide on your objectives and work out ways to achieve them. It won't always be easy to find solutions, but that's part of your job. The best ideas sometimes take a while to surface.
- *Don't be too impatient.* 'Decide in haste, repent at leisure' is good to remember when making important decisions. On the other hand, don't wait until you can make a perfect decision, either.

Step 2: Establish objectives

> 'Vision without action is a daydream.
> Action without vision is a nightmare.'
>
> Japanese proverb

Now it's time to think about the result you want. What must this decision do, or the solution to the problem achieve? What position do you want to be in after you have taken action? How will you know if your action is working?

A clear idea of what the solution to the problem should do (or what the effect of your decision should be) will concentrate your thinking towards a desired outcome and help you in step 5 (when you select the most suitable solution) and step 7 (when you evaluate the effectiveness of your decision).

Box 11.6 shows how stating the problem to answer the question 'How to ...' can help you frame clear objectives.

Reaching a perfect decision or solution to a problem may not be possible, but if you think through your objectives you will at least be heading towards the best possible outcome.

For complex or very important problems, divide your criteria into *musts* and *wants*: what must your decision do for you and, ideally, what would you also like it to do? Establishing these clearly puts you in a good position to select the best alternative and determine how well it is working.

Step 3: Analyse the problem to determine its cause

What is the difference between a problem and a symptom? *Symptoms are the results of problems.* They alert us to the existence of a problem. They do not cause problems. Fixing symptoms and not the real problem is like closing the barn door after the horse has bolted. It leaves the real problem unsolved, to recur again and again, and often creates new problems.

The way to fix a problem is to remove its cause. So your next task is to study the problem, separate it from its symptoms and find its cause. Then you can look for a solution. If you can't solve the problem by removing its cause, decide how best to minimise it and live with it.

Don't jump to conclusions about the cause of a problem. Really think it through and examine it from all angles. Gather facts, ideas and the opinions of others that may help in your analysis. Check out your theories before you act on them. You probably won't be able to get all the facts, but use those you have plus those you can get without too much trouble or expense (see Box 11.7).

Analysing a problem properly can save a lot of time and trouble. In fact, a clear and accurate analysis of a problem will sometimes point directly to its solution. A number of techniques can help you and your work team analyse the problem. We looked at all but the last three in Chapter 9; we look at these final three techniques in this chapter.

BOX 11.6 STATING THE PROBLEM AS A 'HOW TO ...'

- How to reduce the failure rate of portable equipment over two years old.
- How to get more storage space in the administration section.
- How to increase battery sales in stores.
- How to speed up the invoicing process at checkout.

- How to serve customers more quickly during lunch hour.
- How to respond to enquiries for quotations more quickly.
- How to ensure availability of raw materials to the front line when they are needed without tying up extra working capital in stock holding.

This will help you and your team focus on what you are trying to find answers for and keep you on track.

- Pareto charts
- run charts
- stratification charts
- histograms
- scatter diagrams
- control charts
- process capability charts
- cause-and-effect analyses (also called Ishikawa and fishbone diagrams)
- ask 'Why?' five times
- force field analysis

BOX
11.7   **ANALYSING THE PROBLEM**
....

Analyse the symptoms   Car splutters and stops
Identify possible causes   No petrol
                                Faulty points
                                No petrol getting to the carburettor

Check out the possible causes Check the petrol tank for petrol
to see if they are indeed the Check the spark plugs for spark
real cause of the problem   Check the carburettor to see if there is any
                                petrol going through it

Cause-and-effect diagrams

Cause-and-effect diagrams, also known as **Ishikawa diagrams** and **fishbone diagrams**, were first used in quality circles to help employees analyse problems to find their true cause. They are especially helpful with complicated problems where we need to sort out a maze of facts to isolate the most likely cause(s) of a problem.

Diagramming a problem allows us to 'see' it from all angles and identify its most important elements. It is relatively quick to do and usually enjoyable. You can diagram a problem alone or with a small group of people. Either way, you will be relying on the technique of brainstorming (discussed later in this chapter).

To make a fishbone diagram, put the problem in the square at the 'head' of the fish. Then decide the possible categories of causes of the problem and show them as major 'bones' off the central 'spine' of the fish. Figure 11.3 shows a cause-and-effect analysis for the problem of labour turnover. You will see that four aspects of the problem, or possible causes, have been considered: employees, work environment, machinery and rewards. These possible causes may not suit every problem, so choose from the diagnostic areas shown in Box 11.8 or create your own. It is usual to break a problem down into four components, but don't let this constrain you—use three or five categories if you prefer. Do whatever is best suited to analysing your specific problem.

If you think of a possible cause of the problem that could go under more than one category on your diagram, don't worry—put it down somewhere. The main thing is you are looking at your problem from all angles, which is critical to sound problem analysis.

· ·

FIGURE 11.3   THE ISHIKAWA OR FISHBONE DIAGRAM

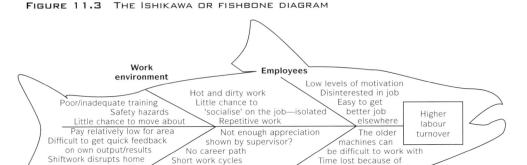

Once your initial analysis is complete, stand back and consider it. Which elements seem most important to you? Circle them to highlight the ones you intend to begin working on or investigating further.

Ask 'Why?' five times

This is a great technique for tunnelling to the cause of a problem. It works like this:
1. Define your problem clearly.
2. Brainstorm possible causes.
3. Decide the most likely cause(s).
4. Ask 'Why?' five times for the most likely causes.

Imagine that labour turnover is costing your department a lot of money. Naturally, you would want to know what's causing it so you can do something about it. Here is how the 'ask why' technique could work.

You define your turnover problem clearly and decide the two most likely causes are poor selection and poor induction. Your 'Why?' chain for poor selection might look like this:

Why?   I've hired the wrong people.

Why?   I'm not applying recruitment and selection techniques.

BOX 11.8

ASPECTS OF PROBLEMS
· ·

These are some of the factors supervisors have found useful in analysing their problems. Choose from this list or use other factors to analyse your problems effectively.

- Employees
- Materials
- Methods
- Job design
- Systems and procedures
- Efficiency

- Machinery, equipment, tools
- Work environment
- Rewards
- Clear goals
- General public
- Internal policies

- Training
- Team support
- Information
- Money and funds
- Customers
- Time

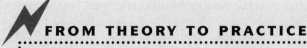

FROM THEORY TO PRACTICE

Look at problems through the eyes of all the stakeholders: customers, competitors, co-workers, management, and so on.

Why?   I'm not confident in them.
Why?   I need more training.

This is the logical end to this 'Why?' chain. Four 'Whys?' are enough to arrive at a possible solution.

Here is the 'Why?' chain for poor induction:

Why?   New employees aren't learning key skills and are not fitting in properly.
Why?   Induction isn't providing the right information and motivation.
Why?   It's too 'hit or miss'—nothing is written down.
Why?   I haven't approached it in a disciplined and systematic way.
Why?   I don't know enough about developing induction programs.

As you can see, by the time you've reached the end of the 'Why?' chain, the solution often becomes fairly clear.

Two: Search for solutions

Step 4: Generate alternative solutions

> 'Nothing is more dangerous than an idea
> when it's the only one you have.'

FROM THEORY TO PRACTICE

- *Work on eliminating the cause of the problem, not just covering up its symptoms.*
- *Know precisely what your solution should achieve.* This helps you see the problem in its wider context.
- *Seek the help of others when you are in doubt.* Ask other people what they think, especially informed people whose judgment you trust. If necessary, seek the help of experts.
- *Examine the problem from all angles and review 'the big picture'.* Relate relevant information: try using a matrix to help you 'see' your data better, create order out of chaos, correlate your information in an orderly way and help you consider the whole system. Learn to cope with 'soft' and limited information. Don't gather data indiscriminately; this wastes time, effort and money. Instead, focus on information that is useful and relevant. Find out only what you need to know.
- *Try to get underlying assumptions out into the open.*

There are three things to remember about finding suitable solutions. First, they never announce themselves with trumpets and drums. They can be elusive and, to find them, we usually need to develop several possible solutions and keep an open mind to all of them. This is not as easy as it may sound. We often have fixed ideas about what might have caused a problem or how it should be solved. This puts us in danger of jumping to conclusions and trying to solve a problem without considering other possibilities, possibly overlooking the best solution without even investigating it.

Second, the best solutions can come not from logical thinking but from creative thinking. Seemingly 'wild' or 'crazy' solutions can lead to some great ideas. This makes it essential to keep step 4, generating solutions, completely separate from step 5, evaluating them.

Third, don't settle for the first action that occurs to you. We need plenty of options to select from. Brainstorming is a good way to tap your creativity and develop lots of options.

Brainstorming

Brainstorming boosts creativity and helps us generate many ideas quickly. We can brainstorm alone or with a group of people (six to eight is a good number).

When brainstorming in groups, use a flip chart to write up the ideas as they are called out. This enables everyone to see them clearly and helps people build on each other's ideas. Seat people informally—in a circle of chairs for example. Box 11.9 gives further tips for brainstorming.

THE **BIG** PICTURE

Are you a 'satisficer'? 'Satisficers' stop at the first answer; they stop searching the haystack when they find the first needle. 'Optimisers' keep searching until they find *all* the needles.

Look beyond the obvious. Question everything, especially your own assumptions. There is always more than one 'right' answer.

FROM THEORY TO PRACTICE

Four guidelines for brainstorming:

1. *Suspend judgment*. Don't worry about whether the ideas are good or even workable. Aim to generate as many ideas as you can before evaluating their worth. This is because even the silliest idea can spark off a really good one through a process known as cross-fertilisation.
2. *Go for quantity*. We'll worry about quality in step 5 when we evaluate alternatives and select the most suitable.
3. *Let your thoughts freewheel* so that a continual flow of ideas streams out. Don't constrain your thinking in any way.
4. *Write them down*. It is surprising how quickly good ideas can be lost and forgotten. Writing them down also aids cross-fertilisation because you will be taking information in through the sense of sight as well as hearing.

TIPS FOR BRAINSTORMING

- Make sure the topic is specific and everyone understands both the topic and the goal of the brainstorming session (e.g. to brainstorm possible causes of a problem, or to brainstorm possible solutions).
- Brainstorm for ideas only: no digressions, discussions or explanations of ideas; this can come later.
- Allow no criticism, verbal or non-verbal (raised eyebrows, groans, etc.). Criticism kills creativity. Evaluate later.
- Write up every suggestion as it comes. Don't edit, 'improve' or change the words used.

- Everyone should be able to see the ideas list being generated. Butcher's paper or an electronic whiteboard are best because they can be saved for future reference. Print the ideas large enough for everyone to see.
- Make sure everyone has a say. Use the round robin technique (see below) if necessary.
- Forget normal constraints and limitations. Be wild! Ideas can be 'sensibilised' later.
- Build on each other's ideas.
- Have some fun! Laughter and fun encourage creativity.

You can generate ideas in a group brainstorming session in two ways. The first is to let everyone call out their ideas as they come to mind. This works well with enthusiastic and involved groups who are experienced at brainstorming. The second is known as the *round robin* method. Here each person calls out their idea in turn, one after the other, or says 'Pass' if they have nothing to contribute when their turn comes up. If you use the round robin method, keep going round until everyone has 'passed' on the same round.

Whether brainstorming on your own or with a group, sit through any 'dry periods'—don't give up at the first sign of the ideas running out. If you wait a minute or two, more are sure to come. A good rule of thumb is to keep going through three dry periods before stopping to evaluate ideas.

Three: Evaluate and act

Step 5: Evaluate alternatives and select the most suitable

Now it's time to evaluate the possible solutions you have developed and decide which will best meet the objectives you set in step 2. This is where problem solving becomes decision making. Every potential solution is likely to have some good points and some bad points. The purpose of evaluating each is to select the one that will achieve your objectives in the best way possible. Box 11.10 lists factors to consider when evaluating alternatives.

Previous experience can help us select a solution, but remember that history does not always repeat itself, especially in today's fast-changing world. What worked before may very well not work this time. Blindly following past experience without considering other possibilities is dangerous. Conditions, technology, people and economic situations all change, and these changes influence what will and will not work.

FROM THEORY TO PRACTICE

Instead of holding a group discussion about why a deadline was missed, a project failed, an account lost, try brainstorming solutions. Ask: 'How can we make sure we don't miss a deadline again?'

EVALUATING ALTERNATIVES

- Will this alternative achieve my objectives? Discard any that will not meet *all* of your *'must'* criteria.
- How will it affect our customers (both internal and external)?
- How will the quality of our product or service be affected?
- How will it affect the task and the team, the rest of the organisation?
- What other parts of the organisation will be affected if this alternative is selected? Check with other sections of the organisation to make sure you have not neglected something. Remember that some decisions create precedents that may involve the total organisation and not just your own section.
- What organisational resources will be required to put this alternative into

practice and what are the costs? Do these outweigh the benefits? If so, revise or discard it.
- Would any problems be created by putting this alternative into operation? What benefits could we expect? If potential problems are serious or outweigh the potential benefits, revise or discard the alternative.
- What could go wrong with this solution? Would it be serious? Could we do something to stop it or to minimise its effects?
- Will employees accept this solution readily?
- Does it fit in with organisational policy?
- Do you feel comfortable with this?

THE **BIG** PICTURE

Keep your 'reptilian brain' under control.

Our higher order thinking functions are located in our neocortex, or thinking brain. But just when we need to use it, our lower brain, or reptilian brain, often takes over and puts us into the fight–flight, panic mode. We may not even know when our reptilian brain kicks in, but when it does fear and aggression dominate our decisions.

This makes the seven-step structured process even more important: it keeps our reptilian brain in check and forces us to use our thinking brain.

THE **BIG** PICTURE

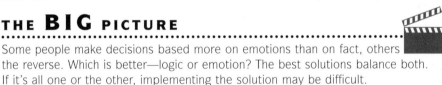

Some people make decisions based more on emotions than on fact, others the reverse. Which is better—logic or emotion? The best solutions balance both. If it's all one or the other, implementing the solution may be difficult.

Step 6: Implement the decision

Now it's time to implement your carefully thought-out solution. There are three things to do:

1. *Plan.* Decide what must be done and how, when and by whom. As suggested in Chapter 5, use the *who, how, what, where, why* and *when* questions to develop your plan.
2. *Safeguard.* Become a pessimist for a short while. What can go wrong? How would you know if it is about to happen? What action can you take now to prevent it happening?

What could you do to recover if it does happen? What will you monitor and how will you monitor it to ensure your decision is working?

3. *Communicate.* How and to whom will you communicate your decision or solution? Include everyone who will be involved or affected. How will you motivate people to accept it and help make it work? Communicate promptly to gain people's support; answer any questions carefully and fully. If people don't support your decision, they can make you, as well as your solution, look pretty silly.

Decisions often result in some type of change that affects one or more employees. We know that people often resist change because it disturbs familiar routines. Take this human resistance into account when planning to implement your decisions for a greater chance of success. (We discuss how to do this in Chapter 12.)

Force field analysis

Force field analysis is a technique borrowed from physics. It is a useful way to safeguard decisions and implement them in a way that will optimise success. Force field analysis helps us to analyse our selected solutions and implementation plans to identify what will help them succeed (*driving forces*) and what will prevent them from succeeding (*resisting forces*).

1 The first step in conducting a force field analysis is to *define both the current and the desired situation clearly*. For example, for the current situation you might describe the problem and its symptoms, and for the desired situation you might describe what you want to be happening instead (steps 1 and 2 of the problem-solving process).

2 In any situation, there will be driving or favourable forces pushing us in the direction we want to go, and resisting forces working against us, holding us back from reaching our goals (see Figure 11.4). The second step is to *identify these driving and resisting forces through brainstorming*. They are likely to come from a large number of areas, including:

●●
FIGURE 11.4   FORCE FIELD ANALYSIS

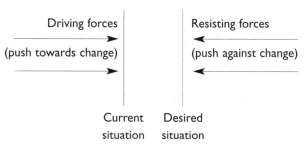

* Internal forces:
  — the task
  — the team
  — individual employees
  — policies
  — procedures
  — organisation culture

* Outside forces:
  — customers
  — technology
  — competition
  — changing government regulations
  — the economic environment

— influential parties (e.g. management or unions)
— administrative practices
— financial and other resources
— leadership styles
— tools and equipment
— time and information.

— changing marketplace conditions
— community pressures.

3 Now you are ready for the third step: *decide which are the most important or significant driving and resisting forces.*

4 The fourth step is to *plan how you will make best use of the most important driving forces* in the implementation of your decision, and *how you will minimise or even remove the significant resisting forces* to give your decision the best chance of success.

Step 7: Follow up and evaluate results

No matter how carefully you have thought through a decision and planned its implementation, things can go wrong. This is why we need follow-up.

Monitoring the implementation of your decision is your insurance. This is not to say that you have to be involved in every detail. But you should never announce a decision, or 'handball' a plan to someone else, and then forget it. Make routine checks to ensure that everything is going as planned; diarise these checks if necessary. They will enable you to catch and fix small deviations before they grow into major problems.

Be prepared to work with your chosen decision to make it succeed. And be prepared to 'let it go' and try something else if it is not achieving its objectives. Box 11.11 suggests some questions to ask in evaluating results.

BOX 11.11 — EVALUATING RESULTS

- Have the desired outcomes been met? If not, why not?
- Can it be rectified?
- Can matters be improved still further?
- What can you learn from anything that worked less well than expected?

- What can you do better next time? What did you learn from the experience? Examining failures and hiccups can highlight errors to avoid in future. If your plan was successfully introduced, analyse what you did that made it succeed and remember it for next time.

CREATIVITY IN PROBLEM SOLVING AND DECISION MAKING

'The problems we face cannot be resolved by the same level lof thinking we were at when we created them.'

Albert Einstein

In today's rapidly changing world, creativity is a vital ingredient to both organisational and supervisory success. Maintaining a competitive edge needs new ways of thinking in all parts of the organisation. Supervisors need to know and use creativity techniques and they need to unleash creativity in their teams to arrive at fresh, useful and actionable solutions to problems or opportunities.

Although some people seem to be more creative than others, everyone is creative to some extent. Yet we often fail to use our inborn creative abilities and this natural skill becomes rusty through neglect. Fortunately, we can learn how to be more creative and we can foster creativity in our work teams.

Barriers to creativity

For a long time, organisations have valued left-brain thinking: logic, reason, rationality. Creativity uses the right side of our brain to think outside the logical box. The limitations that we and others impose on our thinking can stop us seeing anything in other than the usual, accepted way. This 'flat-world thinking' traps us into giving expected answers, stops us from challenging the 'obvious', makes us evaluate any out-of-the-ordinary idea too quickly and negatively, and fixes us on our usual and accepted assumptions.

Habit, laziness and the 'only one right answer' syndrome encourage us to stop at the first answer we think of rather than searching for more and possibly better alternatives. Fixed ideas, especially those that say everything should be orderly and predictable, block our creativity. The fear of sounding silly also restrains our creativity. Focusing on problems, rather than how to fix them, closes our mind to solutions. Lack of willingness to put in the effort needed strangles creativity—coming up with creative solutions to problems can be hard work!

The elements of creativity

'I think there are two keys to being creatively productive. One is not to be daunted by one's fear of failure. The second is sheer perseverance.'

Mary-Claire King

Actually, creative people share five common characteristics or qualities. These are listed below, in no particular order of importance. Although many creative people possess two or even three of these qualities, it would be unusual for even the most creative among us to possess as many as all five or even four of them.

1. *Fluency* is the ability to come up with a large number of ideas. Although not all their ideas are useful, creative people are often able to come up with one new idea after another, seemingly without effort.

FROM THEORY TO PRACTICE

Creative people see what everyone else sees, but see it differently.

Japan Railways (JR) East is the largest rail carrier in the world. When crews tunnelled through Mount Tanigawa in 1978, water gushed out of the tunnel wall at the rate of 60 tonnes a second. As engineers drew up plans to drain it away, a maintenance worker stepped forward with a different idea. He noticed that tunnel workers were drinking the water because it tasted unusually good. He suggested that JR East bottle it and sell it as mineral water. Called *Ohshimizu*, it became so popular that JR East installed special vending machines on its 1000 platforms and introduced a home delivery service. Since then, a range of other *Ohshimizu* products have gone to market including *Ohshimizu* tea and *Ohshimizu* coffee.

THE **BIG** PICTURE

Leading organisations develop initiative and flexibility in their employees. Alan Robinson, professor in the School of Management at the University of Massachusetts, outlines six principles of creativity for organisations to follow:

1. *Alignment.* Make sure employees' efforts are directed at the organisation's main goals so their efforts will benefit the enterprise.
2. *Self-initiated activity.* Let people select the projects they want to work on to increase their motivation.
3. *Unofficial activity.* Encourage informal work on projects, before official sanctions are sought, to reduce censorship.
4. *Serendipity.* Many great 'discoveries' 'just happen', so promote fortunate accidents through strategies that provoke and make best use of them.
5. *Diverse stimuli.* Provide work-related diversions and information and a fun, interesting environment to fire up people's brains.
6. *Communication.* Provide opportunities for employees to interact with each other, face-to-face and electronically, to share ideas and learning.

---

2. Many creative people are *mentally nimble.* Their minds freewheel, or hop easily from one line of thinking to another.
3. They are able to produce *original,* unusual and novel ideas.
4. They are often *helicopter thinkers,* with the ability to see 'the big picture', the wood as well as the trees. They can see the 'same old thing' in a new light.
5. It takes *determination* to be creative. Finding good ideas usually needs persistence and effort. However, creative people are able to carry on despite frustrations. They have the drive to make up another list of alternative solutions when the first list has produced nothing worthwhile. Creative people don't give up, but are willing to try, try and try again.

How to become more creative

For your creativity to flourish at work, you (and your team) need to answer 'yes' to these three statements:

1. I believe I am creative and can think creatively. I don't automatically go with the *status quo,* but approach problems flexibly and imaginatively.
2. I have expertise in my topic—technical, procedural, knowledge.
3. I am motivated. I have an inner passion to solve the problem at hand.

FROM THEORY TO PRACTICE

A Kodak team who would not normally have met each other invented three-dimensional imaging. Each had separately expressed interest in 3-D images at different times and Kodak's Office of Innovation brought them together.

> 'The real creative ideas originate hither and yon in the
> individual members of the staff and no one can tell in advance what
> they will be or where they will crop up.'
>
> Frank Jewett (1879–1949)
> First head of Bell Labs and President of the National Academy of Sciences

One of the most important things you can do to become more creative is to recognise the barriers to creativity within yourself and make a conscious effort to remove them. They stop you believing you are creative and thinking creatively. Are you worried about being criticised for a new idea? Maybe you shouldn't be. Is there a lot of pressure on your time? Take some time out to identify a problem and brainstorm some creative solutions to it. Do you always go for the obvious solution or the one that has worked before? Look for another idea that might work even better.

Wait until you have a long list of possibilities before evaluating them. Don't throw ideas out without a very good reason: 'It will cost too much'; 'The boss will never go for it'; 'It's too big a change'; 'We've tried it before' are not sufficient reasons for abandoning an idea. Stop using 'killer phrases' (see Chapter 2) on yourself and others.

Look for situations in which you seem to be the most creative and observe what you do. Watch creative people to see what good ideas you can pick up from their approach.

> 'The voyage of discovery consists not in seeking new landscapes
> but in having new eyes.'
>
> Marcel Proust (1871–1922)
> French novelist

Try thinking in other 'languages': make mental pictures or think in symbols instead of words. Use all your senses as you approach a problem. Study the elements of creativity listed above and try to incorporate them into your day-to-day behaviour. The effort you spend on this will be well worth it.

FIVE DECISION-MAKING PROCEDURES

1. Voting

A lot of leaders think a vote is a quick way to reach agreement and a lot of people think that a vote is the democratic way to do things. A vote certainly guarantees that a decision will be reached.

Voting, however, has three big drawbacks. It accentuates the differences of opinion between people, which can create a 'battleground' or win–lose atmosphere. This can make some people uncomfortable—especially those in the minority. Also, voting commits people publicly to a position, making it difficult for them to change their mind later without appearing weak and vacillating. Finally, those in the minority, who 'lost' the vote, usually do not carry out the group decision with much commitment or enthusiasm. This is why it is usually better not to take a formal vote, but to work towards consensus instead.

2. Consensus

Voting, although quick, produces 'winners' and 'losers'. As we all know, 'losers' usually feel bad about losing; they often fail to support, and sometimes even undermine, the 'winning' decision. However, everyone usually understands and supports decisions reached by

FROM THEORY TO PRACTICE

Creativity boosters for yourself and your team

- *Abstain from judgment.* Allow ideas to emerge and grow before evaluating them.
- *Follow your passion.* Work in areas you enjoy and that inspire you to do your best.
- *Listen to your subconscious.* Creative ideas often 'bubble up from within' and we need to be able to hear them.
- *Trust the process.* Use creativity techniques and know that creative ideas will result.
- *Stay open and curious.* Find opportunities in the unexpected.
- *Force yourself to approach a problem from different points of view.*
- *Encourage continuous learning.*
- *Work at your cutting edge.* Be challenged, not bored.
- *Balance time allocated and the importance of the task.*

Creativity boosters for your team

- *Match people to the right jobs.* Take advantage of interests, expertise and training.
- *Give people autonomy over the means, if not the ends, of achieving goals.* You decide on the mountain and let the team decide how to climb it.
- *Specify goals clearly.* People need to know where they're headed.
- *Provide enough resources—time, money, space, people, psychological safety, support, etc.*
- *Build a well rounded, diverse team with different perspectives, backgrounds, expertise and thinking styles.* Homogeneous teams may have less friction and 'reach solutions' quickly but they suffer from lack of creativity because everyone is so similar.
- *Provide both positive and constructive feedback.* Without it, enthusiasm and creativity will wilt.
- *Greet new ideas with openness, not scepticism.* Explore new ideas.
- *Encourage collaboration and communication within the team and across the organisation.*
- *Accept mistakes as a route to good ideas.*

consensus. Although it requires more skills from both the meeting leader and group members, and although it is time-consuming, consensus usually results in better decisions and greater commitment. As an added benefit, the process of achieving consensus is usually both educational and motivational.

During the process of reaching a consensus decision, team members hear everyone else's point of view and explain their own. In this way, they can explore differences, see diverging points of view as a way to gather more information and polish ideas. Gradually, consensus is achieved. Not everyone needs to agree 100%, but each person in the group must be able to say: 'It may not be *exactly* what I would have done, but I understand why it has been agreed and I agree with it enough to support it.'

TEAM SKILLS FOR CONSENSUS

Able to:
- listen to others
- articulate a point of view
- communicate empathically
- give and receive feedback
- understand and use problem-solving and decision-making processes
- use creativity techniques and think creatively

- support and encourage other team members
- respect and value diversity and other points of view
- understand and employ consensus-reaching techniques.

To reach genuine consensus, team members must know and apply the team skills listed in Box 11.12.

Achieving consensus

Unfortunately, there is no simple way to reach consensus. It takes time, skills and patience. It also takes practice: as groups become more experienced in participative methods, they usually get better at them. This is especially true if their leader is skilled in meeting management and consultative supervision.

Discussion is a key ingredient of consensus. Ironically, meeting members often report a feeling of going 'round in circles' until a point is reached when, 'suddenly', consensus is achieved and a decision made. Until members become used to this feeling, it can be frustrating and disheartening.

As the leader, your general attitude towards the group can do more to gain group participation than any other single factor. After stating the purpose of the meeting and providing the necessary background information, invite discussion and guide and lead the discussion that follows. The less you participate, the better. It may help to remember that you are there to hear the team's thoughts more than they are there to hear yours. Save your thoughts and opinions until the end so that team members won't feel they must agree with you.

Create an atmosphere that treats what everyone says as important and which values everyone's participation. To get things going, you might have to pose one or two questions. You might invite people to express themselves about one of the points under consideration. Or you might ask a direct question of a group member you know will be able to answer, in order to 'get the ball rolling'.

You can do four things to help a meeting reach consensus.

1. Be very clear about the issue under discussion and the end result you want to achieve: to solve a problem, to come up with a range of options, to analyse and explore a problem to determine its cause.
2. Ensure meeting participants understand and agree with the desired outcomes; if not, discuss this openly and reach agreement, or the meeting will never get anywhere.
3. Summarise frequently, at least each major conclusion or decision.
4. Keep discussion to the stated topic. Don't allow meeting members to become sidetracked by 'rambling shop talk'. If they start to digress, bring them back to the topic under discussion.

Box 11.13 summarises the five phases of reaching consensus.

BOX 11.13 THE FIVE PHASES OF REACHING CONSENSUS

1. *A statement by the leader, identifying the issue(s) to be discussed and the desired outcome(s) of the meeting.* An opening statement might go something like: 'Hello, everyone, thank you for being here. What I intend for this meeting is to explore together how we can best implement the new council policy on providing easier access to information in our department by the ratepayers. I hope that by the end of the meeting, in about an hour's time, we will have come up with a list of possible ways of doing this so that we can all go away and think about them. Then, in our next meeting, we can decide which ideas are the most suitable and plan out how we can put them into place. Is that agreeable to everyone?'
2. *Clarification of the issues and objectives* of the meeting is sometimes necessary, although, more often, a meeting will proceed directly to phase 3.
3. *Discussion by meeting members.* This phase probably accounts for around 80% of the meeting. Focus the group on the topic at hand and ensure that all members have a chance to contribute. As discussed earlier, clearly separate problem exploration, ideas generation and evaluation from each other.
4. *Consensus is reached.* If the issue is controversial, difficult or complex, it may take more than one meeting to reach phase 4.
5. *Action planning.* Here the meeting becomes a planning meeting and decisions are made about who will do what, where, when and how.

3. Groupthink

Without a cohesive team, where individual members feel a strong bond of liking, goodwill and mutual support towards each other, it will be hard to achieve outstanding results. Yet too much cohesion can be counterproductive. It can cause people to feel that the approval of their colleagues is more important than stating an opposing viewpoint, even when it might add new information or provide a better perspective. As a result, a team can reach wrong and even dangerous decisions, or develop policies or strategies that harm the department or organisation as a whole.

Irving Janis, a social psychologist, called this the '**groupthink** syndrome'. He found that groups can become cohesive to the point where their efficiency declines. When this happens, they desire unanimity above realism, and lose their desire to seek and consider alternatives. Such teams ignore negative aspects of their decisions and fail to test them against reality. Conforming to group norms overrides the desire to develop new and better ways and innovative approaches. Those who dare to disagree are seen as 'deviants' or 'traitors' to the group.

The symptoms of groupthink identified by Janis are listed in Box 11.14.

4. Unilateral decisions

Some managers make decisions and announce them. While this is appropriate in some circumstances, consultation and participation usually result in a better decision that is backed

SYMPTOMS OF GROUPTHINK

BOX
11.14

- An unquestioned belief in the 'rightness' of the group, inclining members to ignore the moral or ethical consequences of their decisions and policies and fail to ask experts outside the group for input.
- An illusion of invulnerability, which creates excessive optimism and risk taking.
- Stereotyped views of 'enemies' outside the group, which lead to reluctance to negotiate and underestimating the 'enemy's' ability to counter the group's plans or strategies.
- Limiting discussions to only a few alternatives, focusing quickly on a decision or course of action and looking mostly at its good points.
- An absence of 'censors' to bring to the attention of the group any information or evidence that does not conform to the group's expectations and stereotypes, or

which might shatter its complacency about its effectiveness.
- Discounting or rationalising warnings or signs that the team is operating under false assumptions, making a poor decision or developing a poor strategy or policy.
- A reluctance to reconsider decisions, policies and strategies and search for alternatives.
- Strong pressure on group members to conform to group norms and fall in with the group's stereotypes, illusions and commitments.
- Hesitation of members to air any discomfort, doubts or uncertainties they feel about the group's decisions or policies, so that consensus appears unanimous.

FROM THEORY TO PRACTICE

Research has shown that participative leadership discourages groupthink while authoritarian, or directive leadership, encourages it. To ensure your team does not fall into the groupthink syndrome:

- Invite and consider opposing opinions, objections and doubts.
- Actively look for the weak points in your chosen decision or course of action.
- When developing policies or procedures or making team decisions, brief the group impartially and objectively without advocating your own preferences.
- Develop an atmosphere of open inquiry and careful consideration of alternatives; help the team to explore alternatives impartially.
- Invite experts within the organisation to share their thoughts and ideas and encourage them to challenge team members' views.
- When evaluating alternatives, assign at least one team member to play the role of 'devil's advocate'.
- Know the warning signals that might indicate your decision is failing, and keep alert for them so that you can reconsider your decision if necessary.
- Maintain the group's focus on the task at hand and on the organisation's goals.

by greater understanding and commitment. People will work harder to ensure the success of a decision they have had a part in reaching than if they are merely complying with someone else's wishes. We discuss how to decide whether to involve the team later in this chapter.

5. Factional decisions

Factional decisions are those that are bulldozed through by a minority. These may be the people with the loudest voices, or the most formal or informal influence. Or they may be a few articulate people who are prepared to speak up. The danger with factional decision making is that not everyone's opinion will be heard and considered and some team members will feel left out and uncommitted to the decision reached.

INVOLVING TEAMS IN DECISION MAKING AND PROBLEM SOLVING

Do you think it's quicker and easier to make a decision yourself? Or that you *should* make the decision yourself since you are held accountable for the results?

Think about how a group can provide motivation and help build ideas, how involving people in the decision-making process can enhance the outcome (more brains, better results). Remember that people are more committed to a decision they helped make because their involvement has given them a better understanding of it. This greater understanding will also help them to make it work better.

> **'Men often oppose a thing merely because they have had no agency in planning it, or because it may have been planned by those whom they dislike.'**
>
> Alexander Hamilton (1755–1804)
> A founder of the USA

Does this mean that the work group should participate in every decision? Two types of decision in particular are not suited to a group solution: programmed decisions and those that have no real effect on the work group. If the group has no interest in a decision, involvement would be a waste of everyone's time; the leader should make the decision and announce or explain it.

When to involve the team

If any of the following four factors are present, involve your group in the problem-solving and decision-making process:

1. *The need for acceptance.* The more you need your team to accept the decision, the more you should involve them.
2. *Its effect on the group.* The more the problem or decision affects the group, the more you should involve them.
3. *Their involvement in implementing it.* If the team will be implementing or carrying out the decision, involve them.
4. *The ability and desire of the group to become involved.* If the team wants to become involved, consider involving them, particularly if they have sufficient knowledge or expertise in the issues involved. Even if they do not, involving them could provide useful training and development.

There are many ways, both formal and informal, to involve the group, and many degrees to which you can involve others (see Figure 11.5).

FIGURE 11.5   DEGREES OF INVOLVEMENT

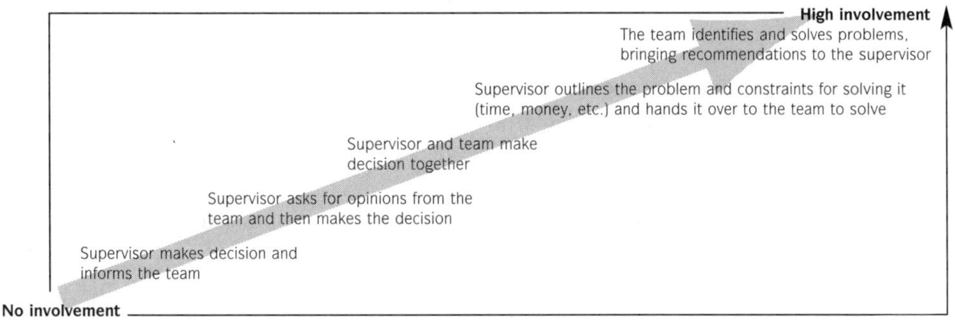

High involvement
The team identifies and solves problems, bringing recommendations to the supervisor

Supervisor outlines the problem and constraints for solving it (time, money, etc.) and hands it over to the team to solve

Supervisor and team make decision together

Supervisor asks for opinions from the team and then makes the decision

Supervisor makes decision and informs the team

No involvement

FROM THEORY TO PRACTICE

- *Involve others*. Bring in the major stakeholders in the outcome of the problem and anyone concerned with or affected by its solution. Seek their information, ideas and suggestions.
- *Listen and pay attention to what others have to say.*
- *Encourage others, particularly the quieter ones, to offer their ideas.*
- *Treat differences of opinion as a way to gather additional information, clarify issues and force the group to seek better information.*
- *Take your time,* don't push too hard—encourage the group to take ownership of the whole process.
- *Keep the group focused on the objectives, on the future and on solving the problem.*
- *Create environments that encourage creativity and motivation—music, activities, colour, space, visual displays.*
- *Don't vote—this only divides people into winners and losers.*
- *Don't make early, quick, easy agreements and compromises—these are often based on wrong assumptions.*
- *Don't foster internal competition.*
- *Don't railroad the group into agreeing with your thoughts and ideas.*

WHEN YOU'VE MADE A POOR DECISION ...

'Many people dream of success. To me, success can only be achieved through repeated failure and introspection. In fact, success represents one per cent of your work, which results from the 99% that is called failure.'

Soichiro Honda (1906–91)
Japanese industrialist

The only way never to make a mistake is to do nothing. That way, we'd be like a ship in harbour but, as William Shedd observed, 'A ship in harbour is safe but that's not what ships are built for.' If we never try anything out, we'll probably never make any mistakes. But we won't make any improvements or learn anything, either!

'Mistakes are inevitable. Learning from them is optional.'

A mind-set that says: 'There are no mistakes, only feedback' is a useful one for supervisors. It frees us to try out new ways of doing things, create exciting hypotheses and test them out or approach a problem from a different angle. The more we try out new things, the more mistakes we're bound to make. And the more successes we're bound to have, too.

As the saying goes, 'Out on a limb is where the fruit is.' People who score a lot of goals also kick a lot of misses. People who shoot a lot of baskets throw a lot of duds. Thomas Edison had thousands of failures before he made a bulb light up. Achievers make more mistakes because they try out more things.

No one can be 100% right all the time. We're bound to make poor decisions: with the rate of change as rapid as it is, we're all facing situations we've never in our lives faced before. So we have to try out new approaches.

When you make a poor decision, and you will, don't ignore it or cover it up, or make excuses or find someone else to blame. Do two things: first, concentrate on ways to rectify it. Analyse what went wrong and decide what corrective action to take. Then take it.

'There are no mistakes, only learning opportunities.'

Second, learn from your mistakes. Ask yourself where you went wrong. Get advice from those around you on what you could have considered that you didn't, what you should have done that you didn't, how else you might have approached it. Think back through the seven problem-solving and decision-making steps—did you omit any, or not work through a step thoroughly? Know what went wrong so that you don't make the same mistake twice.

Finally, get your work team involved if you haven't already. They will have a different perspective on the problem and be able to bring different experiences and background information to it.

RAPID REVIEW

		True	False
1.	Being too hasty or too slow, perfectionism, fear of upsetting people, agonising over every decision and 'decision mania' are common traits of poor decision makers.	☐	☐
2.	We need to be on the lookout for tricks our brain plays on us when we're making decisions.	☐	☐
3.	A programmed decision is one that is suited to developing a standard policy or procedure for dealing with it.	☐	☐
4.	One of the keys to successful problem solving is pinpointing the problem precisely.	☐	☐
5.	Generating and evaluating ideas together saves time and is a good way to proceed.	☐	☐

	True	False
6. Stating what a decision must achieve is a good idea because it helps us select the best alternative.	☐	☐
7. 'Fishbones' help identify the cause of a problem.	☐	☐
8. Considering only one solution is dangerous.	☐	☐
9. Brainstorming can only be done in groups.	☐	☐
10. Force field analyses help avoid potential disasters by alerting you to potential difficulties.	☐	☐
11. Not everyone is creative.		
12. Widespread lack of creativity in problem solving and decision making could lead to real problems for an organisation.	☐	☐
13. A decision reached by consensus is one that everyone fully agrees with.	☐	☐
14. Groupthink occurs when team members like each other so much they fail to disagree, or put forward alternative points of view, or see the potential negative consequences of their actions.	☐	☐
15. Teams should always be involved in all work-related problems and decisions.	☐	☐

APPLY YOUR KNOWLEDGE

1. Why are supervisory problem-solving and decision-making skills even more important now than they were in the past?

2. Referring to the vignette on page 338, imagine Khalid Bibi wants to avoid falling into the decision-making traps discussed. How would he tackle each problem and decision described in the vignette?

3. What does 'being alert for problems' mean? Give an example from your own experience.

4. Give some examples of programmed and non-programmed decisions that you make.

5. Why is it so important to focus on the cause of a problem rather than its symptoms?

6. Why is there nothing more dangerous than a person with only one idea when it comes to solving problems and making decisions?

7. Discuss the things supervisors should consider when selecting the best solution to a problem.

8. Explain what implementing a decision involves.

9. What are some common barriers to creativity you have seen in others or experienced yourself? How did these barriers hold you back from coming up with good ideas?

10. In what ways is consensus better than voting or unilateral decision making? How could factional decision making and groupthink be confused with consensus?

11. Discuss the issues involved in deciding whether or not to involve a work group in problem solving and decisionmaking.

12. Referring again to the vignette on page 338, and using the chapter guidelines on when to involve the team and the degrees of involvement, explain how Khalid should make each of the decisions he needs to make, and why.

Individual activities

1. Using an example from your own experience, illustrate how to go about determining and analysing the 'real' problem.

2. Imagine you are going to rent or buy a new home. Develop a list of 'must' and 'want' criteria for it. How would this list help you in identifying possible homes and making your decision?

3. Have you ever failed an exam or done something less well than you'd hoped? Using a fishbone diagram, brainstorm the possible reasons for this, select the most likely one, and develop an action plan that you could follow to ensure you improve your performance next time.

4. Illustrate the importance of planning, communicating, following up and evaluating in decision making, using a real-life example.

5. Think back over the last few days and make a list of all the problems you solved and decisions you made (however minor or major). Select a suitable problem (i.e. a fairly 'meaty' problem, one that is not a program-med decision and one where you want to fix the cause of the problem to stop it recurring) and apply to it the seven-step problem-solving decision making model described in the chapter.

6. Think of a current or recent problem you have experienced which had many possible causes. Analyse it using a cause-and-effect diagram to determine its most likely cause.

7. On your own, list as many round objects as you can in six minutes.

Time yourself carefully. Compare what you have written to the five elements of creativity described in the chapter. In class, develop a matrix showing how the five elements of creativity are distributed in your class. What conclusions can you draw?

8. Study the barriers to creativity discussed in the chapter and highlight any that apply to you. Select one to work conscientiously at removing over the next four weeks. List some things you could do to overcome the barrier you have selected. Now select two or three of these ideas to apply.

9. Have you ever experienced group-think? Describe the circumstances and its effects. In what ways is groupthink similar to peer pressure?

10. The next time you are part of a social group that is making a decision about something, say, where to go on Friday night, listen and watch as the decision is reached. Is there any evidence of groupthink? Was consensus reached, was a unilateral decision made, was a factional decision made, or was a decision reached by voting? Which of the skills listed in Box 11.12 (*Team skills for consensus*) were used in reaching the decision? Relate the way the decision was reached to the seven steps explained in the chapter. What would happen if decisions were made in a similar way in a work situation?

11. Think back to a problem you solved ineffectively or a poor decision you made. Review it. What can you learn from your mistakes? How will you do it better next time?

Group activities

1. In class, brainstorm a list of essential skills for effective supervisory problem solving and decision making. Then use the nominal group technique to prioritise the top six.

2. In groups of six to eight, conduct a brainstorming session on how to solve a current and relevant problem at your college. Specify the problem carefully to ensure everyone has the same understanding of it. Use the 'round robin' method for the final two minutes of the brainstorming session. Elect a recorder to write your ideas on a flip chart as they are called out. Brainstorm for at least seven minutes. When you have finished, check through the ideas to make sure each is recorded once only; if the same or very similar ideas are listed using different words, combine them as one idea. Then use the nominal group technique to identify the ideas that are the most workable or show the most promise.

3. Divide the class into groups of five to eight. Half the groups should prepare a cause-and-effect diagram that might explain the reasons for an increase in motor vehicle accidents in the college car park which seemed to occur around the end of April. There is no corresponding increase in use of the car park. Identify the reasons that seem most likely. The other half of the groups should use the 'ask why five times' technique to identify causes of the increase in accidents. When all the groups have finished, compare your answers and your experience of using the two techniques. Then develop a list of 'do's' and 'don'ts' for using these two techniques through consensus.

4. In small groups, conduct a force field analysis on why students fail courses. The current situation is '35% of students failing business courses' and the desired situation is '90% pass rate on business courses'.

5. In small groups, conduct a force field analysis on your favourite sports team winning the championship this season.

··········· **CASE STUDY 11.1** ···········

The South Sydney Furniture Company

The South Sydney Furniture Company is a medium-sized manufacturer of bedroom and dining room suites. The company also produces a small line of occasional lounge room pieces such as coffee tables and chairs.

Rather unexpectedly, the purchasing manager, Henry Parden, resigned his job to accept the position of purchasing manager with a manufacturer of upholstered furniture. To fill his position, the company hired Iona Kelford, an experienced purchasing officer from a local kitchen manufacturer. The management team of the

South Sydney Furniture Company felt that Ms Kelford's familiarity with furniture in general, and with the purchasing function, would enable her to assume Mr Parden's duties easily and make a significant contribution to the purchasing department.

When Iona reported for work, the general manager showed her around the plant and introduced her to her secretary, Virginia Bellamy, and to the rest of the team. He also outlined her duties and indicated his plans for reorganising the purchasing department.

The following week, Iona began analysing the operation of the purchasing section and found several disturbing facts. For example, a supply of core stock (timber used as a base for veneers) sufficient to last for 16 months was on hand. In addition, two container loads of core stock had just been received and six more were on the way. All available space at that time was being used to store this material, and she had real doubts as to where the additional stock could be stored. Although she and Virginia searched the files, they were unable to find a purchase contract authorising the shipments. On Wednesday, two urgent calls from the assembly plant informed her that they were out of drawer pulls, hinges and braces for a dining-room suite for a large export order. Unless they could obtain a supply immediately, they would have to stop production of this item and delivery would be late.

Later in the day, the accountant asked Iona to approve a bill from a paint and varnish supplier. On checking, she found that although the material had been received, no purchase order had been issued. She found that Mr Parden's practice had been to allow the paint sales representative to inspect the company's stock and ship whatever supplies the representative thought appropriate. As a result, she estimated that the South Sydney Furniture Company had 18–20 months' supply of various types of fillers, paints and varnishes. Several times during the week, plant supervisors brought Iona bills for brushes, sandpaper, etc., indicating that they had practically exhausted their supplies and had replenished them locally.

Questions

1 List the problems Iona faces and the decisions she must make. Are any suitable for programmed decisions? Should she involve other people in any of them? If so, who, why and to what extent?
2 If you were Iona, what immediate action would you take? Why?
3 What would be your short-term and long-range objectives?

CASE STUDY 11.2

Nipped In The Bud

Alma and her team in finance and corporate services seemed to have everything under control after completing the hectic budgeting period. They settled down to what they hoped would be a routine month of financial analysis and reporting.

It was not to be. Early in the month, one of the customer service reports high-lighted what seemed to be a significant increase in the number of customer complaints. Most of these concerned the length of time customers were kept waiting and the lack of attentiveness from service staff. The complaints had come over the telephone as well as in letters and faxes.

Alma whisked the report down to Siva, who supervised the corporation's field customer service operations. They agreed that they wanted to 'nip this problem in the bud' and set about planning their approach.

Questions

1   Develop a step-by-step plan showing what Alma and Siva should do based on the seven-step problem-solving and decision-making process described in this chapter.
2   What level of input from field staff and their supervisors do you recommend and why?

Answers to Rapid Review questions

1. T   2. T   3. T   4. T   5. F   6. T   7. T   8. T   9. F   10. T   11. F   12. T   13. F
14. T   15. F

CHAPTER 12

INTRODUCING AND LEADING CHANGE

It'll be great?

Linda was thinking about yesterday's announcement on the way to work. Her quasi government organisation, in which she'd risen through the ranks to supervise a large section, had announced it was going to 'corporatise'. On the advice of management consultants who had completed a large organisational investigation project with them, they intended to become a process-driven organisation organised according to key processes, or services, that they provided to the community. Non-essential services and operations would be contracted out.

She could see both upsides and downsides to this. It would mean more responsibility for employees and a lot more interesting jobs. On the other hand, people would need to learn a lot more about the oper-ations of the department, and form new working teams to get the various services delivered efficiently. Certainly, it would challenge them all, and implementing the change would be quite complex.

The changes were to begin next month. All the supervisors were expected to announce what was happening to their teams as soon as possible. They were to reassure everyone that there would be no enforced redundancies, although there would probably be quite a few voluntary separations from the organisation.

How should she approach this? In her experience, people usually resented change and tried to prevent it. She decided to hold a group meeting and announce the plans.

························   OVERVIEW   ························

There probably isn't a supervisor alive who hasn't been involved in introducing and managing change over the past few years. This is a critical time when you can lose or gain the trust, goodwill and cooperation of the people who report to you. In this chapter, you will discover how to lead people through change.

- Are you aware that change is a continuing process, not an event, and that six phases of change continually cycle in all systems?
- Can you explain the organic view of change?
- Do you understand why people often dislike change and try to resist it? Do you know what steps to take to lessen people's resistance?
- Can you explain why communication is central to successful change and do you know *what* to communicate and *when* to communicate it?
- Can you analyse a change initiative and predict whether it will succeed or fail?
- Can you explain how supervisors should introduce change?
- Do you have the qualities and skills necessary for successfully implementing change and helping people adapt to it?

CHANGE IS ALL AROUND US

'Nothing endures but change.'

Heraclitus (600 BC)

How true! Weren't the 1950s different from the '60s, and '70s different again? And weren't the '70s different from the '80s and the '80s from the '90s? It's reasonable to assume, then, that the 2000s will be different too, and that the 2010s will be different from the 2000s.

Just as what worked in the 1950s wouldn't work in the '60s and it won't work now, much of what worked in the 20th century won't work in the 21st. The economy is different; what we know is different; organisations are different; the skills we need are different.

'The future is not what it used to be.'

By the 1990s the half-life of technology was 18 months; in other words, in 18 months, 50% of any brand new technology is obsolete—not old, but obsolete. We process more information in one day than our cave dweller ancestors did in a lifetime. Eighty per cent of the scientists who ever lived are alive today. If you're a young adult, you will probably change your career as many as five times—not just your job, but your *career*. Some are saying that the economy may no longer be global, but instantaneous.

Change is coming upon us faster than ever before in all areas of our lives. Change today, unlike the changes past generations experienced, is revolutionary in nature rather than evolutionary. 'Change', in fact, is a mild word for what we are experiencing. As author Stephen Covey says: 'It's a white water world.'

Organisations must adapt and transform, or die. They must reinvent themselves not once a generation but once every three or four years.

'The only certainty is uncertainty.'

THE **BIG** PICTURE

Jonas Salk, immunologist, physician and discoverer of the polio vaccine, describes the natural order of growth that governs living systems as an S curve. They grow, prosper, plateau and fade. Civilisations do the same. Our grandparents had one S curve per life. We're experiencing many.

Organisations may follow S curves, too. If they are to escape the demise that is the natural order of things they, too, need to make great 'leaps' (see Figure 12.1) and jump the S curve. If we don't keep up, we're falling behind. There's no such thing as staying still.

No doubt vast changes have occurred in your workplace over the last ten years, and it is safe to predict that there will be even more changes in the decade to come—whether we want them or not. Is this exhilarating or unsettling? It depends on your perspective.

DOES CHANGE AFFECT SUPERVISORS?

Change management is no longer a specialised skill but one that every supervisor needs. You will be introducing and managing two types of changes: those you instigate and lead, and those you respond to and manage. Whichever type of change you are introducing, the basic principles discussed in this chapter apply.

These changes can be minor (e.g. incremental improvements to work methods or work flow, introducing new members to the work group, reallocating duties among team members) or it can be transformational change that results in a fundamental change in the way the organisation operates internally and relates to its external environment (e.g. organisation restructuring, changes that result from takeovers and mergers, introducing new equipment or technology).

These widespread changes mean that the role of supervisors will increasingly emphasise people development and coaching, combined with improved strategic and conceptual skills (see also Chapter 1).

FIGURE 12.1   THE S CURVE OF CHANGE

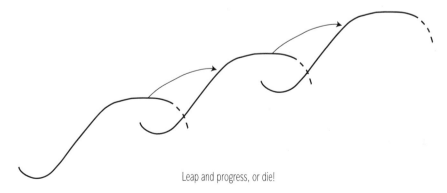

Leap and progress, or die!

THE **BIG** PICTURE
••

The second Australian Workplace Industrial Relations Survey analysed 2000 workplaces with more than 20 employees. Of these workplaces, 81% reported major changes, including changed organisation structure, new technology and changes to working practices and conditions.

'Whosoever desires constant success must change with the times.'

Niccoló Machiavelli (1469–1527)

Italian Statesman and political philosopher

THE CONTINUOUS CYCLE OF CHANGE

As Figure 12.2 shows, we can think of change as a continuing process, and not an event. Six phases of change cycle continually in all systems, although the rate at which they cycle differs from one system, or organisation, to another.

1. Pressures for change

As Box 12.1 shows, pressures for change can come externally or internally.

These pressures can build slowly or come suddenly—for example, due to a change in legislation, a sudden merger or takeover, or an unexpected change to funding arrangements. When enough people perceive the need to change, the inertia of remaining with the *status quo* will be overcome. Pressures for change often need to become quite strong before this happens, since people have many demands on their time and energy, and numerous objectives to achieve to occupy their attention. And, as we learned in the last chapter, the *status quo* has a strong pull.

••

FIGURE 12.2   THE CONTINUING PROCESS OF CHANGE

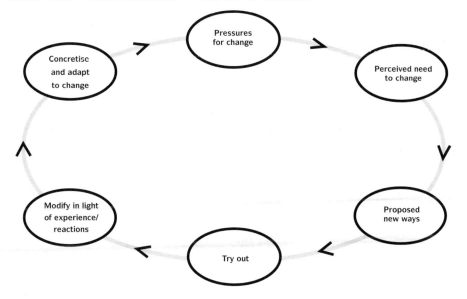

BOX 12.1

PRESSURES FOR CHANGE
••

External pressures
- legislation
- competitor activity
- funding cutbacks
- shareholder demands
- consumer demands (e.g. for more environmental responsibility)
- privatisation
- the breaking up of publicly owned monopolies
- demands for better services at lower costs

Internal pressures
- takeovers and mergers
- technological advancements
- day-to-day total quality management activities
- the need to manage problems (customer dissatisfaction, employee turnover, accident and injury rates, poor performance, etc.)
- new or revised strategic visions
- contracting out for services
- reducing employee numbers
- greater employee participation
- workplace bargaining for individual contracts
- quests for major improvements

2. Perceived need to change

The pressures build and people finally accept the need for change. They are few in number initially and need to rally others to their 'cause'. The 'forces for change' often encounter uneasiness, resistance and 'blinkered thinking' but, eventually, a critical mass of people accepts that there is a genuine need for change. A key factor in a smooth transition to the 'new order' is how quickly this phase gathers speed.

> **'If we don't change our direction, we're likely to end up where we're headed.'**

3. Proposed new ways

People discuss the situation, devise alternatives, review them and revise them until enough people are satisfied that a proposal or combination of proposals will meet their needs. The more people that are involved in this phase, the greater the 'buy in' to the change is likely to be.

4. Try out

The 'new order' is tried out and monitored, sometimes with gusto, sometimes gingerly. This is an uncomfortable time for most people as no one is quite sure what will happen, whether the changes themselves will work, and whether they will work to their advantage. This phase can be unpredictable and sometimes difficult to cope with. Resistance often resurfaces here, particularly if key people, or enough people were not convinced of the need for change in the first place (phase 2) or if not enough people have participated in designing the new ways or fully understand what they entail (phase 3).

> **'You can't just keep doing what works one time because everything around you is always changing. To succeed, you have to stay out in front of that change.'**
>
> The late Sam Walton
> Founder of Wal-Mart, USA's largest retailer

5. Modify

Adjustments and refinements are made to the new ways in the light of experience. The more people involved in modifying and improving the new ways, the faster and better progress is likely to be, both in quality and acceptance. As we saw in Chapter 11, 'two heads are better than one' and resistance is often nine parts lack of consultation.

6. Concretise

The change eventually becomes 'the norm'—that is, until pressures for change build again and the cycle repeats.

THE ORGANIC VIEW OF CHANGE

For the past 300 years a mechanistic view of most things has prevailed. But people, organisations and change aren't machines nor are they like machines. It's probably better to think of them in terms of living systems. This shows that change is a normal part of life. Rather than something mechanistic, disconnected from us and threatening, and therefore to be resisted, this can release us to see change as an ever-present process or cycle that every individual and every organisation goes through.

◢ FROM THEORY TO PRACTICE

Perhaps the main reason that change fails in many organisations is that we introduce it to the majority of employees at the 'try out' phase in the change cycle. If the majority of people in the organisation have not experienced and understood the pressures for change and the perceived need to change, and have not participated in proposing new ways of doing things, how can we expect them to implement the change enthusiastically?

This is why simply announcing a change is seldom enough: people resist change when it is forced on them without their input and with no background information about the whys and wherefores. So, when introducing change:

- Share the problems, pressures and concerns.
- Share both the good and bad news.
- Seek people's ideas and input.
- Build employee feedback into the change process.
- Go for cooperation, not compliance: 'We're all in this together' not 'Do it or else'.

Author and management consultant Dr Margaret J. Wheatley, speaking at the national conference of the New Zealand Association for Training and Development in March 1998, said:

'In recent surveys, CEOs report that up to 75% of their organisational change efforts do not yield the promised results. They ... fail to produce what had been hoped for, yet always produce a stream of unintended and unhelpful consequences. Leaders end up managing the impact of unwanted effects rather than the planned results that didn't materialise.

Instead of enjoying the fruits of a redesigned production unit, the leader
must manage the hostility and broken relationships created by the
redesign. Instead of glorying in the new efficiencies produced by
restructuring, the leader must face a burned out and
demoralised group of survivors.'

An advocate of an organic view of organisations and change, she believes that life is the best teacher on how to introduce change well. To her, the change process is best described not in tidy steps, but as a flowing, tangled web of human interactions.

For Wheatley, the change process works like this: First, the system (an organisation, a community, a person—any system) notices something and is disturbed by it. It circulates the information through its networks and, as the disturbance (pressure for change) circulates, it becomes amplified. As people deal with it, they change it—it grows and accumulates more meaning. Eventually, the pressure for change will swell to such importance that the system can't deal with it in its present state. It needs to change.

In order to change, the system must let go of its current beliefs, structures, patterns, values and behaviours. It enters an unpleasant stage of uncertainty and confusion. But letting go of the way it was allows it to reorganise itself into a new way of operating. It can recreate itself around the new understandings that grew from the initial 'disturbance'. It changes. Change is an obvious and natural thing to do.

The organic view sees change not only as natural but also as mandatory. It's impossible not to change and recreate continually because this would lead to stagnation and death. Systems must change to preserve themselves. If a system can't change, it dies.

Since change is a natural part of life, people don't just want to participate in change, they *need* to. Creating, rethinking, redesigning and reorganising keeps people from dying, psychologically as well as physically. Ignoring people's need to join in will cost us their support. Inviting participation improves the results: while people are working together to create and deal with change, they are also creating the conditions, the new relationships, ways of thinking and working, that will make the change work.

'People support what they create.'

Dr Margaret J. Wheatley

FROM THEORY TO PRACTICE

The need of every system to change and recreate could explain why people never follow directions precisely. They always change a bit here, adjust something there, modify things in some way. This isn't sabotage, stupidity, resistance or rebellion—it's a natural part of life!

People need to be creatively involved in their work. Think about this the next time someone modifies one of your instructions!

PEOPLE HATE CHANGE!

If change is so natural, why do people resist it?

'Better the certainty of misery than the misery of uncertainty.'

Change is about taking people from the known and comfortable to the unknown, frightening and threatening. No wonder it makes most people uncomfortable.

'The only person who likes change is a wet baby.'

The employee who welcomes change with open arms is a rarity, even when the change makes their job more challenging and interesting. Consciously or unconsciously, we think: 'Better the devil we know.'

Change often hits us at core levels. Changes to work groups, for example, usually mean both formal and informal changes. Unofficial group leadership might change and other internal relationships, including the unofficial 'pecking order' and established networks, may shift. Change often violates cherished group norms and routines. People may be anxious about having to work harder, learn new skills or work methods, or become used to new routines or work areas. They may fear the loss of the old job, which they liked, or fear that their new job will be less skilled, less interesting or too demanding. They may resent the implied criticism that the way they have been doing the job is not good enough. They may dislike the thought of outside interference in their jobs or fear loss of control. As a result, the working climate, motivation levels and morale may suffer.

Because of the uncertainties it creates, change causes feelings of dismay, abandonment, anxiety, anger, bewilderment, confusion and a whole host of other emotions. These can lead to such stress responses as sleep disturbances, absent-minded behaviour, withdrawal and restless overactivity. The sources of these feelings and likely responses are shown in Box 12.2. When we're introducing change, we need to be sensitive to the underlying concerns people are experiencing.

'Change is personal.'

As a result, resistance can surface in three main ways:
1. *Passivity:* people may just 'give up' and go through the motions, withholding their energy, efforts and commitment.

THE **BIG** PICTURE

Change usually creates an uncertain future, which produces anxiety. People experience anxiety differently and act in different ways to allay it. But the intent is basically the same: we do something to protect ourselves and preserve our identity.

Therefore, when introducing change, we need to help people understand exactly what will happen to them and around them; help them feel good about it and see where they fit into it; and help them maintain their sense of identity and self-esteem.

BOX 12.2   UNDERLYING CONCERNS REGARDING CHANGE

Uncertainty about the change and its results

People seek to avoid uncertainty; no one enjoys walking in the dark where unknown dangers may lurk. Lack of information or understanding can leave a vacuum that is filled by rumour, speculation, insecurity and anxiety.

Disruption of routine

Many people prefer the well known, familiar and predictable past ways of doing things and don't give them up easily, especially if they worked for them and they don't know whether the new way will work.

Loss of existing benefits

Change might come at a cost that is not balanced by greater benefits resulting from the change. People will resist change that threatens the continuity of their environment, their employment, their career prospects, wages or benefits, or that threatens increased job demands.

Threat to position, power and security

There is often an emotional loss associated with change. Any change that causes a person or group to lose power, status, or prestige will be resisted. Those who have the most to lose will be the most likely to resist.

Disturbance of existing social networks

Friendships, social cliques, informal teams, etc. are often threatened by changes. The stronger the group ties, the greater the resistance.

Challenges to group norms and culture

A group will strongly resist any changes to its norms or culture.

---

2. *Malicious compliance:* people may comply in a way they know will result in undesired outcomes.
3. *Vocally:* people may air their concerns openly, either positively and constructively or negatively and destructively. They may air them to you, their supervisor, or behind your back, to their workmates.

PEOPLE LOVE CHANGE!

... Gary Hamel, Associate Professor of Strategy and International Management at the London Business School, has a different view of change. People love to try new restaurants, new foods, new fashions … we seek the novel.

So why don't we love change at work? In organisations, he says, change has been used as a code word for nasty and unpleasant things. So people hate it.

Supervisors can help people learn to roll with change, not fight it. What sorts of people don't resist change? People who have open minds and want to learn, grow and develop. People who are comfortable with uncertainty and who trust their organisations and their supervisor to 'do the right thing'. People who are willing to step out of their comfort zones and try out new things. People who understand why change is needed and what it entails for them personally, for the organisation and for its stakeholders.

As Box 12.3 shows, supervisors can lead change by helping people to view it in a positive light.

THE PROCESS OF CHANGE

Change management is as much about hearts, minds and behaviours as it is about goals, new systems and structures, and technological practicalities. Change is about *people*. To achieve genuine change, we need to help people's beliefs and behaviours to change.

How you lead and manage change, and support those around you through the change process, will greatly affect its success. In fact, organisation or group change often depends on individual change. For change to cycle smoothly and painlessly, we must achieve attitudinal and behavioural change. The bigger the change, the more important it is to ensure everyone is 'on board'. If we fail to address the people issues, the entire change initiative is likely to fail.

We need strong and sensitive leaders to help people through change at all levels of the organisation. They need to understand the change well and help others understand it. Why is it necessary? Where precisely are we headed? How will it affect people individually? How will people be better off than they were before? Will it require much effort? How much support—for example, training and time to settle in, learn and apply new skills—will we afford people?

This means providing frequent and enthusiastic communication about:

- the purpose and reason for the change;
- an understandable and convincing picture of the desired outcome;
- how the change will take place; and
- each individual's part in the plan and how the outcomes will affect them.

This needs to be communicated in a special way. Supervisors should provide certain types of information at certain times, and these certain times may well be different for different team members.

BOX 12.3 THE UPSIDES AND DOWNSIDES OF CHANGE

The downsides	The upsides
Misery	Learning
Uncertainty	Challenge
Vulnerability	Innovation
Anxiety	Growth
Frustration	Excitement
Doubt	Creating better ways
Confusion	Possibilities
Anger	Fun
Loss	Gain

The hierarchy of adapting to change

Based on extensive research, Jean Hall of the University of Texas has developed a seven-step hierarchy that describes the process people go through in adopting any change. Because it is a hierarchy, we begin at the bottom. Before people can move up to the next level, the questions they have at each stage must be answered fully. This will allay their concerns, releasing them into the next stage. As enough people move through each level, the change is not only introduced but, as you can see from Box 12.4, the change cycle begins again.

BOX 12.4 HALL'S HIERARCHY OF ADOPTING A CHANGE
••

6	*Refocusing*	'I have an idea about something that would work even better.' People begin to see ways to refine the change further and extend its benefits. This may include minor or major changes.
5	*Collaboration*	'I want to work with others to smooth out the process.' People focus on coordinating and cooperating with others to implement the change effectively.
4	*Consequence*	'How are our customers being affected?' People begin to consider the impact of the change on their customers and others in their immediate sphere of influence. Is the change benefiting them and achieving what it is supposed to achieve?
3	*Management*	'I am working hard at doing what this change requires of me.' People focus their attention on the processes and tasks of implementing the change. Issues related to building skills and efficiency, organising, managing, scheduling and time demands are at the forefront.
2	*Personal*	'How will the change affect me?' 'Will you train me and give me enough time to learn?' 'Will you support me until I master the change?' People want to know how the change will affect them and their job, what it will require of them, whether they will be able to meet the demands of the change. They want to know how their existing benefits, formal and informal routines and networks will change (see Box 12.2).
1	*Informational*	'I would like to know more about the proposed change.' People indicate a general awareness of the change and an interest in learning more about it. They seem unworried about themselves in relation to the change and are more interested in the substantive aspects (reasons for the change, general characteristics, effects of the change, etc.).
0	*Awareness*	'I'm not aware of any change.' 'Change? What change?' People's behaviour or comments indicate little concern about, or involvement with, the change.

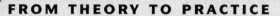

FROM THEORY TO PRACTICE

Hall's hierarchy helps us understand how people are approaching the change at any point in time and tells us what sort of information to offer them. For example, if an employee is at stage 2 and concerned about how the change will affect her personally, it's no good telling her how much the customers will love it. She wants to know how much training you'll provide, how much time she'll have to learn it, what will happen if she has trouble learning it, whether she'll need to move her work station, whether she'll be expected to take on additional duties, and so on.

From the questions they ask and from their behaviour, we can identify where people are in the hierarchy and help them move through it more quickly by providing the information they are interested in when they are interested in it. This will help people accept it more quickly so that it can be introduced more smoothly.

'The barrier to genuine change is people's hearts and minds.'

ELEMENTS OF SUCCESSFUL AND UNSUCCESSFUL CHANGE

According to the Centre for Corporate Change at the University of New South Wales, over 70% of long-term change efforts in Australia fail. The factors associated with successful and unsuccessful change are listed in Box 12.5.

Hazards to avoid

Not surprisingly, change introduced in a climate of poor morale and distrust is almost doomed to failure. Even when employee relations are good, a number of areas remain where mismanagement can obstruct the successful introduction of change. One of the main stumbling blocks is not thinking the change through well enough in advance. Poor planning and, in particular, unclear goals have caused many change initiatives to fail. If you don't know what you're trying to achieve and why, you will have no hope of clearly communicating your wants to your staff and gaining their support.

This leads to another common error: unrealistic objectives. People tend to bite off more than they can chew when introducing change and expect too much too soon. Realism is the key.

FROM THEORY TO PRACTICE

- Are you asking people to meet the same or increased goals with fewer resources (people, money, time, expertise)? If so, this is a clear danger signal that your change efforts will not work.
- Have you put your 'money where your mouth is'? In other words, are you providing enough time, facilities, training and other resources for people to implement the change properly? If so, your change efforts have a good chance of succeeding.

BOX 12.5   SUCCESSFUL AND UNSUCCESSFUL CHANGE

Characteristics of successful change

- clear and measurable objectives and outcomes
- realistic and limited in scope
- constant, honest and clear communication with change leaders
- appropriate strategies used to introduce and manage the change
- good timing—fast enough to give a sense of progress yet not exceeding people's ability to absorb and control it
- participation
- support from key power groups
- use made of existing power structure
- majority support
- competent staff support
- integration of changes with the rest of the system and formal/informal rewards structure
- adequate rewards for those adopting the change
- maintained momentum
- visible successes throughout the organisation
- continuing modification and adaptation in the light of experience

Characteristics of unsuccessful change initiatives

- fuzzy, idealistic or grandiose objectives
- unrealistic and unrestricted in scope
- inadequate information, insufficient warning or involvement
- unclear details in implementation plans so people don't know precisely how to make the desired changes happen
- inappropriate strategies, e.g. prepackaged programs, inadequate resources
- poor timing: e.g. too quick, and people can feel out of control; too slow, and cynicism and disillusionment can result
- authoritarian direction pushing people into changes they don't understand, feel ready for or are not committed to
- lack of support from critical power groups
- lack of management support, e.g. only a few senior managers understand the change and the reasons for it
- people find it hard to give up the old ways, or fall back into them, because there is no incentive for them to move forward
- ignoring or glossing over resistance
- insufficient staff support or other resources available
- change not integrated into day-to-day operations and the system as a whole
- people perceive that the changes impose additional work without removing any work

THE BIG PICTURE

Don't lose momentum! Adapting Newton's Law—'When the forces that caused something to be displaced [the old ways] are removed, it [the organisation] returns to its original position'—shows us how important it is to keep the change moving forward. We can do this in a lot of ways—for example, by celebrating successes, rewarding the people who change and making the changes part of the system and the culture. Failing to do this invites the system to return to its old order.

How long does the Newton effect last? Change needs to operate for its half-life before the tendency to revert to the norm is dissipated. In organisations, the half-life is at least 18 months (based on average turnover of the critical mass).

A third error resulting from inadequate planning is poor timing. We don't want change to proceed too slowly or people will lose heart, yet too quickly and people will feel pushed into things they aren't ready for.

Another mistake in introducing change is authoritarian direction. This leads us into the trap of not providing employees with enough information and not involving them in planning the changes. If people are ever to feel comfortable with the change and move through the three phases of adapting to it (discussed below), they will need plenty of information. Authoritarian direction also ignores resistance and tries to railroad the change through, which only increases employee resistance.

Lack of commitment of supervisors and other key members of the management team is another common problem in introducing change. Any hesitation by the leaders will only increase employees' doubts and therefore their resistance.

The change planning worksheet in Figure 12.4 will help you overcome these hazards.

Dr Ron Cacioppe, professor in the Graduate School of Business of the Curtin University of Technology in Perth, has developed a way to trace problems experienced when introducing change back to their cause. This is shown in Box 12.6. As we saw in Chapter 11, once we know the cause of a problem, it's often clear what we need to do.

 BOX 12.6

DIFFICULTIES IN INTRODUCING CHANGE AND THEIR CAUSES

Problem
- A quick start that fizzles
- Anxiety and frustration
- Haphazard efforts and false starts
- Cynicism and distrust

- People go back to 'the old ways'
- People sceptical, no forward movement

Reason
- No clear shared vision
- Insufficient resources
- No clear action plan
- Leaders not 'showing the way' or 'walking their talk'
- No reinforcement of changes
- No serious evaluation of the change program's results or attempts to improve further

---

THE **BIG** PICTURE

- Does everyone in the organisation have a common view of the future? Can they all answer the questions: 'Who are we?' and 'Where do we want to be?', 'How are we going to get there?', 'What is my role in helping us get there?'
- Is this common view clear and specific (not abstract or vague)? Does it mean something to each individual, personally?
- Is it realistic, given the organisation's marketplace, operating environment, customers, etc.?
- Is the change integrated into the business, not added on 'on top of' everything else people are supposed to be doing?
- Are individual and group concerns being identified and addressed, using Hall's hierarchy?

HOW TO INTRODUCE CHANGE

> 'There is nothing more difficult to carry out, nor more doubtful of success, nor more dangerous to handle, than to initiate a new order of things. For the reformer has enemies in all those who profit by the old order, and only lukewarm defenders in all those who would profit by the new.'
>
> Niccoló Machiavelli

Forcing change on people will lead either to short-term compliance or resistance. Either way, it has little impact on people's attitudes and, therefore, their long-term commitment. Without this, change is unlikely to 'stick'. People will end up working at cross-purposes and without energy.

Here are the eight steps to follow when you need to introduce lasting change to your work group (see Figure 12.3). These apply whether you are initiating the change, or facilitating it on behalf of your organisation.

1. Think it through first

Get clear in your own mind precisely what the change is intended to achieve and what you expect from your team. Analyse the forces for change and those resisting change (see Chapter 11). What support from others will you need? How will you reward and recognise people for adopting the change? (The change planning worksheet in Figure 12.4 will guide you in your preparations for change).

FIGURE 12.3 EIGHT STEPPING STONES TO INTRODUCING CHANGE

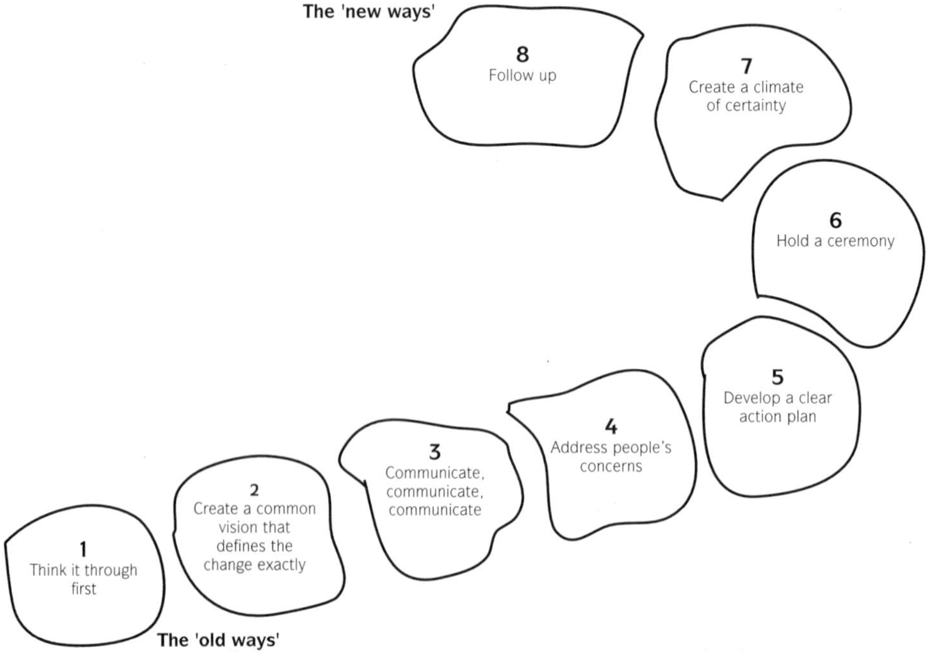

The 'new ways'

8 Follow up

7 Create a climate of certainty

6 Hold a ceremony

5 Develop a clear action plan

4 Address people's concerns

3 Communicate, communicate, communicate

2 Create a common vision that defines the change exactly

1 Think it through first

The 'old ways'

THE **BIG** PICTURE

Consider East Timor, where change of rule to Indonesia was forced upon the people when Portugal moved out. Forced change breeds two reactions: people leave or form underground resistance, which wreaks havoc. This holds true for organisations as well as for countries.

2. Create a common vision that defines the change exactly

Help people understand the need for change and provide a clear vision of what will be accomplished and precisely how people will be affected. Communicate this clearly, and often, to everyone. And believe in it yourself.

Be clear and specific: what is the goal of the change? How will the work team and individuals in it be affected? Precisely what are you expecting of people? If they need to learn new skills, for example, how and when will training be provided? What time frames, measurable outcomes and specific behaviours are you looking for? What will things be like once the change is successfully implemented?

3. Communicate, communicate, communicate

When it comes to change, it is impossible to overcommunicate.

Do you think it's enough to explain something once? It is not! When you consider all the questions people will have at each of the seven stages of adopting a change, it's easy to understand why communication is so important. People need information. They need to know how to get it and where to get it. Much of this information should be from you, their supervisor. Other sources of information are corporate breakfast sessions, divisional meetings, newsletters, other employees who have experienced this or similar change, and an internal change bulletin website. 'Need to know' is out—communicate as much and as often as possible. Then communicate more.

4. Address people's concerns

As we've seen, people will have concerns and questions. Bring them all out into the open and discuss them. The 'formula' is:

- *Surface.* Invite, don't smother, people's thoughts, concerns and questions; brushing them aside will only strengthen them. People may be reluctant at first to air them, so you may have to ask. 'Here's what we need. Do you see any problems? Do you have any concerns?'

FROM THEORY TO PRACTICE

People will look to you, their supervisor, to set the pace and show the way. Do you walk your talk or just talk it? Build trust or your team will sabotage any change efforts.

- *Honour.* Accept what people are saying; their concerns are not 'wrong', 'silly' or the result of 'being difficult'.
- *Explore.* Find out why they feel the way they do. Help them state their concerns as specifically as possible. Ask questions to clarify their thinking. This will help you provide the sort of information people need if they are to come to terms with the change and feel more comfortable with it. Answer their concerns and questions as fully and honestly as you can, giving both the 'good' and the 'bad' news.
- *Recheck.* Make sure their concerns and questions have been addressed in full and people are satisfied with your answers. If they still have doubts, go back and surface them. Ask: 'Anything else?'

Remember, resistance is a powerful part of the human make-up if people fear for their future. Although it may take good listening skills and a great deal of patience, surfacing and discussing people's concerns will help them deal with them and accept the changes more quickly.

5. Develop a clear action plan

Now it's time to involve people in developing clear plans about who will do what, when and how, in order to achieve the vision and make the change work. What specifically must be done to make the change happen?

Brainstorm all the action steps that you can think of that might be steps towards your goal. Now review them and sequence them. Some things have to be accomplished before others; sometimes two things can be done at the same time. Create a possible 'path of progress steps' visually for yourself and the team. Determine what seems to be desirable, even necessary, as a first step. Decide who needs to be involved, and how. How will you know when the steps have been achieved? How will you celebrate achievements along the road to your goal? How will you know if progress slows?

6. Hold a ceremony

Anthropologists have learned that ceremony is one of the most powerful and satisfying ways to achieve closure. Closure gives people permission and enables them psychologically to 'let go' of 'the old' so they can begin 'the new'.

So before asking people to adopt the change, give them a chance to say good-bye to the 'old ways'. Otherwise, they may yearn for 'the good old days' and never fully adopt the change. Holding some form of ceremony, however short and simple, that clearly marks the end of the current stage and welcomes in the next stage helps people to separate, let go and move on.

7. Create a climate of certainty

Since it's the uncertainty that seems to cause the most problems, it's important to build in psychological certainty wherever we can. Here are some ways to do this:

- Tell people what you *do* know as well as what you don't know, even if you don't know all the details yet.
- Explain what *won't* change.
- Set short-term goals for people and groups to work towards and to provide a sense of achievement when they are reached.

- Give plenty of individual and team feedback about how the change is progressing, how people's efforts and support are helping, etc.
- Celebrate successes whenever progress is made.
- Keep communicating. Don't let people hear things from the grapevine or any other way— you should be their primary source of information. Even when you think there's nothing to communicate, people need to hear from you. You can always give a progress report and reiterate the change goals and vision for the future. Even bad news is better than no news.
- Give people a clear path to follow.
- Do whatever you can to provide a sense of stability and routine.

8. Follow up

How is the change progressing? Get feedback from employees about what is working well and what needs improving. Who is still resisting? Why? How can you ease their reservations? Reward those who have changed so that the benefits of change are real and any remaining resisters can see some positive results. Let the group know its progress towards the goal to keep enthusiasm and interest high.

Figure 12.4 shows a change planning worksheet that will help you think through and introduce change.

When the news is mostly bad

There will be changes that can't be couched in positive terms. A factory, shop or bank branch may close, for example, or a large number of people may be made redundant. The more those affected personally identify with what is changing, the more their responses will resemble grief over the loss of a loved one.

When announcing such changes, avoid blaming any one or any thing or exhorting people to see 'the big picture'. Be as empathic and supportive as possible and offer whatever assistance you can on behalf of the organisation (counselling, outplacement consulting, further training, etc.). As discussed above, provide some form of closure that helps people say 'goodbye' so that they can move forward at their own pace.

QUALITIES AND SKILLS FOR LEADERS INTRODUCING CHANGE

'He that would be a leader must be a bridge.'

Welsh proverb

There are three key elements in using these steps to plan and introduce change successfully: sound preparation, clear communication and cooperative participation with those involved in, or affected by, the change. This requires a number of skills. Not surprisingly, the most important of these are empathy and good listening skills. Without these, you will not be able to determine resistance points or potential problems for employees and you will find it difficult to understand and deal with resistance.

You will also need conceptual skills to analyse the proposed change to see how it will affect all aspects of your department's operations and your work team. You need to be able to devise, or lead your team to devise, a sound action plan for communicating, introducing and monitoring the change, one that makes good use of the resources and supports available to you from the rest of the organisation.

• •
FIGURE 12.4   CHANGE PLANNING WORKSHEET

Think of a change you will be introducing in the near future, or are likely to be introducing, to your work team. If you are not aware of any impending changes, think about a change you have introduced to your work team or, at least, have been involved in. Then work through the questions below

Goals
1. What is the goal of this change? What will be different once it's implemented? _____

2. How can you measure whether you have achieved it? _____

3. What is your time frame for introducing the change? _____

4. What specific behaviours do you expect from your team? _____

5. How will you create a common vision and sense of purpose to ensure commitment and acceptance of the change? _____

Planning the change
1. What resources (time, training, space, equipment) will be needed and how will you procure them so that the change will succeed? _____

2. Do the people have the skills and willingness to change? _____

3. Will the leaders of the organisation model the behaviours required by the change and support it enthusiastically? _____

4. How can you involve the team in planning and evaluating the change? _____

5. Is your action plan realistic? Think about scope, pace, supports required. _____

6. How can you ensure several 'small wins' early on, to get the momentum going and allow people to feel a sense of achievement? _____

7. What formal and informal mechanisms will you use to reinforce change? To reward and recognise people who support the change? _____

8. What mechanisms can you put in place to ensure you consult people and communicate frequently? _____

Introducing the change
1. What will be the impact of the change on your team? What will they want to know? Who will react, how and why? (Think through Hall's hierarchy of adopting change and have the necessary information ready at the right time.) _____

2. How will the work group's culture be affected? Formal and informal networks? How can you minimise the effects, make them less 'painful' and more appealing to people? _____

3. Who else will be affected by the change (customers, other departments, suppliers, contractors)? How will they be affected? _____

4. What information will you need to provide? What questions are they likely to ask? _____

Continued . . .

5. What will be the impact of the change on other parts of the system? On your work team's productivity? On quality? On morale? On particular individuals? _____

6. Who are the key parties, both formal and informal? Do you have their support? How can you gain it or strengthen it? _____

7. Analyse the driving forces (for change): task, team, individual, systems, environment. How will you build on them? _____

8. Analyse the resisting forces (against change): task, team, individual, systems, environment. How will you minimise them? _____

9. Do you need any further information? _____

10. How can you build in 'islands of certainty' amidst the change? _____

11. How will you promote the change to win everyone's understanding and commitment? _____

12. How will you provide closure from the 'old ways' so that people can let go and accept the change? _____

Trial test
Is the change big enough or complex enough to need a trial run? Who should be involved? When should it be carried out? How will it be conveyed to the rest of the organisation? What if it fails? How will it be evaluated? By whom?

Keeping up the momentum
1. What communication channels will you use to let people know how the change is progressing? _____

2. How will you maintain momentum for the change?
   - using reward systems, unofficial rewards
   - articulating clear vision/objectives
   - encouraging participation
   - publishing successes throughout organisation
   - using existing power structure
   - integrating with rest of system
   - supporting the supporters
   - providing necessary training
   - communicating and listening
   - tapping into the organisation's value systems
   - using good timing
   - other.

3. How will you gather feedback about how the change is working? How will you gather ideas for making it work better? _____

4. What steps will you take to embed the changes into the way the organisation habitually operates?

You will need marketing skills to promote the change in a way most likely to gain acceptance and cooperation. And you will need conflict-management skills to deal with the conflict that often arises when change is introduced.

Box 12.7 lists some of the behaviours business researcher Tom Waterman found to be important for change leaders.

BOX **12.7** **LEADERS WHO SUCCESSFULLY INTRODUCE CHANGE (WATERMAN)**

- Communicate clear visions and goals.
- Treat everyone as a source of creative input and find ways for everyone to contribute.
- Relinquish some control to team members in order to get results.
- Use facts and information as aids in decision making.
- Keep an open mind and stay alert to new ideas and information.

- Constantly use words such as 'teamwork' and 'trust'.
- Form a solid base of underlying stability and then keep things moving, constantly fighting apathy and proactively building for the future.
- Walk their talk and practise what they preach.
- Inspire commitment and loyalty through their words and actions.

Successful leaders are passionate and persistent about what they are doing. They don't push for change because it's 'best practice' or because everyone else is doing it but because they believe in it at a deep, personal level. They are committed to their vision.

In introducing change, it's the 'soft skills' that are most needed (and, often, most lacking).

- Painting the picture
- Planning
- Consulting
- Building trust
- Finding and sharing relevant information
- Showing confidence in people

Lacking any of these skills is a major barrier to successful change implementation.

Rosabeth Moss Kanter, Professor of Business Administration at Harvard University's Business School, identifies seven essential skills for leading change. These are shown in Box 12.8.

This is a lot to do. Leadership isn't easy.

THE **BIG** PICTURE

According to Kanter's research, there are five reasons for stalling in the middle of a change effort:

1. *Time and resource shortages*, which are often due to poor forecasting; it can be difficult to go back and ask for more.
2. *Unexpected obstacles*; you've never been down that track before so naturally you don't foresee all the obstacles.
3. *Going on to the next project too soon.*
4. *The team gets tired and loses momentum*; change, after all, is hard work. Beginnings are a lot of fun, then reality sets in and spirits lag. Energetic leadership is needed.
5. *Resistance can mushroom* if a leadership vacuum combines with a loss of momentum. Resisters are also likely to attack when the change is nearly a reality, rather than at the beginning when it may never eventuate.

BOX 12.8

SEVEN ESSENTIAL SKILLS FOR LEADING CHANGE (KANTER)

1. The ability to see the big picture and feel the urgency of the need for change, to do things better and be the best, to find problems and fix them. She calls this a '*restless dissatisfaction with the way things are*'.

2. '*Kaleidoscope thinking*' or the ability to see new patterns, embrace new ideas, search for information and knowledge, change perspective and challenge paradigms: take a fresh look.

3. *Build and articulate a clear and compelling vision.* Make one clear, compelling picture. Set the direction. Get people committed.

4. *Build a coalition of influential supporters and backers.* You can't do it by yourself. There are two kinds of allies to help you achieve your vision: (1) power holders, with the resources, expertise, information, legitimacy and political support; and (2) the stakeholders, people who have a stake in the vision and are willing to contribute to its success. Involving others, Kanter says, is the step most often neglected. Sprinkle seeds, walk around, talk about the change, make sure people are familiar with it to build their comfort levels and gain their approval.

5. *Create a team of people dedicated to the vision who feel they own it.* Give them identity as a team and the resources to achieve the vision. Make sure the environment around the team supports it. Give them the resources, space and communication linkages they need with the rest of the organisation.

6. *Persist and persevere.* This is one of the key differences between success and failure in leading change. Learn from your mistakes and keep at it till you make it work. 'Everything looks like a failure in the middle,' says Kanter.

7. *Share the credit and recognition* if you ever want to lead a change again. Recognise and reward people's efforts.

ADAPTING TO CHANGE

When we are confronted with a change, we go through three phases as we adapt to it. How difficult and distressing this adaptation process is, and how long it takes, depends on an individual's make-up (their mind-set regarding change, their ability to respond to it and their personality structure—some people adapt more readily to change than others), how major the change is and how well the supervisor helps them through it.

First, we must accept the need to *make a break* with the old way of doing things, the way things used to be, and then actually make it. This letting go can be very painful, especially if we have a big investment in what we are losing, or strongly identify with it. For example, if our job is made redundant and we gained a sense of self from that job, letting it go is very difficult. When important ties are broken, the world can be a confusing and uncomfortable place. People experience a sense of bewilderment, even horror, during this phase.

This is why a 'ceremony' to say goodbye is so important. Six other ways to help employees through this phase are:

1. Explain the scope of the change so that people are clear about its extent.
2. Make it clear what is not being changed.
3. Make sure people understand precisely how the change will affect them and how you will help them prepare for it.
4. Balance, if you can, what people are losing with what they stand to gain from the change.
5. Keep communicating!
6. Recognise and acknowledge the sadness people hint at or express.

The second phase is the in-between phase of *transition*, a neutral zone where people experience a sense of unreality, emptiness and confusion. People in this phase often 'go through the motions' as if in a state of shock and swing between hope and despair.

Supervisors can help people move through this transition phase quickly by identifying where people are on Hall's hierarchy of adopting change (see Box 12.4) and providing appropriate information. Eventually, a sense of hope will begin to emerge.

This leads to the third and final stage, discovering a *new beginning*. People adopt new goals and start thinking about and planning for the change and the future. All the energy previously spent on resisting the change is now available for dealing with it constructively.

Be aware of these phases when you are introducing change and help employees through them. Without pushing too fast, acknowledge which stage they are in and help them into the next. People will only be willing to change when they're ready to believe it won't make life worse for them, or even that it will make things better. The more quickly people reach the third stage, the more quickly and effectively the change will be implemented.

RESISTANCE TO CHANGE

We may be surrounded by change and most of us manage change in our personal lives all the time, yet we don't seem to have learned how to manage it well in organisational settings. We make it easy for people to balk at change. Some common resistance points are listed below. The more resistance points in any change initiative, the longer the 'battle' for change is likely to continue.

- People become 'stuck' in a phase of adapting to change or on Hall's hierarchy and aren't able to move on
- Hesitation by team leaders or senior management
- Incongruent communication from team leaders or senior management

THE **BIG** PICTURE

Some people will be unable to accept the change and will choose to leave the organisation. While this is inevitable, don't treat it too lightly. When a person leaves, we lose their experience and knowledge and our investment in their training and development.

- Inadequate resources (e.g. time, money, people, equipment, information)
- Inertia, or lack of energy to 'get the ball rolling'
- Changes are piecemeal (not built into the systems, e.g. performance appraisals, operating procedures)
- Lack of rewards for those who adopt the change quickly and well
- Lack of monitoring and evaluation
- Poorly managed conflict at an individual or group level, resulting in the erosion of group or individual relationships and loss of good will.

Resistance usually surfaces during the first two phases of adapting to change when people are struggling to come to grips with it and to avoid real or perceived personal losses. Sometimes, just when everything seemed to be going well, it resurfaces. This often occurs about halfway through the third phase. The two main areas to look out for are:

1. *A crisis in energy.* This may result from apathy, which can develop as a response to stress and cause the change to lose its momentum; or accumulated negative energy might stop the change progressing.
2. *Vested interests.* People who have a lot to lose may step up their efforts to block change or they may combine their efforts and put in a last-ditch attempt to prevent the change going through.

> '**Whether or not we support a solution depends on whether it is done to us or by us.**'

Predicting resistance to change

Figure 12.5 shows a simple model for predicting how successful our change efforts will be. It considers how significant, or fundamental, the change is and how much it impacts on the culture of a group or organisation. The more significant or fundamental the change and the more it affects the way people work together, the more resistance we can expect. Conversely, small changes with little cultural impact are quite easily implemented.

Tips for dealing with resistance to change

Following the five steps to introduce change discussed above will help you minimise any resistance your change efforts meet and make the changes easier for employees to accept. However, some people seem determined to hold on to their resistance, for a variety of reasons. Box 12.9 gives some tips for overcoming the resistance of those who insist on resisting.

FROM THEORY TO PRACTICE

Balance a directive with a cooperative approach:

- Stay enthusiastic; provide clear direction to overcome any inertia or apathy and keep the momentum in the desired direction. Demonstrate the changes you want by walking your talk.
- Involve people through training, discussion, question and answer sessions, etc. to help them develop new attitudes and knowledge

FIGURE 12.5 PREDICTING RESISTANCE TO CHANGE

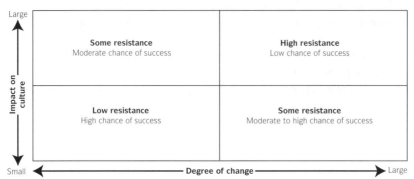

DEALING WITH DETERMINED RESISTERS

- *The road-blocker.* This is a nice, clean type of resistance where the employee just says 'no' in one form or another, usually without giving reasons. Help such employees to be more specific about their objection. Ask: 'What specifically worries you?' or 'What in particular do you object to?'. This will tell you what you are dealing with and give you a point at which to begin discussion. Fully examine the resistance by listening actively and asking questions to clarify. Be sure you have heard and explored fully what the employee has to say before moving on to action planning. When you move to action planning, ensure the employee has clear goals and time lines to achieve.

- *The passive resister.* These people say, in effect: 'Tell me exactly what you want me to do.' This is a hidden form of resistance. If you fall for it, the resister can comply with the bare minimum, but not the spirit, of what you want. Ask: 'Are you quite clear about what is being asked and expected of you?' This should force the resister to accept more responsibility for good performance.

- *The delayer.* 'I'll get on to it first thing Monday morning,' says the delayer. And then, of course, something more important crops up. If you think this is a resistance tactic rather than an honest response, try asking: 'Is there anything preventing you from beginning now?'

- *The reverser.* This form of resistance can be tricky. But if you find yourself being surprised by someone's enthusiastic response ('Wow! What a great idea!'), look for a quick delay as a follow-up. If this happens, you can be fairly sure the employee is telling you what you want to hear but intends to do nothing about it. Say something like, 'I'm really glad you think it's a good idea. What in particular do you like about it?'

Continued . . .

- *The dodger.* 'Let Jane do it' switches the responsibility on to someone else or even another department. If your request is reasonable, don't fall for this tactic. Let dodgers know that it is from them that you are expecting action.
- *The threatener.* These resisters imply that 'the boss' (or someone else) won't approve. This may or may not be true, but don't discuss it now. Say something like: 'I appreciate your concern and I'll check it out. Meanwhile, what I'd like to do is …' or 'I'll bear that in mind. What objections do *you* have?'
- *The sympathy seeker.* These people try to make you feel guilty for asking them to alter their ways and try something new. Empathise with their problem, use active listening techniques and, unless their reasons are very sound, repeat your request assertively.
- *The traditionalist.* This resister says: 'But we've always done it the other way.' Sometimes the old way *is* the best way, but most often the appeal to tradition is straightforward resistance of the 'better the devil we know' variety. Try saying, 'I understand the old way worked very well; however, this situation is unique.' Or 'Yes, the old approach worked well—how can we adapt it to this new way?'

Notice that, with all these responses, you are assertively following the eight steps to introducing change discussed earlier. You clearly communicate the required change, listen to, respect and examine the resistance, and then plan with the employee what action they will take to cooperate. The major difference here is that you are actively inviting the resister to be more open and specific about their resistance and you are assertively repeating your request that a change is made.

Lessen people's urge to resist this strongly by following the tips in Box 12.10.

BOX 12.10 HOW TO LESSEN RESISTANCE TO CHANGE

- Make sure the business vision and strategy are clear, and that the change is clearly linked to it and to the organisation's values.
- Specify the change clearly both in terms of the 'whats' (goals, performance indicators, standards) and the 'hows' (vision, behaviours, culture).
- Explain what success will 'look like' and make sure it is clear how people will benefit.
- Involve people in designing and implementing the change. Make sure everyone is 'engaged' and has a common understanding of the change initiative: where we are, where we want to be, why, and how we'll get there.
- Commit the necessary resources—budget, time, communication, training, etc.
- Build a 'critical mass' of supporters of the change so it can 'take hold'.
- Ensure visible signs of early progress to encourage people.
- Provide communication, training and other opportunities for learning and developing. Direct them all towards the change goals and the business vision and strategy.

Continued . . .

> - Manage the transition from the old to the new carefully. Look after people and help them through the 'discomfort zone' of the gap between 'where we are now' and 'where we want to be'.
> - Monitor progress so you know what is working, what is not working and where the blockages are.
> - Publicise the successes.
> - Support and reward the supporters.
> - Ensure key people are fully supportive of the change.
> - Keep communicating and listening.

RAPID REVIEW

	True	False
1. Change seems to be affecting organisations and employees at ever-increasing rates.	☐	☐
2. Whether they're instigating the change or responding to it and managing it on behalf of their organisation, today's supervisors need strong change management skills.	☐	☐
3. Change can be thought of as a continuous cycle that all systems go through.	☐	☐
4. Most people welcome change with open arms.	☐	☐
5. Once a change is in place and working, supervisors can sit back and manage day-to-day operations.	☐	☐
6. The organic view of change teaches us that people and organisations need to change and need to be involved in change.	☐	☐
7. Change affects people at deep levels, and often results in negative responses to it.	☐	☐
8. If we don't change people's beliefs and behaviours, our change efforts are unlikely to succeed.	☐	☐
9. Hall's hierarchy of adopting a change tells us what questions people want answers to and when they want those answers.	☐	☐
10. Communication is the most important part of any successful change effort.	☐	☐
11. 'Think big' should be our motto when introducing change.	☐	☐
12. A fuzzy action plan for change will result in haphazard efforts and false starts.	☐	☐
13. When it comes to change, you can't overcommunicate.	☐	☐
14. If people resist a change, we should keep up the pressure until they do what we want.	☐	☐
15. Ceremonies, however simple, help people say 'goodbye' to the old ways and make room for the new ways.	☐	☐
16. Since change is coming so frequently, we should just embrace it and jump into it with both feet; planning only slows things down.	☐	☐
17. The three phases in adapting to change involve making a break with the 'old ways', transition and discovering a new beginning.	☐	☐
18. The more change affects the way a work group or team operates, the more resistance we are likely to encounter.	☐	☐

1. 'The 21st century supervisor must be highly skilled in the art of introducing and managing change.' Discuss why this is so and the particular skills and behaviours supervisors need to introduce and manage change.
2. Provide an example to illustrate the continuous cycle of change from your own experience.
3. If change is so necessary and so inevitable, why do people resist it? Discuss the main sources of resistance to change and explain how supervisors can recognise them.
4. Think of a change you have recently experienced. Use Hall's hierarchy of adopting a change to explain how you approached the change.
5. Write a short essay on why it is important for supervisors to create 'islands of certainty' during times of change and suggesting some ways they can do this.
6. Imagine you are Linda, in this chapter's opening vignette on page 372, about to introduce new working methods to your work group. As best as you can, work through the change planning worksheet in Figure 12.4.
7. Discuss the process of adapting to change and illustrate this process with a personal example.
8. Explain how supervisors should introduce change to their department or work group.
9. Use the model in Figure 12.5 to predict how employees at your college would react to a major change.

Individual activities

1. Interview someone who has experienced a major change in his or her workplace. This might be the result of restructuring, a merger or acquisition, a change in funding, new management, job redesign or a move to a new location. Find out all you can about the impact of this change on them, their work group and the organisation's culture. How was the change introduced and managed? What were the obstacles to this change? What resistance to it occurred? Prepare a report analysing how the change was introduced and managed, and the things the supervisor(s) did that helped and hindered the change process.
2. In the vignette on page 372, Linda is about to announce changes to her work group in the way they operate. What concerns would you expect the employees to have? Using the model shown in Figure 12.5, what resistance do you think Linda's organisation will face from its employees?
3. Read the section in Chapter 21 on Maslow's theory of motivation. Relate the three phases of adapting to change discussed in this chapter to Maslow's hierarchy.
4. For Box 12.6 develop a third column called 'Actions' and complete it with what you think are the most appropriate remedial actions to put a floundering change effort back on track.
5. Relate the three phases of adapting to change to Jean Hall's hierarchy of adopting a change. Which stage of the hierarchy relates to which phase of adapting to a change?

6. Interview someone who has experienced a major change at work. Find out how it was introduced and how it progressed. Write an essay analysing this change in terms of how well the characteristics of successful change were met and how the eight steps to introducing change were followed. From your analysis, draw conclusions about how well the change was managed.

Group activities

1. Identify the changes in your life in the past three years. Then identify your reactions to these changes at the time. In retrospect, do you see these changes differently now? Summarise your experiences as shown in the table below and compare them with others in your class.

Change	My reactions at the time	How I see these changes now

2. In small groups, brainstorm the actions a supervisor can take to implement and effectively support people through change. Compare your list with the lists of other groups. Agree on ten or 12 key things supervisors should do when introducing change.

3. In small groups, look at the list of resistance points to change in this chapter. For each, brainstorm as many antidotes as you can think of that a supervisor could use. Compare your list with the other group lists in the class and refine them to your 12 best ideas.

4. In small groups, discuss the following: Why do people embrace change in their personal lives but resist it in their working lives? Ask the person with the longest hair in your group to summarise your thoughts to the rest of the class.

7. Interview someone who has experienced change at work. How did it affect them personally? Analyse their responses to the change using the three-step process of adapting to change.

8. Analyse Case Study 23.2 (Chapter 23), based on the information provided in this chapter. What might be causing the downturn in performance in the office? How should Mary handle it?

5. Imagine an organisation you work for is merging with another organisation. Design an inexpensive ceremony for the employees of each organisation to say 'goodbye' to their old organisation and 'hello' to their new one. Be imaginative!

6. Divide into groups of three with an observer, resisting employee and supervisor. Using the vignette at the beginning of this chapter as the setting, and switching roles every six minutes, the 'resister' should role-play from the types of resisters shown in Box 12.9 while the supervisor explores the resistance as outlined in the chapter. When you have each had a chance to play the supervisor twice, develop a list of 'Do's' and 'Don'ts' for surfacing and dealing with employees who are determined to resist change.

7. In small groups, discuss the following questions and develop a plan of action for Linda in the vignette at the beginning of this chapter: What advice would you offer her about announcing the planned organisational changes to her team and helping them adapt to them? What will she need to be careful to do and not to do? What resistance might she,expect and how should she deal with it?

A Major Change

Chan had been thinking long and hard. As part of the workplace agreement, the organisation would be embarking on a course of job redesign for all non-salaried employees. A major emphasis of this job redesign was to be multiskilling. The goal was to enhance efficiency and job satisfaction. Management also felt that employees held different expectations of their jobs from those of 20 years ago.

In keeping with employee wishes and with the national trend towards industrial democracy, this job redesign was to be undertaken 'participatively'. Team leaders would be responsible for leading the job redesign in their own department. They were to ensure that all employees had a fair input into the process; that EEO, health, safety and welfare issues took a top priority; and that a net 3% gain in output would result. Measures of each department's success would include absenteeism rates, labour turnover rates, grievance rates, output, production costs and other benchmark measures of efficiency and quality.

Chan rolled this around in his mind. Certainly, there were some obvious benefits to the employees: they would have a greater variety of tasks to do and therefore would get the chance to learn more skills and derive more job satisfaction; they would have a greater say in how their department operated (he tried to give them that anyway); they would have better career opportunities and, hopefully, safer jobs. Depending on how the redesign took shape, they would probably even have the opportunity to undertake complete projects and have more responsibility and decision making in their jobs.

And he could see plenty of benefits to the organisation, apart from those stated in the enterprise agreement. More flexible staff, improved occupational health and safety, improved and easier recruitment and retention due to increased levels of job satisfaction, more effective use of technology, improved staff morale … it sounded too good to be true!

What's the downside of all this, then, he wondered.

Questions

1 Analyse and describe how this change might affect individuals in Chan's work team and what their concerns are likely to be. How might it affect the work team as a whole? What should Chan do to deal with their concerns?

2 What do you predict will be the major resistance points or obstacles to this change? How could Chan handle them?

3 If you were to coach Chan on how to plan, introduce and manage this important organisational change in his department, what steps would you recommend he follow and why?

What A Mess!

Linda couldn't understand it. Why were people being so difficult? Couldn't they see the proposed changes to work flow in the department were to everyone's advantage? By placing responsibility for entire processes with small teams, people would be given a chance to extend their skills and feel greater satisfaction for a job well done. Instead, they were stubbornly digging in their heels and refusing to cooperate.

She'd held a group meeting and explained how people would be moved into small teams and how the new work flows would operate. She'd explained how both their internal and external customers would benefit and how the organisation as a whole would benefit. But instead of responding positively and indicating they would rise to the challenge and make the most of the new opportunities, everyone sat there sullenly, giving each other side-long glances and shuffling their feet.

Bruce seemed determined not to cooperate. In fact, he'd simply refused to accommodate the revised team-based processes. He insisted he would continue to perform his tasks as he always had and was completely uninterested in learning any other aspects of the job. 'I'll do what I've been hired to do and what's in my job description,' he stated flatly.

What now? Did he intend to lead the rest of them in refusing to cooperate with the required changes? What should she do to prevent this?

Questions

1   Use Hall's hierarchy to explain why Linda's team is resisting. Based on your analysis, develop a plan for Linda to follow to introduce this change.
2   Should Linda invite her team to participate in designing the specific changes? Why or why not?
3   How should Linda deal with Bruce if he continues to resist?

Answers to Rapid Review questions

1. T   2. T   3. T   4. F   5. F   6. T   7. T   8. T   9. T   10. T   11. F   12. T
13. T   14. F   15. T   16. F   17. T   18. T

CHAPTER 13

CONTRIBUTING TO A WORKPLACE LEARNING ENVIRONMENT

Cutting-edge learning

Gina was excited. An extensive series of in-house, just-in-time learning packages for front-line staff would be offered to employees this week. 'State-of-the-art' training, covering technical as well as interpersonal and customer service skills, would now be available on the intranet and on interactive CD-ROM to all employees, anywhere, any time.

As the leader of a team of front-line customer support staff, she was sure she would find it an enormous help. It would mean she and her team could train any time and anywhere they wanted. During slow periods, this would be especially useful. If it suited them, they could even take the CD-ROM packages home to use on their home computers. The part-timers in particular, she felt, would appreciate this.

Whenever a new product was introduced, which on average was monthly, everyone could 'plug into' the training system and learn the product details at their own pace, where and when it suited them. They could also brush up on their 'soft skills' whenever they had time. Gina had already worked out personal development agreements with most of her team so they could target which packages to work on first.

This training was more than just self-paced learning on a computer screen. It was 'high-tech' interactive software that provided information in a variety of forms and delivered practice situations randomly. Each time a learner used a program, it would be different to the last time, so learners could use each one many times without becoming bored. Along with core scenarios and examples, the programs also randomly delivered a range of additional examples and scenarios each time a learner logged on. Best of all, the software monitored learners' strengths and areas needing further improvement. Depending on these strengths and weaknesses, the software actually selected which information, examples and scenarios to provide more practice on. Learning automatically tailored to each person's needs—a dream come true!

This made 'learning by doing' safe! If people made a mistake, there were no red faces or adverse customer consequences—learners just tried again and kept trying until they were confident and competent.

When a learner completed a module, both Gina and the learner would receive a printout summarising the learner's scores and showing suggestions for further development.

Gina could also print out a summary for her entire team, to get an idea of what further training she would need to provide for them as a group. She could quickly spot who might be having problems in which areas, who was up to date with their learning, and who might need a gentle reminder. She could make sure contractors and part-timers were as well trained as full-time staff, too. No more treating them like 'orphans'!

The opportunities for developing staff seemed limitless. Because she could see who was strongest in which areas, she could pair up people to coach each other. She could use the software as an aid for selection and placement. People could learn individually or in small discussion groups; this would be particularly beneficial, she felt, with the inter-personal skills programs. Best of all, it would put people in charge of their own learning. Isn't technology a glorious thing!

OVERVIEW

An organisation's effectiveness will increasingly depend on its know-how: its ability to identify, gather, manage, store, share, build, retrieve and use knowledge and inform-ation. Does your organisation learn faster than its competitors? Does it spread its know-how around? Does it put it to good use? You'll find out how to do this in this chapter.

- Do you know what characterises a learning organisation and how to contribute to building a learning environment?
- Are you aware of the three types of intellectual capital and how to cultivate and make best use of them?
- Can you describe the ways the Knowledge Revolution is affecting organisations?
- Are you a learning individual contributing to a learning organisation?
- Are you aware of how new working patterns are influencing an organisation's learning climate?
- Can you participate in creating a learning culture?
- Do you know how to learn as you work?
- Do you understand the relationship between empowerment and learning organisations?

THE NEED FOR A LEARNING ENVIRONMENT

Consider this:

- In 1996 there were about 40 million Internet users worldwide; by the end of 2000, it is conservatively estimated that number will be around 500 million.
- More information has been produced in the last 30 years than in the previous 5000.
- The total of all printed knowledge doubles every four or five years.
- One weekday edition of the *New York Times* contains more information than the average person was likely to come across in a lifetime in 17th-century England.
- More than 4000 books are published around the world every day.

As we saw in Chapters 1, 4 and 12, the rate of change is such that yesterday's business model is no longer suitable. The Industrial Revolution of the 1800s has given way to the Information Revolution of the 2000s. It's changing how we work, how we organise enterprises, how we make money, and how we value companies.

It isn't about doing the same things we have always done better, cheaper or faster, but about doing *new* things. How we manage an enterprise, how we motivate and reward people, how we design our systems and processes and relate to our customers and suppliers—all this is changing.

'Any business that thinks it is somehow insulated from the information revolution isn't likely to succeed in tomorrow's economy.'

So said Jay Walker, head of Walker Digital, a laboratory that invents new business methods, and the founder of Priceline, the revolutionary US Internet shopping service.

He goes on to point out that few companies survived the Industrial Revolution or even electrification. Most didn't grasp the need to change the way they made and sold things and therefore failed to make the transition. Will we learn from history or will we see similar patterns with the information revolution?

The new economy is completely different from the old economy. What used to work won't work any more. What do we do when old paradigms are obsolete and the 'old ways' no longer work? Author Margaret J. Wheatley, speaking at the national conference of the New Zealand Association for Training and Development in March 1998, said:

'To create better health in a living system, connect it to more of itself. When a system is failing or performing poorly, the solution will be discovered within the system if more and better connections are created. A failing system needs to start talking to itself, especially to those it didn't know were even part of itself.'

In other words, organisations need to learn. Knowledge rules in the new economy. This has been made possible by advances in desktop computing and the explosion of information and communications technology.

Information and intellectual assets are fast replacing physical capital and assets (real estate, buildings, plant and machinery, stock, money in the bank, etc.). This is why the stock market often values a company at three, four or even ten times its book value (physical and financial assets). Author Charles Handy estimates that intellectual assets are usually worth three to four times the tangible book value of a company; others value

---

THE **BIG** PICTURE

How essential knowledge is to an organisation's success and even survival has hit home belatedly. In the aftermath of the downsizing of the 1980s and early 1990s, many organisations have realised the importance of knowledge and the people who possess it. Salt is rubbed into the wounds as they see companies with significant knowledge assets burgeon.

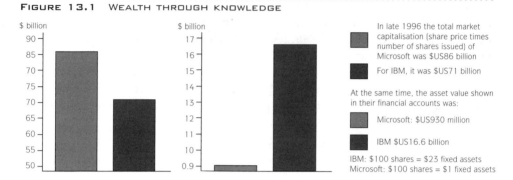

FIGURE 13.1   WEALTH THROUGH KNOWLEDGE

intellectual capital at six to 20 times the value of tangible assets (see Figure 13.1). Some say intellectual capital is the most genuine measure of an organisation's worth and its ultimate asset.

There is no doubt that an organisation's competitive advantage will increasingly depend on intellectual capital. Arie de Geus of Royal Dutch/Shell said:

> **'The ability to learn faster than your competitors may be the only sustainable competitive advantage.'**

FROM THEORY TO PRACTICE

What is intellectual capital? Is it having really smart people working for you? Is it having people with a lot of qualifications working for you? No. It's having people with skills, knowledge and experience in your business working for you. It's having people with good networks, drive and the desire to do a good job working for you. It's having people who are willing to learn, try new things and constantly look for ways to improve working for you. It's building an organisation of committed and dedicated people and supporting them with the culture, tools, equipment, training, facilities and other resources they need to do their jobs well.

THE **BIG** PICTURE

What makes or breaks an enterprise today is not its visible assets but its dynamism, innovation and brains—intellectual capital. Anticipated revenues from inventions, new products, new software, customer relationships and loyalty, brand equity, databases, etc. make an enterprise valuable to its owners, not its buildings. We must find intellectual capital, identify it, recruit it, keep it, build it and 'leverage' it. We must learn to manage it, store it, share it and sell it. We must learn to measure and value it as we value tangible assets.

THE NEW-OLD LEARNING ORGANISATION

:... In a knowledge economy, organisations need to make good use of the knowledge of not just their employees, but also their customers and suppliers. They need to know how to gather, store, transmit, process and retrieve information.

Today, we see enterprises consciously trying to become what is known as a **learning organisation**. This is a term coined by author Arie de Geus to describe organisations that value knowledge and have learned how to acquire and share it for the benefit of their stakeholders. But how new is it really?

Australian Aboriginal societies have successfully done this for millennia, according to Tex Skuthorpe, Aboriginal educator and artist. Addressing the opening session of the 1998 Australian Institute of Human Resources convention in Canberra, he said:

'Aboriginal society is based on knowledge: this is the way we have survived for thousands of years. Processes for spreading and using knowledge are deeply embedded in our way of life and our culture is rich in the processes which achieve this.

'In traditional Aboriginal society, knowledge is not owned or used as a power base. Knowledge carries with it a responsibility to share it and to use it wisely and equally for the benefit of all.'

Three types of intellectual capital

In Chapter 4 we learned that there are three types of intellectual capital (see Box 4.8 in Chapter 4):

1. *structural capital*, or the organisation's knowledge database;
2. *relationship capital*, or the value of its relationships with its customers and suppliers; and
3. *human capital*, or the skills, knowledge and productivity of employees, collectively and individually.

Learning organisations develop these types of knowledge by encouraging and enabling continuous learning—from their own experience, from customers, suppliers, contractors and partners. They cultivate and nurture these knowledge bases, extract meaningful information from them and make them accessible to employees. They spread this learning throughout the organisation so that each business unit doesn't need to reinvent the wheel. Learning is not in isolation. It's shared.

FROM THEORY TO PRACTICE

What opportunities do you have for contributing to your company's general bank of knowledge? What could you do to encourage information sharing in your work team? A learning organisation is not so much a structure as a cultural framework that people work within.

'In order to generate extraordinary value for shareholders, a company has to learn better than its competitors and apply that knowledge throughout its businesses faster and more widely than they do.'

John Brown, CEO of BP, the most profitable of the major oil companies

The goal of learning organisations is to establish full and open access to information throughout the organisation so that individuals and teams can use their initiative within established guidelines and towards agreed visions and goals. This allows an enterprise to adapt to a rapidly changing environment and pass not just information, but more importantly, knowledge and understanding, around an organisation.

Information technology makes this possible but learning organisations are more than sophisticated IT users. IT is about data and information. Learning organisations are about understanding, application, transformation, innovation, creation, cooperation, teamwork and diffusion.

FROM THEORY TO PRACTICE

How can we create an organisation comfortable with change and which embraces continuous learning?

- *Make learning part of the culture so it is expected that people will look for ways to learn and share their knowledge.* For example, supervisors can attend training programs and use what they've learned, read relevant books and share what they've learned with their work teams, train employees and ask them to share what they've learned with the team, hold team meetings and apply Dr Peter Honey's learning cycle to make sure people focus on what they are learning, share it and apply it.
- *Provide technical support so that people can capture and retrieve knowledge easily.* Many organisations (e.g. National Australia Bank, BHP and Cable and Wireless Optus here in Australia) are developing sophisticated information retrieval and sharing software so that people can benefit from the experience of others, share their experiences and insights, and contact others with similar interests to further develop their understanding of a topic.
- *Make the organisation structure as 'minimalist' as possible; let it evolve and keep it moving.* Flat hierarchies distribute responsibilities and therefore experience, encourage people to work together, communicate and share information, and are less formal. This encourages risk taking and trying out 'better ways'.
- *Reward those who learn and share what they've learned.* What gets measured and rewarded gets repeated, so find ways to measure what people are learning and doing as a result of their learning. Find ways to encourage people to share what they've learned and monitor what is shared and by whom. Reward people who come up with new ideas, new ways of thinking or looking at a problem, better ways of doing things, both formally (e.g. through the performance appraisal system) and informally (e.g. with interesting assignments and other 'perks').

Characteristics of learning organisations

An organisation is a learning organisation if its members and stakeholders are continually learning: from their experience, informally from each other and through reading, and formally through formalised educational courses and training workshops. Size is irrelevant. If people seek ways to put what they have learned to good use in their organisations: to improve its products or services and how they are produced, and to improve the way people work together, they are learning individuals contributing to a learning organisation.

There seem to be four key characteristics of learning organisations:

1. They are *learning networks* with a fluid structure. This helps them learn quickly and effectively and helps individuals and entire organisations to source and adapt that learning.
2. They establish *real and virtual relationships*, both internally and externally, that are not hierarchy- or function-based, but based on expertise, interests and process responsibilities.
3. They have *technology, systems* and *structures* that help them gather and disseminate learning, understanding and feedback on individual and business performance quickly.
4. They are made up of *mobile individuals* committed to learning and sharing, not power.

How learning organisations may be evolving

Learning organisations have flatter, more organic, informal, fluid structures (see Chapter 4). As these different organisation frameworks develop, different kinds of jobs and new working arrangements evolve. Box 13.1 summarises some of the new ways people are working, and will continue to work.

HOW TO DEVELOP A LEARNING ORGANISATION

••• If intellectual capital is the ultimate asset and measure of an organisation's worth, it doesn't make sense to leave its development to chance, does it? Whatever their size, organisations need to nurture it methodically and deliberately.

They need to establish formal and informal networks that capture knowledge and channel it throughout the enterprise. Corporate universities are one way to do that. They can instil in employees a desire and willingness to learn, shift their paradigms and update their skills. There are between 1000 and 1500 corporate universities in the United States, including McDonald's Hamburger University, Motorola University, Disney University and Southwest Airlines University for People.

Volvo University has several campuses across the United States and also uses hotels, conference centres and other training facilities to provide set curriculum training programs for employees at all levels in the organisation. Everyone, from the most junior clerk to the President, submits a personal development plan and individual bonuses are based on completing it. Dell Computers' university is entirely online; its virtual campus provides just-in-time learning tailored to meet employees' specific needs. Another approach is Prudential Insurance's Centre for Learning and Innovation. It locates the best ideas and practices in the company and circulates them to all employees.

Other ways to network knowledge include forming interest groups, review groups and learning circles.

BOX 13.1

NEW WAYS OF WORKING

- *Fewer full-time workers.* Futurologists predict that, by the end of 2010, less than half the workforce will be full-time workers. People will become full-time workers at an older age and will retire at a younger age. Those full-time jobs that exist will require about 50 hours a week working.
- *More temporary positions.* About 80% of new jobs in Western industrialised nations are temporary. Non-permanent positions rose by 70% in the 1990s.
- *More temporary full-time and part-time workers.* They will work in a variety of jobs for a variety of organisations.
- *More part-time workers.* Between 1984 and 1990, Australia created 408 000 part-time jobs (compared to 55 000 full-time jobs). Jobs offering seven to 21 hours work a week are growing strongly.
- *Fewer standard-hours jobs.* These will continue to decline until at least 2010.
- *More self-employed workers.* These are the technical, professional and specialised 'knowledge workers' who will contract themselves out for varying periods of time for a specific assignment. For example, there is a central heating specialist in Adelaide who contracts himself to a central heating repair company in the winter and works as a contract gardener for a number of clients during the summer.
- *More domestic workers* such as cleaners and maintenance workers.
- *More 'portfolio' workers* who work at more than one occupation in a variety of part-time jobs that together may make up full-time work.
- *More telecommuters.* Home-based work will continue to grow.

FROM THEORY TO PRACTICE

BP established a Virtual Team Network of PCs in 1995, linking employees, partners and contractors across more than 20 countries and offshore drilling and exploration sites. The network enables people to work cooperatively and share knowledge quickly and easily regardless of time or geographic location. The network contains home pages, technical sites and special interest sites.

Many measurable benefits have been achieved. For example, there has been a big drop in person-hours needed to solve technical problems; a decrease in the number of helicopter trips to offshore oil platforms; and a refinery shutdown was avoided because experts at another location could examine a corrosion problem remotely.

BP estimates that its virtual team network, costing $12 million to set up, produced at least $30 million in value in its first year alone.

As organisations realise the importance of capturing and using the experience, knowledge and learning of their employees, we can expect to see them taking more control of how their employees learn. Some large companies are already offering nationally recognised certificates, diplomas and even degrees through a variety of methods including distance learning, online learning, virtual training seminars and CD-ROM training. Employees are expected to do up to 50% of their training in their own time and take more responsibility for identifying and managing their own learning.

Supervisors in learning organisations will have far more responsibility for ensuring their employees develop their skills, knowledge and experience, share it with others and put what they've learned into practice. Sending someone off to a training course and taking no further action will soon be a thing of the past.

How to spread learning around

Formal arrangements alone aren't enough. Learning organisations need a vision and a sense of direction that gives learning prominence and encourages commitment to the organisation's goals. They need a framework and structure (e.g. a team-based, flat structure), technologies and systems that will support learning. They need to think through and put into place individual training and development opportunities. They need to think about the kind of culture that will encourage and support learning individuals. This includes, for example, rewards and incentives that encourage learning and creativity, a climate of empowerment and trust that encourages and supports the generation of new ideas and initiatives and an attitude that accepts that making mistakes is a necessary part of learning. They need to provide the type of supervision that will best assist employees to participate, use their creativity to innovate and develop new ways of working and use their initiative to achieve the vision (see Figure 13.2).

THE **BIG** PICTURE

Corporations and educational institutions are beginning to forge alliances. For example, Melbourne University, CSR, Edison Mission Energy, Ford Australia, Foster's Brewing Group, Grocon, Mobil Oil, Shell Australia, Solaris, WMC Limited and United Energy support Melbourne University Private. Initial programs commenced in 1999 with additional programs being introduced progressively during 2001. It offers training modules to meet specific corporate needs and a series of modules could make a formal postgraduate qualification.

THE **BIG** PICTURE

How can we capture and distribute what we learn from a major organisational event such as a serious accident, a successful or unsuccessful product launch, a major restructuring, a business breakthrough? This is what organisations are building systems, technologies and cultures to achieve. We are only just beginning to learn how to do this.

FIGURE 13.2 BUILDING A LEARNING ORGANISATION

- Provide a clear vision and direction
- Resource and support it with suitable structures, systems and technologies
- Build a learning culture that encourages and facilitates learning focussed on the vision
- Supervise to encourage participation, creativity and initiative to achieve the vision

THE SUPERVISOR'S ROLE IN LEARNING

A key responsibility of third-millennium supervisors is to learn and help others to learn. There will be no room in learning organisations for supervisors who can't coach and develop their staff. Developing people will be a core activity that cannot be delegated. Some ways to do this on the job are shown in Box 13.2 (see also Chapter 20).

You can expect to supervise employees from all age groups, including 'retired' full-time workers. Some of them will be contract and part-time workers with several contract and part-time jobs. Many workers will not be with you for more than a year.

You will need to be able to encourage them to share your vision and the organisation's vision and help them feel like important, contributing members of the organisation. You will need to understand how people learn and how to establish a culture that encourages them to learn, and know what learning resources are available. You will need to be able to arrange learning opportunities at a moment's notice and in various forms that are flexible and easy to access. You will need to be conversant with the technology that will progressively play a more important role in developing people's skills and you will need to be creative in the way you use that technology. You'll probably need to find your own ways of doing this, as there are few role models around yet.

THE **BIG** PICTURE

People learn individually and act cooperatively in organisations; individuals on their own achieve little.

Two key questions:
1. How can we encourage people to see learning as a lifelong journey and take responsibility for their own learning and development?
2. How can we transform individual learning and knowledge into organisational learning and knowledge?

BOX 13.2 LEARNING ON THE JOB

- Additional responsibilities
- Seconding people to other functions or divisions
- Mentoring and being mentored
- Coaching and being coached
- Projects and special assignments

THE **BIG** PICTURE

Management as we know it began some 125 years ago as an attempt to organise the production of things. Jobs were defined narrowly and procedures spelled out; supervisors planned, organised, staffed, coordinated, reported and budgeted.

Management is shifting to organising knowledge resources. Supervising newer-style knowledge jobs is different. People's added value is measured by what they achieve rather than by the tasks they do. How long they take to do it or where they do it is irrelevant. Since knowledge workers are more in control of their jobs, there is less need for supervisors to direct, plan, etc. Knowledge workers do most of this themselves or in self-directed teams. Command and control supervision is neither needed nor feasible.

Supervising knowledge workers is about articulating a vision, building a culture that will support its execution and eliminating roadblocks that get in the way of achieving it.

THE **BIG** PICTURE

Many employees will work part-time for several organisations at the same time; others will work full-time, rarely for longer than a year. How can organisations offer a vision that captures their imaginations and fills their aspirations? What will you do to ensure that these people have a sense of belonging to your team and can identify with the vision of your organisation? What challenges will you have to meet in ensuring that these people are part of the learning culture?

FROM THEORY TO PRACTICE

How to create and participate in a learning culture
- Accept that your initial learning or foundation training will not see you through the rest of your life.
- Appreciate that learning is a never-ending investment.
- Accept that skills depreciate and need to be upgraded and replaced.
- Gain broad experience, technically and working in cross-cultural teams and in unfamiliar cultural contexts.
- Be prepared for widespread change.
- Develop personal qualities that help you work effectively with others.
- If you specialise, be prepared to leave it behind.
- Consider options beyond working for a single organisation at any one time.
- Adopt best practices and continually try to improve on them.
- Encourage and reward information sharing among staff.

LEARNING EMPLOYEES

> 'In times of massive change, it is the learner who will inherit the Earth, while the learned stay elegantly tied to a world that no longer exists.'
>
> Eric Hoffer, philosopher

Are you a lifelong learner? Do you manage your changing world and make it work for you? Are you flexible, creative and adaptive? Do you respond to changes in the environment with new approaches, new mind-sets and new strategies?

Learning skills include:

- identifying and using learning styles and preferences;
- giving and receiving feedback;
- working with others in a collaborative learning relationship;
- objectively analysing one's own performance in order to improve it, to ask: 'How can I do this better?' and 'Is there some other way I haven't thought of to do this?'
- a mind-set that sees setbacks and mistakes as learning opportunities;
- a discomfort with the status quo; and
- networking with people to achieve goals and share information and ideas, knowing who to go to when new information and ideas are needed.

> 'Anyone who stops learning is old, whether at 20 or 80. Anyone who keeps learning stays young.'
>
> Henry Ford

Learning organisations are made up of learning employees: well trained, highly skilled, experienced and able employees. Learning employees may be full-timers, part-timers, casual or temporary workers, or contractors. They see their careers as self-employed enterprises, providing value-adding services and, at the same time, learning and growing their core competencies.

With a workforce that is becoming more mobile, the responsibility for training and development is shifting from organisations to individual employees, particularly for non-core workers. The days of a large organisation mapping out a person's career and providing the training and development opportunities are long since past. We all must manage our own learning to keep up to date with the rapid changes affecting our lives and work. We must not only manage our own learning, we must be 'obsessed' with doing so in order to remain employable.

Knowledge workers

In the Industrial Age, economic value came from producing things; workers needed muscle-power. In today's Information Age, economic value comes from creating and manipulating information, knowledge and ideas; workers need brain-power (see Boxes 13.3 and 13.4). Futurologists believe that, soon, 70% of workers will be knowledge and information workers. Knowledge work is about planning, supervising, scheduling and managing. Workers at every level, not just managerial, are doing this. This changes the nature of work and transforms the job of supervising.

 FROM BRAWN TO BRAIN

The percentage of the workforce dealing primarily with information is growing:

1900   17%
1996   59%

The percentage of the workforce working primarily with things or delivering services is falling:

1900   83%
1996   41%

THE MOVE TO LEARNING

18th century—self-employed home-based skilled work
19th century—farming and small trade-based enterprises
20th century—manufacturing corporations and employer-based brawn work
21st century—knowledge enterprises and self-employed home-based knowledge work

---

THE BIG PICTURE

The Knowledge Economy is rewriting the rules of business. It is changing organisation structures, roles and employee competencies. The value network is superseding the value chain; intellectual capital is a measurable asset; and organisations are developing strategies to enable employees to learn and share what they've learned.

Employability is rapidly becoming dependent on *ideas, information* and *intelligence*. These three Is will soon describe the essence of the modern organisation and the knowledge and information worker. This means that tertiary-educated people will become more in demand, and lifelong learning the norm, if people are to keep up to date and maintain their 'employability' throughout their careers.

> 'Heavy lifting is out.
> Brains are in.'
>
> Tom Peters, author

How to learn as you work

Think of all the things you have done in the past 24 hours: you may have written a report, studied for an exam, trained an employee, worked on a project, developed or implemented a new procedure, dealt with a customer, problem solved with a supplier. You probably did some of these things very well, some not as well as you could or should have, others in an average manner.

We do things all the time. Because just about everything we do can be done differently and often better, it pays to think through what we have done to see what we can learn from it. This will help us do it better next time.

Dr Peter Honey, a UK-based researcher and educator, has developed a learning cycle that allows individuals, groups and entire organisations to improve their performance by learning from their experience. This cycle is shown in Figure 13.3

First, select an *experience*—something you've done. It doesn't matter whether you were successful or unsuccessful, you can still learn from it. Then *review* that experience: What did you say? What did you do? How did others react? What actually happened? Review it as if you were seeing it replayed on a cinema screen.

Next, draw some *conclusions* about your performance. What did you do well? What did you do poorly? What else could you have done? What worked and what didn't work? From these conclusions, *plan* what you'll do next time you're in a similar situation to improve your performance. This way, you're learning all the time and getting better all the time.

> **'The illiterate of the future will not be the person who cannot read.**
> **It will be the person who does not know how to learn.'**
>
> Alvin Toffler
> Futurologist

Empowerment

Organisations are becoming dynamic and vibrant places to work. Finding ways to use the potential of all employees is becoming increasingly important. The passive 'do as you're told' culture is long gone. Organisations are pushing decision making down the hierarchy and finding ways to increase collaboration and commitment to the organisational vision. Developing effective learning cultures is at the forefront of leading organisations' strategies.

We looked briefly at **empowerment** in Chapter 8. Is it trendy worker participation? Or delegation of decision-making authority to the lowest possible level? It is far more than either of these.

True empowerment is a broad concept. It involves training people to contribute to their maximum potential and providing the necessary conditions and support to allow this to happen. The organisation and all its stakeholders benefit.

FIGURE 13.3   THE LEARNING CYCLE

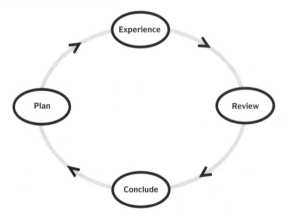

THE **BIG** PICTURE

Culture change is a major issue for organisations. We need to know how to develop cultures that deliver improved results. The challenge is not to see our organisation as moving from one culture to another but as a dynamic learning culture that is capable of continual transformation.

'Empowerment is the creation of conditions within organisations that result in the ability of individuals to contribute their maximum potential energy, creativity, quality efforts and effectiveness to achieving the mission and strategy of the organisation.'

Dr Stephen Covey, speaking at the Sydney Opera House, May 1994

Empowerment is not everyone doing their 'own thing' or making decisions in isolation. It is not about increasing people's responsibilities without increasing their authority, or increasing their authority without increasing their accountability. It is not about 'letting people get on with the job' without support or monitoring of results. It is not something we *give*, but something we *cultivate*.

To do this, we need to provide adequate training and access to people, information, equipment and other resources. Employees need to know what to do and why it is important. They must share the organisation's vision and mission, and understand its strategy for achieving them.

The organisation's systems and reward processes must support individuals and teams as they do their job, together and individually. The operating environment must enable people to communicate with each other, seek and provide information, and alert others to problems and potential problems; it must provide the freedom for employees to make decisions based on informed judgment and a desire to do their best for their customers and the organisation.

Truly empowered people and teams are capable of self-supervision. The function of their team leader or supervisor is to provide support and coaching as needed and to link the team with other teams in the organisation. Empowered teams set their own goals and monitor their own results. They solve their own problems and organise their resources within budget guidelines.

Learning organisations need empowered employees and learning employees need to be empowered.

	True	False
1. The plethora of information available is changing the way organisations operate and how and what they value.	☐	☐
2. If history is anything to go by, most organisations will survive the Information Revolution.	☐	☐
3. Today's valuable corporations are those with knowledge, not real estate.	☐	☐
4. Knowledge organisations have cultures and systems that enable them to identify, acquire, store, manipulate, retrieve, share, grow, and creatively and profitably use knowledge and information.	☐	☐
5. Knowledge organisations are those that use high-tech information technology.	☐	☐
6. Learning networks that spread beyond the borders of the organisation itself are one characteristic of learning organisations.	☐	☐
7. Learning organisations are made up of individuals who consistently learn, both formally and informally, and apply what they have learned to improve the way their organisations operate.	☐	☐
8. Learning organisations are usually hierarchies that allow people to move information up and down the channels.	☐	☐
9. Only managers are knowledge workers.	☐	☐
10. Spreading knowledge around organisations is a third-millennium management imperative.	☐	☐
11. Today, all workers must take responsibility for their own learning and development if they are to retain their 'employability'.	☐	☐
12. Supervisors need to know how to learn and how to help others learn.	☐	☐
13. Continual learning is the order of the day for employees.	☐	☐

1. Write a short essay describing the shift from the Industrial Economy to the Knowledge, or Information, Economy and explain what this means for supervisors and the people they supervise.

2. Discuss the difficulties organisations face in becoming learning organisations. Include in your discussion the complications arising from the need to change business models and other paradigms.

3. Give examples of structural capital, relationship capital and human capital in a modern organisation.

4. Write a short essay describing learning organisations.

DEVELOP YOUR SKILLS

Individual activities

1. Think of three key people in your organisation at different levels in the hierarchy. What specialist knowledge do they have? Who else knows what they know? How would the organisation be affected if this person were to leave suddenly? Prepare a short essay summarising your conclusions.

2. What projects or initiatives has your organisation recently undertaken and what did the organisation as a whole learn from it that it hadn't known before? For example, a recent merger, acquisition, important change, move of premises, opening of new premises, expansion or contraction, development or introduction of a new product, a move into a new market, purchase of new machinery or equipment. What arrangements, if any, have been made to capture, refine and pass on this knowledge? Interview two or three people who were involved and prepare a short essay summarising your conclusions about how organisational learning is, or can be, achieved and used and explaining why it is important to do this.

3. In what ways do learning organisations resemble the organic structures discussed in Chapter 4?

How does an organic view of change, as described in Chapter 12, relate to learning organisations?

4. Refer to the quoted words of John Brown, CEO of BP, earlier in this chapter. Discuss what this means in today's marketplace or for the organisation you work for.

5. Discuss the ways in which the organisation you work for, or your college, does or does not display the characteristics of a learning organisation. List three specific things a supervisor in this organisation could do to help make the organisation even more of a learning organisation.

6. What learning networks have you developed? Diagram them on a piece of paper.

7. How do you rate as a lifelong learner? Prepare a three-step action plan to improve your ability to learn and enhance your 'employability'.

8. List at least ten examples of the 'newer-style knowledge jobs' referred to in this chapter. If you need to, research newspapers and current periodicals, and interview people working in organisations, to find out this information.

Group activities

1. In groups of three or four, research how the Aboriginal Australians shared their knowledge and prepare a paper suggesting ways modern organisations could adapt this to become more effective learning organisations.

2. In small groups, develop a vision for a learning organisation of the future. How will it be structured? Who will work in it, where will they work and how will they relate to each other?

What will be their work patterns? How will they be supervised? You can refer to the sections on *Emerging organisation types*, *Current trends in organisation design* and *Teleworking* in Chapter 4 if you wish. When you have completed your vision, draw this learning organisation symbolically.

3. In small groups, make a list of key responsibilities of a supervisor in a learning organisation. Then list the

key skills and attributes a supervisor will need to contribute to a learning organisation.

4. It was stated in the chapter that employees are becoming more and more responsible for their own learning. This is quite a paradigm shift from seeing organisations as responsible for training and developing their employees. In small groups, discuss the following issues and prepare a short report of your conclusions to present to class.

a) Are organisations still responsible for providing training and development? If so, how much? On what topic areas?

b) Is it only part-timers, contractors and self-employed people who are responsible for their own learning and development or are all categories of employees responsible? Are different categories of employees responsible in different degrees?

c) When is an employee responsible for his or her own learning? When is this not the case?

d) What could happen to employees who don't accept responsibility for managing their own learning?

5. Develop a list of learning opportunities, both on and off the job, that employees can take advantage of. How can supervisors ensure that they, on an individual and a team basis, get the most out of every learning opportunity? What can supervisors do before, during and after the learning opportunity to best help their people? Research your answers and prepare a ten-minute presentation to the class.

CASE STUDY 13.1

The Fluid Team

The charity Shauna worked for asked her to take charge of a to-be-formed team of fund-raisers. Previously a full-time employee with the charity's public relations section, she had recently reduced her commitment to 25 hours per week in order to care for an aged parent. Nevertheless, because of her experience in the organisation and with fund-raising, her employers felt she would be the best person to take on the role of supervising this new team.

She would recruit the team of six from inside and outside the organisation. A staff notice had already been circulated to volunteers and paid employees asking for expressions of interest in joining the team, and a newspaper advertisement had been drafted. It was expected that Shauna's team would be made up of one full-time administrative assistant or two part-time assistants who would job-share, three area supervisors who would look after the city and suburbs, and four funding coordinators. A team of up to 55 volunteer neighbourhood collectors would also join the team as required (see Figure 13.4).

FIGURE 13.4   ORGANISATION CHART

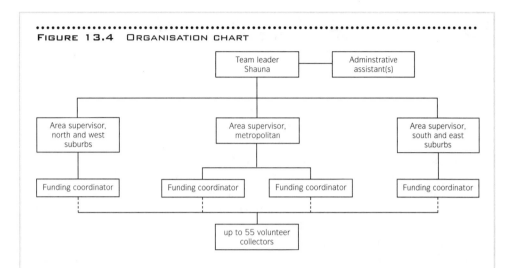

Having accepted the position, Shauna sat down and mapped out a plan of action on a Gantt chart (see Chapter 5). She wanted to be clear in her own mind what she needed to do and when. Then she would discuss this with the chief executive, her boss, to gain final agreement and to work out a budget. She believed that, apart from the volunteer collectors, a mix of about two volunteers for every paid employee would be ideal, although she was prepared to be flexible.

Her vision was to build a loyal and self-motivated team who would enjoy their work and feel proud of it. She knew that people were busy and she couldn't expect too many full-time volunteers, so she planned on a fluid team, with people joining, leaving and rejoining over time. Because of this, she wanted to build in mechanisms to train them efficiently, keep them abreast of the charity's major projects and initiatives, and encourage them to work together, sharing their knowledge, experience and ideas. She believed she should aim for a self-managed team, with her providing overall strategic direction, coordination and support.

Questions

1 Draw a Gantt chart showing what you believe should be Shauna's initial tasks in setting up the team.
2 Discuss the type of staff Shauna might attract (full-time, temporary, part-time, paid, volunteer, etc.) and the implications this has for how she organises and supervises them.
3 Should Shauna set up a learning organisation? If so, how should she go about this and what precisely should she aim to achieve?

CASE STUDY 13.2

On His Own

Brad had his first career shock. After only ten months with the company, it restructured and his position was made redundant. He had joined the organisation as a trainee accountant, expecting to complete his training with the organisation. He had hoped he would be able to stay with them and build a career, but it was not to be.

With a shock, he realised he was on his own. He approached the local TAFE and found that he could complete his studies full-time, beginning next semester. He would be given 'recognition for prior learning' for a lot of the units, so that he would need only two semesters to complete his certificate.

The time would pass quickly, he knew, and he felt he should make some plans for establishing his career soon. He thought about taking extra courses of study to round out his education, and working part-time somewhere to gain further relevant experience. He thought he might have to volunteer his services somewhere if he couldn't find a paid part-time position.

'What else can I do?' he wondered.

Questions

1   If you were in Brad's position, how would you recommend he approach managing his own career? Give some guidelines about the approach he should adopt and some specific suggestions about the steps he should take to improve his 'employability'.

2   What options (e.g. part-time, temporary, contract work, etc.) are available to Brad regarding the types of positions he might find now and when he completes his studies? Map out two possible career paths for Brad based on this. For the first map, imagine Brad is a lifelong learner. For the second, imagine his mind-set is one of, 'I'll find an organisation to look after me and my career.'

Answers to Rapid Review questions

1. T   2. F   3. T   4. T   5. F   6. T   7. T   8. F   9. F   10. T   11. T   12 T   13. T

CHAPTER 14

MANAGING HUMAN RESOURCES

A changed role

Karen Chan's HR department had undergone dramatic changes in the last two years. It had moved from a large and effective operational and administrative service, helping line managers supervise their human resources, to a small strategic unit that outsourced most of the day-to-day HR work such as payroll, training and recruitment. Karen's most important duties had shifted to advising the senior managers and the board on the type and quality of employees it would need to achieve its strategic objectives, how best to attract and retain them, and how to develop the organisational culture into an effective, flexible learning organisation. She was also heavily involved in working out a new team-based structure for the organisation, which would offer employees who were suited, and had jobs that were suitable, the ability to work from home for part of the week.

One of her main goals this year was to broaden the skills of all line managers to help them to take on many of the HR roles that her department had carried out in the past. They would need to improve their range of skills in the areas of participative and supportive supervisory practices and learn new skills to enable them to lead virtual teams and supervise off-site employees. Because of an HRM initiative on pay for performance, they would also need to learn to lead high-quality performance appraisals and performance counselling sessions. As her department wound back on its day-to-day support for line managers, they would also need to become more conversant with legislation, performance management practices and helping their work teams gain and share knowledge. They would need to understand the organisation's goals and values and ensure their staff understood and supported them.

As the supervision and training of all employees was proving to be a key factor in the ongoing success of the business, Karen intended to commission a project to identify the training needs of all other levels of employees, too. She also wanted to focus on the new 'non-traditional' groups of employees, particularly knowledge workers and younger workers, and investigate which HRM practices would best ensure their full support and productivity.

Naturally, Karen continued to monitor important benchmarks of effective HRM practice, particularly employee absenteeism and turnover, safety, training costs and training days per employee by category, and total remuneration investment as a proportion of total operating expenses and return on investment. She was pleased to see that, since the company was seeing its people as a key strategic asset and managing them accordingly, these measures had improved steadily.

Karen had grown and learned considerably in the last couple of years, too. Although it had not been easy or painless, she was glad to have been given the opportunity and the challenge to bring her company to the forefront of HRM best practice.

OVERVIEW

It's a truism to say that people are an organisation's most valuable resource. How they are attracted, retained, remunerated, supported and used is critical to success. In this chapter, you will discover how an organisation does this and find out about the supervisor's indispensable role in the process of managing human resources.

- Do you know what options an organisation has for managing and caring for employees in order to meet its business needs most effectively?
- Do you know the difference between HR's operational roles and its strategic roles?
- Can you explain the role HR policies play in an enterprise's ability to achieve its goals?
- Do you know what HRM functions you will be expected to carry out as a supervisor and why these are growing?
- Can you estimate future staffing requirements?
- Are you aware of the cost of too much labour turnover?
- Can you conduct an informative exit interview?
- Do you know the benefits of job redesign and how to carry out a departmental job redesign?

WHAT IS HRM?

Regardless of size, every organisation has three main groups of resources to work with: finances, plant and equipment, and people. Each person who works in an organisation as a full- or part-time employee or with it as a contractor, consultant or agent contributes to its effectiveness through the quality of their work, their relationships with customers and suppliers, and the ways they gain, use and share their knowledge and know-how. The more content they are with the role they play, the more they understand the organisation's goals and objectives, the more committed they are to achieving them; and the more loyalty they feel towards the organisation, the better their contributions will be. For this reason, looking after an organisation's human resources is critical. This is what human resources management (HRM) is all about.

THE **BIG** PICTURE

As baby boomers retire and the smaller group of Generation Xers take their place, organisations will have a smaller talent pool to recruit from. The workforce will become increasingly more knowledge-based and participatory and expect different things from employers.

Providing enriched jobs, autonomy, flexible remuneration and hours, improved supervisory skills and open communication will become increasingly important HRM challenges.

People as resource groups

The focus of HRM is on employees, not as individuals but as resource groups, or categories of employees. In other words, HRM manages people from a broad perspective while supervisors manage people individually and at closer range. HRM asks: 'How can we manage and care for employees in the way that best meets our business needs?'

As Box 14.1 shows, this entails a variety of activities. If you work for a larger organisation, you may find that it is devolving responsibility for many of these functions to you. Or you may be one of the majority of supervisors employed in organisations too small to afford the luxury of a separate HR department. Either way, you need to understand how to manage human resources. For instance, you will probably be involved in the final stages of employee selection and responsible for carrying out performance appraisals. You will probably carry out induction and other forms of employee training, particularly on-the-job training. You are also expected to be aware of and to observe your organisation's human resource policies and to offer ideas and opinions on these policies. Your role is essential in helping employees align themselves with your organisation's values and goals and providing a workplace culture that people will want to be part of and contribute to.

 BOX 14.1

HRM FUNCTIONS

Staffing: selection and placement
- Forecasting future staffing needs in terms of numbers and type of staff (temporary, casual, part- or full-time, contractors)
- Attracting, selecting and recruiting staff, contractors and other permanent and temporary personnel

- Handling redundancies, retrenchments, retirements and terminations of employment
- Relocating employees (e.g. to other positions or locations or to home offices)

Training and development
- Inducting new recruits to the organisation
- Training and developing existing employees

- Determining the future competencies and skill mix required by the organisation
- Training employees to meet current and future needs

Continued . . .

Career development and knowledge management

- Ensuring that employees develop new skills and are challenged in their jobs
- Determining ways and means to gather, store, share and retrieve knowledge
- Maintaining and monitoring performance appraisal systems
- Maintaining an up-to-date succession plan, particularly for key positions within the organisation

Policy formulation

A variety of policies relating to the human resources of the organisation need to be developed and monitored. These include:

- Security of employment
- Conditions of employment
- Pay scales and methods
- Retirement and superannuation policies, terms and benefits
- Recruitment procedures and standards
- Training and development of employees
- Health, safety and welfare of employees
- Equal opportunity and affirmative action
- Promotions and transfers
- Remuneration
- Discipline procedures
- Grievance procedures
- Absenteeism policies and procedures
- Consultation policy and procedures

Legislation

- Making required government returns (e.g. fringe benefits tax, equal opportunity reporting)
- Ensuring and monitoring conformity with all employment legislation (health and safety, equal opportunity, etc.)

Employee relations and retention

Establishing benefits and policies that will retain the profile of employee the organisation wishes to have to meet current and future needs, for example:

- Communicating relevant organisation information to employees (e.g. results against objectives, vision and values)
- Establishing a supportive and productive organisation culture

Negotiating and liaising with unions, employee representatives and employees in such areas as:

- Legislative matters
- Workforce restructuring
- Industrial democracy
- Enterprise bargaining
- Pay awards
- Employment contracts

Helping managers supervise an increasingly fluid workforce in terms of numbers and types of employees and their changing responsibilities

Employee welfare

Ensuring the health, safety and welfare of all employees through organising or monitoring such things as:

- Conditions of work
- Provision of specialist crisis counselling (e.g. for drug or alcohol abuse)
- Confidentiality of personal employee details

Remuneration

- Pay arrangements
- Compensation and benefits
- Incentive schemes
- Superannuation policy and arrangements
- Performance-based remuneration
- Incentive programs

Organisation and productivity development

- Designing and implementing organisation change initiatives
- Introducing organisation development and change programs (e.g. TQM, benchmarking,

Continued . . .

ISO certification, job redesign, mergers and acquisitions)
- Ensuring the organisation is structured in a way that will achieve its vision and objectives
- Implementing and overseeing internal communication programs

- Creating knowledge management systems
- Designing and establishing performance management systems
- Ensuring suitable job designs throughout the organisation

Miscellaneous

In addition, HR departments often undertake a variety of miscellaneous duties such as:

- Overseeing the company canteen
- Producing an employee newsletter or news video
- Making business-related travel arrangements for employees
- Overseeing the company nurse and doctor
- Liaising with outside consultants and organisations on personnel-related issues

(e.g. arranging for temporary staff and making or recommending charitable contributions)
- Managing and maintaining HR information systems (HRIS)
- Benchmarking HR policies, costs and contributions to ensure the organisation remains competitive

THE CHARTER OF AN HR DEPARTMENT

The HR department is considered to be a *staff function* because it has no real authority to direct others. This makes the HR department a *service* department.

Once upon a time, the role of the HR department was largely administrative and it remains so in many smaller organisations. It advises and assists with operational matters such as recruitment and selection, training and remuneration, and helps to analyse personnel problems and suggest ways to handle them (e.g. high labour turnover or absenteeism rates). Increasingly, however, its focus is on advising on strategic human resourcing issues such as enabling change, how to engage the full efforts of all employees, how to create a learning organisation and how to manage a flexible and changing workforce. Box 14.2 shows some other examples of HRM's operational and strategic roles.

BOX
14.2

HR ROLES

Examples of operational HR roles
- Provide internal and external training programs to meet identified needs
- Help managers understand and comply with regulatory requirements (e.g. health and safety, equal opportunity)

- Help managers resolve personnel issues (e.g. employee complaints and grievances)
- Administer a performance appraisal and planning system

Examples of strategic HR roles
- Help the organisation gain competitive advantage through HRM polices and practices
- Identify and address HR implications of business plans

- Forecast HR requirements
- Initiate moves towards a learning organisation and knowledge management systems

THE **BIG** PICTURE

The current trend is to outsource operational activities and reduce the size of HR departments to a small team offering strategic advice and policy. This means supervisors pick up many of the day-to-day functions formerly carried out by larger HR departments.

'**HR is now considered to be one of the key roles of every line manager.**'

Danny Samson, Professor of Management
University of Melbourne

Supervisors need to add another set of skills to their armoury.

Strategic HRM

Managing human resources is particularly challenging during the changes that organisations are currently experiencing. As we saw in Chapters 1 and 4, the very shape of organisations is changing and different groups and types of workers are being employed.

To manage our human resources effectively, we need to find ways of adequately rewarding and motivating the growing numbers of part-time, home-based, temporary and contract workers. We need to make them feel part of the organisation and willing to be loyal to it. We need to find ways of effectively supervising, supporting and training them, ensuring they are consistently willing and able to meet the organisation's standards of quality and excellence.

'**Today's advanced knowledge is tomorrow's ignorance.**'

Peter Drucker

THE **BIG** PICTURE

Up to 40% of our labour force is involved in knowledge work: producing it, processing it, distributing it and working on its infrastructure. Bill Gates, the world's wealthiest person, is a knowledge worker. As we saw in Chapter 13, knowledge has been called the only competitive advantage. Yet it constantly becomes obsolete.

The productivity of knowledge workers is an increasingly decisive factor in an organisation's success. How should we manage these people and make best use of their knowledge? They are highly paid and highly mobile. They carry their knowledge in their heads. Often, they're not even employees of an organisation but contractors, consultants, part-timers or joint venture partners.

How can we attract the best knowledge workers, align them to our vision and goals, support them, remunerate and retain them?

As an organisation's success comes to depend more and more on what it knows and how its people work together to achieve results, retaining a core of highly skilled, highly productive and highly paid workers with a learning orientation, and managing their knowledge, will become increasingly important. Building multiskilled and cross-functional work teams that work together effectively will become essential. Developing a customer-focused culture of quality is already essential.

The way organisations redesign themselves and their jobs, and the ways in which they supervise people and communicate with them will build or break employee loyalty. Employee loyalty can build or break an organisation. Box 14.3 shows the six most important strategic HRM issues for the next three to five years. This is based on global research from the 1999 international State of the Art/Practice study conducted by the US-based Human Resource Planning Society.

These are all central, challenging and exciting HRM issues. The strategies that organisations develop and the way supervisors implement them will have a direct bearing on their future success.

HRM benchmarking and records

An important aspect of HRM is monitoring the effectiveness of the organisation's employment practices. Collecting and monitoring meaningful statistics can signal potential problems, highlight important trends and be used to plan for the future. These statistics are normally summarised by department, site or branch, and an overall organisation-wide summary made. Key statistics can be used as *benchmarks* for comparison with other organisations and for internal comparisons. Many organisations participate in benchmark surveys and purchase the collated benchmark data from consulting groups and other organisations.

Some common measures of HRM effectiveness include employee turnover, health and safety statistics, absenteeism rates, the number of people applying for jobs, pay levels, numbers of employees from disadvantaged groups employed at the various levels of the organisation, training days and training costs, and remuneration costs as a ratio of operating costs and profitability. Some of these are reported to government annually, others used only internally for monitoring and benchmarking purposes.

Individual employee information such as promotions and transfers, results of appraisal interviews, disciplinary action taken, external and internal training and study undertaken, merit increases, remuneration information and, often, career path information for the organisation's succession plan also needs to be collected and monitored. Health information is often also included, such as blood group and any allergies that may be important in case

---

BOX 14.3 STRATEGIC HRM ISSUES

- Global competition
- Creating greater organisational agility
- Facilitating faster response times
- Valuing people
- Decreasing numbers of skilled workers

- The changing psychological contract (employees feeling less loyalty to an organisation and a greater willingness to change jobs)

FROM THEORY TO PRACTICE

Some larger considerations
- What people issues are most critical to your organisation?
- Where would you put your organisation's HRM capabilities on a one to ten scale if one is terrible and ten is awesome?
- What three HRM areas in your organisation do you see as needing most improvement?
- What do you consider to be your organisation's best HRM practices?

Some questions for supervisors
- What do you do to help develop people's capabilities to enable your organisation to improve?
- What do you personally do to help people align themselves to your organisation's business strategies, vision and stakeholder needs?
- How do you lead or facilitate organisation change and effectiveness in your area?
- What do you do to help your work team be more productive and committed?
- How are you helping to identify and nurture future leaders?
- Can you understand, use and make the best of current and emerging information technology?
- What are you doing to build trust between you, your organisation and your work team?
- What have you done lately to improve work processes?

of injury (e.g. allergy to penicillin), and name, address and telephone number of next of kin. These employee records provide essential information. For instance, if you haven't kept a record of disciplinary action, it can be difficult to determine what step to take next in order to remain within the bounds of the agreed discipline procedure.

Maintaining the many records that relate to the organisation's employees is comparatively easy these days with the advent of computers and many commercially available purpose-designed human resources information systems (HRIS) software programs. This can also be outsourced to specialist agencies.

Because the HRM function is such a broad and far-reaching one, we deal with its various aspects over several chapters (see Box 14.4).

HRM POLICIES

What sort of employer does the organisation want to be? How does it want to treat its staff? What benefits will it provide? How much sick leave, paternity leave and study leave will it allow? What if an employee's aged auntie is ill and there's no one else to care for her—will the organisation allow time off? Can an employee take time off to attend the funeral of their partner's close relative? Will the organisation pay for tertiary studies? If so, will this be during the time of study or only after it is completed satisfactorily? Must the course of study be relevant to the organisation? Will the organisation provide childcare facilities to

BOX 14.4

WHERE TO LOOK FOR HR INFORMATION

■ HR policies	Chapter 14
■ Recruiting, selecting and inducting employees	Chapter 15
■ Retaining employees	Chapter 14
■ Remunerating employees	Chapter 14
■ Training and developing employees	Chapter 16
■ Managing employee health, safety and welfare	Chapter 7
■ Managing productivity	Chapters 8 & 9
■ Organisation design	Chapter 4
■ Job design	Chapter 14
■ Information systems	Chapter 14
■ Workplace relations	Chapter 17
■ Managing a diverse workforce	Chapter 18
■ Strategic HRM	Chapter 14

encourage women into its workforce? Will it want people to work from home? Will it let people work from home if they want to? If business travel is necessary, what class of travel will it be? Who will book it? If an employee is living with another person in a stable relationship but they are not married, will the organisation regard the employee's partner as next of kin for the purposes of insurance, official travel (e.g. a posting overseas) or compassionate leave? These questions need to be answered in light of the organisation's vision and strategies. The way they are answered will affect an organisation's ability to attract good employees and keep them.

In small organisations, the answers often come haphazardly. As the need arises, the policy is developed. This can result in a strange array of inconsistent and often conflicting policies. In large organisations, the answers can give rise to quite complex policies.

FROM THEORY TO PRACTICE

Most organisations have policies to the effect that all employees will treat each other fairly and with respect and that any breaches will be investigated fully and dealt with appropriately. Imagine what would happen if a member of the management team made demeaning and embarrassing remarks to another employee and the HR department (or whoever was responsible for monitoring HR policies in the absence of an HR department) declined to interview the manager involved because the issue was 'too sensitive' and they didn't want to create 'waves'? What messages would this send about how seriously the organisation takes its HR policies and how well it really intends to treat its employees? How long do you think a story like this would take to get around the workforce? And what would the effect be on the loyalty of its employees?

Contrast this scenario with one where the HR department carries out a full, discreet investigation, interviewing each person involved and then taking the appropriate action. The messages are quite different.

Clearly thought-out, consistent HRM policies will help an organisation achieve its vision and mission. They will help to establish the culture of an organisation. The policies and, more importantly, the way they are carried out and kept up to date can set the whole tone of an organisation's dealings with its employees.

HR policies help ensure that employees are treated impartially and in a consistent matter. They outline how matters affecting the employees of an organisation are to be handled and provide guidelines for dealing with employees at all levels. Because they set out the overall, broad results of human resources management, HR policies act as a guide to supervisors in many of the decisions they make concerning staffing matters. They are the starting point for the effective management of human resources and impact strongly on employee morale and loyalty to the organisation. You should be familiar with your organisation's HRM policies because you are responsible for carrying them out in your day-to-day dealings with employees.

ESTIMATING STAFFING REQUIREMENTS

Organisations need to plan ahead to determine their future human resource requirements. This is particularly important in today's quickly changing industrial and economic climate. For example, if your company decides to replace its standard lathes and milling machines with computer-controlled machines, staffing requirements will change from turners and millers to machine operators and technicians. This has long-term recruitment and re-muneration implications, especially if your firm trains its own skilled tradespeople and technicians.

Or your organisation may decide to install a computerised accounting and distribution system. Clerical workers who currently carry out these jobs manually will need to be retrained to operate the computer, and computer programmers and systems analysts may also need to be recruited. Perhaps your organisation will downsize, merge or decide to outsource non-core activities. Perhaps it will decide to cut overheads by requiring employees to work from home. Perhaps the needs of the business will change and more contractors, part-time or temporary workers will be needed.

Someone, then, needs to plan what sort of and how many employees will be needed, when they will be needed and what skills, knowledge and abilities they should have. Even in organisations where the issues involved are not as complex as those cited above, few will have a fixed weekly or monthly output, and variations can affect the number of employees required. Retaining people who are not fully employed is uneconomical, while understaffing leads to a lowering of morale and a decline in quality.

Employee moves between departments and divisions also need to be coordinated. Otherwise, part of the organisation may be reducing employees while another is hiring additional employees with similar skills. Obviously, it would be more economical and better for morale to transfer employees from areas that don't require them to departments that do, if this is possible.

How to estimate the number of employees you require

The following five-step method will help you to estimate future human resources requirements.

Step 1   Determine your product or service *requirements* for the future period—for example, to serve 2000 customers or to produce 2000 ceiling fans next month. Sales forecasts, the business plan and past experience can help you do this.

Step 2   Calculate the number of *hours* that will be required to deliver the service or produce the products. The HRM department or the industrial engineer in the fan factory may have these figures or you may need to rely on your experience. If it takes an average of 17 minutes to serve each customer and you expect 2000 customers will be served, multiply 2000 × 17 then divide by 60 to find out how many hours are required.

Step 3   Work out how many *employees* you will need to provide the service or produce the product. Divide the number of hours required (from step 2) by the number of hours each person will work during the period in question. For example, in steps 1 and 2, you estimated that you will serve 2000 customers next month at an average of 17 minutes per service interaction, requiring 567 hours. In step 3 you will divide this figure, 567, by the number of hours each employee will work over the month. This will be 20 days at eight hours a day, or 160 hours; 567 divided by 160 is 3.54, hence you will need 3.54 service providers.

Step 4   Consider any *support or service* staff for these employees, such as maintenance workers, canteen workers, personnel officers or clerical assistants. Add the number of support staff to the figure arrived at in step 3.

Step 5   Allow for employee *absences*. Your records might tell you that each service provider and support worker is absent for an average of two days per month. Multiply the number of employees calculated in steps 3 and 4 by the average absenteeism rate (in this case 16 hours) and divide the result by the hours that will be worked. This will tell you the number of extra people you will need.

For example, in step 3 we found that we needed 3.54 service providers; step 4 might have shown that 1.5 support workers are needed, totalling 5 employees. In step 5 we found that the average absence for both support staff and service providers was 16 hours per month. Hence 16 × 5 divided by 160 = 0.5 extra employees.

As 0.5 people isn't much, in this example we probably don't need to employ extra people unless our labour turnover or absenteeism is high. Therefore the labour requirement is 5 people. So we need a total of 5 service providers and support staff to serve 2000 customers in a one-month period.

THE **BIG** PICTURE

How to build a workforce for the future:
1. Establish the vision.
2. Determine the key issues that will affect the organisation over the next few years.
3. Decide what sort of workforce you will need (e.g. skill levels, personal characteristics such as an orientation to goal achievement or continuous improvement, customer focus, etc.)
4. Determine the HR strategies that will best attract and retain this workforce.

ATTRACTING AND RETAINING PERSONNEL: THE STAFFING FUNCTION

Effective supervision is the principal factor in retaining high-calibre staff. Important as the quality of supervision is, however, the general quality and tone of HR policies also plays a part. As discussed above, these set the scene for the culture of the organisation and employees' trust and loyalty towards it. Some of the contributions that good human resources management can make to an organisation's ability to attract and retain suitable personnel are discussed below (see Figure 14.1).

Attracting people with the skills we need

An organisation's reputation and image in the marketplace as a 'good place to work', an 'honourable employer' and a respected member of the community help it to attract (or repel) the workers it wants. What springs to people's minds when your organisation is mentioned? Are you proud of the organisation you work for?

Once we've attracted people to our organisation, we need to select the most suitable people and place them in jobs where they can make the most contribution. *Over-recruitment* (hiring a person too well qualified for the job), *under-recruitment* (hiring a person who is insufficiently qualified for the job) and *inappropriate* recruitment (hiring a person unsuited to the type of work) result in people being stuck in jobs they are unsuited to and doing work they dislike. Imagine the effects of consistently poor selection and placement on an organisation's effectiveness and its level of employee turnover! Placing people in the jobs that best suit their skills, abilities and attributes enables them to derive personal satisfaction from their work and make a meaningful contribution to the organisation. This is discussed in greater detail in Chapter 15.

Aligning goals and values

If employees' goals are not the same as the organisation's goals, they will find it difficult to work well in the organisation or even to remain in it. This is why the organisation's vision,

FIGURE 14.1   THE STAFFING FUNCTION

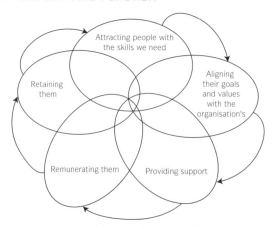

FROM THEORY TO PRACTICE

How does your organisation attract, select and place people? How long do they stay with the organisation? If too many new recruits stay less than three years on average, this is a poor return on investment in recruitment, selection, induction and training. What do you do as a supervisor to induct new people to your section and help retain them in the organisation?

mission and goals need to be clear and communicated in a way that employees will understand and want to commit to. How will the organisation communicate its vision, goals and strategies to employees? How will it ensure that employees understand the benefits of working with *this* organisation as opposed to some other organisation? How will it build loyalty and grow support from its employees? How will it make people feel part of and committed to a larger, worthwhile whole? What formal communication channels will be established to ensure that key messages reach people?

Mechanisms for formal communication with employees to keep them informed about key events in their organisation can help people understand their company and feel an important part of it. Company magazines and newsletters, noticeboards, formal briefing meetings, planned training programs and business conferences, internal vacancy notices, messages and briefing papers from the CEO, corporate videos and handbooks—all these play an important formal role in aligning individual and organisational values. Supervisors play a key role in supporting this strategy and making it work.

Consulting with employees is also important. People need to feel that their voice can be heard and that what they say matters. They want to know that their organisation considers them important enough to keep them informed about what is going on and to find out what they are thinking. Elected employee representatives, union representatives, and health

FROM THEORY TO PRACTICE

When one large company reported a loss for the first time ever, it hired the Melbourne City Hall and invited all employees to attend a meeting. At this meeting, the CEO explained the poor results and, more importantly, precisely said what the company intended to do to improve the figures. Each employee felt a part of something bigger and left the meeting feeling they had an important role to play.

A large Australian public sector organisation embarked on a major cultural change program to empower its employees and heighten feelings of individual responsibility for outcomes. A range of mechanisms—including posters announcing the changes, booklets explaining them, training courses to develop employees' understanding of what was required of them and build the necessary skills—was launched as part of a major communication program.

and safety representatives are all important formal links between an organisation and its employees, although supervisors are undoubtedly the most important link in the communication process. Some organisations arrange regular semi-formal 'informal' meetings between senior managers and employees. Whatever mechanisms are used, effective communication and consultation play a significant role in employee retention.

Providing support

Most people realise that a 'job for life' is a thing of the past. Nevertheless, carefully planning learning and development opportunities is important to attracting and retaining high-quality employees. According to the US Human Performance Practices Survey (1998), leading-edge training practices are clearly associated with an organisation's ability to retain essential employees, employee satisfaction, quality of products and services, customer satisfaction, sales and profitability. What are these best practices? The main leading-edge training and employment practices are shown in Box 14.5.

In addition, the Human Performance Practices Survey found that companies employing best training practices also tend to:
• spend more money on training per employee and as a percentage of payroll;
• train more employees;
• provide more technical skills training;
• use outside providers more often; and
• deliver more training via learning technologies (e.g. CD-ROM training, training via the intranet).

As technology continues to make rapid advances, training issues will become an increasingly important HRM function. With the burgeoning of empowered, participative work teams, an organisation's ability to train its people in the skills of interpersonal effectiveness, and to develop a culture that supports these skills, will become a critical competitive advantage.

Other ways of supporting employees include flexible working arrangements, providing suitable and well maintained systems and procedures, tools and equipment, providing

---

BOX 14.5 LEADING-EDGE TRAINING PRACTICES

Innovative training practices
■ Training resource centres
■ Train-the-trainer courses
■ Mentoring or coaching programs
■ Individual development plans
■ Peer review of performance or 360° feedback
■ Training information systems

Skills training practices
■ Documentation of individual competencies
■ Skill certification
■ Job rotation or cross-training
■ Mandatory annual training time
■ Knowledge- or skill-based pay

Worklife benefits
■ Eldercare and childcare benefits
■ Sick or emergency childcare programs
■ On-site or near-site childcare centres

Flexible employment
■ Flexible scheduling arrangements, e.g. flexitime and permanent part-time employment
■ Job sharing
■ Telecommuting
■ Compressed work schedules
■ Summer and school holiday hours

THE **BIG** PICTURE
....

Training may be gaining even more importance following the massive downsizing of the 1990s. In a longitudinal (over time) study covering 1200 HR managers, the American Management Association found that cutting jobs increases the need to train remaining employees.

A year after job cuts, companies that increased their training activities were more than twice as likely to achieve quality improvements (59% compared with 27%), more likely to increase worker productivity (64% compared with 36%) and more likely to increase operating profits (58% compared with 43%).

---

resources for health and fitness, childcare, evening classes, social clubs and outings, supportive supervision, and professional counselling for employees who run into personal difficulties (e.g. with drugs, gambling or relationships).

The theory behind providing employee welfare and support provisions is that happy, healthy employees contribute more effectively to an organisation than unhappy, unhealthy employees. They can also strengthen an employee's loyalty to an organisation and reduce labour turnover, both of which contribute to the organisation's overall effectiveness.

Coordinating transfers and promotions

Helping employees to identify career opportunities and move smoothly into other jobs or new areas is another important HR support function. In small organisations where vacancies are generally known, it's relatively easy for supervisors to arrange transfers of employees between departments. In large, complex organisations, whose size makes informal communication about job openings more difficult, the logistics usually fall to the HRM department. They may advertise vacancies internally or notify people qualified for the job, and their supervisors, that an opening exists.

Easing an employee's transition to a new job usually involves paperwork—for example, changing pay arrangements, altering conditions of employment or workers' compensation insurance, and adjusting monies withheld for tax and superannuation. If the new job is interstate or overseas, help with the removal process and ensuring that the employee is given sufficient time off, according to the organisation's policy, to settle into the new environment, is also important.

The smooth transition of people posted overseas also needs to be managed. With the globalisation of industry, employees are often asked to work in overseas subsidiaries, parent companies or partner companies for a period of time. Someone needs to work with these employees and their families to make the change as easy as possible, ensure that the remuneration of these employees is adequate, organise work and family visas, establish appropriate allowances (e.g. for housing and schooling), liaise with tax authorities in the countries concerned, and so on.

Remunerating

What pay rates and levels should the organisation offer? Sometimes the answer is, 'We will pay award rates' or 'We will pay award rates plus 10%'. For management and many

---

THE BIG PICTURE
....

People matter. Research has shown a clear link between good people management practices and business success.

In one seven-year study of more than 100 medium-sized manufacturing companies in the United Kingdom, conducted by Michael West and Malcolm Patterson of the Institute of Work Psychology at the University of Sheffield for the Institute of Personnel and Development in the UK, the way employees are managed and developed was found to be far more important to organisational success than the effects of strategy, quality, manufacturing technology, and research and development combined.

People management practices accounted for 19% of the variation in profitability and 18% of the variation in productivity between companies. R&D accounted for less than 9% of the variation; an emphasis on quality, new technology and competitive strategy accounted for about 1% each in terms of their contribution to the bottom line.

The clear conclusion: the more satisfied people are with their jobs, the better their company is likely to perform in terms of profitability and productivity. People really are an organisation's most important asset and main source of success.

What counts as good management practices? In this study it was clear personnel strategy, planned and organised training for people at all levels, skill-based pay, employee share options, profit sharing, periodic monitoring of employee satisfaction, and regular review of people management objectives, strategies and processes, particularly of key areas such as recruitment and selection, performance appraisal, training, reward systems, job design and communication.

---

specialist jobs where there are no awards, and as industrial awards are gradually replaced by enterprise bargaining, organisations will need to discover the 'going rate' for similar jobs in its industry and work out a policy of whether to pay at, above or below the going rate. Generally, 'going rates' are updated by an annual survey and organisations have a policy to pay in the top, middle-upper, middle-lower or bottom quartile range.

Remuneration includes pay (sometimes called compensation) plus benefits such as penalty rates and other allowances, annual leave and sick leave loading, long service leave pay, and so on. The **cost of employment** is often considered to be double this. It includes the cost of remuneration plus superannuation contributions, workers' compensation payments and providing the support infrastructure (pay clerks and the payroll function, injury claims management, superannuation managers, working space and equipment, etc.). It always costs a lot more to employ a person than the amount an organisation actually puts into their pay packet.

The process of agreeing remuneration can be complex. There are three main ways this is done. Remuneration may be precisely worked out with the union and collective contracts agreed. An agreement, known as an individual **employment contract**, can be made between the employer and each employee. Or remuneration can be agreed between the employer and representatives of the employees, often the union, through a process called **enterprise**

THE **BIG** PICTURE

What is the difference between **labour rates** and **labour costs**?

Labour rates are how much an organisation pays per hour (or other unit of time).

Labour costs include productivity—how productive are employees per unit of time? How much do they do (output); how well do they do it (quality and wastage); and how fast do they do it (efficiency)?

It's possible to have high labour rates and low labour costs if the workforce is highly productive. The reverse is also true: low labour rates can result in high labour costs if the workforce is poorly trained and motivated, if labour turnover is high (resulting in high recruitment costs), if workers are inexperienced, slow or less capable than they should be for the work involved.

Highly productive organisations can do things faster, better and in greater quantities than competitors because they have better systems and processes, better cultures, better designed jobs. These factors lower their labour costs, even if they pay more than anyone else.

---

bargaining (see Chapter 17). This results in an employment contract covering a specific group of workers, known as a **workplace agreement,** and specifies a number of critical issues including remuneration and productivity.

As we'll see in Chapter 21, money may not motivate, but it is important in 'getting people in the door'. Flexible remuneration is becoming more important in attracting and retaining employees. Short-term strategies such as bonuses geared to reflect good performance, long-term strategies such as share options and profit sharing, and informal strategies such as tickets to the cinema to show appreciation are important remuneration strategies.

FROM THEORY TO PRACTICE

Many organisations are using pay-for-performance incentives to attract and retain an excellent workforce. Here are some guidelines if you want these incentives to motivate:

- Make it possible to earn up to 10%–15% of the total remuneration package so extra effort is worthwhile.
- Agree clear targets so everyone knows where they stand.
- Establish a clear link to the organisation's goals and performance to ensure efforts benefit the entire organisation.
- Reward effort as well as performance to accommodate degree of difficulty of a task.
- Place the incentives on top of a high base pay—don't use them as a way to transfer business risk onto individuals.

> # THE **BIG** PICTURE
> ●
> Working hours are increasing, to the detriment of people's job satisfaction, personal lives and health. In Australia, 38.1% of men and 13.6% of women work more than 45 hours a week (1994 figures). This is up from 30.2% for men and 9.6% for women in 1985. Are we supporting people enough in their jobs to retain their loyalty and enthusiasm?
>
> Organisations that are introducing family-friendly programs in an effort to counteract increasing working hours are reaping rewards in terms of increased ability to attract new staff, increased loyalty, retention, productivity and morale, reduced stress and improved image. Family-friendly programs include things like job sharing, home-based work, parental leave, carer's leave and breaks and family rooms. (An information package on family-friendly programs is available from the Federal Government's Department of Employment, Workplace Relations and Small Business, Work and Family Unit.)

Retaining employees

Figure 14.2 shows the five key factors in retaining personnel. The first is job design and placement. Well-designed jobs include autonomy, responsibility and teamworking, as well as opportunities to learn and grow, to use skills and contribute ideas. Correct job placement adds the final touch to job satisfaction, high-quality productivity and low labour turnover. To feel satisfied in their job, people need to enjoy the work itself and be temperamentally suited to it (see also Chapters 8, 15 and 19). They also need to feel they are using their skills and, perhaps, being given the opportunity to refine them or learn others.

People also need to feel that what they are doing is worth doing and is valued by the organisation, their supervisor, their customers (both internal and external) and their co-workers. This non-remunerative, or psychological, benefit is critical in retaining staff.

● ●
FIGURE 14.2 RETAINING THE STAFF YOU WANT

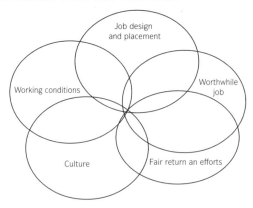

FROM THEORY TO PRACTICE

There are no end of ways to retain workers without adding huge costs to your bottom line. Here is what some organisations are doing:

- Frame customers' letters that praise employees' work and hang them in a prominent place.
- Organise an informal 'lunch (or breakfast) with the GM', department by department. The GM and the group can brief each other on the organisation's and the group's recent successes.
- Send a letter to employees' homes on the anniversary of their joining the company to thank them for their support and to let them know you appreciate their family members' hard work.
- Remember employees' birthdays.
- Offer flexitime, telecommuting, help with childcare and other modern HRM practices.
- Be an organisation that people will be proud to work for, e.g. by supporting your local community.
- Keep employees informed about how the organisation is tracking.
- Provide plenty of learning opportunities.
- Provide plenty of feedback, including the best performers.

Naturally, people need to feel they are fairly paid in return for their efforts and, for many, it helps to be able to see beyond the present job into future possible jobs. *Career pathing* is an important strategic issue in HRM today as organisations are flattening out and promotion paths shrinking. Succession planning linked with training and development plans are one aspect of retaining a qualified workforce.

The fourth factor is satisfaction with the organisation and its culture, which links back to the HRM policies and arrangements discussed above. It includes the type and quality of supervision, the working environment, the level of understanding and commitment to the organisation's vision and goals, and the ways people work together.

The fifth and final part of the total package is providing attractive working conditions. How easy, safe and convenient is it to park your car at work or take public transport to work? What facilities are available on the premises or nearby (childcare facilities, dry cleaners, shops, etc.). How good is the canteen? How flexible are working arrangements (flex time, working from home, time off in lieu, etc.).

Exit interviews

While some turnover of the workforce is healthy, high turnover is damaging and expensive to an organisation and often indicates that something is seriously wrong. As a rule of thumb, the cost of employee turnover is estimated to be one to three times the departing employee's annual salary, depending on factors such as the seniority of the position, and how quickly a replacement can be found and trained. This is made up of direct costs, which include termination payments and replacement costs (recruitment, selection, induction, training) and indirect costs, which include loss of productivity while the position is vacant

---

THE **BIG** PICTURE

According to the US-based International Telework Association and Council, more than 11 million people in the United States, or 6% of the workforce, work from home at least one day a week (1998 figures) and 68% of US companies allow employees to telecommute. Figures for New South Wales, collected by Newspoll on behalf of the Roads and Traffic Authority of NSW, showed that, in 1997, 5% of the workforce telecommuted regularly and 30% said they would choose to telecommute regularly if given the opportunity.

This is not just a nice thing to do for employees, but a strategic decision to help attract and retain the best people. Implemented and managed correctly, it can help an organisation reduce overhead costs and increase productivity. It can save workers' time, reduce stress, increase flexibility and reduce air pollution.

Sadly, research conducted by Christena Nippert-Eng, at the Illinois Institute of Technical Research, found that about one in five telecommuting arrangements fail for one of three main reasons:

1. Selecting people not suited to telecommuting (primarily, the inability to work and solve problems independently);
2. Selecting jobs that don't lend themselves to telecommuting (they need to be jobs people can do at home with only phone, fax and email communication);
3. Supervisors not being able to cope with managing employees at a distance (they need to be comfortable with less 'face time' and 'hands-on' supervision).

Clearly, telecommuting is an important strategic HRM issue.

---

and the replacement not fully trained, the opportunity cost of losing a valued employee, the impact of the employee's departure on workmates, and so on. If ten people earning $50 000 resign over a 12-month period, the cost would be at least half a million dollars. This cost is largely hidden, but it's there nevertheless.

The high cost of excessive employee turnover means that how regularly and why people leave an organisation is an important HRM issue. **Exit interviews** can help determine the causes of turnover. If the person is leaving through choice, the exit interview provides an opportunity to find out the source of dissatisfaction, if any, and perhaps take action to prevent others leaving for similar reasons.

THE **BIG** PICTURE

How much employee turnover is too much? How much is enough? The generally accepted figure is to aim to be in the 25th percentile for your industry in voluntary separations. This means that about 25% of similar organisations have a turnover rate lower than yours. This would put your organisation in the preferred top 25% of organisations to work for.

If the employee is being terminated or retrenched, the exit interview provides an opportunity for the employee and the organisation to part formally and for the organisation to correct any misunderstandings that may have occurred. Any counselling or other form of support that may be required can also be offered at this time.

Someone from the HR department is well placed to conduct these interviews and to keep records of them for future analysis. If there is no HR department, a 'neutral' third party should conduct the exit interviews. This is important, because employees who are leaving an organisation may hesitate to tell their supervisor the real reasons they are leaving but may be willing to tell someone else.

An exit interview should be carried out with everyone who leaves an organisation. Just conducting them isn't enough, of course. We need to do something with the information we collect. Box 14.6 shows some typical questions to ask at an exit interview, which can take anything between 15 minutes and half an hour.

BOX 14.6

SOME EXIT INTERVIEW QUESTIONS

- Can you explain what led to your decision to leave us?
- What are you intending to do?
- What are you most looking forward to in your new role?
- What did you enjoy most about working here? What did you enjoy least?
- If we were able to match (the new salary or other reason given for leaving), would you stay? If not, why not? If we could 'fix this' (whatever is mentioned), would you stay then? (Keep asking until you get a 'yes' response—this will tell you the genuine reason for leaving, not the 'polite' reason.)*
- Is there anything else you would like to mention at this time?

Thank the employee for their time and their honesty.

* You are not offering to match the salary and other things mentioned as an enticement for the employee to stay. You are asking a hypothetical (*what if?*) question. You may want to make that clear at the time of asking the question. This hypothetical series of questions will help you determine the real or most important cause(s) of the employee leaving

---

FROM THEORY TO PRACTICE

What is the employee turnover rate of your organisation? How does it compare to the turnover in your area? In your industry? Is it increasing, decreasing or staying steady? Is it consistent across the entire organisation or are there pockets of high and low labour turnover? Is it consistent across groups of employees or is it higher for some groups (e.g. professionals or minorities) and lower for others (e.g. women or longer-serving employees)? What is causing the turnover? Resignations? Retirements? Retrenchments? Terminations? How does this compare with the industry average?

Asking not only what but also why is important in getting to the bottom of employee turnover.

In attracting and retaining the right people, our focus cannot be solely on full-time employees. Particularly in Australia, we need to consider part-time, casual, temporary and contract workers. In 1996 about 19.5% of our workforce was part of the temporary/casual workforce (compared with 1.9% in the United States, 0.5% in Japan and 1% in Western Europe). Australian supervisors are at the forefront of learning how to align a diverse workforce of employees and contractors.

JOB REDESIGN

Because of the need for organisations continually to restructure themselves to meet the changing requirements of the external environment, job designs are often taken 'back to the drawing board'. The objectives and necessary tasks are examined, streamlined and reallocated so that work can be done more efficiently and to higher standards. Organisations often undertake job redesign as part of an overall workplace change process. It is frequently part of an enterprise agreement.

Job redesign is about analysing and reallocating specific duties, responsibilities and tasks among a group of jobs. In theory, the jobs of a work team or section could be redesigned and tasks reallocated in many ways, most of which would probably work well. These several 'best ways' to redesign take into account the competencies and preferences of each team member. In other words, there is probably no magic formula or one best way to redesign a set of jobs. Whatever design will work effectively and satisfy the needs of the organisation and the team members is a good one.

Although an HR professional usually leads large job-redesign projects, they work best when they are a participative process involving the entire work team. Team-based job redesign incorporates elements of *total quality management*, particularly:
- team involvement and participation;
- targeted problem identification and resolution;
- continuous improvements;
- a focus on outcomes (as opposed to tasks); and
- a focus on customer needs and expectations.

The full process of job redesign usually involves 12 steps (see Box 14.7).

In the early 1990s many public sector organisations went through a process of job redesign as part of *workplace reform*, some successfully, others less so. The less successful attempts merely reallocated existing tasks while the more successful ones used the opportunity to:
- identify problem areas such as bottlenecks, errors, awkward and unnecessary systems;
- improve, streamline and rectify such problems, and thereby enhance productivity and customer satisfaction;
- improve job satisfaction through job enrichment and job enlargement;
- multiskill employees; and
- improve teamwork and participation through a group approach.

When job redesign is successful, a number of benefits typically result:
- productivity gains in return for remuneration increases;
- tasks are redistributed to achieve multiskilling, job flexibility and more satisfying, challenging jobs;

- an ongoing and long-term means of achieving a flexible workforce is achieved;
- the culture of the organisation shifts towards participative, democratic management styles in line with trends towards industrial democracy and participation;
- training and development needs of employees are identified, and appropriate training programs are designed and introduced; and
- the skills of the organisation's first-line and middle managers are upgraded and updated.

In this way, the organisation, its customers and the jobholders all benefit.

BOX
14.7

THE JOB REDESIGN PROCESS
•••

Stage 1   Perceived need and preliminary arrangements

1. Problems are experienced in completing work in a timely and efficient manner, absenteeism and low morale is evident, and job requirements are changing due to changes in the external and/or internal environment.
2. The HR department establishes a framework to provide training in, and oversee, the job redesign process.
3. The management team is briefed on the redesign program and objectives; priorities, a timetable and budget are agreed upon.
4. Work teams meet and are briefed on the job redesign process, its objectives, timetable, etc. and questions are answered. Arrangements are made for training and assistance and a series of regular work-team meetings to conduct the job redesign is agreed.

Stage 2   The redesign

5. At these team meetings, members consider such issues as:
   - Who are our customers and what are their expectations of us?
   - Could our team objectives be stated more clearly? Are they being achieved?
   - How could our effectiveness be improved?
   - Where are the bottlenecks? How could the work be better organised?
   - Which tasks could be done differently?
   - Could we organise the sequence of tasks differently, or improve the work layout?
   - Could decision-making responsibilities be placed closer to the work area?
   - What skills do we need?
   - Do we really need all the records we keep?
6. Work teams form preliminary conclusions and recommendations about how their tasks and duties could be carried out more effectively and meet customer needs more satisfactorily. They use techniques such as brainstorming and force field analysis to identify obstacles to change.
7. They pass their recommendations to management.

Continued . . .

Stage 3 **Implementation**

8. After approval from management for the redesign, HR specialists help the work team to revise workflows, develop procedures and prepare job descriptions and personnel specifications.

9. Training needs for each team member are identified based on the personnel specifications. A training plan is developed for the work team and priorities identified.

10. Team members receive the necessary training to carry out their revised job roles.

Stage 4 **Evaluation**

11. Management, staff and unions (if applicable) evaluate the process and plan how to use the lessons they have learned.

12. They all live happily ever after because: team members know each other better and have found working together was fun and achieved results; a participative organisation culture was strengthened; job satisfaction and morale increased while absenteeism fell; the quantity and quality of work improved as staff developed a sense of ownership of their work and felt that their opinions mattered; customers were better satisfied because their needs were more reliably met.

.... RAPID REVIEW ....

	True	False
1. Whether or not an organisation has an HR department, the human resources of the organisation still need to be managed.	☐	☐
2. The HR department has direct authority to hire and fire people.	☐	☐
3. Due to the changing nature of organisations, the HRM function is currently undergoing a basic and important shift of emphasis toward strategic issues.	☐	☐
4. HR records and statistics can alert supervisors and HRM specialists to trends and potential problems. If there is no HR department, supervisors should keep and monitor a few basic HR records themselves.	☐	☐
5. HRM policies can set the tone for morale and loyalty in an organisation.	☐	☐
6. When it becomes important to estimate future staffing requirements, there are clear guidelines to follow.	☐	☐
7. The specific ways in which an organisation manages its people will have an effect on how easily it can recruit and retain high-calibre staff.	☐	☐
8. There are four elements to the staffing function: attracting people, aligning their goals and values with the organisation's, providing training and other support, and remuneration.	☐	☐
9. In order to retain the people we want, we need to offer them worthwhile and well designed jobs and put the right people in them, pay them fairly, and offer an appropriate working culture and working conditions.	☐	☐

	True	False
10. Exit interviews aren't important since the employee has already decided to leave.	☐	☐
11. The more organisations change in order to respond to the needs of their external environment, the more job redesign projects supervisors can expect to be involved in.	☐	☐
12. Because there are clear 'best ways' to design jobs and organise the work to be done, supervisors should undertake job redesign projects themselves.	☐	☐

·   **APPLY YOUR KNOWLEDGE**   ·

1. Discuss the reasons why supervisors are becoming more responsible for many of the HRM functions traditionally done by a personnel or HR department, and the skills they will need to do this successfully.

2. What purpose do employee records serve? Who should keep them?

3. Give three examples of HRM policies and explain how they help supervisors manage people effectively.

4. 'The more an organisation depends on its people, the more care it must take with its HR policies.' Discuss.

5. Prepare an example illustrating how you would estimate HRM requirements.

6. Consider the tourism industry. One chain of hotels has an HR remuneration policy that states it will pay people at rates applicable to the top 25% of the industry. Another chain has an HR remuneration policy that states it will pay at the rates of the bottom 25% of the industry. What effect would you anticipate each of these policies would have on the ability of each chain to attract and retain staff? How would these policies affect the quality of work and customer service? What part would the effectiveness of each chain's supervisors play in retaining good staff?

7. What do you expect would happen if an organisation paid extremely well but failed to provide the other elements that contribute to attracting and retaining staff?

8. How can exit interviews be useful to supervisors?

9. Which do you think is more crucial to the staffing function—supervisors or HRM departments? Why?

·   **DEVELOP YOUR SKILLS**   ·

Individual activities

1. Interview two people: someone from an HR department and a practising supervisor. Find out the HR duties of each. How do they differ? Prepare a short report to present to your class.

2. Compare the HR functions of the supervisor you interview with the HR functions of the terminal supervisor whose job is partially described in Box 15.3 in Chapter 15. How do they differ? How are they similar? What conclusions can you draw about the HRM duties of supervisors?

3. Interview an HR manager about the HR policies of their organisation. Find out what the broad objectives of the HR department are and what

its overall strategies to achieve them are.

4. Based on the example in this chapter on estimating future employee numbers, calculate the number of employees required using two successively higher figures for labour absenteeism. What does this tell you about the cost of absenteeism? About the importance of good supervision in keeping an organisation's labour costs down?

5. Analyse your college or place of work using the five factors explained in this chapter that are important in attracting and retaining staff. What conclusions can you draw? What is done well? What opportunities for improvement are there?

Group activities

1. Divide the class into three groups. Each group will find out what the standard working conditions and HR policies are for organisations in your area. One group should concentrate on private sector organisations, another group on not-for-profit organisations and the third group on public sector organisations. Compare the working conditions and HR policies of these three types of organisations and see what general conclusions you can reach.

2. Some people dislike the term 'HRM', preferring the older term 'personnel'. They believe that treating human beings as a mere (inanimate) resource like any other (money, time, raw materials, plant and equipment) is demeaning and dehumanising. Others believe that employees must be carefully managed and monitored, like all other resources. Debate this issue in class.

3. Management guru Peter Drucker suggests we manage organisations as though they're communities of volunteers. Why do you think he says this? What might this mean in practice from an HRM perspective and an individual supervisor's perspective? Draw up two lists to discuss with the full class.

4. Research clearly indicates that treating people as valuable resources pays off. On this basis, HR should be a central function of all organisations. Yet in many it is still relegated to a peripheral role. Discuss the dangers in this and come up with a clear and specific rationale for bringing HRM into a pivotal role.

5. In the international study quoted in this chapter that determined the six key strategic HR roles over the next three to five years (Box 14.3), Australia received a 'pass' in bench-marking terms. In other words, we're okay but there's lots of room for improvement. Discuss the implications of this from a supervisory point of view: if Australian supervisors don't improve their HR skills, what will happen?

St Mark's Job Redesign

Betty Jones is the admissions supervisor at St Mark's, a large city hospital. She has built a team of diligent and competent workers. Morale is high and the work group has a reputation for cooperating with each other and with other departments to make sure that patient admissions are processed cordially, swiftly and accurately.

Recently, St Mark's HR department supervised a benchmarking study of all the departments in the hospital with other large hospitals. Much to the credit of Betty's skills as a supervisor, the admissions department ranked in the top 25% of all large hospital admissions departments on almost every criterion.

Because of St Mark's focus on customer satisfaction, however, the board decided to invest in new technology to lift Betty's department into the top 5% of all large hospitals' admissions. Although the staff levels would be much the same, the proposed new technology would mean that most of the jobs would see dramatic changes in both duties and skills required.

Clear objectives have been established, but the decision on the allocation of the new jobs to the employees has yet to be made.

Betty's immediate supervisor feels that she should provide a written job analysis, job description and personnel specification for each job to help select the most suitable employee for each job. Betty disagrees because, as she says, she has a very good work group that likes to participate in decision making. She would prefer to make the group aware of the objectives and let them determine who will accept which duties, and in this way balance out the workload between them. 'If,' she tells her supervisor, 'you still require a written job description, each of the staff will write their own after we have the new set-up working. Then we will know exactly what each of the employees is doing.'

Questions

1   Who has the more appropriate approach to redesigning the jobs, Betty or her supervisor? Give reasons for your choice.
2   How would Betty's approach enhance the hospital's customer satisfaction focus? How would it build the team and the individual skills of her staff?
3   Prepare a plan for redesigning the jobs in the admissions department based on the stages described in this chapter.

Whatever Next?

A group of first-line managers met in the canteen to share their thoughts. Benny was concerned about the rumours of Karen Chan (see the vignette on pages 432–24) working on a new organisation structure. They were all to become 'team leaders' and take on responsibilities such as recruiting their own team members, keeping basic HR information records and dealing with a lot more of the day-to-day issues they had always relied on Karen's department for. Since her department had been downsized, they really had been thrown in at the deep end, although of course Karen was always there in a real emergency.

Margaret chipped in: 'I think that's fine. I have no problem with picking up some of the things Karen's people used to do. It's mostly good common sense and some record keeping. I tell you what *is* worrying me: How in the world are we going to supervise people who work from home? We'll lose all sense of what's going on!'

'This whole team business concerns me,' said Dave. 'Not just the virtual team side of things, but leading a team instead of a bunch of individuals. Nothing will stay the same! I don't know anything about any of that stuff!'

'And what about this pay-for-performance we've been hearing about? How is that supposed to work?' said Francis. 'I can just see what will happen if we're responsible for assessing people's contributions and skills and deciding their pay rates! What a recipe for World War III!'

'My main problem is all the part-timers and contractors that work in my section. I tell you—talk about just being here for the beer! They seem to have no idea what we're trying to achieve and I can't do anything about it—after all, the contractors are here for a fixed period of time and the part-timers—well, what can I do—fire them? They'll be too hard to replace; their skills are very specialised and …'

Suddenly, they all went quiet. Karen Chan had come into the canteen and was walking over to them. 'I was hoping I'd find a group of supervisors here,' she said. 'I've got a few things I'd like to ask your opinions about. You've probably heard about some of the changes we're making, and …'

Questions

1 If you were these supervisors, what would you like to ask Karen?
2 What do you suppose Karen wants the supervisors' opinions on?
3 How do you think Karen can best help these supervisors come to terms with their changing roles?
4 How do you think the supervisors can best help their teams come to terms with their changing roles?

Answers to Rapid Review questions

1. T   2. F   3. T   4. T   5. T   6. T   7. T   8. F   9. T   10. F   11. T   12. F

CHAPTER 15

RECRUITING, SELECTING AND INDUCTING EMPLOYEES

The thousand-dollar question

Wai sat at her desk, thumbing through the HRM manual. 'Where to begin?' she wondered.

Her most experienced cost accountant was leaving at the end of the month and she wanted to find a replacement as soon as possible. The manual said that a job analysis should begin the recruitment process. What goals did she want the job to achieve? What tasks were to be carried out? What were the key responsibilities? Could she rearrange duties within her department to eliminate the need to recruit? Or to recruit someone with a different set of skills to the person she was replacing?

From there, she should update the job description as necessary and then develop a 'personnel specification' describing the 'ideal job-holder'. She should submit these to the firm that the company outsourced its recruitment work to so they could prepare the vacancy notice for the internal intranet and the advertisements for the newspaper and their web site for her approval.

The recruiters would handle the details of placing the vacancy ads and internal notices, screening the applicants and interviewing suitable applicants, and provide her with a short list of three to five candidates that best met her personnel specification. She would interview them and make the final selection.

Before interviewing them, she would refresh her skills by reading the section on recruitment interviewing in the manual. One thing Wai didn't delude herself about was her ability (or lack of it) to judge people's character and abilities, so she certainly intended to review that section at least once!

She could see this process would take longer than four weeks. This meant she would also need to make some arrangements for temporary help. 'Better fill out the form for that first,' she thought.

This chapter explains how to recruit effectively. This will reduce your stress and increase your chances of hiring the right person for the position and the organisation. It will add to your skills package in a mobile employment marketplace and save your organisation unnecessary expense.

- Do you know how to use the three basic tools of effective recruitment?
- Can you select a suitable source from which to recruit?
- Do you know how to ensure a good fit between a candidate and a vacancy?
- Can you find out reliable information from and about applicants?
- Can you conduct an effective recruitment interview and avoid its dangers?
- Do you know how to ask questions that will generate *real* information?
- Are you familiar with the legal requirements of recruitment?

- Can you participate effectively in panel and group interviews?
- Are you familiar with the range and uses of selection tests?
- Are you able to design and conduct a helpful induction program? Do you know how to cater for workers with special needs?
- Are you familiar with the 'cobber' system and when to use it?
- Do you know why and how to conduct performance reviews for new recruits?

THE SUPERVISOR'S ROLE IN RECRUITMENT

Making the correct decision about who to employ is important. The wrong decision can be costly in terms of labour turnover, lowered productivity, extra training time, unhappy employees, time wasted interviewing and checking references, and money wasted advertising the vacancy. As we saw in Chapter 14, these costs add up to one to three times the departing employee's annual salary.

Do you think recruiting employees is the responsibility of the HR people? That's a common misconception. In smaller organisations, supervisors are usually involved in the recruitment process from the beginning. They complete the job analysis and write the job description and personnel specification, place the advertisement for the vacancy, vet the applications, conduct the initial interviews, and select, place and induct the most suitable candidate.

In large organisations, the HR department may do much of the early work in the recruitment process, leaving the supervisor to select recruits from a short-list of suitable job applicants. Increasingly, organisations of all sizes are outsourcing recruitment to external providers, leaving line managers to supervise the process and make the final selection decision.

Learning how to recruit and interview effectively will reduce your stress and increase the chances you will hire the right person for the position and the organisation, saving you future heartache. And it will add to your skill package in a mobile employment marketplace.

THREE BASIC TOOLS FOR RECRUITMENT AND SELECTION

:... The three basic recruitment tools are the job analysis, the job description and the personnel specification.

Job analysis

A **job analysis** studies the way a job is carried out and what it is intended to achieve. A formal job analysis thoroughly investigates the job and its environment. It involves:

- observing the job being done;
- talking to the people doing it; and
- studying the training document for the job—someone else may have already done the job analysis for you.

You probably won't need to analyse the job to this degree every time a person leaves. However, you should think about how you might reallocate or recombine duties and responsibilities in order to make better use of employees' skills and abilities and their wishes to take on additional duties or responsibilities. The job analysis can also help you spot where changes to the job will help get results more smoothly. Once you have made any changes you want to make, you can write the job description and the personnel specification. (You can also use job analyses to prepare job breakdowns for training and for developing **standard operating procedures (SOPs)**.)

Job descriptions

The **job description** specifies the duties, tasks and activities to be performed—that is, what is to be done and, often, the standard to which it is to be done. It should also list the internal and external relationships, responsibilities and accountabilities and any other information that is relevant to the job. Additional information might include the requirement to work overtime, to lift heavy loads or to travel away from home.

It's always a good idea to involve the job-holder in writing the job description. You might also want to enlist the help of the HR department.

Box 15.1 shows a sample job description for a milk deliverer. Box 15.2 shows a sample job description for a sales representative in a different, briefer format.

Box 15.3 shows part of a job description for a grain storage terminal supervisor. (Other key result areas of this job description that are not shown are: financial management and administration, environmental health and safety, operations and inventory management.) Notice that it sets the standards of performance by describing what must be done in objective observable outcomes; this is known as a **competency-based job description**. When a competency-based job description is available, there is often no need to prepare a separate personnel specification because the job description already contains the skills and abilities required of the job-holder. You can also use a document like this in performance appraisal and training needs assessment for the individual job-holder.

From these examples, you will see that job descriptions are written in many formats. Choose the one best suited to your needs or follow your organisation's standard format, if there is one. (See Chapter 16 for a further discussion on competency.)

Jobs change over time and job descriptions can become out of date, so you should conduct a job analysis and update job descriptions periodically.

BOX 15.1 JOB DESCRIPTION FOR A MILK DELIVERER

Job title: Milk deliverer
Reports to: Depot Manager
Responsible for: Vehicle, goods delivery, products, sales and debt collection
Job purpose: To provide an efficient milk and food products delivery service to customers in the designated rounds area. To increase sales at every opportunity through increasing sales per customer and/or increasing the number of customers. To ensure that monies owed are collected weekly. To maintain a positive company image through friendliness and courtesy.

Key result areas

1. *Customer product queries.* Answer customer queries concerning storage, ingredients and general production methods.
2. *Vehicle care and loading.* Load the vehicle in a safe and efficient manner according to company policy. Check oil, water, lights, brakes and tyres daily. Drive in accordance with legal requirements at all times.
3. *Bookwork.* Update rounds book weekly in accordance with the company system.
4. *Delivery.* Complete all deliveries efficiently and courteously according to customer orders.
5. *Sales.* Increase sales to new and existing customers to targets agreed with the depot manager.
6. *Credit.* Collect monies owed to the company on a weekly basis, allowing a maximum of four weeks' credit per customer and collecting at least 80% (or other figure as may be agreed with depot manager) each week.

BOX 15.2 JOB DESCRIPTION FOR A SALES REPRESENTATIVE

Relationships

Reponsible to: Area Manager
Responsible for: Managing time, territory and customer relationships
Other contacts: Liaise with technical adviser and regional products adviser

Job purpose

- To obtain maximum penetration of the company's products into potential industrial users in the sales area to agreed sales and profitability targets.

Job content

- Identifies industrial and commercial users of our products in sales area and contacts them in order to maintain and expand current levels of business.
- Builds strong relationships with existing customers.
- Works with specialist colleagues to provide an effective problem-solving service for users' technical problems and to meet their requirements through our products.

COMPETENCY-BASED JOB DESCRIPTION

BOX 15.3

Position: Terminal Supervisor   **Location:** Central Terminal

Pay scale: 14A   **Date prepared:** 11/1/99

Purpose of this position: To supervise all daily operations of the terminal to contribute to the achievement of our overall business goals.

Position reported to: Operations Manager

Reporting positions
1 documents clerk, 1 general hand, 5 terminal attendants (2 casual, 1 part-time), 1 mechanic (casual)

Special requirements
Ability to successfully negotiate workplace agreements based on current industrial relations practices; ability to move about the terminal and inside silos (reasonable physical fitness); able to work long hours during harvest in order to meet expected results; able to recognise, analyse and store grains correctly; able to follow poisonous substances regulations; able to fight spot fires and follow emergency procedures.

Education, qualifications or licences required for this position
Current fire fighting certificate; current hazardous and poisonous chemicals certificate.

Key result areas	Duties and responsibilities	Training needs assessment	
		Competent	*Training required by (date)*
HR management	**Deputise for reporting roles** Acts in place of reporting staff when they are absent.	☐	☐
	Self-development Maintains qualifications required; undertakes further training as needed to maintain effective skills and knowledge to perform current job and prepare for further responsibility.	☐	☐
	Annual performance review Participates in own annual review and conducts annual review for all reporting staff.	☐	☐
	Training needs analysis Conducts an initial and annual formal TNA and prepares a training plan for all reporting staff.	☐	☐
	Training resources and budget Provides or organises training resources according to training needs analysis; plans, prepares and recommends an annual training budget responsive to various needs.	☐	☐

Continued . . .

Training plan
Ensures reporting staff are trained
according to training plan.   ☐   ☐
Recruitment
Recruits suitable staff.   ☐   ☐
Induction
Inducts new staff according to
company induction kit to achieve safe
productive work outputs in the
minimum time.   ☐   ☐
Pastoral care
Provides care for reporting staff when
important personal needs become
known. Reports important issues to
appropriate parties.   ☐   ☐
Communication
Maintains open lines of
communication between all parties
and departments to ensure wide
understanding of key business issues. ☐   ☐
Performance counselling
Counsels or recommends counselling
of reporting staff whose performance is
substandard; maintains full records of
reasons for, and results of, counselling. ☐   ☐
Wage review
Recommends wage reviews annually
according to guidelines.   ☐   ☐
Termination
Terminates employment of reporting
staff whose performance is substandard
according to all company procedures
and requirements.   ☐   ☐
Roster management
Manages staff roster to achieve
equitable and effective labour
availability.   ☐   ☐
Leave management
Approves leave applications and plans
alternative delegation of duties to
maintain performance levels and
terminal operations.   ☐   ☐
Team leadership
Provides effective leadership to enable
staff to share and achieve company
goals.   ☐   ☐

Continued . . .

	Staff management Manages the work of all reporting staff to the best standards of practice to achieve company goals.	☐	☐
Sales and marketing	**Represents company** Represents the company at nominated customer, industry or community functions.	☐	☐
	Company image Develops the appropriate image through customer service and responsiveness to customer needs.	☐	☐
Customer service/ quality management	**Quality management meetings** Convenes or participates in QM meetings as scheduled and performs assigned roles.	☐	☐
	Product and service quality Ensures hygienic and correct storage of all grains at all times.	☐	☐
	Customer service standards Complies with all customer service standards applicable to role.	☐	☐
	Calibration and hygiene Conducts calibration and hygiene checks on all measuring devices and grains according to documented procedures.	☐	☐
	Quality records Maintains quality records for all grains as required by the quality management system.	☐	☐
	Customer feedback Solicits and responds to any customer feedback, particularly complaints, as a top priority by taking all reasonable steps to resolve any dissatisfaction. Reports any significant customer feedback to operations manager.	☐	☐
	Telephone Answers the telephone promptly and politely, assesses the caller's need and responds appropriately.	☐	☐
	Nonconformance reports Raises or acts on quality system nonconformance reports on issues that affect or could affect hygiene and quality.	☐	☐

Personnel specifications

Once you have determined the job description, the next step is to describe the person best suited to do the job. You do this in a **personnel specification**. You can list the **competencies** a person requires to do the job well—in other words, list what the job-holder must be able to do, under what conditions, and the standards they must reach. Competencies consist of skills, attributes and knowledge and are discrete, observable behaviours. Or you can include a greater depth of detail by specifying the *skills*, *knowledge* and *attributes* that underlie the competencies needed to do the job well.

The personnel specification describes an imaginary, ideal job-holder. Develop it by referring to the job description: *what must the job-holder know or be able to do in order to do this job well?*

It can be tempting to rush too quickly through preparing the personnel specification. Poorly constructed or vague specifications are a major cause of over- or under-recruitment of staff and subsequent poor job performance, so take care to prepare them carefully.

Make sure the job description and personnel specification accurately reflect the needs of the job. If you set them too high, you may have difficulty finding people to fill your vacancies. Alternatively, you may fill your vacancies with people who are overqualified and who may become bored and resign, or you may have to pay them more than the job itself merits. The reverse is also true. You don't want a mediocre employee in a job calling for an expert.

Box 15.4 hows a sample personnel specification for a milk deliverer. Box 15.5 shows a sample personnel specification for a technical sales representative.

FROM THEORY TO PRACTICE

Always base the personnel specification on actual job requirements and not on any extraneous or irrelevant personal factors. Include only job-related skills and abilities, never information that is not directly relevant to the job, such as age, sex or marital status. This will help to ensure you neither over-recruit (recruit a person whose abilities and ambitions extend beyond your vacancy) nor under-recruit (recruit someone without sufficient skills or motivation to do the job well). It will also help you to ensure a good job fit.

BOX 15.4 PERSONNEL SPECIFICATION FOR A MILK DELIVERER

Work conditions	Personnel requirements
1. Physique	
(a) Outdoor work, all weathers.	Free from chest complaints, arthritis, etc.
(b) Long distances to be walked, stairs to be climbed.	Free from chronic leg ailments, flat feet and other complaints.
(c) Loads to be lifted on and off a vehicle; crates with bottles of milk and produce to be carried when walking and climbing stairs.	Of at least average fitness and strength. Free from back troubles, arm or leg deformities.

Continued . . .

(d) Need to read from and write in rounds book in varying grades of light.

Normal eyesight/corrected vision; free from 'night blindness'.

(e) Deal with customers.

Acceptable personal appearance and manner.

Above-average standard of general health and fitness. Acceptable standard of appearance.

2. Attainments

(a) Education.

Legible handwriting. Basic communicating skills and education.

(b) Driving licence.

Must hold a current driving licence, covering the type of vehicle job-holder is to drive.

(c) Relevant experience.

Outdoor work; work involving driving, contact with public, handling cash.

(d) Employment record.

Sound, dependable record in paid or unpaid activities.

3. Aptitudes

(a) Handling cash.

Mental arithmetic sufficient to cope with simple accounting procedures. Ability to handle cash.

(b) Rounds book to be maintained accurately and up to date.

Administrative skill to maintain rounds book.

4. Intelligence

(a) Company policies.

Must be capable of learning and understanding company rules and pricing structure.
Must be capable of understanding various grades of goods to communicate such details to customers.

(b) Bookkeeping.

Must be capable of learning and administrating simple bookkeeping systems: cash, goods ordering, etc.

Ability and willingness to absorb new information and to use company paperwork and bookkeeping systems.

5. Disposition

(a) Early rising is necessary.

Willingness and ability to adjust to this must be shown.

(b) Must be regular and prompt in attendance.

Check on past time-keeping and general attitude.

(c) Working on own.

Prepared to accept responsibility and working on own. Check previous jobs.

(d) Customer relations.

Friendly and helpful approach.

(e) Selling.

Positive attitude towards selling and dealing with customers.

(f) Adaptability.

Adaptable to rounds changes, rest days, traffic, etc.

(g) Active, outdoor work.

Compare with jobs previously held.

Dependable, friendly and helpful, able to work on own.

6. Interests

(a) Conflict of interests.

Check for possible conflict of interests between job and outside activities, especially early starts and evening cash collection.

(b) Transport.

Own transportation an advantage; if not available, check suitability of public transport.

Need/desire for security, permanency of employment; domestic arrangements.

BOX 15.5 PERSONNEL SPECIFICATIONS FOR A TECHNICAL SALES REPRESENTATIVE

General appearance	Neat, well-groomed appearance.
Education	HSC or equivalent, including Mathematics and English; technical subjects an advantage.
Interests and hobbies	Depth of interest and achievement in more than one activity. Interest in mechanical things. Assertive behaviour, e.g. competitive at sports and social pursuits. History of successfully encouraging/persuading others.
Work experience	Proven ability to work with others from varied backgrounds. Has persevered with success in disagreeable tasks. Sales experience and experience of organising own work would be advantageous. Evidence of success in the face of difficulties or under pressure.
Plans and ambitions	Has worked towards a career in selling. Awareness of business environment. Has taken steps to make a realistic career plan. Has shown keenness to absorb technical data. Positive preference for selling to industry. Results-oriented.
Circumstances	Able and willing to move about and be away from home. Driving licence.
Key competencies	Assertiveness. Ability to overcome problems and withstand stress. Sociable. Clear speech. Able to persuade. Able to work on own.

Once you have thought through the job and are clear about its nature and requirements (job description) and the sort of person who will be able to do it well (personnel specification), you can begin the recruitment process.

SOURCES OF RECRUITMENT

Newspaper and other printed media advertising

Advertising job vacancies in newspapers is a popular method of attracting applications. You might select a local newspaper if you're looking for a part-time clerical assistant and a national newspaper if you're seeking a more senior staff member or someone with specialist skills. Newspaper advertisements can be expensive and need to be written carefully to attract suitable applicants and deter those who are not suitable.

Specialist journals can also be effective ways to reach potential applicants. If your vacancy is for someone who might belong to a professional or trade body that publishes its own journal, an inexpensive advertisement will reach your precise target audience.

Internet advertising

There are currently 150–200 Internet recruitment sites in Australia and analysts estimate that online recruitment will double between 2000 and 2003. Many recruitment agencies, dedicated Internet recuitment sites and employers have interactive web sites that list current employment opportunities. These are not yet replacing traditional recruitment methods but are becoming an increasingly important tool in modern recruitment. Twenty per cent of Internet users do not read a newspaper, so advertising vacancies on the Internet reaches people an organisation might otherwise miss, and research estimates that 98% of job seekers would use the Internet to look for employment.

Intranet advertising

Many organisations have their own intranet on which they post vacancies along with other organisational information. This may take the place of, or be in addition to, a central notice-board where vacancies are posted.

Recommendations from existing staff

If your organisation or department has an established, well motivated group of employees, you may find it helpful to encourage staff members to recommend their friends for job vacancies. Being familiar with the nature and requirements of the job and the workplace culture, existing staff will often recommend suitable people.

Past employees

If your organisation's HR policies do not prohibit the re-employment of former employees, you could seek or consider applications from past employees who had a satisfactory employment record.

Casual or part-time staff

People who are, or have been, employed satisfactorily on a casual or part-time basis will be familiar with the type of work and the organisation. Because you know them, you can easily assess their ability to meet the requirements of a full-time position.

Employment agencies

Recruitment agencies provide services for placing people in suitable employment. If you give them precise information about the nature of the work to be done (a job description)

THE **BIG** PICTURE

Internet recruitment seems to offer four additional factors to the world of recruitment:

1. *Speed.* Electronic recruitment that bypasses 'snail mail' and 'telephone tag' can bring recruiters and applicants together more quickly.
2. *Accuracy.* It seems to be easier for the organisation and the applicant to provide greater detail, which helps them both be more discerning and selective.
3. *Breakdown of geographical constraints.* Organisations can reach a far-flung pool of applicants and people can locate and target opportunities wherever they are in the world.
4. *Improved communication.* Without the constraints of geography and time, people can form stronger communication links.

and the type of person required (a personnel specification) they can usually provide several candidates with the required skills from whom to make a selection.

Some employment agencies can be expensive, so the benefits of using them will need to be weighed against their costs. The benefits of using employment agencies include a professionally placed job advertisement, the ability to maintain client confidentiality, the saving of your own time and effort in conducting the initial interviews and advice about comparable rates of pay and duties in your industry.

Radio advertising

Some organisations have found that announcing vacancies on a popular radio station is a good way to attract suitable candidates. Use a radio station that the people you want to target listen to.

Educational institutions

Schools and tertiary educational institutions can often assist with the provision of candidates, especially where specialist training is required. They can also provide useful references. Brief them clearly on the type of people you are looking for.

Previous applicants

HR departments, or those carrying out the HRM function, often build up a file of potential employees from those who have applied or been interviewed for other positions, and from those who have written to the organisation asking to be considered when future vacancies occur. They are time-consuming to search through but it can be worth the effort.

Direct approaches

When specialised skills are needed for a job, or when the methods outlined above have been unsuccessful, it may be necessary to approach people known to have the required skills but who are not actively seeking a job change. 'Head-hunting' is not a common method of recruitment except at senior levels or for specialised jobs. Nevertheless, supervisors should be on the lookout for suitable people, both inside and outside the organisation, who could be approached directly when a vacancy occurs.

A GOOD JOB FIT

Before appointing new employees, it is important to find out as much as you can about their skills and abilities so that you can compare them with the job requirements. If you know what **competencies** the job requires you can match them against each applicant's competencies. Competencies describe the skills and attributes a person must have in order to do a job well. They include manual skills, knowledge and attributes. If you cannot find a perfect 'fit', as will often be the case, competency-based recruitment shows you precisely what training and information you will need to provide the successful candidate.

> 'Formal qualifications are a minimum for consideration; their absence disqualifies the candidate automatically. Equally important, the person and the assignment need to fit each other.'
>
> Peter Drucker
> *HBR*, July/August 1995

Also, make sure there is a good 'fit' or alignment between a candidate's values and the organisation's values, the candidate's working style and the job requirements, and the type of work the candidate enjoys doing and the type of work that is being offered. Unlike competencies, these can't really be acquired through training, but are a 'go' or 'no go' signal.

SOURCES OF INFORMATION ABOUT APPLICANTS

You can obtain information about an applicant from four sources:

1. the applicant's initial letter and sometimes an enclosed work history, also known as a *résumé* or *curriculum vitae (CV)*;
2. the application form;
3. the employment interview; and
4. reference checks.

The applicant's initial letter and résumé

People write to organisations in reply to an advertised vacancy or sometimes 'on spec' (i.e. on the chance that there may be a suitable, unadvertised opening). Their letters should give you some basic information about their educational and other qualifications (e.g. apprenticeships, equipment they are trained to operate), their employment history and why they are seeking a job move.

THE **BIG** PICTURE

Nucor Corporation is the most successful steel company of the last 30 years. It builds plants in farming communities because that is where they believe they will find a strong 'work ethic'. 'We can teach steel but we can't make lazy people productive. A work ethic can't be taught' is their credo.

The moral: hire people who want to be productive and share your core vision. In the case of Nucor, this is: to be an organisation whose workers and management share the common goal of being the most efficient high-quality steel operation in the world, thereby creating job security and corporate prosperity in an industry ravaged by foreign competition.

FROM THEORY TO PRACTICE

Claudio Fernandez-Araoz, a partner in Egon Zehnder International, an executive search firm, believes that a second opinion of a candidate reduces the possibility of hiring error from 50%–10%, while a third opinion practically guarantees a sound selection decision—providing all interviewers are properly briefed on the ideal candidate profile and are properly trained in behavioural interviewing techniques.

You will base your decision about whether to interview the applicant on this information. Such things as the neatness and accuracy of the letter, the way it is laid out and how logically the information is presented can tell you quite a lot about the applicant.

The initial telephone discussion

Occasionally, an advertisement asks prospective employees to telephone for 'a chat' about a vacancy. This replaces the initial letter as a first point of contact. It serves as a 'screening' interview to eliminate clearly unsuitable candidates. You can arrange a time with those who seem suitable to come in for an interview and thank those who do not seem suitable for their interest, explaining that you are looking for someone with different skills.

This technique can save you time reading through written applications and conducting initial interviews. It can be particularly useful when recruiting people for jobs that involve direct contact with the public, as it allows you to make an early assessment of the applicant's communication skills.

The application form

The application form should be designed so that it presents a precise and logical summary of the job applicant's education, work history and any other factors relevant to the position being applied for. Such information, collected in a standardised way, makes it easier for you to compare applicants. Familiarise yourself with each applicant's completed application form before the interview, as it will provide you with clues to the sort of questions to ask during the interview.

A sample application form is shown in Figure 15.1, although every organisation's form will differ to meet its own specific requirements. Later in this chapter, information you can and cannot legally request is detailed under the heading 'Legal requirements'.

The employment interview

Job interviews are the most commonly used method of employee selection. They give both the prospective employee and the employer a chance to learn about each other. The interviewee can get a feel for the working environment and climate of the organisation while the interviewer can learn more first-hand and detailed information about the candidate. Some organisations hold as many as three interviews:

1. a screening interview to eliminate those applicants who are obviously unsuitable. As mentioned, this first interview is sometimes conducted on the telephone;
2. a preliminary interview to select a short-list of suitable candidates; and
3. a final interview with the prospective supervisor, who will make the decision about which candidate to appoint.

Employment interviews can be *structured* or *unstructured*. Unstructured interviews are favoured by people who have never been properly trained in how to interview. They are more like a series of meandering questions aimed at nothing in particular. 'Tell me about yourself', 'What are your strengths and weaknesses', 'Are you familiar with Power Point?' Structured interviews have a significantly higher chance of making a successful selection decision and are also more positively viewed by candidates, who feel they are more relevant and thorough. Behavioural interviews (see below) are the most reliable type of structured interview.

FIGURE 15.1   SAMPLE APPLICATION FORM

APPLICATION FOR EMPLOYMENT

POSITION APPLIED FOR . . . .

SURNAME . . . . GIVEN NAMES . . . .

MR/MRS/MISS/MS . . . . ADDRESS . . . .

. . . . POST CODE . . . .

PHONE NO. BUS. . . . . HOME . . . .

PREVIOUS EMPLOYERS (show last or present employer first)

Employer	Dates		Wage	Duties performed	Reason for leaving
	From	To			
1.					
2.					
3.					

EDUCATION	Schools, colleges and universities attended	Dates		Full- or part-time	Examinations passed
		From	To		

Trade or professional qualifications (show dates gained)

INTERESTS	Membership of professional, community organisations, etc.	Hobbies, sporting activities, etc.

Referees (show name, employer, position, phone no.) . . . .

. . . .

. . . .

When are you available to start? . . . .

APPLICANT'S SIGNATURE . . . .

DATE . . . .

Reference checks

The purpose of reference checking is to validate your selection decision. In order to protect the organisation's interests, a reference check on the chosen candidate should always be carried out. The HR department or employment agency normally does this. If there is no HR department or if you are not using the services of a recruitment agency, you should do it yourself.

A reference check usually takes 20 to 30 minutes and should be done over the telephone. The procedure is as follows:

1. Give your name, position and organisation and explain the reason for your call. Some referees may want to ring you back to ensure that you are who you say you are. (This is good practice and you should do the same if you are ever approached to act as a referee. Make sure you ring back through the switchboard and not to a direct line.)

2. Briefly explain the key tasks of the vacancy and your main selection criteria (from the personnel specification). Ask questions directly related to your requirements and to clarify and substantiate the information you obtained from the candidate during the interview.

3. Thank the referee for their time and end on a positive note.

In short, telephone reference checks are mostly concerned with:

• confirming factual information given by the candidate concerning the employer in question (e.g. dates, wages, nature of duties); and
• probing important areas of the personnel specification and in what specific ways the candidate matches or fails to match these important areas. Box 15.6 shows some sample questions for telephone reference checks.

EMPLOYMENT INTERVIEWING

•••• Can you imagine hiring someone without having first met and talked to them? Or accepting a job without having met your boss-to-be and seen where you'll be working? As notoriously unreliable as recruitment interviews are there is really no substitute for them.

The drawbacks of interviews

We all like to think that we have good 'people sense' and a rare ability to pick the right person. Unfortunately, most of us don't. Unless we take great care in the employment

---

BOX 15.6 SAMPLE QUESTIONS FOR TELEPHONE REFERENCE CHECKS

- Confirm that dates of employment, pay and any other important details given are correct.
- In what capacity was X (the candidate) employed?
- What did you/X's supervisor think of X?
- How well did X perform the job?
- How closely did X have to be supervised?
- Did X have any contact with the public? (if relevant)
- Was X dependable about quality of work? Time keeping? Attendance?

- How would you rate X's general conduct?
- Why did X leave?
- Would you re-employ X? Why or why not?
- What would you say are X's strong points? Weak points?
- Did you form any opinion of the work for which X is best suited?
- How did X get on with people?
- How much potential/initiative, etc. did X show?

interview, research has shown that we could make just as good a selection decision by choosing at random from among the applicants!

Why is this so? We all have our own biases and prejudices, our own way of sifting and filtering information so that it fits in with what we expect or wish to hear. In addition, the **halo/horns effect** and the fact that the first impression, although often incorrect, is a lasting one mean that we often—wrongly—make up our minds about an applicant during the first few minutes of an interview and spend the rest of the interview looking for 'evidence' to confirm our first impression.

Other common mistakes are not asking each candidate the same questions, not relating questions to job requirements, not knowing what an 'acceptable' answer is, and asking questions in a way that makes the 'acceptable' answer obvious.

What to look for in an employment interview

Look for as close a match as possible between a candidate and your personnel specification. The best way to do this is to ask good questions and then listen! You will never find out anything about an applicant while you are talking, so aim to listen for 60%–80% of the interview and talk for only 20%–40% (depending on the job and how much information you need to provide).

Listen closely to everything each applicant says and decide how well it matches your personnel specification. Your judgment can be important here but, in most cases and with practice, it will be fairly evident whether or not you have a close match between a candidate's competencies and those required for the job.

Behavioural interviewing

People tend not to change a great deal. Even as we grow older and more mature, we keep the same basic behaviour patterns that we have always had—things like the ability to act responsibly, our degree of shyness, how thorough or lax we are in the things we do, whether we like to have a lot of people around us we can chat to or prefer to work quietly on our own. Personality traits like these, if they are relevant to the job, can greatly affect a person's ability to do it well.

A skill or ability, once developed, also tends to stay with us. Similarly, knowledge gained stays with us. This means that, by asking the right questions and listening carefully to the answers, you can find out the sort of things applicants have done in the past, use this to predict what they will do in the future and decide how closely this matches your personnel specification. This is **behavioural interviewing**.

THE **BIG** PICTURE

A lot of people spend their working lives frustrated because they're doing jobs that don't make the best use of their talents and capabilities. This is nothing to do with intelligence or ability but preferences in ways of working, of thinking, of communicating. Putting the right person in the right job is critical.

FROM THEORY TO PRACTICE

If you are recruiting a junior clerk to work in a large open-plan office in a job that requires frequent contact with others both inside and outside the department, you may decide that one attribute you will look for is an outgoing, friendly approach. If one applicant spends her spare time reading, listening to music, riding her pony on her own and doesn't belong to any clubs, you may conclude that she will not be as outgoing and friendly as another applicant who regularly plays golf with a group of friends, was president of his school photography club and currently coaches a junior cricket team. Which candidate sounds more promising to you so far?

One of the clerk's duties will be to file information accurately for easy retrieval. Perhaps an applicant has had experience of filing in other jobs or filing information to assist his studies at college. As the interview progresses, you may find out that, although he has had filing experience, he finds the task mundane and boring. Another candidate may have had no previous filing experience but has used her abilities to organise information methodically in other ways. Now which candidate sounds more promising?

As an interview progresses, other information or evidence will come to light. In a behavioural interview, ask questions to find out as much as you can about what an applicant has done, enjoyed and learned in the past and compare it with the job requirements.

Behavioural interviewing is based on the premise that the best predictor of future behaviour is past behaviour. Finding out what candidates have done in past situations similar to situations they will face in our job is a far better way to assess suitability than how well someone 'performs' during an interview.

Behavioural interviewing has four distinct advantages. It helps you assess candidates more objectively, based on specifics rather than 'gut feel' or 'general impressions'. Asking each candidate the same series of questions helps you compare 'apples with apples'. It helps you select and eliminate candidates for job-related reasons only. And questioning past behaviour helps ensure answers are based on fact and gives you a better insight into a candidate's experience, knowledge, values and motivation.

Public relations in interviewing

Every employment interview is, in part, a public relations exercise. You want each interviewee to leave your premises with a positive impression of your organisation and the feeling that the interview has been fairly and professionally conducted. This means that, even if a candidate has somehow slipped through the preliminary screening procedure and is clearly unsuitable, you will be polite and considerate and not obviously and tactlessly cut the interview short. Remember, each person you interview is a potential customer or user of your organisation and so are their friends.

CONDUCTING THE EMPLOYMENT INTERVIEW

In many ways, employment interviews are not very different from the other sorts of interviews that supervisors conduct. As with any interview, you will want to prepare for it carefully. Decide on your objectives and what questions you will ask, and establish a sequence for the discussion to follow. The more planning you do and the better prepared you are, the better the interview will go and the happier you will be with the results. Remember the Australian Army saying from Chapter 5?

'Prior planning prevents poor performance.'

A useful interview outline, which can be adapted for other types of interview, is described below and summarised in Figure 15.2.

1. *Prepare for the interview.* Before the interview, plan your opening questions and a few key questions carefully. Think of job-related questions that will bring out the information you need. Jot down an interview outline or plan. Gather any information you need: pay, conditions, hours. How will you arouse interest and enthusiasm in your vacancy? In your organisation?

    Prepare for each applicant. Review the information you have on the candidate and list additional questions to ask and points to cover. Study each applicant's initial letter and work history, and the completed application form if you have it. What clues does it give you? What information would you like to follow up? What evidence is there that the candidate fits your personnel specification?

    Select a suitable interview room, one that is reasonably private and free from distractions such as outside traffic noise or noise from a factory or canteen. It should also be one that will give a favourable but realistic impression of your organisation.

    Consider the seating arrangements. Will you sit behind a desk or be less formal and perhaps less intimidating and invite the candidate to join you at a low coffee table? Try to ensure that your chairs are of the same height, and that telephone calls or visitors will not interrupt you. Inform anyone who needs to know when, where and for what job you will be interviewing. Ask the receptionist to hold all your calls or switch your phone through to another number. Put a 'Do not disturb—interview in progress' sign on your door if necessary. Make sure the interviewee will not be blinded by the sun or other harsh lights.

FIGURE 15.2   THE SIX STEPS TO RECRUITMENT INTERVIEWING

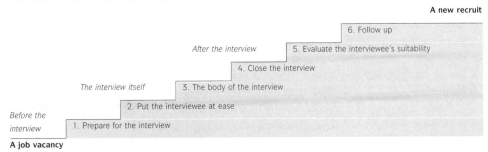

A new recruit

6. Follow up
After the interview   5. Evaluate the interviewee's suitability
4. Close the interview
The interview itself   3. The body of the interview
2. Put the interviewee at ease
Before the interview   1. Prepare for the interview
A job vacancy

2. *Put the interviewee at ease.* Once the interviewee has arrived and is sitting in front of you, do everything you can to put them at ease. Nervous interviewees will not be able to tell you much about themselves, so your goal is to get them to relax as quickly as possible. Continuing to write up notes from your last interview, studying the application form or being otherwise 'engaged' is taboo.

Thank the candidate for coming and take a few minutes to build rapport. Once you can see that the interviewee is relaxed and talking, continue with the 'real' interview.

Give the interviewee the benefit of your full attention for the next half to three-quarters of an hour. Give evidence that you are listening: eye contact, periodic summaries, active listening responses.

3. *The body of the interview.* This is where you give the applicant a little bit of information about the job and your organisation and then listen. Encourage the candidate to 'open up' by asking open-ended questions, those that can't be answered by 'yes' or 'no'. These might include: 'Tell me about your last job'; 'What made you decide to become an engineer/word processor/operator/trainee accountant/factory worker?' 'What attracts you to the hospitality industry?' After you ask a question, be sure to give the applicant enough time to think and respond. Don't jump in to fill the gap of a thoughtful silence.

Remain neutral, whether you agree or disagree with the candidate's statements. Question with a purpose. Build up a picture of what the candidates have done in the past to predict what they will do in the future. Explore past performance under various headings based on your selection criteria. What do candidates need to know and be able to do (competencies) in order to perform the job well? Get specific evidence of each candidate's ability (or lack of it) to meet your criteria.

Don't make a decision about applicants during the interview. Leave this until afterwards when you can compare them properly against your personnel specification.

Box 15.7 shows a typical running order for the body of a recruitment interview.

4. *Close the interview.* When you are satisfied that you have all the information you need, answer any questions the candidate may have. Then explain what the next step is (e.g. another interview) and when and how you will be in touch. Never leave a person hanging, wondering what is to follow. Thank the interviewee for coming and for the interest they have shown in the job and your organisation. Then ask if they are still interested in the vacancy. Stand up and show them to the door or out of the building.

Every candidate should leave feeling they have been fairly treated and with a positive image of your organisation.

5. *Evaluate the interviewee's suitability.* Although you will have made a few notes during the interview itself, take a few minutes now to gather your thoughts. What was your overall impression? In what ways did the person match the personnel specification? In what ways was there not a match? Write down anything you will need to help you recall the interviewee and his or her suitability for the job; you will probably be seeing several people and it's easy to become confused between the candidates if you have not made clear notes.

Then compare the candidates. Which best meet your selection criteria? Some organisations check references for the preferred candidate at this point before making their final decision. Other organisations make a job offer to the preferred candidate,

---

BOX 15.7 SUGGESTED RUNNING ORDER FOR THE BODY OF AN INTERVIEW
....

1. Applicant's background
- Key tasks: Assess match in:
  — skills
  — knowledge
  — abilities
  — aptitudes
  — experience
- Get behavioural examples: what *did/does* the candidate actually do that shows match/mismatch to your selection criteria?
- Find out about what the candidate did/does, not how the job was organised or what the previous employer's systems and policies were.

2. Educational experiences and interests
Educational experiences may not be relevant with older candidates, but may be with younger ones, especially if their work experience is limited.

3. Circumstances
These should *only* be probed if they are clearly relevant to the job requirements. For example, childcare arrangements are unlikely to be relevant to job requirements unless the job-holder is required to work overtime or to be on 24-hour callout (e.g. a maintenance fitter).

---

making it clear that the offer is subject to reference checks. When the job offer is accepted, reference checks are carried out before the candidate begins work.

6. *Follow up.* Once your decision has been made, make a written offer to the candidate you have selected. Inform whoever needs to be informed (e.g. HR, salary administration, your boss, your organisation's nurse). Once your offer has been accepted, tactfully let the unsuccessful candidates know in writing, thanking them once again for their interest and wishing them success in their careers. Be sure that the letter of offer and contract of employment are sent to the new employee's home or are ready on their first day of work and that the new recruit knows when, where and to whom to report on their first day.

Keep the details of all applicants for the job confidential. Don't discuss them with anyone other than your manager or the HR department. Just as you wouldn't want your personal details made known to others, neither do applicants to your organisation.

QUESTIONING TECHNIQUE

An interview is an artificial situation where people just talk. They don't *do* anything. Yet it is basically on how well a person 'performs' in an interview that our selection decision is made (with the assistance of reference checks and any test results). This makes it imperative that we find out as much worthwhile, job-related information as we can during the course of the interview. Our questioning and listening skills are paramount. These are best developed through practice. Meanwhile, here are some guidelines on questioning technique.

FROM THEORY TO PRACTICE

Should you give the applicant information about the job first, and then find out about the applicant, or the other way round? There are pros and cons for each. There are two main benefits in giving the job information first. The first is that the candidate, after hearing about the job and the organisation, may decide to withdraw, thus saving you the trouble of proceeding with the interview. This is not likely, but has been known to happen. The second benefit is that it gives interviewees a chance to settle down, collect their thoughts, survey their surroundings and generally relax.

The main drawbacks are, first, that a clever candidate, after hearing what you have to say about your organisation and the vacancy, may be able to slant their answers towards what you want to hear (and away from the real truth). The other difficulty is that once you are in 'talking mode', explaining about the job and the organisation, it may be difficult to stop talking and proceed to the listening part of the interview. Many an interview has been totally spoiled by an interviewer going on and on, in far too much detail, about the job or the organisation. *The more you talk, the less you learn about the applicant.*

If you give the candidate a chance to talk followed by a short description of the job and the organisation, the candidate will not be able, based on anything you have said, to slant information in the way that best suits the vacancy. Starting off the interview with the candidate doing most of the talking also means that, part-way through, the candidate won't suddenly have to switch from listening to talking mode. This is not an easy switch for many interviewees.

So which is it to be—talk first then listen, or listen then talk? The correct answer is the one that works best for you. Decide for yourself, based on your own experience and a weighing up of the pros and cons of each approach.

Focus your questions to obtain job-relevant information that relates directly to the personnel specification and the candidate's ability to carry out the tasks listed on the job description. This will help you to avoid questioning in areas not related to the candidate's ability to do the job, and enable you to conduct a more time-efficient and productive interview. In general, ask all candidates the same questions and give them the same information about the job. Ensure at all times that there is no discrimination, overt or implied, intended or unintended, against or in favour of candidates on the basis of their sex, age, ethnicity, marital status, religion, sexual preference or physical or mental impairments.

As a guide, do not inquire into family circumstances, relationships, partner's situation, family planning or childcare arrangements. If you need to know whether the candidate will be able to get into work on time, or to work overtime, ask directly! Other areas you should not ask about include national or ethnic origin, mother tongue, religious affiliations, trade union activities and sexual preference.

For example, don't ask the following questions:
- Are you married?
- When are you going to start a family?
- What country were you born in?
- What clubs and organisations do you belong to?

If a vacancy has special requirements, address these directly. For example:
- Are you able to work overtime at short notice?
- Will you be able to spend three days a month travelling?
- This job involves working on Saturday mornings from 8 am to 12 noon. Are you able to do that?
- This job requires you to work overtime most Tuesday and Thursday nights until 7.30 pm. Are you able to do that?

Questions such as these should relate specifically to job requirements and they should be asked of each candidate.

Take great care at all times to ensure you are truly and objectively matching a person's skills, knowledge and attributes against the job requirements. Plan your questions carefully to make sure you cover all the relevant aspects of the job. Start with the job description and personnel specification. Think about the skills, knowledge and characteristics you are looking for. Consider how you want the job duties to be performed so you can determine the behaviours you want. Then find out whether the candidate has displayed these behaviours previously (or whether the candidate hasn't displayed them). Use a lot of follow-up and probing questions and don't accept vague or incomplete answers.

Ask **open questions** that require more than a 'yes' or 'no' answer and ask them in a non-threatening way. Avoid 'leading questions' that flag the answer you're looking for or that lead the candidate into answering what they think you want to hear. Avoid hypothetical questions that ask the candidate to imagine what they would do in a given situation.

A variety of questions can help you gain information about a candidate's competencies that relate to job requirements. Use the questions in Box 15.8 as a guide to help you develop your own questions to target a specific job-skill requirement. Bear in mind that you are seeking behavioural examples of a candidate's past performance and conduct. With enough thought and practice, you will find that you are able to 'think on your feet' and ask relevant questions that will target the information you need. Box 15.9 gives some additional 'Do's' and 'Don'ts'.

Have a probationary period of one to three months for junior positions and six to 12 months for key appointments if your organisation policy allows this.

Don't over-rate the last person you interview—they often look better simply because your own interviewing skills have improved with practice.

LEGAL REQUIREMENTS

:...Australia and New Zealand, like many other countries, have enacted legislation that prohibits discrimination on the basis of race, colour, age, marital status, religion, sex and sexuality, and national or ethnic origin in all areas of employment. This includes

BOX 15.8 EXAMPLES OF INTERVIEWING QUESTIONS

- What responsibilities do/did you have in your current/last job?
- What did you like most about your last job?
- What did you dislike about it?
- Describe a difficult customer you have encountered and how you handled him/her (for customer service positions).
- What has been your greatest success/biggest achievement so far?
- What has been the most difficult job you have ever tackled?
- What has been the most rewarding job you have ever done?
- What made you leave your last job?
- Tell me about the largest account you have landed and how you did it (for sales positions).
- Give me an example of a recent typical day and explain how you planned it.
- Describe a time in your last job when you needed to work without supervision.
- Tell me about a time when you had to use spoken communication skills to get a point across.

- Give me an example of an important goal that you have set in the past and tell me about your success in reaching it.
- Which of your achievements are you most proud of?
- Describe the most frustrating/enjoyable part of your job.
- Describe a situation in which you were able accurately to 'read' another person and deal successfully with her or him.
- Of the jobs you have had, which did you enjoy the most? The least?
- Why? Give me an example of that.
- Describe a difficult problem you have confronted and how you handled it.
- Tell me about ...
- What did you do then?
- Exactly what happened?
- Give me an example ...
- Have you ever ...?
- What happens when ...?

BOX 15.9 DO'S AND DON'TS WHEN ASKING QUESTIONS

Do
- Ask questions that draw out specific behavioural information that can be related to job requirements.
- Ask questions that are directly related to job requirements.
- Ask neutral questions and use neutral language.
- Stay focused!
- Keep the flow of the interview moving smoothly.
- Encourage quiet candidates to provide detail.
- Allow the candidate sufficient time to answer.
- Find out whether the candidate is *motivated* to do the job as well as whether they *can* do it.
- Aim for a conversational flavour to the interview, not a rigid question-and-answer session.

Don't
- Don't ask 'cute' or trick questions like: 'Tell me about yourself' or 'Why should I give this job to you?' These don't draw out specific behavioural information that could relate to job requirements.
- Don't ask illegal or discriminatory questions geared around gender, race, age, nationality, disabilities, etc.
- Don't unduly pressure the interviewee or put them under contrived stress to measure their tolerance.
- Don't ask 'loaded' questions ('You *will* be able to work overtime, won't you?').
- Don't ask hypothetical questions: 'What would you do if ...?'
- Don't allow interruptions or distractions to spoil your interview (e.g. telephone calls).
- Don't make snap judgments.

employment interviews. So what can you legally ask an applicant? Each state and country has slightly different laws but there are some fairly clear guidelines:

- Only ask questions that relate directly to job requirements.
- Do not treat females or minorities differently from the way you treat others.
- Don't ask questions of applicants from a particular group that you don't ask of all the others. Ask the same job-related questions of all applicants—men and women, minority and non-minority.
- Avoid implying or subtly indicating that you are biased for or against a particular group with your questions or statements.
- Don't state or imply that women or men, Aborigines, Samoans or Europeans have traditionally held particular jobs.
- Standardise the forms you use during an interview to record questions and answers. This will help you keep an unbiased record.

The important thing to remember is that you have a responsibility to both your organisation and to all the applicants to pick the person best suited to the job. To do this, you must be careful to ensure that personal prejudices, which have no bearing on a person's ability to do the job, do not affect your choice. Antidiscrimination laws protect the interests of both employers and applicants. You should be aware of these and how they affect you in the recruitment process. They are discussed in more detail in Chapter 18.

WHICH CANDIDATE TO HIRE?

This is never as easy as it may sound. You interview several applicants and find that each has some strong points and some weak points when you compare them with the personnel specification. Which candidate do you hire? There is no sure way to tell which candidate will best suit the vacancy in advance, but you will increase your chances of hiring the right person if you do the following:

- Have clearly in mind the skills, experience, knowledge and abilities needed to perform the job well. Review the personnel specification before the interview and examine each applicant's scores in aptitude tests (if these are used). (Aptitude tests are discussed below.)
- Immediately after the interview, write down the strong and weak points of the applicant. You may find it useful to do this point by point, following your personnel specification. Some interviewers use a numerical 'scoring' system for this.
- Follow up the applicant's prior work experiences. With the applicant's permission, call previous employers to establish work experience and aptitudes.
- Put all the data from the above three points together and, based on this, make your final choice. You will probably pick the best applicant.

It is unlikely that anyone will match your personnel specification absolutely perfectly. Your aim is to make the best possible match. With that in mind, two good rules to go by are: (1) never settle for the best of a bad bunch; (2) when in doubt, the answer is 'no'. Your subconscious has probably picked up some evidence that you can't put your finger on. Listen to any 'nagging doubts'. A wrong decision is too costly in terms of time, money and morale.

POINTS TO REMEMBER WHEN INTERVIEWING

Applicants don't want to know every detail of your organisation, the method of wage or salary calculation, how workplace agreements are made, or every last detail of the job they will be carrying out. They want to know that you are a fair and considerate employer, how often wages are paid, how often overtime is required and what the people with whom they will be working are like. They want a brief outline of the duties and responsibilities, and anything unusual about them. Box 15.10 indicates the sort of information you should consider giving. Follow the KISS principle: Keep It Short and Simple!

Be as honest and factual as you can. Don't oversell or undersell your organisation or the job. An oversell may mean a dissatisfied employee within a few days. An undersell may mean that you will lose a potentially excellent employee.

Applicants are also interested in the organisation in general, so tell them briefly about it. Use this opportunity to build up some goodwill for your organisation—this is part of the public relations aspect of recruitment interviewing.

Give the candidate your complete attention. This is an important step for both of you: you want to find out if the candidate will be a good employee and the candidate will want to know if you will be a good supervisor. Provide any information that will be helpful. If you clutter up an interview with distractions, such as shuffling papers, jotting down ideas or taking telephone calls, this will not only disrupt your train of thought but also tell candidates that you don't think they're important enough for you to give them your undivided attention. As a consequence, you'll fail to get the information you need.

Don't give away any negative feelings by scowls or grunts. If you do, the applicant will get the message and you may not get the full picture. A relaxed candidate will always be more forthcoming with you. To achieve your objective of drawing out lots of job-related information, you must help the interviewee relax. You are not trying to trap anyone or trip them up, but to achieve a good match between the candidate and the vacancy. Don't drum your fingers on the table or tap your pencil or your foot. Such things signal impatience and a desire to get the interview over with. Instead, keep quiet, be pleasant and let the applicant answer your questions. Don't fall for the halo/horns effect by letting one negative trait of the candidate influence your assessment of their other traits. Don't jump to conclusions.

PANEL AND GROUP INTERVIEWS

Many supervisors find themselves part of a panel of interviewers where two or more people are involved in the selection interview and decision. Panel interviews require preplanning to

BOX **15.10** AN OVERVIEW OF A JOB

- Duties and responsibilities involved
- Job title and relationship with other jobs
- Activities involved in doing the job, such as standing, walking or sitting, or if the job involves working alone or in a group
- The degree of authority and responsibility the employee will have
- Promotion prospects
- What kind of equipment and materials will be handled and any health hazards involved
- The environment or working conditions where the job will be performed
- Pay and related benefits

determine who will chair the interview and the procedure by which each panel member will ask questions so that it will proceed at a steady, orderly pace and cover the desired area of applicant response.

Group interviews involve several applicants being interviewed together as a group, by one or more interviewers. This type of interview usually takes the form of the applicants interacting with each other as well as with the interviewers. This technique is often used where the personnel specification requires 'people skills' such as good communication, poise, tact, resourcefulness, leadership and the ability to cope with stressful situations.

When running panel and group interviews, interviewers should meet and carefully review the job description and personnel specification to ensure that everyone understands the selection criteria in the same way. They should agree on the running order, or outline, of the interview and the approximate time for each area, and then allocate an area or areas of the interview outline to each interviewer to cover. In other words, one person looks after opening the interview; another explains the job; another probes the candidate's work history, and so on. Consider assigning the role of recorder to one person, as it can be very off-putting to candidates to have several people jotting down notes!

With group and panel interviews, as with one-on-one interviews, the aim is for a smoothly run, well orchestrated, professional interview. Interviewers jockeying for control of the interview, interrupting each other to ask questions, not following a clear interview outline but asking questions randomly and hopping from one to another will give a poor impression of the organisation and is unlikely to result in a sound selection decision. So prepare thoroughly—it will be time very well spent.

SELECTION TESTS

There are many commercial psychological and skills tests available to help you reach a selection decision with confidence. People qualified to do so must administer many of these; in some cases, they require the supervision of a registered psychologist. Pre-employment testing falls into three categories: aptitude and skill tests, psychological tests and medical tests.

Aptitude and skill tests

Aptitude tests determine whether an applicant has the basic skills or aptitudes to carry out a job. For example, a keyboarding speed and accuracy test is often given to applicants applying for positions requiring well-honed keyboarding skills. Trade-based tests can assess whether an applicant has the training, knowledge and dexterity necessary for many factory jobs. One chain of department stores requires that applicants for lift operator jobs spend a day in a lift to ensure they can cope with the motion involved. Spatial and mechanical comprehension, numerical ability and the aptitude to program computers are other aptitudes that can be tested. These practical work tests are usually given at the screening or preliminary interview.

Psychological tests

Psychological tests seek to find out if the applicant has the potential or capacity to handle the requirements of the job and the attributes needed to do it well. They include psychometric tests, which measure personality traits such as extroversion/introversion, sociability and values. If used correctly, they can provide useful information to compare with the personnel specification and can be valuable in ensuring a good job fit between the candidate and the organisation.

Medical tests

Medical tests are routinely used in selection, especially when there is clear-cut evidence that certain health or fitness traits relate directly to job requirements. They can help to determine whether an applicant is physically capable of carrying out the job. For example, if you were employing a person to work in a boiler room, foundry or glass factory, you would need to ensure that the candidate is medically fit to withstand high temperatures. Other information that can be obtained from a medical test may cover eyesight, physical strength, colour blindness, allergies, hearing and overall health. Medical tests provide baseline medical information for future reference and can indicate the type of work to which a person is best suited.

THE IMPORTANCE OF INDUCTION

Having spent time and effort on making a selection decision, we want to do everything possible to ensure the new employee feels 'at home' and begins making a meaningful contribution as quickly as possible. This is the role of **induction**. Starting employees off 'on the right foot' helps them become valued contributors to your department's success more quickly.

Induction is important for another reason, too. Just as we often take on a new employee on a probation or trial basis, employers are also on trial. New employees will determine during their first few weeks whether the job and the organisation live up to their expectations. If not, they will soon withdraw their efforts or seek other employment. Most employees who leave their jobs do so in the first three months, often due to poor induction rather than poor selection.

It is your responsibility to see that induction is properly carried out for each employee who joins your department. Good induction is more than just introducing new employees to their job and workmates. It is the process by which you help a new employee fit into a job, a work team and an organisation as smoothly as possible. It is a way of helping people settle in and find their feet. It involves making a person feel welcome and important. It means anticipating all the questions the new person might have but doesn't know who to ask or doesn't feel confident enough to ask. It is about shaping their approach to their new job.

Some of the advantages of good induction are listed in Box 15.11.

Anyone who is new to your department should receive some sort of induction training. Sometimes it will be people totally new to your organisation. At other times, it will be people who have transferred into your department from other sections of the organisation. Whoever your new employee may be, make sure you provide induction training.

FROM THEORY TO PRACTICE

Southwest Airlines welcome new employees with a celebration, for example, a pizza party. What do you do to make new employees feel welcome?

BOX 15.11 THE ADVANTAGES OF GOOD INDUCTION

- Good induction helps to give new employees a favourable impression of the organisation and contributes to their overall enthusiasm for their new job. In this way, it can be an important factor in reducing labour turnover and employee dissatisfaction and in developing good morale.
- Induction gives you the opportunity to establish a good working relationship with the new person. It lets you explain their job in relation to others in the organisation. You can carefully explain rules and regulations to minimise future misunderstandings.

- Good induction helps to remove people's apprehension when starting a new job. As you probably remember from your own experience, the first few days in new surroundings are often awkward ones.
- Induction can also reduce the time spent ineffectively by new employees by providing a sensible program to follow during the first few days on the job. Asking too much or too little of a new employee can be frustrating and destroy confidence. You can avoid this with a well thought-out induction program.

What should induction cover?

Induction can generally be split into two distinct parts. The first is *induction to the organisation*, which the HR department often carries out. This part of the induction program covers general items such as pay arrangements and employee benefits and activities, and deals with the organisation as a whole: how it is structured, where the new recruit will fit in, the organisation's history, and its products, services and customers. HR departments of large organisations sometimes have induction videos or probide this information on its intranet and/or in booklets.

Induction to the department is the second part. Supervisors usually do this, although they may delegate some aspects to others such as a leading hand or a 'cobber'. The key is to explain the rules and regulations, and any special duties and responsibilities involved in the job. Box 15.12 outlines the sort of information that an induction program should cover.

The supervisor's responsibility for inducting new employees

Supervisors are responsible for inducting new employees, although the HR department, if there is one, often assists. They may also provide you with a checklist of items to cover when inducting a new recruit into your department. If your organisation has no HRM function, you will need to ensure that you cover both company and departmental induction yourself. Develop your own induction checklist and keep it on file so that you can use it with all new employees.

Setting up an induction program

The first step in any induction program is to make a list of the topics you will need to cover. Once written down, you can put the topics into a suitable sequence and use this induction program again for each new employee, with occasional minor updates.

Don't bombard a new employee with too much information at a time. Facts and figures, rules and regulations—in fact, information of any sort—is difficult to remember if it is given all at once. Put yourself in the recruit's shoes. What would you want to know? How much information would you be able to retain? Provide information in small 'bite-sized' chunks.

BOX 15.12 INFORMATION TO INCLUDE IN AN INDUCTION PROGRAM
....

Induction to the organisation

- General background information about the organisation: its history, vision and mission, structure, products, customers, competitors, promotion opportunities, scope to acquire new skills
- Introduction to lines of communication, both formal and informal
- General industry information
- Information on the overall working environment of the organisation, its policies, rules and work practices
- Details of relevant awards and enterprise agreements, systems of pay, superannuation
- Sources of advice and assistance within the organisation
- Organisation policy on smoking, alcohol, misconduct, holidays, what to do if you're late or ill
- A tour of the organisation: other departments, main functional areas
- An overview of the grievance procedure and other relevant policies

Induction to the department

- Give them a physical work space or station and somewhere to put their personal things
- Health and safety requirements of the job and the department
- Hours of work, breaks, finishing time
- Time-keeping and recording procedures
- Security systems; e.g. fire drills, fire warden, location of extinguishers, warning signals, procedure in case of an accident
- Amenities: washrooms, lockers, canteen, café bar, car park
- Department tour: the work layout, location of toilets, kitchen, fire escapes, etc.
- Review of job description
- Introduction to workmates, leading hands, worker representatives (e.g. union representative, health and safety representative) and other people they will be working with or 'seeing around the place'
- Outline of training to be given
- Pay: how and when the employee is paid, pay rates, deductions, premium pays, saving opportunities
- Everything about the employee's job—what tools, equipment and supplies will be used and how these can be obtained, safety requirements, housekeeping, where the job fits into the overall organisation vision and goals, your expectations of them, what others expect of them, and so on.

In general, provide the information of most *direct relevance* to the new employee before proceeding with more *general information*. People want to know things that affect them immediately first, such as the location of the toilets, where to park and how their pay is calculated. Information to provide later in the induction program includes the names and responsibilities of senior managers, how superannuation is calculated and the overall structure of the organisation.

You might spread the induction program over one week or one month, depending on the amount of information you need to cover and how much time you can spare at any one time with each new person. Be sure not to let it drag on for too long, though, or both you and the new employee will lose interest.

It is up to you to choose what your induction program will cover and how you will cover it. Your general approach to induction, however, is critical. Show interest in new employees and make it clear that you want to help make the transition to their new job a smooth and painless one. This increases your chances of a successfully executed program. You will have set the scene for a well-motivated team.

The 'cobber' system

Sometimes there are so many new recruits that if supervisors were to carry out the entire induction program themselves, they would have little time for their other supervisory duties. If you find yourself in this position, you could consider adopting the Australian Army's 'cobber' system. 'Cobbers' are experienced workmates who are willing to assist new employees during their first few days or weeks of employment. They should be mature, organisation-minded people who are fully conversant with rules, regulations and procedures, and who will be able to answer most questions a new employee will have. Appointing a 'cobber' can take some of the load off your shoulders.

WORKERS WITH SPECIAL NEEDS

Make sure you give special attention to inducting members of disadvantaged groups. Some groups of workers are more at risk than others. Take their specific requirements into account when designing or delivering induction and other training programs.

Accident rates are higher and tend to be more serious for *young workers*, for example. While young people are not all the same, their physical, emotional and social factors can put them at special risk. Many lack workplace experience, which can lead to accidents if they don't fully understand potential dangers and the need for special precautions. Make sure you provide full information on health and safety matters and workplace hazards. Try assigning an experienced worker or cobber to ease them into their new job.

Induction information, safety signs, operating instructions for machinery, and so on, tend to be printed in English, which can disadvantage and place at risk people from *non-English-speaking backgrounds*. To help them, you can obtain many health and safety publications printed in a variety of languages such as Arabic, Assyrian, Cantonese, Croatian, German, Greek, Italian, Turkish and Vietnamese from the Occupational Health and Safety Authority in your state or territory. Encourage these employees to participate in committees and make sure they have access to information that affects their employment. Make sure all workers can easily understand the symbols used in the workplace.

We also need to accommodate *people with disabilities*. Aids such as magnifiers, telescopes and closed circuit television can assist *visually impaired* people. Speak to them directly and do not raise your voice. Ask what assistance you can provide and give clear spoken directions indicating surface condition, direction or activity in the room. Make sure the workplace is free of obstructions and easily accessible and allow them to practise their new job under careful supervision.

Communication is the most significant problem with people with *hearing impairments*. Many are able to lip-read if you speak clearly and directly to them. You can also use visual clues and write down your message as a backup. Use the 'show me' technique to check you have presented the information clearly. Make sure lighting is adequate so that anyone with hearing impairments is able to see people's faces and what is happening around them.

Intellectual disabilities can vary. The main objective in inducting and training people with intellectual disabilities is to create independence. While the style of learning depends on each individual trainee, you will need to think through the induction and training program carefully. Record the progress they are making. Ensure that trainees with learning difficulties demonstrate their understanding practically with the 'show me' technique throughout their training.

People with *movement problems* may have difficulty walking up stairs, kneeling or grasping objects. Some adjustments to the workplace such as additional machine guarding, rails on stairs and ramps, and machine control points may assist people with motor impairments and those who are amputees. Analyse their individual needs carefully.

Many workers are hampered by *literacy problems*. Over one million adults in Australia have problems with basic reading and writing. This means that one in seven workers do not have the reading and writing skills they need to work efficiently and safely. In some industries this figure is higher. For example, in the construction industry, one in four workers have basic literacy problems and 50%–80% of workers in the food industry have been found to be 'functionally illiterate'. These people have trouble acquiring job-related skills and knowledge, completing forms and understanding their rights and responsibilities in the workplace. They may have difficulty understanding machine operation manuals, emergency procedures, safety instructions and precautions. Take special care to induct and train them fully and completely.

PERFORMANCE REVIEWS FOR NEW TEAM MEMBERS

Conduct monthly performance discussions with new team members for the first few months. Let them know how they are progressing and fitting in. Ask if the job is proving to be what they had expected and whether they are enjoying it. Highlight any area of concern, explaining why it is a problem. Analyse with the employee why the problem exists. Make sure there are no misunderstandings at this early stage. Note these discussions in your diary or in their personal file. (See also Chapters 8 and 24.)

RAPID REVIEW

	True	False
1. A poor decision on which person to hire can be a costly one.	☐	☐
2. Accurate job descriptions and personnel specifications based on a sound job analysis are important tools in successful recruitment.	☐	☐
3. There are many sources of recruitment other than newspaper advertisements.	☐	☐
4. Competency-based recruitment is about matching required job competencies with the competencies of applicants.	☐	☐
5. A candidate's letter of application doesn't provide much useful information.	☐	☐
6. It makes sense for the interviewer to read through a candidate's application form with the candidate.	☐	☐
7. Interviewers need to guard against the halo/horns effect and against making up their minds about a candidate prematurely.	☐	☐
8. Good interviewers talk more than they listen.	☐	☐
9. Competency-based interviewing involves finding out what candidates have done in the past and using it to predict what they will do in the future.	☐	☐
10. It doesn't matter if an unsuitable candidate gets a bad impression of the organisation since they won't be getting the job anyway.	☐	☐
11. Apart from small talk at the beginning of an interview to relax a candidate, all discussions should be job-related.	☐	☐

	True	False
12. Interviewers need to find out if young female applicants have a boyfriend and plan to get married and start a family because this will affect their decision about whether to hire them.	☐	☐
13. References should be checked on all candidates.	☐	☐
14. References need only be checked if you are uncertain about whether or not to hire someone.	☐	☐
15. As much detail as possible about the organisation and the job itself should be provided during the first interview.	☐	☐
16. Panel and group interviews require special preparation.	☐	☐
17. To induct new employees properly, all a supervisor needs to do is introduce them to their workmates, show them around the department and set them to work on their new job.	☐	☐
18. The HR department will often take over supervisors' responsibilities for inducting new employees and do it for them.	☐	☐
19. Supervisors should develop an induction checklist and save it for use with all new employees.	☐	☐
20. People who transfer into a department don't need to be inducted.	☐	☐
21. Some groups of workers—such as young people, those with disabilities, people from non-English-speaking backgrounds and people with literacy problems—need special attention during induction and training.	☐	☐

························   APPLY YOUR KNOWLEDGE   ························

1. Discuss the role of job analyses, job descriptions and personnel specifications in the recruitment and selection process.

2. List 11 sources of recruitment and explain which would be suited to various positions in your own organisation or college.

3. What information can we learn from an applicant's initial letter?

4. What are the main dangers or disadvantages of an employment interview? How can these be overcome?

5. Describe the process a recruitment interview should follow. What should interviewers do before and after the interview?

6. Why is it so important to listen carefully when conducting an interview? Discuss at least six other tips you would follow when interviewing.

7. 'History repeats itself.' Discuss this in relation to behavioural interviewing.

8. In what way is recruitment a public relations exercise?

9. 'An interviewer's dilemma is treating each applicant fairly while at the same time meeting the organisation's need to find the best person for the job.' Discuss.

10. Write an essay outlining the benefits of thorough induction and job training to: (1) the trainee, (2) the supervisor, (3) the work team and (4) the organisation.

11. List the specific points a thorough induction program to your organisation and department (or your college) should cover.

Individual activities

1. Conduct a job analysis and develop a job description and personnel specification for a job you have access to (e.g. a job where you work or in your college or a job you are interested in applying for).

2. Go back to Chapter 10, question 1 under *Individual Activities*. Based on how you answered this question, what knowledge, skills and attributes would you expect to see on a personnel specification for the customer service position you were thinking of?

3. Look through the advertised vacancies in a newspaper. Select at least a quarter-page advertisement and, from the information given, prepare a brief job description and personnel specification.

4. Write a competency-based job description for the role of full-time or part-time working student. Try to use the following format: 'under (these specific conditions) the job-holder will do (these tasks) to (these) standards'.

5. The next time you are in a fast food outlet or department store, carefully observe the people who are serving customers. Do you notice anyone who seems particularly good at the job? Is anyone not very good? Based on your observations, develop some criteria for selecting customer service staff in this establishment. What questions could you ask to determine a candidate's suitability for a job here?

6. Some supervisors say they will only take people who have the experience and competencies they are looking for. Others say they would rather hire a person with the right 'approach', or attitudinal skills, and train them themselves. Who do you agree with? Why?

7. Develop a telephone reference check for the position you described in question 1 above. Note what you would say at the beginning of the call and list the questions you would ask.

8. Referring to Case Study 20.1 in Chapter 20, do you believe Robert Nicosea would make a good manager in a Bob's Ozzie Burgers outlet? Explain your reasons.

9. Go back to Case Study 9.1 and develop an induction checklist showing the topics that should be covered for the people who will be recruited to work the second shift.

10. Prepare an induction checklist to use with new students at your college, indicating time frames for completing each element on it. Include any special considerations that would be needed for students confined to wheelchairs and for people with a hearing impairment.

11. Describe the steps you would take in preparing an outline to use in a monthly performance review with new employees.

Group activities

1. Look through the advertised vacancies in a newspaper and find a customer service position where the job-holder will deal with people on the telephone. Prepare a short job description and personnel specification. Develop a series of questions to ask in an initial telephone discussion. Also develop a standard form for the interviewer to record key points from each discussion.

   Select someone in the class for the role of 'telephone interviewer'. Take turns 'phoning in' for an initial discussion. Applicants should be themselves during this role-play.

   Once you have completed the telephone interviews, draw up a list of candidates to invite for interview, explaining why you believe these people are suitable for a further interview.

2. In small groups, analyse the job of full-time or part-time working student and design a job description and personnel specification for it, stating the competencies required.

3. In small groups, develop a job description and personnel specification for the president of your college's students' association. Compare them with the others developed in your class and agree on a job description and personnel specification that satisfies you all.

   Prepare an interview outline and a few key questions. In groups of three, conduct an interview for the position with one person being the interviewer, another the candidate and a third the observer/coach. The candidates should be themselves. The candidate and observer/coach should give feedback to the inter-viewer on what they did well and

how they could improve. Then switch roles and interview again. Each person in your group should play each role at least once. If you wish, candidates can fill out the sample application in Figure 15.1 to provide the interviewer with some initial information before the interview begins.

   Based on this exercise, develop a list of 'do's' and 'don'ts' for interviewers with your entire class.

4. Conduct a panel interview for the job of the president of the students' association as described in activity 2 above.

5. Form into groups of three with an interviewer, an observer/coach and a person to role-play Ralph Lewis from Case Study 15.2 on page 487. Take turns in each of these roles as described in activity 2 above, and interview Ralph Lewis for the job of manager of the Vancetown outlet.

6. Referring to Box 1.6 on page 16, randomly divide and assign the skills and attributes to class members. Develop questions to draw out and assess an interviewee's competencies in the skills and attributes you have been assigned. Then in pairs or threes, test these questions out on each other. How effective are they? How can you improve them?

7. Interview someone with special needs (e.g. someone with a non-English-speaking background, a young person entering paid employment for the first time, or a person with a disability) in your organisation or college. Find out how their supervisor was able to help them adjust and fit in to the organisation. Could anything else have been done that would have helped? Discuss your findings in class.

Sam's Recruitment Problem

After lengthy discussions with his manager, Sam Tomayko was convinced that success in staff selection depended upon a supervisor's skills in recruitment. As Sam became more aware of the need to choose replacement staff carefully, he began to look at his existing employees to determine what made them successful. Choosing the best of them, Sam suggested that they ask their friends to apply for positions he knew would soon be vacant.

This approach seemed to be successful as Sam received word from a number of prospective applicants. He then interviewed those who appeared to have the experience and personal qualities needed.

He applied his own ideas about the way interviews should be conducted. He usually fitted them into the normal day's activity, with the telephone ringing constantly and people dropping into the office for advice, to leave messages or even to have Sam make one of his 'on-the-spot' decisions. Between these interruptions, Sam would carry out the interview, dominating the time available by talking about the job, the opportunities in the organisation and his own impressions of what made a successful applicant.

Throughout the interview, he made notes and symbols on the applicant's form. He also liked to make a decision as to whether the applicant had the job before the interview was over so he could let them know on the spot. This saved tedious letter writing.

Then Sam found himself being called to his manager's office to discuss the personnel problems developing in his department. It seemed that new recruits were not suitably qualified for their jobs, while applicants who were known to have the necessary skills had been informed at their interviews that they were not the type of employee the organisation was seeking or that the job would not suit them or their background.

Sam's manager decided to work out an action plan whereby Sam would develop his skills in recruitment and selection. They sat down to decide together what to include and how it could best be covered.

Questions

1   Was Sam's manager wasting her time? Why, or why not?
2   What were the specific problems with Sam's interviewing technique?
3   How would you explain to Sam the way a selection decision should be reached?
4   What topics should be included in the action plan to develop Sam's skills? How would you suggest they be covered (e.g. through reading books, attending evening classes, coaching from the HRM manager, role playing)?

CASE STUDY 15.2

East-West Oil

The East-West Oil Company is a growing company with a progressive management team. Brian Vawn is in charge of the company's retail outlets (service stations). In general, the company tries to locate a service station in towns with a population of 15 000 or more, but location also depends on competition, a suitable site and business potential.

Each of East-West's service stations is leased to a local manager who operates within broad company guidelines and minimum direct supervision. Every station is required to sell petrol, oil, tyres, batteries and related products. Additional products can be sold and many stations carry lines such as soft drinks, grocery items, confectionery and 'fast food'. With company encouragement, most stations operate a service centre where minor car repairs are carried out. Most of these centres, for example, give motor tune-ups, correct minor electrical troubles, reline brakes, and balance and align wheels.

The manager of the Vancetown station has notified Brian Vawn that he will be giving up his lease. Located in an area with a population of 88 000, this is one of East-West's most profitable and best equipped stations. Situated at the intersection of two main highways, the station attracts a great deal of passing, as well as local, trade.

The station has eight pumps and operates two wash pits, two lubrication bays and a large service centre employing four full-time mechanics. With the exception of the service centre, the station is open 24 hours a day. In the last ten years, turnover has climbed steadily.

Finding the right person to replace the station manager has been difficult, but Vawn is encouraged by the background and record of one applicant, Ralph Lewis. Lewis is a first-rate motor mechanic who has been employed for the past 12 years with a local transport firm. He has a good record with that company and at present is in charge of a fleet of 12 trucks. He has also worked as a transmission mechanic, a tune-up specialist and a front-end expert.

Questions

1 On the basis of the above information, develop a brief job description and personnel specification for the vacancy.
2 If you were interviewing Ralph Lewis, what facts would you need to know to make a decision about hiring him?
3 Prepare an interview outline showing several behavioural questions to be used at each stage of the interview.

Answers to Rapid Review questions

1. T   2. T   3. T   4. T   5. F   6. F   7. T   8. T   9. F   10. F   11. T   12. F   13. F
14. F   15. F   16. T   17. F   18. F   19. T   20. F   21. T

CHAPTER 16

TRAINING EMPLOYEES

Off to a great start!

Khee Moon had just had his final monthly performance review with his supervisor. It was his third and last one for another 12 months. Each month, since he had joined the company, he and his supervisor had met to review his progress against the training plan, talk about any areas needing improvement (fortunately, there had been only one, a technical matter he had difficulty grasping initially). His supervisor also asked him how he was fitting in, whether the job was meeting his expectations, and so on, each time they met.

At this last meeting, she had also asked him to tell her about an off-the-job training course he had attended. It had been on *Crystal Clear Communication* and she wanted him to tell her what he had found most interesting, what he had found most useful and how he planned to apply what he had learned on the job. She seemed pleased with his report, because she asked him to tell the others in the team about what he had learned and how they could all use it at their next team meeting.

She also told him about another course that was coming up. This one was on health and safety, focusing on emergency procedures. She explained that this was an important one to attend because everyone was responsible for knowing what to do in the event of an emergency. She outlined what he could expect to learn and set a time with him to go over what he'd learned the week following the course.

Khee Moon felt these discussions had given him the opportunity to get to know his supervisor a bit better and understand how she worked. He also found them quite motivating in the sense that they made him feel as if he really 'did matter'.

His job training had progressed quite well, to the point where his supervisor felt he would easily reach experienced worker standards within six months. They concluded the meeting by reviewing the job training he still needed to complete.

OVERVIEW

Training is an important part of every supervisor's job. New recruits, transfers, people who need to improve their skills—the need for training will never disappear from a supervisor's workload. In this chapter you will find out how to carry out this important function effectively to boost your work group's morale and multiply your section's efficiency.

- Can you state the benefits of effective training?
- Do you know what the trend towards competency-based training is about and how it differs from 'traditional' training?
- Are training courses and programs the only way to train or are there alternatives? When should you use them?
- When should training be done away from the job and when should it be done 'on the job'?
- Can you tell when someone needs training?

- Can you recognise and cater for individual learning styles so that people learn easily?
- Can you plan a training program for the individuals in your department?
- Can you ensure your employees receive the training they need, and do you know what to do to support that training?
- Can you provide quality training yourself when necessary?
- Do you know how to assess the effectiveness of training?
- Do you know the importance of keeping your own training up to date?

THE ADVANTAGES OF TRAINING

Not everyone's performance is perfect all the time in every aspect. Taking steps to see that performance is consistently as good as it can be is an important part of a supervisor's job. Organisations that invest in training and learning are regularly shown to have a healthier bottom line and better all-around performance. For example, a US study called the 1997 Human Performance Practices Survey found that organisations that invested an average of US$900 per employee on professional development outperformed organisations that invested an average of US$275 per employee. They achieved:

- 57% higher net sales per employee;
- 37% higher gross profit per employee; and
- a 20% higher ratio in market-to-book values.

THE **BIG** PICTURE

Systematic job training was first introduced during World War II when large numbers of new factory workers needed to be trained to replace the experienced tradespeople who had gone off to war. Systematic training helped many factories to reduce the length of the training period from four years to 12–18 months without any loss to quality or speed.

Systematic training shortens the learning period and reduces the length of time it takes new employees to reach what is known as *experienced worker standard*. This saves time and money and cuts down on waste. It also reduces the unit cost of your goods or services and can increase quality.

Training can also improve the job performance of employees in their current jobs and increase their skills and ability to take on other jobs. It can reduce accidents, minimise customer complaints and update skills. It can show people more efficient ways of doing the job and better ways of working together. Training in correct and safe work methods also develops proper attitudes towards safety and helps people understand their duties and responsibilities and the reasons for them. As an investment in the future, training makes sense.

Training is not just about providing, updating or upgrading technical skills. There are also the all-important people skills. The Karpin Report (see Chapter 1) identifies training in interpersonal skills as one of the most needed types of training in Australia. It can improve employees' ability to work cooperatively with others, communicate clearly and be part of a high-performing team. People-skills training at all levels is a significant factor in achieving organisational excellence.

Training also shows employees that you are concerned about them and their welfare. It helps to meet people's needs for recognition and self-development (see Chapter 21). Employees develop new skills and polish existing skills. Training adds to people's abilities, enhances their earning ability and job interest, and makes them more valuable to the organisation. This boosts morale. Good training is often reflected in indicators of employee satisfaction such as timekeeping, absenteeism and turnover. Organisations that develop a reputation for providing good training are able to attract and retain the best employees.

Training, then, is a critical workplace issue and should be regarded as a core business expense, not something to do only in the 'good times'. Our economic future depends on a

---

THE **BIG** PICTURE

According to Thomas A. Stewart in *Intellectual Capital: The New Wealth of Organisations*, a 10% increase in the educational level of the workforce increases productivity 8.6%. Compare this with a 10% increase in plant and equipment values, which yields a 3.4% increase in productivity. Which would you invest in?

THE **BIG** PICTURE

Do you think training is expensive? Think about how much it would cost *not* to train!

The *1995 Australian Workplace Industrial Relations Survey* found that 72% of larger workplaces provide training while only 51% of smaller workplaces offer training. This means the majority of Australian employees, who work in smaller organisations, may be missing out on training.

skilled and adaptable workforce. Training is a means of improving our country's competitive standing and our organisations' competitive edge.

> 'How central is training to the role of all forms of human endeavour? Every time we watch an athlete win a gold medal for performing some amazing feat, or breathe a sigh of relief when someone we know recovers from an operation, or wonder how builders can build buildings with everything working and in the right place, or enjoy a meal in a restaurant, or buy a product—we are experiencing the results of training.'
>
> Annie Macnab
> Centre for Management Studies, Central TAFE, WA

The supervisor's role in supporting learning

Everyone needs training at times. People who are new to your department and the organisation need both induction and job training. Experienced workers often need training to update their skills and knowledge or to improve their current performance standards. Modern organisations are continually changing methods and technology. Each change means that additional training must be provided to ensure that employees are able to cope with the new circumstances. People who transfer into your department also need training on the jobs they will be doing.

Your involvement in training is therefore an ongoing process. The report of the Australian Mission on Management Skills took particular note of the key role played by line managers in training employees.

The best training in the world won't be effective unless you support it. This applies to both on-the-job training and off-the-job training. If you send employees in your section away on a training course, you still have a responsibility to make the training effective. The two things that most influence the effectiveness of training are under the control of supervisors: what the supervisor does before and after the training is critical.

Before the training, set some time aside to discuss it with the employee. What will the training cover? What do you expect the employee to learn? How do you expect them to use it on the job?

After the training, sit down and discuss it with the employee. Show some interest. What did they learn? How do they plan to use it? How can they share what they have learned with others? Support and encourage employees to use their newly learned skills, whether they are technical skills or people skills. Show that you have noticed when employees use their newly acquired skills. If you fail to do this, employees will think using their new skills is not important. They will stop using them and go back to their old ways of doing things. Their time and effort, and the organisation's investment, will have been wasted. Don't ignore this essential aspect of support for training.

BEST PRACTICE TRAINING

Most organisations spend less money and train fewer people than the pace-setting organisations. Nevertheless, these forward-looking organisations provide us with a benchmark to measure ourselves against and perhaps aspire to. How much do leading-edge organisations spend on training? Up to 10% of payroll. They also train a larger percentage of employees and have more trainers. They tend to make greater use of training technology such as interactive CD-ROMs and video, multimedia, intranets and electronic performance support systems. They make greater use of innovative training practices such as mentoring, coaching, 360-degree reviews and individual development plans, and provide more training supports such as training resource centres, training information systems and train-the-trainer courses. They empower employees through self-directed teams, employee access to key information and employee participation. They reward their employees through profit sharing, stock ownership plans, team-based pay and incentives.

The Human Performance Practices Survey (HPPS) cited above shows a solid relationship between an organisation's performance and its learning and development practices. It also found that about 25% of leading-edge organisations' training is to update employees' job-specific technical and computer skills. They also provide a lot of product and service training and teamworking training. Other training includes induction training and training in management and supervisory skills.

Most training is still classroom-based and instructor-led, although the more a company uses competency based training and high-performance work practices, the more likely it is to use innovative training practices such as learning technologies and self-paced learning. The HPPS and a US Bureau of Labor Statistics survey found out what types of courses are being offered and the percentage of organisations offering them; the summary is shown in Box 16.1.

Unfortunately, comparable Australian figures are unavailable. However, we know from the 1995 Australian Workplace Industrial Relations Survey and the 1997 Small Business Changes at Work survey that 78% of public sector and 64% of private sector organisations provide formal training. We also know that:
- 68% of managers;
- 60% of paraprofessionals;
- 47% of professionals;
- 46% of plant and machinery operators and drivers;
- 44% of sales and personal service workers;
- 41% of tradespersons;
- 31% of clerks; and
- 30% of labourers and related workers

were offered off-the-job or classroom training. Full-time and part-time employees are equally likely to receive training and young employees receive more training than other categories of employees.

How does your organisation measure up?

THE **BIG** PICTURE

Best practice training is firmly focused on the needs of the organisation, on outcomes and on performance. It is supported and followed up by management. How do you rate your organisation against best practice enterprises? What examples can you cite to support your rating?

BOX 16.1 TYPES OF COURSES

- **Induction**, e.g. information about the organisation and its operations, mission, functions, policies, compensation, benefits, work requirements and standards, rules, safe working habits; offered by 94%.
- **Management and supervisory skills**, e.g. conducting performance appraisals, implementing regulations and policies, managing projects and processes, planning, budgeting; offered by 93%.
- **Computer literacy and applications**, e.g. how to use computer software, spreadsheets, databases and graphics, both off-the-shelf and company-specific; offered by 91%.
- **Job specific technical skills**, e.g. procedures, technology, service delivery, machinery; offered by 88%.
- **Occupational safety and compliance**, e.g. safety hazards, procedures, regulations; offered by 84%.
- **Teams**, e.g. individual and group training to improve communication, collaboration and teamwork, conflict resolution, decision making; offered by 77%.
- **Quality, competition and business practices**, e.g. TQM, business process re-engineering, benchmarking, business fundamentals; offered by 76%.
- **Customer service**, e.g. maintaining and improving customer relations, call centre operations; offered by 76%.
- **Awareness**, e.g. EEO, affirmative action, workplace diversity, sexual harassment, AIDS; offered by 74%.
- **Professional skills**, e.g. specialised knowledge and applications in accounting, engineering, manufacturing, computer science, information systems management, law, consulting; offered by 73%.
- **Product knowledge**, e.g. product specifications, repair, upgrading, maintenance for sales and service professionals; offered by 70%.
- **Executive development**, e.g. performance management, strategic planning, creativity, global marketing; offered by 63%.
- **Sales training**, e.g. the attitudes, skills and habits needed to influence the purchasing decisions of prospects and customers for franchises, dealers and salespeople; offered by 53%.
- **Basic skills**, e.g. remedial training in literacy, reading comprehension, maths and English as a second language; offered by 50%.

COMPETENCY-BASED TRAINING

Although it has been around for a long time, we have seen a strong move towards **competency-based training** (CBT) in the last decade. The shift to CBT has profound implications, moving us away from a view of training in terms of *time spent learning* to training based on *outcomes*.

A lot of people are still confused about CBT, though. This is largely because of the terminology, or 'jargon', involved in CBT (discussed below) and the highly procedural approach that must be used for CBT to work satisfactorily.

A **competency** is the ability to perform an activity to the standard expected in a job context. Job-holders are assessed as competent when they can demonstrate that they have the required skills. A competency states exactly what is to be done, to what standard and under what conditions. Competency includes:

- the ability to perform individual tasks (*task skills*);
- the ability to manage a number of different tasks within a job *(task management skills)*;
- the ability to respond to irregularities and breakdowns in a routine (*contingency management skills*); and
- the ability to deal with the responsibilities and expectations of the work environment (*job and role environment skills*), including working with others.

The word 'skills' brings us to our first main confusion regarding CBT. Psychologists have traditionally divided human behaviour into three groups, described as *cognitive, psychomotor* and *affective* behaviours (or knowledge, skills and attitudes). Based on this, 'skills' has come to mean manual skills for many people. However, skills as used for competency purposes means more than this. For example:

- The ability to multiply two three-digit numbers together is a *knowledge skill*.
- Hammering a nail into a piece of wood is a *manual skill*.
- Accepting the need to arrive at work on time is an *attitudinal skill*.
- Driving a car legally to a destination on time in heavy traffic combines knowledge, manual and attitudinal competencies.

Expanding the term 'skill' in this way allows us to talk about *knowledge, manual* and *attitudinal* skills. It also allows us to talk about a great variety of skills we use in our daily lives—for example, communication skills, interpersonal skills, study skills and thinking skills.

Traditional training versus competency-based training

Let's examine competency-based training by contrasting it with traditional training. Most of us have experienced *traditional training* at school (although many progressive schools are now beginning to use CBT). With traditional training, we (the trainee or student) spend a fixed period of time undergoing training that follows a course curriculum. Everyone spends the same amount of time studying the same subject. The training is *content-based*. The teacher or trainer directs or controls the class.

We join our class or course with learning needs different to everyone else, with our own learning styles and our own personal issues. Yet we go through the same training or teaching content as everyone else. We might get sick or lose concentration or, for other reasons, miss some of the training. At the end of the training period, we might 'pass'; we might not, or we might just scrape through. *The outcome of traditional training varies.*

Most of us also experienced *competency-based training* when we learned to drive a car. We studied road laws and test examples and then passed a competency test to show we knew the rules of the road. In South Australia, we had to achieve a 60% pass or better on Part A of this test and 100% on Part B. We could take as long as we needed to do this. Once we

BOX 16.2

THE MAIN DIFFERENCES BETWEEN
TRADITIONAL TRAINING AND CBT

···

Traditional training	*Competency-based training*
■ time is fixed	■ time is variable
■ outcome is variable	■ outcome is fixed
■ trainer/teacher is in control	■ learner is in control
■ content-based	■ skills-based
■ time-based	■ performance-based
■ group-paced	■ individual-paced
■ group needs	■ individual needs
■ delayed feedback	■ immediate feedback
■ textbook and workbook based	■ modules and media based
■ limited field experience	■ learning in the field
■ lectures, demonstrations	■ assistance of a resource person
■ general objectives	■ specific objectives
■ subjective criteria	■ objective criteria
■ final grades	■ learner competence

could do it, we could get a learner's permit and learn to drive a car. We got our licence when we could demonstrate the required competency by driving the car on a public highway under test conditions without losing more than eight demerit points. It was clear *what* we had to do and *how well* we had to do it. Learning took as long as we needed in order to demonstrate our competency.

With CBT, the *training time is variable*: the time that we take to learn a certain skill is different from the length of time others take to learn it because we're all different. Our training, or learning, will continue until we can demonstrate a specific competency—that is, that we have learned to do something to a specific standard under certain conditions.

This means that the *outcome* of training, not its duration, is fixed. Training continues until the standard is achieved. We, the learner, control the training. We learn for as long as it takes for us to achieve the predetermined performance standards, or competency. We can study and practise as much or as little as we need to. We can study when we are able and in the way that suits us best.

Everyone has different learning needs and learns in different ways. We can select from a variety of methods to help us learn. These include self-directed learning, projects and individual learning such as reading, watching a video, learning from an interactive CD-ROM or interviewing an expert.

'Training is for cats and dogs.
People learn.'

Dick Dusseldorp, founder of Lend Lease

Recognition of prior learning

We all have different life experiences and begin training with varying levels of skills. CBT recognises this. Recognition of prior learning (RPL) allows us to 'fast track' through some training for skills we already possess. We don't need to go through each training module, or all of any one module. If we can prove a competency by performing the task to the required standard under the specified conditions, we can receive credit for what we already know and can do and move on to other areas of training where we need to develop our skills further.

Assessing competency

Assessors are people who have been trained to determine accurately whether we have displayed a competency. The person who determined whether you were able to drive a car well enough to obtain your driving licence was an assessor. Your college teacher who assesses your papers to determine how well you meet the competency criteria set down in the relevant training module is also an assessor. In industry, supervisors are often assessors. To assess a person's competency, an assessor might just watch a person work or review a project they have completed.

Costs and benefits of CBT

Organisations benefit from CBT's fixed outcomes: guaranteed minimum standards of performance. Competencies are identified and written down. Everyone knows what they are expected to be able to do and how they will be expected to 'prove' that they can do it.

People who know the job in question usually develop *units* and *elements of competence, performance criteria* and the *range of variables* through a thorough **job analysis** (see Chapter 15). It can take a long time to get these right, but the time taken pays off. Trainers can use this information to design training; assessors can use it to determine people's competence; job-holders can use it to determine their level of skills and decide whether they need further training; careers guidance teachers can advise students on careers based on their interests and aptitudes.

The major drawback of CBT is the cost (time, people, money) of getting the system up and running. Some critics of CBT say it has a narrow focus. CBT trains people to demonstrate specific skills in a particular environment, while education attempts to develop a range of knowledge and skills and the ability to learn. Education develops the 'whole person' and can teach us to think and apply our knowledge in a variety of situations.

Other critics believe that CBT is best applied to specific manual and mechanical occupations and point to the difficulties in applying it to more complex occupations such as the law, psychology, engineering or architecture. Attitudinal and knowledge competencies can be difficult to 'pin down'.

Understanding the jargon

Many *units of competence* make up an occupation (plumber, flight attendant, machine operator, waiter, supervisor). Units of competence are broken down into *elements of competence*. These elements are the building blocks of related sets of skills. Box 16.3 shows some units and elements of competence for supervisors, or front-line managers. The units have been grouped into 'themes'. These competencies were developed by the Australian National Training Authority and endorsed by the Standards and Curriculum Council in June 1996.

Performance criteria set the standard to which each element of competence must be carried out. Since performance criteria assess the quality of performance, they must be objective. To be able to do something 'well' is too vague. The standards required need to be

BOX 16.3 UNITS AND ELEMENTS OF COMPETENCE FOR FRONT-LINE MANAGERS

Theme	Units of competence	Elements of competence
Leading by example	1. Manage personal work priorities	1.1 Manage self 1.2 Set and meet own work priorities 1.3 Develop and maintain professional competence
	2. Provide leadership in the workplace	2.1 Model high standards of management performance 2.2 Enhance the organisation's image 2.3 Influence individuals and teams positively 2.4 Make informed choices
Leading, coaching, facilitating and empowering others	3. Establish and manage effective workplace relationships	3.1 Gather, convey and receive information and ideas 3.2 Develop trust and confidence 3.3 Build and maintain networks and relationships 3.4 Manage difficulties to achieve positive outcomes
	4. Participate in, lead and facilitate work teams	4.1 Participate in team planning 4.2 Develop team commitment and cooperation 4.3 Manage and develop team performance 4.4 Participate in, and facilitate, the work team/group
Creating best practice	5. Manage operations to achieve planned outcomes	5.1 Plan resource use to achieve profit/productivity targets 5.2 Acquire resources to achieve operational plan 5.3 Monitor operational performance 5.4 Monitor resource usage
	6. Manage workplace information	6.1 Identify information needs 6.2 Collect, analyse and report information 6.3 Use management information systems 6.4 Prepare business plans/budgets 6.5 Prepare resource proposals
	7. Manage quality customer service	7.1 Plan to meet internal service and external customer requirements 7.2 Ensure delivery of quality products/services 7.3 Monitor, adjust and report customer service
	8. Develop and maintain a safe workplace and environment	8.1 Access and share legislation, codes and standards 8.2 Plan and implement safety requirements 8.3 Monitor, adjust and report safety performance 8.4 Investigate and report non-conformance
	9. Implement and monitor continuous improvement systems and processes	9.1 Implement continuous improvement systems and processes 9.2 Monitor, adjust and report performance 9.3 Consolidate opportunities for further improvement
Creating an innovative culture	10. Facilitate and capitalise on change and innovation	10.1 Participate in planning the introduction of change 10.2 Develop creative and flexible approaches and solutions 10.3 Manage emerging challenges and opportunities
	11. Contribute to the development of a workplace learning environment	11.1 Create learning opportunities 11.2 Facilitate and promote learning 11.3 Monitor and improve learning effectiveness

described. Box 16.4 shows some performance criteria for the first two competence elements of front-line managers.

A *range of variables* states the conditions under which a skill is to be performed. These tell us the breadth and depth of both the competency and the training that must be provided. It is one thing to do a job well under perfect conditions and another to do it well under difficult conditions. Box 16.5 shows some of the ranges of variables for the first element of competency for front-line managers at *Australian Standards Framework* (ASF) level 3. This is the lowest of three supervisory levels.

BOX 16.4 EXAMPLES OF PERFORMANCE CRITERIA ••

Element of competence	Performance criteria
1.1 Manage self	a. Personal qualities and performance serve as a role model in the workplace.
	b. Personal goals and plans reflect the organisation's plans, and personal roles, responsibilities and accountabilities.
	c. Action is taken to achieve and extend personal goals.
	d. Consistent personal performance is maintained in varying work conditions and contexts.
1.2 Set and meet own work priorities	a. Competing demands are prioritised to achieve personal, team and organisation goals and objectives.
	b. Technology is used efficiently and effectively to manage work priorities and commitments.

BOX 16.5 EXAMPLES OF RANGES OF VARIABLES •••

Element	Range of variables
1.1 Manage self	At ASF level 3, front-line management will normally be engaged in a workplace context in which they;
	• have some autonomy for operation;
	• work under limited guidance;
	• may have a broad guidance and autonomy if working in teams;
	• have responsibility for others;
	• may have team coordination responsibilities;
	• apply a broad range of skills to a range of tasks/roles;
	• operate in a variety of workplace contexts;
	• are involved in some complexity in the choice of actions;
	• use competencies within routines, methods and procedures; and
	• use some discretion and judgment in using resources, services and processes to achieve outcomes within time constraints.

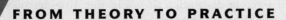

FROM THEORY TO PRACTICE

BHP introduced competency-based training for supervisors in its Long Products Division. A national team developed supervisory competencies. They then designed performance criteria and ranges of variables for each element of competence. Based on these, they developed a curriculum and designed a series of learning modules to assist supervisors develop the required competencies. To support the modules, they developed learning activities such as undertaking projects, attending workshops, learning from videos, working through self-paced study guides, joining study groups and reading selected texts and articles. A senior trainer coordinates a support system of mentors, coaches and assessors at each work site.

Supervisors meet with a coach to identify their training needs. They answer a series of questions to pinpoint skills and knowledge gaps. Based on how they answer these questions, the supervisor and coach design the supervisor's learning program, selecting modules and learning activities best suited to each individual supervisor.

Within a generous time limit, supervisors can take as long as they need to complete each module. Their competency is assessed through a series of 'assessable tasks'. When supervisors have completed enough modules, they are awarded a nationally recognised Certificate or Diploma in first-line management.

Getting started with CBT

We need the commitment and support of all the interest groups before CBT can be successfully introduced. These include the relevant trade unions and management, as well as the employees themselves.

Some organisations are able to use the CBT system set up by their industry body. The government has established *Industry Training Boards* (ITBs) to formulate competencies for each industry. Other organisations develop their own system. As mentioned above, this takes a lot of time and effort.

First, a team is formed and trained to develop CBT systems. Then they agree on the specific jobs and tasks they will start with. From there, they identify the specific *competencies* required for these tasks and then the *elements* that make them up. For example, some of the elements in driving a car are reversing, parking, three-point turns and hill starts. Then they agree on the *performance criteria* and conditions under which these competencies can be measured. The *range of variables* describes the workplace conditions under which the task is to be performed. The team then verifies the competencies and develops learning methods. Finally, they run a pilot to make sure they are on the right track and put supporting mechanisms in place: coaches, assessors, trainers and coordinators. Then they fine-tune the whole system.

Competencies in job descriptions and training

Competency statements are also useful ways to write position, or job, descriptions. Describing job responsibilities and activities as competencies has the advantage of providing a consistent framework of language throughout an organisation and a basis for job grading and remuneration. The partial position description shown in Box 16.6 describes a retail salesperson's customer service responsibilities in competency terms.

The job-holder and supervisor can use the job description to conduct a training needs analysis by comparing existing skills with skills required. They can prepare the training plan by referring to the training courses available for various competencies. The close link between on-the-job performance and off-the-job training is clear, which encourages individual skills development. Both the organisation and individual job-holders benefit.

BOX 16.6 CUSTOMER SERVICE PORTION OF A RETAIL SALESPERSON'S JOB DESCRIPTION

Competency unit	Competency element	Key tasks/responsibilities
Customer service	Greets customers	Greets/acknowledges customers promptly and politely whether face-to-face, by phone, or other means of communication
		Puts customers at ease by making them feel welcome
	Answers telephone	Answers the telephone politely and efficiently
		Directs calls to the appropriate people
		Deals with messages promptly
	Listens	Listens carefully to customer needs/requirements
		Observes both product/service and personal needs
		Checks understanding of customers' needs
	Questions	Asks questions to clarify needs/requirements
		Uses open and closed questions to determine needs without intimidating customers
	Provides and explains information	Offers information and explanations about product and service, responding to customer needs
	Empathises	Demonstrates an understanding of the customer's situation
		Always offers the product/service solutions that are best suited to the customer
	Acts with honesty	Provides accurate, complete and reliable information/recommendations that suit the customer's best interests

TYPES OF TRAINING

There are many ways to train. The choice depends on how much time and money are available, the nature of training needed and the number of people to be trained. Most organisations, however, use a combination of five main formal methods to train their employees: on-the-job training, classroom training, coaching, self-paced training and off-the-job training. Action learning is a sophisticated training method that is popular in many organisations.

On-the-job training

Supervisors usually provide on-the-job training at a person's workplace or workstation. In large departments where there might be several trainees, supervisors may delegate this duty, for instance, to a 'cobber'. Whoever carries out on-the-job training should be trained to break a job down, teach it following the four-step process and encourage trainees, as described later in this chapter.

On-the-job training is best suited to teaching specific job-related and technical skills requiring less than two or three weeks' training. If the training period needs to be longer, classroom training (see below) is normally provided.

Other ways to train people on-the-job are through special assignments and secondments, job rotation, joining committees (e.g. a health and safety committee) or attending meetings. Provided you supervise on-the-job training carefully (as discussed above), it can be a very effective and inexpensive way to develop people's skills.

Classroom training

Classroom training is used most frequently where a number of employees—such as machine operators, word processor operators, bank tellers, technical salespeople, some customer service personnel (e.g. retail salespeople and telephone support staff), and so on—need to be trained in the technical aspects of their job, and when the training period required exceeds three weeks. This form of training takes place away from the job in a classroom set aside and equipped for training. Work conditions are duplicated as much as possible, with machines and other equipment set up as needed. As with all forms of off-the-job training, classroom training allows people to make their mistakes and learn in a 'safe' environment, away from customers and where their mistakes won't reflect badly on themselves or their organisation.

Coaching

Often, one person can help another to learn, develop their skills and improve their performance. This can take several forms: coaching, mentoring, close supervision, working with a more experienced person or meeting with selected professionals (e.g. accountants, MIS specialists). These people can open doors to new information or further develop the skills and knowledge an employee already has. The coach and employee usually meet several times and the emphasis is on building the employee's skills. This may be done by providing information, suggesting books to read, other people to talk to or courses to attend, or just conversing and asking questions to help the employee think things through.

As with any other form of training, you can coach people to improve their existing job duties or to gain new or delegated tasks or knowledge. Aim your coaching efforts at an identified need.

Self-paced training

In the aftermath of downsizing, many organisations are finding it difficult to release employees for blocks of training. Self-paced training is an increasingly popular remedy to this difficulty. People can learn on their own from specially designed learning modules, workbooks and study guides; also useful are activities such as reading books, periodicals and trade publications, and working with interactive CD-ROMs and audiovisual training programs and videos.

Supervisors can help people to learn by acting as positive role models. Similarly, you can identify role models for yourself, people who do things well, and learn by emulating them. Networking is another good way to increase your learning opportunities.

Off-the-job training

Off-the-job training is most frequently used for developing conceptual skills and people skills, such as problem solving, planning, decision making, leadership, performance management and communication skills. It can also extend employees' technical understanding of aspects of their job.

Parts of induction programs may take place off the job, but we tend to think of off-the-job training in connection with in-depth knowledge that provides an understanding of principles and how to apply them in practice.

Off-the-job training can be residential, in-house or off-site. It can last for one day to two or more weeks. It can be only for employees of a particular organisation or employees can attend courses open to the public. Both allow participants to share and learn from each other's experiences as well as from their course leader. Examples of off-the-job training include:

- night-school courses—for instance, on supervision;
- English as a second language courses;
- post-trade training;
- day-release for tertiary studies;
- public or in-house seminars on specific topics such as health and safety or employment legislation which last one day or more;
- public or in-house workshops on topics such as computer applications or appreciation, time management, or sales and negotiation skills;

THE **BIG** PICTURE

Take responsibility for your own training and development. Despite the recommendations of the Karpin Report, organisations are tending to provide only as much training as they 'have to' to keep employees' skills up to date. This usually means on-the-job skills training. Personal and management development is increasingly left to each employee to arrange.

What steps are you taking to identify and learn the personal and management skills you need to stay ahead of the crowd?

- public or in-house management and supervisory development programs, which typically last from two to five or more days and cover a range of management skills;
- conferences and lectures organised for the public or by professional bodies for their members and guests;
- two to three day in-house team-building workshops;
- one to two day public or in-house seminars and workshops on interpersonal skills such as communication skills, conflict resolution or assertiveness; and
- satellite or video conferences, which are good for reaching large numbers of people dispersed geographically.

A variety of teaching and learning techniques are used in off-the-job training. Some of the more commonly used training methods include short lectures and experiential techniques such as case studies, specially designed 'games' and 'learning experiences', role playing, group discussions, simulation and practice of the techniques and concepts being taught based on trainees' job and real-life issues.

Training can also combine off-the-job and on-the-job elements. Plant visits, study tours and secondments to other organisations fall into this category. Plant visits can open trainees' eyes to other ways of doing things and extend their general knowledge. Study tours and secondments can be time-consuming and expensive, so they need to target learning needs carefully and be well followed up.

Case studies

Case studies might involve the use of a realistic situation or problem that illustrates a topic or theory and shows why and how it can be used in real life. They are a good way of learning to apply skills to topics such as leadership, negotiation, problem solving, project management and introducing change.

'Games' and learning experiences

Many trainers provide 'games' and other learning experiences to extend trainees' skills, knowledge and experience. On the surface, they may seem to have nothing to do with the trainees' jobs. However, with carefully guided discussions after the experience, trainees can learn about themselves and each other, how to work in groups to solve problems or achieve a goal, how to improve their own work style, or develop useful working procedures. Outdoor training and many indoor and outdoor team-building activities make extensive use of such 'games' and learning experiences.

Role plays

Role plays are also used extensively in off-the-job training. Two or more trainees act out a situation—for example, a recruitment or performance counselling interview—which has been described to them. The trainer may design the role play or the trainees themselves might 'set the scene' based on their own experience or current real-life situations. Role plays allow people to apply theory and practise skills in a 'safe' environment where they can get constructive feedback from observers and other role players. Sometimes, a role play is repeated two or three times to allow trainees to refine their skills based on feedback they've received. Sometimes, roles are reversed so that the 'supervisor' plays the 'employee' and vice versa. This helps to increase empathy for the other's point of view.

Group discussions

Discussions are another good way of learning. We all have a great deal of knowledge and experience to share, and discussions, when led by a skilful trainer, are excellent ways to help trainees consider other viewpoints, share experiences and learn from each other.

Simulation

Also used in classroom training, simulations allow trainees to perform a task under 'virtual' conditions. For example, a machine that simulates driving conditions can test and improve your driving reflexes and skills through lifelike practice. Flight simulator programs not only provide home entertainment, they are also used to train real pilots. Many organisations are investing in CD-ROM simulation training for their staff, particularly if they have large numbers of trainees or if the training required is very technical or sophisticated.

Business games are another example of simulation. A computer simulates market conditions, while trainees operate the business and make decisions about such key things as how much to buy, what the selling price should be and how much money to spend on advertising and new product development.

With role plays, case studies, simulations, 'games' and learning experiences, we learn from *doing*, rather than 'talking about' something. This usually makes learning quicker, more enjoyable and longer lasting.

Hi-tech training

Many production houses produce training videos and CD-ROM training for use in classrooms and off-the-job training situations, with small groups and for individual self-paced study. Fortunately, there is an ever-increasing number of Australian- and New Zealand-produced videos and CD-ROMs on the market, which are generally more acceptable than overseas productions to audiences 'down under'. If you work for a large organisation, contact your training or HR department; they may have a library that you could draw on for your own personal development and that of your work team.

Some large organisations also produce their own training videos. These may present general information—for instance, for induction or to introduce a new corporate strategy, vision or policy—or they may be technical in nature, aimed at either skills or knowledge development.

Some sophisticated interactive CD-ROM training packages, using **fuzzy logic** and realistic scenarios, put the learner in the 'hot seat' and provide 'hands-on' virtual practice in a range of technical and interpersonal skills (e.g. supervision, project management and conflict management). People can learn in a situation that is nearly 'live' without their mistakes having serious repercussions. Some companies are producing interactive videos, too.

Private training organisations and tertiary educational institutions are also beginning to offer training online, over the Internet. Many take advantage of interactive capabilities for learning and assessment and some provide dedicated chat rooms with a tutor available at specified times. (In fact, this book has a web site where students, teachers, invited experts and others can interact with each other and find out more information.)

Although videos and CD-ROMs and other hi-tech training methods can be expensive, they have advantages. They are transportable and flexible: small groups and even individuals can be trained economically. Also, people learn at different rates, and they can review and repeat learning points on videos or CD-ROMs in a way that is not possible with classroom training.

Their main drawback is that the viewer/learner can become passive: lean back, get comfortable and mentally 'switch off'. If this happens, learning is unlikely to take place. Good training videos are designed to involve the learner and stimulate thinking throughout the video as well as after viewing, and the best CD-ROMs are fully interactive.

To be cost-effective, this type of training must be used, not shelved; this requires an effective administration system, publicity to let people know that videos are available and monitoring to ensure they are used effectively.

Action learning

Action learning uses team projects to provide learning opportunities and, at the same time, improve the organisation's performance. A team works to resolve real workplace problems and issues and learn at the same time. Trainers and other expert resources support learners throughout the life of a project, which typically lasts six to 12 months. Team members are selected, based not only on what they can bring to the team but also on their learning needs. This dual focus makes action-learning teams different from quality or project teams which focus only on improvements.

Action learners use the learning cycle (see Figure 16.1) to reflect on and learn from what they do.

FIGURE 16.1   LEARNING STYLES

FROM THEORY TO PRACTICE

How do you help employees benefit from their training and put it to good use? How do you help them 'spread it around' to other employees?

LEARNING STYLES

It's a good thing there are lots of ways to learn, because people learn in different ways. Figure 16.1 shows the four learning styles suggested by Peter Honey, Alan Mumford, David Kolb and others who have worked with this learning cycle over the years to help people identify how they learn best and learn how to learn better.

Activists like to roll up their sleeves up, get 'stuck in' and learn as they go. They enjoy trying new things and having new experiences. *Reflectors* prefer to observe others doing something before having a go themselves and like to think about what they're learning. *Theorists* learn well from concepts and models and think about what they are learning in abstract terms. *Pragmatists* want to know how to apply what they're learning 'in the real world'.

When training staff, find out which learning style they prefer and make sure you incorporate it, or you'll lose your learner. Having said that, although we all have a preference for one learning style, learning is most effective when all four styles are used. This means you should try to incorporate all four learning styles into any training you do. You can do this by asking questions to help the learners think through what they're learning in each of the four ways (e.g. 'Explain what you are doing as you use this procedure' (Activist); 'What did you find easy/difficult in using this procedure?' (Reflector); 'What conclusions can you draw about …?' (Theorist); 'How can you use this to improve your productivity and make your job easier?' (Pragmatist)). You can also give activists plenty of opportunity to try out new ways of doing things and explore for themselves how to do something (within health and safety constraints). You can ask reflectors to keep a learning journal, and theorists to develop new and better ways of doing things. Make sure pragmatists understand the relevance to their jobs of what you are asking them to learn, and enlist their help in making things easier and more practical.

IDENTIFYING TRAINING NEEDS

Many large organisations have training staff who can assist supervisors in identifying and meeting the training needs of their departments. Whether or not an organisation has training specialists, however, supervisors are ultimately responsible for ensuring that employees are adequately trained.

Although training is not the solution to all problems, there are signs to watch for that indicate a need for training. Box 16.7 lists some common indicators of both supervisory and employee training needs. Whenever any of these symptoms appear in your department, it is time to check on the need for additional or refresher training for yourself and your staff.

Training needs can result from organisational changes, job changes or individual performance shortfalls. They are normally identified through a **training needs analysis**. This identifies any shortfalls between the required performance (competency) and what a person or team is able to do. These performance gaps can relate to skills, knowledge or attitudes. Once the gap is identified, we need to determine whether it can be remedied by training or whether there is some other, better solution, such as improving systems, procedures, tools or equipment, providing more time or information, or better teamwork (see Chapter 8). If we think training is the best answer, we can plan what type of training is most appropriate.

BOX 16.7 INDICATORS OF EMPLOYEE AND SUPERVISORY TRAINING NEEDS

Indicators of employee training needs
- High scrap or rework
- Low production
- High accident rates
- Need for excessive overtime
- Excessive customer complaints
- Excessive absences

Indicators of supervisory training needs
- Too many resignations or dismissals
- Unusual lateness or absenteeism in department
- Need for excessive overtime
- Poor employee morale
- Lack of employee cooperation
- Poor productivity of the team or individuals

In this way, training needs analyses help supervisors plan logically for the training and development of their work teams and can also help identify other ways to improve performance.

Identifying training needs means gathering factual information about current performance or results and desired performance or results. There are many ways to conduct a training needs analysis:
- by observing staff as they carry out their duties;
- by comparing expected performance with actual performance;
- through specially designed questionnaires and competency checklists;
- by analysing customer feedback and metrics such as quality measures and accident reports;
- through group meetings where the team brainstorms their training needs; and
- by analysing business records, business plans, performance appraisals and exit interviews.

The identified training needs are then turned into a training plan, which broadly outlines the objectives of the training and the specific skills, knowledge or attitudes to be taught or developed, and shows who will be trained and when and how the training needs will be met. Training plans can also indicate any priority areas and how the effectiveness of the training will be assessed.

PLANNING TRAINING

Training plans are an important tool for supervisors. One good way to conduct a training needs analysis in your department and develop a training plan is to draw up a matrix. List all the key tasks and duties in your section across the top of a sheet of paper and the names of all your employees down the left-hand side of the page. If appropriate, estimate what will be required in the near future. At the bottom, show the ideal number of people that should be available at all times to carry out each task. This will result in a grid, or matrix (see Figure 16.2).

FROM THEORY TO PRACTICE

What is the 'ideal number' of people able to do a job? Probably more than just one! Don't forget to allow coverage for holidays, sick and other leave, busy work periods, time taken off for training, even lunch breaks.

FIGURE 16.2 TRAINING NEEDS ANALYSIS/TRAINING PLAN FOR A MILK BAR

Task duties

	Stock shelves 1	Price goods 2	Order goods 3	Take inventory 4	Make change 5	Operate cash register 6	Deal with customers 7
Jean	✓	✓	+	+	✓	✓	+
Yunhua	−	−	✓	✓	✓	✓	✓
Alf	+	✓	+	+	+	+	−
Morgan	✓	✓	✓	✓	✓	✓	✓
Terry	✓	+	+	+	✓	+	+
Actual number able to perform task	3	3	2	2	4	3	2
Ideal number able to perform task	5	3	2	3	4	4	5

Key
✓ can do well
+ can do but needs more training/experience
0 cannot do and does not need to do
− cannot do and should be trained to do

Place a tick (✓) where each employee can already carry out a task or duty competently and a cross (x) against any tasks or duties people don't need to know how to do. Then compare the number of people who can do each task with the ideal number of people who should be able to do it. This will show you how many people you need to train and in which tasks.

You now have a good indication of which people require training and the degree of urgency and priority you should give to individual training needs. You can also encourage employees to discuss the jobs they would like to learn with you.

For instance, you will see in Figure 16.2 that all jobs except 1, 4, 6 and 7 have adequate job cover and that, of these, 4 and 6 can be covered with a minimum amount of training. This means that special attention must be given to training for jobs 1 and 7. In addition, we can see that Morgan, a very able employee, can do all required jobs; perhaps we should think about additional training and development for her so that she will not become bored and her performance level drop. We can also see that jobs 2 and 3 are potentially overstaffed, leading us to speculate that perhaps the milk bar itself is overstaffed. One possible place to make a cutback or to allow natural attrition would be in Alf's position, where few skills are required.

A chart like this (Figure 16.2) will help you to analyse your training needs and also act as a training plan. Just add target dates to each person's square showing when you intend to have training on that job completed. For instance, if you want to have Jean fully trained in job 7 by 4 September, you would write 4/9 in that box.

Now you are ready to develop a training program. First, decide the objectives of the training in terms of the competencies to be achieved. Then decide the methods of training you will use, and how you will assess whether the training objectives have been attained. You should also develop or obtain any training materials you will need and determine what equipment you will use.

JOB BREAKDOWNS

Job breakdowns are your memory-jogger. They help you do a better job of instructing. You should always develop a job breakdown and follow it when you give any on-the-job training. This helps to ensure that you teach the job in the most logical sequence (*stages*) and that you include all important considerations (*key points*). Once you have developed a job breakdown, you can use it over and over again.

A job breakdown consists of stages and key points. *Stages* are usually natural breaks in the action, activity or process of the job. They help you teach a job in the most logical sequence and ensure there is not too much information for the learner to master. A job

⚡ FROM THEORY TO PRACTICE

Always prepare a job breakdown while you are actually doing the job so that you do not miss out anything important. In other words, do the job and make notes as you go. It is no good thinking about how you would do it or how you have done it in the past.

The acid test of a good job breakdown is being able to do the job using only the stages you have written in the job breakdown.

breakdown should have a maximum of seven stages; more than this is too much for most learners to remember all at once. If a job has more than seven stages, break it down into separate units and teach each separately.

Key points are anything about a stage that might:
• affect safety;
• affect quality;
• cause injury;
• make the work easier; and
• provide any special information (e.g. special knacks or 'know-how').

Safety factors are always key points. If you find that a stage contains more than five key points, break it down into two stages.

To prepare a job breakdown, go through the job and break it down into stages. The seven stages in cooking scrambled eggs, for example, might be:
1. Assemble utensils and ingredients within arm's reach.
2. Grease pan.
3. Place pan on burner.
4. Crack eggs into bowl.
5. Beat eggs.
6. Add eggs to pan.
7. Cook eggs.

Next, determine the key points for each stage—things that will make each stage easier for the learners to remember and carry out correctly, efficiently and safely. For example, in the second stage of cooking scrambled eggs—grease pan—the key points might be:
• Use one tablespoon of oil per egg.
• Swirl oil around the bottom of pan to cover.

In the third stage—place pan on burner—the key points might be:
• Set burner temperature to high.
• Point pan handle away from you.

In the fourth stage—crack eggs into bowl—the key points might be:
• Make a short, sharp crack across middle of each egg.
• Grasp egg gently between fingers and thumbs—break egg with thumbs along crack.
• Empty contents into bowl.
• Dispose of shells in organic waste bin.

The completed job breakdown might look like the one shown in Box 16.8.

Stages and key points speed up the learning process and help trainees remember what is important in doing the job correctly and safely.

GIVING INSTRUCTIONS

Once you have your job breakdown, all you need do is use it to follow these four steps to good training:

Step 1 Prepare   *Step 3* Try out
Step 2 Present   *Step 4* Put to work

BOX 16.8 JOB BREAKDOWN: COOKING EGGS

Stages	Key points
1. Assemble utensils and ingredients within arm's reach.	■ Pan ■ Spatula ■ Oil ■ Fork ■ 3 eggs ■ Bowl
2. Grease pan.	■ Use one tablespoon of oil per egg. ■ Swirl oil around bottom of pan to cover it.
3. Place pan on burner.	■ Set burner temperature to high. ■ Point pan handle away from you.
4 Crack eggs into bowl.	■ Make a short, sharp crack across the middle of each egg. ■ Grasp egg gently between fingers and thumb—break egg with thumbs along the crack. ■ Empty contents into bowl. ■ Dispose of the shells in organic waste bin.
5. Beat eggs.	■ Make rapid, circular stirring movements with fork. ■ Eggs should become uniformly coloured. ■ Paste-like consistency.
6. Add eggs to pan.	■ Pour in quickly.
7. Cook eggs.	■ Approximately 4 minutes. ■ Turn eggs with spatula every 8 seconds. ■ When mix begins to dry and colour lightens, the eggs are cooked.

FROM THEORY TO PRACTICE

You can easily adapt job breakdowns into standard operating procedures (SOPs). These step-by-step guides are handy references for employees to turn to. When turning your job breakdowns into SOPs, make sure you use the active voice (grease the pan, not the pan should be greased) and use the same terms throughout the SOP (don't say pan in one place and saucepan in another).

Step 1: Prepare

Stage	Key points
Gather materials	• Job breakdown; other training aids.
Tidy workplace	• Clean, tidy and free of tools and equipment that are not required.
Relax trainee	• A nervous person will not be able to learn.
Explain	• Explain the job you are going to teach and your aim—what you expect trainee to be able to do after your training
Can they do it?	• Know anything about the job? Ever done anything like it? • If yes, build on existing knowledge and make associations with the trainee's past experiences to make learning easier.

Stage	*Key points*
	• If trainees say they can do the job, ask them to demonstate. (You may not need to teach it, or you may find gaps in skills and knowledge that need filling.)
Motivate trainee	• Give a reason to learn. A person who wants to learn is the easiest to teach.
	• Explain why the job is important, how it fits into the overall scheme of things, the benefits the trainee will gain from learning it.
Ensure correct position	• Trainee must be able to hear and have a clear view of the job you are about to demonstrate.

Step 2: Present

Stage	*Key points*
Create understanding	• Use your job breakdown as a guide.
	• Carry out the job yourself stage by stage, emphasising the key points.
	• Instruct patiently, clearly and slowly. Not too fast.

Step 3: Try out

Stage	*Key points*
Ask trainee to do the job	• Exactly the way you have just demonstrated.
Ask trainees to tell you, out loud, what they are doing	• Listen to make sure the trainee repeats the key points back to you.
	• If any are missed, ask trainees what they have just done, in order to draw out the key points.

FROM THEORY TO PRACTICE

Each time you give an instruction, be sure to refer to your job breakdown to ensure that you present all, and only relevant, information.

FROM THEORY TO PRACTICE

Most inexperienced trainers make the mistake of instructing too fast. Let the trainee 'chew and swallow' each stage before moving on to the next one. Look at the trainee when you finish demonstrating each stage and watch for a nod or some other sign of understanding before moving on.

Another common mistake is to talk about other things when the trainee is trying to concentrate. Ask them how their weekend was later!

Stage	*Key points*
Stop trainee if they make a mistake, or if you can see a mistake is about to be made	• Tell trainees they did something that was not quite right and ask if they can identify it. It is much better for trainees to work out their mistakes than for you to tell them.
Continue until satisfied	• Have trainees continue doing the job for you, explaining what they are doing, until you are satisfied they have learned it correctly.

Step 4: Put to work

Stage	*Key points*
Application	• Leave trainees to practise their newly acquired skills and gain experience and confidence. • Indicate precisely what you expect the trainees to do: for example, complete 12 forms over the next $2\frac{1}{2}$ hours; form 17 U-bends per hour over the next 3 hours. • Always provide a target to aim for to help trainees assess their own performance.
Any problems?	• Indicate to whom the learner can go if a problem arises.
Check back	• Go back and check as often as necessary to ensure the job is being done as you have taught it: safely, efficiently and correctly.

Can all jobs be taught in this way?

Use a job breakdown and the four steps to training described above to teach any job that has an element of manual skill in it. You may, however, need to use your imagination and

FROM THEORY TO PRACTICE

If you have written a clear and complete job breakdown of seven or fewer stages with no more than five key points per stage, the trainee will probably need to perform the job for you only one, two or three times. When you are satisfied that the job is being done correctly, move on to the fourth step.

FROM THEORY TO PRACTICE

Regardless of how well the learner appears to be handling the new job, you must implement a regular follow-up program to ensure they continue to do the job in the required manner and to the required standard. You don't want any bad habits to creep in. Your follow-ups can become less frequent as the trainee gains experience.

adapt the four steps in order to teach some jobs. For example, what about long, complex jobs? Many jobs have more than seven stages. Break these down into units of instructions, each with no more than seven stages. Some units will be easier to learn than others. Sometimes, you can teach the easiest units first, gradually moving onto the more difficult ones. Sometimes, this won't be possible—for example, the job may need to be carried out in a particular sequence. If this is the case, complete the job in its correct sequence; as you come to them, teach the trainee the easiest units while you complete the more difficult ones. As the trainee masters the easier units, progressivley teach the more difficult ones. In this way, trainees build their skills until they can complete the entire job.

Group instruction

Group instruction is broadly similar to individual instruction. You still use your job breakdown and instruct following the four steps described above. However, when you come to the third step ('try out'), give each trainee a turn at doing a stage of the job. Ask them to tell you out loud what they are doing while you listen for key points.

The other important point with group instruction is to ensure that the whole group can hear and see what you are doing in the 'present' step. This isn't always as easy as ensuring that just one trainee can see you.

FROM THEORY TO PRACTICE

Here are some other practical tips to remember when instructing:
- Smile and use a friendly tone of voice.
- Speak slowly and clearly.
- Follow your job breakdown strictly.
- Use examples, exaggerated movements, repetition and changes in voice tone or speed (louder, softer, quicker, slower) to stress key points.
- Explain and reinforce basic workplace terms as you train.
- Make it clear that if trainees have finished the task you set them, they should not just 'sit there' but ask what to do next, read any product manuals, SOPs, etc.
- Don't step in and take over if learners make a mistake. Help them figure out what they've done wrong and rectify it.
- Assess the learners regularly, and keep a record of how they are doing against the goals; review it together often.
- Build learners' confidence with lots of positive feedback and constructive encouragement.
- Have frequent breaks.
- Keep the training practical and non-theoretical.
- Relate the training to the learners' prior experience and knowledge.
- Keep learners involved and active, not just sitting there watching you!
- Review what you've covered often. This increases learning significantly.
- People tend to recall what they've heard first and last, so pay special attention to emphasising, reinforcing and reviewing the middle bits.

THE CHARACTERISTICS OF A GOOD TRAINER

It is difficult to remember how confusing something can be before we learned it. That's why it's not easy to give good instructions about something we know well and why it's important to take the time to plan training and prepare for it thoroughly. Ideally, you will carry out on-the-job instruction yourself but, occasionally, you will want to delegate your instruction duties to someone suitable and qualified to carry out training. The following description of an effective trainer therefore applies either to you or to the person you delegate to carry out training.

> 'The secret in education lies in respecting the student.'
>
> Ralph Waldo Emerson (1803–82)
> US author, poet and philosopher

Good trainers need to be patient people who are interested in helping others to learn and in passing on their skills and knowledge. They need to be good communicators and genuinely interested in others, in the organisation and in the jobs they will be teaching. They should be safety-conscious and trained not only in safe working methods but also in instruction techniques: how to prepare job breakdowns and how to follow the four-step instruction plan.

They should be able to think quickly on their feet and they should be outgoing and friendly. They need to be tolerant yet firm and have an empathetic understanding of the difficulties encountered by trainees. They should be interested in training and should practise what they preach.

Does this sound like you?

The most common error in instructing

The most common error is trying to teach too much at once. Distinguishing between *must know*, *should know* and *could know* will stop you from giving the learner too much information to absorb all at once (see Figure 16.3).

'Must know' refers to the stages and essential key points of a job—all the basics that the learner must know in order to be able to do the job. The job breakdown should contain only 'must knows'.

FIGURE 16.3 'MUST KNOW', 'SHOULD KNOW' AND 'COULD KNOW'

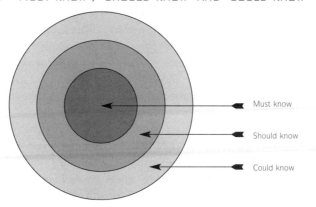

Must know

Should know

Could know

Once the learner has mastered the basics of the job, after step 4, *Put to work*, you can then explain the 'should knows'. These are the things about the job that the learners really should know about, but which are not, strictly speaking, essential for them to understand in the early stages of learning.

When the learner has become proficient in the job, it is time to add the icing on the cake, to explain the 'could knows' or 'nice to knows'. These are the details that add job interest and round out a person's job knowledge.

With the example of cooking eggs used earlier, the 'must knows' are all contained in the job breakdown. 'Should knows' might include egg sizes, various egg-beating techniques and how to test eggs for freshness. 'Could knows' might include pan sizes, materials and thickness, additional flavourings and optional ingredients, and why the eggs are cooked on a high temperature.

LEARNING PLATEAUS

People learn at different rates and almost everyone has periods when their performance isn't improving, regardless of the effort they are putting into the job or the quality of your training. This is called a *learning plateau*. It is as if the learner becomes saturated with new skills and knowledge and subconsciously 'switches off' in order to consolidate what they have recently learned.

Most people experience a plateau during the learning process. The difficulty for trainers lies in identifying learning plateaus because they occur at different times for different people and will last for varying lengths of time for different people and tasks.

All trainers should be aware of this difficult part of learning. Try to recognise it and assist the learner to move on from the plateau. Slow down and stop pushing if you suspect a learner has reached a learning plateau. It is only temporary and will pass.

LEARNING BEHAVIOUR

Many principles of learning have evolved from research into education and training methods. Apply them whenever you train employees. These learning principles are shown in Box 16.9.

MEASURING THE EFFECTIVENESS OF TRAINING

Most major organisations and many smaller ones have formalised training programs for both management and non-management workers. Numerous surveys have shown the impact that such training has on various parts of an organisation. Drops in customer complaints, accidents, employee absenteeism, grievances and turnover, and increases in production and sales have all been shown to follow successful training programs. Quantifying the improvements made directly as a result of training is often difficult, however.

How can you prove that a dollar spent on training returns more than a dollar in benefits? There are several ways to evaluate the effectiveness of training programs.

One way is through self-reports. You can gather the opinions of employees who have been trained by asking them personally, or give them an evaluation form to complete. Another way is to assess the skill of employees before and after training through skill or competency tests or interactive CD-ROMs, or by measuring their performance on the job before and after training. Comparing key measures such as quality, wastage, unit costs, incentive earnings and safety can be useful, depending on the type of training you are assessing.

BOX 16.9 LEARNING PRINCIPLES

- People of all ages and intellectual capacities have the ability to learn new skills and behaviours.
- People must be motivated to learn. This motivation can take a variety of forms, such as personal development, promotional possibilities or financial incentives. Find out what will motivate your trainees best. People often learn most when they can see how training relates to their personal goals.
- Learning is active, not passive. Get the learner involved (e.g. in the third step of training, 'try out').
- People tend to acquire knowledge more rapidly with guidance. Trial and error is too time-consuming and inefficient and too easily results in poor and unsafe work habits. Give plenty of feedback and set clear targets that trainees can work towards and use to assess their progress.
- Offer lots of positive reinforcement of correct behaviours to cement desired behaviours. Be liberal with your praise and encouragement.
- Good training materials and teaching aids are important. Use job breakdowns, case studies, discussion questions, diagrams, videos and readings appropriate to the skill and knowledge being taught.
- Provide time to practise the learning. People need time to internalise and assimilate what they've learned, in order to build confidence.
- Vary training techniques to offset fatigue and boredom.
- The learner must feel satisfied with the learning. Take into account each trainee's desires and expectations.
- Actual learning represents a change in behaviour and all changes require adjustments. Give people time to adjust and build confidence.
- Allow for individual differences in the learning process. What some people can learn easily may be difficult for others because of differences in basic abilities, previous experience or background.
- Learning is a cumulative process. What has been learned in earlier sessions or through previous experience conditions and modifies a person's reactions to any training session.
- People learn complex tasks and skills more slowly and simple skills more quickly.
- Learning requires attention and concentration. Avoid distractions.
- Learning involves long-term retention as well as immediate acquisition of knowledge. Help trainees learn and retain information by ensuring understanding and building plenty of practice into your training sessions.
- Accuracy generally deserves more emphasis than speed during the learning process. Speed can be built up later.

THE **BIG** PICTURE

Some companies calculate the return they get for their training dollars. Motorola, for example, calculates a return of over $50 for each dollar spent on employee training. Training, if well planned and effectively carried out, actually saves more money than it costs.

This isn't always a truly scientific way to evaluate a training program because we cannot always be sure that improved performance is due to the training. It may be due to better supervision, better raw materials, economic conditions or better production planning. For example, if sales representatives sell more after a sales training program, is this because of the training or would sales have increased anyway? Or if they sell less after sales training, does this mean the training failed?

To find out, you would need to compare the output of the group of employees who were trained with the output of another group who were not trained (a control group). This might show, for example, that the group who were trained increased their sales by an average of 12% while the average sales of the control group declined 8%. This would indicate strongly that the training was worthwhile.

Often, the purpose of training is to enhance employees' interpersonal skills and behaviour on the job. The effectiveness of this type of training is more difficult to measure. Tests might show that employees have learned something or they may report that they liked the course, but this does not guarantee they will use this knowledge in their job. As discussed earlier, supervisors can help to ensure that employees put their training to use on the job by discussing the training with them beforehand and afterwards. If competency-based training methods are used, assessors will be able to assess whether the trainees are able to apply the skills they learned on the course.

SUPERVISORS NEED TRAINING TOO!

People aren't born supervisors! Training in management techniques such as problem solving, decision making, planning and time management, and in interpersonal skills such as leadership, interviewing and performance counselling can help develop their skills. Training extends and upgrades the skills and natural abilities of management employees just as it does for non-management employees.

As we saw in Box 16.7, supervisors need training to overcome problems that may crop up in their department. They also need general supervisory training and development and interpersonal skills training to update and enhance their existing skills and knowledge, and technical training to keep up with technological innovations. Once a person becomes a supervisor, they usually need less technical job-related training (apart from update training) and more training in the management, people and conceptual areas. This type of training falls under the heading of personal and management development.

Personal and management development

Underlying the *Enterprising Nation* report of the Karpin Committee is a consistent theme: we must pay closer attention to equipping managers at all levels to ensure they operate effectively in an increasingly complex environment. The report identifies the development of front-line managers as a primary need in Australia. As managers at all levels move from styles involving coercion, command and control to styles encouraging cooperation, consensus and commitment, they need to upgrade their skills, particularly in the areas of interpersonal skills, strategic thinking, leadership, and flexibility and adaptability to change. Training to develop these skills is often referred to as *personal* and *management development*.

It includes conceptual and skills training in techniques such as planning, problem solving, decision making and business finance, and in interpersonal skills such as communication, performance counselling, negotiation and conflict management. Well developed skills in these areas are critical to an organisation's effectiveness.

> 'Learning is not attained by chance. It must be sought for with ardour and attended to with diligence.'
>
> Abigail Adams (1744–1818)
> Former US First Lady

Supervisors and team leaders are a significant organisational resource because they play an important role in delivering workplace change and improving productivity and product and service quality and timeliness. Despite this, the Karpin Report is critical of the training provided for supervisors. A number of research projects conducted on behalf of the Committee led to the criticism. Professor Vic Callan of the Graduate School of Management at the University of Queensland, for example, surveyed 200 managers and found that:

- when first placed in a management role, two-thirds believed they were not very effective;
- half of them learned about the process of managing the 'hard way', through experience;
- the main challenges they faced were learning to change personal beliefs, learning to live with not being on top of things, accepting personal limitations, dealing with conflict and disciplining employees;
- they underestimated the challenges of managing people; and
- three-quarters were surprised by the amount of personal learning that occurred in becoming a manager.

As a result of its research, the Karpin Committee recommends that training for front-line managers include a focus on quality, managing a diverse range of employees, empowering workers and workplace leadership. It must meet the needs of the organisation, be long-term in its approach and help establish a learning culture.

Residential or off-the-job training programs are common forums for personal and management development. The HR or training department, if there is one, normally arranges this training. The organisation itself may run it (in-house programs) or it may send staff to a public course. The main advantages of in-house courses are that they can be designed specifically to meet organisation needs, and participants are able to extend their knowledge of how the organisation operates and their networks within it. This in turn serves a team-building and motivational function and helps to strengthen the organisation's culture. Public courses, on the other hand, expose participants to a wide range of experience, opinions and thinking, often from both public and private sectors.

Other forms of personal and management development include participation in committees, advisory groups or project teams, mentoring or coaching by a senior manager, planned job rotation, part-time tertiary studies, day-release courses, self-paced learning and delegation. On-the-job experience, action learning programs, job assignments and work with other organisations can also be effective.

	True	False

1. Good training saves time, money and waste, and leads to better safety, efficiency and quality standards. ☐ ☐
2. Many companies find that training more than pays for its costs. ☐ ☐
3. Supervisors play a crucial role in delivering and supporting training. ☐ ☐
4. A competency is a set of skills that includes manual skills, knowledge skills and attitudinal skills. ☐ ☐
5. Competency-based training is really no different from traditional training. ☐ ☐
6. Recognition of prior learning means that trainees get 'credit' for what they already know and don't have to attend training programs on it. ☐ ☐
7. People generally can't gain recognition for prior learning until an assessor has assessed them as competent in any given task. ☐ ☐
8. An occupation is made up of units of competence that are broken down into elements of competence which must be carried out to a specified standard called 'performance criteria' and under specified conditions called a 'range of variables'. ☐ ☐
9. On-the-job training isn't used much today. ☐ ☐
10. Self-paced training caters well for individual needs and is extensively used in CBT programs. ☐ ☐
11. After conducting a training needs analysis, supervisors make a training plan, which outlines when and how the training needs will be met. ☐ ☐
12. Job breakdowns only need to be followed if the instructor is unsure of how to do the job. ☐ ☐
13. The four steps to training manual skills are: Prepare, Present, Try out and Put to work. The final step can be skipped if the trainee has caught on quickly. ☐ ☐
14. Good trainers are patient and clear communicators who are genuinely interested in the job, the trainee and the organisation. ☐ ☐
15. When trainees hit a learning plateau, they should be encouraged to try harder. ☐ ☐
16. True learning requires practice to build and retain skills. ☐ ☐
17. Not all managers need training. ☐ ☐

---

1. Write an essay outlining the benefits of systematic job training to (1) the trainee, (2) the supervisor, (3) the work team and (4) the organisation.

2. Discuss supervisors' responsibilities in supporting off-the-job training and explain how they can meet these responsibilities.

3. Contrast competency-based training with traditional training and describe how CBT could be applied in your own organisation or college study program.

4. If your work department or college decided to establish competency-based training, how would they go about establishing a CBT program?
5. Describe the five methods most frequently used to train employees.
6. Describe how supervisors can identify training needs and plan to meet them in their department.
7. What is a job breakdown used for? What are its main elements?
8. What happens when a trainee reaches a learning plateau? What can supervisors do to help?
9. Discuss the principles of learning and how supervisors can apply them when training employees.
10. What topics would you like to see covered in a management development program you are about to attend? Why?

·   ▰▰▰ **DEVELOP YOUR SKILLS** ▰▰▰   ·

Individual activities

1. Get examples of CBT programs from organisations in your area or from one of the industry training bodies. Highlight and provide definitions for the CBT terminology used.
2. Describe an occasion in your life when you underwent competency-based training. What did you like about it? How did it aid your learning? How was your competency assessed?
3. Write competency elements, performance criteria and a range of variables for the competency unit of writing an essay.
4. Prepare and complete a training needs analysis using the matrix format suggested in this chapter, either for your department at work or for running a household. If the training needs analysis is for your work area, use the actual employees to complete your analysis and discuss it with your manager. If it is for running a house-hold, use the people who live in it to complete your analysis and discuss your findings with members of the household.
5. Prepare a job breakdown for a simple manual skill.
6. Describe a time when you reached a learning plateau.
7. Refer back to the vignette and second case study in Chapter 14 on pages 423 and 450. What topics would you recommend be included on an in-house management development program that is being designed specifically to meet their needs? Explain your reasons for suggesting these topics. How could Karen Chan confirm these needs and identify any that you have missed?

Group activities

1. Form into groups of three. Take turns using the job breakdown you prepared in activity 5 above to give instruction to one of the people in your trio, following the four steps to instruction described in this chapter. Ask the third person to join your 'trainee' in critiquing your effective-ness as a trainer and make a list of things to do to improve. Switch roles twice so you each have a chance to be learner, trainer and coach. Then switch groups and train someone else, incorporating your list of things to do to improve. Switch roles again, so that you each play learner, trainer and coach in your second group, too.
2. List the competencies required of an effective job trainer in your organisation. Compare it with the lists prepared by others in your class.

3. Review the vignette on page 488. In small groups, discuss how Khee Moon's supervisor approached his training. Clearly, she invested considerable time in training Khee Moon. What benefits do you expect she will reap as a result? Prepare a list to discuss with the rest of the class.

CASE STUDY 16.1

Kendalls Department Store

Kendalls Department Store was established in 1903. Originally a piece-goods and shoe outlet, it soon branched into other merchandise and, by 1908, it had become a department store. Living up to its motto of 'Satisfaction Guaranteed or Your Money Back', Kendalls prospered.

In 1921 a second Kendalls opened in a nearby town and, during the next 19 years, seven stores were opened in other communities. By 1980, after a few 'ups and downs', Kendalls represented a chain of 22 stores in country towns, with each employing an average of six front-line managers.

One of the problems experienced in this growth pattern was that of recruiting and selecting adequately trained store managers and department supervisors. Until recently, Kendalls' policy had been to hire people with prior managerial experience in other retail outlets. The current managing director of the chain, Louisa Kendall, great-granddaughter of the founder, had questioned this practice for some time. She felt that it was costly because Kendalls had to pay more to lure a good employee from another store and, in addition, the employee had to be retrained in Kendalls' methods—a further expense.

In January 1995, Louisa Kendall contracted with Alison Decker, an experienced training consultant, to outsource employee training. Alison's first priority was to develop an in-house training program for prospective and newly promoted store supervisors.

Questions

1 What method of analysing supervisors' training needs and what methods of training would you suggest for Kendalls' supervisory training program? Why?

2 Develop a checklist indicating the topics that might be covered in a training program for prospective and newly appointed store supervisors that you think Alison would find satisfactory. Give reasons for your choice of topics. If you have completed Chapter 15, develop a brief job description and personnel specification to base your training program on.

The Trouble With New Equipment

For the past nine years, Loree had supervised the staff in a large general office providing support to a national manufacturing, distribution and retailing organisation. She had always advocated an on-the-job training approach for new staff and for updating the skills of existing employees. She believed that the best way for a person to become efficient in a job was to work beside those who could do the job until they became proficient.

The introduction of new technologies and information management systems had not improved efficiency as much as she had hoped. Moreover, staff turnover was increasing and morale was suffering as employees became frustrated by their inability to maintain the required levels of work output.

Before the latest upgrades, management suggested that all staff be sent on a training course to familiarise them with the correct operating procedures. Loree said they would learn more quickly on the job and selected a few of the longer-serving staff members to attend. They would teach the others, which would cost less and create less disruption. She felt there would be the added advantage of being able to control how the rest of the employees were being trained, and she would be able to place everyone in the job where they appeared to be the most productive.

Those who went to the training course found the new skills required were quite different from those they had developed over the years and it took them longer than expected to grasp the new terminology and methods. As a result, they were still feeling their way when the new equipment was installed and they were expected to start teaching their colleagues who had not attended the training course. This meant that the development of these employees was not as rapid as Loree had expected.

Now it appeared that those trained off-the-job were not accepting the instruction they had been given and were doing the job the way they thought was best. This resulted in increased errors, duplication of many jobs and confusion as to what was really required.

Questions

1   What mistakes did Loree make? What should she have done instead?
2   What should Loree do now to get output up to the required levels as quickly as possible?

Answers to Rapid Review questions

1. T   2. T   3. T   4. T   5. F   6. T   7. T   8. T   9. F   10. T   11. T   12. F
13. F   14. T   15. F   16. T   17. F

CHAPTER 17

WORKPLACE RELATIONS

A steep learning curve

Things were a lot different now than when George Anders first started supervising 15 years ago. Then, he could issue instructions and know they would be followed. Now he needed to listen to the people he was used to giving instructions to and take their opinions and ideas into account. He had found they cared about their jobs and wanted to be involved. In fact, he had learned that the more he involved people, the more they seemed to care.

George readied his papers for the enterprise bargaining meeting, the second this week. Things were going well, he thought, now that he had 'learned the ropes'. The HR manager and an adviser from the Employers' Chamber, working with the union representatives, had handled the last agreement. He had gathered it was a pretty difficult exercise for everyone concerned because it was the first time the company had tried something like this. It went reasonably well, although from his point of view there had been a few difficulties in implementing parts of the agreement.

Clearly, others thought so too, because this year three supervisors were brought onto the negotiating team. He found the process quite enlightening. One thing he quickly learned was that it was more important than ever to listen to people. If they were going to reach agreement on productivity improvements, job flexibility, improved working conditions and pay, everyone needed to be involved. That was his job: to keep people informed, listen to them, take their thoughts back to the negotiating table and help work out ways that everyone could be satisfied. This wasn't 'old school thump-the-table' industrial relations—this was 21st-century problem solving!

He was confident that a good agreement would be reached. He also knew that it would be realistic and easy to implement, thanks to his input and the input of the other supervisors on the bargaining team. He also knew that, because everyone was kept well informed, there would be genuine commitment to the agreement.

OVERVIEW

The workplace has changed markedly over the years. It is more empowered, open and flexible. The workplace of the Information Revolution demands different skills of supervisors and offers them different challenges. This chapter explains what you can do to cultivate cooperative workplace relations.

- Do you know how to make the most of industrial democracy and employee participation? Can you effectively employ consultative supervisory methods? Do you know how to share information and what information to share?
- Can you describe how workplace relations legislation affects supervisors and workplace practice?
- Can you explain how the role of industrial awards changed in the latter half of the 1990s?
- What rights and obligations do employers and supervisors have when dismissing employees?

- Can you describe the process of workplace bargaining and how workplace agreements are reached?
- Can you add value to your organisation's enterprise bargaining process?
- Do you know what has happened to a union's right to strike?
- Do you know how to work effectively with trade unions?
- Are you familiar with how unions are structured and financed in Australia and New Zealand?

INDUSTRIAL DEMOCRACY

In the 1960s **industrial democracy** became a political goal. In June 1967 the federal government set up its tripartite National Employee Participation Steering Committee and since then a variety of federal Acts and papers, policy documents and accords from political, industry and trade union bodies have followed. The Australian Workplace Industrial Relations Survey 1995 shows increases in direct and indirect forms of employee participation since 1990. The number of joint consultative committees, for example, has more than doubled since 1990.

We have seen a remarkable consensus on the importance of *employee participation* in Australian organisations. In 1983 the Australian Labor Party–Australian Council of Trade Unions Accord focused on *consultation* as a key factor in bringing about some needed changes in Australian industry. In 1984 the tripartite National Labour Consultative Committee published its *Guidelines for Information Sharing*. Also in 1984, the Arbitration Commission on Termination, Change and Redundancy obliged employers to inform and consult employees over major technical and organisational changes. In 1986 the federal government published a policy discussion paper called *Industrial Democracy and Employee Participation* and in 1988 the Confederation of Australian Industry and the ACTU published a joint Statement on Participative Practices. Throughout the early 1990s, government, industry and the trade union movement continued to cooperate in achieving real workplace change through the consultative process of **enterprise bargaining**.

This has added to the strong momentum that has built up for a more open, participative style of supervision and management. Participation is now a fact of organisational life.

Participation aims to give employees the opportunity to influence decisions that affect them, their work and their work environment. We can contrast it with **consultation**, which is a process by which management seeks employees' views before reaching a decision. Both participation and consultation are ways to make better use of people's skills, knowledge and experience, to increase the motivation and commitment of all employees and to make organisations more effective.

Participation is a style of supervising, not something a supervisor does once a week or only when it is convenient. It requires skills in listening, questioning and confidence building. Knowledge of how to lead the meetings and discussions that are indispensable to participation is also needed. To paraphrase Shakespeare:

> 'Some supervisors are born with participative skills, some achieve participative skills and others have participative skills thrust upon them.'

Fortunately, the skills of participative supervision can be learned. These are summarised in Box 17.1 and discussed below.

1. Communication, information sharing and consultation are fundamental to any participative process; in fact, participation cannot be achieved without them. Are you a clear communicator, willing and able to identify and share relevant information, and able to use consultative and participative styles of leadership?
2. All employees should have the opportunity to influence decisions on issues that directly affect them at work. For this to happen, you must be able to listen to what is *really* being said, and to encourage even the most reserved employees to offer their ideas and opinions.
3. There should be short chains of command, delegation of responsibility and decision making, and established mechanisms for communication and consultation. These are three main conditions for effective participation. If your organisation has set up consultative procedures and committees, you should be familiar with them and know how to use them effectively.
4. Consultative and cooperative approaches to conflict are needed. 'Win–win' approaches are becoming increasingly necessary and are taking over from the traditional adversarial or 'win–lose' approach. Can you recognise the need for, and employ, conflict resolution techniques, and use collaborative group techniques to achieve win–win outcomes?

BOX 17.1

PRINCIPLES OF PARTICIPATION

1. Communication, information sharing and consultation
2. The opportunity to influence decisions
3. Short chains of command, delegation of responsibility and decision making, and use of established mechanisms for communication and consultation
4. Consultative and cooperative approaches to conflict
5. Participation is not a panacea
6. Joint understanding and shared objectives
7. Must be desired by management and employees alike

5. Participation is not a panacea. It is a better way of supervising and managing organisations, but it would be unrealistic to say that participation will cure all organisational ills. Yet it is an important ingredient of effective organisations. Are you prepared to invest the time, effort and patience required to introduce participative methods and see that they are used well? Determination and commitment are needed from all parties.

6. Shared understanding of objectives is essential for successful participation. Can you communicate the organisation's aims and objectives clearly, and motivate and enable your team to share them and work towards them?

7. Management and employees alike must want participation. All groups at all levels in the organisation must be committed to participation as something that will make their work life more productive and satisfying.

21ST-CENTURY WORKPLACE RELATIONS

To compete in the world and maintain our standard of living, Australia needs to be a flexible country. We need flexibility to deal with a changing employment mix (e.g. more female, casual, service and knowledge workers and fewer permanent jobs) and deregulation, lowered tariff protection and privatisation. Attaining the flexibility we need has been a major concern of our last two Coalition and Labor governments and, as a result, the last 20 years have seen profound changes in Australia's workplace relations environment.

THE **BIG** PICTURE

Flexibility is a scale, not an on-off switch. In a totally unregulated employment market, we could send ten-year-olds down mine shafts for 12 hours a day. In a totally regulated market with no regard to commercial reality, the economy would eventually crumble.

Here are five forms of flexibility:

1. *Flexibility within the organisation* to move people around, assign different work, different hours, etc. The *Workplace Relations Act 1996* targets this through Workplace Agreements.

2. *Flexibility to hire and fire*, without legal, administrative or fiscal (e.g. redundancy pay) restrictions. Unfair dismissal regulations have made it more difficult to employ and shed workers as circumstances change, and proposed changes to federal legislation are seeking to strengthen this type of flexibility.

3. *Real wage flexibility*, to change pay as business conditions and demands for labour change.

4. *Relative wage flexibility*, to change relative pay in different trades, occupations or sectors in line with market conditions.

5. *Flexibility of workforce*, a function of training and educational levels. Australia has traditionally had problems in this area which means workers can't be moved around as easily as in, say, Germany or Japan, where training and education levels are higher.

Beginning with **award restructuring** in the 1980s, which attempted to reduce the number of trade unions and **demarcation disputes**, legislation has continued the push to increase Australia's competitiveness and flexibility. Employment legislation is changing on two key fronts. First, it is shifting from a social and protective role to one of promoting the efficient functioning of labour markets. Second, it is moving from setting employment pay and conditions collectively to agreeing them at enterprise level. This represents a fundamental shift in the paradigm of Australian labour law.

WORKPLACE RELATIONS LEGISLATION

Like the *Employment Contracts Bill* of New Zealand, the Australian *Workplace Relations Act 1996*, the *Workplace Relations and Other Legislation Amendment Bill 1997*, and its part 2 legislation, *Workplace Relations Legislation Amendment (More Jobs, Better Pay) Bill 1999*, which is before Parliament as this book goes to print, recognises that Australian industry must become more globally competitive if we are to maintain our high standard of living. One way to increase our competitiveness is to limit many restrictive labour practices in order to improve workplace flexibility, efficiency and productivity.

To this end, the current government continued down the path of workplace relations reform established during the 1980s. Throughout the 1990s it maintained the trend towards decentralised workplace relations and enterprise level agreements, labour market efficiency and links between pay and productivity.

The *Workplace Relations Act 1996* attempted to move workplace relations from an adversarial approach towards strategic human resources management based on shared goals of employers and employees. It made a number of far reaching adjustments to the nature of workplace relations and workplace practices in Australia. The key initiatives are summarised in Box 17.2.

The 'second wave' workplace relations legislation

The so-called 'second wave' of coalition government industrial legislation was introduced to Parliament on 30 June 1999 as the *Workplace Relations Legislation Amendment (More Jobs, Better Pay) Bill 1999*. As this book goes to press, it is still under discussion.

The Bill proposes further changes to awards, Australian Workplace Agreements, industrial action, right of entry and the structure and function of the Industrial Relations

---

THE BIG PICTURE

Enterprise unions predominate in Japan. Most employee benefits are directly related to profitability and there is extensive joint consultation, usually through monthly meetings, with interchange of information on various matters such as company policies, production plans, working conditions and benefits. Management not only relays decisions to keep workers informed but also uses these meetings as an opportunity for open discussion.

Union membership rates have fallen from about 50% of the workforce in the 1940s to 28% (1986 figures). This is similar to Australian membership rates.

BOX
17.2
SUMMARY OF KEY INITIATIVES OF THE WORKPLACE RELATIONS ACT, 1996

The **Australian Industrial Relations Commission** (AIRC) (likely to be renamed the Workplace Relations Commission) was given a generally reduced role. For example, it lost its powers to restrict the number or proportion of part-time, casual and junior workers, to set ratios of apprentices to tradespeople, and to set maximum and minimum hours of work for part-time employees.

Awards: The AIRC continues to supervise awards, which were simplified and 'confined in their scope to providing a safety net of fair minimum wages and conditions'. Its powers to make new awards and arbitrate existing ones were limited to 20 designated areas, mainly safety net pay adjustments and other award minimums (see Box 17.3). It must 'ensure that awards are suited to efficient work performance according to the needs of particular workplaces or enterprises'. Access to the AIRC for arbitration became a last resort and confined to an enterprise basis.

Australian Workplace Agreements (AWAs) and Certified Agreements: All other employment conditions are now decided through a new system of contracts agreed through *workplace bargaining*. This places responsibility for workplace relations and conditions of employment with each organisation and its employees.

Industrial action: The AIRC received wider powers to recommend that industrial action not occur or stops. If the recommendation is ignored, it can make an order, enforceable in the courts, to prevent or stop the action. Employers were given greater scope to file civil actions against unions, union officers or employees for damage to their business caused by industrial action. There can be no strike pay unless the action involves a reasonable concern about health and safety matters.

Unions: The Act removed the automatic recognition and encouragement of trade unions as key participants in the regulation of employment conditions and limited union powers. Union involvement must be by invitation of a member of the workforce who is also a member of the union. The request to participate in the bargaining process or to represent an employee or group of employees must be in writing.

The Act banned compulsory unionism ('closed shops') and the ability of employers to state a preference for hiring union members. Individual employees are free to join or not join a union and they can join the union of their choice, not necessarily the union selected by the AIRC under the 'conveniently belong' rule.

The Act encouraged the creation of *enterprise unions* and *autonomous enterprise branches*, where members are drawn from the same enterprise, regardless of skill, trade or function. The majority of a union's members must vote, by secret ballot, to establish an autonomous enterprise branch. The anticipated advantage of enterprise unions and autonomous enterprise branches is that a prosperous enterprise would be in the interests of members.

Right of entry was restricted to unions with members who have invited them into their workplace. Right of entry now depends on a written invitation by at least one employee who is a union member. The union must give the employer 24 hours notice before they enter an employer's premises, and they have no automatic right to inspect or view an Australian Workplace Agreement (AWA) or any document related to an AWA.

BOX 17.3 **DESIGNATED AWARD AREAS**
....

- pay rates
- piece rates and bonuses
- classifications
- hours of work
- overtime
- loadings
- penalty rates

- leave issues such as long-service leave, holidays and parental leave
- award dispute-settling procedures
- redundancy
- termination
- stand-down provisions
- types of employment

Commission. A summary of the proposed changes is shown in Box 17.4. You will see that these are not all straightforward and many are open to interpretation. This is why organisations have lawyers and workplace relations specialists to help supervisors deal with workplace relations issues!

Some difficulties

Genuine bargaining needs to have parties of roughly equal power and some industrial lawyers feel that the proposed Amendment Bill shifts the balance of power too far in favour of employers. They have three main concerns about the pending legislation in this regard.

They say it will make it almost impossible to organise legitimate industrial action. This undermines the free bargaining process as unscrupulous employers may now make 'take it or leave it' offers to employees when negotiating workplace agreements.

The 'no-disadvantage' test (i.e. employer offers of terms 'no less favourable' than the relevant award which are now 'bottom line' only) could erode employees' terms and conditions of employment, or at best make it difficult to improve them.

The severe downgrading of the authority, status and role of unions and the Industrial Tribunal further shifts the balance of power in favour of employers.

AWARDS

..... The *Workplace Relations Act* largely overturned the Australian **collective bargaining**, **award** and **conciliation and arbitration** system. Awards no longer comprehensively regulate employment conditions but set out in detail the legal minimum 'safety net' conditions of employment for a particular job or occupation. Instead of awards, which set conditions of employment for groups of workers at a national level, terms and conditions are agreed at workplace and individual level.

There have traditionally been two types of award: a *minimum rates award* and a *paid rates award*. Minimum rates awards are based on the value of the job, not the individual filling that job, and sets the minimum pay and conditions of employment. Workers can be paid at 'above-award rates' if they or their representatives can negotiate a better deal with their employer than the minimum award. As these awards are based on the value of skill required for one job compared with another, over-award payments to one group of workers have in the past resulted in pressure to increase the awards of other groups.

Over-award payments cannot be made under a paid rates award. Current legislation prohibits new paid rates awards, and existing paid rates awards will be converted to

BOX 17.4 A SUMMARY OF PROPOSED 'SECOND WAVE' LEGISLATIVE CHANGES

Australian Workplace Agreements and Collective Agreements. Reaching agreements and getting them approved will be simplified and no longer need a formal hearing to be ratified. A hearing will only be needed if an agreement clearly fails to meet statutory requirements or is requested by one of the parties concerned. The Employment Advocate, instead of the Commission, will assess AWAs. AWAs will override CAs. Employers will no longer have to offer identical AWAs to comparable employees.

Awards. Before awards can be altered and used for safety net purposes, they must be simplified and cannot maintain internal relativities between classification-based rates of pay.

Allowable award matters. The list will be shortened by removing matters covered by other legislation such as long-service leave, notice of termination and matters deemed to be more suitably decided at each workplace such as jury service and union picnic days.

The Industrial Relations Commission will be restructured and renamed as the Workplace Relations Commission. Its compulsory conciliation powers will be limited to disputes relating to allowable award matters after the bargaining period has expired, demarcation disputes and 'unfair dismissal' cases. Where both parties agree, it may also conciliate on other disputes on a fee-for-service basis of $500. The parties can also select an independent mediator.

A mediation adviser will be appointed to promote the use of mediation and establish and maintain a list of accredited mediators.

Industrial action. Lawful industrial action can take place during a statutory bargaining period if a majority of employees at the workplace consent to industrial action in a secret ballot. Notice of intended action is extended to five days. The procedures dealing with secret ballots are highly technical and based on a complex timetable, which will increase the difficulty of taking industrial action. The Commission will be required to attempt to stop or prevent proposed industrial action within 48 hours of receiving notice of proposed action.

Union entry. A system of certificates will be used to protect the identity of the union member who has invited a union official to enter an employer's premises.

Unfair dismissal. Employees who can use the federal Act to obtain amends for unfair dismissal will not be able to seek redress under other legislation. If employment is terminated on grounds that include the operational requirements of the business, it cannot be regarded as harsh, unjust or unreasonable.

Constructive dismissal. Employees will need to prove that the employer either indicated to them that they would be dismissed if they did not resign or they did something that was intended to force the employee to resign.

Conciliation. The Commission will be able to require an applicant to lodge money in advance as security in case costs are awarded against them.

Failed conciliation. The Commission will recommend an appropriate settlement if a claim is not conciliated successfully and can prevent the claim from proceeding to arbitration if it believes an applicant has a poor case.

simplified minimum rates awards after consultation with the parties concerned. As paid rates awards disappear, minimum rates awards will be pared back and simplified to meet a safety net of minimum standards.

The *Amendment Bill* currently before Parliament makes it clear that the role of awards is now 'to help address the needs of the low paid'. It expressly states that awards must not provide for wages and conditions of employment above the 'safety net'. Unions call this *award stripping*.

UNFAIR DISMISSAL

Recent legislation and regulations have also overhauled and simplified unfair dismissal laws. Certain minimum conditions continue to apply before an employer can terminate a person's employment. For example, it is still illegal to terminate a person's employment for discriminatory reasons or without providing notice, warning the employee about alleged unsatisfactory behaviour or performance, or giving the employee an opportunity to respond. In other words, there must still be a valid reason to terminate a person's employment. However, less rigid conditions are placed on the interpretation of unfair dismissal claims, which can now only be made by people who were earning less than $64 000 per annum. The onus is now on the employee to prove that the dismissal was unlawful, and the focus is now on whether the termination itself was fair and justified and less on whether a strict procedure was followed.

The AIRC and not the Industrial Relations Court (which the 1996 Act abolished) currently hears claims. The AIRC will attempt to settle claims, initially by conciliation, then by arbitration. It will consider whether a termination of employment was harsh, unjust or unreasonable. When determining the remedy for an employee who has been unfairly dismissed, the AIRC will have to take the potential impact of the remedy on the viability of the employer's business into account. The remedies it orders, including reinstatement and monetary compensation, are enforceable in the Federal Court (which takes over the role of the Industrial Relations Court).

Applications regarding unfair dismissals must be lodged within 21 days of written notice of termination and there is now a $50 lodgement fee, which may mean that fewer 'frivolous' claims are made. If a claim is found to be vexatious, the claimant will be required to repay the legal costs of the employer.

Employees have access to federal jurisdiction (the system described above) only if they are on a federal award, are Commonwealth public servants or Territory employees, or are employed by incorporated private sector organisations on an AWA. Other employees must use their state legislation.

WORKPLACE BARGAINING AND WORKPLACE AGREEMENTS

We are swiftly moving away from a workplace relations system based on a centralised national collective industry-based bargaining system and awards, to a decentralised local workplace agreement system. A key feature of the *Workplace Relations Act* was a new arrangement for **workplace bargaining** called Australian Workplace Agreements (AWAs). Employers and employees (or their representatives) can now negotiate terms and conditions that suit their particular workplace. This places the onus for workplace relations squarely on the organisation and each of its employees and gives the parties involved greater influence over the nature and content of their employment relationship. The intention is to allow greater flexibility—for example, in working arrangements such as hours of work, job sharing, and so on. This has the potential to allow organisations to plan changes and introduce them rapidly. They are a way of building better, more productive business environments and assuring our standard of living by helping enterprises in Australia be more internationally competitive. The goals of workplace agreements are to:

- allow organisations to introduce more relevant productivity measures and pay for productivity;
- create a climate conducive to good communication between the workforce and the employer;
- provide processes for better workplace understanding of the key issues affecting remuneration and business operations;
- provide stability for long-term business initiatives;
- create more flexible working arrangements;
- improve the skill levels of the workforce; and
- allow the smooth introduction of new production methods.

Workplace agreements are reached during a process of bargaining that takes place between an employer and its employees (or their representatives) at a work site. The work site is known as the **single bargaining unit**. Employees and employers can appoint people to be their bargaining agent in making, approving, varying or terminating AWAs. This appointment must be in writing and one party cannot refuse to recognise a bargaining agent appointed by the other party. Four other criteria that AWAs must meet are that they must be in writing, must specify an expiry date no longer than three years, must include provisions relating to antidiscrimination and must contain a dispute resolution procedure. AWAs may be terminated or varied by either party by agreement.

Workplace agreements give management and employees a way of getting together to decide how to improve the operation of their enterprise and how to share in its success. Everyone can benefit, in both unionised and non-unionised workplaces. Employees can gain a better deal in conditions and pay, based on productivity, better skills development and job security. Employers can become more competitive and profitable through better productivity, improved work practices and reduced labour costs. More jobs and a healthier economy can result.

THE **BIG** PICTURE

Most organisations want to measure the benefits resulting from workplace agreements. They can select a variety of indicators, depending on their main activities. They might include, for example, quality of products or services, customer satisfaction, after-sales service, absenteeism, staff turnover, health and safety measures, output levels and waste reduction. (See Chapter 9 for a discussion on best practice benchmarking.)

Workplace agreements are usually linked to the wider issue of workplace change. They also incorporate a clear and agreed vision and goals for the future of the enterprise to which all employees can feel committed. These goals are translated into specific, time-framed actions and targets that everyone in the workplace will work towards. As such, these agreements are far more than just a way to give or receive a wage increase. In addition to remuneration, workplace agreements cover other HRM issues such as job design, communication and consultation, employee welfare, career advancement and skills development. They provide opportunities to motivate employees and increase their commitment, develop a skilled and multiskilled flexible workforce, reduce the level of industrial disputation and provide greater job security. Each agreement is unique and so is the process that creates the agreement.

Successful workplace agreements rely heavily on the quality of the relationships between management and employees. They need to be based on a realistic understanding of current workplace processes and marketplace constraints, and open communication between employer and employee representatives.

Three bargaining streams

Employers can choose between three streams of agreements.

1. *AWAs.* AWAs must be based on consultation between employers and employees (or their agents). They replace the previously relevant awards, although they must at least meet the minimum 'safety net' provisions of the award that would otherwise cover the employee. Individual contracts or collective agreements (which cover a group of employees) can be reached with or without union involvement or AIRC scrutiny. Whether the AWA is collective or individual, each employee must individually sign such an agreement. If you haven't signed an AWA, you aren't bound by it. Once they have been signed by an employer and one or more individual employees, and filed with the Office of the Employment Advocate, they become binding and enforceable.

2. *Certified agreements.* CAs can be negotiated either with unions or directly with employees. For unions to be involved, a member of the union must request union representation. Industrial action is prohibited during the negotiating period.

THE **BIG** PICTURE

An efficient bargaining process leads to a high-quality workplace agreement.

The bargaining process shouldn't drag on for too long because this drains resources and frustrates people. It needs to be focused and cooperative, not shoot off in unexpected directions or become adversarial. The process to follow, based on a problem-solving model, should be agreed at the beginning of the discussions.

A high-quality outcome is one that people are committed to achieving. People can't commit to agreements that are vague, wordy, ambiguous and difficult to understand or to agreements that fail to address the real concerns of the parties involved.

CAs can be made with the approval of the majority of employees. If you haven't signed it, you are still bound by it if the majority of employees have signed it. CAs should be registered with the AIRC, which must be satisfied that the majority of employees have genuinely endorsed the agreement. Like AWAs, CAs must meet minimum 'safety net' conditions and include dispute prevention and settlement procedures and must not discriminate against employees on the grounds of union membership or any of the 14 other grounds specified in the Bill. Under current legislation, certified agreements must meet certain minimum conditions such as equal pay for equal work, 12 days sick/care leave, 12 months parental leave, and long-service and jury service leave. (As mentioned earlier in the chapter, some of this may change if the amendment legislation currently before Parliament is approved.)

3. Offering employees **state agreements**, either individually or collectively, which will override federal awards.

Employers can mix and match these bargaining streams by negotiating certified agreements for groups of workers while offering selected employees individual employment contracts (AWAs). Employers and employees may also agree to remain on federal awards, although the proposed legislation removes the incentive to do this.

The bargaining path an organisation chooses will depend on many factors including its level of unionisation, the union's and employees' approach to workplace change, the degree of trust between its management and workforce and the organisation's culture. In the short term, many organisations are likely to continue negotiating with the unions. ICI, Concrete Constructions, BHP and many other companies have already achieved positive change by working with unions to reach workplace agreements.

The upside of workplace agreements

Workplace agreements can help develop trust and improve communications and productivity. They can make organisations more democratic and help them restructure

---

THE BIG PICTURE

How to reach agreement:
1. Nominate employee and organisation representatives. Involve supervisors as well as HR specialists, since supervisors will be implementing the agreement.
2. Agree on the process.
3. Consult with those who will be signing the agreement to keep them abreast of developments.
4. Set clear goals that aim to make improvements to the organisation and employees' working life.
5. Listen, discuss and explore.
6. Develop a range of options.
7. Agree on the best of them and write them into the final agreement.
8. Make sure the final agreement is clear and easy to understand.
9. Have the workplace agreement signed by the employees.

and become more adaptable to compete in today's demanding environment. Those organisations that can win the trust and confidence of employees have an opportunity to replace confrontationist workplace relationships with something better and more productive. They have a genuine opportunity to transform themselves into more flexible, efficient, globally competitive businesses.

The downside of workplace agreements

Enterprise bargaining has been successful in many ways but there are still problems. Old adversarial thought patterns are hard for some employer and employee representatives to break. Many have failed to improve productivity or hold initial productivity improvements. There is evidence of increased levels of third party involvement, which goes against the intentions of the legislation. Negotiating procedures remain complex in many organisations.

THE RIGHT TO STRIKE

The right to strike during negotiations for new workplace agreements (AWAs and CAs) remains legally protected. Notice must be given of such action and it must be taken only after a genuine attempt to reach agreement has been made.

If the employers and employees have agreed that industrial action will not occur during the life of their agreement, employers can take action against unions who engage in industrial action during that time. The *Workplace Relations Act* strengthens the AIRC's powers to address illegal workplace disputes and prohibits strike pay. It also reintroduces sanctions against secondary boycotts (industrial action taken 'in sympathy' with another union) through the *Trade Practices Act* in order to reduce the incidence of 'wildcat' and 'downstream' strikes where workers of one industry strike in support of another group of workers. Primary boycotts (affecting exports) are also outlawed.

The AIRC is no longer able to insert clauses into awards prohibiting industrial action. Instead, employers can apply to the AIRC for a direction for unlawful workplace action to cease. These directions will be legally enforceable in the Federal Court, which can issue injunctions requiring employees and unions to observe the AIRC directions, and fine employees and unions who fail to comply.

WORKING WITH UNIONS

Whether directly or indirectly, most supervisors have some involvement with unions or employee associations. Although union membership is declining, about one-quarter of Australian employees are members of a union. All or some of the employees you work with may be members of a union or employee association. Your organisation may depend on other businesses whose employees belong to unions. Because they are an integral part of the work scene, you need to understand and work with unions effectively.

Types of trade unions

A trade union or employee association is an organisation of employees set up to represent the interests of its members. There are six basic kinds of union.

Craft unions represent workers who possess a particular skill, regardless of the industry, its location or the size of workplace groups. Members of craft unions are usually people who have completed an apprenticeship.

Industrial unions represent people working in a particular industry, regardless of the level of skill or the type of worker involved in that industry. An industrial union will try to have all workers in a particular workplace as members, whereas a craft union would try to enlist only those workers with the particular skill or training relevant to that union.

There are few true craft unions or true industrial unions in Australia and New Zealand. In fact, most unions have elements of both types in them.

General unions recruit members without any regard to skill or industry and represent a diverse range of occupations. Most general unions have been formed by the amalgamation of several smaller unions and they are often, as a consequence, very large, possessing pockets of great strength.

Sectional unions represent workers performing similar types of work, such as marine cooks or university technicians.

White-collar and *professional unions* represent non-manual workers. They may be organised as sectional unions or industrial unions.

Demarcation lines and disputes

In the past, demarcation disputes often arose between unions. They sometimes argued among themselves about which union a group of workers should join, or they argued over which jobs 'belonged' to which union. Issues concerning where the boundaries of one stopped and where the other started were known as **demarcation disputes**.

Demarcation lines once meant, for example, that bricklayers could lay bricks but they couldn't carry them—only brickies' labourers (who belonged to a different union from the bricklayers' union) could carry the bricks. Demarcation lines between unions often created inflexible and inefficient working methods.

Because several unions could be represented in the one workplace, supervisors had to be careful that they did not unintentionally ignite a demarcation dispute by asking someone to do a job that 'belonged' to an employee from a different union.

Because of the disruption such disputes caused industry and the economy, the governments of Australia and New Zealand have sought to limit demarcation disputes. In encouraging individual enterprise agreements, enabling organisations to become more flexible and multiskilled, demarcation disputes in New Zealand and Australia are virtually a thing of the past.

The objectives of unions

The trade union movement is undergoing changes in structure, style and size in response to marketplace and legislative changes and the changing needs and expectations of members. The change in the mix of the workforce, with more casual and part-time employees, more knowledge workers and greater use of contract labour is reducing the unions' traditional employment base.

Unions continue to seek to protect and advance the economic, social and political interests of their members. This has traditionally meant wages, hours of work and working conditions. However, most modern unions are concerned with a broader array of member-oriented issues, including such things as:

- hiring and firing procedures (redundancy schemes have become a major feature of the work of some unions);

- superannuation arrangements;
- the extent of the employer's control over job content and methods;
- the proper way for supervisors to approach employees;
- promotion systems;
- the rights of unionists and union officers;
- the health, safety and welfare of members;
- social issues such as nuclear disarmament;
- education and training; and
- enterprise bargaining and productivity.

People join unions because, as a coordinated group, they have a greater bargaining power with employers and government than they would as individuals. Despite the changes to the workplace relations legislative environment that began with the *Workplace Relations Act* in 1996, unions will still help their members to gain the best possible deal with respect to terms and conditions of employment. However, they will do this through contract negotiations at workplace level (if they are asked by their members to act in this role) rather than collectively. This may mean that unions need to operate more like a consultancy, providing information to members on remuneration and working condition benchmarks, what should go into an employment contract, and so on. They will arm their members with knowledge to equip them to enter negotiations to help balance the scales.

The structure of Australian unions

Unions typically have a pyramid structure. There are three basic levels: the plant or shop level, the local level (usually a regional or state branch) and the national level.

The shop level

At the base of the pyramid is the rank-and-file membership—the people who often comprise a supervisor's work team. They usually elect a *delegate* from their ranks to represent their viewpoint and interests to both the union and management.

Delegates' activities vary from union to union, but generally involve enrolling new members, processing grievances and acting as spokespersons for their members in their day-to-day dealings with management. For example, if workers are unhappy with a change that a supervisor makes to the nature, timing or location of their work, they might ask the delegate to present their objections to their supervisor if the change appears to be outside union conditions or workplace agreements.

The local level

At the local level are *union organisers*. They are paid officials who liaise with delegates and assist members and delegates if a dispute occurs.

Unions meet regularly and form bodies known as *Trades Hall Councils* or *Trades and Labour Councils*. The general objectives of these councils are to:
- negotiate industry-wide agreements;
- prevent or control workplace disputes;
- ensure that the union movement is represented in the federal and state parliaments; and
- present the aims and principles of trade unionism.

Delegates affiliated with councils attend meetings to discuss a wide range of political and workplace matters and elect council representatives to bodies such as workers compensation boards and university and technical college councils. Council decisions are usually made by a majority vote of delegates.

The national level

At the national level, a large union typically provides two services. *Industrial* and *research officers* provide information to back up negotiations with employers. *Elected officials* devise policies and implement the decisions of the union's general meetings. These officials usually include a president, one or more vice-presidents, a secretary, an assistant secretary and a treasurer. Together with other executive members, these officials are responsible for the day-to-day management of their union at state and national level, subject to the decisions of the appropriate policy-making body (*conference* or *congress*) which normally meets annually or biannually.

Three of the most important functions at the national level of union organisation are:
1. negotiating with national or industry employer representatives;
2. representing union members on the question of wages and other conditions of employment; and
3. making representations to government on matters affecting their members.

The major national body dealing with trade union matters is the Australian Council of Trade Unions (ACTU), founded in 1927. It coordinates the industrial policies of the union movement and, in particular, presents the union's case in major proceedings. It has also acted as a mediator and negotiator in major disputes, although this role may decrease as individual workplace agreements become the norm.

The objectives of the ACTU are:
1. socialising industry—that is, its production, distribution and exchange; and
2. using the resources of Australia for the benefit of the people—ensuring full employment with rising standards of living, real security and full cultural opportunities for all.

The ACTU executive consists of a full-time president and secretary elected by and from its congress (policy-making body), two vice-presidents elected by and from congress, six delegates elected by and from each of the ACTU state branches, and seven other delegates, one elected from each of seven industry groups. The executive conducts the business of the ACTU between congress meetings and has the power to initiate and deal with all matters affecting the interests of the trade union movement.

The structure of New Zealand unions

The pyramid structure also holds true in New Zealand. At the shop level are the *rank-and-file members* of the union and their representatives—the *union delegate* or the *shop steward*. These names appear to be interchangeable, and effectively mean the same thing: the representative of the workforce at the workplace elected from their own membership.

The *organiser* is employed by the local branch of a union and has responsibility for a number of companies within a geographical area. These companies are usually assigned on the basis of locality or alphabetical order. In New Zealand, unions cover a fairly wide geographical area; for example, the Wellington branch of the New Zealand Engineers Union could cover the bottom half of the North Island and have organisers operating out of Wellington, New Plymouth and Napier.

At the top of the pyramid is the *national union office*, responsible for formulating policy, negotiating national awards and agreements and liaising with other national unions, government departments and employers' organisations.

The New Zealand Council of Trade Unions (NZCTU) is set up much along the lines of the ACTU. It was established in the late 1980s and replaced the New Zealand Federation of Labour. The functions of the NZCTU are similar to those of the ACTU.

How unions are financed

Membership fees, usually a joining or initiation fee and an annual contribution, finance most union activities. Union delegates are responsible for collecting union dues and enlisting new members, and are sometimes paid a small commission. In addition, some governments make grants to the trade union movement to assist in its operations.

Most union officials are paid. The secretary, usually the most important official, is nearly always a full-time salaried officer in state branches. Other full-time administrative, research, legal and clerical staff, not necessarily drawn from union membership, are employed in the main offices of the larger unions, and some unions also employ full-time organisers to visit factories and work establishments to enrol members and organise union activities.

Unions and political parties

Australian trade unions generally affiliate (link) with their state branch of the Australian Labor Party (ALP). This allows them to send delegates to the state conferences of the ALP where policy is formed. The unions contribute to the strength, membership and finance of the ALP, which appears to try to limit the influence of unions by seeking support from a wide range of groups in the community. There have also been strong traditional links between unions and the New Zealand Labour Party through financial contributions and the establishment of working relationships.

Many trade unionists win seats in Parliament and a large number of former union officials now sit in Parliament. Not all union members share the political affiliations of their trade union, though. A particular political party cannot rely on the voting support of all the members of the unions affiliated with that party.

SUPERVISORS AND UNION DELEGATES

... As a supervisor you will probably have dealings with the union delegate, if there is one in your workplace. In one sense, this simplifies your job because delegates usually know the employees and have a 'feel' for their opinions. If you develop a good working relationship with the delegates, they will be able to give you an informed view and share their opinions on matters regarding working conditions, safety equipment, how to operate an employee suggestion system, and so on.

Clearly, the roles of delegates and supervisors are different. Nevertheless, many of their concerns overlap; for example, both supervisors and delegates should be concerned with the interests and welfare of employees. These shared concerns mean it is in your best interests to develop good working relationships.

Ensure that you become familiar with the conditions, awards and agreements that cover your workplace. Unions and management are not 'enemies'. In fact, both have a shared interest in ensuring that the organisation operates as efficiently and effectively as possible. If the organisation is unable to continue to offer work, then the very reason for the union's existence would disappear.

How do unions and workplace agreements affect workplace practice?

Workplace agreements, awards and workplace practices can place constraints on what supervisors can and can't do. You should be aware of your organisation's awards and agreements so that you don't inadvertently violate them. If you ask an employee to perform a task that requires greater skills than the job the employee has been doing, the union delegate or the employee may demand a higher job classification. If you wish to retrench two or three employees because business is slow, you may not have the freedom to dismiss who you like but may have to follow the termination procedures set down in the relevant award or workplace agreement.

Many larger organisations have moved the authority to make certain decisions away from supervisors and centralised it in a workplace relations or human resources department. For example, supervisors may no longer control a small change in work methods or the way a complaint is handled. This is to ensure that decisions do not violate an award or workplace agreement or cause a grievance. In multi-plant companies, this centralisation can be quite noticeable because management wants decisions made with all locations in mind, rather than allowing individual supervisors to make a decision for only one department.

This is particularly true with grievances handling. The procedure for handling grievances agreed to by employers, unions and the government often specifies that the first point of contact in a grievance will be between the delegate or employee representative and the supervisor. If your authority to handle a grievance has been transferred to the workplace relations department, you should check with them before giving an answer.

To prevent a supervisor from doing something that could cause a dispute, management has, in many instances, virtually taken away from supervisors the authority to discipline on the spot. In matters of grievances and other procedures where there are agreements made with the unions or employee representatives, you need to be very clear on precisely what these agreements are and stick to them. To avoid complications, you should also be clear about the extent of your authority in a given situation.

How changing workplace practices affect supervisors

We are faced with decreasing markets for our traditional rural and primary products, rapid advances in technology and the increased competitiveness of our overseas trading partners. Our traditional adversarial system of industrial relations, marked by collective bargaining and awards, has led to workplace practices that have reduced our ability to compete globally.

These have recently been overhauled by federal legislation, with implications for supervisors' day-to-day work practices and the way they manage operations.

We all play an important role in workplace relations. The skills of supervisors and managers will be tested, particularly in relation to establishing a climate of trust and cooperation with the rest of the workforce. To do this well, many will need to enhance the range of skills they possess and change many of their workplace relations paradigms.

Supervisors will be at the forefront of implementing and managing many of the changes in their workplace. They will need to encourage and help employees learn new skills and adapt to the changes being brought about by workplace agreements focusing on productivity improvements, multiskilling and cross-skilling. They will need to learn how to work with people taking advantage of more flexible working arrangements. They will need to act as a bridge between their organisation and their work team, explaining the new workplace relations arrangements and helping people work effectively within them.

As management, employees and the unions direct their attention towards the common goal of increased workplace efficiency, supervisors' roles will involve more coordination than before, and there will be a greater emphasis on communication, participation and consultation. If the goal of greater flexibility is to be achieved, supervisors will also need to take increased responsibility for scheduling and implementing on-the-job training programs and creating learning environments.

We can expect that an increased range of skills will result in increased job satisfaction and levels of pay. Organisations will benefit from quick adjustment to technological and other changes, and costs will be reduced. Australian society will benefit from greater demands for our goods and services, increased output and reduced unemployment.

RAPID REVIEW

		True	False
1.	An important aspect of industrial democracy is worker participation, which allows everyone an opportunity to have a say in matters that affect them.	☐	☐
2.	The *Workplace Relations Act* in Australia and the *Employment Contracts Bill* in New Zealand both seek to make the economy of their country more globally competitive and replace collective bargaining with workplace bargaining.	☐	☐
3.	The award system of collective bargaining and unfair dismissal laws are currently being overhauled in Australia.	☐	☐
4.	Federal awards are likely to be gradually replaced by state awards and workplace agreements covering most employees in Australia.	☐	☐
5.	Workplace agreements and employment contracts are making important changes to workplace practices which affect the way supervisors manage and work with employees.	☐	☐
6.	Since the numbers of unions and the numbers of people joining unions are decreasing, supervisors don't need to worry about working cooperatively with the union delegate any more.	☐	☐
7.	The differences between the types of unions are clear-cut.	☐	☐

	True	False
8. Unions have traditionally been concerned with conditions of employment such as wages, working hours and other working conditions. Many are also concerned with a range of other issues such as superannuation, nuclear disarmament and education for their members.	☐	☐
9. Most unions are bureaucratic in structure.	☐	☐
10. The ACTU and NZCTU are the peak national bodies to which unions can affiliate.	☐	☐
11. Most unions have no political affiliations.	☐	☐

APPLY YOUR KNOWLEDGE

1. Explain the seven basic principles of participation and the skills you'll need to apply them.
2. Discuss the main ways in which the *Workplace Relations Act* and the *Workplace Relations Amendment Act* have affected workplace relations in Australia, and explain the key mechanisms they apply to achieve their objectives.
3. What types of awards are there? Which type will supervisors be likely to deal with in the near future?
4. What benefits can we expect from workplace bargaining?
5. How might multiskilling of employees change the supervisor's role?

6. How might workplace agreements or individual employment contracts affect the day-to-day activities of supervisors?
7. Describe the six basic kinds of trade unions.
8. What are some common objectives of trade unions?
9. Diagram the three levels of union organisation and explain how they relate to each other.
10. Discuss how trade unions affect supervisors and the relationship that should exist between the supervisor and the union delegate.

DEVELOP YOUR SKILLS

Individual activities

1. Ask the Department of Industrial Relations for booklets explaining the *Workplace Relations Act* and the *Workplace Relations Amendment Act* and prepare a report summarising the main provisions of the *Workplace Relations Amendment Act*.
2. Interview a human resources manager to find out how their organisation has been affected by the Australian *Workplace Relations Act* or the New Zealand *Employment*

Contracts Bill. If the Amendment Act has passed through the Australian Parliament, find out what its effect has been.
3. Prepare a short report summarising the provisions of the current legislation regarding unfair dismissals.
4. What awards, if any, operate in your workplace or college? Who do they cover? How are they made?
5. Find out about the main provisions of the workplace agreement in your organisation or another you are familiar with.

6. Compile a portfolio of media articles on workplace relations.
7. Interview an employee or employer representative who has negotiated a successful workplace agreement. Find out all you can about the process itself and how effective it has been. Prepare a report for class and combine your findings to draw general conclusions about the process of workplace bargaining and what makes it effective.
8. Interview an industrial officer at your local employers' association and find out all you can about the process of developing workplace agreements. What factors help agreements to succeed? What factors work against them? If you can, find out about a specific workplace agreement and write it up to present as a case study to the class.
9. Contact the local office of a trade union and find out what its objectives are and what help it offers its members in reaching workplace agreements with their employers. Find out what the union's primary sources of finance are and how it expects to change over the coming years, particularly in the services it provides its members and the way it delivers these services.

Group activities

1. As a group, prepare a list of factors that help and hinder workplace bargaining.
2. Simulate a participative meeting intended to reach an agreement on how best to alter roster arrangements so that the office is staffed by at least four people during the lunch hour. Assign people to the following roles:
   - *Supervisor:* you are skilled in leading participative meetings and genuinely want to reach a consensus on this matter.
   - *Annette:* you don't want to staff the office during lunchtime because you have lunch every day with your boyfriend who works in the building next door.
   - *Beth:* you don't care when you work or don't work as long as someone tells you!
   - *Greg:* you don't think your supervisor should get everyone involved in this because it just starts trouble and generates ill will—supervisors should make the decisions they are paid to make.
   - *Anton:* you think it's great everyone is having a say in making this decision and you're prepared to be flexible.
   - *Robin:* you're quite happy to go along with just about anything but you don't really like to talk much 'in public'.
   - *Andy:* you're not concerned about whether or not you work over lunch, but you would really like to discuss improving the lunchroom facilities.
   - *Craig:* you're happy to participate in this meeting to reach a consensus.
3. How important is trust between a supervisor and work team? Compile a list of specific actions supervisors can take to build trust in their work teams. Now make a list of actions that would break down trust in work teams. What can you conclude about how easy or difficult it is to build trust and to destroy it?
4. Form the class into two panels to debate the proposition: 'Unions and management are on opposite teams.'

5. Mary was stunned. All her training as an employee of the state for the past 17 years hadn't prepared her for this! Her department was being reorganised along private sector lines and employees were being urged to move from collective bargaining to individual employment contracts. There were advantages to both systems from her point of view, as far as she could see, and advantages to her now semi-autonomous department with both systems, too. She felt quite torn—feeling somehow 'betrayed' on the one hand and excited by the possibilities on the other.

Working in small groups and referring to the above paragraph, make a list of reasons for Mary feeling positive and feeling negative about the changes. Decide how you would advise her to deal with her feelings. Then decide how you would deal with Mary if you were her supervisor.

CASE STUDY 17.1

Happy Hotel's Workplace Agreement

Penny Lee Paleca, the employee relations supervisor at the City branch of the Happy Hotel, was on a roll! Four months ago she had assembled a representative group of the hotel's employees to begin work on a new workplace agreement.

Their objective was to ensure that their hotel benchmarked in the top 10% of their chain and comparable chains in a variety of productivity and customer and staff satisfaction measures, including waste reduction, billing efficiency, repeat business, absenteeism and staff turnover. Specifically, they decided that their agreement would address the following issues:

• ensuring all individuals and groups employed at the hotel had a say;
• establishing arrangements for flexibility in working hours and leave provision;
• establishing flexible pay;
• agreeing an internal dispute prevention and settling procedure;
• implementing the pay-for-skills plan developed by corporate head office;
• ensuring that a minimum of 40 hours training per year would be provided for all employees to upgrade their skills and increase their job satisfaction;
• establishing ongoing quality teams to examine and recommend on ways of working more effectively; and
• monitoring their progress.

In forming the committee, Penny had taken care to include a range of employees representative of the hotel and the community it served. Members came from all levels and shifts of the hotel and included men, women, young people and people from non-English-speaking backgrounds. The atmosphere at their regular meetings was cooperative and results-focused. Members reported regularly to their work groups on the progress the committee was making, and came to each meeting with fresh ideas and viewpoints.

All in all, Penny couldn't be more pleased with the way things had gone so far. Having said that, agreeing on methods for flexible work hours had proved somewhat problematic at first, given the nature of their business. The committee's overriding concern had been to ensure that customers would receive a high level and quality of service regardless of whether it was night or day, summer or winter, or a public holiday. They also wanted to increase flexibility for employees with family and other personal commitments, be able to adapt to seasonal demands and customer requirements and reduce overtime costs.

They considered a number of options, including averaging ordinary hours over extended periods via a 76-hour fortnight instead of a 38-hour week; varying the length of the working week according to seasonal needs; varying the hours of core time; staggering start and finish times; accruing time off for working public holidays in place of penalty payments; and rostering shiftwork. In the end, they worked out arrangements that would satisfy just about everyone and not result in any increase to wages costs.

Working to an agreed agenda and timetable, they were now ready to write the agreement. Penny Lee's job was to liaise with their corporate head office to ensure they were meeting all the requirements of the *Workplace Relations Act* and that the dispute-settling procedure they had agreed on was acceptable to the chain as a whole. Once the agreement was written, a series of team meetings would be held to discuss and ratify it. When it was finalised, Penny would lodge the agreement with the AIRC for approval.

The committee would continue to meet every two months to keep track of productivity changes and customer and staff satisfaction measures. Penny would post summary graphs on the employee noticeboards and send copies to head office for their records.

Questions

1 Review and comment on the process of developing a workplace agreement to date.
2 Given the way the committee appears to be working together so far, how do you predict its success in writing the actual agreement and getting it accepted?
3 Imagine that the committee could not agree on arrangements for flexible working hours—what might have happened then? What could have been done to get the process back on track?

Industrial Democracy
The Hard Way

Simon Low supervised a work team made up primarily of clerical officers. New to the position, one of the duties he liked least was leading team meetings. He usually managed to get through them quite quickly, informing team members of any changes that might affect them, letting them discuss them and then closing the meeting, often with no progress being made or answers provided to concerns raised.

Last week, his manager indicated that she wanted to discuss his meeting leadership style at their biannual performance review coming up at the end of the month. She gave him a copy of the department's policy on worker participation and industrial democracy and asked him to think about what it meant in practice.

'Simon,' she had said, 'you are responsible for supervising your work team in a participative manner. We really need to draw on everyone's opinions and ideas and hear their problems. I consider this to be an important part of your job.'

Questions

1   What skills will Simon probably need to develop to lead his team participatively?
2   Might he need to change his attitude towards participation?
3   How could his supervisor help him most constructively?

Answers to Rapid Review questions

1. T   2. T   3. T   4. T   5. T   6. F   7. F   8. T   9. T   10. T   11. F

CHAPTER 18

MANAGING A DIVERSE WORKFORCE

The selection problem

Al Duncan and Joe Ziskos are discussing the appointment of a new supervisor.

'Well, if it comes right down to it, Al, I suppose we'd have to say that Eileen is the best qualified for the job. She really knows her stuff, gets on with everyone in the department, and she's solid and dependable.'

'Isn't she the young girl who got married a couple of months ago?' said Al.

'Yes, that's her—lovely girl.'

'Well, you know, Joe, I have a real problem with appointing a girl to that job. What we need is someone who will take good control of things out there, someone we can depend on. I'm not sure she's the best person for the job. Anyway, she'd never be able to put in all the overtime that's required.'

'She's always been semi-in-charge, Al. Everyone listens to what she says and what she says usually makes good sense. What is it you're really worried about?'

'I guess another thing is that she's bound to go off and start a family one of these days. I'd really like to have a dispatch supervisor we can depend on, one who will be with us for a good few years. Who else is there we could promote?'

'The only other suitable person is Neil McCann, but I'm not too sure about him. He seems to take a lot of sick leave and he isn't as familiar with the work as Eileen. And he's only been with us 14 months.'

'So we're in a tricky situation. Either it's Eileen, who's bound to go off and start a family and couldn't put in the overtime anyway, or it's Neil, who we're not too sure about. What shall we do, Joe?'

OVERVIEW

In many ways, strength lies in diversity. In this chapter you will find out how and why to make the best use of a varied workforce.

- Can you state the benefits of diversity to an organisation, its employees, its customers and the country?
- Can you explain the sources of discrimination and why it occurs?
- Do you know why legislation has been introduced to prevent discrimination and who in particular it is trying to help?
- Can you explain the five types of discrimination the antidiscrimination legislation is trying to prevent, and how it is attempting to prevent them?
- Can you recognise discrimination when it occurs?
- Can you explain the role of equal employment opportunity measures and the two important principles on which they are founded?

- Do special measures and equal employment opportunity measures need to cost an organisation a lot of money?
- Is there a difference between not discriminating and encouraging diversity at work?
- How can supervisors make the best use of the talents of people with disabilities?
- Do you have any prejudices or make any assumptions about people that could affect your ability to be an effective supervisor?
- Do you know what to do to prevent harassment and bullying? Do you know who is most at risk?

WHAT IS DISCRIMINATION?

We live in a big country, filled with an assortment of people, each with the potential to make meaningful contributions to our economy and to society. Some are members of groups that experience higher levels of unemployment than the population in general, and many face barriers in their employment and other disadvantages throughout their working lives.

Many organisations have yet to tap this reservoir of potential. The Karpin Committee has recommended that we capitalise on their talents. How can we make sure everyone contributes as best they can? Why haven't we done this fully?

As we learned in Chapter 15, people tend to recruit people who are like them. People also tend to recruit people who are most like others successfully doing the same job. By the same token, people also tend to promote and offer opportunities to people most like them and like those doing similar jobs. This perpetuates a *status quo*: men do trades; women become secretaries; Asians work with computers; Greeks open restaurants ... Added to this, we often unwittingly act on the basis of unfair and inaccurate stereotypes such as older workers don't learn as quickly; people with disabilities don't work as productively; people from non-English-speaking backgrounds do unskilled work. This results is many people from these groups being excluded and treated differently and less fairly than they should be. This is often unintentional but results in discrimination against certain groups of people. It also means we aren't making full use of the talent available. So the government has put legislation in place to encourage people to look beyond the *status quo* to harness the abilities of all Australians. It has made discrimination illegal.

The International Labour Organisation has defined **discrimination** as:

'... any distinction, exclusion or preference made on the basis of race, colour, sex, etc. which has the effect of nullifying or impairing equality of opportunity or treatment in employment or occupation.'

Eliminating discrimination and learning to supervise a variety of people effectively will assist us to reap the benefits of a diverse workforce.

Five ways to discriminate

Discrimination can be either overt or covert. **Overt discrimination** is direct, clear discrimination on the grounds of sex, race, social origin or one of the other factors listed above. If someone says, 'We don't want to employ a woman because a woman couldn't handle the pressure' or 'Don't employ an Aboriginal—he'll go walkabout on you', this is overt discrimination.

There are two main types of **covert discrimination**:

1. It can be based on characteristics that belong to or are connected with a group of people (e.g. women, Aborigines, young people). For instance, because women bear children, they have often been obliged to take breaks in their careers in order to stay at home to look after their young families. This has placed women at a disadvantage in employment both before, and often after, they have children. If an employer assumes that a younger woman will be having a family and will be leaving paid employment to do so, they may be reluctant to promote, train or otherwise invest time, money or effort in her. Then, when women have had a family and return to the job market, they may be seen as having outdated or rusty skills or perceived as lacking confidence in their abilities.

    It is illegal to base promotion, training and other employment decisions on characteristics that may be linked to some members of one group or another. It is often unsound logic to do so; for instance, in the example cited above, statistics show that women have a similar—and in many cases lower—turnover than men (despite their child-bearing role).

2. A second type of covert discrimination can be based on characteristics that are incorrectly or unfairly associated with people of a particular group. These are normally assumptions based on stereotypes. For example: 'Men are ambitious and logical, while women are emotional and better at interpersonal relations'; 'Aborigines are lazy'; 'An employee with a physical handicap would make the rest of our staff feel uncomfortable'; 'Asians are best at detailed work requiring fine manual dexterity.'

FROM THEORY TO PRACTICE

Is an organisation that offers insurance benefits to the married partners of employees being discriminatory? Probably, since this would discriminate against people in de facto and homosexual relationships.

Covert discrimination is often subtle and difficult to spot. People who discriminate covertly by making these assumptions are often unaware that they are discriminating.

Direct discrimination can be either overt or covert. An example of *overt direct discrimination* is a clear statement of refusal to hire people with particular characteristics (e.g. disability, gender, marital status). *Covert direct discrimination* can be more difficult to identify. A consistent failure to hire suitably qualified and competent applicants who have impaired mobility may be a sign of direct covert discrimination.

Indirect discrimination occurs when policies or practices that appear on the surface to be neutral actually have an adverse impact on a particular group of people. It often results from assumptions that everyone is the same as the policy makers—assumptions that are embedded in an organisation's policies, practices and procedures.

Here are three questions to ask to see whether indirect discrimination is occurring:

1. Are people with a particular characteristic expected to comply with a requirement or condition that the majority of people without that characteristic can comply with more easily?
2. Are people with a particular characteristic expected to comply with a requirement or condition that it is not possible for them to comply with?
3. Are people expected to comply with unreasonable requirements or conditions?

FROM THEORY TO PRACTICE

Towards the end of the 1980s, Australian Iron and Steel Pty Ltd had a 'last on first off' redundancy policy at its Port Kembla steelworks. The High Court held that this discriminated indirectly against women even though, on the surface, it appeared to be a neutral policy. However, because of past discriminatory hiring practices that favoured men, a higher proportion of female workers were retrenched. (*Australian Iron and Steel Pty Ltd v Banovic and Others, 1987*)

FROM THEORY TO PRACTICE

Is an organisation being discriminatory when it offers training that increases promotion opportunities only at weekends? That depends: can all employees easily attend training at weekends? What about people with childcare responsibilities, such as single parents? They might find it difficult to arrange child minding at weekends, so they could allege their employer is discriminating against them indirectly. Are married men less likely to have childcare responsibilities and therefore be able to attend the weekend training more easily? If so, a case could also be made that this policy discriminates against women. Could the organisation consider providing training during working hours or arranging childcare at the weekend training?

THE BIG PICTURE

Can you imagine ...

■ Women being forced to resign from government jobs when they get married?
■ The amount of money people earn being dictated by their sex?
■ Access to superannuation based on sex?
■ Skin colour dictating what jobs a person is allowed to do?

Sounds terrible. Yet this describes the employment situation in Australia in the 1970s.

Systemic or **structural discrimination** is the result of longstanding direct and indirect discrimination. It's been common practice for so long, it seems to be the 'natural order of things', not discrimination. The gender segregation of occupations is an example of systemic discrimination. If a manufacturing company, for example, consistently trains only male machine operators to set machines when a vacancy for a setter-operator opens, or if only female applicants for secretarial positions are considered seriously, we might well be dealing with systemic discrimination. What other gender-linked occupations can you think of? Might they be examples of systemic discrimination?

Much of the discrimination that has occurred in the past (and is unfortunately still occurring) is overt. Far more difficult to recognise, and potentially of greater sensitivity and difficulty to deal with, however, are actions that are based on longstanding employment practices and on unchallenged assumptions about individuals from particular groups.

ANTIDISCRIMINATION LEGISLATION

There are nearly 20 million people living in Australia and New Zealand. About half are either in work or looking for work. How effective are we in using their skills and abilities?

Like many governments, those of Australia and New Zealand have legislated to encourage us to make the best use of everyone's skills and abilities. This legislation allows us to select people from the varied talent pool available to us so that we draw on the talents and skills of all members of society. It makes discrimination in the workplace illegal. The intention is to make our enterprises and our economies stronger and more competitive.

FROM THEORY TO PRACTICE

Does the sales manager who has never considered recruiting a woman because 'women won't want to travel' think that he is discriminating? Is the office supervisor who has never considered hiring a clerical worker with a disability knowingly discriminating? Probably not.

What assumptions do you make about people that may not be true and which may disadvantage them? How might these assumptions prevent you from making the best use of a diverse workforce?

The Australian Commonwealth Government has legislated to ensure there is no discrimination in employment and occupation on the following grounds:

- race
- colour
- sex
- religion
- age
- criminal record
- sexual preference
- trade union activities
- political opinion
- national extraction
- social origin
- physical or intellectual disability
- marital status
- medical record
- nationality
- parental status (including pregnancy).

State legislation is also aimed at ensuring that every member of Australian society is given a fair go.

Discrimination is also illegal in New Zealand. Legislation states that employers must not base employment and related decisions on a person's colour, race, ethnic or national origin, sex, marital status, religious or ethical beliefs, age or disability. Employers cannot refuse or omit to employ people based on these factors. They must offer terms, conditions and benefits of employment and opportunities without regard to these factors. They cannot dismiss or subject any person to any detriment on the grounds of these factors.

The legislation of both countries is designed to help us make the best use of our diverse workforce. Known collectively as **antidiscrimination legislation**, it seeks ultimately to stop discrimination by providing a means to rectify or compensate for acts of discrimination.

Australian legislation provides for a conciliation phase. A person appointed by the government, usually a commissioner, will listen to both sides and then try to help them reach an agreement or compromise that is satisfactory to both parties. This is done at a hearing.

If agreement is not reached, or if either party is unhappy with the outcome, the legislation provides for recourse to tribunals and then to courts, which, in most cases, have powers to enforce their decisions. Findings in favour of the person who has been discriminated against may include the payment of compensation, reinstatement and/or other action that is felt appropriate. Hearings by a commissioner are in private and are relatively informal. Tribunals and courts tend to be public and more formal.

Here are two more points to bear in mind:

1. You cannot discriminate against someone who has threatened to take, or is in the process of taking, action under antidiscrimination legislation (e.g. you cannot terminate their employment or make working life so difficult for them that they resign).
2. If a person can show that discrimination has been even a very minor factor in the way they have been treated, there has nevertheless been discrimination and they could win damages from an arbiter or the courts.

Who is antidiscrimination legislation trying to help?

The National Committee on Discrimination in Employment and Occupation has identified the following four groups in Australia as being disadvantaged:

- women
- Aborigines and Torres Strait Islanders

* migrants
* people with disabilities.

This doesn't mean that every person who belongs to one or more of these groups is disadvantaged. Rather, the laws recognise that people who belong to one or more of these groups are far more likely to be disadvantaged than those who do not. Statistics show, for example, that individuals who are members of such groups tend to be:

* concentrated in low-paying, low-status jobs;
* concentrated in a limited range of occupations;
* excluded from the labour force for reasons not related to their ability to perform a job;
* limited in their opportunities for career progression;
* more likely to be unemployed; and
* more likely to face prejudice, not only when applying for a job but also at many other times during their working life.

The legislation covers full-time as well as part-time employees, temporary employees and contract workers.

Discrimination in practice

Here are some examples of situations that used to occur in the past but which are now unlawful because they are discriminatory:

* offering a woman, a migrant or an Aboriginal Australian less money or fewer 'perks' than other people doing the same or a similar job;

FROM THEORY TO PRACTICE

How to supervise people who don't yet speak English well:

* List tasks step by step, in the correct order (see Chapter 16).
* Speak slowly and clearly, in complete sentences (pidgin English is often considered insulting).
* Don't add unnecessary words or distract with small talk, etc. while giving instructions or training.
* Avoid complicated and lengthy sentences and explanations.
* Avoid slang.
* Pause every few sentences to allow time to process what you've said.
* Use examples, hand movements, models and graphs to emphasise important points.
* Explain and reinforce the basic vocabulary of the workplace often.
* If possible, arrange for others who speak the person's first language to support them.
* Make it easy to ask questions and be aware they might be hesitant to do so because of looking 'stupid' or feeling embarrassed.
* Ask for your instructions to be repeated in their own words to make sure you have communicated clearly.

- not offering a person a job, training or promotion because of an assumption that the person will leave and have a baby, go walkabout, take too many days' sick leave, be unreliable, not be able to relocate or not be promotable;
- asking different questions of people applying for the same job;
- insisting on qualifications such as physical factors (weight, height), academic training or years of experience that are not directly related to job requirements and are likely to place certain people at a disadvantage; and
- offering different conditions or terms of employment to different people doing similar jobs.

If discrimination occurs, the person discriminated against can turn to the law for help. They can file a complaint with the federal Human Rights and Equal Opportunity Commission or State Antidiscrimination Board/Equal Opportunity Commission. If the complaint is upheld, the offending party can be ordered to pay compensation and refrain from further discrimination.

EQUAL EMPLOYMENT OPPORTUNITY

Figures published by the International Labour Organisation indicate that Australia has the lowest percentage of women in management and one of the most gender segregated workforces in the industrialised world. Women are employed in a narrower range of industries and occupations than men and are clustered lower down the organisational hierarchy. They are offered less training than men and are overrepresented among the long-term unemployed. We find similar patterns in other groups of Australians such as migrants, older workers and people from non-English-speaking backgrounds.

Because of this, equal employment opportunity (EEO) measures have been introduced. These provide us with a means to identify and stop discrimination before it starts. The best known EEO measure is equal employment opportunities for women or **affirmative action**. Federal legislation requires employers of more than 100 people to develop programs to promote equal opportunities for women and monitor and report annually on their progress. This ultimately seeks to remove discrimination against women in the workplace through actions designed to eliminate the present effects of past discrimination.

FROM THEORY TO PRACTICE

A blind man worked in a large organisation for many years as a desk clerk. He carried out his duties well. An opportunity for a transfer to another job arose, a job that the blind man was able to do and would have liked to do. He was refused the transfer on the grounds that, although he could carry out the duties of the transfer position, he was not suitable for promotion to the next job up the line because that position required a sighted person. That was discrimination. Failing to transfer the blind man was discriminatory and unlawful because more than the required skills and abilities of the job in question were taken into consideration.

THE **BIG** PICTURE
Antidiscrimination legislation and EEO are about common sense and fair play. They aim to help us select the best person for the job. They help us make objective decisions relating to hiring, firing, paying, transferring, promoting, retrenching, training and developing employees. We can achieve these aims by basing our decisions on two important principles:
1. taking into account job-related characteristics only, especially skills and abilities; and
2. making merit the sole consideration in employment decisions and ignoring irrelevant factors such as age, sex and nationality.

The aims and benefits of EEO

EEO aims to reduce stereotyping of roles, skills and abilities; for example:

- Women are better with words, more intuitive, less ambitious and more emotional than men.
- Men are less patient, and better with numbers, decision making and problem solving than women.
- People with physical handicaps don't learn as quickly as able-bodied people and are harder to talk to.
- Aborigines won't be committed to the organisation's goals or work hard at doing a good job.
- Asians are more manually dexterous and have better mathematical skills than people from other races.

Some of these stereotypes may be accurate sometimes, but no stereotype is accurate all the time. Some women are more intuitive than some men but, equally, some men are more intuitive than some women. Some people with disabilities don't learn as quickly as some able-bodied people but, equally, some able-bodied people don't learn as quickly as

THE **BIG** PICTURE
EEO does not mean that you or your organisation loses your right or obligation to choose and train the best available person for the job. In fact, antidiscrimination and EEO legislation help us do this by *encouraging us to select the best person for the job* in terms of those skills and abilities that are essential for carrying out the work most effectively. In eliminating irrelevant criteria, we can make fair and more meaningful employment decisions. We treat people equally, whatever their individual differences. By not limiting our range of candidates, and basing our decisions on merit, we increase our chances of selecting and benefiting from a diverse workforce.

some with disabilities. Such stereotypes not only do *us* a disservice but also the people we attribute them to.

EEO aims to help us get the best out of female employees and others from disadvantaged groups by reducing the tendency for them to be employed in low-paid, low-status jobs and to be promoted to less responsible positions than non-disadvantaged people. It aims to eliminate differences in employee benefit plans, conditions of employment, pay, perks, transfers, promotions and a host of other job-related conditions.

EEO helps us broaden the range of employees in an organisation and attain a workforce representative of the community at large. This can help organisations to be more flexible, more in tune with all their customers and suppliers and more adaptable to future requirements. The payoff will come not only in the morale and adaptability of the whole workforce, but in all other aspects of the organisation's effectiveness.

The open and fair employment practices encouraged by EEO measures and the legislation are consistent with most organisations' commitment to developing the skills and talents of their workforce, selecting the best people for jobs, giving regular feedback on how people are doing and other good management practices.

Special measures

Equal treatment doesn't always result in fair treatment and sometimes it isn't enough simply to cease to discriminate. Sometimes **special measures** need to be taken—actions aimed at

FROM THEORY TO PRACTICE

How can you make it easier for people to work with you? How can you make your employment practices more inclusive? Here are some ideas:

- Introduce family-friendly working arrangements such as unpaid personal leave, job sharing, paid parental leave and workplace childcare facilities.
- Recognise that family needs go beyond childcare. It includes elder care and household management (shopping, cooking, cleaning). Requirements to work overtime or long hours (paid or unpaid), travel, work at home on weekends, etc. assume that someone can look after home duties. (When you work extra hours, who does your ironing?)
- Have a dry cleaner collect and deliver at your workplace.
- Arrange with a greengrocer or supermarket to fill orders and deliver to your workplace.
- Negotiate with a cleaning company to provide discounted household cleaning.
- Extend your organisation's cafeteria or arrange with a local caterer to fill orders for healthy take-home meals.
- Provide laptops with fax modems so people can work from home when children are sick, or when employees have to stay home for a tradesperson or to accept a delivery.

Provide support like this to everyone equally and encourage everyone to make use of it. If it's offered only to women or seen as supporting female employees, they will be seen as different and more costly to employ.

THE **BIG** PICTURE

What barriers to career advancement do women face? Here are a few of the main ones:

- corporate cultures that favour men;
- stereotypes and preconceptions of women;
- lack of women on boards of directors;
- exclusion from informal networks; and
- management's perception that family responsibilities will interfere with work.

What barriers do those from 'disadvantaged' groups face? Here are a few of the main ones:

- exclusion from informal networks;
- stereotypes and preconceptions based on race and ethnicity;
- lack of mentoring opportunities;
- lack of role models; and
- perceptions that corporate cultures favour people from white Australian backgrounds.

What are the best ways to eliminate these barriers? Here are some ideas:

- CEO support for women and people from disadvantaged groups in professional and senior roles;
- more dedicated efforts to recruit and retain senior females and people from disadvantaged groups;
- formal mentoring programs; and
- education for all employees based on diversity.

---

redressing discrimination that has occurred in the past. Special measures fall under the general heading of equal employment opportunities. They aim to help people from disadvantaged groups 'catch up' quickly so they can compete equally for jobs, training and promotion. In Australia, special measures are not quotas, positive discrimination or any of the hundred and one other devices you may have heard about.

One example of a special measure is the English as a Second Language courses now provided by many TAFE colleges. Another is the Australian government's legislation on affirmative action or equal employment opportunities for women. This is an attempt to ensure that women get a fair go at every step in employment and occupation, from career choice to retirement benefits.

Special measures may also mean the modification of conditions of employment in order to accommodate cultural, religious or special personal needs. The government recommends the following practices:

1. Provide information on paternity leave.
2. Where flexibility in working hours and conditions is possible without detriment to efficient operations, efforts should be made to accommodate the special needs of individual employees.
3. Provide advice to employees on company policy in relation to such matters as leave for training, blood donations or jury service.

4. If your workforce is composed of people from different cultural backgrounds, be prepared to give and receive information on likely special needs such as the observance of prayer times and religious holidays, the observance of mourning periods for a deceased relative or the wearing of traditional dress.

5. Help employees whose first language is not English by encouraging them to attend one of the many English language courses available and, if necessary, use different languages on signs and for explaining an employee's rights and responsibilities.

6. Provide co-workers with information to assist their understanding of the special circumstances and needs of their workmates.

7. Modify the work environment where necessary to enable people with disabilities to achieve their potential.

DIVERSITY AT WORK

People with 160 different ethnic origins, speaking more than 1000 languages, make up Australia's population. Almost 25% of our population was born overseas, more than half in non-English-speaking countries. One or both parents of 20% of Australians were born in a

FROM THEORY TO PRACTICE

World Vision Australia realised it needed to do something to retain its younger female employees. When they went on maternity leave, they failed to return to work and this represented an enormous loss of the organisation's investment in recruitment, training, knowledge and experience. In response, they introduced family-friendly initiatives on a tiny budget ($10 000). Here are some of them:

- flexible start and finish times and rostered days off;
- children can be brought to the office in an emergency (e.g. during school holidays);
- a parents' room is available to care for sick family members;
- job sharing is allowed;
- a nursing mothers' room is available;
- six weeks paid maternity leave is offered;
- modems and terminals are offered to staff on maternity leave so they can stay in touch via email;
- part-time employment is offered;
- a mother's support group meets every six weeks;
- staff on maternity leave are encouraged to attend training courses paid for by World Vision;
- paid sick leave can be used for family illness and needs; and
- optional vaccinations are arranged for staff and their families.

Success: 79% of women returned to work after having children in the first three years of these initiatives, representing huge savings to World Vision by retaining valuable resources. The working climate has improved significantly and is more positive despite a high-pressure working environment.

THE **BIG** PICTURE

How silly is discrimination? How well do special measures work?

Let's pretend it isn't a white Anglo-Saxon male dominated world but a short people dominated world. Everyone in power is under 1.65 m (5'5") and the most powerful people are usually under 1.6 m (5'3"). After years of discrimination, tall people demand equity. Short people agree and try out three remedies.

- *Assimilation.* The short people teach tall people to try to act like short people. 'Bend over to get in through doorways,' they urge. 'Breathe in to fit into small chairs in the conference room.'

- *Accommodation.* The short people fix some of the structural barriers that get in the way of tall people. They make the doors at the back of the building higher; they make some of the desks bigger so the tall people's legs don't have to squeeze in underneath them. They even create less demanding career paths called 'tall people tracks' for those tall people who can't or won't fit into the short people's world.

- *Celebration.* Some short people celebrate the differences of their tall colleagues. They point out the advantages that tall people have (they stand out in a crowd; they can reach things on high shelves). They decide to place them in jobs where their advantages can be used: they put them in warehouses where there are tall shelves, they ask them to help design products for tall people.

Do these three approaches sound familiar? Are you aware of programs that teach women to be more like men? (Speak up! Use the word 'I' more! Learn to play golf!) Are you aware of organisations that accommodate the unique needs and situations of women (formal mentoring programs to compensate for women's exclusion from informal networks, flexible work arrangements, maternity leave, etc.)? Have you heard of programs that celebrate diversity (teaching men to listen more and work in a team cooperatively, channelling women into jobs where their 'special skills' can be used)?

These made a difference in the early days when discrimination was more obvious. But they've gone about as far as they can. Now we're left mostly with the nearly invisible systemic discrimination. How do we rid ourselves of this?

Source: Harvard Business Review, Jan–Feb 2000, 'A Modest Manifesto for Shattering the Glass Ceiling', by Professors Debra E. Meyerson and Joyce K. Fletcher, building on work begun by Professor Lotte Bailyn of MIT and Rhona Rapoport, Director of the Institute of Family and Environmental Research in London

non-English-speaking country. Women comprise 52% of our population and about 42% of the workforce. There are almost 305 000 Aboriginal Australians or Torres Straight Islander people, almost 50% of whom are under 21. We will benefit from a diverse workforce that reflects our diverse country.

The Australian Council on Population and Ethnic Affairs has stated:

'**Multiculturalism has given us the chance to build a remarkable nation, with a distinctive and meaningful blend of cultures. The approach we adopt as a nation towards the many diverse individuals who make up our** society ... will be one of the critical factors determining what Australia will offer its people for the rest of this century and beyond.'

Workplace diversity goes beyond the EEO idea of rectifying the disadvantages of women, Aboriginal Australians and Torres Strait Islanders, people whose second language is English and people with disabilities. It recognises the positive contribution that a diverse workforce can make to organisational effectiveness and morale. Box 18.1 shows some measures of workplace diversity.

Workplace diversity also offers us the opportunity to employ people from a variety of backgrounds to enhance our organisation's performance and competitive advantage. Valuing diversity helps us to discover new perspectives, tap different knowledge and experience bases and generate new ways of doing things. People with different experiences, ideas and approaches can contribute in wider and more diverse ways than employees who come from only one or two homogeneous groups. Given the right conditions, diverse teams can actually perform better and more creatively than teams of people with similar backgrounds.

Changing from a closed to a diverse organisation culture opens the door to capitalising on the range of talent and viewpoints available. Diversity means we have access to wider information and ideas about our marketplace and greater understanding of all our customers. A multicultural workforce can provide access to new markets and help develop internationally successful products and services. Nine out of ten of Australia's fastest growing export markets are now non-English-speaking countries. Using the talents of a diverse workforce effectively will be an important source of competitive advantage.

Non-discriminatory practices mean we select the best person for a job regardless of their age, sex or ethnic origins. Open and fair employment policies and practices boost morale and motivation. If you know you are working for an employer who cares about you as a

---

BOX
18.1

SOME MEASURES OF WORKPLACE DIVERSITY

Characteristics identified in EEO legislation
- Gender
- Age
- Race and ethnicity
- Disability
- Parental status
- Religious belief
- Cultural background
- Sexual orientation
- Language

Other measures
- Literacy and numeracy skills
- Personality style
- Personal values
- Outside-of-work commitments
- Educational level
- Socioeconomic background

- Marital status
- Carer commitments

How does your organisation measure up?
- Numbers and patterns of participation, including seniority levels
- Distribution across occupations and salary levels
- Casual and part-time participation
- Dispersal across the organisation
- Recruitment and promotion numbers
- Retention and separation rates
- Returns from maternity leave
- Numbers affected by downsizing and reorganisation
- Training patterns
- Complaints and grievance patterns
- Absenteeism

⚡ FROM THEORY TO PRACTICE

How diverse is your workplace and college? Think about:

- gender
- age
- language
- religious beliefs
- personality profile

- ethnicity
- cultural background
- sexual orientation
- carer responsibility
- value systems

- people with physical disabilities
- people with intellectual disabilities
- marital status
- socioeconomic background
- life experiences

person, regardless of your sex, colour, national origin or whatever, you are more likely to return this respect.

Human resources management practices based on diversity principles represent progressive management and can have positive effects in the short term and, especially, in the long term. Following these practices will help you and your organisation to make the best use of its employees.

Building an environment where everyone is valued, recognised and allowed to develop to their potential is a major ingredient in the success of a modern organisation. Diversity is not an end in itself, but a sensible way to achieve organisational objectives.

People with disabilities

Did you know that you have about an 18% chance of becoming disabled at some time during your working life? People with disabilities are Australia's largest minority group, representing both genders and all ethnicities, age groups and social and educational backgrounds. Although 18% of the population have disabilities, which is 15% of the potential workforce, their participation rate in the workforce is about half that of the non-disabled. Why is this? Do they not want to work? Or do we not want to hire people with disabilities?

We've all heard the excuses: 'It will cost too much to accommodate their needs', 'They won't fit in', and so on. But these excuses are just that—excuses. It is unlikely that any expensive workplace adjustments will be needed and, if they are, 80% will cost less than $500, which can be paid for by the Government. These excuses are preventing us from benefiting from the experience, abilities and ideas of one million people. According to Ian Walker of Diversity@work, a government-funded employment and training agency, this could be costing the country $18.8 billion.

THE **BIG** PICTURE

All organisational policies, practices and processes that touch the lives of employees are potential diversity issues. They include recruitment and selection, promotion, training, performance appraisals, career development, arrangements for leave and further study.

THE **BIG** PICTURE

Our workforce is changing and growing more diverse. As the baby boomers retire and there aren't enough Generation Xers to replace them, we will need to extend our recruitment pool. Over the next few decades, we will be employing more people with disabilities. That makes good sense, as research shows that people with disabilities have above average productivity and retention rates, and below average absenteeism.

Building a diverse workforce

You have the responsibility to choose the best person to hire, train and promote. There are many things you can do to make sure you fulfil these obligations, beginning with the selection process. You must know exactly what the job requires. To ensure you select the best person and that you give everyone a fair go, base the job description and personnel specification solely on the requirements of the job. In most cases, factors such as race, colour, sex, age, religion, political opinion or criminal record will be irrelevant to how well a person can do a job. If you think one of these factors is relevant to a vacancy you are trying to fill, you may be required to prove how and why this is the case.

When advertising a vacancy, mention only requirements that are necessary for the performance of a particular job and which do not have the effect of excluding members of a particular group or sex. Avoid gender-linked job titles—that is, those that describe the job or occupation in terms of one particular sex (e.g. salesman, waitress, draftsman). Use titles with no gender attachment (e.g. sales representative).

Ask the same questions of all applicants and be certain that these questions relate directly to job requirements. Be aware also of any underlying assumptions you may be making about people from particular groups. Make sure that your questions do not imply unfair or partial attitudes to race, colour or sex. Offer information about the position in the same way to all applicants.

Boxes 18.2 and 18.3 outline some of the key things to keep in mind when hiring and terminating staff.

FROM THEORY TO PRACTICE

Do any of the human resource policies and practices of your organisation contain prejudices or assumptions that are unrelated to job requirements? If a job requires skills and abilities A, B, C and D (say, reading, writing, arithmetic and the ability to stand on your feet for eight hours a day), then recruit someone with those abilities. If a person's religion, marital status, sex, colour or national origin are not related to their ability to perform the job successfully (in this case, to do A, B, C and D), then disregard these factors.

BOX 18.2 WHAT YOU CAN AND CANNOT ASK

General information to collect on an application form
- Position applied for.
- Surname, given names.
- Contact details.
- Educational qualifications, other qualifications, special skills, training, etc.
- Employment history and any other relevant experience.
- Referees' names and contact details.

Other information that may be relevant for certain jobs

The following information should be sought *only* where it is job-related:

- Age: Has minimum age been reached or is the applicant below any maximum age that may apply to employment law?
- National or ethnic origin: Is the applicant legally entitled to work in Australia?
- Languages: Questions on which languages the applicant speaks, reads or writes might be relevant in such jobs as police constable or airline flight attendant.
- Religion: Is the applicant willing to work a specified work schedule?
- Physical disability: Would a disability preclude the applicant from performing the duties of the job, be hazardous to the safety of the applicant or co-workers, clients or the public?
- Medical information (e.g. someone with chronic back pain may not be able to sit

(or to stand) for as long as the job requires, or may not be able to lift loads required by the job).
- Height and weight.
- Criminal record/traffic convictions and accidents: Someone convicted of larceny may not be suitable for some jobs which would place them in a position of trust (e.g. a job dealing with money or giving them access to people's homes).

Information that may not be requested
- Marital status: You may, however, ask applicants if they are willing to travel, be transferred, work weekends, shifts or overtime.
- National or ethnic origin: This includes references to birth place, mother tongue, nationality or foreign residence.
- Organisations: You may not ask applicants to list the clubs and organisations to which they belong.
- Photographs: These may not be requested prior to an interview.
- Race or colour: This includes complexion, colour of eyes, hair and skin.
- Relatives: No information concerning relatives, including names, addresses and relationships, may be required of an applicant. The names and addresses of person(s) to be notified in the case of accident may be required after the selection decision has been made.

FROM THEORY TO PRACTICE

Be aware of any prejudices or assumptions you hold about groups of people in our society. Do you have any tendency to stereotype people by age, sex, background, etc.? Avoid making decisions based on those stereotypes. Our tendency to stereotype is heightened whenever a person stands out as different from 'the norm'. For example, we're likely to consider a white male applying for a managerial job and a female applying for a secretarial position on their merits, yet assess a female from a non-English-speaking background applying for a managerial position, or a male body builder applying for a secretarial job, according to our stereotypes.

BOX 18.3   TERMINATION OF EMPLOYMENT

You cannot terminate employment on the basis of:

- union membership or participation in union activities outside working hours or, with the consent of the employer, within working hours;
- seeking to become, acting as or having acted as an employees' representative;
- filing a complaint or participating in proceedings against an employer involving alleged violation of laws or regulations;
- race, colour, sex, marital status, family responsibilities, pregnancy, religion, political opinion, national extraction, social origin or sexual preference;
- absence from work due to maternity leave;
- temporary absence from work because of genuine illness or injury, provided appropriate advice has been given and the period of absence is not unreasonable in the circumstances; or
- time off work while on workers' compensation.

You can terminate employment on the basis of:

- an employee's failure to conduct himself or herself in a manner appropriate to the job;
- retrenchment due to the operational requirements of the business;
- redundancy as a result of the introduction of new technology or organisational changes; or
- inability or failure to do the job adequately (provided you have discussed the problem with the employee, offered remedial training and given the employee an opportunity to improve).

Encourage other supervisors to be aware of the antidiscrimination legislation and how it affects them and the organisation. This is not something only the HR manager or general manager needs to know about—all supervisors must be familiar with this legislation.

Think over your employment practices. Gather some statistics that will show whether people from certain groups are or are not being recruited, being trained, being offered interesting assignments and committee work, being promoted. Does your organisation employ members of all groups in the full range of jobs or are people from some groups concentrated into a few types of jobs? Are some groups of people concentrated in a few levels of the organisational structure? Are any groups or individuals disadvantaged or excluded? If so, in what ways? Do the requirements of the jobs involved justify these disadvantages or exclusions?

An inability to penetrate informal networks lies at the root of lack of diversity in many organisations. Who are you including in your informal networks? Who are you excluding?

To gain the diversity advantage, develop a work climate that values everyone's contributions and that acknowledges, respects and makes the most of individual differences. Create an environment where everyone can perform effectively. Build on the strengths of everyone in the work team. Set a good example by valuing each person as an individual.

By being familiar with the contents of this chapter and bearing in mind the aims and principles of the legislation and EEO measures and the value of a diverse workforce, you will be in a position to ensure that both you and your organisation are equal opportunity employers and act within the requirements of antidiscrimination legislation.

Flexibility in a diverse workforce

More women with higher education and aspirations are joining the workforce than in previous generations. More men in the workforce are married to such women. More people from non-English-speaking backgrounds are seeking employment. Part-time and casual employment and the use of contract labour is growing. We need to manage this changing and diverse workforce, not just as groups of people but as individuals, each with their own unique needs and preferences. One set of rigid policies cannot work across today's highly diverse employees.

Flexible workplace arrangements such as job sharing, flexitime and telecommuting are growing in popularity in response to the needs of the marketplace and workforce. Other flexible arrangements that we might see more of in the future include:
- compressed work weeks: the standard 40-hour week compressed into less than five days;
- V-time programs: time and income trade-offs that allow full-time employees to reduce work hours for a specified pay reduction;
- flexible working years: working hours are specified for a whole year and employees can choose their working times to fill the yearly quota; and
- work-based childcare.

Such arrangements acknowledge the non-work responsibilities and outside interests of employees. Box 18.4 shows some common ingredients of diversity policies.

DIGNITY AT WORK

Harassment

Harassment is unwelcome and uninvited behaviour that is offensive to 'reasonable' people. It may be verbal or physical behaviour that causes a person to feel offended, humiliated or intimidated. It can be based on gender, pregnancy, marital status, race, religion, disability, age or sexuality. It can happen to anyone and can occur in the workplace or away from it, for example at a conference, a business trip or a business function. Here are some examples of harassing behaviour:
- derogatory comments;
- personally offensive remarks;
- smutty jokes;
- unnecessary touching;
- repeated comments;

BOX 18.4 COMMON INGREDIENTS OF DIVERSITY POLICIES

- The recognition that each employee has individual skills and contributions to make and should have equal access to employment opportunities.
- The application of the merit principle for all employment-related decisions.
- The accountability of all employees in management roles to uphold the policy with respect to recruitment and selection, performance management, training and development, promotion, reward and recognition.

- Clear steps to take to deal with breaches in fair treatment and where to seek assistance.
- How complaints will be investigated and resolved.
- Confidentiality.
- How any offenders will be dealt with.
- Formal or informal procedures.
- Every employee's responsibility to recognise and value the differences of the employers, customers and suppliers they work with.

- suggestions or remarks about a person's alleged sexual activities or private life;
- persistent unwelcome social invitations or telephone calls from workmates at work or at home;
- patting, pinching or touching; and
- display or distribution of offensive material, for example 'girlie' posters (either on hard copy or electronically).

Harassing behaviour may be based on unexamined assumptions and be unthinking rather than malicious. Nevertheless, it can produce feelings of anger, resentment, fear, powerlessness, humiliation and entrapment, hindering a person's ability to perform a job effectively and reducing their job satisfaction. Whether or not harm is intended, such behaviour creates an unpleasant working environment that can become hostile, demeaning or intimidating.

Harassment has probably always occurred but until recently it had no name and its victims suffered silently; it was 'invisible' or dismissed as a personal problem for those involved. It is now recognised as a significant and costly problem in many organisations.

Surveys have shown that 50%–88% of all working women feel they have been sexually harassed at some point in their working lives. We're probably all familiar with the overt 'grab and grope' forms of **sexual harassment**. More subtle forms of sexual harassment also exist. Sexual harassment is unwelcome or unwanted sexual advances, requests for sexual favours or unwelcome sexual conduct. It includes verbal as well as non-verbal behaviour and innuendo. Some of this behaviour may fall within society's norms, with such conduct being acceptable at some parties or in some clubs. But what may be acceptable behaviour at some social gatherings is not acceptable in the workplace if the victim feels unable to prevent it because of fears for their job, promotion or perks. At a party, we can walk away from behaviour we find offensive; at work, this is often not the case.

Although the majority of victims of harassment are female, males can also be affected. Harassment has to do with dominance and the exercise of power, real or perceived, in the workplace. People who are harassed have no power—if they did, they would not be harassed. This is why it is often young people employed in positions lower down the organisational hierarchy who are the victims of harassment. Such people find it difficult and awkward to make complaints about the treatment they are receiving. Supervisors of young people need to be particularly alert to the possibilities of harassment taking place.

People who are upset by unwelcome sexual conduct normally complain to their supervisor first. Treat them with empathy and understanding: it takes courage to come forward, and many don't—they lose their motivation and commitment and often 'vote with

FROM THEORY TO PRACTICE

Sexual harassment in a nutshell
- Is it *unwelcome*?
- Is it *sexual in nature*?
- Is it *reasonable that the victim feel* intimidated, embarrassed or offended?

THE **BIG** PICTURE

Harassment isn't just boss to subordinate.

1. One employee may not harass another employee in the same organisation. For example, a manager may not harass an employee; a group of employees may not harass another employee; one employee may not harass another employee.
2. An employee of one organisation may not harass an employee of another organisation during the course of their work. For example, a technician servicing a client's equipment on the client's premises may not harass that client's employees. Both the client and the technician's employers have a responsibility to see this does not occur and to stop it if it does.
3. An employee or group of employees of an organisation may not harass an employee of another organisation who visits to provide goods or services. For example, the employees at the client company may not harass the technician in the above example.
4. A person may not harass another person when providing goods or a service. For example, a hairdresser may not harass a customer.
5. Employees may not be harassed by the people they are providing goods or services to. For example, a customer may not harass a hairdresser.

If any of these types of harassment take place, the employer has a responsibility to protect the employee from harassment and to prevent their employees from harassing others.

---

their feet'. Organisations lose valuable employees as a result. Know your organisation's process for dealing with a complaint and follow it.

If the employee is dissatisfied with the outcome, they can complain to an independent body. The Commissioner for Equal Opportunity has the power to investigate and deal with complaints. Generally, conciliation is tried first before a complaint is referred for a formal hearing at the Human Rights and Equal Opportunity Commission under the federal *Equal Opportunity Act*. Penalties may be substantial and can include payment of compensation, reinstatement, transfer of the harasser, an apology, or the development of an internal sexual harassment policy.

Prevention is better. Be aware of your obligations and alert to your own unexamined assumptions and actions based on these assumptions. Be alert to the actions of others that may cause unnecessary discomfort, embarrassment or unpleasantness.

Bullying

Bullying is a particular form of harassment. Although they tend to be male, bullies can also be female. They are people who manipulate others using aggression. They purposefully ride roughshod over people to get their way and to feel 'one up'. They often act illogically and don't respond to reason. Bullies may have low self-esteem themselves and try to enhance their self-worth by demeaning others. They delight in making others uncomfortable. They often begin their careers as bullies in childhood and carry the behaviour over into adulthood

FROM THEORY TO PRACTICE

Supervisors have a clear obligation to investigate any occurrences of harassment and to take steps to remedy the situation and prevent any further occurrence. To ignore harassment is to condone it. Here are some steps you can take to prevent it:

- Discuss it at team meetings: what it is, what is and is not acceptable behaviour, etc.
- Counsel employees individually if they need it.
- Distribute literature on the subject (e.g. government pamphlets).
- Post your organisation's harassment policy and discuss what it means with employees.
- Train yourself to recognise early signals of harassment and step in quickly.
- Make sure everyone understands where to go for advice and support and how to make a complaint.

and their working lives. Bullies may be people in positions of authority and victimise people with less power. Bullies may also bully their peers. They often bully competent, successful people who make them feel inadequate or threatened in some way.

Because they have had so much practice, bullies are masters of verbal abuse. They use verbal hostility to wield power over others and often terrorise them. Their need to dominate and put others down means they deny or ignore the feelings, experiences, values, opinions, accomplishments and plans of those around them. They invalidate people, humiliate them and undermine them. Unlike physical abuse, it doesn't leave marks that you can see, but it's just as painful. Bullies gradually wear their victims down, eroding their self-esteem and self-confidence with a constant stream of ridicule and petty fault-finding.

FROM THEORY TO PRACTICE

There are two types of bullies: the obvious and the subtle.

- The boss or colleague who shouts and swears at you, constantly criticises or ridicules you in front of others.
- The boss who gradually erodes your duties and responsibilities, constantly sets unrealistic goals and impossible challenges, sets you up to fail by not giving you important information, calls a meeting when you are unable to attend and then castigates you for not attending, criticises you for minor mistakes and ignores your successes, or continually sabotages your work. These are consistent, not one-off incidents.

'She would time me when I went to the toilet.'

'He would tear strips off me at meetings, in front of my peers.'

'People used to cower when he entered the room.
Some people literally jumped.'

'My work was never good enough, no matter how hard I tried. And I
know I was doing what I was expected to do, as well as everyone else.'

'She'd set an impossible deadline and then say something like: "Just
remember. Jobs are no longer for life." '

Bullying usually consists of continual demeaning, aggressive, non-sexual remarks and has a similar range of negative effects as harassment. Like harassment, bullying makes the victims' working life miserable and can cause physical illness as a result of the stress. Like harassment, bullying is unacceptable in the workplace. Every employee has a right to be treated with dignity and respect. And, like harassment, the costs are often hidden. People may take sick days, lose their concentration and perform less well than they could, or leave the job altogether, particularly if they see no other recourse. Organisations pay in terms of morale, productivity and reputation.

'Keep away from angry, sore-tempered men,
lest you learn to be like them and endanger your soul.'

Proverbs 15:18

Since many bullies show a charming face to others, their victims are often reluctant to speak up for fear they will not be believed. Bullies will continue to bully as long as people let them. Don't suffer in silence or let your team members suffer. Don't ignore it or turn a blind eye. Address it. Make the bully aware that their behaviour is not acceptable. Often, they lack the interpersonal skills to deal with people differently, so they need to be shown what type of behaviour is acceptable in place of bullying. Because bullying is a long-established habit, one discussion is usually not enough. Each time the bullying behaviour occurs, it should be addressed and an alternative method of dealing with the person or problem discussed. Box 18.5 lists tips for dealing with a bully and Box 18.6 shows some common ingredients of dignity policies.

THE **BIG** PICTURE

There is a growing acknowledgement of the existence of workplace bullies. Recent separate surveys by the TUC (the peak union body in the UK) and the Institute of Personnel Development in the UK indicate that, in the past five years, as many as one in eight people have experienced bullying at work. Bullying is estimated to account for between one-third and half of all stress-related absenteeism in the UK with an annual cost of about $2.6 billion. In Europe and the United States, high-profile court cases are hitting the headlines and, in 1998, Britain had its first High Court bullying case, for psychiatric injury caused directly by bullying, brought against the Ford Motor Company.

BOX 18.5 DEALING WITH A BULLY

If the bullying behaviour is not trivial but persistent and intentional, try these tips:

- Use the bully's name, often. This gets their attention.
- Use the word 'you' (in other circumstances, we would say 'I', but 'you' makes them accountable. 'I' statements don't work with bullies (see Chapter 24).
- Name the behaviour and tell the bully what to do instead. For example, *don't* say 'I don't like it when you interrupt me'; *do* say 'John, you're interrupting. Let me finish.'
- Remember that, to a bully, silence is acceptance.

BOX 18.6 COMMON INGREDIENTS OF DIGNITY POLICIES

- A statement defining harassment and bullying.
- A commitment to a workplace environment that values people and dignity.
- Clear standards regarding acceptable behaviour, with the stated objective of ensuring dignity for everyone and creating a positive working environment.
- An outline of the responsibilities of all executives, managers, supervisors and employees in applying the principles.
- A clear framework for taking action to report unacceptable behaviour, both informal and formal, including access to an independent external investigator.
- A list of people to approach to discuss the problem (including union representatives, if appropriate).
- A commitment to prompt action if harassment or bullying is alleged.

- 'Champions' of the policy at senior level, scattered throughout the organisation to promote and give credibility to the policy.
- Accessible 'supporters' across the organisation at all levels, who have been trained to give confidential emotional support both to people considering taking action and to the alleged bully.
- A clear range of responses to deal with offenders, beginning with counselling and ending with termination of employment.
- Incorporation of dignity-at-work issues into training programs; respect accepted as a core value of the organisation.
- Every employee's responsibility to treat other employees, customers and suppliers with dignity is made clear.

THE **BIG** PICTURE

Is the stress of restructuring and downsizing and the need for fewer people to achieve more with less leading to more incidences of bullying and harassment? Some people think so. Professor Cary Cooper, who is leading a major study in the UK into workplace bullying, believes a new type of bully is emerging. He calls them the 'overloaded bully', someone who is under pressure and unable to cope with the demands put upon them. They don't have the deep-seated need to humiliate others—bullying is just how they cope with pressure.

It certainly seems that bullying is an issue organisations cannot afford to ignore.

FROM THEORY TO PRACTICE

How approachable are you? How easy would it be for one of your employees to discuss with you the fact that they were being bullied or sexually harassed?

RAPID REVIEW

	True	False
1. Failing to employ a diverse group of people at all levels in our organisations means that we miss out on people's talents and the unique contributions they could make.	☐	☐
2. Antidiscrimination legislation seeks to prevent us from taking into account gender, race, ethnic origin or other factors unrelated to a person's ability to do a job when making employment decisions.	☐	☐
3. Saying, 'I don't want to employee a man for this job because he won't have sufficient interpersonal skills and sensitivity' is an example of covert discrimination.	☐	☐
4. A person who feels discriminated against can seek help under federal or state law.	☐	☐
5. All women, Aborigines and Torres Strait Islanders, migrants and people with disabilities have been identified as disadvantaged.	☐	☐
6. EEO seeks to remove discrimination against women in the workplace by giving them unfair advantages over others.	☐	☐
7. Organisational policies and procedures, particularly in the HRM area, should be examined for any unintentional discrimination.	☐	☐
8. Because everyone is different we should ask different questions of different job applicants. For example, while it is reasonable to ask a woman whether she has adequate child-minding arrangements, it would be silly to ask a man this question.	☐	☐
9. In order to get the best value from employees, we should ensure our employment practices are fair to everyone.	☐	☐
10. Sexual harassment is unwelcome or unwanted sexual advances, requests for sexual favours or unwelcome sexual conduct. Young people and those in less senior positions are particularly at risk.	☐	☐
11. There is a growing acceptance of the existence of workplace bullies, who habitually demean and degrade others and create an unpleasant and even hostile work environment.	☐	☐

APPLY YOUR KNOWLEDGE

1. What is discrimination? Give two realistic examples each of the five types of discrimination discussed in this chapter.
2. Why do you think the federal and most state governments have felt it necessary to pass antidiscrimination legislation?
3. Antidiscrimination legislation helps 'victims' as well as organisations. It can also help perpetrators (those guilty of discrimination and harassment). Discuss.
4. What are the two main principles of EEO? What do these mean in practice and how do organisations benefit from following them?
5. What are EEO, special measures and diversity programs trying to achieve? How do they relate to antidiscrimination legislation?
6. What are 'special measures' and when might they be necessary?
7. What are some specific actions supervisors can take to comply with EEO and diversity goals?
8. What are some benefits of a diverse workforce?
9. How do EEO measures and the antidiscrimination legislation affect recruitment and selection? Training and development? Promotions and transfers? Pay, benefits and conditions of employment? Dismissal, discipline and grievance procedures?
10. What actions can supervisors take to help remedy the effects of past discrimination in their organisation? To eliminate any discriminatory practices that may still exist?
11. What is harassment? What is bullying? Who is vulnerable to each? Why?
12. What is a supervisor's responsibility if they become aware that one of their employees is being harassed or bullied?

DEVELOP YOUR SKILLS

Individual activities

1. Referring to the vignette on page 548, what specific mistakes is Al making when considering Eileen for this appointment?
2. Provide an example of each of the following forms of discrimination in terms of opportunity or treatment in employment: exclusion, preference and distinction. State whether the example you have given is of overt or covert discrimination and whether it is direct or indirect. Explain also whether the examples you have given might be systemic in nature.
3. Interview someone from a disadvantaged group. Find out whether they have ever been affected by overt or covert discrimination. If they have, find out how they were disadvantaged. How might the discrimination have affected the discriminator?
4. What are the key provisions of the Commonwealth antidiscrimination laws? Gather information from the library, employer organisations, the government printer and/or trade union offices.
5. Gathering information from the sources listed above, identify the key provisions of the antidiscrimination laws in your state. Compare and contrast them with Commonwealth legislation.
6. Find out about any EEO and special measures a large employer in your

area takes. Why have they taken these steps? Prepare a report for class.

7. Do a literature search in your library for recent articles on the topic of bullying in the workplace and prepare a short report summarising this issue.

Group activities

1. In small groups, brainstorm the effects of discrimination on the person who discriminates, their organisation, people who are discriminated against, other workers and society. Summarise your thoughts under the headings below and compare your thoughts with other groups in your class.
    Discriminator
    Organisation
    Those discriminated against
    Other workers
    Society

2. How does a diverse workforce benefit all the stakeholders in an organisation? Discuss this in small groups and summarise your thoughts to the rest of the class.

3. Has anyone in your class ever been sexually harassed or bullied? What happened? What were the effects? What was the outcome?

4. In small groups, brainstorm the effects, both positive and negative, of a homogeneous workforce and the effects of a heterogeneous, or diverse, workforce. How can good supervisory practice guard against the negative effects of diversity?

5. Referring again to the vignette on page 548, discuss, in small groups, the mistakes Al and Joe made when considering possible candidates for the dispatch supervisor vacancy. How should they have approached this?

CASE STUDY 18.1

Promotion On Merit?

A middle-aged supervisor arrived home looking drawn and tired after a particularly bad day at work. His wife asked him what the trouble was. He replied, 'You won't believe this, Marion, but I've been summonsed to appear before the Commissioner for Equal Opportunity. Someone has made a complaint against me under the *Racial Discrimination Act.*'

'Oh no, that's awful—what's it all about?' she said.

'You remember that key process operator we're trying to recruit? That's a really critical job and I need someone I can rely on. Well, an Aboriginal applied for it, internally—a guy from another department. It would mean a promotion for him. When his supervisor came to see me to ask if I'd consider him—well, I naturally said I couldn't. He knows as well as I do that these fellows aren't dependable and I just have to have someone who will turn up regularly for this job. It's for the good of the company, really ...'

Questions

1 What mistakes has this supervisor made?
2 Was he really acting in the company's best interests?
3 What advice would you give this supervisor for the future?

CASE STUDY 18.2

Carmen's Problem?

'Come in, Carmen, and sit down. I want to talk to you about how you're getting on here. You seem a bit nervous and edgy lately and I'm worried that it seems to be affecting your work performance. Is anything wrong?'

'No, everything's fine ... (pause) ... It's just, well—oh, it's nothing, really. Not important.'

'I'd like to hear what it is, Carmen, although of course I'll understand if it's personal and you'd rather not tell me.'

'It's stupid—you'll think I'm just being silly ...'

'It seems to be bothering you, whatever it is. Why don't you tell me about it?'

'Well, you know how the men fool around and make jokes and things.'

'Yes, I know they all get along well together. What is it you mean, Carmen?'

'Well, they tease us a lot. It doesn't seem to bother the other girls much, but it makes me upset. I'm not used to that sort of thing. I don't know what to do about it.'

'What do you mean, they "tease" you?'

'For instance, when we have to climb up those ladders to get at the things stored up there, they make remarks. I don't always understand what they say, but they always laugh loudly and I get embarrassed. I sometimes drop things and they laugh even louder.'

'Is this only with you, or does this happen with the other women too?'

'Oh, no, it isn't just me—they tease them, too. I don't think they really like it much either, but they pretend to laugh back.'

'I see ...'

Questions

1 If you were Carmen's supervisor, what would you say now?
2 What action would you take?
3 How difficult do you think it was for Carmen to talk about this?

Answers to Rapid Review questions

1. T   2. T   3. F   4. T   5. F   6. F   7. T   8. F   9. T   10. T   11. T

PART III

MANAGING PEOPLE

Organisations are constantly looking for ways to improve. In Parts 1 and 2 we looked at how managing workplace practices and operations can help organisations and their stakeholders to achieve their goals. In Part 3 we learn how leading and working effectively with people contributes to organisational success.

Effective people management and building and maintaining strong relationships with others, internally as well as with external supplier organisations and customers, is a critical ingredient of any organisation's success.

It is both a skill and an art. It is a skill because we can learn the basic theories about leadership, motivation, conflict resolution, performance counselling and appraisal. We can study how to induct and train employees, provide work instructions and

delegate duties. The art lies in how we adopt and adapt this knowledge and put it into practice in our own unique way.

Most supervisors are knowledgeable about the technical aspects of the jobs they are supervising: office supervisors are familiar with the clerical and administrative procedures they supervise; nursing supervisors are able to carry out the duties of the nurses they supervise; manufacturing supervisors can operate the machines and equipment of their sections; service supervisors can perform the duties of the front-line staff they supervise. Indeed, many supervisors once performed the jobs they are now supervising.

Yet managing people is perhaps the skill supervisors need the most. Weak people skills contribute directly to lost productivity and ineffectiveness. The interdependence of today's work relies on leaders and supervisors who know how to get the best out of people. Without the cooperation and support of their team, supervisors cannot succeed in achieving the task.

How can we learn the art of managing people? Most of us aren't born leaders or motivators. We must learn and develop these skills. Watching and learning from role models, those who are skilled in the art of working effectively with people, is one good way to learn and develop your own people skills.

Observe them, analyse what they do and make their strong points your own. Reflection helps, too. Review your own leadership experiences and experiences of working with others, draw conclusions about what worked and what didn't and plan to do it better next time.

The information covered in this final section of *Supervision* will provide you with a framework for leaning from role models and from your own experiences. It includes the basic theoretical information you will need to develop these all-important skills of managing people.

CHAPTER 19

MANAGING EFFECTIVE WORKING RELATIONSHIPS

Seeds of doubt

Technically, Marta felt she knew her job and she believed she supervised her staff well. Yet, although she wouldn't admit it to anyone, she sometimes felt that the job did get on top of her. Lately she'd been waking up worrying about things she needed to do, decisions she had to make, things people had said ... And her partner seemed to think that recently she had become more short-tempered than usual.

In truth, a number of issues were troubling her, like the need to confront a staff member about poor work habits, and the fact that her boss didn't seem to value her opinions. Sometimes she felt she might be 'rubbing her staff up the wrong way', but she couldn't quite put her finger on it. Deep down she sometimes wondered if she really was as good a supervisor as she thought. Or was she just kidding herself?

Can you develop and sustain effective working relationships with people? If you can't, you will not succeed as a supervisor. This chapter shows you how to work effectively with people by developing your understanding of yourself and enriching your personal skills base.

- Do you know what you most value and what motivates you to succeed?
- Would others agree that you 'mean what you say, say what you mean', and 'walk your talk'?
- Are you self-aware and open or secretive, self-absorbed and unaware of your affect on others?
- Do you know what type of working situations you excel in?
- Do your mind-sets empower you or hold you back?
- Who is in charge of your behaviour— yourself, or other people and circumstances?

- Can you figure out where other people are 'coming from'?
- Do you know what the 'psychological contract' is and why it's important to honour it?
- Can you recognise how other people would like you to communicate with and relate to them?
- Do you respect others before expecting them to respect you?
- Are you a clear and assertive communicator?

WHO DEVELOPS EFFECTIVE WORKING RELATIONSHIPS?

.... Have you ever worked with someone who was confident and assured; who showed respect to others and who gained their respect; who communicated with people in a clear and direct way that made them feel good about themselves? People like this invariably have effective working relationships. Others enjoy working with them because they know they can trust them and depend on them to say what they think and keep their promises. They respect them because they do their work well and achieve results. They work in 'give and take' relationships, from which everyone benefits.

People like this understand themselves and others. They share similar mind-sets, or ways of looking at the world and their place in it. They have well developed interpersonal skills and, usually, good job and conceptual skills, too. This helps them work effectively with others.

How do people become like this? Some develop these skills by attending personal development workshops. Others read books from the self-development section of book-shops and libraries. Others try to emulate the people they respect most (role models). While each of these approaches can work, a combination of them is probably the best way to cultivate your personal skills so that you can develop and maintain effective working relationships.

In this chapter, we will look at several of the elements involved in this (see Figure 19.1). You can use this information as a basis for your own development and future success as a supervisor.

FIGURE 19.1   ELEMENTS OF EFFECTIVE WORKING RELATIONSHIPS

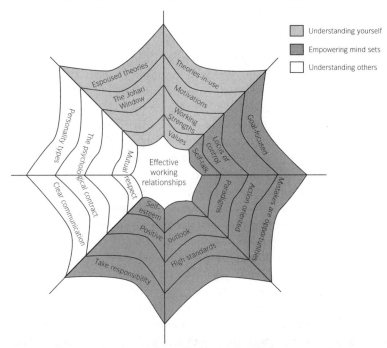

UNDERSTANDING YOURSELF

Effective supervisors understand themselves. They know their values and motivations and they know their strengths and limitations. This is the foundation of their ability to develop satisfying relationships with others and their ability to achieve goals, both their own and their department's. It is also the foundation for understanding others.

Values and motivations

In Chapter 3 we looked at the importance of values—knowing what you believe is important and worthwhile and what you are willing to stand up for. Knowing and acting on our values and making decisions based on them builds our integrity and self-respect. It helps us act in consistently ethical ways. It earns us the respect of others.

Ah, but does it? Newspapers frequently carry stories about those who act on their values of self-interest and having more at all costs. We all know a supervisor or manager who values self-preservation or self-promotion more than anything else. This is still value-directed behaviour, isn't it?

In Chapter 21, we examine what motivates us, and others, to do what we do. Understanding our values and the source of our own motivations helps us to set personally worthwhile goals and direct our behaviour and communications in productive directions.

Espoused theories versus theories-in-use

Have you ever known anyone who says one thing and does another? A supervisor might say: 'I believe in participation and I really value the contributions of my work team.' This is what

Chris Argyris, retired Harvard professor of Industrial Psychology, calls their **espoused theory**— what they say. The way a person behaves is their **theory-in-use**. If this same supervisor fails to listen to team members' ideas or suggestions, his theory-in-use might be something like this: 'People don't have any ideas worth listening to or valuable contributions to make.' Or another supervisor might say: 'My team is great. I've taught them all they know and I really respect them' (espoused theory) yet constantly check on the quality of their work and avoid delegating work to them (theory-in-use: 'I can't really trust my people and need to check on them').

Are these supervisors hypocrites? Possibly. More often, a conflict between an espoused theory and a theory-in-use is due to one of three other reasons. They may really *value* participation and *want* to believe that people are reliable (their espoused theories) but their mental models, on which they base their day-to-day behaviour, haven't caught up with their values yet. Or these values might be part of their organisation's values and culture, but not their own, and so the supervisors feel pressured to say they believe in these things when they really don't. Possibly, another value overrides the value in question; for example, a supervisor in an organisation that punishes mistakes might value participation but values staying out of trouble more and doesn't want to take the risk of involving the team. Either way, their espoused theories—what people say—and their theories-in-use—what they actually do—don't match. As a result, what they do contradicts what they say.

When people say one thing and do another, they are difficult to work with. This is often part of a person's blind spot: others see their inconsistency but they don't. Supervisors who have too many discrepancies between their espoused theories and theories-in-use lose credibility with their work teams and colleagues and fail to develop effective working relationships.

People are happiest and work best when their own values and the values of the organisation they work for agree. That way, there is no conflict. Managers at all levels need a strong sense of their own values and their organisation's values. This helps them act with integrity and consistency and earn the respect and confidence of others. This is central to effective working relationships.

The Johari Window

Joe Luft and Harry Ingham developed a model for self-awareness which they called the **Johari Window**. It shows two dimensions to understanding ourselves:

1. aspects of our behaviour and style that are *known* or *not known* to us (*self*); and
2. aspects of our behaviour and style *known* or *not known* to those we have contact with (*others*).

A combination of these two dimensions reveals four areas of knowledge about ourselves. These are shown in Figure 19.2.

The top left box is the public self, or *arena*. It is that part of ourselves that everyone knows. It includes such information as our name, job and experience in the organisation.

The *blind* area, in the top right box, contains things about ourselves that others can see, but of which we are unaware. This could be about anything—for example, the way you ask questions: you might believe your questions stem from curiosity or a desire to know something, but the manner of your questioning irritates others who feel they are being cross-examined.

FIGURE 19.2   THE JOHARI WINDOW

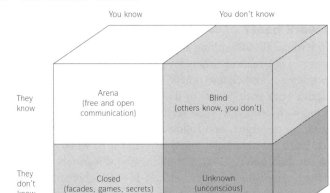

The *closed* area in the bottom left contains things that we know about ourselves but which others do not—secret things. For example, your boss might keep you standing during informal meetings and this annoys you but you say nothing and keep standing; this would fall into the closed area if your boss remains unaware that you would prefer to sit. Most of us have many thoughts and feelings in our closed area that we choose not to reveal to others. Sometimes, there is good reason for this privacy. At other times, it is our own fear of rejection that causes us to keep information to ourselves when, in reality, telling others could improve communication, trust and teamwork.

The final area is the *unknown* area. This contains information that is unknown to both others and ourselves. This is the vast area of the unconscious.

Although the model in Figure 19.2 shows these boxes of equal size, for most people they are not. The relative size of each box is different for different people. Some people have a much larger closed area than others; these are often the people that colleagues find puzzling, secretive and difficult to communicate with. Other people have large arenas; people enjoy

FROM THEORY TO PRACTICE

Try to increase the size of your *arena* and shrink your *blind* and *closed* areas to promote effective working relationships. This increases communication and trust. You can shrink the *blind* area through self-reflection and asking others for their feedback on how they see you. You can shrink the *closed* area by showing more of yourself to others you trust. Thinking about the content of each area, taking risks and revealing more of yourself to others and asking for feedback will help to move some of the content of the *blind* and *closed* areas to the open *arena* and strengthen your relationships with others.

Be aware of the public aspects of yourself such as your facial expressions and body language and their impact on others.

working with them because they are open in their communications, work well with others and develop honest and trusting relationships.

How do you work best?

Here are some questions about working styles. If you know the answers to them, you will be able to select working situations where you can use your strengths, avoid those that will highlight your weaknesses and choose others to build areas you need to strengthen.

Do you prefer to work with people or do you work best with things, or perhaps ideas? If you like working with people, in what relationship—mutual interdependency in a team situation, as a leader, a colleague, or a follower? Near people, but working independently? How do you best grasp information—when you read it or when someone tells you about it? Do you learn best by listening, doing, thinking about it or talking it through out loud? What kind of environment do you perform best in—a highly structured and predictable one, or a hectic and unpredictable one? Do you perform best in a large or a small organisation? Are you more comfortable in hierarchies or in informal, relaxed structures?

Management guru Peter Drucker says most of us know what we're *not* good at but not many of us know what we *are* good at. This is silly, he says, because we perform best from our strengths, not by just avoiding our weaknesses.

He advises us to monitor our own performance. He uses a 14th-century technique called **feedback analysis**. Whenever he has an important decision to make, or does something important, he notes down what he expects will happen. Nine to 12 months later, he compares his actual with his expected result. He has been doing this for 20 years and says he has learned many surprising things, including the types of people he works best with.

Feedback analysis shows where we need to improve our skills or acquire new ones (often to further strengthen skill areas). It also shows where we have no strengths, talent or skill— areas to stay away from! Don't waste time developing these, as you'll have little chance of becoming even mediocre. An analysis like this will also highlight our bad habits; once we know them, we can take steps to remedy them.

EMPOWERING MIND-SETS

What do you believe about yourself, others and the world around you? These **mind-sets** colour everything you say and do and are important ingredients in the quality of working relationships you are able to develop and maintain with others.

Paradigms

Paradigms are our mental models of the world and how it operates. These unquestioned and strongly held beliefs are so much a part of us that we may not even be aware of them. Nevertheless, they have a strong influence on our behaviour and our ability to work effectively with others.

A supervisor whose paradigm about employees is that they are basically irresponsible, lazy and untrustworthy will behave quite differently to employees than a supervisor whose paradigm says that they are basically responsible, hard working and trustworthy. Each supervisor will develop different working relationships with their employees.

Paradigms form **self-fulfilling prophecies**. They not only guide our actions, but also attract outcomes that confirm them. This means they are strong yet invisible and unconscious influences in the workplace.

THE **BIG** PICTURE

Teams, organisations and entire industries can form collective paradigms. In the 1970s the managers of America's car industry had a mental model that said, 'Our customers only care about how a car *looks*' and nearly lost their business to the Japanese car manufacturers who offered reliability. If we do not bring our mental models to the surface and examine them regularly, entire companies, not just individuals, could end up operating according to a set of outdated paradigms.

**'We are all captives of the pictures in our head—
our belief that the world we have experienced
is the world that really exists.'**

Walter Lippmann (1899–1974)
US author and journalist

Supervisors need to be aware of their own mind-sets and those of their work teams and try to keep them up to date and based on facts. Imagine a purchasing department of an organisation with a paradigm that says: 'Suppliers are out to provide the least they can get away with at the highest possible price. We have to watch them and constantly push to lower their prices or they'll take advantage of us.' This mind-set will make it difficult to form effective working relationships with the suppliers and the organisation will suffer as a result.

Self-esteem

How do you feel about yourself? Do you value yourself as a worthwhile individual? Are you self-confident and self-assured? Do you respect yourself enough to state your opinions and desires clearly? Are you comfortable with who you are?

Our **self-esteem** describes our mind-set about ourselves. Some people have high self-esteem while others have low self-esteem. People with low self-esteem feel unworthy and uncomfortable within themselves. They lack self-confidence and the ability to state what's on their mind.

Self-esteem is a major determinant of a person's behaviour and, thereby, their effectiveness. Like paradigms, it becomes a **self-fulfilling prophecy**.

Take, for example, a supervisor who believes she makes a lot of mistakes, doesn't communicate well with others and has few skills to offer; she will behave quite differently, and get quite different results, from another supervisor who believes she is likeable,

---

THE **BIG** PICTURE

Most employees adopt the work-related attitudes and paradigms of their supervisor. This is why it is so important that supervisors are positive role models to employees.

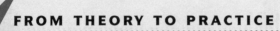

FROM THEORY TO PRACTICE

Do you think positively or negatively about yourself, your abilities, your personality, your appearance and your future? Get into the habit of being your own best friend, not your biggest critic.

communicates well, makes decisions easily and is a natural leader. Whether or not these beliefs accurately reflect reality, they reflect these supervisors' self-esteem and act as a self-fulfilling prophecy as each unconsciously finds ways to make them come true.

Imagine that the two supervisors described above are each asked to make a presentation at a meeting. The first, believing she is a poor communicator and makes a lot of mistakes, will be nervous and unsure of her ability to make an effective presentation. This will hinder her from giving the good presentation she would probably like to give. The second person, on the other hand, will be more likely to give a good presentation because she believes in her own abilities.

We sometimes hide these convictions from ourselves, but they guide our behaviour nonetheless. A positive self-regard helps build effective working relationships in another way, too. People with high self-esteem tend to build the self-esteem of the people around them. This strengthens everyone's ability to maintain effective working relationships.

Self-talk

Whether we are aware of it or not, we are constantly talking to ourselves. Psychologists have estimated that we talk to ourselves at least 50 000 times a day. Sometimes we are aware of this **self-talk** as we hold a little conversation with ourselves: 'Should I or shouldn't I?'

Much of our self-talk contains messages, or instructions, about how we should behave. Sometimes we're aware of them; at other times these conversations and instructions take place in the blink of an eye, far too quickly for us to be conscious of them. But they 'hit home' just the same and our subconscious makes sure we carry out our 'instructions'. Remember the self-fulfilling prophecy:

FROM THEORY TO PRACTICE

Have you ever 'known' you were going to fail a test or fail to kick a goal? Even if you were mentally and physically able to do so, your own thoughts would probably have prevented you from succeeding.

Elite athletes, sportspeople, business people and lots of others mentally rehearse a first-class performance before the actual event. This increases the likelihood that they will achieve excellence.

What do you imagine about an upcoming important event: do you see yourself falling flat or sailing smoothly through? What does this tell you about your self-talk?

'Whether you think you can or you think you can't—you're right!'

Henry Ford

Imagine the self-talk of the first supervisor described above: 'Oh no, I'll never make a good presentation! I'll forget what I'm going to say; I'll be really nervous. No one will pay any attention to me and I'll look like a fool.' In contrast, the second person might say: 'Well, this will be my first presentation. I'd better think it through carefully and practise it a few times so that it makes sense and people will listen to me. They usually do, anyway; this is really no different from a conversation with several people. I'll practise and do a really good job!'

Our self-talk reflects our self-esteem: high self-esteem leads to positive, empowering self-talk; low self-esteem leads to negative, limiting self-talk (see Box 19.1). It combines with our other mind-sets to produce our behaviour and guide our relationships with others. Positive or negative, it can help us or hinder us in establishing and maintaining effective working relationships.

Supervisors need positive self-talk to help them get through their usually hectic days with grace and ease. Negative self-talk only makes things more difficult.

Box 19.2 shows some of the different behaviours of 'winners' and 'losers'. Who would you rather work with?

FROM THEORY TO PRACTICE

The most important voice you'll ever hear is your own. Listen to self-talk. Do you give yourself encouraging messages that build your self-esteem and boost your confidence? Or are they limiting messages that hold you back and stop you from being as effective as you can be? If your self-talk is tearing you down, change it so it builds you up.

BOX 19.1 EXAMPLES OF HURTFUL AND HELPFUL SELF-TALK

Hurtful self-talk	Helpful self-talk
I always get things wrong.	Next time I'll put more effort into it.
I'll never understand this.	I'll really need to concentrate.
It's too complicated for me.	I'll work this through logically and carefully.
I'm always awkward around people I don't know.	I'll make an effort to be really friendly.
I'm terrible at things like this.	I haven't learned to do that well yet, but I'm getting better.
I'll never get it right.	I'll stick with this until I master it.
Isn't that just like me to do something stupid! What a clod I am!	That isn't like me—I usually do things better than that.
I never do anything right.	I need to watch where I'm going.
	That's not like me. Next time, I'll ...

WINNERS AND LOSERS

A winner says: 'Let's find out.'

A winner who makes a mistake says: 'I was wrong.'

A winner goes *through* a problem.

A winner says: 'I am good but not as good as I could be.'

A winner learns from those who are more skilled.

A winner says: 'There ought to be a better way to do it.'

A winner makes commitments.

A loser says: 'Nobody knows.'

A loser who makes a mistake says: 'It wasn't my fault.'

A loser never gets past it.

A loser says: 'I am not as bad as a lot of other people.'

A loser tears down those who are more skilled.

A loser says: 'That's the way it has always been.'

A loser makes empty promises.

Locus of control

Do you ever react without thinking? Do you let others 'make' you angry? In short, do you let others dictate your behaviour, or do you 'call the shots'? Do you do things because you 'have to' or because you 'want to'? Where is *your* **locus of control**?

People with an *external* locus of control let other people and outside events determine their behaviour, while people with an *internal* locus of control decide how they will behave.

If you let someone else's bad mood bring yours down too, it is a sign that your locus of control is outside yourself. If someone is rude to you and you're 'rude right back', that's also a sign your locus of control is external. Someone or something else, not you, is controlling your behaviour. Low self-esteem is usually accompanied by an external locus of control.

If, on the other hand, you can remain cool, calm and collected when those around you panic, if you can ignore the rainy day and be happy anyway, if you can do what you want to do and ignore 'peer pressure', your locus of control is probably internal. *You* are in charge of your own behaviour, not circumstances or other people. High self-esteem is usually accompanied by an internal locus of control.

An internal locus of control also helps people build and maintain effective workplace relationships. Supervisors need an internal locus of control so that they, not other people or events, are in charge of their behaviour and communications. This helps them appear more mature, self-contained and 'in charge'. Others naturally trust them and look to them for guidance and leadership.

FROM THEORY TO PRACTICE

Develop an internal locus of control by learning to take a few deep breaths and thinking before responding. Ask yourself: 'What do I really want to do here?' Maintain your professionalism, regardless of how people around you are behaving.

High standards

Think of the best boss or the best teacher you've worked with. Did they bring out the best in you? Did they help you achieve things beyond what you thought you were capable of? Did they stretch you and extend you?

People who establish effective working relationships usually have high standards. Whatever they attempt, they try to do it to the best of their ability. They expect others to do the same and, thanks to the self-fulfilling prophecy, this brings out the best in everyone. Since people enjoy stretching themselves and working at their potential, most of us are glad of the opportunity to work with people like this, which strengthens working relationships.

Supervisors who have high standards for themselves and others establish effective working relationships and get results. Others respect them and enjoy working with them.

Goal-focused action orientation

A goal-focused and action-oriented mind-set encourages us to set realistic yet challenging goals. Instead of daydreaming or 'wishing' we could achieve things, we can proactively and persistently work towards making things happen.

What turns a daydream into a goal? Action! The more concrete steps we take towards a goal, the more likely it is we'll achieve it. Do you want to pass an exam? You'll need to attend class, pay attention, take notes, study them, buy the textbook, read it, take more notes and revise them several times. These are all actions that will help you pass the exam. Wishing you would pass it, but doing nothing, practically guarantees failure.

Establishing a clear vision and goals that employees can understand, share and feel good about contributing to, is part of a supervisor's responsibility in establishing effective working relationships. Their behaviour sets the pace for how action-oriented and goal-focused their work teams are and what they are able to achieve.

Focusing on our goals combined with action helps us achieve them, especially when progress is slow or we run into difficulties. With a goal-focused mind-set, we can look for ways around problems.

> 'The road to achievement in relationships and in work is paved with obstacles that are used as stepping-stones.'

A mind-set that focuses on goals and finds ways around problems usually helps build effective working relationships. Box 19.3 lists some tips on how to set goals.

Taking responsibility

People who establish effective working relationships take responsibility for developing and nurturing them, just as they take responsibility for setting and achieving goals. Similarly,

 BOX 19.3

HOW TO SET A GREAT GOAL

- Set a few and state them simply, so that you will be able to keep them in mind and focus on them.
- Make them specific. Know precisely what you want to achieve.
- Make them achievable and at the same time, a little bit 'stretching'.
- Set target dates.
- State them in positive terms—say what you *do* want, not what you *don't* want.

just as they don't wait for their goals to be achieved with no action on their part, they don't wait for effective relationships to develop without helping them along.

When things go wrong, they don't blame themselves, others or circumstances. Instead of fixing blame, they take responsibility to fix the problem. This makes them a pleasure to work with, both at a personal level and at a work level. It's easy to establish effective working relationships with people who have a mind-set of taking responsibility.

A positive outlook

> 'There are those who bring joy wherever they go.
> And those who bring joy whenever they go.'

People who establish effective working relationships bring joy wherever they go. Their positive outlook is refreshing. It attracts people to them and it rubs off on others.

On the other hand, people who bring joy *when*ever they go have a negative outlook that is depressing. Others avoid them. Their sagging spirits can easily bring those around them down, too. This isn't the way to work effectively with others.

Mistakes as learning opportunities

Do you know anyone who will deny that a problem exists, even when something has clearly gone wrong? Or who blames other people or circumstances if things aren't working out perfectly? Or who is paralysed by guilt if they do something wrong and dare not take further action in case of making another mistake?

They should listen to Soichiro Honda, founder of the Honda Motor Corporation:

> 'Success is 99% failure.'

Making mistakes is natural and normal.

> 'Mistakes are inevitable. Learning from them is optional.'

What we need to do is learn from mistakes and help the people who report to us learn from theirs.

As we saw in Chapter 13, acknowledging and learning from our mistakes helps us get better all the time. It moves us out of the past, and feeling bad, and into the future, where we focus on how to improve. It also helps us establish and maintain effective working relationships because it makes us the sort of people others want to be around and take their lead from.

UNDERSTANDING OTHERS

Understanding a little about where others are 'coming from' and why they do the things they do makes it easier to develop effective working relationships with them. It makes it easier to fulfil the psychological contract and work with people cooperatively and in a way that is mutually satisfying.

The psychological contract and mutual rewards

The **psychological contract** is a package of unwritten and usually unspoken expectations and norms about how we will work with others. When all parties honour it, it works fine.

When someone violates it, trust is eroded and relationships suffer. Supervisors need to ensure the psychological contract that exists in a work department is a healthy one that respects individuals and their contributions. A healthy psychological contract ensures relationships will be cooperative and mutually rewarding. It focuses people's efforts on the vision and goals they are all trying to achieve. It includes all the stakeholders.

For example, a department may have a psychological contract that expects people to help each other out when they have completed their own work, to share knowledge and information freely, to treat each other and customers with respect, and to have fun and enjoy each other's company while working towards achieving their goals. A contract like this would lead to cooperation and mutually rewarding behaviours. Someone who breaks this pact would find it difficult to establish effective working relationships until they honoured it.

Personality types

Wouldn't it be nice to know how people prefer to relate to others and deal with information? Putting such knowledge to use would really help us work effectively with them, wouldn't it? It would put the finishing touches on our ability to develop and maintain effective working relationships. It would help us handle people with sensitivity and help our teams to thrive.

Carl Jung pioneered the study of **personality types** in the early 1900s. People, he said, face the world in two basic ways. *Introverts* are happiest when they are by themselves, doing their own thing. Although not necessarily shy, they do not seek out social or group activities. *Extroverts* love mixing with others and feel lost when by themselves. Most of us fall somewhere between the two, leaning more towards the extrovert or towards the introvert.

Jung also concluded that people receive and deal with information in four ways: *thinking, intuiting, feeling* and *sensing* (see Box 19.4). For most of us, one of these four is dominant while one or two are semi-developed and one is underdeveloped.

BOX 19.4   FOUR WAYS OF RECEIVING AND DEALING WITH INFORMATION

- *Thinkers* are strong on clear, logical reasoning; they are methodical and enjoy analysing problems. They are less effective when it comes to implementing solutions and are sceptical unless we give them facts and sound, rational information. At work, we often find thinkers working with facts and figures, in systems analysis or research.
- *Intuitors* are good at using their imagination to come up with ideas. They enjoy playing around with ideas and theories; they see the 'big picture' easily but often miss out on the details. The hunches of intuitors are often correct. At work, we find them strongest at long-term planning and creative tasks.
- *Feelers* see things according to their personal values and gut reactions rather than from a technical weighing up of 'pros', 'cons' and facts. They are warm and outgoing, and work best in groups because they are perceptive about people's moods, feelings and reactions. We need feelers to organise, build teams and harness people's enthusiasm. They make good counsellors and public relations people.
- *Sensors* are down-to-earth, energetic and hard-working, preferring action to words or ideas. They are practical people with a lot of common sense and are the first to roll up their sleeves and say, 'Let's get on with it'—often before thinking a problem through. 'Try it, then fix it' is their motto, because they are impatient and like to get things done. At work, sensors are usually well organised and are good at 'getting the ball rolling', setting things up, negotiating, trouble-shooting and converting ideas into action.

FROM THEORY TO PRACTICE

Use these ideas to concentrate on your strengths and work more effectively with others:

- Work out what your strengths are—doing (*sensor*), organising (*feeler*), analysing (*thinker*) or creating (*intuitor*).
- Ensure your weaknesses are covered by building a well balanced team. If you are a thinker, make sure you have feelers, intuitors and sensors around you so all the bases are covered.
- Keep out of situations in which your weaknesses are likely to be continually exposed and which will erode your self-confidence and self-esteem.
- If you have been given a task that requires a strength in which you are underdeveloped, pick the brains of a colleague or delegate the job to someone you can trust.
- Remember, however, that you cannot avoid all situations that challenge your underdeveloped areas; sometimes you must cope as best you can and learn to improve.

Katharine Myers and Isabel Briggs developed Jung's work further, and distinguished 16 personality types. Their type indicator is used extensively in organisations to help people understand themselves and each other better and develop more effective working relationships.

By being aware of how we deal with others and with information, we can try to place ourselves in situations where we will feel most comfortable and able to contribute. Similarly, if we are aware of how others operate, we will know how to work with them more effectively. We will be able to give them information in the way they prefer and try to place them in situations where they will feel most comfortable and be best able to contribute.

Mutual respect

When we understand a bit about others' needs and preferences when working with people and information, it's easier to relate to them in ways that they prefer. This helps us develop effective working relationships. This understanding also makes respecting their needs and wishes easier. When we respect others, it's easier for them to respect us. Cooperative and effective working relationships are based on mutual respect.

Clear communication

Effective working relationships require honesty and openness tempered with mutual respect. People need to know what's on our minds and we need to be able to express it with consideration and tact. People who can do this are called assertive. To be truly assertive, we need:

- high self-esteem;
- positive self-talk;
- an internal locus of control;
- mental models that include self-respect and respect for others; and
- clear and strong values including openness and honesty with others.

Assertiveness is a style of communicating and relating to others that enhances mutual respect and allows clear, open, direct and honest communication to take place. It is a combination of learned verbal and non-verbal skills that becomes most apparent in the way we communicate with others, both orally and through our body language. Assertiveness is self-enhancing (it increases self-respect) and is not hurtful to others. It is a main ingredient of establishing and maintaining effective working relationships.

AGGRESSIVE, PASSIVE AND ASSERTIVE BEHAVIOURS

There are three broad styles of communication: **aggressive**, **passive** (also called *submissive*) and **assertive**. These are shown in Figure 19.3.

Aggressive and passive styles are part of the **fight–flight response** that all animals, including human beings, are born with. When faced with danger, our instincts tell us either to stand our ground and fight, or to flee—to turn and run. Blood moves from our brains into our muscles, and adrenalin courses through our bodies to provide the energy we need.

Although most of us are seldom placed in the life-threatening situations for which this fight–flight response was originally useful, it is still part of us. Our early training and the role models around us often further strengthen our inborn ability to behave passively and aggressively. Our ability to behave passively or aggressively often shows up in the way we communicate and in the types of relationships we develop with others.

Assertiveness is a quite different style of behaviour and communication. Unlike aggression and passivity, assertiveness is not inborn. It is made up of verbal skills and non-verbal signals that we must learn and practise. We can further strengthen assertive behaviour by observing the way assertive role models behave and communicate with others.

The rights involved in assertiveness

There are several basic human rights that assertive people claim for themselves and extend to others. Those listed in Box 19.5 are a sample from the rights contained in the *Universal Declaration of Human Rights*, and there are many others. You could, for example, make lists of the rights of employees, the rights of supervisors and the rights of employers.

When someone is behaving assertively, they will seek to uphold both their own rights and the rights of others and work towards an outcome or solution that satisfies both or all parties. This is called a **win–win position**: I win and you win too.

Someone behaving aggressively will be primarily concerned with maintaining their own rights and achieving an outcome that they alone are happy with. This is called a **win–lose position**: I win and you lose. On the other hand, someone behaving passively is more

FIGURE 19.3   STYLES OF COMMUNICATION

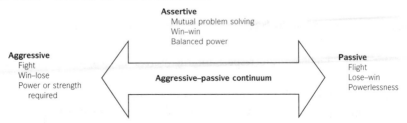

BOX 19.5 A SELECTION OF HUMAN RIGHTS

We all share the right:
- to refuse requests without feeling guilty or selfish;
- to have our own needs considered equally with the needs of others;
- to be treated with respect and to maintain our dignity;
- to life, liberty and security of person;
- to recognition as a person;
- to freedom of thought, opinion and expression.

concerned with upholding the rights of the other party and reaching an outcome that makes that person happy. This is called a **lose–win position**: I lose and you win.

Recognising aggressive behaviour

Think of someone you would call aggressive. Do they fail to respect other people's rights by speaking in a very direct, demanding, dominating manner that often comes across as a 'verbal assault'? Do they use hostile remarks (e.g. sexist or racist remarks) and sarcasm to drive home their point and ride roughshod over others? Do they express their opinions as facts and make their requests sound more like demands or threats? Do they criticise, blame, call people names, label their behaviour, praise people evaluatively, question people excessively or inappropriately, offer unasked for advice or make threats a lot?

Non-verbally, do you observe glaring eyes, set jaw, a jutting chin, clenched or thumping fists and finger stabbing? Do they invade other people's personal space—which others might call 'standover tactics'? Is their tone of voice firm, abrupt, hard or strident? If so, you have correctly identified this person as aggressive!

Recognising passive behaviour

Contrast the above with someone you know who is an 'eager-to-please, make-no-waves' person. Do they fail to respect themselves by apologising for what they say, seeking permission for their thoughts or actions, and frequently justifying themselves or their statements? Do they devalue themselves and their opinions, use put-downs of themselves ('I'm hopeless') and dismiss their own needs as unimportant ('What would *you* prefer?')? Do they talk in a rambling, hesitant, singsong or whining manner in a soft, dull or monotone voice? Do they seldom express their feelings, opinions and preferences or express them in an indirect way, for example, through hints?

Do you observe 'ghost' smiles on their face when they are expressing anger or being criticised, and evasive, downcast eyes? Is their body posture tense and accompanied by hand wringing, hunched shoulders, nervous movements, or shrugs and shuffling feet? If so, you have identified a passive or submissive person!

Recognising assertive behaviour

Now think of someone you would call assertive. Do they make statements that are clear and to the point, and which indicate respect for themselves as well as for others? Do they distinguish between fact and opinion and make suggestions rather than give 'advice', orders or demands? Are their suggestions constructive, free of judgment and blame? Do they seek ways to get around problems and differences of opinion? Do they express their feelings, needs, opinions and legitimate rights in a way that doesn't punish or threaten others or ignore or discount others' rights? Do they seem comfortable, relaxed, flexible and open? Are they accepting and tolerant of others?

When you observe them, do you notice that their voice is steady and firm, clear and neither too loud (aggressive) nor too soft (passive)? That there are no awkward hesitations, but a steady, even pace in the way they speak? That their facial expressions and other body language accurately reflect their feelings and what they are saying—that is, they are *congruent*? Is their eye contact appropriate and hand movements open, emphasising key points? Then this person is assertive!

ASSERTION SKILLS

Assertiveness really comes from inside—from our beliefs, or mind-sets, about ourselves and others. When we respect both ourselves and others, and claim and extend the basic human rights to each other, we will behave assertively naturally.

Nevertheless, most of us need to learn how to be assertive. We can do this by looking at the ways assertive people behave and communicate and emulating what they do. In this way, we can develop a set of assertion skills.

Here are some of the main verbal assertion skills that help to build effective working relationships. We can divide them into two groups. The first group is an *all-purpose* group, useful in most situations. The second group contains *self-protective* skills that are particularly helpful when someone is ignoring or infringing your rights, especially when they are behaving aggressively towards you. The skills in the second group help you to stand your ground assertively and maintain your rights without violating the rights of the other person. If you use these self-protective skills inappropriately, they will be counterproductive and regarded as aggressive and disrespectful rather than assertive.

With all verbal assertion skills, it is important that your body language and tone of voice are congruent with—that is, agree with—your verbal statements. For example, if you deliver an assertive message in a soft, hesitant voice, with downcast eyes while wringing your hands, it is unlikely that others will take your message seriously. Similarly, delivering an assertive message in an overly forceful, aggressive manner is likely to appear aggressive and antagonise the receiver rather than encourage cooperation.

All-purpose assertion skills

Self-disclosure
This skill involves revealing how you are:
- *feeling*
  —'I feel angry and disappointed to have to bring this up again; however ...'
  —'I feel uncomfortable discussing this with you right now.'
  —'I'm at a loss to know what to do.'
  —'I feel great—on top of the world!'
- *thinking*
  —'I think it would be a good idea to take a break and continue our conversation this afternoon.'
  —'As I see it, there are two options open to us right now ...'

—'Our next step appears to be . . .'

—'I think we've made excellent progress.'

• *reacting to something*

—'It seems to me we're going round in circles.'

—'I'm confused—would you go over that again?'

—'I'm too upset to discuss this right now. Can we meet this afternoon?'

—'I really appreciate that. Thank you.'

Self-disclosure sometimes requires trust and courage, and willingness to take a risk to build a better working relationship.

Open-ended questions

As we saw in Chapter 2, this skill involves asking questions that encourage the other person to give more than a 'yes' or 'no' answer. Such questions help you to understand the other person's point of view and open up the communication between you. You will find that they are valuable in work discussions and interviews as well as in social situations.

'I' language

'I' language involves taking responsibility for your own feelings. Compare 'I feel angry when ...' with 'You make me angry when you ...'. In the first example the speaker has taken responsibility for a feeling, while in the second there is a suggestion of blame that is likely to make the other person feel defensive and start an argument. If you are just learning assertion skills, you might find the 'I' message formula shown in Box 19.6 helpful.

Active listening/summarising/asking questions to clarify

These important communication skills were discussed in Chapter 2. They are assertive because they show that you respect the other person's point of view enough to listen to it carefully and to make sure that you have understood what they have said. This in turn will help you communicate your own point of view more clearly and develop effective working relationships.

BOX 19.6 THE 'I' MESSAGE

1. **The action**	When (*objective, non-evaluative description of the other person's behaviour*)
2. **My response**	I get/become/feel (*a no-blame description of your own feelings or the effect of the action on you*)
3. **My preferred outcome**	I'd prefer (*description of what outcome you would like without telling the other what to do*)

Example:

1. When your report is late, as it was today ...
2. I get annoyed and frustrated because it holds up my work.
3. I'd like to work out a system so that this won't happen again

Negative inquiry

This skill involves prompting the other party to give you more information that you hope will prove useful. Alternatively, if the person is just being aggressive or 'stirring', it will quickly exhaust the topic. Negative inquiry involves an assertive, non-defensive, non-accusatory request for more specific information. It is useful in situations where you want to find out more about someone's criticisms, and it helps the critic to be more direct and assertive with you. Box 19.7 gives an example of how you can use negative inquiry.

BOX 19.7   NEGATIVE INQUIRY

Employee	'You're a hopeless trainer!'
Supervisor	'What is it about the way I train that you don't like?'
Employee	'Well, you don't seem to explain things slowly enough.'
Supervisor	'If I slowed down a bit, would that help?'
Employee	'Yes, that would help a lot!'
Supervisor	'What else do you think I could do?'

Self-protective assertion skills

Broken record

This skill involves calmly repeating your position over and over again, like a broken record. It enables you to persist in what you want without becoming sidetracked or 'talked around' and without giving excuses, explanations, reasons or apologies. It effectively stops aggressors in their tracks and is particularly useful when your position, opinion or needs are being ignored. An example of using the broken record technique is shown in Box 19.8.

Fogging

With fogging, the assertor deflects criticism that is unimportant, irrelevant or poorly timed by acknowledging that there may be some truth in it, without agreeing, disagreeing or apologising. When faced with this type of criticism, you acknowledge that there is a possibility that what your critic says has some truth to it, without commenting on it further. This effectively cuts off the criticism and closes that aspect of the conversation. An example of this is shown in Box 19.9

BOX 19.8   BROKEN RECORD

Supervisor	'I noticed you were 20 minutes late this morning. That's the third time this month and we've spoken about this before. I really need you here on time.'
Employee	'Oh, it's my car. It's still giving me trouble.'
Supervisor	'Well, I still need you here on time.'
Employee	'Yes, well, I'll be getting it serviced in a couple of weeks.'
Supervisor	'And have you arranged something to make sure you get in on time until then?'

BOX 19.9 FOGGING

Employee	'You're holidaying on a houseboat? That sounds pretty dull to me!'
Supervisor	'Yes, it sure isn't everyone's cup of tea.'
Employee	'Why don't you do something exciting and fun? How about trekking in Nepal?'
Supervisor	'Perhaps I'll consider that for my next holiday!'

Negative assertion

Negative assertion means assertively accepting and acknowledging your errors or mistakes without feeling guilty, apologising, asking for forgiveness or becoming defensive (e.g. by offering explanations or excuses, denying the mistake, or counterattacking). It is useful when criticism is justified—when you have made a mistake or are in the wrong—but choose not to discuss it right now. Box 19.10 gives an example of using negative assertion.

BOX 19.10 NEGATIVE ASSERTION

Employee	'Well, you certainly didn't explain that very well at this morning's meeting!'
Supervisor	'You're right, I didn't give enough background information.'
Employee	'Yeah, you really had us all confused.'
Supervisor	'Yes, I noticed that too. I plan to explain a bit more about it at our next meeting.'
Employee	'Yes, that's a good idea.'

How does assertiveness help?

Supervisors need to be assertive in their workplace communications. Assertively stating their own point of view while respecting the rights of others earns them respect and a reputation for having the 'courage of their convictions'. It builds effective working relationships.

There are many situations when being assertive can be useful. Examples include:

- initiating conversations
- expressing annoyance
- responding to criticism
- turning down requests
- accepting a compliment
- offering a compliment
- asking for a favour
- making a complaint
- making a request
- saying positive things about yourself.

FROM THEORY TO PRACTICE

What are some situations in which your working relationships would benefit from increased assertiveness?

	True	False
1. People undertake personal development activities to help them develop more effective working relationships.	☐	☐
2. Since a lot of our values and motivations are unconscious, we needn't worry about them.	☐	☐
3. One of the keys to working effectively with others is shrinking the blind and closed areas and expanding the arena in our Johari Window.	☐	☐
4. If we understand the way we work best, we can make more effective use of our strengths and learn ways to compensate for our weaknesses.	☐	☐
5. Paradigms are mind-sets that silently guide our behaviour and our working relationships.	☐	☐
6. People with high self-esteem are arrogant.	☐	☐
7. Self-esteem and self-talk are important because they shape our behaviour, and lead to a self-fulfilling prophecy.	☐	☐
8. An internal locus of control helps us control our behaviour and choose how we respond in difficult situations.	☐	☐
9. Supervisors need high self-esteem if they are to be really effective in their jobs.	☐	☐
10. Feeling good about yourself and helping others feel good about themselves is a good way to build effective working relationships.	☐	☐
11. A goal without an action plan is just a wish.	☐	☐
12. People who complain about problems and difficulties but don't do anything about them find it difficult to establish and maintain effective working relationships.	☐	☐
13. A positive outlook that finds ways around problems, learns from mistakes and stays focused on goals helps people develop effective working relationships.	☐	☐
14. Since the psychological contract is unwritten and unofficial, we don't need to adhere to it strictly.	☐	☐
15. According to Carl Jung, people tend to deal with information in one or two of four ways: thinking, intuiting, feeling and telling.	☐	☐
16. Mutual respect is a cornerstone to effective working relationships.	☐	☐
17. Assertion can be mistaken for aggression if the assertor isn't careful to respect the other person's rights as well as their own.	☐	☐

1. How could the Johari Window be used to develop teamwork in an organisation?

2. List ten words that you believe accurately and fairly describe you. Now list ten words that you believe describe your work mates, your work team or your study group. Now list ten words that you believe describe the world around you. Look carefully at the words you have written: what do they tell you about your mind-sets?

How realistic are they? Are they likely to help you or hinder you in developing and managing effective working relationships? How will they affect the people you supervise?

3. In what ways do our mind-sets guide our behaviour and influence the results we get?

4. How do self-esteem and self-talk affect a supervisor's ability to develop effective working relationships? Develop two or three examples to illustrate your answers.

5. Why is it important for supervisors to have an internal locus of control?

6. Discuss the mind-sets that help supervisors establish and maintain effective working relationships with their staff, their colleagues and their customers.

7. Give an example of a psychological contract and explain how understanding and honouring it helps people's working relationships. What is the supervisor's role in establishing and maintaining the psychological contract?

8. Outline the differences between assertive, aggressive and passive behaviour.

9. Write short notes to explain the following techniques and give an example of each:
   (a) broken record
   (b) fogging
   (c) negative assertion
   (d) negative inquiry.

10. Discuss the ways in which assertiveness is essential to a supervisor's ability to establish and maintain effective working relationships.

11. List the relationships and situations in which you typically communicate in an assertive, submissive and aggressive manner. For those relationships and situations where you typically communicate in a submissive or aggressive manner, list the benefits of behaving this way. Now list the potential benefits of communicating assertively in these situations or with these people. Now list the specific things you could do to behave assertively in these situations or with these people.

· DEVELOP YOUR SKILLS ·

Individual activities

1. From your own experience, give an example of someone's espoused theory being contradicted by their theory-in-use. What effect did this have on those around them? On how others felt about this person? On their effectiveness? How could you have tactfully drawn the contrast to this person's attention? How could they have become aware of it themselves?

2. What could you do to increase your arena (see Figure 19.2)? What would be the risks of doing this? What would be the benefits?

3. For the next two weeks, consciously listen to your self-talk. Keep track of the messages you are giving yourself: are they mostly positive and supportive or negative and undermining? Each time you give yourself a negative message, say: 'Stop!' and change it to a more supportive message. For example, if you catch yourself saying: 'I'll never be able to remember this. I'm so stupid!' say something like this instead: 'I'll be able to remember this as long as I concentrate. I can do whatever I set my mind to.' You may want to keep a journal of your self-talk.

4. Write an essay discussing the principles involved in developing and maintaining effective working relationships. To what extent are these dependent on a person's maturity and integrity?

5. Think back over the various things you have done over the past two months. Write them down in two columns, one column of those where you were pleased with the results, the other where you wished for better or different results. Referring to the information under the 'How do you work best?' heading in this chapter, draw some tentative conclusions about your strengths, limitations and preferences. Keep a feedback analysis diary to validate your conclusions.

6. Consider Jung's system of personality typing. What are the dangers in categorising people? In what ways can it be helpful?

7. Emerson said: 'What you are shouts so loudly in my ears, I cannot hear what you say.' What we are communicates far more eloquently than anything we say or do. Discuss this in relation to the concept of developing and maintaining effective working relationships and relate your thoughts to the role of the first-line manager.

Group activities

1. Think of five values or beliefs that guide and motivate your actions as a supervisor or as a student. Compare your list with the rest of your class. What similarities are there? What differences? How do these values shape your behaviour? How do they affect the relationships you build with others?

2. What is the difference between high self-esteem and arrogance? Discuss this question and present your thoughts to the rest of the class.

3. Form into groups of two or three with people you know reasonably well. Review the rules of giving helpful feedback. Then share something about yourself with the others that is in your closed area of the Johari Window. Then take turns giving each other some feedback on the blind area of the Johari Window. Confine your feedback to objective, non-evaluative statements. Follow the outline below:

    (a) Something you don't know about me is ... (share something from your closed area).

    (b) Something I really like about you is ... (aim for something that might be in your partner's blind area).

    (c) I think you might be more effective if you ... (aim for something that might be in your partner's blind area).

    If you wish, change partners every 10–15 minutes to give you an opportunity to get feedback from several people and practise your skills of offering and receiving feedback several times.

4. In groups of three or four, develop a strategy to establish and maintain effective work relationships with your peers and colleagues. (If you are not working, develop a strategy to establish and maintain effective work relationships with other students and with your teachers.) What specific behaviours will you need? What specific action steps will you need to take?

5. Imagine two supervisors—one highly effective and well respected by staff, colleagues, customers and management, the other not as

effective or respected. List as dot points the following information for each supervisor:

(a) level of self-esteem

(b) typical examples of self-talk

(c) their locus of control

(d) some of their values

(e) some of their mind-sets

Now describe how each of these supervisors might approach:

(f) developing their own staff

(g) delegating work to their staff

(h) securing a promotion to their retiring boss's job.

6. Mentally label each of the four corners of the classroom, Thinker, Feeler, Intuitor and Sensor, so that each of these ways of dealing with information has its own corner. In turn, each student should stand in the quadrant they believe is most like them. They should ask for feedback from others on where the others would have placed them, and why. (They should feel free to change groups based on feedback they get from others.) Then, in groups of Thinkers, Feelers, Intuitors and Sensors, discuss the questions below. Appoint someone to summarise the discussions to report back to the other groups.

(a) What kind of work and tasks do you enjoy the most and find most interesting and challenging?

(b) What kind of work and tasks do you least enjoy and find the most boring and difficult?

(c) What sort of information do you like to have when making an important decision?

(d) What sort of people do you get on best with?

(e) What sort of people annoy you?

(f) What are your limitations?

(g) What are your best qualities?

7. In small groups, select three occupations. How would a Thinker behave in each occupation? A Feeler? An Intuitor? A Sensor? Summarise your responses to compare with the other groups.

8. Form into small groups and read out the Walter Lipman words quoted earlier in this chapter. What do you think he is saying?

CASE STUDY 19.1

Glenys's Dilemma

Everyone knew that Les would be retiring at some time during the next 18 months and Glenys decided that she wanted to be offered his position as section supervisor. She was determined to make a positive bid for the job and, if successful, to use it as a stepping stone to further her career in the organisation, which, after all, boasted about being an equal opportunity employer.

As one of the longest serving members in her section, Glenys had experienced no real problems on the many occasions she had been called upon to act in Les's position when he was away on leave and she had no doubts about her ability to do the job from a technical point of view. But she suspected she needed to develop more solid working relationships with her peers and would-be staff, and the other supervisors whom she hoped would become her peers.

Her first step in achieving her plan was to read up on the skills and techniques that forged effective working relationships. She found several books on these topics in her local bookshop and learned that effective working relationships are more about understanding oneself and others, and a collection of attitudes that underpin interpersonal skills and techniques.

The information she got from these books and put into practice really did seem to make it easier to get along with people—staff and management alike. Of course, it wasn't easy and she often felt uncomfortable, but, as she had read, people will never improve their skills if they don't take risks and try out new things.

She then turned her attention to learning about assertiveness. More books, some evening classes and more practice … this was getting to be hard work!

Management and staff alike seemed impressed with the changes in her and in her overall performance and Glenys herself was amazed at how much easier it was to work with people now. It came as no surprise when she was appointed to succeed Les as supervisor. To her delight, she found she was able to handle her new responsibilities. She was even able to get funds for extra staff and equipment at the last budget allocation session—not an easy achievement! It seemed to Glenys that all her hard work had paid off.

Questions

1   Glenys had clear goals and a plan to achieve them. Describe the key elements in her plan to develop more effective working relationships with others.

2   In what ways would Glenys's learning plan and activities have aided her in her goal to become the section supervisor?

CASE STUDY 19.2

Delusions Of Grandeur?

David finally got the break he had been hoping for. He was appointed as team leader of the technical trainers of his company's learning and development unit. Now he would really have a chance to show management what he was made of! His career was about to begin!

First, he intended to make some important changes in the way the team operated. He called a team meeting and announced that, from now on, there would be strict adherence to the standard working hours. Also, he intended to check everyone's expenses quite carefully when they returned from their frequent interstate field training trips. Under no circumstances did he intend to let the budget blow out! The trainers pointed out that their frequent travel was often done in non-working hours and a lot of their preparation for training was undertaken in their personal time. They saw some of the 'relaxed' timekeeping when back at head office as *quid pro quo—* normal give and take. David replied that, on the contrary, this was a normal part of the job and they'd better start getting used to it. Seeing which way the wind was blowing, the trainers kept the rest of their thoughts to themselves.

The next item on David's agenda was the training program he had run last week. The training manuals and training aids hadn't turned up. 'Sheila is supposed to send them and, as usual, she messed up. I intend to find a replacement for her as soon as possible. I won't have the unit looking unprofessional like that in front of the trainees.'

Later, in the canteen, the trainers had quite a few things to say among themselves. 'Fancy him checking up on our expenses—*he's* the one who is well known for over-claiming!' They all agreed on that point. 'David always says one thing and does another. And if he thinks I'm doing any travel or preparation in my own time, he's got another think coming!' Once again, agreement all around.

'What really gets me,' said Margot, 'is that the only way David seems to feel good about himself is by putting others down. He even does it in training sessions.'

'He's always flying off the handle, too! I've even seen him let rip into trainees if they don't understand what he was showing them first time around! All the trainees hate him—what in the world could management have been thinking of when they made him team leader?'

'Perhaps they just wanted him out of the training room!' suggested Andy, only half-jokingly. 'Yeah, great, so now he can take all his moods out on us!'

'Poor Sheila. She never makes mistakes on *our* programs—only David's. That's because he leaves her such poor instructions about what he wants. I wonder what we can do to help her?'

'He'll never listen to us. He's always got to be the one with the answers and the good ideas. We may as well forget about suggesting anything or pointing anything out to him. I think I'll go check the want ads!'

'Me too! He's such an aggressive little fella! I don't want to stay around here any longer than I have to!'

With that, the technical trainers ambled off back to their workstations.

Questions

1 Analyse where David is going wrong in his working relationships with his team.
2 What advice would you give David if he is to develop more effective working relationships with them?

Answers to Rapid Review questions

1. T   2. F   3. T   4. T   5. T   6. F   7. T   8. T   9. T   10. T   11. T   12. T
13. T   14. F   15. F   16. T   17. T

CHAPTER 20

PROVIDING LEADERSHIP

Sandra's china and glassware team

Sandra is the supervisor of the china and glassware department of a large city store. She has five staff reporting to her:

- Bill, 22, a management trainee attached to her department for three months;
- Angie, 35, who, with three years' experience, is the most senior sales assistant in the department;
- Dave, 17, who has been with the store for six months, four of those months in Sandra's department;
- Kylie, a young 16, straight from school and three weeks in the department;
- Marie, a part-timer in her mid-40s, who has worked in china and glassware for nearly a year.

We join Sandra on a Monday morning late in October as she parks her car and walks towards the store. 'I must organise something really special for my team before the Christmas rush starts; they've got a long hard period coming up. Of course, Kylie is new, but she seems all right—as long as you tell her every little detail of what you want done. But that's to be expected ...

'Dave's coming along well, but I must impress on him the need for the "daily dust" in his area—customers don't want to handle dusty glasses! For the most part, though, you tell him what you want done and why you want it done and he's just fine.

'Not like Angie—all she needs is a little help here, a small suggestion there, and things happen like magic. Best move I could have made, delegating the display work to her—seems to have given her a new lease on life.

'Bill's coming along well now, too. He even comes up with the odd good idea; he's a fast learner—just explain what you're doing and he catches on quickly. He likes to discuss things.

'And then we have Marie, a real brick! You can always count on Marie to raise spirits and liven everyone up.

'Which reminds me, I must call a meeting over lunch to discuss how we can use the extra floor space we've been allocated for the Christmas period. I'll begin by thanking them for their hard work—our sales are up 8% and it's largely because of this increase that senior management has given us that extra space.

'Oh, and I must thank Marie for staying behind yesterday to clear up that backlog of credit slips ...'

Good leaders can always get the best from their work group. This chapter discusses what it takes to be a good leader. You will discover the characteristics and behaviours great leaders share and what to do to develop them in yourself.

- Can you define leadership?
- Can you distinguish between the main schools of thought on leadership and extract useful information and tips for yourself from them?
- What are the four main styles of leadership and which is best?
- Should a leader be concerned more with the task to be achieved or with the people doing the task?
- What is functional leadership?
- How does the self-fulfilling prophecy affect a leader's behaviour and results?

- What information can situational leadership theories add to the leadership equation?
- Is leading different from managing?
- What will the 21st-century leader be like?
- In what ways are leaders really servants?
- Is leading a team different from leading individual contributors?
- Are you the type of leader employees want?

WHAT IS LEADERSHIP?

Even when organisations have access to identical plant, technology and equipment, they do not get identical results. As we learned in Chapter 13, it is their employees who provide the real competitive advantage for most organisations. This makes people who can lead others valuable. Good leadership is worth more than modern technology, new buildings or a favourable quarterly result.

Leaders have always had a major influence on a work group's performance and a direct effect on an organisation's success. Yet the challenges presented by today's dynamic environment make effective leadership more important than ever before. It is now a core competency that supervisors must possess.

> **'A leader articulates and embodies a vision and goals and enables others to share and achieve them.'**

People need clear, challenging and worthwhile goals to strive towards. Good leaders express them clearly and precisely. More than this, they supply the vision, the 'light at the end of the tunnel', the overall sense of purpose, that makes work take on a special significance.

People will do something when they feel it is in their best interests. Leaders understand this. They communicate the vision and goals in a way that enables others to feel part of them so they will work willingly and cooperatively towards achieving them. Leaders coach and support others in their efforts, and develop positive and respectful working relationships with employees. Their followers admire them and know they can count on them. Leaders 'practise what they preach' and act as a positive role model that others want to emulate.

> **'Leadership is not about *making* people work.**
> **It's about *letting* people work.'**
> Lee Doricott, Manager, New South Wales

This is leadership. A true leader asks not 'what can my followers do for me?' (to paraphrase the late US President, John F. Kennedy) but 'what can I do for my followers?' A leader is not a teller but a guide.

> '**Leadership is like air.**
> **Necessary for life but impossible to see or touch.**'
> Japanese proverb

Leadership is both an elusive quality that inspires others to perform, and a skill that enables a person to persuade others to accept directions and goals willingly. This helps them lead their teams to achieve significant results. Here are some other definitions of leadership developed by a group of managers from all over Australia. They gathered at Uluru to examine leadership and find out how they could become better leaders.
- 'Leaders have an ability to control, motivate and direct people and ideas.'
- 'Leaders have the courage of their convictions and are fair and just in achieving their goals.'
- 'Leaders communicate and achieve goals and plans effectively.'
- 'Leaders help others to achieve a shared goal without relying on position or power.'

There is no one definition that covers all situations. The definition each of us adopts has to be 'right' for us.
- 'The leader is the servant of all, able to show a disarming humility without the loss of authority.' (Sir Edward 'Weary' Dunlop)
- 'Leadership is about achieving enterprise goals through the work of others.' (David Karpin in the Karpin Report)

Leaders, then, are people who can influence the behaviour of others for the purpose of achieving a goal.

Leadership is like a piece of string ...
How is leadership like a piece of string? Here is one answer:

> '**If you take a piece of string, roll it in your hands**
> **and drop it on the table, it will not settle the same way twice.**
> **Leadership is the same. No two technical problems are the same,**
> **no two customers are the same, no two staff problems are the same.**'
> John Bongenaar, Manager, Taumaranui, New Zealand

Here is another:

> '**Like a piece of string, leadership has no beginning and no end.**'
> Richard Davidson, Manager, Adelaide

Fortunately, we can all learn how to become more effective leaders. Our knowledge about leadership has been added to over the years, through careful observation and research. What we know about leadership today may not be the whole story, but it will help us to become more effective leaders if we apply it. In this chapter, we look first at theories about leadership and then at ways in which you can put these theories into practice.

Many theories reach similar conclusions by different paths. The task for you is to pick the most important points from each and build your own understanding of leading others.

There are three main schools of thought on leadership—the trait, behavioural and situational approaches.

THE TRAIT APPROACH

Most primary school teachers will tell you that some children seem to be natural leaders and others don't. Can we learn what makes a person a leader by studying the physical, intellectual and personality characteristics of leaders? If we can find certain qualities among all or most leaders, all we have to do is find people with these qualities and make them leaders (or so the thinking goes).

Some studies have indicated that, on the whole, successful leaders are taller, brighter and better adjusted, and have more accurate social perceptions than non-leaders or poor leaders. One study found that successful leaders have physically larger heads than non-leaders! Many researchers have suggested that successful leaders display self-confidence, a desire to influence others, abundant energy and high levels of job knowledge.

However, these traits do not hold true in all or even the majority of cases and this approach has, on the whole, been disappointing. The researchers who analysed the results of over 100 leadership studies found that, of the many traits identified for successful leaders, only 5% of them were reported in four or more of the studies.

The three most commonly found traits are intelligence, initiative and self-assurance. According to a number of studies, intelligence should be above average (but not of genius level) and should include particularly good skills in solving complex and abstract problems. Initiative involves independence and inventiveness and the capacity to see what needs to be done combined with the desire and ability to do it. Self-assurance has to do with self-esteem and setting challenging personal goals.

The trait approach is generally considered an oversimplification of a very complex subject, for four main reasons:
1. No one can have all the leadership traits identified by the research.
2. Many traits are so ill defined as to be useless in practice.
3. There are too many exceptions: many successful leaders do not display the 'necessary' leadership traits.

THE **BIG** PICTURE

Sir Edward 'Weary' Dunlop developed his 'empathic' approach to leadership in the Japanese POW camps during World War II. He identified 11 desirable aspects of leadership:

- Motivation
- Courage
- Decisiveness
- Selflessness
- Responsibility
- Initiative
- Integrity
- Loyalty
- Judgment
- Knowledge
- Ability to communicate

He was thinking of military leadership. Would these characteristics also help business leaders, not-for-profit leaders and public service leaders?

4. Even the 'top three' traits of intelligence, initiative and self-assurance, while important, are not sufficient in themselves to make an effective leader.

Speaking at the Second Annual Worldwide Lessons in Leadership series at Faniel Hall in Boston, Massachusetts, USA, Geoffrey Colvin, the editorial director of *Fortune* magazine, had this to say about leadership:

> **'Leadership isn't a job description; it's a trait, a state of mind ... Leadership is about vision, spirit, and character; getting diverse individuals to work together as a team.'**

Despite the lack of hard data to support the trait approach to leadership, it has wide, popular appeal. Is this because we intuitively 'know' there is 'something to it'?

Evolutionary psychologists look at how the brain is 'hardwired'. People have individual differences and we are born with many character traits and predispositions that harden as we age into adulthood. Some personality traits, they believe, are inborn in the form of deep-rooted inclinations. They are finding in favour of the notion that some people are born to lead while others are born *not* to lead.

An important attribute for leadership, says Nigel Nicholson, professor of organisational behaviour and dean of research at the London Business School, is the desire to lead.

> **'The motivation to lead is the baseline requirement for competent leadership.'**

Reluctant leaders are invariably poor leaders. We can train managerial skills and competencies, but not the passion to lead.

Transformational leadership

Research in Australia and overseas indicates that organisations need a special type of leadership, especially at senior levels, to lead them through these times of rapid change.

FROM THEORY TO PRACTICE

Jim Dawson joined Zebco at a time when high-quality yet inexpensive Asian imports began to flood the American market, threatening the company's viability. Because workplace relations between employees and management were poor, it was difficult to make the necessary increases to productivity that would save the company.

As an 'outsider', Dawson knew trust would be an important issue in rebuilding workplace relations. He chose two highly visible and symbolic actions to reduce 'class differences' between workers and management. He discontinued the reserved parking spaces for management and instituted the President's Club—anyone with 100% attendance won a reserved parking space. And he walked into the factory one morning and smashed the time clock with a crowbar.

Productivity increased threefold. Today, Zebco is the world's largest fishing tackle company.

THE **BIG** PICTURE

Kerry Sanderson joined the Fremantle Port Authority as chief executive in 1991 when it was reporting losses of $11.5 million, a debt-to-assets figure of 89%, a workforce of 670 and huge port charges. By 1999 she had transformed it into an organisation winning the praise of the Bureau of Industry and Economics and the Australian Quality Council. Port charges declined by 21%, the debt-to-assets figure dwindled to 30%, container trade doubled and, in 1998, the FPA made an after-tax profit of $7.5 million with 176 employees.

How did she transform the FPA? She restructured the organisation to make it leaner and flatter, developed a vision and strategy, which she communicated in a personal way to port staff and customers, and helped everyone to feel included in achieving it. She modelled a genuine commitment to customers and reversed the old 'command-and-control' culture. She trained employees and made them accountable and responsible. She instituted a culture of 'fix the system, don't fix blame' and introduced peer feedback to alert employees to their strengths and weaknesses.

One employee put it this way: 'You are going to be far more innovative, because a lot of pressure goes off you when you know you can make a mistake and won't lose your job—or at the very least risk being berated by the boss.'

Transformational leadership is a term coined by the political scientist, James MacGregor Burns. He defined it as looking beyond present constraints, striking out in new directions, taking risks, influencing beliefs and values.

Transformational leaders *develop a clear and compelling vision* for their organisation, one that all employees understand and can commit themselves to. These leaders *guide* their organisation through *revitalising change*, redesigning it from top to bottom. Their goal is to make it more efficient, responsive and effective, better able to meet the changing

FROM THEORY TO PRACTICE

Professor Jay Conger of the London Business School has been studying charismatic leadership for a number of years. He believes we can all develop elements of it. Here are some ways:
- Take courses to improve your speaking skills.
- Learn to stage events that send powerful messages.
- Learn to think more critically about the status quo and its shortcomings.
- Do more to motivate your team.
- Be passionate about what you do.
- Learn to become comfortable with taking risks and standing up for your convictions.
- Learn to communicate your goals and future vision clearly, and make them attractive and attainable.

requirements of the marketplace and society. They *drum up enthusiasm* for these changes throughout the organisation. These are the three most significant functions of transformational leaders.

Transformational leadership might be thought of as a modern variation of the trait approach. Transformational leaders seem to possess a number of important core traits: high levels of energy, a strong goal orientation, well developed conceptual abilities and high levels of personal integrity and trustworthiness. They are dynamic and *charismatic*. They are excellent communicators and master motivators. They are strategic thinkers who take the broad overview and set clear visions, missions and goals. They have the courage of their convictions and the ability to inspire people throughout the organisation. Their drive and enthusiasm set the pace for others to follow. Which of these characteristics do you possess?

THE BEHAVIOURAL APPROACH

The trait approach looks at what effective leaders *are*. Behavioural theories of leadership concentrate on what effective leaders *do*. Leadership is thought of as a set of behaviours. Effective leaders do things that poor leaders do not.

Let's begin by looking at the commonly referred to styles of leadership and then move on to five behavioural theories: (1) Tannenbaum and Schmidt's continuum of leadership styles; (2) Blake and Mouton's managerial grid; (3) Likert's concept of consideration and structure; (4) Adair's functional leadership approach; and (5) McGregor's Theory X and Theory Y. Each of these offers useful insights and practical ways of looking at the issue of leadership.

Leadership styles

Leadership is often categorised into four styles:
1. dictatorial
2. authoritarian
3. democratic
4. laissez-faire.

Dictatorial leaders are negative leaders who rule through force. They hold threats of punishment over the heads of people to compel them to perform. This may get results in some work situations but, generally, the resulting quality and quantity do not remain high for very long. Instead, dictatorial leadership usually creates unrest and dissatisfaction. Sooner or later, employees 'revolt' by doing the bare minimum of work or transferring to another job.

Authoritarian leaders exercise strong control. They avoid employee participation and withhold information from their followers, preferring to make decisions themselves. Authoritarian leaders retain all the power and issue orders with no questions allowed and no explanations given. This tends to make followers dependent upon them for decisions and directions, and can result in the group feeling 'lost' in the leader's absence.

> 'You do not lead by hitting people over the head.
> That's assault, not leadership.'
>
> Dwight D. Eisenhower, former US General and President

While dictatorial and authoritarian leaders are task-centred, *democratic leaders*, or participative leaders, are people-centred. They encourage participation. They ask for people's opinions and suggestions and involve them in solving work-related problems. Because employees are well informed and used to solving problems themselves, they can function effectively when their leader is absent.

The fourth style of leadership is *laissez-faire*, or non-directive. These leaders do not appear to give active leadership at all. They provide the group with information and possibly some general direction and then let them get on with the job with little or no interference.

Laissez-faire leadership can be very effective when the work group is highly skilled and motivated and the work is complex or unstructured. This may be the case when supervising professionally qualified employees. However, when established standards and goals need to be met on a regular basis, this is probably not the most suitable style of leadership.

Tannenbaum and Schmidt's continuum of leadership styles

In the late 1950s Robert Tannenbaum and Warren H. Schmidt attempted to integrate ideas about leadership and developed what they called a *continuum of leadership styles*. They saw leadership behaviour ranging from leader-centred strategies to employee-centred strategies, as shown in Figure 20.1. In this model, authoritarian leaders fall towards the left end of the continuum, laissez-faire leaders far up on the right end and democratic leaders somewhere in the middle.

Blake and Mouton's managerial grid

In the 1960s Robert Blake and Jane Mouton developed what they called the *managerial grid* (see Figure 20.2). They concluded that leaders could focus their attention on one of two key factors: concern for *people* or concern for *output*. These combine to give five possible leadership styles. A specially developed questionnaire ranks how much attention a leader pays to each of these on a scale of 1 (low) to 9 (high).

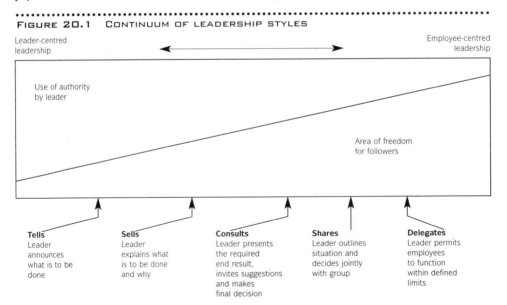

FIGURE 20.1 CONTINUUM OF LEADERSHIP STYLES

Leader-centred leadership

Employee-centred leadership

Use of authority by leader

Area of freedom for followers

Tells
Leader announces what is to be done

Sells
Leader explains what is to be done and why

Consults
Leader presents the required end result, invites suggestions and makes final decision

Shares
Leader outlines situation and decides jointly with group

Delegates
Leader permits employees to function within defined limits

FIGURE 20.2   THE MANAGERIAL GRID

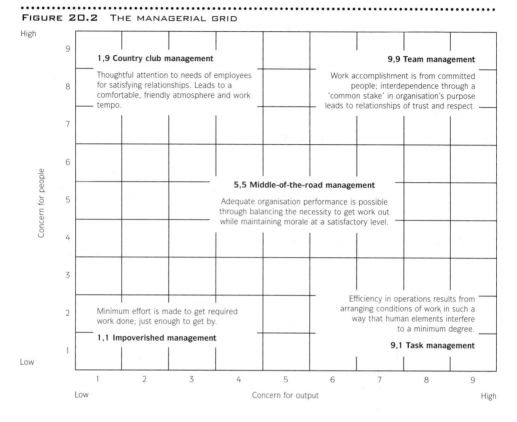

1,1 Impoverished management. Leaders who score 1,1 are those with little concern for either people or production. They are leaders in name only and make little effort to perform or encourage their work group towards high performance. People often describe them as laissez-faire leaders.

9,1 Task management. Here the leader's main concern is the accomplishment of the task, getting the job done. Little concern is shown for the needs and welfare of employees. People often describe these leaders as authoritarian or dictatorial.

5,5 Middle-of-the-road management. These leaders show some concern for both employee satisfaction and job performance, but only enough to get by.

1,9 Country club management. The country club leader's main concern is employee satisfaction and keeping good relations in the group. These leaders seek a friendly atmosphere and a comfortable work tempo. Like the impoverished leaders, they are sometimes described as laissez-faire.

9,9 Team management. A supervisor with a team style of leadership involves all the members of the work group in planning and making decisions. These supervisors seek understanding, agreement and commitment. They listen to and encourage people, aiming at a creative approach to getting the job done. The team management style is similar to the democratic style of leadership discussed above. Team leaders are participative leaders.

Blake and Mouton originally believed that a 9,9 or team management leadership style was most appropriate in all situations. However, we now know that this is not the case. Sometimes task management will work better—for instance, when supervising repetitive work being done by unskilled, inexperienced and/or unmotivated employees. Similarly, country club or 1,9 management often works well with highly skilled, experienced and motivated staff. It is probably safe to say, however, that the impoverished 1,1 leadership style is unlikely to work in any situation!

Likert's concept of consideration and structure

At about the same time that Blake and Mouton developed their managerial grid, Rensis Likert and other researchers also identified two dimensions of leadership concern. They labelled these *consideration*, or concern for people, and *structure*, or concern for task (see Figure 20.3).

Consideration includes behaviour that indicates mutual trust, respect and rapport between supervisors and the work group. Consideration does not mean a superficial pat on the back, but rather a deeper concern for group members' needs. Leaders high in consideration will, for instance, encourage two-way communication and participation in decision making.

Supervisors high in consideration (as measured by specially designed tests) operate towards the right end of the leadership continuum and are more democratic in their approach to employees than are leaders who score low in consideration.

Leaders high in *structure* tend to organise and control group activity and their relationships with their followers. Such leaders explain what they need from each group member, assign tasks, plan ahead, establish precise ways of getting things done and push for high production. We could expect leaders who are high in structure to operate towards the left end of the leadership continuum and in an authoritarian manner.

Like Blake and Mouton, Likert has given us a two-dimensional model of leadership. Unlike them, however, he did not recommend one particular approach. Instead, he noticed from his research that some successful leaders are high in consideration and low in structure, while others are high in consideration and high in structure. It seems that high consideration, whether combined with high or low structure, is important for effective leadership. Consideration is associated with such indicators of effective leadership as low

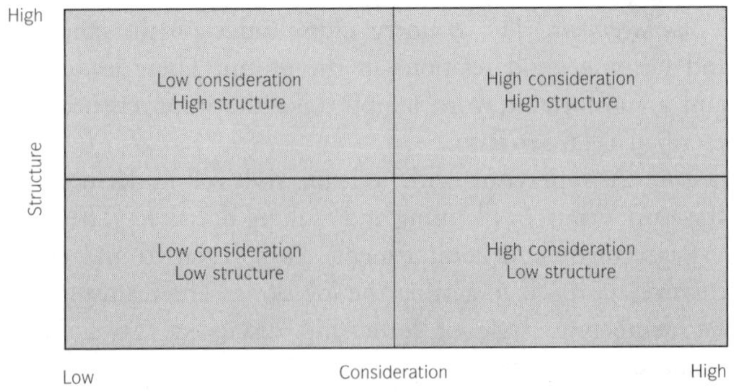

FIGURE 20.3   LIKERT'S CONSIDERATION AND STRUCTURE MODEL

labour turnover, few grievances and high levels and quality of output. This shows us that effective leaders need to have strong people skills.

Adair's functional leadership approach

John Adair's approach to leadership is called *functional leadership* or *action-centred leadership*. He bases it on his observation that, to be effective, a leader must ensure that three distinct areas of need are satisfied:

1. *task needs*—the need to succeed in achieving set goals: achieving the task;
2. *team needs*—the need for the group to work as a team: building the team; and
3. *individual needs*—the need for individuals to feel satisfied with their work: developing and motivating individuals.

As shown in Figure 20.4, ignoring any one area of need will have an adverse effect on the other areas. For example, supervisors who fail to build strong, cooperative teams will find that individual team members are not as motivated and the task is not achieved as well as it would be if they had taken the time and effort to build the team.

Box 20.1 shows the sorts of things supervisors need to do to meet task, team and individual needs. A leader who meets all three areas of need is probably acting as a 9,9 or team manager and is likely to be 'high' in both consideration and structure.

FIGURE 20.4 OVERLAPPING NEEDS

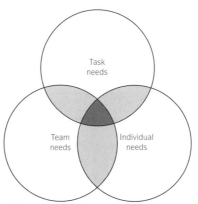

FUNCTIONAL LEADERSHIP

How do you rate at functional leadership?

Task needs

Do you:

Plan
- by seeking all available information?
- by making a workable plan?
- by establishing priorities?
- by checking resources?

Initiate
- by briefing the team on the task?
- by explaining why the task is necessary?
- by delegating tasks to group members?
- by checking understanding of individuals?

Support
- by reporting progress?
- by maintaining standards?
- by maintaining morale?

Monitor
- by keeping discussion and actions relevant to the task?
- by influencing work pace?
- by clarifying or defining policy when required?
- by summarising progress?
- by reviewing objectives?

Team needs

Do you:

Plan
- by involving the team and sharing commitment?
- by consulting and agreeing on standards?

Initiate
- by setting and maintaining group standards?
- by obtaining feedback?

Support
- by coordinating team efforts?
- by reconciling conflict?
- by encouraging and developing ideas and suggestions?
- by relieving tension with humour?

Monitor
- by prodding your group to a decision or action?
- by summarising progress?
- by disciplining individuals who are threatening to disrupt the group?
- by answering questions?
- by assessing group performance?
- by recognising success and learning from failure?

Individual needs

Do you:

Plan
- by establishing any special knowledge or skills possessed by individuals which are relevant to the task?
- by clarifying aims?
- by gaining acceptance of goals?

Initiate
- by setting targets?
- by delegating?

Support
- by encouraging and expressing appreciation for individual contributions?
- by reconciling or airing disagreements?
- by listening, enthusing, advising and reassuring?
- by recognising effort?

Monitor
- by noting progress?
- by training and guiding?
- by checking the feasibility of an idea?
- by assessing performance?

McGregor's Theory X and Theory Y

Douglas McGregor found that leaders' opinions of followers determine their leadership behaviour. He identified two contrasting beliefs or mind-sets that leaders can hold about employees' approach to their job: **Theory X** and **Theory Y**.

Theory X

Leaders with a Theory X mind-set believe that workers have an inherent dislike of work. They work only because they have to and will do as little as possible for their pay. It therefore follows that leaders must continually coerce workers, direct their efforts, keep tight controls on them and use threats of punishment to keep them in line. Theory X leaders believe that most people actually prefer this type of supervision because they lack ambition and want to avoid responsibility. Workers, they believe, are interested only in job security and good wages.

Theory Y

Leaders with a Theory Y mind-set believe that work is as natural as rest and play. They believe people want to do their jobs well, and that they will seek responsibility, challenge and self-direction if they are committed to the overall objectives of their department or organisation. They believe people want to be committed to goals and visions and want to learn new skills. They believe that employees want to use initiative and imagination in their work.

This theory implies that supervisors can only successfully change their leadership style by changing their attitudes and beliefs about why people work. If you relate this theory to the **Pygmalion effect**, you will see that both Theory X and Theory Y leaders are correct! The Pygmalion effect is a self-fulfilling prophecy. It is a process by which we impose fixed labels

FROM THEORY TO PRACTICE

Do you think a Theory X approach means that a supervisor will use a dictatorial style of leadership? Not always. A Theory X country club leader might think: 'If I'm really nice to employees, they'll help out when I need it.' Or a Theory X leader might 'help' their team members excessively because they believe they are incapable of superior performance and it would be too risky to let them work on their own, without assistance.

FROM THEORY TO PRACTICE

Does Theory Y leadership sound like laissez-faire or country club leadership to you? Not necessarily. Because they hold their work team in high regard, Theory Y leaders often set high standards for them to meet. In this sense, Theory Y leaders can be team leaders. They are also participative, democratic leaders.

on people, either positive (**halo effect**) or negative (**horns effect**). People then live up or down to our expectations and predictions.

Negative labels such as 'he is lazy' or 'she is stupid' are powerful and damaging. Positive labels such as 'she is bright', 'they are cooperative' or 'he is hard-working' predict success and growth. Having stuck a label on a person, we proceed to give them feedback, in very subtle ways, based on our labels and, as we 'know' they will, they begin to respond in the way that we 'expect'. This is how some supervisors become trapped in a vicious circle of poor performance: they take a Theory X attitude and treat employees as if they are lazy, untrustworthy, irresponsible, stupid, good-for-nothing layabouts. They are then not surprised when their employees begin to show signs of acting that way. This makes it difficult to hold a genuine performance improvement discussion.

Supervisors with positive beliefs of their employees, on the other hand, find it much easier to encourage good performance. These are the Theory Y supervisors who set high standards and expect employees to attain them—after all, they are perfectly capable, intelligent, responsible and hard working, so there is no reason why they should not attain high standards. Leaders who believe their followers are bright, hard working and dedicated will treat them that way and their followers will tend to live up to their expectations.

What beliefs do you hold about other people's performances?

What do the behavioural theories tell us?

Behavioural theories of leadership are useful for showing us that leaders need to do certain things to succeed. But they are not very useful in telling us *when* a leader needs to do them or in *what situations* they should be done. For instance, when would authoritarian leadership or task leadership work well? Could country club leadership ever be effective?

There must be another piece to the puzzle, so let's look at the situational approach.

THE SITUATIONAL APPROACH

We have seen that the behavioural school of leadership examines what leaders do. Authoritarian leaders, for example, use a lot of directing behaviour: they frequently tell their subordinates what to do. Sometimes this is effective, sometimes it isn't.

Situational leadership shows us that effective leaders sometimes behave in an authoritarian manner, sometimes in a participative or democratic manner and sometimes in

---

THE **BIG** PICTURE

Have you heard the saying, 'Horses for courses'? This applies to leadership, too. Some situations need leaders high in dominance while others need leaders high in empathy and tact. Still others need leaders with finely honed negotiation abilities. There are as many types of leaders as there are leadership situations. The thing that unites successful leaders is not their particular set of skills as much as the fact that their personality profile meets the demands of the situation, and that they *want* to lead.

a laissez-faire manner. The situation dictates which is most effective. This means that, if you want to be an effective leader, you need to be able to use each style and know when to use them. This will increase the range of situations in which you can lead effectively. The styles of leadership available to choose from are those discussed above.

Leaders who are not familiar with situational leadership theory, or who are not flexible enough to adapt their leadership style to suit the circumstances will lead effectively in some situations and poorly in others.

Let's look at three models of situational leadership: (1) Fiedler's contingency theory, (2) Hersey and Blanchard's task readiness theory, and (3) Tannenbaum and Schmidt's elements of leadership theory, which builds on their continuum of leadership styles.

Fiedler's contingency theory

Fiedler's contingency theory identifies three factors that determine the appropriate leadership style in any given situation. These are:

1. *Leader–member relations.* How much do the followers trust, respect and have confidence in their leader? We can subjectively assess this as high (good) or low (poor).
2. *Task structure.* Must established procedures be followed (high structure) or do employees have discretion in carrying out the task (low structure)?
3. *Position power.* How much power and influence goes with the leader's job—the power to hire, fire, reward and punish? This may be high (strong position power) or low (weak position power).

According to Fiedler's contingency theory, an autocratic, telling style of leadership—one that emphasises a high concern with task—works best in situations that are either favourable or unfavourable for the leader. In a moderate situation, a more democratic, people-centred approach is more successful. The most favourable or easiest situation for a leader is one characterised by:

• good leader–member relations
• a highly structured task
• strong position power.

In contrast, the least favourable situation for a leader is characterised by:

• poor leader–member relations
• low task structure
• weak position power.

Hersey and Blanchard's task readiness theory

Leadership styles

Hersey and Blanchard also recognise two dimensions of leadership behaviour: *directive behaviour*, or how much task focus and supervision a leader provides, and *relationship behaviour*, or how much support and encouragement a leader provides.

Directive behaviour includes setting objectives, developing plans, programs and schedules related to the employee's work, structuring the task that is to be performed and directing the way in which it is to be carried out, training people on-the-job, and maintaining close and frequent supervision of the task.

Relationship behaviour concerns how much a leader shares with the employee those task activities described above: objective setting, development of plans, programs and schedules directly related to the employee's work, and so on. It also relates to how much the leader shares problem solving and decision making about the way the task will be carried out and how much coaching, counselling and encouragement the leader provides.

Using this model, four styles of leadership are possible (Box 20.2). Notice that these four leadership styles are similar to Tannenbaum and Schmidt's continuum of leadership behaviour.

Task readiness level

How does a supervisor know which of the four leadership styles to use? The task readiness level of each employee for each task provides the answer. Hersey and Blanchard suggest that a leader's style should vary according to each employee's task readiness level.

Two things make up a person's **task readiness level**. The first is their *competence*, or *ability* to do a particular task. This is a combination of skills, knowledge and experience in doing a particular task. The second is their *willingness* to take responsibility for doing the task. It is a combination of motivation and self-confidence.

The concept of task readiness level relates to one task only. This means that someone's readiness level can be high on some tasks and low on others. Therefore, their leader will use different leadership styles with them for different tasks.

- *Readiness level 1 (or R1)*. Low competence and low willingness to do a task unsupervised—this person needs direction and so an S1 or *telling* style of leadership is called for.
- *Readiness level 2 (or R2)*. Growing competence and willingness—this calls for an S2 or *explaining* style of leadership.

BOX **20.2**   **HERSEY AND BLANCHARD'S LEADERSHIP STYLES**

- Style 1 (or S1)—high directive/low relationship behaviour.   'I'll decide.'
- Style 2 (or S2)—high directive/high relationship behaviour.   'We'll talk; I'll decide.'
- Style 3 (or S3)—high relationship/low directive behaviour.   'We'll talk. We'll decide.'
- Style 4 (or S4)—low relationship/low directive behaviour.   'You decide. I'll be available.'

Style focus		Behaviour
S1:	the task at hand	telling
S2:	both task and relationships with team members	explaining
S3:	supporting and helping team members	participating, coaching, encouraging
S4:	monitoring tasks and relationships	delegating

- *Readiness level 3 (or R3).* Satisfactory competency but low willingness based on lack of confidence or lack of motivation—this person needs support and so an S3 or *participating* or encouraging style of leadership is called for.
- *Readiness level 4 (or R4).* High levels of competence and willingness—this calls for an S4 or *delegating*, 'hands off' style of leadership.

Figure 20.5 shows ways of recognising employees at different levels of task readiness.

Use Figure 20.6 to help you determine which leadership style is most appropriate for each of your staff. First, consider the task readiness level of an employee in relation to the particular task and assign a readiness level from 1 (low) to 4 (high). Now draw a line vertically up to intersect the bell curve in one of the four leadership styles (S1, S2, S3 or S4). This will indicate the most suitable leadership style for this staff member in relation to that particular task. You can also apply the concept of task readiness level to a work group to get a feel for the overall leadership style you should use with them.

Using the task readiness level approach, you can see that your behaviour towards employees should change as they develop skills, experience and confidence. You need flexibility in your styles of leadership!

FIGURE 20.5 ASSESSING TASK READINESS LEVEL

Readiness level 3	Readiness level 3 (regressing)	Readiness level 2
How does this look? Can I run this by you? I'm not sure if I can.	I'll do it later. It's someone else's turn. What? Me again! Been there, done that.	Show me. I'll have a go! I'm not sure. I don't know how but I'll give it a try.
Readiness level 4 I've already done it. Leave it to me. No worries! Here, let me help with that.		**Readiness level 1** I don't know how. I can't do it. I did my best, but ... I've never done this before.

FROM THEORY TO PRACTICE

As an employee's task readiness level increases in terms of accomplishing a specific task (not the entire job), begin to reduce directive behaviour and increase relationship behaviour. This should continue until the employee reaches a moderate level of readiness. As the employee begins to move to an above-average job readiness level, you should decrease both directive and relationship behaviour. As task readiness levels increase still further, employees want to see a corresponding reduction of close supervision and an increase in delegation as a positive indication of your trust and confidence in them.

FIGURE 20.6 TASK READINESS THEORY

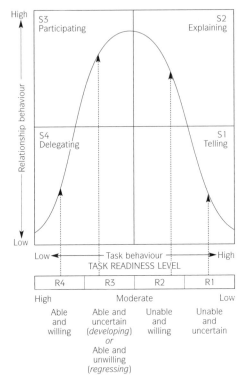

Regression

Is that the end of the story? No. As experienced supervisors know, employees sometimes 'go off the boil' or 'lose the plot'. A once skilled and motivated employee can turn into a disgruntled, uncooperative bludger. They *know* how to do the job but they no longer *want* to do it.

This happens when they lose their motivation, or willingness. This could be for any number of reasons, ranging from personal problems to poor supervision to poor working relationships within the team (see Chapter 8). Whatever the reason, the person has moved backwards (regressed) from being a skilled and willing readiness level 4 employee to a competent but unwilling readiness level 3 employee—someone who has the *competency* or knows how to do the job but lacks the *willingness*.

Look at Figure 20.6. Locate R3 on the task readiness level part of the chart. Follow the line up to see what leadership style to use with an R3 regressing employee. You will see that they need low-task high-relationship behaviour. Telling the person what to do or providing further training would be a waste of time because they already *know* what to do. High-task behaviour is not the answer (although it is usually the first refuge of inexperienced supervisors or poor leaders).

The R3 regressing employee needs supportive, participative relationship-building behaviour. Sit down and have a chat. Ask questions. Find out what the problem is. Try to see things from the disgruntled employee's point of view. You may find that boredom has set in and they want a new challenge. Or they feel unappreciated and neglected. Or you may find that faulty tools or equipment or poor work systems hinder them to the point where they have given up trying. Whatever the cause of the problem, you can't do anything about it until you find out what it is.

Tannenbaum and Schmidt's elements of leadership theory

The third situational theory of leadership incorporates Tannenbaum and Schmidt's continuum of leadership styles and adds three situational dimensions to take into account when deciding which leadership style to use.

Based on their findings, here are some guidelines to help you select the most appropriate leadership style.

1. *Consider the task.* For example, is there one best way to do it or are there many possible alternatives? How routine or complex is it? How critically important to the organisation is the issue? Is there a high degree of risk involved? Is time short?

    A small, highly skilled team performing a fairly flexible task in a changing environment would respond best to democratic, people-centred leadership.

    On the other hand, a leader facing a situation where time is critical, or where a large work group is involved in carrying out precisely specified, routine work would probably achieve better results by using more directive behaviour. (Remember that directive behaviour needn't be rude or harsh; it can be polite and helpful!)

    If the issue or task at hand is highly critical or sensitive, the leader would need to retain a reasonable amount of authority and probably would not go further than consulting the work team.

2. *Consider the employees.* For example, what style of leadership are they used to and comfortable with? How much independence and responsibility do they want? How many followers are there? How competent and willing are they? Are they directly affected by a decision or involved in its execution? How experienced are they at working together? How confident are they? Do they understand and identify with the organisation's goals?

    If people are used to, and expect, participative leadership and have high readiness levels, an autocratic leader would find it difficult to gain their loyalty and win cooperation. Similarly, if a work team is used to highly directive leadership, a sudden change to democratic, consultative leadership would almost certainly fall flat, at least initially.

3. *Consider the leader.* Don't forget yourself in this! What style of leadership are you most comfortable with? What styles of leadership have you experienced yourself? Who are your role models? How confident are you about using each of the leadership styles? What is the expected leadership style in your organisation—its cultural norm of leadership? What are its values, traditions and policies? How dispersed are its work units?

    No matter which style of leadership you choose, it is important that you feel comfortable with it. Some people would never be able to act convincingly in an autocratic telling style, while others would feel too uncomfortable in a delegating or sharing style.

WHICH STYLE OF LEADERSHIP IS BEST?

:... These situational approaches show us that one style of leadership is no 'better' or 'worse' than any of the others. The art is to be able to use each of them appropriately, at the right time and in the right place.

Most experienced and successful supervisors agree that they need to vary their leadership style according to the demands of the situation. Box 20.3 summarises some of their thoughts.

As Box 20.4 shows, effective leaders need to be comfortable operating along the full range of the leadership styles continuum, using each as the situation warrants. In the long term, though, the best results in terms of team spirit and performance are usually associated with leadership styles along the participative end of the continuum.

This is, no doubt, why most organisations in Australia and New Zealand are moving towards **participative management** and **industrial democracy**. They need leaders at all levels who are trained in and willing to use selling, consulting, sharing and delegating styles of leadership and who know when to use each.

LEADING VERSUS MANAGING

:... We examined some of the differences between leaders and managers in Chapter 1. Here is what many supervisors consider to be the 'bottom line':

'Manage yourself.
Lead others.'

BOX 20.3 WHEN TO BE 'HANDS ON'; WHEN TO BE 'HANDS OFF'

Laissez-faire 'hands-off' leadership is fine when:
- everything is going well
- followers understand the task clearly
- followers are committed to the task
- followers are skilled and experienced

Teams need a strong 'hands-on' leader when:
- there is a crisis
- the goal is unclear
- followers are unskilled or inexperienced
- time is tight
- followers are confused or uncertain

BOX 20.4 WHICH LEADERSHIP STYLE?

Tells_____ Sell _____ Consults _____ Shares _____ Delegates

One best way	Many alternatives
Critically important to the organisation	Not critically important to the organisation
High degree of risk	Low risk
Time shortage	Plenty of time available
Large numbers	Smaller numbers
Less skilled, experienced or motivated staff	Highly skilled, experienced or motivated staff
Low involvement or effect on employees	Highly involved or affected employees

'Leadership is of the Spirit, compounded of personality and vision.
Management is of the mind, more a matter of accurate calculation, of
statistics, of methods, timetable and routines. Its practice is a science.
Managers are necessary. Leaders are essential.'

Field Marshal Lord Slim

'Leadership is the art of achieving more than the science of
management says is possible.'

Colin Powel, retired US General and Chief of Staff

Today's organisations need less management and more leadership. Why?

- Today's leaders have more responsibility and wider spans of control.
- Technology can simplify and even take over many of the planning, monitoring, scheduling and reporting functions that managers used to do.
- Flattened organisation structures have greater need for local decision making, judgment, creativity, ethics, risk management and leadership skills that have little or nothing to do with traditional management skills.
- Globalisation exposes every organisational weakness; strong and dynamic leaders are needed to create strong and dynamic organisations.
- Organisational success depends less on what we do than on how we do it. It's the people that make the difference and people need leaders. Good leadership gets the best out of people.

Leading and managing clearly require different skills sets. Today's supervisors need to apply both leadership and management skills.

THE 21ST-CENTURY LEADER

:···As we saw in Chapter 1, leadership and management are changing. The autocratic and even dictatorial styles of leadership, acceptable as recently as the 1960s, are no longer acceptable. Authority derived from position power (see Chapter 3) no longer rules. As organisations evolve, the old-fashioned leadership roles of controller, commander, dictator, ruler, decision maker and judge are becoming less and less effective. Leadership is no longer about dominance, authority and power, but influence and persuasiveness. It is about communicating principles, not setting rules. It is about being a guide, not a teller.

FROM THEORY TO PRACTICE

How to be more of a leader and less of a manager
- Know yourself realistically—your strengths and limitations, your preferences, blind spots, etc. (see Chapters 3 and 14). Do you know what yours are?
- Be willing to learn continuously, refining your leadership abilities. Are you willing to learn continuously about leadership and work to get better at it?

Today, we expect leaders to be participative and democratic. We expect them to empower their work teams, to coach them, motivate them and support them. We expect them to create a sense of purpose, lead the way by example and introduce and manage change sensitively. We expect them to innovate and maintain an unwavering customer focus. We expect them to inspire loyalty, dedication and commitment. We expect them to build teams, resolve conflicts and act as mentors, enablers and inspirers. Quite a tall order!

'Leadership is not magnetic personality—that can just as well be a glib tongue. It is not "making friends and influencing people"—that is flattery. Leadership is lifting a person's vision to higher sights, the raising of a person's performance to a higher standard, the building of a personality beyond its normal limitations.'

Peter Drucker

Servant leadership

One of the most interesting developments in leadership thinking is the idea of the servant leader.

'Be interested in the people whom you serve and your life will be happy.'

King Akathol of Egypt's advice to his son, the future king, 2200 BC

The Chinese philosopher Lao-Tsu (6th century BC) said:

'To lead the people, walk behind them. For the best leaders, people do not notice their existence. When the best leader's work is done, the people say, "We did it ourselves."'

THE **BIG** PICTURE

Because of the changes taking place in the environment that organisations operate in, leaders will increasingly be found at all levels of the organisation, not just the top. Often, they won't have a formal title, or position power, to support them but will rely on their personal power (see Chapter 3).

Peter Senge, director of the Center for Organisational Learning at Massachusetts Institute of Technology's Sloan School of Management, believes leadership in any sphere is the same at the core. He views leaders as people who bring forth new realities. Senge identifies three types of leaders:

1. Local line leaders, e.g. business unit managers, who introduce and implement new ideas.
2. Executive leaders, the top-level managers who mentor local line leaders, steward cultural change and manage the strategic aspects of an organisation.
3. Internal networkers, people with no formal authority who move inside the organisation to spread new ideas and practices and generate commitment.

Servant leadership is unselfish and not built around a person's ego or desire for fame and glory. It is a genuine desire to help people achieve their potential. One of the best known contemporary writers on servant leadership is Robert K. Greenleaf. His concept evolved from his Christian faith, particularly words attributed to Jesus:

> **'The greatest of you should be like the youngest and the one who rules like the one who serves.'**
>
> Luke 22:26

There are perhaps very few leaders who can demonstrate this quality in the real world. For this reason, servant leadership is sometimes thought of as an untested ideal. In essence, servant leaders help followers to grow and reach their potential in their job. They release potential and bring out the best in people.

Franco Bernabe is the CEO of ENI, the Italian industrial group. He transformed it from a debt-ridden, government-owned and politically controlled and corrupt utility into a competitive and profitable publicly traded corporation focused on energy in just six years. Here is what he has to say about leadership:

> **'Leadership is fundamentally about humanity. It is about morality. Your primary job as a leader is to see what is good for your organisation and what is good for the people who work for you, and to create something for the well-being of your fellow citizens.'**

Perhaps servant leadership is more than an untested ideal after all. Here are some of the main attributes of servant leaders:

- They develop strong, energising and empowering visions on which their followers can focus their efforts, and they live their vision in their daily actions.
- They listen carefully and non-judgmentally to others' thoughts and opinions, and reflect on what they have heard.
- They make informed decisions based not on short-term benefits for a few but on long-term repercussions. This requires courage and self-denial, since sometimes the best decision will be unpopular.
- They are prepared to learn from others.
- They are committed to the truth regardless of the cost.
- They have and display empathy and compassion.
- They reconcile conflicting ideas.
- They right wrongs.
- They protect those who cannot protect themselves.
- They are persuasive and convincing.
- They think conceptually, describing the big picture that is in their mind in words and feelings so that others can share it.
- They are not concerned with protecting their own position but with doing what is 'right' according to their own values and standards.
- They have foresight and the ability to predict a likely outcome based on perception, judgment and intuition.
- They adopt the principles of stewardship: being responsible for the longer-term welfare of others.

- They are decisive and flexible: having weighed up the alternatives they commit to a path of action unreservedly while remaining open to new information.

Servant leadership is easier to describe than to practise. Each of us can exercise these qualities. The greatest of us will exercise them consistently and to the benefit of the greatest number.

Team leadership

Tomorrow's leaders are likely to be team leaders. These are leaders who work with their teams to establish and achieve goals. They focus on building strong, cooperative teams, enabling the team and its members to excel at their tasks, satisfying internal and external customers, and producing or providing service to a high-quality standard. Here are some of the key attributes of team leaders:

- They have a high tolerance for uncertainty.
- They are open to new information and ideas.
- They are able to see an issue from other viewpoints—for example, those of customers, competitors, team members and the organisation's management.
- They are able to develop multiple options and solutions for win–win outcomes.
- Their focus is conceptual, based on outcomes and results, not tasks.
- They are able to select the right people for the task at hand.
- They identify, develop and use individual team members' talents.
- They know how to reward people for their efforts.
- They are teachers and coaches.
- They empower their team to make the decisions they are trained and equipped to make.

We examine team leadership in greater detail in Chapter 22.

WHAT TYPE OF LEADER DO EMPLOYEES LOOK FOR?

No two people are exactly alike and so we cannot single out one type of leader as the ideal for which everyone is looking. One person looks for guidance and encouragement, while another prefers to be left alone to get on with the job. What do you look for in a leader?

THE **BIG** PICTURE

Is leadership in business the same as leadership in the sciences, the arts, or education? Superficially, they may seem different. Yet, according to Peter Senge of MIT, they are essentially the same.

Speaking at Faniel Hall in Boston, Massachusetts, USA at the Second Annual Worldwide Lessons in Leadership series, in October 1997, he said: 'The phenomenon of leadership is the phenomenon whereby human communities bring forth new realities.'

How do you think this definition applies to leadership in business, the arts, sciences and education?

Despite individual differences, there are some specific behaviours that most employees look for in a leader. Most, for example, want a leader who lets them know clearly what is expected of them and how they are getting on. They want a sincere pat on the back when they deserve it. They want training, and guidance when they are having difficulty achieving their objectives. They want a leader who is approachable and keeps them informed about what is going on.

Employees want leaders who let them know honestly where they stand and what their chances of advancement are. They want leaders who give them a sense of importance, who make them feel they are valued members of the team and that they are doing a worthwhile job. They want leaders who create order and structure, who have well defined objectives and who organise resources efficiently.

People want supervisors who emphasise the positive rather than the negative aspects of their performance and who listen to their ideas. Employees want supervisors who are fair, impartial and consistent in their dealings, and who set a good example.

HOW GOOD A LEADER ARE YOU?

Figure 20.7 will help you assess your leadership skills. Work through it, asking yourself, 'Do I do this?' and 'Would my team members say that I do it?'

Leadership is personal. We must each build our own leadership model and grow it as we grow. Leadership is a lifelong journey.

'Leadership and learning are indispensable to each other.'

In a speech prepared for delivery in Dallas by John F. Kennedy
on the day of his assassination, 22 November 1963

FIGURE 20.7   ASSESS YOUR LEADERSHIP SKILLS

	Do I do this?		Would my team members agree that I do this?	
Communicating	Yes	No	Yes	No
Let others know about decisions, changes, etc.	❑	❑	❑	❑
Provide specific, accurate and constructive feedback	❑	❑	❑	❑
Clearly communicate my own opinions and feelings	❑	❑	❑	❑
Show concern for others' opinions and feelings	❑	❑	❑	❑
Listen effectively and ensure I've understood	❑	❑	❑	❑
Set clear, challenging and worthwhile goals	❑	❑	❑	❑
Clarify objectives and targets	❑	❑	❑	❑
Provide a vision and sense of purpose	❑	❑	❑	❑
Keep confidences	❑	❑	❑	❑
Communicate in an honest, fair and impartial way	❑	❑	❑	❑
Communicate in a positive way	❑	❑	❑	❑
Develop rapport and empathy with each team member	❑	❑	❑	❑
Keep team members informed about what is going on	❑	❑	❑	❑
Empowering				
Treat everyone as a VIP	❑	❑	❑	❑
Inspire commitment	❑	❑	❑	❑
Think of myself as my team's biggest supporter and helper	❑	❑	❑	❑
Delegate effectively	❑	❑	❑	❑
Encourage others to solve problems	❑	❑	❑	❑

Continued . . .

··

FIGURE 20.7 (CONTINUED)

	Yes	No	Yes	No
Seek team members' comments and ideas	❏	❏	❏	❏
Ensure people feel they are valued members of the team, doing a worthwhile job	❏	❏	❏	❏

Managing change

	Yes	No	Yes	No
Explain it in a positive light	❏	❏	❏	❏
Help others understand the reasons for the change	❏	❏	❏	❏
Explain clearly and specifically what it will mean to the team and what is required of them	❏	❏	❏	❏
Answer questions fully and honestly	❏	❏	❏	❏
'Paint the big picture'	❏	❏	❏	❏
Try to understand their feelings by putting myself in their place	❏	❏	❏	❏
Engage their assistance in making the change work	❏	❏	❏	❏

Coaching

	Yes	No	Yes	No
Help team members develop their knowledge and skills	❏	❏	❏	❏
Offer improvement suggestions	❏	❏	❏	❏
Encourage effort	❏	❏	❏	❏
Recognise and acknowledge effective contributions	❏	❏	❏	❏
Provide guidance when it's needed	❏	❏	❏	❏
Conduct regular performance reviews	❏	❏	❏	❏
Give sincere and specific compliments	❏	❏	❏	❏
Train staff systematically and regularly	❏	❏	❏	❏
Delegate to increase skills and job interest	❏	❏	❏	❏
Praise progress	❏	❏	❏	❏

Commitment to quality

	Yes	No	Yes	No
Focus on customer needs when making decisions	❏	❏	❏	❏
Demonstrate and encourage commitment to quality	❏	❏	❏	❏
Look for continuous improvements	❏	❏	❏	❏
Solve problems by addressing their cause	❏	❏	❏	❏
Organise resources to give the team what they need to do their job	❏	❏	❏	❏

Leading participatively

	Yes	No	Yes	No
Work towards consensus whenever possible	❏	❏	❏	❏
Work to develop teamwork	❏	❏	❏	❏
Practise what I preach	❏	❏	❏	❏
Remain open to ideas	❏	❏	❏	❏
Encourage everyone to share their ideas and opinions	❏	❏	❏	❏
Set aside time for team-planning and problem-solving meetings	❏	❏	❏	❏

RAPID REVIEW

	True	False
1. Good leaders are vital to organisations.	☐	☐
2. We can learn how to be better leaders.	☐	☐
3. The trait approach to leadership focuses on what leaders *are*, while the behavioural approach focuses on what leaders *do*.	☐	☐
4. Transformational leaders help lead and guide their organisation through times of turbulent change.	☐	☐
5. To be an effective leader, you must be participative.	☐	☐
6. Dictatorial leaders use fear to achieve their goals.	☐	☐
7. Today, we know that team leaders are the most effective leaders.	☐	☐
8. Leaders can have two primary concerns: the task and people.	☐	☐
9. According to Adair, leaders should focus on one of three things: the task, the team or the individual.	☐	☐
10. Theory X leaders have a mind-set that says people are basically lazy and need to be supervised closely.	☐	☐

	True	False
11. The situational approach to leadership shows us that different styles of leadership are appropriate in different situations.	☐	☐
12. Most theorists agree that a leader cannot focus both on people and the task at the same time.	☐	☐
13. Task readiness level is task-specific. It is not as useful when it is generalised to cover a person's competency to do an entire job.	☐	☐
14. Sometimes, employees will 'go off the boil': even though they *can* do a good job, they have lost their willingness to.	☐	☐
15. Tannenbaum and Schmidt's research indicates that leaders should consider the task, the followers and their own inclinations when selecting a leadership style.	☐	☐
16. Leading and managing are much the same thing.	☐	☐
17. The concept of the servant leader places the leader in the service of the team.	☐	☐

APPLY YOUR KNOWLEDGE

1. What is a leader? Illustrate your answer using each part of the following definition: 'A leader articulates and embodies a vision and goals and enables others to share and achieve them.'

2. Discuss the strengths and weaknesses of the trait, behavioural and situational approaches to leadership.

3. How do task, team and individual needs relate to each other? Illustrate your answer with examples from your own work or study experience.

4. What is the difference between being a leader and being a supervisor? Discuss the job of a supervisor from a leadership point of view, and from a managing point of view.

5. 'Leaders can only lead if the followers are willing to follow.' Discuss the implications of this statement for supervisors.

6. 'While all supervisors must be leaders, not all leaders can be supervisors.' Discuss.

7. 'Manage yourself. Lead others.' What does this mean to a supervisor?

8. Referring to the vignette on page 636 in Chapter 21, analyse the situation of each supervisor in it using Fiedler's contingency theory. Assume that leader–member relations are good and position power is weak. What leadership style do you believe is indicated and why? Use other leadership theories to support your position if you wish.

DEVELOP YOUR SKILLS

Individual activities

1. The supervisor in the vignette on page 605 said she wanted to organise something really special for her team before the Christmas rush began. Analyse the wisdom of this using Adair's functional leadership model.

2. Referring to the vignette at the beginning of this chapter, analyse the readiness level of each member of Sandra's team. Explain your reasons.

3. Refer to Case Study 14.1 (page 449, Chapter 14). How would you describe Betty's leadership style? Given the information presented in the case study, is her style appropriate? What evidence do you have for your answer?

4. How would you assess Sandra's readiness level in Case Study 2.3 (page 76, Chapter 2)? What leadership style is her supervisor, Linda, using? Is this appropriate? Why or why not?

5. Review Case Study 2.2 (page 75, Chapter 2). Is Simon a leader or a manager? Why? Based on what you have learned in this chapter, what advice would you give Simon to help him become a better supervisor?

6. Give an example of each of the four styles of leadership from your own experience.

7. Select a theoretical approach to leadership and discuss how you could use it to improve your own leadership in a real-life situation.

8. Are you more a Theory X or Theory Y leader? How do you know?

9. Select and apply a situational leadership theory to four common situations in your workplace.

10. What does an analysis of your work situation tell you about the leadership style you should adopt?

11. How do you rank your own task readiness level for the key tasks you are responsible for? If you have any staff, how do you rank their readiness levels for the key tasks they perform? Are you using appropriate leadership styles?

12. Do you know (or know of) anyone who sounds like the transformational leader described in this chapter? Write a short essay describing this person. Do you think their abilities are inborn traits or learned competencies? Support your answer with evidence from your own experience and study.

13. Compare the concept of servant leadership with the quotation from Andrew Carnegie on page 638 in Chapter 21.

14. Do supervisors need to be both leaders and managers? Which set of skills do you think the most successful supervisors would rely on the most?

Group activities

1. In small groups, make a list of some effective leaders that you know of or know personally. What makes them effective? Make a list of their characteristics. Once your list is complete, identify which are skills, which are behaviours, which are attitudes and which are personal qualities. What does your list tell you about leaders and leadership? How does it relate to the theories discussed in this chapter?

2. Working in groups of four to six, and referring to the lists you developed above, agree on your own definition of leadership.

3. Complete these sentences in small groups: 'An effective leader is …', 'Things effective leaders do …'

4. On your own, spend three minutes answering the question: 'How is leadership like a piece of string?' Then compare your answers.

5. 'Unless you know how to follow, you can't be a good leader.' All supervisors need to be both leaders and followers at times. Working in small groups, develop a list of the skills and behaviours needed to be a good follower. Provide a short explanation of how these skills and behaviours would help you to be a good leader, too.

6. In small groups discuss how Theory X leaders and Theory Y leaders can *both* be right. Develop some examples to illustrate this.

7. 'Leadership is not something we do but who we are. We can't separate the act from the person.' What does this mean? Do you agree with it? Discuss in small groups and present your conclusions to the class.

CASE STUDY 20.1

Bob's Ozzie Burgers

As managing director of Bob's Ozzie Burgers, Bob Johnson was always on the lookout for potential managers. The chain had grown from one outlet in 1996 to its current 17 outlets in two states, with plans for further expansion. It was known as the leader in its field, and no small part of its success was due to the shrewd and capable management of Bob and his management team. In his words, 'Our most valuable asset is our employees. And our most valued employees are qualified leaders who can manage our food centres.'

His latest applicant was a young man named Robert Nicosea. Robert's experience was not too exciting: work in a supermarket as a checker, and summer work during school holidays as a construction labourer and as a clerk in an accounting firm. Not too impressive a record, but what struck Bob was Robert's burning desire to get ahead—to succeed, to make something of himself.

Robert's job in the supermarket had been head checker responsible for training and supervising the 11 other checkout staff. The job also entailed checking out each register to ensure that the tapes and the money tallied. When Bob telephoned the store manager for a reference check, she gave a glowing account of Robert's job performance.

At his first interview with Bob, Robert exhibited an almost contagious enthusiasm for honest work, belief in others and a desire to succeed. According to his application form, Robert Nicosea was the leader and informal spokesperson for his local trout fishing club and president of his town's youth fellowship group.

Bob asked Robert why he wanted to be the manager of one of his outlets and why he thought he would be a good leader. Robert thought for a moment, then replied: 'First of all, I know I can do the job. I've had experience in food handling in a supermarket and I know figures and bookwork. Also, I think I know how to handle employees. I believe that people like to see their boss have a strong hand and exercise sound and strong control. They like a supervisor who is not afraid to make decisions and who will make them quickly. They like a boss who runs a tight ship. And I think that all of these things apply to me. I'm not afraid to make a decision. And I certainly don't mind telling an employee to do something. Furthermore, if an employee isn't performing, I don't mind giving a reprimand. And I don't believe in "suitcase management"—carrying people who aren't pulling their weight.'

He paused, and went on. 'I believe that I'm a born leader. I've always wanted to tell others what to do. Even when I was little, I always wanted to lead the rest of the kids on my street—to tell them what we would do, to be the captain of the team.

'For these reasons, Bob, I know that I could be one of your best managers within a year. I'm sure that I can run one of your outlets and increase business and profits. I'm a hard worker. I don't mind long hours, hard work and tough goals. Give me a chance and I will prove to you that I can get results.'

Thanking Robert for coming to see him, Bob indicated that he was interviewing several other candidates and would let him know his decision in a few days. The two shook hands and Robert departed.

Questions

1   What leadership qualities do you see in Robert Nicosea? Are they the type of qualities that would be effective in a fast-food outlet?
2   Choose two leadership theories presented in this chapter and use them to analyse Robert's leadership style as he described it.

CASE STUDY 20.2

A Question Of Style

Helen Goodman had been maintenance foreperson at the local telephone service centre for six years when a deputation of her staff confronted her. After a few comments by their nominated spokesperson, they presented a long list of complaints. She took the list and thanked them.

The group impressed her—they were not militant, but quite serious. She could not shrug off the incident as insignificant. Through the years, her theory had always been that 'the complaining soldier is the happy soldier'. She had thus frequently passed off an employee complaint as a superficial gripe from a basically happy employee.

As she thought back on her work at the service centre, she recognised that from time to time she had received complaints from individual employees, perhaps more than the normal number. She had dismissed them casually because she did not believe they were serious. Now confronted by a long list of complaints from all the staff, she really 'sat up and took notice'.

The complaints varied. The following are typical examples:

- We're concerned that you don't seem to understand us or maintenance work.
- You are distant—we would like to get to know you better.
- We are never sure you pass our suggestions up the line.
- We believe you show partiality to the female employees.
- You appear to us to be more concerned with the show that the maintenance department will make than with supervising.
- You follow the rules too strictly.

Questions

1 Judging from the list of complaints, what major problems exist for Helen Goodman?
2 What corrective action should she take? Why?
3 Do you think she has the potential to continue as a successful leader? As a supervisor? Why, or why not?

Answers to Rapid Review questions

1. T   2. T   3. T   4. T   5. F   6. T   7. F   8. T   9. F   10. T   11. T   12. F   13. T
14. T   15. T   16. F   17. T

CHAPTER 21

MOTIVATING OTHERS

A motivating situation

Sara, Leslie, Frances and Norm were enjoying a cup of coffee in the canteen following the monthly supervisors' meeting. The message the general manager had delivered during the meeting was brief but very clear. Sales were declining; costs were rising; output was not up to the quality standards. Worst of all, the company was unable to keep up with the innovations of the opposition in an industry where, only a few years ago, it was the acknowledged leader. 'What is needed,' said the general manager, 'is for you supervisors to get out and motivate yourselves and your people to get this company on the go again!'

'It's all right for you,' said Sara to Leslie, the sales supervisor. 'All you have to do is run a sales competition with a weekend of skiing in the Snowy Mountains or sunbaking on the Gold Coast for the winner. The rest of us don't have the opportunity to find that sort of money, and money and bribery are what motivation is all about.'

'It's not as easy as that,' replied Leslie. 'The main difficulty I have motivating staff is that my people operate quite independently of my control. There are some of my salespeople I don't see for three or four weeks at a time. When they are making sales they are generally self-motivated. But when they come face to face with a customer's complaint about something that has not been attended to correctly by accounts or delivery, then not even money will motivate them. No, I think that people are easier to motivate when you have them under constant observation so you can see any change in their attitude and do something about it right away.'

'That's relying too much on human relations theories, which work okay in the textbooks but not in the work-place,' replied Sara. 'My staff are best motivated when they are faced with the challenge of keeping up with the work going through the office. If people know exactly what is expected of them they are easy to motivate. That's why the easiest people to motivate are those in the assembly area. Daily and even hourly output is easy to measure and the workers know where they stand in relation to expected performance against established standards.'

'Not exactly,' replied Norm. 'My people are semi-skilled and do a monotonous job. The only way to motivate them is by using fear—a sort of spear and whip approach. I don't like to be an autocratic type of manager, but if the boss wants motivated staff I'll probably have to sack a few whose work is not as good as the rest in the hope of improving overall performance.'

'My problem of motivation is quite different from the rest of you and nothing that you have suggested will help motivate my people,' said Frances, from the research and development section. 'My team are highly qualified from long periods of study in their respective fields. They work independently of each other most of the time and it's personal achievement that motivates them.

'As for motivating ourselves, that might be all right for the younger supervisors who are seeking promotion. But I'm happy with my position and I don't particularly want to go any higher. As a matter of fact, more meetings like today's and I'll be happy to go back to the bench and let someone else supervise the section! My motivation comes from looking forward to being around long enough to retire and collect my superannuation!'

OVERVIEW

People won't work any harder than they choose to. As the saying goes: 'Ya gotta wanta'. In this chapter you will discover ways to make people want to work.

- Can you distinguish a motivated from an unmotivated employee?
- Does fear motivate? How about money?
- Is there any such thing as an unmotivated person?
- What are people looking for from their work and what happens if their needs are not met?
- Does everyone share the same basic needs?

- Do the same things motivate everyone?
- Do you know how to build people's motivation?
- Do you know what causes people to lose motivation?
- Will people work harder if they think their chances of success are low or high?
- What motivates you?

WHAT IS MOTIVATION?

Supervisors are paid to ensure that jobs are done to a standard of excellence and, many would say, to build healthy teams and develop leaders for the future of their organisation. To do this well, they need to promote a climate in which people can become motivated.

Most employees, when they join an organisation, sign some sort of 'job contract' which details the hours to be worked, the rate of pay and other benefits, and the job to be carried out. It doesn't say how hard the employee is to work, how much effort or cooperation they should put into the job, or how favourable or positive their attitudes towards the organisation must be. In short, the job contract doesn't indicate how motivated the employee must be.

Supervisors set the scene for their staff to do that little bit extra, to do their job as well as it can be done, to look after the tools and equipment of the organisation as well as they can—in other words, to do the thousand and one little extras that make a workplace productive and efficient and ensure its future. This is motivation.

In return, people expect that the organisation will do certain things for them, that it will meet some of their needs. Supervisors have a lot of control over whether or not these needs are met. The more an individual's needs are met, the more the person will be motivated. (This is the basis of the **psychological contract** we discussed in Chapter 19.)

However, just as we can lead a horse to water but can't motivate it to drink, we cannot motivate anyone. *People motivate themselves.* Motivation is like an internal engine that gets a person 'moving'. Supervisors can set the scene that will start the engine and allow people to do their best.

HOW IMPORTANT IS MOTIVATION?

Andrew Carnegie, the great steel magnate of the 1930s, was at one time the wealthiest man in America. At one point, he had 43 millionaires working for him. ($1 million in those days would be worth more than $20 million today.) They weren't millionaires when they began working for him. They became millionaires as a result of working for him. When asked how he developed them to become so valuable, he replied:

> 'Men are developed the same way gold is mined. When gold is mined, several tons of dirt must be moved to get one ounce of gold. But one doesn't go into the mine looking for dirt. One goes in looking for the gold.'

Charles Schwab was the first person to earn more than $US1 million a year in Andrew Carnegie's steel mills. When asked what equipped him to earn $US3000 a day—was it his vast knowledge of steel?—he replied, 'Nonsense! Lots of people work here who know lots more about steel than I do. I can inspire people. I consider my ability to arouse enthusiasm among employees the greatest asset I possess.'

All supervisors are motivators; either they're doing it poorly or they're doing it well. Some supervisors really know how to bring out the best in people, to get that extra effort. They have a knack for inspiring people: they are skilled in the art of motivation. Such supervisors are valuable assets to any organisation.

LAZINESS AND FEAR

Have you ever watched the way some people rush off home at the end of their shift? How many anglers do you know who will leap out of bed at 3 am to go on a fishing trip? How many skiers are happy standing in freezing temperatures waiting for the chair lift, anticipating the run down the mountain? The answer: Plenty! People are willing to do things because they are motivated to do them. Doing these things gives them something in return.

> 'There are no unmotivated people, only unmotivated employees.'

Most people aren't inherently lazy. Your challenge is not to transform lazy, unmotivated workers into industrious 'workaholics', but rather to channel their existing energies into a desirable work performance. You probably don't like being lethargic and bored; neither do most employees. People welcome supervisors who can help them enjoy their job and get satisfaction from it.

Is fear a good motivator? Threats such as losing your job or being reprimanded may work in the short term but generally the effect doesn't last long or work very well. Positive motivation works best. Today's successful supervisor does not rule through fear or threats. Supervisors who attempt to motivate through fear should remember three things:

1. The employee motivated through fear must be subjected to constant supervision.
2. Fearing the consequences of not doing the job reduces in importance once the employee has become accustomed to such threats.
3. Fear sets off an automatic adrenalin response in the body that triggers our ancient 'fight–flight' response. Employees instinctively want either to hit supervisors who manage through fear or run from them!

In the long run, fear, power and force as motivators are unsuccessful. They are outdated forms of motivation. Other motivation methods that may have worked in the past, particularly money and competition, are also less effective than they once were for most workers. Today's motivators are job design, work-related goals, self-improvement, participation and, increasingly, working conditions that are 'family friendly'.

> 'Motivation isn't about lighting a fire under a person.
> It's about lighting a fire within.'

DOES MONEY MOTIVATE?

Economic rationalists tell us that human behaviour is rational. People calculate how much effort they will put into a job based on how much money they receive in return for their efforts. Despite the popularity of this theory, there is no evidence to support it.

Study after study shows that money does not motivate, at least not for long periods of time. Satisfaction and respect motivate; the money follows as a result of good performance. People will forego moving jobs to one that pays substantially more in order to remain working in a place where they can use their skills and talents and can work with others in an atmosphere of mutual respect.

Think about it: your manager walks up to you tomorrow and says: 'My friend, in recognition of your excellent performance and because we think you're a terrific person, we have decided to double your pay.' Naturally you would be very pleased and, perhaps, in gratitude, work really hard for three, four or five weeks. However, if you're like most of us, you would quickly learn how to spend your increased earnings and come to take them for granted. They would then cease to motivate you (although the fear of losing them might motivate you for a little while longer).

As we'll see below, money for most people is what is known as a *hygiene factor* and helps to satisfy our physiological and security needs. There are exceptions, of course. Some people really do come to work just for the money. This may be because they need it badly. Or they may consciously choose a high-paying but not necessarily satisfying job for some other reason—for example, because they are getting most of their psychological, higher-order needs met away from the workplace. However, such workers are probably in the minority.

Does money ever motivate? It can be a strong motivator sometimes. Money (in the form of a pay rise, bonus or incentive), if it is *clearly* being paid in recognition of good performance, can motivate. In this case, though, it isn't so much the money itself that is acting as a motivator, but rather what it symbolises—recognition of good performance.

So if money doesn't motivate, what does? Intangible things: a sense of achievement in doing the work itself; the recognition of managers and peers; career advancement, job challenge; management trust and support; an enjoyable work environment, using your skills and talents; meaningful work; some degree of autonomy; feeling appreciated—these are what research identifies as motivators. These are the higher-order, psychological needs identified by Maslow and Herzberg (see below). Work climate, culture and content are far better motivators than money.

MOTIVATING OTHERS

There is nothing simple about motivation. As a maintenance manager in Sydney remarked shortly after his first appointment to line management:

> **'People can be a source of joy**
> **or an absolute misery.'**

He was talking about supervising people. Motivating others is one of the biggest challenges that supervisors face.

To learn how to motivate people, we need to understand something about what makes them tick. There are three questions relevant to motivation:
1. What are people's basic needs?
2. What do they need from their work?
3. What happens if these needs are not met?

Answering these questions is fundamental to good supervision. It will help you establish and maintain effective working relationships. It will help you ensure the job is done to a standard of excellence.

OUR BASIC NEEDS

Values are powerful motivators for most people. As we've seen in Chapters 3 and 19, values are beliefs about what is right and wrong, good and bad, important and not important. We act in ways that are consistent with our values.

Basic needs also motivate us. Although we are all unique individuals, with different backgrounds, experiences and values, we're also alike in many ways. Psychologists believe we share the same basic needs and that these needs also guide or motivate our behaviour.

We examine three theories that are particularly helpful in explaining the basic needs most of us share. These needs motivate all of us, although for most of us they are unconscious. Like many of our values, we are not aware of them in our day-to-day lives. Maslow described these needs in his hierarchy of needs.

Maslow's hierarchy of needs

According to Abraham Maslow, human beings have certain physiological and psychological needs. We can think of these needs as drives or impulses that cause us to act in ways we

FROM THEORY TO PRACTICE

If you were really hungry and we offered you a large, delicious meal in return for doing something for us, you would probably be motivated to do it in order to get the meal. But once you'd eaten, hunger would no longer motivate you. Unsatisfied needs motivate; once satisfied, they cease to motivate. We move on.

believe, consciously or unconsciously, will fulfil our needs. We must fulfil our needs if we are to function well.

Maslow grouped these needs into six categories and arranged them into a hierarchy. This means that lower-level needs must be reasonably well satisfied before needs at the next higher level can emerge.

Maslow proposed that unsatisfied needs motivate people. Once a need is satisfied, it no longer motivates a person; then the next level of needs comes into play.

Maslow's hierarchy, illustrated in Figure 21.1, shows the six levels of needs, with physiological needs being the most basic.

Physiological needs

We cannot live without air, food and water. If we are short of any of these basic necessities, they become very important to us and we spend most of our time and energy trying to attain them. Other basic physiological needs are sleep, shelter, sex and a comfortable temperature.

> 'There are people in the world so hungry that God cannot appear to them except in the form of bread.'
>
> Mahatma Gandhi (1869–1948)

FIGURE 21.1   MASLOW'S HIERARCHY OF NEEDS

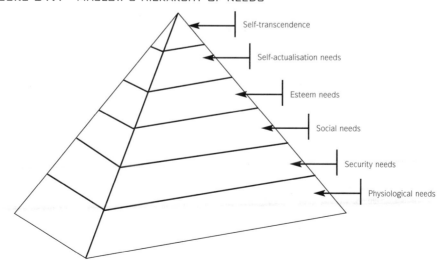

Organisations help to meet our basic needs by paying us a wage we can live on and providing basic working conditions such as a safe and secure building, and ventilated and temperature-controlled air.

Security needs

Once our physiological needs are satisfied, we can turn our thoughts to satisfying our security needs: ensuring continuity in our food and water supply, providing clothing for ourselves and more permanent, safe and secure shelter that protects us and our possessions from outside threats, such as the elements and other people. Organisations help to meet our needs for security through a safe working environment and fair and just human resources policies.

Social needs

Once we have satisfied our physiological and security needs, we turn to social needs. We begin to seek acceptance, affection and a feeling of 'belonging'. This need expresses itself, for example, in the need to be loved and to have someone to love, to be a friend and to have friends. Work helps to satisfy some of our social needs by providing an opportunity to be in the company of others and build friendly working relations.

Esteem needs

Some esteem needs are internal, such as the need for self-respect, autonomy and achievement. Others are external, such as the need for appreciation and the respect of others, and for status, recognition and attention. Work is an important way for many people to satisfy both their internal and external esteem needs.

Self-actualisation needs

This is the need to improve ourselves, to learn, develop and grow, to use our abilities and skills to the full and reach our potential. Maslow believed self-actualisation is difficult to achieve fully. People always try to better themselves and react against situations that prevent them from doing so. For example, if we find that our job is dull and boring, we might try hard to make it interesting and challenging. If this is not possible, we look outside work for opportunities to develop and grow as a person. A challenging job where we have the

FROM THEORY TO PRACTICE

Although we tend to move *up* the hierarchy for most of our lives, we sometimes move back down it. Think, for example, about what would concern a person most who is nearing the age of retirement: many will become concerned with security needs again. Think about a young couple who have just taken on a large mortgage: what might their primary concerns be? Think about someone who has a safe and secure place to live, an income sufficient to cover their main needs, a group of friends they enjoy spending time with, and an interesting job that provides learning opportunities and the opportunity to help others. Suddenly this person loses this job and their income. What might motivate them now?

FIGURE 21.2   MASLOW'S HIERARCHY OF NEEDS AND THE WORK ENVIRONMENT

Need	*Examples of how the needs relate to the work environment*
Self-transcendence ⇑	Feeling that we are making a contribution to society and the organisation, doing worthwhile and meaningful work.
Self-actualisation ⇑	Challenging work allowing creativity, opportunities for personal growth and advancement, freedom to make work-related decisions.
Esteem ⇑	Title and job responsibility, praise and recognition for work performed, opportunity for advancement, competent management, status symbols, privileges, merit awards, participation in decisions, authority.
Social ⇑	Friendly work relations, supportive supervision, organised employee activities, trust, feedback, being informed, helping others.
Security ⇑	Superannuation and insurance schemes, job security, safe and healthy working conditions, dependable supervision.
Physiological	Pay, benefits and working conditions (e.g. rest periods, labour-saving devices).

opportunity to use our skills and learn new ones can provide us with a major channel for satisfying our needs for self-actualisation.

Self-transcendence

In Maslow's later years he refined his hierarchy of needs and included self-transcendence as the ultimate goal of human beings. This is the desire to rise above the self and become part of the greater whole.

Although we are never fully satisfied at any level, some satisfaction at the lower levels is necessary before most people will seek to satisfy upper-level needs.

Atkinson's and McClelland's theories

Whereas Maslow's theory stresses an innate, or inborn, hierarchy of needs, David McClelland believed that some needs are learned or acquired socially as we interact with our environment. To a large extent, he says, our early training and learning impact upon and modify our innate needs and, in this way, our environment plays a significant part in the strength of each need.

John W. Atkinson developed this thinking further. His model relates behaviour and performance to three basic motives:

1. *Power motive* —the need for control. Some individuals have an intense desire to be in charge and in a position of authority. Others have a low need for power. Many supervisors have a high need for power.

2. *Affiliation motive* —the need or desire to be with others or to belong to a group. Some people have a strong need to be part of a group and accepted by others. For others, this is less important. Customer service staff and those who deal constantly with the general public often benefit from a high need for affiliation.

3. *Achievement motive* —the need to achieve and accomplish. People with a strong achievement motive are somewhat independent and gain personal satisfaction from performing a task well. Supervisors and many employees with a strong achievement motive often excel in their work.

We all have each of these needs to some extent. The strength of each need relative to the other needs gives each of us our own unique 'needs profile'. Can you see a relationship between these learned needs and Maslow's innate needs?

McClelland related Atkinson's model directly to business drive and management. For example, his research showed how a high need for achievement was related to how well individuals were motivated to perform their work tasks.

WHAT DO WE NEED FROM WORK?

....Herzberg's two-factor theory

Frederick Herzberg adapted Maslow's theory to an industrial setting. But, unlike Maslow, who saw motivation operating across a single continuum of needs from physiological to self-transcendence, Herzberg divided people's needs into two groups of factors operating along two different continuums. He called them hygiene factors and motivation factors.

The first group of factors, the **hygiene factors**, operates across a continuum from dissatisfaction to no dissatisfaction. As Figure 21.3 shows, the hygiene factors relate to the *environment* in which we do the job. An organisation that meets the hygiene needs of its workers will eliminate dissatisfaction, but will not motivate its employees to work harder. This is where the motivation factors come into play.

The second class of factors, the **motivation factors**, operates across a continuum from not motivated (no job satisfaction) to highly motivated (job satisfaction). From Figure 21.3, we can see that it is the nature of the *work itself*, not the surrounding environment, that provides job satisfaction and motivation. Motivators come from the job itself. This means that a person's motivation can come from their job, provided their work surroundings

FIGURE 21.3   HERZBERG'S TWO-FACTOR THEORY

Hygiene factors

Dissatisfaction ◄——► No dissatisfaction

Economic

e.g.   Wages and salaries
Superannuation
Insurance
Parking facilities
Company canteen

Status

e.g.   Job classification or title
Privileges
Company status

Security

e.g.   Job security
Grievance procedure
Fairness, consistency
Policies and administrative
practices

Motivation factors

No job satisfaction ◄——► Job satisfaction

Meaningful and challenging work
Recognition for good work and skills
Feeling of achievement
Responsibility
Opportunities for learning, growth and advancement
The work itself

Job knowledge

e.g.   Job instructions
Shop talk
Newspapers, bulletins

Physical

e.g.   Job layout
Work demands
Equipment
Health, safety and welfare
arrangements

Interpersonal relations

e.g.   Friendliness
Coffee groups
Office parties

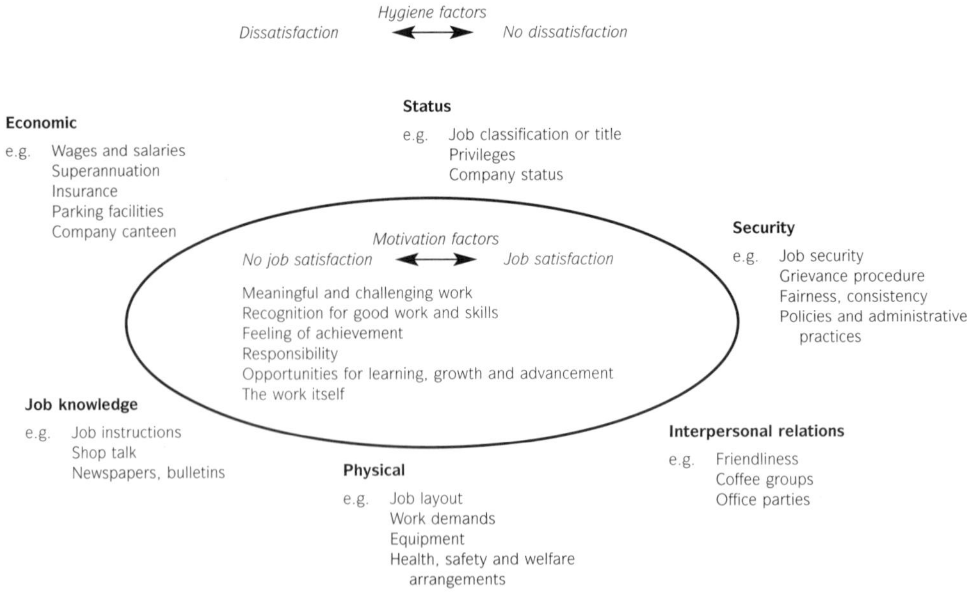

(hygiene factors) are adequate. Although hygiene factors do not motivate themselves, they are a prerequisite to motivation.

As you can see from Figure 21.4, there is a close relationship between the theories of Maslow and Herzberg. Herzberg's hygiene factors relate roughly to the lower three levels of Maslow's hierarchy (physiological, security and social needs) and the motivators relate to the top levels (esteem, self-actualisation and self-transcendence).

Herzberg says that employees expect that the organisation they work for will satisfy their hygiene needs. If it does not, dissatisfaction and demotivation will result. If the organisation satisfies hygiene needs, employees will not be motivated, but will be in 'neutral'. Then we can motivate people by providing a job that offers meaningful and challenging work and is interesting to do.

We tend to take hygiene factors for granted unless they do not meet our standards. If they do not meet our expectations, they will cause dissatisfaction and come to dominate the behaviour not only of individual employees but also of the work group. This means organisations must continually strive to be competitive in these areas (working conditions, remuneration, training, health, safety and welfare, a friendly working environment, comfortable and attractive office furnishings, etc.) to attract and retain quality staff. So even though they don't motivate, hygiene factors are important.

They are often easier to provide than the intangible motivating factors that come from an interesting and challenging job. Herzberg noted that most organisations attend to the hygiene factors, providing good pay, benefits and suitable working conditions, but tend to give inadequate attention to the motivating factors.

Three tiers of motivation

Warren Mills, a Melbourne-based management consultant, has developed a working model of motivation based on his own experience and observations (Figure 21.5). Three sets of

FIGURE 21.4   HOW MASLOW'S AND HERZBERG'S THEORIES RELATE TO EACH OTHER

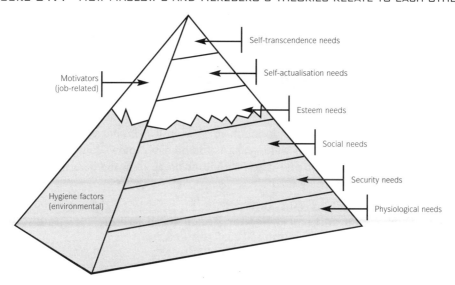

Motivators (job-related)

Self-transcendence needs

Self-actualisation needs

Esteem needs

Social needs

Security needs

Physiological needs

Hygiene factors (environmental)

FIGURE 21.5 A THREE-TIERED MODEL OF MOTIVATION

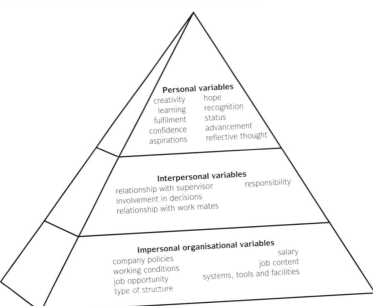

Personal variables
creativity hope
learning recognition
fulfilment status
confidence advancement
aspirations reflective thought

Interpersonal variables
relationship with supervisor responsibility
involvement in decisions
relationship with work mates

Impersonal organisational variables
company policies salary
working conditions job content
job opportunity systems, tools and facilities
type of structure

factors, *impersonal organisational variables, interpersonal variables* and *personal variables* combine to motivate or demotivate people. Mills believes that the personal variables are the strongest motivators, although, like Maslow, he believes they must be built on a foundation of the impersonal and interpersonal variables.

This theory is interesting because it shows us that what Herzberg called the hygiene factors create the conditions where motivation can occur. Motivation comes from both a personally satisfying working environment (the interpersonal variables) and personal growth, or self-actualisation (the personal variables).

WHICH NEEDS ARE THE BEST MOTIVATORS?

The lower-order needs, or hygiene factors, are part of the job environment. As we've said, they do not motivate but will demotivate if they are not satisfied. They are sometimes called *push factors* because, through fear of losing them, they push an employee towards doing the job. Because they are external, they are weak. As you probably know: doing a job for fear of what you will lose if you don't do it usually means doing only the bare minimum, just enough to get by without being fired.

'If you want to build a ship, don't drum up people to collect wood and assign them tasks and work. Rather, teach them to long for the endless immensity of the sea.'

Antoine de Saint-Exupery
French author and aviator

For most of us, the higher-order, psychological needs motivate better. These are often called *pull factors* because it is the interesting nature of the work itself that pulls a person towards doing a good job. These motivators, or pull factors, are internal. For this reason, they can be strong motivators indeed. People will do a job to the best of their ability simply because they enjoy doing it or enjoy the satisfaction of doing it well. Thus it is the higher-order needs, those to do with the job itself, that motivate best. Box 21.1 lists some non-financial incentives supervisors can use to motivate employees.

Vroom's expectancy theory

According to Victor Vroom, the strength of our motivation depends on two things. The first is *how strongly we believe that we can succeed*. For example, if a salesperson believed his chances of making a sale to a prospect were extremely low, he would probably not feel motivated to spend a great deal of time and effort on that prospect. He would look for prospects more likely to buy and focus his efforts on them. Similarly, if we asked a machinist to produce a high-tolerance piece of work on an old, broken-down lathe, she would probably not feel highly motivated to do it, knowing that her chances of success were minimal. If we asked you to write a 5000-word essay on the relationship between chaos theory and quantum physics, you might not be too motivated to write it unless you happened to have a good understanding of the subject or a keen interest in it.

The second part of expectancy theory looks at the likelihood of *receiving something we value in return for our efforts*—that is, the likelihood of some of our needs being met. If we

---

NON-FINANCIAL INCENTIVES

- Treat employees as individuals.
- Offer sincere praise and recognition, for example:
  — letter of thanks
  — an on-the-spot 'Thank you'
  — gift vouchers
  — recognition in company publications.
- Provide learning and development opportunities.
- Give feedback on performance.

- Encourage participation.
- Carefully orient and induct new employees.
- Train them well.
- Communicate.
- Increase accountability of individuals for their own work.
- Give people complete units of work where possible.

THE **BIG** PICTURE

A study by Response Analysis in Princeton, New Jersey, USA, of 1600 employees found that:

- 52% will give their best if they're given responsibility;
- 42% will give their best if recognised for their success; and
- 39% will give their best if their strengths are suited to their duties.

What would you estimate would be the figures in Australia and New Zealand?

offered you $50 000 to write that essay on chaos theory and quantum physics, you might be more prepared to put a bit of effort into it. Or perhaps the guarantee of a promotion to a job you would like would be a better motivator for you. Vroom's theory also tells us that what we offer in return for good performance must be equitable, or worth the effort. You might not knock yourself out to write that essay for 5 cents! Or the incentive of a promotion might not appeal if you're not interested in one.

To motivate people, we must first help them believe they can succeed and then let them know they will receive something they want in return for succeeding. In short, people ask themselves: 'What's in it for me?' If the answer is something they value and there is a good chance of success, they will be motivated to work hard.

WHEN MOTIVATION NEEDS ARE NOT MET

You may know someone for whom 'life begins at five o'clock'. These are the people who hate their jobs and do them only for the money. Their days drag; they are miserable. They probably do only the minimum of work, and may become dissatisfied troublemakers. How sad. Being unhappy for 40 hours a week will add up to a large chunk of their life.

If only their supervisors could find a way to place them in a job they would enjoy and provide them with some satisfaction. If only they would make them feel their job is worthwhile and valued and their efforts appreciated. If only they would find out what they wanted from their jobs and try to provide it. If only their supervisors knew something about motivation!

We all have needs. If our job doesn't satisfy them, they don't disappear or take a back seat. We must look elsewhere for them to be met. While a job can't meet all our needs, it should meet many of them. The fewer needs that are met by our job, the more we will turn our attention outside work, or towards other, often undesirable channels at work to satisfy them.

When motivation needs are not met, people tend to ask for more pay, better superannuation plans and long-service awards, better lighting or air-conditioning, and so on. In other words, they tend to focus on the hygiene factors (Herzberg) or the physiological and safety needs (Maslow). Under these circumstances, if you 'give people what they ask for' and they still complain or fail to be motivated, it may be that what they ask for is not really what they want. After all, it's more usual to strike for more money than to strike for more respect and recognition!

Any attempt to satisfy needs at the lower levels will only return the situation to 'neutral'. Hygiene factors don't motivate people. The motivation factors do.

FROM THEORY TO PRACTICE

When you want an employee to do something, think: What's in it for them? Which group of needs would best apply—social? esteem? self-actualisation? What can I supply in return for good performance? Recognition? Further training? More job challenge?

Two things, then, can happen when employees' needs are not being met by their job.

1. *They can try to satisfy their needs off the job.* Take the case of Ken. He likes to organise people and things. His job provides no scope for his organising abilities, but Ken satisfies his desire to organise (which in turn helps meet his needs for responsibility) by running a local youth group. This may work out well for Ken, but employees who find it necessary to meet many of their needs outside work usually end up withdrawing from their job and becoming 'nine-to-fivers', doing only what is specified in their job contracts and no more.

2. *They can become frustrated.* This frustration can be expressed in a range of ways on the job. Linda, like Ken, also likes to be an organiser but her job provides no outlet for this. So she has become the informal leader of a group of disgruntled workers and a thorn in the side of her supervisor.

If you are to avoid these two situations, try to ensure that jobs provide outlets for people's needs. If you don't, they may rebel, withdraw their cooperation or engage in subtle acts of sabotage and 'malicious compliance'. Ken's and Linda's supervisors could build elements into their jobs that used their organising skills.

JOB PLACEMENT AND MOTIVATION

If the job itself is an important factor in our level of motivation, it follows that job placement can provide significant motivation (or lack of it). Working at a job we enjoy, with people we like, feeling confident about what we do and appreciated for our efforts, being given the opportunity to contribute fully and develop our skills is probably the most important aspect of motivation. Fortunately, supervisors have a great deal of control over these things and play a major part in meeting these motivation needs.

Place people in jobs that allow them to satisfy some of their strongest needs. This may mean redesigning a job to make it more complex, more challenging and more satisfying in order to meet a worker's responsibility and growth needs. Or it may mean transferring an employee from a job that requires working in isolation to one that allows working with a group to meet social needs.

FROM THEORY TO PRACTICE

Organisations largely meet people's lower-order needs. As we've seen, these don't motivate so much as provide a neutral base line. Higher-order needs motivate. These are largely under your control.

Try to match people with jobs that offer the greatest opportunity for satisfying their particular needs. Then make sure they understand precisely what is required of them. Try to ensure that they realise how their needs can be met and that they will receive rewards they value through good job performance. Always recognise their efforts. This will help you to get the best out of your people.

HOW TO USE THE MOTIVATION THEORIES

Both Maslow's and Herzberg's theories show us that everyone has similar needs. Yet each of us has our own unique combination of needs and they express themselves differently, according to our personalities. We also have our own expectations of how our needs should be met. To complicate matters further, different motivational need groupings operate in each of us at different times in our lives and careers.

So what motivates Fred will not necessarily motivate Jane. Fred may value recognition from his supervisor (esteem) and friendly relationships with colleagues (social) while Jane may value job training (self-actualisation) and a space in the company car park (esteem). Or perhaps Jane and Fred are both motivated by a need for power but with Fred this is expressed as a need to dominate and control others, while for Jane it appears as a desire for independence and decision making in her work.

Similarly, what motivates Fred for one day, or one month, or even for one year will not necessarily motivate him the next day, month or year. People's needs change over time. What a person aged 20 needs and expects from work is usually very different from what a person aged 50, approaching retirement, will look for. All these factors mean that you should get to know as much as possible about the feelings and attitudes of the people you work with. This will put you in a position to try to satisfy whatever needs you think motivate them.

Vroom's theory shows us that it is necessary to understand employees so that you can reward them in ways that are important to them. It is up to you to make the required performance levels clear to everyone and let them know that good performance will pay off for them.

Since motivation comes from within, there is no standard package for motivation other than this one: try to determine what people want from their work. Then try to see that they get it in return for good performance.

Many studies in Australia and overseas have shown that those who supervise others are often unaware of what motivates their staff. Don't fall into the trap of assuming you know

FROM THEORY TO PRACTICE

What do your people want from work? What do they want to avoid? Why do they come to work—or take a 'sickie'? Do their jobs satisfy and motivate them? What about career progression? Salary and working conditions? Status? Power? Sense of achievement? Sense of security?

Given that different things motivate different people at different times, you will probably need to talk to your employees and get to know them as people, to find the answers to these questions.

If you find the answers fall mainly into the lower-order needs and the 'push' category, you'd better do something about the hygiene factors at your organisation or you are likely to be faced with motivation problems. If your answers fall mainly into the higher-order needs and the 'pull' category, pat yourself on the back and keep up the good work!

what people want from their jobs. And remember, a need, when satisfied, ceases to be important and thus ceases to motivate.

Research clearly indicates that most employees want to be motivated by their work. Basically, most people want the following:

- to do a meaningful and worthwhile job that provides enjoyment and satisfaction (esteem and self-actualisation needs);
- clear standards and objectives (achievement needs);
- adequate job training (achievement, self-actualisation, growth);
- supportive supervision (social, recognition);
- feedback on performance (esteem, recognition);
- opportunities for advancement (responsibility, growth);
- being treated as a worthwhile individual (social, esteem, recognition);
- safe and healthy working conditions and adequate remuneration (safety and physiological needs);
- to work with tools, equipment and work systems that support, not hinder, their best efforts (security and achievement); and
- to work for someone who 'practises what they preach' and behaves with integrity, honesty and fairness (security, social, esteem, self-actualisation).

Figure 21.6 summarises this.

MOTIVATING YOUR EMPLOYEES

Supervisors have many opportunities to motivate their employees. The following tips are not luxuries. They are necessities.

Treat employees as individuals

Be genuinely interested in employees. Find out about each of them: their families, what they do in their spare time, what their ambitions are. This will provide clues to what motivates them best.

Remember that different people need different supervisory approaches. Some need close supervision, others need independence, others lots of recognition. Suit your style to the person. They each have different experience levels and different expectations.

FIGURE 21.6   THE MOTIVATING CIRCLE

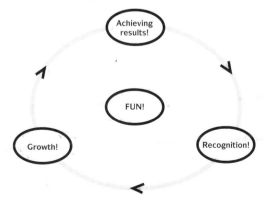

Provide a vision and 'paint the big picture'

An inspiring vision to work towards, and knowing how they personally contribute to achieving it helps energise employees. *Take a few extra moments to explain* and watch motivation and productivity rise.

Set high standards and make your expectations clear

Don't settle for second best—*expect the best from employees.* Set challenging goals and make sure everyone knows and understands precisely what you require. Make your expectations clear, quantifiable and time-framed.

Make the work interesting and worthwhile

Monotonous, boring jobs lead to a lack of interest and motivation. Although the surroundings and their fellow workers may be congenial, dull jobs can lead to problems. *Identify boring jobs and make them more satisfying.* Providing variety, interest and challenge can be difficult but the benefits from increased motivation are great. Job redesign, job enrichment, job enlargement, job rotation and participation are all possibilities. Being able to carry out the whole job from beginning to end, or at least knowing what the whole job is can also help, as can frequent feedback and visible results of performance.

You've probably heard the saying, 'If a job is worth doing, it's worth doing well.' But think of this:

'Only a job worth doing is worth doing well.'

People need to know that what they are doing is worth doing well. *Make sure your people know that their contribution is important to the department and the organisation.*

Give responsibility

Most people respond well to being given some responsibility and control over their own work, their goals and the monitoring of their own results. *Delegate as much as you can.* Don't oversupervise.

Develop people's skills

The opportunity to learn and use skills will motivate many employees. *Provide growth opportunities* through *multiskilling, upskilling* or *cross-skilling.* This may mean encouraging someone to attend training programs, or delegating some of your tasks to give workers a chance to develop skills not used in the day-to-day job routine. Broadening people's skills and knowledge makes them more valuable to the organisation and builds a strong work

---

THE BIG PICTURE

Remember Sisyphus? The gods condemned him to ceaseless effort rolling a rock up to the top of the mountain, whence it would fall back down. They believed there is no more dreadful punishment than hopeless and futile labour.

Is there any hopeless and futile labour where you work? What is it? What could you do to eliminate it or improve it?

team. The individual concerned will be motivated and others will see that there are possibilities for growth and will be motivated as well.

Seek and give feedback

Talk openly and honestly with your staff. This builds trust and confidence, meets part of people's social needs and makes them feel important and valued. Give feedback on how they are doing, the progress they are making and any problems that crop up. If a task wasn't done quite right, ask what could be done to improve the situation and what can be done to ensure it is done correctly next time. Chances are, they will know. If necessary, offer an improvement suggestion in a helpful manner, not in a threatening or demeaning way. Seek feedback on how you can give better support and help to your people.

Reward people

Work out what is important and reward people in a way that means something to them. That way, the behaviour will be repeated. Box 21.2 shows some commonly used rewards. Tailor these rewards to suit the individual or team so that they are valued and appreciated and will motivate the recipient(s) to continue. Don't reward every high-performance behaviour every time. Occasional rewards work better. Make sure to tell the recipient precisely what the reward is for. Vary your rewards for maximum motivation.

Say thanks

Have you ever done something really well at work and your boss never mentioned it? Did you feel motivated? Did you want to 'keep up the good work'? Even if you were well paid, you would probably start looking around for another job if this happened repeatedly.

The routine remark, 'Thank you for your effort' can be a bit superficial, although it is better than no thanks at all. Try to be more specific. Whatever you mention will be repeated. *Genuine praise and recognition for a job well done* shows people you've noticed and flags what is important. It helps to meet esteem and recognition needs.

'The deepest principle of human nature is the craving to be appreciated.'

William James, psychologist

When people *improve their performance*, make sure they know you've noticed. This is especially important with employees new to a task; as we learned in the last chapter, the lower a person's task readiness level, the more important the praise. When someone does

---

 BOX **21.2** **WAYS TO REWARD**
....

Praise (Personal/public, informal/formal)	**Material rewards**
Thank individuals or groups	Gift or cinema vouchers
Send brief thank you notes	Flowers, chocolates, etc.
Recognise and celebrate achievements in formal meetings and informal gatherings	Retention of frequent flyer points
	Organisation logo items
Present plaques and certificates	
Employee or team of the month program	
Performance management system	

something *especially well*, make sure they know you've noticed. And when someone *consistently* does something reliably and well—you guessed it—make sure they know you've noticed.

The rules are: be genuine in your praise and recognition of people, and recognise good performance as soon as possible after it occurs. Nothing can shrink motivation more than thinking your efforts go unnoticed.

Remove barriers to good performance

If staff aren't performing as well as they should, find out why (see Chapters 8 and 24). The 85:15 rule tells us that, 85% of the time, the reason will be out of the employee's control. Poor or faulty tools and equipment, poor work methods, lack of time and lack of information are frequently at the root of poor performance. All the competence and motivation in the world can't overcome these. *Find out what blocks good performance and remove it.*

Build self-esteem and confidence

Only people with high self-esteem and confidence perform at their best. This self-fulfilling prophecy is one of the unrecognised keys to motivation. Those who are expected to achieve usually do.

> 'Trust men and they will be true to you.
> Treat them greatly and they will show themselves great.'
> Ralph Waldo Emerson
> US poet and philosopher

Make everyone a winner

Nothing succeeds like success. *Give every employee the opportunity to be successful, or at least a significant part of success.* Give credit to everyone who contributes.

Promote participation in decision making

People like to be 'in' on what is happening, not only in their own work area but also in the rest of the organisation. This helps them to feel part of things and builds loyalty. Taking part in decision making helps boost social, esteem, recognition, responsibility and growth needs. So, *invite employees to help set realistic targets and have a say in decisions that directly affect them and their jobs.* People are committed to decisions they've had a say in. (See also Chapter 11.)

If you can, empower your work team

There is a big difference between employee involvement and employee **empowerment**. With the first, the supervisor still calls the shots. As we learned in Chapter 20, sometimes this is appropriate. Sometimes, empowerment is appropriate.

Empowerment is not abandonment. Nor is it giving people permission to do something they haven't been trained to do. Empowerment involves giving people responsibility and accountability in line with their **task readiness level** (see Chapter 20) in such areas as decision making, planning, goal setting and quality assurance. This flexibility and choice helps to meet responsibility and self-actualisation needs and increase commitment.

Recent US studies show that motivation, productivity and performance improve most when:

- work is organised so that employees have the training, opportunity and authority to participate in decision making;
- they have assurances they will not be criticised or ostracised for airing unpopular ideas;
- they know they will not lose their jobs as a result of productivity improvements (you can't work on self-actualisation while removing the lower-order need for security); and
- they know they will receive a fair share of any performance gains (**gainsharing**).

Find out how the team and each team member wants to interact with you. Find out what sorts of problems and decisions each wants to help you with. Agree how each will update you and keep the others informed. Giving people responsibility and a 'say' motivates.

Promote cooperation and team support

Knowing that they belong and are vital members of the team helps satisfy employees' social, recognition and esteem needs. The basic mateship system encourages one person to help another. Encourage employees to ask for and offer help and assistance. *Structure your team in a way that invites an exchange of ideas, interdependence and mutual support.* Promote this sort of teamwork in any workplace where groups of employees deal with each other.

Listen to your staff

Everyone has feelings and opinions they want to express. Find time to listen. Use these discussions to point out the importance of a person's work to the organisation's progress and success. Such actions on your part will help fulfil employees' achievement, recognition, social and esteem needs.

Make sure you understand what they are saying and comment constructively on their ideas. Don't hesitate to question when you don't understand. *Listen to employees.* This shows them they are important and makes them more willing to listen to what you say.

Keep promises and build trust

Trust is a special quality that develops between people and among work teams. It takes time and effort to develop, and seconds to destroy. Promises made but not kept are powerful demotivators because they break down the trust that has been built between supervisors and work groups or organisations and employees. *Walk your talk. Keep your promises. Honour your commitments. Set the example for your team to follow.* This is essential to a motivating environment.

Resolve conflict and complaints

With good judgment, empathy and honesty, conflicts and complaints can be resolved. Allowing them to linger saps motivation and productivity. *Focus on solving conflict to everyone's satisfaction rather than sweeping it under the carpet or assigning blame.* Attempt to understand the problem and search for the best solution. When conflict arises, use a problem-solving win–win approach to resolve it.

Always control your temper. 'Count to ten', take time to think, and then discuss it in private with the person who has done something 'out of line'. Calmly explain why you are angry; then listen to their point of view. If you have made a mistake, admit it.

Set a good example

Lead from the front. Don't ask people to do anything that you do not or would not do yourself. This applies to everything to do with the job—timekeeping, good housekeeping, following safety procedures. *Insist that your staff keep to the rules as you do.*

HOW TO MOTIVATE YOURSELF

There are times when we all need 'a bit of get up and go'. Sometimes it's to do a task we dislike. At other times it's to start a conversation we're not looking forward to. Sometimes we just need 'energising'! Since the strongest motivation comes from inside, it's up to us to motivate ourselves.

We need three things to want to 'get moving':

1. desire to reach goals;
2. self-confidence to take action; and
3. commitment to put in the effort.

Desire

We must have a *clear goal* in mind and *want* to achieve it. There has to be some value in it for us and, perhaps, for others, too. If we really want to do something, we will find a way. If you're lacking motivation, try asking yourself: 'What positive outcome will there be in accomplishing this?' 'What will happen if I don't do it?' 'What will be my reward for achieving this?' 'Why is it important that I do it?'

There's a big difference between *wanting* to do something and *having* to do it. Try changing your language. Instead of saying: 'I have to do this (groan)', try saying 'I want to do this because ...' Having to do something often leads to half-hearted attempts while wanting to do it produces whole-hearted efforts and a better result. Set a clear, positive and specific goal for yourself.

Self-confidence

Self-confidence is important, too. As Vroom's expectancy theory shows, we must have a reasonable expectation of success before we will attempt anything whole-heartedly. Do you believe you can do this thing well? Have you been trained? What help and support might you need to organise for yourself? Think about your self-talk (see Chapters 3 and 19). Are you giving yourself limiting, negative messages that you won't succeed? If so, change them. Self-confidence stems from positive self-esteem. It gives us the will to act to achieve our goals.

Commitment

The third factor in motivating yourself is commitment. Are you committed enough to be willing to put in the time and effort required? Are you committed to trying again and again until you succeed? Are you committed enough to forego something else in order to achieve it? For example, part-time study while working at a full-time job requires a lot of commitment. There are many pleasurable personal, family and social activities you may need to pass up in order to study or attend classes. How willing are you to do this? Looking only at immediate, short-term drawbacks can blind us to the more fulfilling longer-term rewards and lessen our commitment.

In addition to these three elements of self-motivation, it can also help to project yourself into the future and mentally 'see' yourself succeeding at the task. 'Feel' your success. Savour it. Knowing how worthwhile it will be can supply much-needed motivation (see also Chapter 19).

Jot down a simple plan for approaching your task if it is a big one. Set yourself realistic yet challenging goals and time frames. Then you won't have a head full of 'loose ends' but a clear plan of action on which to concentrate (see also Chapter 3).

Try listing the major 'push factors' associated with the task. How can you turn them into 'pull factors'? List your ideas. Think about what else might be stopping you from beginning or working on your task. What can you do to remove these barriers? For instance, it can be difficult to study in a noisy environment. What could you do to make it quieter? Could you study in a different environment, one more conducive to thought and concentration?

RAPID REVIEW

	True	False
1. It is fair to say that people lacking in motivation will never produce excellent work.	☐	☐
2. Supervisors don't motivate people. People motivate themselves if the conditions are right.	☐	☐
3. Fear is an effective motivator.	☐	☐
4. Supervisors need to understand what people want from their jobs and try to provide it if they want them to be motivated.	☐	☐
5. Since each of us is different, our basic needs are different.	☐	☐
6. According to Maslow, unsatisfied needs motivate.	☐	☐
7. Esteem needs include self-respect as well as the respect of others.	☐	☐
8. Atkinson identified three areas of need which are at least partially learned: the needs for power, affiliation and achievement.	☐	☐
9. Herzberg says that hygiene factors are environmental and are strong motivators.	☐	☐
10. Herzberg's motivators are to do with the job itself.	☐	☐
11. Money is the main motivator for most people.	☐	☐
12. Vroom says that people will be most motivated when they believe they can succeed and when they expect their success will earn them something they value.	☐	☐
13. If people's jobs fail to motivate them they are likely to become either 'nine-to-fivers' or troublemakers.	☐	☐
14. Job placement cannot motivate.	☐	☐
15. What motivates people can change over time.	☐	☐
16. Motivation is an ongoing process all supervisors need to be involved in.	☐	☐

1. List and explain the six types of needs that Abraham Maslow believes we all have. Give examples of how each need relates to work and to study. Do all employees respond to higher-order needs? Give some examples to illustrate your answer.

2. 'A person does not live by bread alone.' Discuss in relation to Maslow's motivation theory.

3. Draw a bar chart which you believe illustrates the relative strengths of your own needs for power, affiliation and achievement. Ask someone who knows you well in a work or study situation whether they agree and why. Now ask someone who knows you well in a social situation whether they agree and why. Are their answers similar or different? What could account for this?

4. 'The organisation looks after hygiene factors. The supervisor looks after the motivation factors.' Discuss.

5. Discuss the needs that relate to how employees are motivated, according to David McClelland.

6. Describe two things that can happen if a person's needs are not satisfied by their work. If you can, give examples from your own experience.

7. List at least ten things that you as a supervisor can do to raise the motivation level of your employees.

8. What motivates you at work? In your studies?

9. Look back through Chapter 8 and the five keys to building productivity and performance. Write a short essay explaining how having all five keys 'in place' will help motivate employees. Use Herzberg's, Vroom's and Mill's theories to explain your thoughts

Individual activities

1. Think of someone you have worked with whom you would call highly motivated. Describe this person. Think of someone with little motivation. Describe this person. How did their differing levels of motivation affect how well they did their work?

2. Thinking about the motivated and unmotivated people you described in the question above, what factors in their environments might help to account for their differing levels of motivation? What internal factors might help to account for it? Relate this to the statement made in the chapter that people are motivated to do something when they can see it is in their own best interests to do it.

3. Think of these motivated and unmotivated people and apply the theories of motivation discussed in this chapter to each of them, using the theories to explain their level of motivation.

4. Refer to Case Study 20.1 (Chapter 20), Bob's Ozzie Burgers. Analyse Robert's motivational needs using Maslow's and Atkinson's theories. How motivated do you think Robert would be working for a supervisor who supervised his work closely and didn't involve him in decision making?

5. Use Maslow's theory of motivation to analyse which of your needs are satisfied in a work or home setting.

6. Based on Maslow's and Herzberg's theories of motivation and thinking

about the higher-order needs at the top of the pyramids and the lower-order needs at the bottom (see Figures 21.1 and 21.4), what do you think would be the primary motivators of employees in Australia and New Zealand? Would the same things motivate workers in an economically less advantaged country devastated by floods, such as Mozambique was in February and March 2000? What about a country like India where people might be very wealthy, middle class, or so poor they barely subsist?

7. Give examples of your own needs based on Herzberg's two-factor theory of motivation.

8. Draw up your own three-tiered model of motivation, based on Mills' model as described in this chapter. What is in each of the three tiers for you?

How well are your needs being met by your current lifestyle and job?

9. Analyse the strength of your motivation as a student using Vroom's expectancy theory of motivation.

10. Relate Vroom's theory to the task readiness theory described in Chapter 20.

11. 'Leadership and motivation go hand-in-hand.' Based on what you have learned from Chapters 20 and 21, explain this statement. Illustrate how supervisors can meet employees' motivational needs by using the appropriate leadership style.

12. Think of three things you want to accomplish over the next three months. What 'push' factors are involved? What 'pull' factors are involved? What can you do to turn the 'push' factors into 'pull' factors?

Group activities

1. If we all have the same groups of needs, why do they surface in different forms? Discuss and present your conclusions to the class, citing relevant examples to support your conclusions.

2. Discuss and agree on at least 12 specific things supervisors can do to apply Vroom's expectancy theory.

3. Think about these two words: *cooperation* and *compliance*. What do they mean in terms of motivation? Give examples of each and indicate which form of motivation is the strongest. Illustrate your answer with a personal example from someone in your group.

4. Divide a large piece of paper in half down the middle. Head one side, 'HAVE TO' and the other side, 'WANT TO'. In small groups, brainstorm the

effects of 'having to' do something versus 'wanting to' do something. How does this relate to motivation? How does it relate to the push and pull factors of motivation discussed in this chapter? Summarise your findings by concluding what they mean for supervisors and their employees.

5. What do you think the quotation from Gandhi earlier in this chapter is referring to? Discuss in relation to Maslow's hierarchy of needs. Contrast it with the quotion in question 2 in the *Apply your knowledge* section above. Can they both be correct?

6. Using your college as an example, analyse its environment (from an employee's point of view) using Herzberg's two-factor theory.

The Keen Supervisor

Gregory Kean is one of Manly Manufacturing's most promising engineers. He was top apprentice six years ago and has always been a keen and willing worker, eager to get ahead.

Because of his efforts, clear thinking and organising abilities, the company promoted Gregory to the position of supervisor of the general maintenance department. He and his team of five are responsible for the general day-to-day care and maintenance of the plant, buildings and grounds of the company. When Gregory was promoted, he became more determined than ever to show senior management his capabilities. His level of motivation was high and he decided to make a clean sweep of general maintenance and really 'smarten up their act'.

Prior to Gregory's promotion, general maintenance had a reputation as an 'easy-does-it' department. The work was done and, by and large, done well. However, as far as Gregory could see, the previous supervisor didn't really 'supervise' at all.

So in Gregory Kean went, tightening up on systems and procedures, making sure they were followed, ensuring lunch breaks weren't extended, continually monitoring everyone's work, handing out jobs each morning and generally ruling with the proverbial iron hand. Plenty of time to get to know the team better later, thought Gregory, once I've established the new order of things around here!

Now, four months later, the best tradesperson has quit, another is openly looking for another job and the team is no longer functioning as a unit. The four who are left seem to have withdrawn their cooperation, use no initiative and do only what Gregory tells them to do.

Gregory's supervisor has decided it is time to have a chat with Gregory to get to the bottom of what can only be described as a crisis in motivation.

Questions

1 What, specifically, do you think led to this crisis?
2 Using the information in Chapter 20 on leadership, what leadership style would you say Gregory is using? Is this style appropriate? Give evidence for your answer.
3 Which motivational theory might Gregory study to help him correct the situation? Show how the theory you suggest could help him.
4 Gregory has focused on task issues rather than people issues. Many new supervisors do this. Why can this be a mistake?

The Transfer Problem

According to his previous supervisor, Dana had always been a conscientious and accurate worker with a pleasant and willing attitude. Yet, ever since his transfer, his error rate had been above average, he seemed sullen and generally exhibited a 'couldn't care less' attitude. Andrea was at a loss to know what to do. She had spoken to Dana about his performance twice in the four months since he had joined her department. After the first discussion, his performance had improved slightly, only to fall off again about two weeks later. The second time they discussed the problem, his performance improved dramatically and remained excellent for about three weeks. Now it is back to its original low level.

Andrea has gone to the personnel officer for advice on how best to deal with Dana. As far as the personnel officer can determine, Dana's jobs in Andrea's department and in his previous department are similar, although the former job may have allowed for greater discretion in decision making and a greater degree of freedom regarding how the work was actually carried out. The only other difference, and this so far is just guesswork, is that in his old department Dana had built up a reputation of 'knowing what he was doing' and was regarded by the other members of the work group as something of an 'expert'. Even though he is clearly capable of meeting the requirements of his present job, he just doesn't seem to want to.

Questions

1   What motivational needs seem to be missing in Dana's new department? What could Andrea do to meet them?
2   If you were Andrea, what would be your next move?
3   From the information in the case study, and referring to the information on task readiness level in Chapter 20, what would you assess Dana's overall readiness level to be? Is Andrea's style of leadership appropriate? Why or why not?

Answers to Rapid Review questions

1. T   2. T   3. F   4. T   5. F   6. T   7. T   8. T   9. F   10. T   11. F   12. T   13. T   14. F   15. T   16. T

CHAPTER 22

LEADING WORK TEAMS

Trouble in the team

'My team has the most terrible attitude—they drive me to distraction with their constant whingeing, whinge-ing, whingeing. It's their attitude—their attitudes are all wrong. They think they're here for a picnic!'

'How do you mean, John?'

'Well, it's just … well, for instance, when I hold a group meeting, which is about once a fortnight, we always spend the first 20 minutes listening to everybody's complaints. They just won't settle down 'til they've had their moaning session … And it's always such petty stuff. You wouldn't believe it—last week they were actually griping about wilted lettuce at the canteen salad bar!

'And another thing—they never help each other out. Like, you know, if Alice or Tom get loaded down, which they often do, wouldn't you think one of the others would offer to give them a hand without being told to? But no, no, they'd rather have their long lunch breaks. They've just got no sense of responsibility.'

'That sounds pretty bad, all right. What action have you taken to try and swing things round a bit?'

'I'm a bit stumped, really, Joan. I don't know what I can do. Some days, the chit-chat gets so loud, you can hardly hear yourself think. So they must have a bit of team spirit, I guess. But when it gets out of hand, I have to tell them to pipe down.'

'Does their chit-chat stop them from working?'

'Well, no, of course not, but it would just sound bad if someone were to come into the area.'

'It does sound like you've got a problem there, John. Let's put our heads together and see what we can come up with to build them into a high-performing team.'

Do you supervise a team or a group of individuals? Today's supervisor needs to be skilled at developing teams and helping them to perform well, whether they all share the same work area or are scattered across the continent or the globe. In this chapter you will discover the real power of teams and how to lead them.

- What is the difference between a work team and a work group?
- What goes on in teams and what does it mean to *be* a team?
- How can you help a team develop identity and synergy? How can you help team members work well together? How can you build a strong team culture and positive norms?
- Why is being a member of a successful team so enjoyable, satisfying and motivating?
- What types of teams are you likely to be supervising in the workplace?
- When should you step in and show leadership and when should you be a 'hands off' team leader?

- How do teams change and grow over time?
- Can you analyse the dynamics of a team?
- Why can new team members 'upset the apple cart' and how can you prevent it?
- Do you know whether you are an effective team leader and how you can improve your skills in this area?
- What formal and informal team roles are you aware of?
- How should you lead a team whose members seldom or never meet face-to-face? What if your organisation merges with another—how should you lead a merged team?

THE MOVE TO WORK TEAMS

As modern organisations have become more streamlined and team-based, the nature of supervision has changed. Today, many supervisors lead teams. They need to know how to mould and empower teams so they can direct themselves with reduced input from management and achieve the results their organisations need from them.

Leading teams is about managing a diversity of people. It is about forging individuals, with their own needs, abilities, interests and confidence levels into a cohesive, cooperative whole that is more effective than the sum of its individual parts. Communication and a sense of team spirit are essential. These, combined with clear and challenging goals and well-trained, motivated team members, enable teams to achieve **synergy**. This is the ability of the whole to be more than just the sum of its individual parts.

FROM THEORY TO PRACTICE

- Can everyone in your team express the essence of your organisation's vision and main goals?
- Do they demonstrate understanding of how they contribute to it?
- Do they demonstrate understanding of your organisation's performance and the issues affecting it?

If so, congratulations. If not, what can you do to help them answer these questions?

Understanding what goes on in teams, and what it means to *be* a team, will help you to influence and help your work team to become a high-performing team. You will need a sound understanding of group dynamics and individual and group behaviour, combined with skills for diagnosing team needs, developing teams and managing productivity. We have already examined much of this in other chapters in this book. In this chapter, we concentrate on the formation, functioning and development of teams and on how to create and lead a high-performance team.

How teams began

> 'We're a pack animal. From earliest times, we have used the strength
> of the group to overcome the weakness of the individual.
> And that applies as much to business as to sport.'
>
> Tracy Edwards, yachtswoman who skippered
> the first female crew to circumnavigate the globe

When you think about it, not much can be done without the cooperation, support and assistance of others. Joining together to achieve more than we could achieve alone is natural. Most people enjoy being part of a group, particularly a successful, high-achieving team. Think of how much time and effort people are willing to put into being part of a winning sports team or a successful community project team. Think of how much satisfaction they get from being part of it. Teams are enjoyable and motivating.

Widespread use of teams in organisations began in the 1980s in the face of growing international competition and economic pressures. Large manufacturing industries began forming quality circles to help cut defects and reduce rework. Public sector organisations began combining people into multiskilled teams responsible for achieving objectives in an effort to increase job interest and customer satisfaction. Not-for-profit organisations brought people together to maximise their use of resources to combat funding constraints.

When organisations needed even greater improvements, many introduced re-engineering programs to redesign work processes from top to bottom. A by-product of this was cutting out layers of middle management, pushing work and decisions down the organisation. Work teams are a natural way to produce more with fewer people.

Today, teams are becoming increasingly popular. Some manufacturing organisations have forsaken assembly line principles to follow 'cell manufacturing' principles, where small groups of workers make entire products from start to finish. Many service and public sector organisations are organised around team principles. Not-for-profit organisations often rely on teams to accomplish their objectives in a way that individuals working singly would not be able to achieve.

A GROUP OR A TEAM?

A group is a collection of individuals. There is no sense of group identity or team spirit. A group of individuals standing in a bus queue is just that—a group of individuals. A team is different. It is made up of individuals who come together for a shared purpose.

Working in the same area doesn't make you a team. A work group becomes a team only if people depend on each other and the unique contributions each can make towards achieving their shared objectives. Teams need common goals, a sense of shared purpose and identity, and interdependence. If it is a high-performing team, its members will work cooperatively to achieve goals.

> 'A team is a small number of people with complementary skills who are committed to a common purpose, set of performance goals and approach, for which they hold themselves mutually accountable.'
>
> Jon R. Katzenbach and Douglas K. Smith

Leading a group of individuals is one thing. Building and leading a highly motivated, high-performing work team poses additional challenges and demands even greater skills.

TYPES OF TEAMS

Quality circles

Quality circles were an early form of team. Typically, they meet for a few hours a week to identify, analyse and rectify problems, particularly problems to do with workflows and systems. To participate effectively in a quality circle, people need specialised training in problem identification and resolution and in statistical and other total quality management (TQM) tools such as Ishikawa diagrams, brainstorming and flow charting (see Chapters 6 and 9).

With management support, training and resources, many quality circles have made measurable improvements to quality and productivity. Morale can also improve as a result of individual skills development, team membership and the pride that comes from achieving results. Box 22.1 lists the main characteristics of effective quality circles.

Multifunctional or cross-functional teams

Multifunctional or cross-functional teams are responsible for delivering an entire product or service, from design to manufacturing, marketing, delivery and after-sales service. They usually include people from all functions of an organisation—marketing, manufacturing, engineering, quality assurance, finance and human resources.

Problem-solving teams

A problem-solving team is a popular type of temporary team made up of knowledgeable people who meet to solve a specific problem and then disband.

BOX 22.1   CHARACTERISTICS OF EFFECTIVE QUALITY CIRCLES

- Clear, shared goals and purpose
- A systematic approach focused on what to do and how to do it
- Supportive systems and work environment
- Fully trained and willing members
- A knowledgeable leader
- Frequent feedback
- Team Identity

- A climate of mutual respect
- Fun
- Cooperation
- Sense of achievement
- Rewards for achievement
- Knowing how each individual fits in and contributes to the team as a whole

Management teams

Management, or leadership, teams consist of managers from various functions like sales, production, finance and human resources, who coordinate work and strategy across the organisation.

Work teams

More work teams are being introduced every day. Members work together to achieve results. When they are empowered to make their own decisions, they are called self-managed teams.

Self-managed teams

Self-managed teams can achieve impressive results based on their authority and ability to organise their work and make production-related decisions. They often manage their own budget, have the authority to reorganise work systems and work flows, and hire their own team members. Because of their broad responsibilities, they are usually kept informed about how their company is faring in the marketplace and the health of its balance sheet.

Leadership of a self-managed team may rotate according to a set schedule, members may elect their own leader or leadership may move between members informally, according to team needs. When they are first set up, an official leader with supervisory experience is often appointed to help the team learn how to manage itself—what needs to be done, how it can be done, how they can best work together to achieve their aims.

Virtual teams

Team members of virtual teams are from different locations, often scattered across offices, regions, states or even countries. Technology enables them to communicate by fax, email, teleconferencing and videoconferencing. Members meet in person as needed and often take turns leading the team.

Matrix teams

In an organisation with matrix teams, people are members of several teams, each made up of members from different functions. For example, an organisation might have a regional sales team whose members are also part of specialised product-type teams. Industrial engineers might be part of two or more production teams while also being part of a product launch team, working with customers, suppliers, marketing and finance specialists, and research and development engineers to design and launch a new product.

Merged teams

Today, acquisitions, mergers and takeovers are normal. Employees from once competing organisations are being asked to work together cooperatively for the common good of the new company. This presents special challenges as people mourn the loss of the old, struggle to come to terms with the new and cope with new ways of working and a host of new people, procedures and systems.

THE BENEFITS OF TEAMS

There is no doubt that well led teams can achieve cost savings and remarkable gains in productivity, innovation and responsiveness to customer needs. Companies that have introduced team-based organisations have reported up to 40% gains in productivity, smooth transitions to customer-responsive organisations, and manufacturing and design flaws cut by half. Other organisations have reported massive cost savings as a result of recommendations by quality circles, work teams and problem-solving teams.

Teamwork can improve job satisfaction through harmonious working conditions and by providing people with more control over their jobs. It can increase efficiency through reduced layers of management. Teams are an excellent way to use the skills and knowledge of people effectively. They can increase morale and spur innovation.

THE TROUBLE WITH TEAMS

One of the best known examples of self-managed work teams is Volvo, which introduced them in its car factories in Kalmar and Uddevalla. Work became more interesting but also more costly. Eventually, Volvo closed down these experimental plants and concentrated production at Gothenburg using the traditional assembly line. Clearly, teams are not the answer to everything.

It is not that teams don't work, but there are a lot of obstacles. There are problems with introducing teams into the workplace and with managing and supporting them. There are problems associated with encouraging people to participate fully and effectively. It can be difficult to maintain high levels of cooperation and creativity. Let's look at the most common problems with teams.

Developing a culture that rewards team performance is not easy and requires management to lead the way. There are dilemmas about how to remunerate and reward teams most effectively. Should members be paid individually or as a group? Paying people individually does little to encourage teamwork, yet paying the team as a whole could frustrate star performers.

Many organisations have rushed into creating teams for the wrong kind of job, or have created the wrong kinds of teams. Not all jobs and activities are best handled by teams, and teams are often introduced when they aren't really needed or when another solution (e.g. automation) would be more effective. Some types of teams are better suited to certain activities than other types. If self-managed teams are called for but the concept seems too 'radical' for the organisation, quality circles may be introduced instead and management can be left wondering why they are not achieving the expected results.

Teams introduced in isolation usually fail to achieve the expected results. They are often formed without clear objectives and given insufficient training and support. Endless meetings can result, with people wondering what they're supposed to do, and how. Effective team membership requires skills, training and practice. Teams often need special support

---

THE **BIG** PICTURE

When are teams the best option? When are they not needed?

Teams are needed when they produce something together that members could not produce individually. They are needed when the collective skills, experience, knowledge and abilities of team members will contribute in different ways and at different times to team leadership and direction setting. Teams are not needed when the leader really does know best.

from the organisation such as changes in work design, new forms of monitoring and reward systems, or technology such as email to help communication between them. These supports are costly and time-consuming but, without them, frustrations can mount.

Yet these difficulties are no reason to give up on teams.

AN AUSTRALIAN CASE STUDY—FROM CONFLICT TO PARTNERSHIPS

Penrice Soda Products Pty Ltd is an Adelaide-based company producing soda ash and bicarbonate of soda, which is used in making glass, paper products, domestic and industrial powder cleaners, stock feed, pharmaceuticals, laundry bleaching powders, cakes and biscuits, and in the mining and metals industries. Workplace relations between management and workers had traditionally been more 'adversarial' than 'cooperative'. This began to change dramatically in 1998 when self-managing work teams were introduced in the mechanical maintenance service section. Three teams of 12, ten and seven people made up this section.

The turnaround began when one of the teams was given the opportunity to relieve for their supervisor as a team. They were trained in issues and questions relating to work teams and a two-month trial commenced. One month into the trial, a second maintenance group began a similar process and, the following month, team members conducted an evaluation of the two trials. They concluded the pilot was working and made formal presentations to the Penrice Leadership Team and other key stakeholders to gain support for an extended pilot program. A six-month pilot was launched with all three teams, and a memorandum of understanding with specific targets and performance measures was drawn up. Further training to support the work teams began.

One year later, the company and work teams reported the following successes:
- positive attitudes of team members;
- major maintenance overhauls completed within budget and more efficiently;
- quicker response times and less downtime;
- greater interaction and improved communication with internal customers;
- improved relationships between management and shop floor;
- greater understanding of the company and its strategic direction;
- more involvement in decision making;
- innovative approach to work and problem solving;

THE **BIG** PICTURE

Create constellations of teams. Teams need to work with other teams if they are to be truly effective. For example, Boeing had three layers of over 200 cross-functional teams working on its 777 project, all pulling together to design a passenger jet which flew its first successful test flight in 1994. It had fewer than half the number of design problems of earlier projects. The 'flap team', 'tail team' and 'wing team' all communicated with each other through their team leaders who communicated with the overall cross-functional project management team.

- identification of cost-saving targets;
- greater motivation due to higher levels of empowerment; and
- enhanced image for the maintenance group.

TASK AND PROCESS ISSUES

Two issues relate to the success of any team. The first is **task**, the subject matter or job that they are working on—*what* is being done. Task issues relate to the team's purpose and the goals it sets out to achieve. As we saw in Chapter 8, you need to make this crystal clear to all team members.

The way a task is done, the operating procedures or the steps taken to complete a task is often referred to as its **process**. In group dynamics, process also relates to *how* a task is

---

THE BIG PICTURE

In 1998, 68% of US manufacturing organisations were using self-managing work teams as a fundamental part of their structure (up from 28% in the same survey five years prior). Self-managing teams, it seems, are on the rise. Australian figures are not available, but informal surveys suggest we are moving in the same direction.

FROM THEORY TO PRACTICE

Here are three ways to jump start a new team's task achievement:

1. *Develop a team mission statement.* Ask team members to write their ideas on four flipcharts headed: We do; We could do; We won't do; and We can't do. Discuss themes and reach agreement on the contents of the four charts. Using the 'Do' and 'Could do' charts as the major direction for the team, develop a mission statement that encapsulates them and fits in with the organisation's vision and mission.

2. *Develop metrics* (measures) so that members can assess their performance. These measures should show the connection between the team's work and the overall organisation's success measures. The team can even help design its own measures of success.

3. *Train people properly.* Effective team membership is based on clear communication skills, teamworking skills and respect for others. Train in these skills as well as in decision-making and technical cross-training. People don't just have to learn new skills; they must also unlearn traditional roles and behaviours. Matrix and multifunctional teams in particular often need extra training, especially in organisations with a tradition of poor cooperation between functions. The best training in the world will be useless, however, unless you help and encourage team members to use the skills, too.

Spreading training over a period of time is a better option than intensive training in teamworking skills. Training a team before it actually forms is a poor option because people don't know what they need to learn.

done. This is the second important factor in a team's success: how is the team going about achieving its task? How are people working together to achieve results?

Figure 22.1 shows how leaders and teams need to balance their focus between *task* and *process*. Too much concentration on either the task or the process will cause a team to flounder.

Team building and team maintenance

Unfortunately, many teams overemphasise their focus on the task. Ironically, the task itself suffers in the end. This is because process issues have a more dramatic influence on task achievement than anything else! Since poor team processes are a major cause of ineffective teamwork and poor results, an awareness of process issues will help you to diagnose problems early and deal with them more effectively.

If a team isn't succeeding in its task, look at its group dynamics. Think about doing some **team building**. This means working with the team to define its purpose (task issues) and strengthen the way team members work together to achieve it (process issues). This is often done by means of a two to three day off-site team-building workshop. Specially designed activities help the team to focus on the way they work together and identify areas for improvement. Time is taken to explore the team's purpose and goals and discuss specific ways of working together more effectively to achieve them. Usually, team members give meaningful feedback to each other about what they are doing that helps the team, and what they could do to be even more effective. The shared experiences of a team-building session strengthen the ties between team members, help members see each other in a different light and appreciate each other's differences and contributions. It builds up a store of shared experiences that help to establish or strengthen the team's culture. Team building often helps to create a high-performing team.

Once a team is 'built', the work doesn't stop. It must be maintained at peak performance. **Team maintenance** is about ensuring the team continues to function effectively. Periodically, teams need to discuss both their task objectives and the way they are going about achieving them with a view to making further improvements (or getting things back on track, as the case may be).

FIGURE 22.1   TASK AND PROCESS ISSUES IN A TEAM

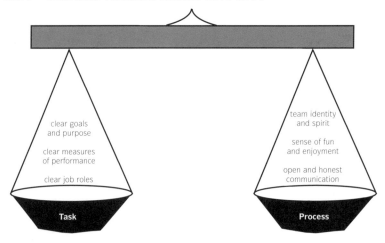

FROM THEORY TO PRACTICE

How does your team look at how they are working together? Do they freely discuss 'the way we are working together' at team meetings? Are any deviations from the agreed way of working together aired and discussed openly? Do you periodically review your team's mission and goals and make sure they still support your organisation's overall vision and goals? Do they take time out to have some fun and participate in enjoyable non-task activities where they can enjoy each other's company away from work (e.g. at a sports event or a team picnic or over a game of cards at coffee break)?

You can't afford to ignore team maintenance if you want to lead a successful high-performing team.

A balancing act

Do you think you should be a traditional leader and tell the team what to do and how to do it? Or should you be 'hands off' and empower your team? According to research into teamwork, neither approach works. Team leaders should offer a balance of both approaches. Be very clear about the team's objectives (high task) and let the team decide the means to those ends as much as possible (high process).

TEAM CULTURE AND NORMS

As a team's processes, or ways of working together, become established habits, a team **culture** and **norms** develop. Through its traditions, time spent together and the experiences it has had as a group, a team acquires an identifiable difference from other teams. It has its own unique ways of operating, getting things done, solving problems and airing disagreements. As teams develop, the accepted behaviour patterns and ways of doing things become clearer and more recognisable. It is these behaviours that new team members struggle to understand and become part of, and it is these that 'newcomers' can disrupt.

It is easier to experience a team's culture than to describe it. This is because the rules and codes of behaviour that influence team members to behave in certain ways are usually *implicit*, or not stated, whereas the task issues are usually *explicit*, or clearly stated (or they should be!). Box 22.2 contrasts the culture of two teams, one a high-performing team and the other a poorly performing team.

FROM THEORY TO PRACTICE

What if a crisis occurs? Should a leader still balance task with process? No. The leader will almost certainly need to focus primarily on task issues and restore the balance when things have calmed down.

What if things are going really well? Should a leader still balance task with process? Now is the time to relax a bit, congratulate yourselves and attend to team process.

The 'balance' isn't always constant (see also Chapter 20).

TWO TEAM CULTURES

BOX
22.2

A poorly performing team

Feelings

- threatened
- in personal 'danger'
- low self-esteem
- poor team image
- low team identity

Behaviours

- excessive politeness/open conflict
- excessive competition between members
- latent or expressed hostility
- some members withdraw, others dominate
- lack of cooperation
- in-fighting
- personality 'clashes'
- gameplaying
- decisions are put off
- 'busyness' without achieving much
- blaming, scapegoating
- focus on problems

Results

- stress
- lack of enjoyment
- poor participation
- formation of cliques
- stereotyping
- hidden agendas
- poor team spirit
- poor results
- dominant leadership

A high-performing team

Feelings

- secure, unthreatened
- strong team identity
- sense of fun and enjoyment
- enthusiasm
- trust
- energetic

Behaviours

- energies/abilities are task-directed
- open and honest communication
- open disagreements without personal attacks
- active listening
- respect for individual differences
- win–win approach
- focus on solutions
- anticipation of others' needs
- self-discipline

Results

- task achievement
- camaraderie
- enjoyment
- team spirit
- change introduced smoothly
- creativity
- mutual acceptance
- 'hands-off' leadership
- empathic relationships
- smooth coordination of effort
- commitment to goals and the team itself

FROM THEORY TO PRACTICE

What is the standard of dress in your work team? What style of language is used? How do people speak about the organisation? How do they speak about their customers? How much effort do members put into their jobs? How much do they focus on quality and customer satisfaction? Do they strive to get things right first time, or is there a 'she'll be right' or 'close enough is good enough' approach?

These attitudes and behaviours can either support or work against the team, the supervisor, and the organisation and its other stakeholders.

If you want your team to be a high-performing team, take the time and trouble to examine its codes of behaviour and make them explicit. If you find they are hindering, rather than helping, the team to achieve its task, discuss this openly and agree on more helpful ways of working together.

Trust

Teams can't work without trust. They must trust their own team members, their leader and their organisation. One of the biggest factors in breakdowns of trust has been broken promises that no retrenchments would result from productivity and process improvements.

> **'Trust cannot develop in the absence of trustworthiness.'**
>
> Dr Stephen Covey, speaking at the Sydney Opera House, May 1994

Building trust takes work, honouring promises and setting the right example. Impartiality, fairness, full communication, participation and politeness go a long way to building trust (see also Chapter 3).

GROUP DYNAMICS

The way a team works together greatly influences both the quantity and quality of its output. **Group dynamics** refers to the unique pattern of forces operating in a group that affects the interactions between people and their relationships with each other. Group dynamics are forged from the way that individuals, their leader, the task and the environment combine. They influence how the team goes about doing the task—the official job that everyone is there to do. The main elements of group dynamics are discussed below.

Communication patterns

These are easy to observe but far from simple. What words do group members use? What tone of voice do they use with each other? What does their body language say? What symbols are important to them? How are their communications timed? Are they clear? What channels are used? Who talks to whom? When? Where? For how long? Who is left out? Do members really listen to each other?

Observe these patterns because they reveal something about the informal status and power of group members. Communication patterns indicate how effectively the group is using the skills of its members to get the job done. They influence a team's efficiency, how well it does its work and the satisfaction and morale of the members.

THE **BIG** PICTURE

According to Sirkka L. Jarvenpaa of the University of Texas at Austin and Associate Professor Dorothy E. Leidner of INSEAD in Fontainbleu, France, trust develops in three stages:

1. *Deterrence-based trust:* at first, team members do things because they fear punishment if they don't.
2. *Knowledge-based trust:* develops when team members know each other well enough to predict each other's behaviour with confidence.
3. *Identification-based trust:* building on empathy and shared values emerges as members begin to identify with the team and each other.

Can you see how important a team's process is to building trust?

Decision making

Groups are constantly making decisions. What are they about? How are they made? Does everyone have a say or do only a few people express opinions? Is silence mistaken for agreement? Are issues discussed so that consensus is reached or does one person make the decision? Ensure everyone in the team understands and follows effective decision-making procedures.

Climate or atmosphere

Do members feel free to express themselves and share their feelings? Do people support each other? Are people free to contribute to the group goals in the best way they can? Is there a sense of enjoyment as the team gets on with the task at hand? These things are signs of a positive climate, one that is understanding, trusting and accepting. Groups like this find it easy and enjoyable to complete their tasks and achieve their goals.

A climate can also be controlling, rigid and punishing. This makes task achievement difficult. You will influence the climate of your work team for better or worse by the example and standards you set.

Informal leadership and other roles

Everyone wants to have a 'role' in the group, whether it is being known as the spokesperson, the expert, or the clown. Is there any friction over who holds these roles? How strong is it? Observe your team to get a feeling for who the informal leader is and who holds the other informal roles, because these have a significant influence on the group's attitudes, behaviours and results. For example, the clown can be disruptive or a valuable tension-reliever. The gatekeeper can shut people out or make sure everyone has a say. The devil's advocate can pour water on good ideas or point out potential problems and how to fix them. We examine roles in greater detail later in this chapter.

Cohesion

Cohesion relates to how tightly bound as 'one mind' the members of a group feel. It relates to the 'attractiveness' of the group to its members. Some teams stick together like glue and have a real sense of 'us', while others are more like a haphazard collection of individuals.

Since cohesive groups are more likely to work well together to achieve their task, try to develop the cohesiveness of your team. Help members to develop a sense of group identity and team pride. Provide opportunities for them to get to know and respect each other as diverse individuals.

But beware! High cohesiveness, if combined with other poor group dynamics, particularly poor group decision-making processes, can lead a team into **groupthink**. This is a phenomenon that occurs when members of a team get along so well that individuals are loath to contradict what appear to be the wishes of the majority. This prevents them from becoming high-performing teams and makes them a danger to their organisation. If you think the team you are leading may be suffering from groupthink, find out more about it in Chapters 6 and 11 and take steps to minimise it.

Participation

Who are the high participators? Who are the low participators? How are those in each category treated? Who is left out and why? Who generates enthusiasm and 'keeps the ball rolling'? Who contributes ideas and suggestions? Who is the first to notice something going wrong and bring it to the team's attention? These things give you clues about the team's priorities and what it values.

Power and influence

Who influences whom? How? Who has the power to 'tell' others what to do? Who is listened to when they speak? Is anyone ignored? Who do others copy? Admire? If those wielding informal power and influence are doing so in ways inconsistent with organisational goals, trouble is brewing!

Together with team norms (discussed above) and a team's maturity (discussed below), these are the main aspects of group dynamics. Be aware of them and observe them. Think through the questions listed in Box 22.3. You may not know immediately what a behaviour, a comment, or a seemingly small 'incident' means, but put it 'on hold' and one day it may be seen as an important piece of a puzzle about why your team is or is not working well.

INFLUENCES ON GROUP DYNAMICS

The following factors influence group dynamics:
- factors within each individual group member;
- factors in the immediate (or associated) environment;
- factors within the job or task;
- factors within the group itself; and
- the leader.

Together they determine how a team organises itself and how well it functions. Monitor them and try to ensure that each contributes in a positive way to the team's operations.

BOX 22.3   ASSESSING GROUP DYNAMICS

- Do team members communicate openly, honestly and respectfully with each other and with their supervisor?
- Are team members respected and valued as individuals?
- Do team members communicate readily and easily with all other members?
- Are team members friendly and helpful towards each other?
- Do team members feel close to the others?
- Will one member go to the aid of another?
- Is information shared readily?
- Do team members know each other on a personal level?
- Do the members resolve issues on a win–win basis?

- Does belonging to the group satisfy individual team members' needs?
- Do team members feel a sense of responsibility for getting the job done?
- Is the climate of the group helpful and friendly?
- Are people interested in and involved with each other, each other's jobs and the department's objectives?
- Are members clear about team goals?
- Is there an easygoing camaraderie among team members?
- Do group norms support the department's goals?

'Yes' answers to most of these questions indicate that the dynamics of the work team are likely to lead to successful task achievement.

Be particularly watchful if any one of these factors changes, because a shift in the dynamics of the group as a whole could occur.

Factors within each individual

Each team member's abilities, skills, experience, attitudes, values, role perceptions and personality—all the things that make a person unique—determine what they are willing and able to contribute, their level of motivation, methods of interaction with other group members, and degree of acceptance of group norms and the organisation's goals.

Factors in the environment

Environment determines what can and cannot be done in a broad sense. It includes the organisational culture, the closeness and type of other teams, the organisational reward system, the formal patterns and styles of authority, the power structure within the organisation, the resources (e.g. tools, time, space, information) available, and the quality and type of leadership. These things establish the boundaries within which the team must operate and thus shape the dynamics that are possible within a group or team.

Factors within the job

The design of the job and the technology being used are important because, to a large extent, they control the freedom of team members to make decisions concerning their work and the amount of interaction that is possible between them. The layout of the department

FROM THEORY TO PRACTICE
....

Train members in skills that will allow them to be useful members of the team. Find out what motivates them and try to ensure their needs are met through their participation in the team and their contributions to it (see Chapter 21). Make sure everyone knows how important their contributions are, and recognise those contributions. Recruit team players and make them feel welcome by inducting them carefully and fully into the team. Take time to make sure they understand what you expect of them both in terms of job goals and performance indicators (task) and how you expect them to work with others (process). Experienced supervisors know that 'one bad apple can spoil the whole barrel'. Don't tolerate 'bad apples' in your work team. Instead, expect and insist on 'the best' from each team member.

FROM THEORY TO PRACTICE
....

How will your team and your organisation benefit when you ensure your team has the resources it needs to do the job well? When you make the effort to establish good working relationships with other groups in the organisation? When you use leadership styles consistent with people's task readiness level (see Chapters 8 and 20)?

FROM THEORY TO PRACTICE

As far as the job allows, involve employees in decisions that affect their jobs. Streamline the work flow and organise it in a way that allows people to work together and everyone's contribution to show. If you can, make the team as a whole responsible for the quality and quantity of its output.

What improvements could you make to the way you involve employees in these things? What's stopping you?

and individual workstations, and the type of work involved, also affect the dynamics of the team.

Factors within the group

The dynamics of the team itself have a powerful effect on how well it functions. Size is important, too: ten or 15 people work better and enjoy it more than larger teams. Communication between team members and between members and their supervisor is less complicated with fewer people and they can help one another more easily. It is also easier for each member to get to know the others. Turnover of membership (how rapidly people leave and enter the group) is also important because 'newcomers' are likely to change team dynamics.

The extent to which members all have similar education, training, experiences and backgrounds is called its *homogeneity*. This also affects dynamics because a homogeneous team, while it can be cohesive and supportive, often has difficulty in adapting to change and in being creative. Homogeneous teams are also more prone to groupthink.

While teams need to be homogeneous in their understanding of their goals, roles and procedures, they need to be heterogeneous in their mind-set, approaches and ways of thinking. This diversity leads to insight, creativity and strength.

The leader

How does the team leader influence the group? As we've seen throughout the book, employees take their cue from their leader. The leader sets the pace for work, establishes what is important and what isn't (quality, customer service, timekeeping, etc.), and establishes the working climate for the team. In short, without a leader who 'paints the picture' and shows the way, a team is left to flounder and become dependent on its informal leader. Then it's 'luck of the draw' whether it will perform well.

FROM THEORY TO PRACTICE

Work to develop a positive team climate and team spirit. Develop a team that respects and values individual differences. Try to ensure the team is composed of people with different personality groupings (see below) so that each member can contribute in important ways to the team's process. Build and maintain the team at a high-performing level. Allow the team as much freedom as you can to establish its own work rhythms and patterns.

Whether a self-managed team selects its own leader or the organisation appoints one, effective leadership is a vital ingredient of a successful team.

'On the face of it, the conditions that foster team effectiveness are simple and seemingly straightforward to put into place. [Yet setting up the conditions that make for successful teams is] more a revolutionary than an evolutionary undertaking.'

Professor J. Richard Hackman
Harvard University

HOW EFFECTIVE IS YOUR TEAM?

Do these characteristics describe your work team? An effective, mature work team:

❑ has a clear understanding of 'why we exist' (vision and purpose) that all members are committed to;
❑ has a clear understanding of 'how we work', the team's internal structure and working arrangements;
❑ has clear, shared goals and objectives that are quantified and time-framed, demanding yet achievable, which the team may be involved in setting;
❑ integrates individual members' goals with team goals where possible;
❑ has group norms that align with and support the goals of the department and the organisation;
❑ receives frequent, clear feedback on how well they are achieving their goals and how well they are working together;
❑ makes the best possible use of its resources and the individual talents of its members to achieve its goals;
❑ has clear roles and procedures;
❑ continually monitors its performance and even designs its own performance measures;
❑ brings problems out into the open;
❑ treats mistakes as opportunities to learn;
❑ encourages and shares ideas freely and enthusiastically;
❑ has a strong sense of team identity;
❑ tolerates and respects individual differences;
❑ has a climate of mutual respect, fun and cooperation;
❑ doesn't necessarily wait for the supervisor to tell them what to do and who should do it, but is willing and able to sort out many of these things for themselves;
❑ has open, free-flowing, accurate and cooperative communication;
❑ balances communication between task and process and examines the way it functions;
❑ uses appropriate decision-making procedures;
❑ has a supportive environment and supportive work systems (tools, equipment, time, information) to help the team focus its efforts to best effect;
❑ has members who show loyalty and support for each other, the leader and the organisation, and who encourage and compliment each other;
❑ has high participation by all group members—everyone gets involved and derives personal satisfaction from their involvement and the team's achievements;

❑ sees controversy and conflict as positive reflections of members' involvement and deals with it constructively and collaboratively;

❑ has a strong sense of cohesiveness, enjoyment and team spirit;

❑ is made up of members who constantly seek ways to improve their operations;

❑ has members who are 'multiskilled' and can step in for each other when necessary; they can also work singly, or in any subgrouping or as a total unit;

❑ has members who know they are valued members of the team, making a worthwhile contribution in both a task and process sense;

❑ has members who talk to each other on a personal level as well as about task matters and enjoy each other's company; and

❑ has members who feel like 'winners' and enjoy a sense of achievement.

Use this as a checklist to see how effective your work team or study group is.

STAGES OF TEAM GROWTH

A team's maturity has nothing to do with how long it has been a team or the age of its members. It has to do with how effective the team is at its task. Mature teams, whose members understand and contribute fully to the team's goals, are effective.

> **'A team is like a spiral. It's always moving. Either it's moving up and getting better, or down and getting worse. Which way it moves depends on the team members and their leader's abilities and skills.'**
>
> Croydon Hall, Team Leader,
> Perth, Western Australia

Just as people go through a life cycle from infancy through childhood, adolescence and adulthood to old age, teams also grow, develop and change. As an adult behaves differently from a child and has the capacity to cope with different and more complex tasks, teams are also characterised by the different behaviours of their members and different team capabilities at each stage of their development.

A team's 'life cycle' has five predictable stages. Be aware of your work team's maturity, or the stage of development it has reached, because this relates directly to its success. You can do a lot to help your team 'mature'.

THE **BIG** PICTURE

Psychology professor, J. Richard Hackman of Harvard University, says work teams cluster at opposite ends of the success continuum. Many teams are high-performing; many fail miserably. Few are in between

What makes the biggest difference? Two things: how they are led and whether their organisation provides the support they need.

FROM THEORY TO PRACTICE

Give teams in the forming stage a 'feel' for what they are supposed to be doing and where they are headed. Set the scene for how team members should work together, how formal or informal their relationships should be and how much focus there should be on the task at hand.

If a new member joins your work team, make them feel welcome, give them a defined role to fill and a contribution to make, and help them get to know the other team members as quickly as possible.

1. Forming

Forming is the first phase in a team's development. 'Strangers' come together for the purpose of carrying out a task or activity. A group of individuals is faced with sorting out exactly what its purpose is, what their relationships to each other are, where each will fit into the team 'pecking order' and what each can contribute.

Task issues take a back seat to personal feelings: anxiety, apprehension, wondering what the group and its leader will be like and how to behave. People are cautious, careful and conscious of themselves and each other. They watch for clues about appropriate behaviour. Polite, impersonal discussions revolve around 'why are we here?' and getting acquainted. The need for group approval is strong at this stage and group identity is low or absent.

A modified version of forming also occurs when new members join an established team. They will usually feel pleased to join yet anxious, uncomfortable and uncertain about how to behave and where they will fit into the team. Team productivity often falls when a new member joins as members adjust their relationships and roles.

2. Storming

The *storming* phase describes the conflict and in-fighting which surface as people explore their differences in values and working styles. Team members are tense as they vie for informal leadership and other roles and deal with the difficulties of formulating common goals, aims and working principles and procedures. Leadership may be challenged and power struggles may develop. Productivity remains low.

Storming teams often seem to be 'stuck' in some way. This may be due to these internal conflicts or to a 'crisis of energy', where team members seem to lack their earlier spark and

FROM THEORY TO PRACTICE

No matter how bad the storming gets, keep team members together and talking until they feel comfortable. This can take months. Storming teams need strong leadership, direction and organisational support in defining boundaries and setting clear guidelines. Continue to show confidence in the team and help new members adjust and fit in so that the team can develop and become more productive.

enthusiasm. There may be disagreements about what the group should do or how they should do it, or a sense of reluctance to 'get stuck into it'. Disillusionment and frustration with the team and its capabilities may surface.

3. Norming

If the team survives storming, the *norming* phase begins. Codes of behaviour, norms and policies about 'how we do things around here' are established both formally and informally. Teams settle how they will function and make decisions. The roles each team member will play are clarified as members learn to understand and appreciate each other's individual differences and talents. Each team member learns where they stand in relation to the others and gains a clear idea of their role and the contributions they can make. As team members organise themselves, the level of trust and openness grows.

Don't be alarmed if task matters seem to take a back seat at this time. As team members settle into working rhythms, patterns and relationships and begin making progress on the task, a renewed sense of hope and a short period of 'play' and celebration of their new-found working arrangements often occurs.

The team will get down to work more seriously as the norming phase progresses. They will begin to depend less on the leader, although they will continue to need your guidance and confirmation that things are progressing in the right direction. A sense of 'who we are' as a team and a team identity will emerge towards the end of this phase. There will be less 'me' and more 'we'.

4. Performing

Many teams (but not all) are fortunate enough to become *performing* teams. They achieve synergy, creativity, harmony and high productivity. Members work together as a nicely balanced whole to achieve more than would be expected from them individually. Performing teams are mature teams whose members can work together, independently or in any combination to achieve their goals. They draw on each other's unique strengths and have learned to compensate for each other's weaknesses.

High productivity on the task side and high satisfaction and team spirit on the process side are evident. High morale, loyalty and cohesion exist. There is open communication, close teamwork, flexibility, trust, resourcefulness and innovation. There is a team spirit that you can practically feel. High-performing teams are a team leader's dream come true!

When teams reach the performing stage, their leader becomes a colleague and a resource to help the team achieve its goals. The team itself is capable of setting, monitoring and achieving its goals with little direction from the leader. This is when you will be able to use leadership style 4, delegation, or 'hands-off' leadership (see Chapter 20).

FROM THEORY TO PRACTICE

Ensure that appropriate team norms develop during the norming stage. Norms such as: *'We insist on high quality'*, *'We put the customer first'*, *'We listen to each other's views'* and *'We turn up on time'* are essential if your team is to reach the next stage, performing.

....
FIGURE 22.2 THE STAGES IN TEAM DEVELOPMENT

Stage 1 Forming
Key questions	Who is in this group?
	Do I want to be in this group?
	What are we supposed to do?
	What are our goals and objectives?
Process issues	Dependence on leader to provide structure and guidance, and set ground rules
Task issues	Orientation to team purpose, objectives and tasks
	Dependence on leader
Key issues	Who am I in this group?
	What can I offer it?

Stage 2 Storming
Key questions	Who's in charge?
	How much power and influence do I have?
	Who has the formal/informal power?
	How will decisions be made?
	What are the coalitions in this group?
Process issues	Conflict, hidden or out in the open
	Leadership, power, authority, roles
Task issues	Organising
Key issues	Conflict or crisis of energy may make the group seem 'stuck'
	Disillusionment
	Leader should show confidence

Stage 3 Norming
Key questions	How will this group operate?
	What are the ways to behave in this group?
	What is the protocol?
	What are our policies, rules and procedures?
Process issues	Cohesion, 'in' groupness, 'we' versus 'they'
	Shared ideas, information, feelings
	Emerging openness and trust
	Striving for harmony
Task issues	Data flow
	Making progress
Key issues	The team may abandon the task and 'play' a while, enjoying their cohesiveness
	Leader should ensure appropriate norms develop

Stage 4 Performing
Key questions	What is the best way to do my job well?
	How can I contribute to the team's task?
	How can we improve our effectiveness and efficiency?
	Are we getting the best results possible?
Process issues	Interdependence
	Members can work singly, in any combination of subgroups or in the team as a whole unit
Task issues	Problem solving
	Harmonious collaboration
	Task goals clear to all
	High commitment to the team and its tasks
	Continuous improvement
	Let's get on with the job and do it well!
Key issues	Achievement

Stage 5 Adjourning or mourning
Key questions	How will I feel when I (or others) leave or when we disband?
	What are the consequences of leaving or disbanding?
Process issues	Feelings of impending loss, anxiety about what comes next
	I feel both sad and excited
	Excitement about 'going it alone'
Task issues	Final winding up to ensure achievements won't be lost
Key issues	Formal closure and goodbyes

As mentioned, when a new member joins, a team regresses to an earlier stage. A new member joining a performing team can destroy the feelings of camaraderie and team spirit that built up as the team developed. It must regress and grow again to the performing stage, carrying the new member along in the process. Usually, this means you will need to become more 'hands-on' for a while.

'The most successful leader in business is not the man who goes around giving detailed instructions to his subordinates. It is the man who gives his subordinates only general guidelines and instils confidence in them and helps them do good work.'

Akio Morita
Chair of Sony and author of Made in Japan

5. Adjourning

Adjourning, or *mourning*, is the final stage of some teams. Temporary teams disband, work sites close down, a team or part of a team merges with another team, a team is made redundant and its work contracted out. This leaves a 'hole' or sense of emptiness in its members' lives, with feelings of loss and sadness. Many work teams never reach the full adjourning stage but, if a team member leaves, a form of mourning occurs, usually marked by a sense of impending loss and promises to get together in the future.

Some sort of official closing celebration or 'ceremony' can help a team through this difficult phase—perhaps a shared meal or informal get-together (see also Chapter 12).

The stages of team development are not always distinct but often merge into each other. Although they have been described in a linear sequence, teams can move back and forth between them as new members join, new challenges emerge or changes are introduced. Team growth is a complex process.

Helping teams to grow and keep growing

After the initial 'honeymoon' period, teams can lose momentum. Box 22.4 has ten tips to avoid this. You can also use these tips to get a team that's in a slump back on track.

Managing changes in team membership

Whenever a team member leaves or a new member joins, the team is disrupted. Goodbyes and hellos can be sad. Each time a member leaves a group, a kind of 'grieving process' occurs. Each time a member joins a group, the forming, storming and norming processes must begin all over again. Loyalties and alliances may shift as the new member settles in and learns the routine and rhythm of the team, which may be interrupted, at least temporarily. Group norms and morale may be threatened or changed. Dynamics often change irrevocably.

Use your understanding of the team life cycle and of group dynamics to help your team remain as productive as possible during this time. As soon as you know a team member will be leaving, bring the team together to discuss the departure and the reasons for it. Members may be proud of a team mate's promotion, sad about the loss, or anxious about an increased work load. Step in to provide the necessary team support and rebuild the team. Be clear, decisive, open and willing to listen.

Discuss how each team member and the team as a whole might be affected and what can be done to diminish the negative effects of the departure. Discuss how team

BOX 22.4 AVOIDING TEAM 'MID-LIFE CRISIS' ··

1. *Support the team.* Clearly define team goals and other expectations. Recognise and celebrate team success. Rotate team member duties. Make sure the team has ways to evaluate its progress in both task and process.
2. *Publicise the team's successes.* Make sure the rest of the organisation hears about how well your team is doing.
3. *Keep training team members.* Involve the team in deciding their own training needs and what training new team members will need.
4. *Keep reviewing the team's mission.* This may well change in light of changing organisational priorities. If it doesn't change, the review will serve to refocus members. Set new goals to challenge the team so members don't become bored.
5. *Keep working on team process and procedures.* It's easy to forget the team guidelines set when the group was established. This means important process matters may slide. Periodically review and update team guidelines.
6. *Rotate assignments.* If there's any chance members' tasks could become monotonous once mastered, rotate them. This not only keeps interest and morale high but ensures members are cross-trained.
7. *Encourage as much participation in decisions that affect them as possible.* Can your team determine the materials and equipment it needs or the best way to do the job, for example?
8. *Compensate the team.* If team membership is additional to a person's work and not a full-time team membership, make sure they are compensated for the extra work and time they will need to contribute.
9. *Keep communicating.* For example, hold monthly business reviews about developments, customers, new initiatives and so on to ensure a steady flow of information.
10. *Keep team membership balanced.* As we see in the section below, on individual differences, make sure you have a balance of skills and personalities in the team.

performance can be kept on track and what projects or tasks might be at special risk. Discuss when and how the team member will be replaced and the new member inducted into the team.

Do all you can to make new members feel welcome and find their place in the team quickly. Once the 'new team' moves forward into norming, allow it to explore its new identity. Ensure the goals remain clear and that new team members have plenty of feedback on their performance and how they are fitting in. As the team moves into performing, step back into your former role of support.

FORMAL AND INFORMAL LEADERS

The organisation appoints the **formal leader** who has some formal authority or *position power*, which they usually need to supplement with their own *personal power*. **Informal leaders**, on the other hand, are 'appointed' by the work group itself, usually because of their referent and/or expert power (their personal qualities and job knowledge).

It's possible, but not usual, for a supervisor to be both the formal and informal leader of the group. More often, work groups have two leaders: the informal and the formal. This does not necessarily mean that the supervisor is not supervising properly. It may mean that the informal leader is meeting certain team and individual needs that the formal leader cannot or should not meet.

The informal leader may be the person who can produce the most or who serves customers best or who has the most expert knowledge. Or it may be the most articulate and dissatisfied person leading a group of discontented workers.

Team members look to informal leaders just as much as they do to their official team leader, to see how things should and should not be done. The cues of informal leaders about such matters as rate of output, dress, level of cooperation with the supervisor, acceptable language and degree of courtesy to customers are far stronger than official policy or procedures about these things. This makes informal leaders' role an important one in establishing and maintaining group norms. They 'set the pace' and this 'pace' can be in your favour or in direct opposition to what you're trying to accomplish.

If the 'pace' the informal leaders set is, for example, one of lower productivity, poorer quality or service, or less cooperation with management than you would like, you have a problem on your hands. You can talk and cajole, but the work group will continue to behave in line with its norms and the 'pace' set by the informal leaders—until the team itself decides to change things.

Who is the informal leader of your work group? Does he or she support you, the organisation and its objectives? Since informal leaders usually have as much (and often more) influence on a group's output as the formal leader, it is important to know this. Don't try to eliminate any informal leaders in your work group, but ensure that they are working with and not against you.

The standing of informal leaders is precarious. Being an informal leader today and a non-leader tomorrow is not unusual. This is especially so if the composition of the work group changes frequently or if the work location, product or task changes. As a group's needs change, so does its choice of informal leader.

FROM THEORY TO PRACTICE

To identify the informal leader in your work group, look for the person others go to for advice, assistance or just a chat. Who is the person who speaks for the group, the person who is able to 'get the ball rolling'?

SKILLS CHECK FOR TEAM LEADERS

'Anyone who wants to lead the orchestra must be willing to face the music.'

Are you willing and able to face the music? Here is a checklist of skills and attributes that team leaders need:

❏ Willingness to share control
❏ Willingness to be 'of' and not 'above' the team
❏ Conflict resolution skills
❏ Motivation skills
❏ Team-building skills
❏ Coaching skills
❏ Change-facilitation skills
❏ Networking skills
❏ Communication skills
❏ Interpersonal skills
❏ Trustworthiness, honesty, personal integrity
❏ Able to understand how the team thinks and feels

❏ Job knowledge
❏ Able to inject some fun
❏ Able to get people to share your vision
❏ Able to build pride in individuals and the team
❏ Approachable
❏ Able to unite people
❏ Able to empower people
❏ Empathy and caring for team members
❏ Emotional intelligence
❏ Action- and results-oriented
❏ Willingness to learn
❏ High self-esteem

ROLE THEORY

In the discussion above, we mentioned team member **roles**. Roles are the 'parts' we play in any situation. 'Playing a role' does not mean that we are acting or in any way behaving 'unnaturally'. Rather, it means we are behaving according to a personally held set of concepts that defines for us how we should behave in a particular situation. This personal set of concepts is called **role perception**.

We develop our role perceptions by watching and reading about others (**role models**) in similar situations. The family we grew up in, our friends and the organisation in which we work all contribute to our role perceptions.

We 'fine-tune' our role perception to conform to the **role expectations** held by others around us—the expectations others have about a particular role. 'Others' may include other supervisors, senior management, workmates and even families. In some organisations, for example, supervisors dress very informally while in others the expected dress is 'smart casual' or a business suit. Some organisations expect supervisors to be strictly task-oriented while other organisations place importance on supervisors attending to process issues in a team. Role expectations such as these will alter the role perceptions of the supervisors affected by them. Role perceptions and role expectations are often stereotypes.

You probably have a role perception of how a supervisor should act and behave, the sort of attitudes supervisors should hold, how they should dress and so on. This role perception may be slightly different from the role perception you hold for a team leader. Your perception of acceptable supervisory behaviour might alter if you moved to an organisation with a different culture and working climate, and you might change some of your behaviours in order to fit into different expectations.

⚡ FROM THEORY TO PRACTICE

How do you see the role of a team leader? As controller, commander, ruler and decision maker? Or as delegator, coach, champion, catalyst and guide?

Some of the roles people play help their group to function more effectively. Other roles are *dysfunctional*—that is, they hold the group back from working effectively. Box 22.5 shows some functional and dysfunctional roles found in teams. They have been divided into task and process roles but, in practice, many roles serve a dual purpose.

Role conflict

If there are no major differences between an individual's role perception and the role expectations of others, there is no problem. But if they differ, there is **role conflict**. There are two types of role conflict. The first results when others' expectations about us differ from our own ideas of what we think we should and can do.

BOX 22.5 FUNCTIONAL AND DYSFUNCTIONAL ROLES IN TEAMS

	Functional roles	Dysfunctional roles
Task roles	information seeker	ideas squasher
	opinion seeker	dominator
	analyser	competer
	information giver	aggressor
	opinion giver	critic
	idea builder	enthusiasm deflater
	coordinator	dissenter
	summariser	stubborn donkey
	ideas person	subject changer
	systems organiser	saboteur
	standard setter	manipulator
	initiator	special interest speaker
	clarifier	sympathy seeker
	teacher, coach, trainer	complainer
	follower	show-off
	consensus builder	
	mediator	
Process roles	tension reliever (clown)	disruptive clown
	gatekeeper	approval seeker
	encourager	withdrawer
	compromiser	yea sayer
	harmoniser	sarcastic remarker
	friend	wool gatherer
		recognition/status seeker
		sniper/cynic
		conflict avoider/seeker

FROM THEORY TO PRACTICE

Be aware of the principal roles in your team. Who plays which roles most often? How do they help or hinder group processes and task achievement?
  Strengthen the way your team operates by helping people become aware of the roles they play and the effects these roles have on the task and team process. As people become more sensitive to, and aware of, how they can help a team function more effectively, their skills improve.

The second occurs when two or more of the several roles people play conflict with each other. Take Leslie, for example. She is a single parent with three children still at school and the sole provider for the family. She has no income other than what she earns from work outside the home. She is also secretary of the local school's parents association, which meets every month, and she actively follows the leisure and sporting activities of her children. During busy periods, Leslie's supervisor wants her to work overtime almost every night of the week. Leslie is very keen to have the extra income, but she feels she is letting her children down, as they have to prepare their own evening meal and occupy themselves without her guidance. Supervisors need to be sensitive to role conflicts like this.

Another example of role conflict is the school leaver who begins her first job wearing clothing or a hairstyle that does not conform to the role expectations of her organisation regarding appearance. A more serious example is the employee for whom the wearing of standard safety protection gear is not part of his role perception. This could result in a serious accident if role expectations and role perceptions are not brought into line. Supervisors need to determine when it is important that role perceptions and role expectations match. In the wearing of safety gear, it is clearly important that they do. Sometimes, however, a matching of role perceptions and role expectations makes little difference to how well a task is performed.

Role clarification

As we saw in Chapter 8, making expectations clear is an important supervisory function. This is called **role clarification**. On the task side, ensure members of the team understand clearly what is expected of them in their job role. On the process side, make explicit the behaviours you expect of all members of a work group. You can do this through formal and informal individual and team discussions.

Some of these expectations are written down formally (e.g. in the job description) while many are informal expectations that people must infer or 'pick up'. If you are introducing a new employee to your department, make sure you do not leave any important role expectations for the new person to 'pick up', but explain them clearly. This will save a lot of misunderstanding, errors and embarrassment.

INDIVIDUAL BEHAVIOUR AND DIFFERENCES

In Chapter 19 we saw that people have different personalities and ways of working. The most effective teams are made up of a variety of people who can each contribute in their own special way to the group. Here we examine four basic personality groupings needed in any team.

1. The first is *leaders*, both formal and informal. Someone needs to set direction and 'get the ball rolling'. Someone needs to set the pace and focus on results. Every team needs strong-willed people who will take the initiative, speak up, make decisions, solve problems and challenge the *status quo*.
2. The second grouping is *encouragers*, people who add enthusiasm, spirit and a sense of fun to the team. These are socially outgoing individuals who enjoy coming up with fresh ideas and trying out new and better ways of doing things. They see the 'big picture'. They are energetic, talkative people whose innovative, creative, flexible, positive

approach compensates for their lack of concern for detail. They create a motivating environment and enjoy working with and helping others.

3. Teams also need *team players*. These easygoing, relaxed, consistent people are the glue that binds a team together. They may not be 'balls of fire' but they are patient, willing, cooperative and reliable. They are comfortable taking a 'back seat'. They are good listeners whose stable, quiet manner calms excited people. Team players work steadily; they prefer regularity and no sudden 'surprises' or changes in direction or goals. Their loyalty and helpfulness make them valuable to any team.

4. Every team also needs *systematic organisers*. Someone must look after the details and check things carefully. These are deliberate, well organised people who are good at analysing and thinking through problems. They weigh up both sides of an issue and examine alternatives carefully. They are detailed, accurate, thorough and exacting. We can depend on systematic people to keep to time, work conscientiously and produce accurate, detailed information.

These individual differences are essential to an effective team. Yet they also have the potential to create conflict. Some people can't understand why everyone isn't like them and are scornful of those who aren't. Team leaders need to show them that everyone is different and that it is the differences that make individuals valuable and necessary to the team. Make sure you instil respect for different styles of operating and the varied contributions each team member makes. Create an environment where people can make the most of their differences to enhance collective results.

LEADING VIRTUAL TEAMS

Some team members in today's organisations have never met face-to-face. Leading virtual teams or teams where people often or always work from home or off-site presents additional challenges. These teams may be made up of employees, contractors, agents and office-based employees at various locations, or a mixture of all of these. They are not like football teams or traditional work teams where people work together all the time in order to win. They're more like orchestras or medical teams which train and do some work independently, and then come together for a final effort.

FROM THEORY TO PRACTICE

Resist any urge to recruit people who are 'like' the other team members or you'll end up with too many or too few people from a particular personality type. Too many *leaders* will fight among themselves for control, while too few can mean a team has difficulty making decisions and lacks energy. Too many *encouragers* can mean a team has lots of fun but achieves few results, while too few can dampen team spirit and creativity. Too many *team players* without a leader can cause a team to stagnate and fail to improve, while too few willing hands to do the work can mean it never gets done. Too many *systematic organisers* can cause a team to suffer from 'paralysis by analysis' while too few can mean the important details are overlooked.

You will need to establish policies and procedures for the team to follow for things on-site employees normally take for granted. For example, what couriers should they use? Are there any specific times everyone should be available for telephone calls and meetings? How should they obtain general office supplies and materials? Since email will probably be one of your main channels of communication, you should agree an email protocol for how the team will operate the system: how often should people check their email? How quickly should messages be answered? How should emails be prioritised and acted on?

You'll need to be willing to transfer most of your 'control' to the employees themselves. You won't know whether they're working by looking up from your desk—this increases the importance of frequent communication, feedback and trust. Establishing clear individual and team goals is essential. Base goals on results, not time spent at a desk or on a telephone. Schedule regular face-to-face or virtual reporting meetings between you and individual team members and you and the entire team.

Building trust with people you don't see very often (or ever) can be a tough task. Responding quickly to email and phone messages (at least within half a day) will help. Resist the urge to get straight down to business on the telephone or in emails. Without the usual body

FROM THEORY TO PRACTICE

How can you best supervise telecommuters (people who work all or part of the time from home) and make them effective members of the corporate team?

- Make sure they understand the work flow of the entire team and how they contribute to it.
- Alter performance measures to reflect the new ways of working.
- Be clear about the results you expect. Leave the 'how to's' and time needed to achieve them up to the teleworker.
- Agree a procedure for monitoring performance—it's easy to miss someone floundering if you can't see them. How will you know when someone has done something of value?
- Give plenty of clear and specific feedback.
- Keep them in the information loop through regular formal and informal contact (telephone, email, etc.)
- Encourage teleworkers to communicate with each other and share information, ideas and 'tricks of the trade'.
- Make sure they have the tools and training they need to produce and communicate.
- Create opportunities for get-togethers, both social and work-related, to develop and build relationships.
- Know what the difficulties are and how you will help people adapt to a new style of work and new ways of communicating.
- Train off-site employees to work effectively off-site: time management, communication with co-workers and customers, how to set up a home office, how to separate work from private life, how to inject some social contact into your working day, etc.
- Train on-site employees to work effectively with off-site employees.

language clues, this could be interpreted as impatience or criticism. Spend a bit of time getting to know people. Beware jokes and humour, which can often be misinterpreted from a distance.

Because team members seldom meet face-to-face, you need to work extra hard to keep lines of communication open. Email, telephones, periodic face-to-face, online or video-meetings will help, particularly if they are based on a top-of-mind desire to keep people informed. Schedule monthly teleconference or face-to-face meetings and distribute the agenda prior to each meeting. Make sure company information and knowledge is accessible and members are able to plug into the formal and informal networks.

There are other important issues to think about. How will you build and maintain the morale and team identity of out-of-sight employees? Gossip, rituals, common beliefs and values are all more difficult to establish at a distance. How will you identify and recognise good performance of individuals and the team as a whole? How will you recognise and deal with below-standard performance?

LEADING A MERGED TEAM

Mergers have become commonplace, which means you may well find yourself leading a merged work team. Aligning individual members towards the new organisation's vision and goals, helping the team deal with the changes and move quickly through the stages into performing will be a top priority.

THE **BIG** PICTURE

Trust develops differently in virtual teams. The three types of trust discussed in *The big picture* earlier in this chapter exist but, instead of evolving slowly over time, trust tends to be established—or not—right at the beginning, and the type of trust established at the start usually sticks. The first interaction of the team members is decisive in establishing which kind of trust will become the norm for the team.

Communication is always a critical factor and, in virtual teams, communication is primarily through email. The first electronic messages set the tone for trust. Introductory messages that imply a lack of trust will set the scene for a virtual team plagued by low morale and poor performance while those that establish a set of rules for 'how we will work together' leads to deterrence-based trust.

Jarvenpaa and Leidner's research tells us that virtual teams with the highest level of trust share three traits:

1. They begin their interactions with a set of social, getting-to-know-each-other messages. Members introduce themselves and provide some personal background before focusing on the work at hand. This helps establish knowledge-based trust.
2. Each team member's role and function in the team is made clear, which helps identification-based trust.
3. The messages of team members are best described as eager, enthusiastic and action-oriented.

The initial contacts and the way they are handled sets the tone. The pattern set at the outset quickly hardens.

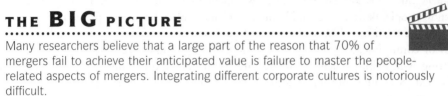

THE BIG PICTURE
....

Many researchers believe that a large part of the reason that 70% of mergers fail to achieve their anticipated value is failure to master the people-related aspects of mergers. Integrating different corporate cultures is notoriously difficult.

Communication is a must. Keep the lines open between employees and yourself and act as a conduit of information from the organisation as a whole. Know what the new organisation's vision and objectives are and make these clear to everyone, over and over again. The more you communicate, the more you will defuse the rumour mill. Listen as well as talk, and deal with issues quickly (see also Chapter 12).

TEAM BRIEFINGS

Some organisations are using **team briefings** as a way to ensure employees regularly and systematically receive information about the organisation. The intention is to provide details that are relevant to the employees so they will feel more in tune with the organisation's operations and progress towards its objectives.

Team briefings follow a *linking pin* model (see Chapter 4). Beginning at senior level and cascading through the organisation, each team leader briefs their team on:

- *Progress:* How the organisation/division/team has performed overall in relation to key measures and areas such as quality, safety and customer satisfaction.
- *People:* New appointments, visitors.
- *Policy:* Any changes to corporate or divisional policy.
- *Points for action:* What's coming up, what we will do to respond to other points.

Sessions are usually weekly or monthly, depending on the organisation's needs. Because they are face-to-face, team leaders can ensure people understand what is happening and why, and can ask questions and explore issues that affect them. They give team leaders an opportunity to reinforce their 'management message' and keep lines of communication open. Some benefits of team briefings are shown in Box 22.6.

You need to know exactly what information you want to relay and then present it clearly and concisely. This takes preparation. Here are some pointers:

- Use short sentences that you can say in one breath.
- Avoid long words, rambling repetition, jargon and any technical terms that may be unfamiliar to the team members.

BOX 22.6 THE BENEFITS OF TEAM BRIEFINGS
....

- Raise awareness of organisational and divisional issues and results
- Increase commitment
- Reduce misunderstandings
- Improve consultation with employees
- Reduce reliance on the grapevine

- Make key points clearly to minimise misunderstandings.
- Leave a short, three to five second pause after each key point to let it sink in.
- Emphasise key points by slowing down, saying them more softly or loudly, emphasising key words or phrases, using descriptive adjectives and action verbs, drawing an analogy or a word picture.
- Make really important points three times, in three different ways.
- Avoid tired clichés like: 'Let's go for it!'
- Deliver difficult messages in a tactful, non-threatening way.

TIPS FOR TEAM LEADERS

'Team leaders need to be parent, teacher, and referee all at once.'

Experienced team leader from Christchurch, New Zealand

Treat all your employees not only as important individuals but also as valuable team members. Build and maintain the team's sense of importance. Discuss anything affecting the team in a way that involves all members. Make sure the best performers know how important they are to a new organisation.

Analyse your team's behaviour patterns whenever the members are not performing to your expectations. First ensure that the group understands what needs to be done and what is expected of it. Then ask yourself if any problems could be interfering with the group's output. Are machines running properly? Are raw materials up to standard? Is the quantity of work unusually high? Is a team member's absence or lack of training or experience putting pressure on the rest of the team? If nothing emerges here, ask yourself if the group has had enough training to perform to standard. If it has, think about why the team is not performing as well as you want it to. Are internal power struggles in the group hindering its effectiveness? Has a newly normed group taken time out to 'play'? Is its current performance rewarding to members in some way? Is poor performance more rewarding than 'better' performance?

The team needs to understand how achieving the expected goal will benefit it and how it will help members achieve their personal goals. Ensure that good performance is more

FROM THEORY TO PRACTICE

Should you sit or stand to deliver a team briefing? Sitting is less formal and usually looks less rehearsed and 'prepared'. It conveys you are open to discussion and questions and puts you on a more equal footing with team members. More feedback, opinions and discussion usually result.

Standing seems more formal and prepared. It is also more authoritative, saying: this is important. People grant more control to you if you stand, but it may look as if you don't want feedback or discussion. This means that negative comments might be saved until after the session, for the corridors and café bars.

You could have it both ways—stand for the information-giving part and then sit for the discussion.

rewarding than average or poor performance. (Remember that rewards come in many forms, not just money.) Be aware of the group dynamics discussed above so that you can empathise fully with the group and deal with it successfully.

Box 22.7 summarises additional tips developed by over 200 experienced team leaders in Australia, New Zealand and South-East Asia. What tips can you add to this list?

BOX 22.7

TIPS FOR TEAM LEADERS

- Offer improvement suggestions: what to do *next* time or *from now on*
- Ask, don't tell
- Find out how you can help members achieve their goals
- Improve employees' skill levels
- Encourage, don't police
- Expect the best
- Build self-esteem
- Begin with the end in mind—paint the picture
- Strive to understand all points of view
- Set a good example
- Find something to compliment specifically and sincerely
- Help everyone use their skills and talents
- Think before you act or speak
- Show appreciation often
- Give plenty of compliments
- Be approachable and listen to people
- Have some fun!
- Address problems quickly; find the root cause so that you don't treat symptoms
- Help the team fix its own problems—don't always do it for them
- Have contingency plans
- Listen before deciding and without judging
- Smile and be friendly
- Communicate often
- Give them a treat!
- Stay flexible
- Give moral support
- Correct with care
- Empower the team
- Know and understand yourself
- Accept feedback
- Learn from mistakes
- Keep team members up to date
- Be available and responsive to people's problems

- Ensure work is allocated according to members' capabilities and interests
- Delegate work that is not essential for you to do
- Agree on high-quality standards and targets with the team
- Always look for ways to improve performance
- Involve the team in problem solving and decision making
- Be alert to any team member who seems left out; try to find a positive role for them
- Avoid setting up situations of extreme competition
- Rotate jobs within the team to increase individual skills and strengthen group identification
- Identify everyone's responsibilities clearly
- Set clear goals
- Create a positive, 'can do' atmosphere
- Help group members get to know each other
- Use group incentives wherever you can
- Focus on solutions and goals (what you *do* want), not problems (what you *don't* want)
- Don't fix blame, fix the problem. Ask: *How can we …?* or *What can we do to …?*
- Get rid of the 'lemons', people whose sourness brings everyone down
- Don't keep everyone on board—just the winners
- Spend equal amounts of one-to-one time with team members, even if it's just a ten minute coffee break
- Keep track of anniversaries and birthdays Let people leave early on the day, if work allows; take them to lunch or bring in a cake to celebrate
- See training as an investment in the team's future and a way to build loyalty

	True	False
1. Today's supervisors need to know how to build high-performance teams capable of directing themselves with less input from management.	☐	☐
2. Understanding team dynamics is essential for successful team leadership.	☐	☐
3. Coming together in groups is a natural way for people to derive satisfaction and achieve goals.	☐	☐
4. Widespread use of teams began in the 1800s.	☐	☐
5. A group is different from a team.	☐	☐
6. A problem-solving team is an example of a temporary team.	☐	☐
7. Many teams fail to achieve the desired results because of poor introduction and inadequate training of team members.	☐	☐
8. The real cause of a team failing at its task is often a team failing at its processes.	☐	☐
9. Once a successful team has developed, the team leader can sit back and relax.	☐	☐
10. Team leaders can safely ignore group dynamics if things seem to be going well.	☐	☐
11. Informal leaders set the 'pace' of a work group and influence its productivity and quality.	☐	☐
12. An effective team never argues or has disagreements.	☐	☐
13. Role perceptions and expectations are often stereotypes.	☐	☐
14. Role clarification is a key duty of supervisors.	☐	☐
15. All teams need leaders, encouragers, team players and systematic organisers.	☐	☐
16. Through clever leadership, teams can skip some of the stages in their life cycle and reach the performing stage quickly.	☐	☐
17. If a new team member is highly skilled at their job, there is no damage to the way the team functions.	☐	☐
18. Effective team leaders are always on the lookout for ways to improve team performance.	☐	☐
19. Two types of teams that supervisors need to learn how to manage are virtual teams and merged teams.	☐	☐

1. In your own words, describe what it means to be a modern team leader and discuss the types of teams they find themselves leading.

2. Outline the benefits to organisations, team members, team leaders and their customers that can be expected from high-performing teams. What needs to happen in order to achieve these benefits?

3. Write a short essay describing and giving examples of task and process issues in a team and explaining how a team leader can monitor and influence them.

4. Thinking about its group dynamics, the way it goes about achieving its task and how well the task is achieved, how do you rate the effectiveness of your own work team or study group? Why?

5. What would happen if a team leader's role expectations differed from the role perceptions of the team members? What could be done to bring them into line? Why would this be important?

6. Describe the four personality groupings needed in any team.

7. Outline the stages in a team's growth

and apply these to your own class or work group.

8. Discuss the possible effects of a change in team membership.

9. Who are the informal leaders of your class and study group and your work team? How do you know this? Considering both their personal qualities and the function they perform in the group, why do you believe they have become the informal leaders?

10. Discuss the special considerations that team leaders must take into account when leading virtual and newly merged teams.

· **DEVELOP YOUR SKILLS** ·

Individual activities

1. Think of a *high-performing team* you have been a member of. What were the goals it set out to accomplish? Were they quantifiable, time-framed, visible, worthwhile, challenging and shared by the whole team? If so, how did this come about? How well were the goals achieved? How did members work together? What were each person's task and process roles in the group? What sort of task and process feedback was available?

2. Thinking about the differences between a group and a team, do you know of a group that became a team? How did this happen? Discuss the significant events that led to this group becoming a team.

3. Describe the group dynamics of your work team, study group or class.

4. The words of Professor J.R. Hackman quoted in this chapter seem to be pessimistic regarding the ease with which organisations can establish successful teams. Why might he be saying this? Do you agree with him?

5. Describe the culture of your work team or class in one or two

sentences. Now write down how you would *like* the culture to be. List some of the norms in your work team or class. Would you like any of them to be different? How?

6. Observe your study group, class or work team. List the task behaviours you notice. List the process and team maintenance behaviours you notice. What behaviours aided task achievement? In what ways did the task succeed or suffer because certain behaviours were or were not used? In what ways did the team succeed or suffer from the process behaviours that were or were not used? What stage of development would you say the team has reached? Who played what roles most often and how did these help or hinder group processes and task achievement?

7. Referring to the checklist in the section, *How effective is your team?*, analyse the effectiveness of your own work team or study group.

8. Refer to the description of the four personality groups needed in any team. Identify the people in your

work team or study group according to these four groupings. How do they contribute to the team's effective functioning? What would the team be like without them? Are any of the four types missing? What is the effect of this? What could the team leader do about it?

Group activities

1. Working alone, list all the teams and groups you have belonged to over the last ten years. Include community groups, sports teams, church groups, committees and family groups. Now divide these into high-performing and low-performing teams and note the characteristics that made them so.

    Now form into groups of five or six. Compare your lists and combine them to come up with a list of characteristics of high-performing teams and a list of characteristics of poorly performing teams. Put this on butcher's paper to compare with the other groups in your class. Use the format shown below.

Characteristics of high-performing teams	Characteristics of poorly performing teams

2. In small groups, brainstorm the skills and behaviours required of team members and team leaders. Record your answers on butcher's paper to compare with the rest of the class. Some examples are shown below.

    Skills and behaviours required by:
    Team members
    - be open and honest
    - look for ways to improve

9. Think back to your first class at college or to the formation of a study group. Write a short essay tracing the 'life cycle' of your class or study group using the information given in this chapter. Give specific examples of people's behaviours at each stage.

    - help others
    - participate
    - be dependable

    Team leaders
    - clear focus
    - get everyone contributing
    - develop individual skills
    - be enthusiastic
    - celebrate task achievement

3. In small groups, list words that describe how you perceive the role of a supervisor. Do the same to describe how you perceive the role of a team leader. Are there any differences? What could account for them? Use your role perceptions to come up with a definition of 'supervisor' and a definition of 'team leader'. Share your definitions with the other teams in your class. How similar are your role perceptions?

4. In small groups, analyse the stage of team development that John's team in the vignette on page 662 seems to have reached. Be prepared to cite supporting evidence for your conclusions. Based on your analysis, what are five things that John could do to help his team progress to the next stage of team development?

Richardson's Group Problem

Ted Richardson was still angry when he related the following story to his family on Friday night. According to Ted, the 14 employees of the bearing assembly team which he led had worked together for 26 months without any problems. Their work had been of good quality, and productivity and team spirit high. Jim Johnson, one of the longer-serving members of the group, was an especially good employee and Ted had recommended him for promotion. His recommendation was accepted and, although the team had been sorry to see Jim leave, they were happy about his promotion.

When Jim left, Ted made several changes within the team. A few duties were shifted around and a new employee, Elizabeth Jennings, joined.

Things had appeared to be settling down to normal but that morning 'all hell broke loose'. The team rejected 23% of its output for poor quality, an all-time high. Accusations started flying. Several employees blamed the poor quality on Elizabeth Jennings. Three of the women in the group came to Elizabeth's defence. Some of the men accused the women of sticking together and not putting the blame where it lay.

At this point, Ted stepped in and told the group that if both quality and quantity of output did not improve, he would replace *all* the poor employees. His actions smothered the flame of anger but in no way was it extinguished.

Later that afternoon, something happened within the group that really caused tempers to flare. Heated arguments led to an unofficial work stoppage. Even employees on other teams stopped their work to watch all the commotion. Ted moved in and ordered everyone back to work, standing by to make sure his orders were followed. The team reluctantly resumed work for the last 45 minutes of the day. Afterwards, some of the old hands told Ted that they couldn't work under such tension and would be applying for a transfer if he didn't do something.

As Ted explained to his family: 'It all happened because I worked to get a promotion for one of my best employees.' Ted pondered his best course of action. How could things have gone so wrong so suddenly?

Questions

1 Analyse the factors you believe led to the problems in the bearing assembly team. Use both team stages and group dynamics to explain your answer.
2 To what stage in its life cycle does the bearing assembly team seem to have regressed?
3 What specific steps can Ted take to develop the team?

Jean's Teams

Jean Hubbard had been in business for four-and-a-half years. Opening up her office supplies store with virtually no capital, she had worked night and day to make it a success. It had grown and was well accepted in the community.

Jean employed seven full-time and two part-time staff. Four of the full-timers worked in the back office, dividing the invoicing, stock ordering and billing work between them as it came in. If anything out of the ordinary occurred, they called on Jean for assistance. They had all been with Jean for the past three years and got along together quite well.

The others, three full-timers and the two part-timers, worked 'front of store', dealing directly with customers and inquiries. Jean could usually be found here, too. The longest serving of these employees had been with Jean for 12 months and the two newest for three months and two weeks, respectively. Jean had noticed that the front of store staff seemed to keep a lot more to themselves than the office staff. They waited to be told what to do and didn't seem to help each other out unless she asked them to.

Jean wished she could now afford to work less and enjoy more. But things didn't work out that way. There always seemed to be problems that she personally had to solve—a customer who didn't get what he ordered, an employee with a personal complaint or grievance, staff not showing up for work at the right time—the list went on.

Jean really didn't know what to do. She wanted to give her employees authority to make decisions in the store operations, but she didn't feel that she could rely on them to do what she hired them to do. It seemed that every one of them had complained about his or her job, indicating they were all overworked and not appreciated. She always laughed when they started talking this way, telling them that what they needed to do was to roll up their sleeves and get to work. This usually shut them up and they returned to their jobs.

In fact, this was one of the things that always annoyed Jean—her employees were always complaining, telling her that they needed a better washroom, or that they wanted an area where they could sit down for a coffee break or eat their lunch. She laughed at such ideas, telling them that this was a place of work, not a home where you could lounge around. To Jean, her employees just didn't seem to appreciate all that she was doing for them. They always wanted more!

Jean wanted to have a prosperous business. She wanted her employees to like her and each other. But she didn't know how to go about telling her employees what she wanted from them. She had never been 'good with words' and she figured that her actions would tell them a whole lot more than any fancy words, anyway.

Questions

1 What teams does Jean have in her store? What stage of development has each reached? What is your evidence? What factors in Jean's leadership style may explain this?
2 What steps could Jean take to improve the teamwork in her store?
3 If you have completed Chapter 21, analyse the motivation levels of Jean's employees using Herzberg's two-factor theory. What is going on here?

Answers to Rapid Review questions

1. T   2. T   3. T   4. F   5. T   6. T   7. T   8. T   9. F   10. F   11. T   12. F   13. T   14. T   15. T   16. F   17. F   18. T   19. T

CHAPTER 23

PROVIDING WORK INSTRUCTIONS AND DELEGATING DUTIES

The end of the financial year

The end of the financial year is always a tough time. Stocktake is a major task. Numerous reports have to be prepared and the auditors are always sniffing about checking on things. Everyone feels under pressure and overworked.

Derek Walsh, the warehouse supervisor, is in charge of the stocktake. He understands the importance of an accurate count and takes the task very seriously. Everyone is involved in the count, from senior management to factory hands, and Derek is number one on stocktake day.

Derek is finalising his memo to all staff on how to carry out the count. He wonders how he should—or if he should—change his style when telling the managing director how to do the count compared with the way he tells the people who work for him in the warehouse.

A large part of every supervisor's job is giving work instructions and delegating duties. Supervisors also need to be able to receive work instructions and accept delegated duties. In this chapter, you will learn what to do when you are on the giving end, and the receiving end, of instructions

- How can you achieve cooperation and commitment and avoid compulsion and coercion when giving instructions?
- Do you know the six types of work instructions and when you should use them?
- Can you help employees accept instructions?
- What should you do if someone refuses to carry out your instructions?

- How and when should you put instructions in writing?
- Who should give work instructions to your employees?
- Do matrix organisations undermine the unity of command principle?
- How should you receive instructions? What if you disagree with an instruction?
- How can you delegate without losing control? What should you delegate?

LET'S DEFINE OUR TERMS

The dilemma of giving work instructions

A large part of every supervisor's job is giving work instructions and delegating duties. Supervisors also need to be able to receive work instructions and accept delegated duties.

In today's empowered and participative organisations, the need to give work instructions can lead to confusion and misunderstanding. 'Yesterday's' supervisor was the supreme order-giver. Is a supervisor who gives orders today a relic from the past? Or a strong, decisive leader?

People often criticise the laissez-faire style of leadership as 'do-nothing' leadership. Is the supervisor who fails to give work instructions a 'do-nothing' leader? Or a strong, empowering leader?

The dilemma of giving instructions is not just a question of leadership style. For many, it has connotations of dogmatic, dictatorial leadership. Others see it as a way to lose the valued friendship, cooperation and support of their work team.

In all this confusion, it is no wonder that people sometimes back away from the concept of giving work instructions. Let's begin by defining what we mean when we talk about giving work instructions and delegating in this chapter. We're not talking about issuing instructions in a dictatorial way (see Chapter 20), an approach that makes most modern supervisors feel uncomfortable. Nor are we talking about the 'power-mad' supervisors who become carried away and bark out commands without thought or respect. Giving instructions that leave no room for discussion, or giving unnecessary instructions, are two quick ways to lose the goodwill and support of your staff.

The concept of giving instructions is not used here in its militaristic context or its harsh, 'commanding' context, but rather in the sense of *assigning duties to a team or team member*.

Does this detract from empowerment? In its strictest sense, full empowerment means that members of a work team have a great deal of autonomy and work out many issues for themselves. If it is also a high-performing team, it will have synergy and its members will be competent and willing (see Chapter 22). Teams like this really don't need anyone to tell them what to do. The supervisor or team leader guides them, using a questioning approach to help team members work things out for themselves.

Strictly speaking, supervisors who are trying to develop fully empowered work teams would probably avoid giving instructions; they would delegate and help the team to decide how to proceed. However, the road to full empowerment is a long one and most supervisors are still expected to give work instructions at some time or other along that road.

Delegating

If you have completed Chapter 20, you will remember a leadership style called 'delegating'. For a supervisor to be able to delegate appropriately, the employee must be fully trained and competent, willing and confident. Using the delegating style of leadership with someone not fully trained or willing is an incorrect use of that style.

In this chapter, the term 'delegate' isn't used in the strict sense required by the leadership style of the same name. We use it in the sense of *assigning one of your own duties or responsibilities* to a member of your work team. This may be someone who is already competent and willing to do the job; or it may be someone who does not know how to do it, and you will need to train them.

COMMAND AND COERCION VERSUS COOPERATION AND COMMITMENT

How do you prefer to receive orders? Most people respond more willingly to a request than to a command. It is usually the circumstances and the recipients that determine how you should give directions, but you should always aim for cooperation, not mere compliance. There is a big difference—employees who are cooperating with you will carry out the order to the best of their ability; those who are only complying will do just as you ask, no more and no less.

Whether you use the term 'order', 'request', 'direct', 'instruct', 'bid' or 'ask', the words you use, your tone of voice and your body language will make a big difference to the way people 'hear' and respond to your instructions. Mutual respect will help you to give work instructions in a way that encourages cooperation. Respecting both yourself and the person you are directing will come across in the way you give the instruction. You will win commitment and avoid mere compliance.

If you have supervised for any length of time, you have probably already found out that telling someone to do something isn't enough. We need to know how to give instructions and directions that others will follow willingly. This results from the combination of three skills: good leadership, the ability to motivate and clear communication. These can be learned and are covered in other chapters (see Chapters 2, 19, 20 and 21, for example).

SIX TYPES OF WORK INSTRUCTIONS

Work instructions come in various strengths. How strongly you make a request depends on the situation and the employee.

Some situations, for example emergencies or highly critical situations, require prompt action. These call for clear, decisive instructions; you may not even have the time to explain them. At the other end of the extreme are situations where there are lots of possible options and plenty of time. Here, you can afford to take a more 'relaxed' approach.

The people you work with may have different expectations of their jobs, too. Some are highly motivated and self-directed. They generally respond best to instructions that state the end result and allow them the freedom to decide the best way to achieve it. Others might be just learning a job and would prefer you to spell out directions step by step. Still others lack motivation and need frequent guidance. Box 23.1 summarises the main types of work instructions you can give.

Direct and explicit work instructions

There are occasions when supervisors must use a direct approach, or revert to their authority, when giving instructions that must be followed without question. For example, when an employee is engaged in an unsafe work practice, prompt action is required and you may need to resort to giving a direct order. Occasionally, there may be employees who, because of past experiences or the attitude to the job, only respond to direct instructions.

Explicit instructions state both the 'what' and the 'how'. They state the end result or goal and describe, step by step, how to achieve it. Explicit instructions are good to use with new, unskilled or inexperienced employees.

Generally, though, under normal working situations, these types of instructions cause resentment. Too many commands and direct orders often reflect unsure or immature

---

BOX 23.1 SIX TYPES OF WORK INSTRUCTIONS
....

Direct work instructions	These are commands, leaving no room for discussion. They are useful if time or ramifications are critical. Use for health and safety matters; for example, you might say: 'You *must* close the machine guard *fully* before proceeding', or '*Always* put on a hairnet and wash your hands before handling food'.
Explicit work instructions	State clearly and precisely *who* is to do *what, when* it is to be done, *how* it is to be done and *where* it is to be done. Use with people who are limited in their experience and/or abilities or with those who lack a sense of responsibility or commitment to the job.
Request work instructions	These begin with 'Would you', 'Will you', etc. Use these with nervous, sensitive, skilled or motivated workers.
Implied work instructions	Here your order is implied, or not explicitly stated; for example, 'We need to …'. Use with people who readily accept responsibility or where improved methods are sought.
Undirected work instructions	These call for volunteers. Use them when a job is 'beyond the call of duty' and state not only *what* is required but also *why*.
Conditional work instructions	These allow latitude, limits, judgment and initiative in the how, when and what areas. They help maintain cooperation and commitment and should be used whenever possible.

supervisors and seldom achieve more than grudging compliance. When a spirit of cooperation is lacking, employees will rarely do more than what you specifically tell them. This stifles initiative, creativity, suggestions and ideas and you then face the problem of directing reluctant staff. So try to avoid giving direct and explicit instructions if you can take another approach. If you use them only occasionally, employees will know it is for a particularly good reason and will respond better.

Request and implied work instructions

Most employees expect and deserve more than the one-way situation of 'I tell—you do'. Often, because of their education, specialist skills or experience, employees are capable of modifying or improving an instruction. Requests and implied orders allow this latitude. They are also useful when you are giving directions that require some change. Giving employees the opportunity to express their opinion or contribute to implementing a change will help overcome resistance.

Request and implied work instructions are particularly useful in complex situations and when employees are capable and willing. Asking 'Would you …' or 'Could you …' or saying 'We need to …' are polite ways of softening work instructions and encouraging cooperation. They allow some discretion and initiative in carrying out the request which encourages people to put their skills and experience to use.

Undirected work instructions

Occasionally, you may need someone to do something 'above and beyond the call of duty'. When this is the case, explain the task and ask for a volunteer, rather than selecting an employee and giving a direction. The opportunity to volunteer can provide an employee with the motivation needed to do the job, especially if in doing so the person is able to satisfy one of their own needs or goals.

Conditional work instructions

With experienced and responsible employees, it is often best to explain the overall objective you require and allow them to determine how best to achieve it. Conditional orders state the end results required but leave the method of achieving them to the employee.

This approach is best for experienced and willing employees. It can also be used to good effect when training and developing employees in order to upgrade their skills, although you should talk through with them how they will approach the task, rather than just letting them 'get on with it'.

People with low levels of task readiness (see Chapter 20) are unlikely to be able to carry out a conditional instruction successfully, either through lack of skills or lack of willingness, so this approach can be dangerous with inexperienced or unreliable staff. Neither should it be used when you are not able to give a specific objective or sufficient background information.

HELPING EMPLOYEES TO ACCEPT INSTRUCTIONS

Some orders that supervisors give originate at more senior levels in the organisation. If you are uncertain of the reasoning behind them or if you are not in agreement with them, they can be difficult to pass on. The same applies to your staff's reactions. If they can't see the reason for your directions or don't agree with them, there is little hope they will be carried out with full cooperation and to the standards you expect. This means that the best instructions are those that explain fully what you want done and why it is important. People usually prefer to see things in their wider context—it gives them a better understanding of what you require and they feel more committed to it.

Follow these guidelines for giving effective instructions:

- *Be clear and specific in what you expect employees to do*. If you are not, there is little chance that employees will know what you require. Always establish specific objectives and communicate these and other relevant information clearly.
- *Sequence your instructions in the most logical order possible*.
- *Select the right person for the job*. Choosing someone with both the ability and the desire to carry out the task will help to ensure your instructions are carried out effectively.
- *Be confident and calm in your delivery*. Your confidence will be contagious.
- *Use the following headings*:
  WHAT is to be done in terms of:
  - quality
  - quantity
  - time
  - safety.
  WHY that person is being asked to do it.
  WHY the task is important.
  HOW to do it (for direct and explicit work instructions only).
- *Make sure your instructions are understood fully*. If necessary, repeat them. We all misunderstand sometimes. If an employee who has not carried out a direction to your satisfaction says, 'I didn't know that was what you wanted', you have not communicated clearly or sufficiently.

  Give the employee ample opportunity to ask questions, to clear up any areas of uncertainty or doubt. Better still, ask the employee to repeat your instructions back to you. This will highlight any doubts or misunderstandings so that you can clarify them.
- *Give reasons for the directions whenever possible and encourage suggestions* on how to achieve the objectives. This recognises and uses the skills and knowledge of the employee.
- *Ensure you give the directions at an appropriate time*. It is unwise, for example, to give work instructions when angry. Other examples of poor timing are when employees are about to go to lunch or knock off for the day, or when the direction comes on top of an incident that has lowered the morale of the group.

  Occasionally, you may need to pass down an order from upper management at a time when it could cause friction among your work group. Supervisors need to be constantly aware of the level of group morale so that they can anticipate the reaction to an instruction and time it so that it will be accepted.
- *Monitor progress* so that if things start to go wrong you will have enough time to rectify the situation and check on the final result to ensure it is in line with the objectives you set.
- When appropriate, *praise or thank employees for their efforts* and ensure that your feedback is timely and specific.

Box 23.2 lists some useful pointers for giving work instructions.

SOME DO'S AND DON'TS FOR GIVING WORK INSTRUCTIONS

BOX 23.2

DO
Be sure you know exactly what you want before giving instructions.
Be sure you know the employee has the ability to carry out the assigned task.
Give orders and instructions only when needed.
Distribute tasks and instructions evenly among employees.
Be consistent with what is to be done and the standards required.
Ensure the order is understood and will be carried out willingly.
Follow up to see that your directions have been carried out in the desired manner and to the specified or expected time and quality standards.

DON'T
Assume that after you have given the order, it will be carried out to your satisfaction.
Be careless or offhand if you want employees to take you seriously.
Assume an employee can do the job or understands what is expected— double check!
Get order-happy. Make sure one task is completed before giving more. Don't give orders unnecessarily to make yourself appear important.
Give all the good jobs or the unpopular jobs to the same people all the time. Overwork some because they will accept your directions with less fuss than others.

HANDLING A REFUSAL TO CARRY OUT DIRECTIONS

One approach may be to refer the offender to your manager, like a teacher sending a naughty student to the head-teacher for punishment. Another approach may be to try to enforce your authority or use bribes to gain compliance. None of these would be very effective in getting the job done or ensuring future cooperation and they could make a hero of the erring person in the eyes of workmates.

Both parties might 'lose their cool' and get into a heated argument. This won't help at all. So the first advice to follow is: keep calm, count to ten and give yourself time to consider whether the order was a reasonable one. Is the employee clear about what you are asking? Does the person receiving the work instruction have the skill, ability and time to carry it out in the required fashion?

If you cannot understand why an employee won't do what you ask or instruct, try a direct approach. Ask what the trouble is and find out why they don't agree with your suggestions. Maybe they have a good reason for not doing what you requested. Maybe they misunderstood. Maybe something you said or the way they interpreted it annoyed them. A questioning approach can help you find out.

If an employee still refuses to follow your instruction, what should you do? You can, of course, suspend the employee on the spot if the request was a reasonable one and if the workplace agreement permits. This is punitive action, however, and is likely to cause ill will that might affect other employees as well as cause longer-term difficulties with the suspended employee. You could modify your instruction. This might get the employee back

⚡ **FROM THEORY TO PRACTICE**

● ●

Consider your options carefully before deciding what action is necessary to resolve the situation. Start with a 'whisper' and slowly escalate as necessary, keeping a cooperative, win–win approach uppermost in your mind. Questioning or spending more time explaining what you require, the importance of the task and why your directions need to be carried out, are 'whispers'. If this doesn't work, escalate to other options such as modifying your request to get the job done in the short term. Further escalation might be holding an appraisal or performance counselling interview. As a last resort, you may need to bring out the 'loud hailer'. Let the employee know that appropriate disciplinary action may result. Do this only when everything else has failed.

After dealing with the immediate situation, carefully think through what happened so that you can learn from it and ensure that a similar situation does not occur in the future.

to work, and you can talk privately and constructively later. Remember that your job is to get work accomplished with the help of other people; to do this well, you need to work with, not against, your team.

The north-bound bus approach

If an order or instruction is reasonable, particularly when a change in policy or procedure is concerned, many supervisors find 'the north-bound bus' approach works well. When we get on a bus going north, we will go north, too. If we don't want to go north, we should get off that bus and try another one.

Organisations often alter course to head in a new direction: they might introduce a new customer service philosophy, establish new procedures and work methods based on a new technology, or reorganise and change established reporting structures. Symbolically, they are now heading 'north'. Some employees may have trouble accepting this new direction. If, after following the advice given in Chapter 12, an employee still refuses to 'head north' with everyone else, the north-bound bus approach may be a last resort. Clearly, this is a 'loud hailer' method that should only be adopted when other approaches have failed.

HANDLING NON-COMPLIANCE

Figure 23.1 will help you to select the best course of action. Each square suggests a possible cause and a possible approach. In the first square, the employee is willing but has insufficient job knowledge or skill, so training may be the answer. In the second square, the employee is willing and has sufficient knowledge or skills, so you will need to look to the environment or the *chance to* key (see Chapter 8) for a clue: perhaps the employee has insufficient resources (tools, equipment, time or information) or is working with cumbersome systems.

In the third square, the employee lacks not only skills and knowledge, but also willingness. This suggests that you should examine your selection procedures or job placement (to stop this happening in the future) and consider transferring the employee to

● ●

FIGURE 23.1   A CARELESS ATTITUDE—OR IS IT?

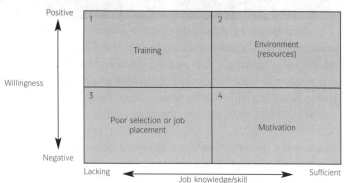

other, more suitable work. As a last resort you may have to consider termination of employment. In the fourth square, the employee has sufficient job knowledge but lacks willingness, so the problem is a motivational one.

WRITTEN WORK INSTRUCTIONS

Some supervisors think that putting an order in writing is enough to ensure that it will be understood and carried out. As we saw in Chapter 2, written communication is one-way communication. Because there is no immediate feedback, we have no guarantee that the receiver has understood or even read our message.

Supervisors who insist on putting all instructions in writing are often trying to compensate for their own shortcomings. They feel that if a job is not done or completed correctly, they can blame the person to whom the written instructions were given. Excessive use of written instructions can lead employees to disregard them, or delay the information getting to the people it is intended for. When employees receive most instructions by memo, they may come to treat urgent requests in the same way as routine ones.

There is, however, a place for written instructions. Give or confirm in writing directions that fall into these four categories:

1. *Permanent change of procedure*. When the direction is to change a policy or procedure or to introduce a method or plan that will be used from now on, a written confirmation following a verbal explanation can be referred to until everyone is familiar with the new routine. These are usually called 'standing instructions'.

2. *By precedent*. Where certain instructions have always been given in written form (e.g. confirmation of holidays or temporary changes to normal policy), continue to give these in writing.

3. *Complexity*. Written orders are helpful when the directions are complex and it will be useful for both you and the team to be able to refer back to them.

4. *Same message to a number of people*. When the same instructions must be given to a number of people in different places or at different times to ensure standard adherence, putting them in writing will save a lot of time that would otherwise be spent repeating the same information.

WHO SHOULD GIVE WORK INSTRUCTIONS TO YOUR EMPLOYEES?

When Henri Fayol established his 14 principles of management, he included the principle of **unity of command** as one of the more important (see also Chapter 4). This states that employees must receive their instructions about a particular task from only one person. Fayol believed that if employees were responsible to more than one supervisor, conflict and confusion would arise as to what to do and whose directions should have priority. Therefore, try to ensure (as far as possible) that you are the only person who gives orders to your employees.

A **matrix organisation** is a relatively new form of organisation structure that seems to go against this principle. Instead of the predictability of one boss, employees must learn to cope with the ambiguity, conflicting priorities and excitement of having two or more managers. This need not necessarily go against the unity of command principle if each supervisor manages only clearly defined, and different, aspects of a person's job. When this is not the case, confusion and conflicts can arise.

Responding to more than one manager is a difficult task for many, however. Matrix organisations prosper when people are able to deal with the ambiguity resulting from reporting to more than one manager and invest their personal energy, enthusiasm and creativity in dealing with multiple projects and challenges.

RECEIVING INSTRUCTIONS

What should you do when you are on the receiving end of work instructions? Most important of all, make sure you thoroughly understand what needs to be done. Don't be shy about asking questions! You want to minimise any chance of misunderstanding and doing something that was never wanted in the first place. Clarify all areas on which you have any doubt.

Ask for guidelines on timing, quality, quantity and so on. There is no need to ask your boss to do the job for you or to explain it step by step, but specific operating parameters will ensure that you both know what is required. Are there any constraints, such as time or money, that you will be expected to work within? Check these out and plan accordingly. Assumptions can be dangerous.

Have all the relevant people been made aware that you have been asked to carry out these instructions? Will you need to enlist the cooperation of others or temporarily acquire any special authority?

Be positive in your attitude and show, through your words as well as your actions, that you are willing to carry out the instruction.

DISAGREEING WITH AN INSTRUCTION

You will often be required to relay instructions and information from your manager to your work team. Occasionally, you will not agree with them, or you may believe that they will result in an adverse reaction from your work team.

An easy response to such a situation would be to take sides with the employees and accuse senior management of being 'out of touch' or unaware of the repercussions and to pass on the information or instructions, adding something like: 'I know it's crazy and won't work but that's the way they want it done.' Rather than creating harmony within the work group, such a negative attitude only makes it harder to enlist the cooperation of employees.

Negative supervisors are usually those who are unable to see 'the big picture' or understand the overall reasons behind an order or a change in policy or procedure. They cannot understand that sometimes a 'tough' decision must be made, despite the fact that it is likely to be unpopular.

Thoroughly talk through with your manager any instructions you don't fully agree with. State your opinions calmly, slowly and clearly. Cite any relevant examples, facts or figures to illustrate your points. Avoid being purely negative—try instead to be constructive in your remarks. In other words, don't just say, 'It will never work.' Explain why you think this and offer some alternative approaches.

If, at the end of the discussion, your manager still requires that you relay the instructions, it is your job to do so, provided that no organisational policies or legal issues are contravened. If you believe that rules are being breached, raise the matter again with your manager or, if necessary, with your manager's manager. If there is no breach of the law or corporate policy, carry out the order or pass it on to your team, explaining the reasons behind it as fully as possible. Remember that, as a supervisor, you are part of the management team and must be a supportive member of that team.

DELEGATION

Giving work instructions involves directing people to carry out duties and tasks that are part of their job. Delegation involves giving people the authority to carry out tasks that are normally your responsibility. You give someone else the **authority** and **responsibility** to carry out a specific task while you retain the **accountability** for it.

Accountability is being held answerable for work for which you have been given authority and responsibility. You can delegate authority and responsibility, but you cannot delegate accountability.

In other words, you may delegate one of your tasks to an employee together with the authority to do it, and hold the employee responsible for getting it done correctly and on time, but you cannot delegate your own accountability to your manager and the organisation for getting the task done safely and correctly.

Delegation or abdication?

Some supervisors delegate a task and leave the employee, floundering, to 'get on with it'. They mistakenly believe that this 'sink or swim' approach is delegation, that it is a way of training staff, and that it is an acceptable way to 'test an employee's mettle'. This is not delegation, not staff development and certainly not a fair way to 'test' someone. Delegating a task to someone and failing to ensure that they will approach it properly or failing to monitor their progress is not delegation. It is abdication.

Don't be under any illusions about delegation. It is not a quick and easy way to off-load your work onto someone else. Always delegate according to the five keys (see Chapter 8). When you delegate a task to someone, make sure they will be able to do it; that they have the training and the resources (time, equipment, information) they need; that they are clear about what you are asking them to do, and why you are asking them; and that they will approach the task correctly and efficiently. Most often, this means talking it through with them first, stressing the results required and the importance of the task.

The importance of delegation

Delegating effectively helps you get the maximum benefit and output from your employees and frees up some of your time to do other things.

Some supervisors resist delegating, saying that 'the buck stops with me' or 'it's quicker and easier to do it myself'. They don't want to spend the time training their employees or they don't trust them to do the job to the required standard. Others fear 'letting go' or 'losing control', or worry that passing on knowledge will weaken their power base or value to the organisation. Some use the easy tasks as relaxation or as a way to avoid doing other parts of their job. These are just excuses.

Delegating is a good way to involve others and build an effective team. It can give employees a sense of participation. It can be a great source of job enrichment and is a good way to develop, train and coach employees on the job. Sharing knowledge and skills can also be a great motivating influence. It can make employees feel that they belong, that they have some say in things and that they are not just cogs in a wheel.

Delegating is also a good time-management tool. It will give you time to look ahead—time to plan your work and your department's work more effectively. You won't be troubled by today's problems all the time. Effective delegation can free you from details, giving you time to be sure that your department is operating smoothly, output is integrated and synchronised, and you are attaining your key objectives in a manner that is both effective and efficient.

What happens if you don't delegate?

If you don't delegate, you will probably end up doing everything yourself. You will be the kind of supervisor who is always pushing carts around the floor, photocopying memos, cleaning a machine, relieving an operator, filing the day's typing and doing a thousand other tasks, rather than your own job of supervising. In short, you'll be so busy doing odd jobs that your overall job will suffer. Your desk will be overflowing and your employees will be in a state of confusion because you haven't organised things properly.

If this sounds like your situation, then your basic problem is probably that you don't understand what delegation is or how it makes for good supervision and can be a 'sanity-saver'. You can't do it all yourself. Give some authority and responsibility to your work team to make decisions and do things where they have the necessary training, experience and information. Wise delegation helps you get on with your job of supervising the work and workers in your department.

Remember, supervisors get things done through others. If you find yourself using any of the excuses in Box 23.3 for not delegating, think again. They are not sound!

Five steps to effective delegation

Delegating involves assigning a suitable task to a suitable person, providing the right information and training, and following it up effectively.

BOX 23.3 COMMON EXCUSES FOR NOT DELEGATING

- My staff are too inexperienced to do this. I have to do it myself.
- It takes more time to explain the job and farm it out than it does to do it myself, so why bother?
- I can't afford to have my staff make a mistake for which I will be responsible.
- This job is different. It demands my personal attention.
- My workers are all busy, too, and don't have time for an additional load.
- I don't have anyone who will take the responsibility for work like this.
- I got where I am today doing this type of work, and I don't plan to stop now.

- If I pass it on to an employee, I'll lose control of the job. I won't know what's going on.
- People will think I'm lazy—that I'm just passing the buck.
- No one knows exactly how I want this job done.
- If you want a job done well, you've got to do it yourself.
- This job is too important to trust to an employee.
- This is my occupational hobby, and I don't plan to turn it over to someone else.
- I've got to OK the final product anyway, so why not do it to begin with?

Step 1: Decide what to delegate

Use the work delegation plan in Figure 23.2 to help you decide what tasks you could or should be delegating. When new work comes into your department, ask yourself whether you could delegate it.

FIGURE 23.2   WORK DELEGATION PLAN

Recurring and routine tasks	Who can do it now?	Who could be trained to do it?
Tasks that would increase or develop an employee's skills or knowledge	Who can do it now?	Who could be trained to do it?
Occasional duties or tasks	Who can do it now?	Who could be trained to do it?
Tasks I do that are in someone's area of expertise or interest	Who can do it now?	Who could be trained to do it?

Step 2: Decide who to delegate to

You could choose a person who is already clearly able and willing to take on the responsibility for doing a task or has a flair for it. Or you could choose an employee who wants to learn the task in order to develop or extend their skills or make their job more interesting or challenging. It could be that you have planned to develop someone's skills for future promotion or to extend job interest, and delegating a task or duty to them is a good way to do this. Or perhaps an employee has shown interest in a particular type of work and you decide to delegate it to them so that they can decide whether they really like it.

If the task requires a fine eye for detail, who enjoys this type of work? If it requires working with others cooperatively, who is good at that? If it is a repetitious task, who would enjoy doing it? If the unexpected might occur, who would handle it well? Try to achieve a good match between the person and the task (see also Chapters 15 and 19). Whatever your reason for delegating a particular task to an employee, make sure you are clear about it so that you can communicate it to the employee.

Step 3: Delegate

As with giving instructions, delegate using the following headings:
- quality
- quantity
- safety
- time
- why you are delegating this task to this person and why it is important.

Don't leave employees wondering why you have selected them, how important the job is, by when or how often the task is to be done, the standards or end result you expect, or whether there are any constraints such as time or money.

Train or coach as necessary to fill in gaps in knowledge or skills. Discuss how the employee will approach the task (don't insist that it be done in the way you used to do it or would have done it). In other words, delegate according to the results desired, not according to the methods to use, unless these are very clear-cut and specific and really are the best way to approach the task. Explain the time frame and available resources. Make sure they know they can come to you for help or advice and you'll help them think it through. Discuss how you will monitor the task to ensure that it is being completed effectively.

Once you have delegated, don't hound the employee, trying to keep on top of every last detail. Worse still, don't take it back and do it for them. Let them get on with it and monitor only the critical control points you have agreed.

 FROM THEORY TO PRACTICE

If the employee seems a bit daunted by the additional responsibility, focus their attention at the beginning of the task to help them get started. For example, instead of saying, 'This needs to be ready in six weeks' say, 'When do you think you'll have the outline ready for me to have a look at?'

Step 4: Inform others if necessary

Sometimes you will need to inform the employee's colleagues, other supervisors or senior managers that you have delegated a particular task or duty to someone else, particularly if that employee will be liaising with others in order to carry it out. Let them know, too, that you have complete confidence in the employee's ability to succeed in the task.

Step 5: Monitor results

Although you delegated responsibility and authority for the task, you retain accountability, so you must ensure the results are meeting expectations. Is the task being carried out efficiently and effectively and to the standards you require? Monitoring allows you to make any necessary adjustments to the way the task is being done. If the employee is making mistakes, use them as opportunities for training and guidance.

Every once in a while, discuss what the employee is learning and how they are enjoying the task. Make sure they understand how it fits into the 'big picture' and how they can use the skills they are acquiring in other aspects of their job.

Does delegation mean losing control?

If you follow the steps to delegation outlined above, you will monitor results (step 5). This will ensure that things stay in control and that the job is done correctly. Your monitoring should alert you in plenty of time if things are going off the rails, enabling you to take swift corrective action.

If the person you have delegated to gets it wrong, review what went wrong and turn the mistake into a learning opportunity. When you delegate, you also delegate the right to make mistakes. We all make mistakes from time to time.

Monitoring delegated duties

One of Murphy's best known laws of management is:

'In any field of endeavour, anything which can go wrong will go wrong.'

You can't afford to delegate a task and hope for the best. Keep tabs on it to ensure the employee is carrying it out as safely, correctly and efficiently as expected and progressing satisfactorily towards the goal. Do this by monitoring **critical control points**. Examine results at certain key stages and compare them with the expected or desired results. If there is a gap between the results required and what is achieved, discuss what corrective action can be taken.

To monitor delegated duties, set up a systematic method of measuring progress against targets that will alert you and the employee to any deviations from the requirements. You can set up this system so that the employee gets the information directly and comes to you only if there is a deviation (**management by exception**); this works well with highly skilled and motivated employees. Or you can arrange it so that the actual results go directly to both you and the employee for comparison with the desired results. (The results should never go only to you because this will make the employee overly dependent on you and reduce their motivation.) Either way, you will need to do two things when setting up a monitoring process:

1. Decide what needs to be monitored. What is important? Production? Quality? Costs? Sales? Expenses? Monitor only what is important.

2. Establish the target or standard—the gauge against which you will both measure performance. Follow the formula for SMARTT targets; make sure they are:

Specific

Measurable

Achievable

Relevant (related to the organisation's key measures and goals)

Trackable

Time-framed

Try to measure *positive*, not negative, data. In other words, measure what you do want, not what you don't want; for example, set a target and measure the percentage of items passing quality control inspection rather than items failing inspection. Try to monitor **lead indicators** rather than **lag indicators** (see Chapter 5).

Use the system shown in Figure 23.3 to monitor results. It involves three steps, although you won't need the last step when the employee is carrying out the delegated task correctly. As the figure indicates, this monitoring process is a continual cycle.

Step 1   *Measure actual performance.* Keep the information you gather to a minimum, but make sure it is key information. What you are after is clear, quick, low-cost information.

Step 2   *Compare actual with target.* Preferably, management by exception should bring to your attention only performance that is outside expectations.

Step 3   *Correct any deviation.* Encourage employees to work out for themselves what corrective action would be best; only if they are really stuck should you tell them. This is not to make life awkward for the employee, but to ensure that the task is not delegated back up to you. It also helps people learn from their errors.

Five levels of monitoring

You can select from five levels of monitoring, depending on the employee's level of skills and experience and their willingness to do the task.

Level 1   *Just do it!* This is for employees who are competent and willing. You can safely assign them the work and let them get on with it, provided you have warning signals in place that will alert you to any potential problems.

FIGURE 23.3   THE MONITORING CYCLE

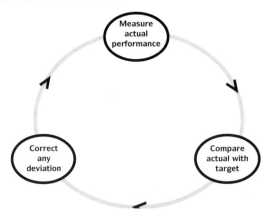

THE **BIG** PICTURE
··
Remember that getting things done is not the only thing that's important. Allowing others to learn, even if the task is not accomplished as quickly, efficiently or effectively, is also important.

Level 2   *Keep me informed.* This is for employees who are dependable but slightly less skilled, experienced or willing. They can carry on, but should keep you informed of certain key information so you can satisfy yourself things are progressing well.

Level 3   *Check back first.* Ask the employee to check back with you before proceeding at certain critical points. That way, you can assure yourself that things will be done correctly.

Level 4   *Let's talk it through first.* Ask the employee to decide what to do and then come and talk it through with you before acting. This is an expanded version of level 3 and lets you review how the employee is thinking and approaching the task. It gives you a chance to coach and develop their skills.

Level 5   *I'll walk you through it.* This is for employees new to a task. Use the training approach discussed in Chapter 16.

Suitable tasks for delegation

Let's start with those tasks that are clearly not suitable. Don't delegate tasks that are well beyond employees' training or experience. Setting people up to fail is the worst possible kind of supervision. Do not delegate sensitive or confidential matters such as discipline, performance counselling or pay. Keep matters dealing with organisational policy or security and any high-risk or high-cost tasks in your own hands. Avoid delegating boring 'gofer' jobs and jobs that you don't like to do yourself, especially unpleasant or otherwise disagreeable tasks. Don't delegate planning and monitoring activities, or anything that needs to be done quickly.

That leaves most other tasks as suitable for delegation. Recurring and routine duties, tasks that would be particularly suitable for training, developing and stretching employees and tasks that would make their jobs more interesting in some way are all suitable for delegation. So are tasks that require special skills that you may not have and tasks that need to be done but you can't squeeze into your schedule. Small projects, data collection, research and portions of larger projects can all be delegated. Tasks that don't require your personal input are also good to delegate.

Common mistakes in delegating

Do you recognise any of these common delegating mistakes?
- delegating all the plum jobs to the staff member you like best;
- not delegating to people who have excellent skills and commitment for fear of being shown up;
- as a new supervisor, failing to let go of the old job;

- failing to thank employees who have completed a delegated task enthusiastically and/or well; and
- forgetting that you can't delegate accountability.

Employee reactions to delegation

Not all employees respond positively when you delegate a task to them. One person might say, 'I already do enough' and this may be true—they may be overworked. On the other hand, they or the department may be poorly organised. Another employee may complain: 'I never know what I'm expected to do!' If this happens, ask yourself whether you have delegated completely and clearly and provided all the necessary information. Or perhaps the employee lacks confidence or is worried about what your reaction to mistakes will be.

An employee may complain: 'You knock yourself out and never a word of thanks!' In this case, you had better review the information on managing performance and motivation (Chapters 8 and 21) and learn to give positive feedback. Someone else might say: 'Tell me exactly what you want me to do.' This may be because you have always thought for them and told them exactly what you wanted them to do, step by step. Perhaps they don't want to take on this task at all, and this is their way of telling you.

'I can't do it!' might mean 'I lack confidence and need a bit of help', while 'Why should I bother?' or 'Why should I be doing your job for you?' may mean 'You don't reward me enough' or 'There's no point in my doing it—I'm going nowhere in this job anyway!' or 'Why should I help you out—you never do anything for me?'.

Deal with these reactions tactfully. Use your **active listening skills** and ask clarifying questions to make sure you fully understand the employee's objection to taking on the task you want to delegate. The responses may be valid or they may signal a deeper morale and motivation problem.

Tips for delegating

If you follow these tips, you will discover the 'art' of delegation.

1. Don't wait until the last minute. Delegate early. Take a step back and plan your delegation. Look at the deadline and work back from there.
2. Be sure that you delegate to the right person. Before you delegate, consider their skills, experience and motivation with respect to the new job. Don't delegate more than is justified by the employee's capabilities and experience.
3. Make sure that you give your reasons for selecting the employee for this particular job. It is important to show that you have confidence in your choice.
4. Explain clearly and check you've been understood. Clarify what you are delegating and why. Define at the outset what the job is all about. If you can't delegate the whole job but only a part of it, explain where it fits into the whole picture. Explain exactly what has to be done, the limits of the authority and how you will measure results. Unless you need to train the employee to do the job, you don't need to specify how to do it, but make sure you clearly state the results you expect.
5. Ensure the employee understands the importance of the task.
6. Give any guidance and support that is necessary without oversupervising or criticising. Pass on any information relevant to the performance of the job that the employee will need to know.

7. Make sure you provide the necessary resources.

8. Agree review methods and dates.

9. Delegate, don't abdicate. Keep control through feedback. Get periodic reports and offer suggestions or advice only if it is warranted.

10. Inform others who need to know what you have delegated and to whom.

11. Don't overdo it. Don't pile so much on your employees that they become overburdened.

12. Don't hover. There is a fine line between interfering and helping. Let the employee get on with the new task.

UPWARDS DELEGATION

Some employees have a habit of shifting their responsibilities upwards, to their supervisor. People sometimes do this if they are unsure about what they are supposed to do. Or they may feel unable to carry out some of their tasks due to lack of training or experience, or because of environmental barriers such as poor or unsuitable tools and equipment, awkward systems, or lack of time or information. Sometimes, an employee is simply unmotivated. If any of these situations apply, you may well find tasks being subtly passed up to you.

This can happen in many ways. For example, employees may ask for your help. If this happens, make sure you don't end up doing their job yourself. If some particular operation (or machine) is not working smoothly, the employee may ask you to see what is wrong. You promise to think about it and say you will be back in touch. Through this simple manoeuvre, the responsibility for sorting it out has been shifted on to your shoulders. Situations like these can add up and when they do you will find yourself solving your employees' problems and doing their work instead of supervising the department.

Upwards delegation can eat away at the time you have to run your department. It can result in dependent employees who can't think for themselves or act without permission. Supervisors can end up doing everyone's job except their own.

What should you do when an employee approaches you for help? Be courteous, listen to the problem and help any employee who really needs it. You will have to be the judge. For those employees who are trying (perhaps without even being aware of it) to get you to solve their problems for them, let them know that you have every confidence in their ability. Let them know that it is their job and that you are confident they will come up with an excellent solution. Talk the difficulty through with them if you think it appropriate to do so. Later, check back to see what the employee has done. Offer suggestions if you wish and give praise where praise is due.

	True	False
1. Giving too many work instructions is just as dangerous as not giving any at all.	☐	☐
2. Giving instructions means telling people what to do.	☐	☐
3. Supervisors don't often need to give instructions in a fully empowered organisation.	☐	☐
4. Delegating is a leadership style as well as a supervisory action.	☐	☐
5. Depending on how you give an instruction, the result can be mere compliance or full cooperation.	☐	☐
6. Different types of work instructions should be given to different people and in different situations.	☐	☐
7. Supervisors have the right to direct any employee to do anything.	☐	☐
8. An employee who refuses to carry out an instruction should be suspended immediately.	☐	☐
9. If employees make a mistake or have trouble carrying out an instruction, the supervisor should take the task back or give it to someone else until they have learned to do it properly.	☐	☐
10. Putting instructions in writing protects supervisors if the instructions are carried out incorrectly.	☐	☐
11. Delegating may not result in more motivated workers if it only adds to the list of boring tasks people have to do.	☐	☐
12. Generally speaking, only a person's direct supervisor should issue directions to them.	☐	☐
13. If you disagree with an instruction, you should refuse to carry it out.	☐	☐
14. Supervisors should not delegate tasks that they enjoy doing themselves or that they are good at.	☐	☐
15. Once a task is delegated, supervisors can safely forget about it and move on to other things.	☐	☐
16. If an employee says 'I'm too busy to take on this task' about a duty a supervisor wants to delegate, it may or may not be true.	☐	☐
17. Although delegation is a good time-management tool, supervisors should take care not to overuse it.	☐	☐

APPLY YOUR KNOWLEDGE

1. 'Nowadays, it is necessary to give the reasons behind your instructions if you want them to be carried out willingly.' Do you agree? Why, or why not?

2. Give some guidelines on when supervisors should use each of the six main ways of giving directions.

3. List and explain at least eight tips which, if followed, will help ensure that your employees accept your instructions.

4. What should you do if someone refuses to obey your directions? List your options ranging in strength, indicating which should come first and why.

5. What are four possible causes of instructions not being executed

correctly? Explain the remedies each suggests.

6. Summarise the circumstances under which instructions should be put in writing.

7. What should supervisors do if they are asked to pass on a decision or an instruction with which they disagree? Develop some action guidelines based on the information provided in this chapter.

8. What is delegation and how does it help a supervisor achieve results and develop staff?

9. What should you do if an employee makes a mistake on a task you have delegated?

10. What should you do if an employee asks for help with a problem?

DEVELOP YOUR SKILLS

Individual activities

1. You are a supervisor who wants to ensure that the customer service counter is tidied up and made fully presentable before tomorrow's visit by a senior manager from interstate. What type of instruction would be appropriate? Give your reasons for selecting that type of instruction and write down what you would say.

2. You have just seen an employee in your section carrying out an unsafe work practice. What type of instruction is appropriate to rectify this and ensure it doesn't happen again? Give your reasons for selecting that type of instruction and write down what you would say.

3. Write a short essay contrasting the principle of unity of command with matrix organisations and suggest how the problems of unity of command can be overcome in matrix organisations.

4. Your manager has just asked you to pass on a new policy to employees, banning smoking anywhere on company premises, including outside the building. You are concerned that employee resistance to this will be high as people are in the habit of stepping outside for a smoke throughout the day. Formulate a response to your manager.

5. Interview a practising supervisor to find out which of their duties they delegate and how delegation has helped them in their job. Have they run into any problems when delegating their duties? What advice can they offer?

6. Prepare a plan to delegate a recurring paperwork duty that involves liaising with supervisors in other departments. Incorporate the five steps to delegation outlined in this chapter. Outline a suitable monitoring procedure to follow up this delegated duty to ensure it is carried out correctly and on time.

Group activities

1. In small groups, discuss whether Derek (in the vignette on page 701) should change his style when telling the managing director how to do the stocktake count or whether he should use the same style he uses with the people who work for him in the ware-house. Try to refer to the theories presented in Chapters 20 and 21 on leadership and motivation if you have studied them. When you present your thoughts to the class, include the rationale behind your conclusions.

2. In pairs, take turns giving this order to each other: 'Robin, can you do

this now, please.' Experiment to see how many different inflections you can put on these words and see how each is received by your partner. Which would work best if Robin were a negative, uncooperative employee? Which would work best if Robin was willing but not fully trained in the duty concerned?

3. Following the exercise above, the person playing Robin should refuse to carry out the instruction. Role-play how you would deal with this using the information provided in this chapter. Get some feedback from 'Robin' on what you said and did that worked well and how you could improve.

4. Referring to question 1 under *Individual activities* above, assume that the employees in the section are responsible and helpful. Pair up and take turns giving the necessary order, using each of the six types of orders. Which works best in this situation? Why?

5. Referring to question 6 under *Individual activities* above, role-play delegating this duty to someone in your class. The person should react in one of the negative ways discussed in this chapter. Deal with it, then ask for feedback from the person playing the employee. Did you deal with their reaction effectively? Will the way you dealt with it ensure their continued cooperation?

CASE STUDY 23.1

The Untimely Overtime

When her department had a special order to complete by the following day, Ann Turnbull asked all the staff if they would be prepared to work overtime that night. All agreed except Tony Small. Tony claimed he had made prior arrangements for that evening and wasn't interested in the overtime anyway because he would lose more than half of what he earned in income tax.

'Besides,' he said, 'our workplace agreement requires that we be given 24 hours' notice of being required to work extra hours.'

Ann tried to explain that it was an emergency and she could not have given prior notice, but Tony remained unmoved. Ann allowed herself to be provoked into insisting he work overtime or run the risk of being dismissed.

When the normal finishing time came, all the staff started their overtime on the special order except Tony, who left in full view of the staff, saying in a loud voice, 'You can't make me work overtime if I don't want to.'

Questions

1 Apart from meeting the deadline on the order, what new problems will probably face Ann Turnbull?

2 What action should Ann take when Tony arrives for work the next day?

3 How should Ann have handled Tony's refusal to work overtime?

A Poor Appointment?

Charlie Simmons' resignation from the position of office administrator came as a shock to the organisation. Charlie had run the section for the last ten years and was not expected to retire for another eight, so nothing had been done about developing a successor for his position.

Charlie had always let it be known that it was his department, and his long years of experience and knowledge of the organisation had allowed him to adopt an autocratic leadership style that his staff accepted without question.

The appointment of Mary Williams to the vacant position was met with mixed feelings by the office staff. Mary had been with the organisation for only two years but was by far the best academically qualified person for the job, especially in view of management's decision to introduce new technology into the office procedures—a plan that had been strongly resisted by Charlie Simmons.

When Mary took over her new position, she began to put into effect many of the new procedures that had been discussed at the appointment interview. So that there would be no confusion about what was expected of individual staff members, Mary intended to tell each of them how the changes would affect their jobs and give each one written details of how their new job should be done.

With so many changes occurring, management saw the opportunity of introducing some new ideas, too, and gave these to Mary to implement urgently. Mary felt that many of these schemes were not practical. However, when the staff complained that they were unworkable, her only explanation was, 'This is what management wants us to do.'

It wasn't long before work in Mary's section was falling behind schedule. Many of the new instructions appeared to be in direct conflict with each other. Standards and reliability of information declined, deadlines were not met and morale began to drop. In fact, management began considering Mary's appointment to be a poor choice. Although she appeared to have many good ideas, they thought she lacked the ability to carry them out. They were considering replacing her with a more experienced worker and reverting to the old system, which had at least provided adequate results.

Questions

1 What do you see as the basic problem in this office? What has probably contributed most to this situation?
2 If you were Mary, what steps would you take to rectify the situation? What support would you need from management?
3 What approach should Mary have taken in giving and passing on instructions?

Answers to Rapid Review questions

1. T   2. F   3. T   4. T   5. T   6. T   7. F   8. F   9. F   10. F   11. T   12. T   13. F
14. F   15. F   16. T   17. T

CHAPTER 24

MANAGING CONFLICT AND GRIEVANCES AND COUNSELLING POOR PERFORMANCE

Revving up Jed

As Susan got ready for work, she thought about how she would handle the performance improvement interview she had scheduled for first thing this morning with Jed, her '2IC'. She had appointed him about eight months ago, knowing that she would have a lot of on-the-job training to do. She was convinced she had done this well because, until recently, he had been doing a good job, gradually getting better and better, as one would expect.

Lately, however, he seemed to have lost some of his initial enthusiasm. For example, he was no longer at his desk, 'ready to roll', ten or 15 minutes before starting time, although could she, in all fairness, bring that up? No, it was more than that. The all-important weekly activity summary for the department had been late twice in the last six weeks and there had been two serious errors in last week's report. He had let several key tasks slide over the last six weeks, too, notably the forward-planning

schedules, which were now behind by three weeks.

Worst of all, one of the employees who reported to Jed came to her earlier in the week to complain that Jed wasn't assigning work so that they had time to complete it properly by the deadline. He seemed to be leaving things to the last minute and, when she pointed this out to him, he told her to spend less time complaining and more time working. She had been quite offended by his attitude and wanted to register a formal grievance

As Susan reflected on Jed's performance, she decided to get to work a bit early and make a list of the points she wanted to discuss with him. She knew he realised the importance of all these tasks and could do them adequately, so why had his performance slipped? She also knew that he normally had a good 'way' with people and she was surprised by the complaint of one of his team members. She should get to the bottom of this before things got any worse. She just hoped she hadn't left it too late.

Conflict management, grievance handling, performance counselling—your skills in all these areas will contribute significantly to a harmonious and productive workplace. This chapter looks at how to manage conflict and grievances and how to help employees turn around poor performance. We also learn what to do if an employee has a personal problem and how to terminate employment.

- Can conflict ever be useful? Is the absence of conflict a good sign?
- What causes conflict? How does it grow?
- How can you recognise conflict and deal with it before it becomes a crisis? What happens if conflict goes unresolved?
- What is your preferred conflict management style? Is this the best one in every circumstance?
- What skills, mind-sets and behaviours will help you manage conflicts effectively?
- What is the difference between a conflict and a grievance?
- How should you respond to grievances?
- What should you do when an employee's performance slips below the acceptable standard?
- Do you know the common signs of poor performance that supervisors must address?
- What are the most common causes of poor performance? Do you know the

five indispensable keys to good performance?
- What are the rules of giving and receiving feedback?
- What can you do if an employee has 'the wrong attitude'?
- Can you describe the five stages of a performance counselling session?
- What should your overall aims be in performance counselling?
- What are two key skills you will need to conduct an effective performance counselling meeting?
- How should you document your efforts to improve an employee's performance?
- How should you terminate someone's employment if this becomes necessary?
- Should supervisors become involved in personal counselling? How can they help employees with personal problems if they decide to?

THE SUPERVISOR'S ROLE IN MANAGING CONFLICT AND GRIEVANCES

Who do you know who has never had a conflict with anyone? No one? That's not surprising. Some conflicts, of course, are merely minor irritations that we can quickly and easily forget. Others are more serious and can do lasting damage if we don't handle them carefully and skilfully.

Good communication helps us avoid some conflicts. Other conflicts, though, are inevitable and we should resolve them effectively so that they do not cause lasting damage to relationships, or become counterproductive and costly to the organisation.

The responsibility for managing conflict in work teams usually falls to the team leader, or supervisor. Supervisors are also called upon to resolve conflict between work teams within the organisation and, occasionally, between an employee and the organisation. As organisations strengthen relationships with suppliers and customers and everyone works more closely together, supervisors may have to manage apparent conflicts with them. They may also have to resolve conflict with other supervisors in the organisation if the needs of their respective departments seem to be at odds. Skill and sensitivity are important factors in reaching a resolution acceptable and beneficial to all parties.

We begin this chapter by examining conflict, what causes it and how to manage it. We then examine grievances, a form of conflict, before turning to the topic of how to counsel people if their performance falls below acceptable standards.

WHAT IS CONFLICT?

We can define conflict as verbally and/or non-verbally expressed disagreement between individuals or groups. It may occur, for example, between two individuals—between supervisor and employee, or manager and supervisor. It can occur between an individual and a group, between groups in the same organisation or between organisations. Conflict can even exist within an individual—for example, when one part of you wants to stay at home and rest while another part of you knows you should get up and go to work.

Can conflict ever be useful?

Conflict can lead to resentment, quarrels, clashes of will, power struggles, self-righteousness, the formation of 'camps' (taking up strong stances) and either/or thinking. It can be disagreeable, disruptive and stressful. This is the negative face of conflict, because conflict of this sort leads to anxiety, anger and frustration. It can harm morale and productivity and weaken an organisation.

> 'Heat and animosity, contest and conflict may sharpen the wits, although they rarely do; they never strengthen understanding, clear the perspicacity, guide the judgement, or improve the heart.'
>
> Walter Savage Landor (1775–1864)
> Poet

However, the absence of conflict is not necessarily good. Lack of conflict can indicate that a relationship is stagnating or that the parties are not sufficiently interested in it to resolve their differences. The fact that people argue means they have a stake in the issue and care about it and each other. In fact, a certain amount of conflict is healthy and can be productive if we handle it well. Conflict can move a relationship out of a rut. It can develop confidence in and even enhance a relationship. It can result in a better way of doing things. It can allow people to discover the best resolution to a situation and it can bring hidden feelings out into the open so they can be dealt with constructively.

In fact, no conflict at all is often a more worrying sign than the presence of conflict. Conflict itself isn't the problem. How we *resolve* it can be.

ASSERTIVENESS AND CONFLICT

It is safe to say that supervisors who handle conflict *assertively* are far more successful in the long run than supervisors who deal with differences of opinion in an aggressive or a passive manner. (See Chapter 19 for more information about assertiveness.)

Supervisors who adopt an aggressive 'win–lose' approach ('I win–you lose') meet with hostility, resentment and compliance rather than good will and cooperation. They need to rely on threats and their formal authority to deal with difficult situations.

Some supervisors take the opposite attitude, one of passiveness or submission. Their attitude is 'don't make waves', 'sweep it under the carpet', 'peace at any price'. These supervisors often find that people take advantage of their 'good nature', and difficult issues remain unresolved until resentment builds up to such an extent that an aggressive 'explosion' occurs.

The skill of assertiveness enables supervisors to confront conflict openly and deal with it constructively. It allows them to go for a 'win–win' approach, exploring all options until they find the one that is most satisfactory to all parties.

CAUSES OF CONFLICT

Many conflicts are due to *poor communication*. Barriers such as prejudice, selective hearing and preconceived opinions, as well as such poor communication skills as lack of empathy, inability to listen actively, poor summarising skills and unassertiveness, have led to many unnecessary conflicts and caused others to escalate.

Fear is another common cause of conflict. Fear of what we might lose (including face) can cause us to take an aggressive stance, lessening the likelihood that we will resolve the conflict in everyone's interests and achieve a positive outcome.

> 'People don't get along because they fear each other.
> People fear each other because they don't know each other.
> They don't know each other because they have not properly
> communicated with each other. '
>
> Martin Luther King (1929–68)

Differences in values underlie many conflicts. For example, if you value good timekeeping as a sign of responsibility and motivation, and an employee's attitude is 'What's a few minutes here or there? I get my job done, don't I?', it doesn't take a genius to predict that the two of you will soon be in conflict over timekeeping!

People often disagree over *content matters*, such as who said what, and over policies, plans and priorities. Disagreement over *perceptions* lies at the heart of many conflicts: for example, who knows best, who has authority, whose job it is, and so on.

Differences in goals, wants, needs, expectations and *clashes of personality* can also cause conflicts. *Competition for limited resources* is another common starting point for conflict. *Role pressures* and *emotional issues* also play their part.

Since conflict can begin so easily, smart supervisors think through the ramifications of any actions they plan. They make sure they don't unwittingly open a 'can of worms' and set off unnecessary conflict. They spot potential conflicts and act to ensure they don't arise or, at least, to minimise them.

COMMON RESPONSES TO CONFLICT

Responses to conflict fall into three categories: a person's *internal* responses, *hindering* responses and *helpful* responses.

Many people have never learned to deal effectively with conflict and therefore would prefer, if at all possible, to avoid it. Because they lack assertiveness skills, their internal response is either 'fight' (aggression) or 'flight' (submission). Both these responses cause stress. Some of the stress responses that people have are 'butterflies' in the stomach, a thumping heart, tightening of the vocal chords (resulting in a higher than usual, or shrill, voice or the need for repeated throat-clearing), clenched fists, tightening of the jaw, grinding of teeth and shortness of breath.

Repeated conflict situations that go unresolved or are resolved unsatisfactorily can cause long-term stress responses such as ulcers, problems associated with tension or substance abuse, and domestic problems.

Box 24.1 summarises responses to conflict that hurt and that help. Hindering responses can create deadlocks, interfere with mutual understanding, and leave losers resentful and even inclined to sabotage. Helpful responses can unlock creativity, build relationships and achieve mutually satisfying outcomes. We look at the helpful responses and the skills they require in more detail later in this chapter.

HOW CONFLICT GROWS

Each conflict is different. Having said this, we can identify certain predictable phases, or stages of conflict, ranging from minor to major. These are shown in Figure 24.1.

The first stage of conflict is *discomfort*. We feel uncomfortable about the situation or a person, although we may not be able to put our finger on why. We may not even be conscious that there is a problem or, if we are, we are unsure of exactly what it is.

If we don't address and sort out these feelings of discomfort, we may reach the next stage of conflict: an *incident*. Here, a short, sharp exchange may upset and irritate both parties. However, there is no lasting damage if we can resolve the conflict at this stage.

The next level is where *misunderstandings* of a more serious nature occur. We often confuse, misperceive or wrongly attribute motives and facts to the other party. Our thoughts may return often to the problem.

BOX 24.1

HURTING AND HELPING RESPONSES TO CONFLICT

Hurting responses	*Helping responses*
■ avoiding it	■ trying to understand the other's point of view
■ personal attacks	■ being willing to listen
■ getting angry	■ keeping calm
■ changing the subject	■ knowing what you want
■ apologising inappropriately	■ assertively stating your position and goals
■ playing the martyr	■ isolating what you are disagreeing about
■ pretending to agree	■ getting a 'referee'
■ giving up and giving in	■ looking for mutual goals
■ trying to turn the conflict into a joke	■ a win–win mind-set
■ a win–lose mind-set	■ respecting the other party
■ 'either/or' thinking	■ knowing your own limits
■ unwillingness to compromise	■ willingness to resolve
■ unwillingness to explore options	■ agreeing on clear goals or outcomes
■ lack of empathy	■ empathy
■ refusal to see the other's point of view	■ assertiveness
■ being negative	■ mutual respect
	■ being positive

FIGURE 24.1   STAGES OF CONFLICT

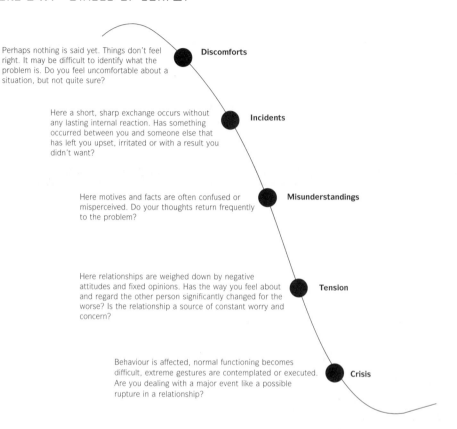

Perhaps nothing is said yet. Things don't feel right. It may be difficult to identify what the problem is. Do you feel uncomfortable about a situation, but not quite sure? — **Discomforts**

Here a short, sharp exchange occurs without any lasting internal reaction. Has something occurred between you and someone else that has left you upset, irritated or with a result you didn't want? — **Incidents**

Here motives and facts are often confused or misperceived. Do your thoughts return frequently to the problem? — **Misunderstandings**

Here relationships are weighed down by negative attitudes and fixed opinions. Has the way you feel about and regard the other person significantly changed for the worse? Is the relationship a source of constant worry and concern? — **Tension**

Behaviour is affected, normal functioning becomes difficult, extreme gestures are contemplated or executed. Are you dealing with a major event like a possible rupture in a relationship? — **Crisis**

Source: The Conflict Resolution Network, PO Box 1016, Chatswood, NSW 2057 (phone (02) 9419 8500)

If we do not deal with the conflict at this level, it is likely to move on to *tension*, where we feel uncomfortable whenever we think of the situation or whenever we see or think of the other party. The relationship between the parties becomes weighed down by negative attitudes and fixed opinions.

This can lead easily to the final stage of an unresolved conflict, that of *crisis*. Normal functioning between the parties can be very difficult and extreme gestures are often made or contemplated. Often, a major 'scene' occurs which can result in the disruption of the relationship—for example, quitting your job in the heat of the moment or saying something you are certain to regret later.

THE DANGERS OF UNRESOLVED CONFLICT

You will notice that the stages of conflict in Figure 24.1 are shown against a curved line. Think of this line as a hillside and think of the conflict as a ball. As it moves down the hill, it gains momentum and becomes more and more difficult to stop. Like the ball, conflict gains momentum and becomes more difficult to deal with as it progresses through the stages. This is why it is important to recognise and address conflict early on, when you become aware of it. Delay only makes it difficult.

Supervisors who ignore conflict do so at their peril. Conflict that goes unresolved usually deepens and moves through the levels until it reaches a crisis point. Sometimes a 'scene' is not possible, so one or both of the parties may 'vote with their feet'—for example, by resigning. Or they may become irritable, moody, sulky, depressed, impatient or intolerant. Scapegoating, gossiping and backbiting are other signs of underlying conflict. Direct or indirect aggression, such as malicious compliance and passive compliance, are other consequences and signs of unresolved conflict.

CONFLICT MANAGEMENT STYLES

'Mankind must evolve for all humankind a conflict method which rejects revenge, aggression and retaliation.'

Martin Luther King

Kenneth Thomas and Ralph Kilmann have devised a model that identifies the behaviour of an individual or group in a conflict situation. The model is based on our intentions along two dimensions: how much effort or energy we put into satisfying our *own concerns* and how much energy we devote to cooperation and satisfying the *concerns of the other party*.

As Figure 24.2 shows, this approach leads to five different styles of managing conflict. Each style is appropriate in some situations and inappropriate in others, so supervisors need to be able to use all of them, and also know *when* to use them.

Competing

Competing is uncooperative. It is usually aggressive because you pursue your own concerns at the expense of the other person. This win–lose method of managing conflict is based on power. People using this style of conflict management use whatever power seems appropriate (their ability to argue, to pull rank, to use economic sanctions) to impose a solution

FIGURE 24.2   CONFLICT MANAGEMENT STYLES

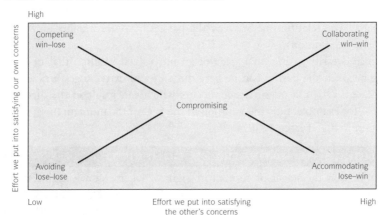

on the other party. The usual response to this is resentment, antagonism, hostility and lack of cooperation.

Supervisors who continually compete in conflict situations are often surrounded by 'yes men'. Others consider such supervisors 'hard to get on with' and say they don't know when to admit they are wrong. Those who compete habitually find it difficult to build up cooperative working relationships.

> **'Adversarial power relationships work only if you never have to see or work with the bastards again.'**
>
> Peter Drucker

This is not to say, however, that we should never use this method of dealing with conflict. When speed and decisiveness are at a premium, as they are in emergencies, it might be an appropriate style. When you are in conflict with parties who refuse to cooperate and who are trying to take advantage of you, managing the conflict competitively may be your best option. When safety issues are at stake, or you need to make a difficult or unpopular decision, a competitive stance may be necessary. Situations where the issue is more important than the relationship tend to call for a competing style. However, when making this choice, be aware that you are likely to damage the relationship.

When you must use a competing style, remember to behave assertively, not aggressively. This will help to reduce the negative responses a competing style brings out.

Accommodating

Accommodating is cooperative—the opposite of competing. It is often passive or submissive, because you are putting the other party's wishes before your own. Accommodating might take the form of selfless generosity or charity, agreeing to another person's request when you would prefer not to, yielding to another's point of view against your better judgment, or resentfully carrying out another's wishes.

Even when they are sure they are right, some people don't like taking a stand. Supervisors like this may be uncomfortable about using their power or afraid of losing the friendship or cooperation of their staff. The danger of this approach is that their staff often do not take them or their ideas seriously.

When the issue is less important than the relationship, we might choose accommodating behaviour. When building a relationship is more important than the issue, or when your 'stake' in the conflict or issue isn't high, accommodating may be a good option. When you have no hope of having your wishes met, you may also decide to accommodate as a way of minimising your losses and maintaining a climate of cooperation with the other party.

Avoiding

Avoiding is uncooperative. You pursue neither your own concerns nor those of the other person, but 'let sleeping dogs lie', pretending the conflict isn't there or perhaps hoping it will go away. Inappropriate avoidance of issues leads to resentment, displacement of feelings (the proverbial 'kicking the dog') and griping, general discontent and gossiping.

Of course, avoiding might also take the form of diplomatically sidestepping an issue, postponing discussion until a better time, or simply withdrawing from a threatening situation. So avoiding can have its uses, especially if neither the *relationship* nor the *issue* is important to you. Many potential conflict situations are just not worth the time and effort of becoming involved. Or you may want to collect more information before taking action. Sometimes temporary avoidance is the best policy to let everyone 'cool down'. Avoidance is also a good choice when it is more appropriate for others to handle the conflict—when it isn't really your place to become involved.

Collaborating

Collaborating is cooperative. It is the opposite of avoiding. Collaborating involves attempting to work with the other party to find a solution that satisfies both of you. It might take the form of exploring a disagreement to learn each other's positions, perceptions, wants and needs, and putting your heads together to come up with a satisfactory resolution.

This is not easy. It requires practice and skills in problem solving as well as good communication skills, particularly in the areas of empathy and assertiveness.

Collaboration takes time, effort and skill, but is particularly useful in situations where both the *issue* and the *relationship* are important and where an outcome that satisfies both parties is desirable. It is appropriate when we need all parties to be committed to the solution and when we need a creative solution.

Compromising

Compromising is intermediate in cooperation. It involves 'splitting the difference' to arrive at a solution partially acceptable to both parties. This falls on middle ground between competing and accommodating, where you give up more than in competing but less than in accommodating. It addresses issues more directly than avoiding but doesn't explore them in as much depth as collaborating.

Compromising can be quick. Although it leaves neither party fully satisfied, it can be useful in situations where time is running out or when collaboration or competition have failed. It can also provide a temporary, short-term solution to a conflict while collaborative discussions continue. Sometimes, settling for a workable compromise is the best you can do.

WIN–LOSE, LOSE–WIN AND WIN–WIN

When what you want differs from what someone else wants, how do you approach it. Do you want to have your way no matter what? Would you do just about anything rather than have an open disagreement over it? Or do you try to put your heads together, to figure out how you can both be satisfied?

The first describes a win–lose approach to conflict: 'I win—you lose'; 'me versus you' or 'us versus them'. The second describes a lose–win approach: 'I lose—you win.' The third describes a win–win approach: 'Let's both win if we can.' The focus is 'us together versus the problem'.

How we direct our *energy* is different. With win–lose and lose–win, it's directed towards total victory or total defeat. With win–win, we direct our energy towards establishing an atmosphere of constructive cooperation and search for outcomes desirable to both parties.

Empathy is different, too. With a win–lose mind-set, people can see the issue only from their own point of view. With lose–win, we see it from the other's point of view. A win–win mind-set helps us to appreciate the other's viewpoint as well as our own. The *focus* also differs: the emphasis is on reaching a solution with win–lose and lose–win; and on goals, outcomes and longer-term issues with win–win.

A win–lose approach often *personalises* the conflict. A win–win approach treats it *objectively* and impersonally. In win–lose, the parties are *conflict-oriented* rather than *relationship-oriented,* as they are with win–win. The immediate disagreement takes priority over the long-term effects of the conflict and its resolution.

Box 24.2 summarises the mind-sets of win–win, lose–win and win–lose supervisors.

FOUR STEPS FOR RESOLVING CONFLICT

Step 1: Initiate a discussion

Deal with the issue openly and honestly. This does not mean start an argument! Attacking or demeaning the other party, or communicating blame or judgment in any way, will only result in a defensive response that blocks successful conflict resolution.

Begin the discussion by making a short, clear statement that 'sets the scene' and explains to the other party what you want to discuss. This is called **framing** the discussion. Before you begin, make sure you have enough time to discuss the problem.

BOX 24.2   WIN–LOSE SUPERVISORS, WIN–WIN SUPERVISORS AND LOSE–WIN SUPERVISORS

Win–lose supervisors	*Win–win supervisors*	*Lose–win supervisors*
■ Me against you	■ We're in this together	■ You against me
■ We're on opposite sides	■ We're on the same side	■ We're on opposite sides
■ I want total victory	■ Let's see if we can both be satisfied	■ You are the victor
■ This is how it is	■ Here's my point of view; what's yours?	■ We'll do it your way
■ I want a quick fix	■ We both need to be satisfied long-term	■ I want a quick fix
■ My goals are most important	■ Let's see if we can meet your goals, too	■ Your goals are most important
	■ What are our common goals?	
■ I'll 'attack' you personally if I have to	■ Let's deal with this objectively	■ Let's not argue
■ This is a fight	■ Let's deal with this amicably	■ Let's not fight
■ I must win this battle	■ Let's solve our problem	■ You win this one
■ 'My way or the highway'	■ How can we resolve this?	■ Your way is the way we'll go

---

FROM THEORY TO PRACTICE

Think of conflict management as agreement management. How can you best reach agreement on this issue? How can we move towards the same side? How can we reach a joint understanding? How can we prevent problems or misunderstandings from occurring again?

FROM THEORY TO PRACTICE

Should you say anything or not? Think about the issue and your goals, and your relationship with the other person. How important to you is each one? Say something when both your goals and the relationship are important to you. Say something when the issue alone is extremely important to you. Save your breath when neither is that important.

Step 2: Give good information

Then clearly state your point of view. The techniques involved here are '**I' messages** and '**I' language**. Use neutral, objective, non-emotive language to explain the tangible or real effects the conflict has on you. Be sure to state your own point of view accurately, assertively and congruently—look as if you mean what you say.

Step 3: Gather good information

Listen to the other's point of view. Use empathy and active listening to make sure you really hear the other person's viewpoint. Avoid becoming defensive, attacking the other person, telling them what to do, or taking a hard-line approach. These will only harden your 'position' and increase the conflict. Instead, ask clarifying questions and summarise your understanding whenever you can. Remember—you only have to *understand* how the other person sees it, not necessarily *agree*. Before moving on, be sure you understand each other's point of view.

Step 4: Problem solve

Once both parties have had their say and been heard, it is time to turn to problem solving. The steps are as follows:
(a) *Summarise the problem.* What is the issue? Where does each party stand? What are the facts, feelings and concerns of each party? Don't define the problem as a conflict between competing solutions, but rather in terms of conflicting needs. And don't be in a hurry: be sure you have fully explored the problem before trying to solve it. Frequently, as we discuss a problem we redefine and shed new light on it.
(b) *Search for mutually acceptable solutions.* Generate as many possible solutions as you can before evaluating them and deciding which one to adopt. The more solutions you have to choose from, the more successfully resolved your conflict is likely to be.

FROM THEORY TO PRACTICE

If the discussion becomes heated, stop. Ask for some time out. For example, say, 'I'd like a minute or two to digest what you've said. How about a short break?' Better still, suggest a break if you feel yourself tensing up or becoming angry, before tempers flare.

BOX 24.3 GENERATING SOLUTIONS

■ brainstorming	Collect as many ideas as possible.
■ currencies	What is cheap for you to give and valuable for the other to receive, and vice versa?
■ chunking down	Break the problem down into smaller parts. Is it possible to fix part of the problem if not all of it?
■ chunking up	Look at the problem from a wider perspective.
■ more information	If answers will not come, do you need more information?
■ what if?	Ask yourself: if we find no solution, what alternatives do I have?

Box 24.3 gives ways of generating solutions. This is the creative part of problem solving. It can be difficult to come up with a good solution right away, which is why patience and determination are important ingredients in conflict management.

(c) *Evaluate the possible solutions.* Generally, it will become apparent when to move on to this step. Remember: you are trying to reach a good, workable solution, not just any solution.

Are there any flaws in any of the possible solutions? Any reasons why a solution might not work? Will it be too hard to carry out or implement? Is it fair to each party?

(d) *Decide together.* Choose the solution most acceptable to both parties. Shared commitment is essential. Don't make the mistake of trying to persuade or push a solution onto the other party. If people don't freely choose a solution, chances are it will not be carried out.

Plan the implementation of the solution together and don't forget to evaluate it after it has been in operation for a while. If it isn't working, begin the problem-solving process again at step 1.

SKILLS FOR MANAGING CONFLICT SUCCESSFULLY

Two skills are essential for opening a discussion. The first is the ability to prepare and deliver a framing statement. The second is the ability to give good information by stating your point of view assertively—for example, with an 'I' message.

The ability to hear the other's point of view, respect it and respond to it requires skills of empathy, listening, clarifying and summarising. Problem solving to reach a mutually acceptable outcome needs assertiveness, empathy, negotiation and idea-generating skills.

FROM THEORY TO PRACTICE

Have you managed the conflict well? Here are four ways to tell:
1. You are both satisfied with the outcome.
2. You can work even better together now.
3. You will be able to manage any further conflicts more effectively.
4. You have a deeper appreciation and understanding of each other.

Discussion skills, such as self-disclosure about how the conflict is affecting you, or what you are feeling or thinking right now as you are discussing the conflict, can often help to bring things back into perspective. It can also result in a similar response from the other party and thus lead to greater understanding of the issues involved in the conflict. The same is true for relationship statements, where you express what you think or feel about the person with whom you are in conflict. For example, you might say, 'I'm really uncomfortable discussing this with you (self-disclosure) because I'm worried that it will damage the good working relationship we have and which I'd really like to see continue (relationship statement).'

Stick to behaviour descriptions so the other person doesn't feel under attack. Describing your feelings, perhaps with an 'I' message, can encourage the other party to see things from your point of view and increase their willingness to collaborate. Making an interpretive response (to check your understanding) is similar to active listening. It is particularly useful when the other person is using jargon or speaking indirectly or vaguely.

TIPS FOR SETTLING CONFLICTS

- *Keep all 'weapons' out of reach.* Then you won't be tempted to use them. Pulling rank, threatening, point scoring or hiding behind a clearly outdated or irrelevant corporate 'policy' only add fuel to the fire.
- *Search for common ground.* Once you have identified something you both want, or want to avoid, you have set the scene for working together, not against each other. Once you have found your common ground, work towards it.
- *Stick to the facts.* Becoming personal really heats up the conflict!
- *Bring in a trusted third party.* Mediators can often help both parties to clarify the issues and deal with the conflict calmly and objectively.
- *Try tackling the easier problems first,* not as a way of avoiding the tough ones but because the progress you make can encourage you to find solutions to the tough problems too.
- *Keep early discussions informal.* It's always easier to 'toughen up' than 'soften down'.
- *Emphasise the relationship.* If you are both clear that you want a continued good relationship, then you will work harder towards that end.
- *Limit each discussion to a few issues,* otherwise the 'mountain' will appear insurmountable.
- *Keep a long-term view in mind.* This helps to keep things in perspective.
- *Look for and foster flexibility and creativity.* How can you *both* get what you want? Don't limit yourself by grasping the first solution that suggests itself.

THE **BIG** PICTURE

After you've resolved a conflict, review it and learn from it.
- What caused it? Have you removed the cause so it won't occur again?
- What helped you resolve it? What got in the way?
- What signs were there that the conflict was brewing? Would identifying and addressing it earlier have helped? What could you have done? What should you bear in mind for the future?

- *Listen carefully and summarise frequently.* Summarise the other's point of view, especially before disagreeing. Make sure the other person feels you have heard and understood their point of view.
- *Adopt a problem-solving approach.* See the dispute as a problem to be solved rather than a battle to be won.
- *Test your assumptions.* Bring them out into the open and verify them. State your position and your understanding of the other's position clearly. Making assumptions about what the other party does or doesn't know or want can be a recipe for going round in circles.
- *Respect the other party.* Putdowns and personal attacks damage the relationship and lessen the likelihood of successful resolution. Make no demands on the other person.
- *Agree on the process.* Right at the beginning, agree how you will approach the conflict and the discussions.
- *Agree on the content.* Make sure you are both talking about the same thing.

GRIEVANCES

Handling **grievances** is an important supervisory duty. Grievances are complaints or dissatisfactions that an employee has *formally registered* with the supervisor, some other manager or the union. They usually arise when an employee thinks an injustice has been done and when more subtle, less formal expressions of dissatisfaction have been continually ignored.

Grievances usually start with an employee informally expressing a complaint or dissatisfaction, usually to the supervisor but sometimes directly to the shop steward or someone from the HR department. Whether or not the complaint actually has substance, the employee probably genuinely feels it is true. Supervisors who treat such complaints as 'whingeing' are inviting them to blow up into full-sized grievances. The best time to reach a mutually satisfactory solution is early on, before frustration, anger and bad feelings escalate.

If the grievance is initially between the employee and the supervisor, and the supervisor's answer does not satisfy the employee, he or she may then go 'up the line', following the organisation's formal grievance process.

Dealing with grievances

If employees genuinely believe they are being treated unfairly and bring the problem to you, be relieved! They trust you enough to come to you with a problem, which is far better than brooding and saying nothing.

- *Listen attentively to the grievance.* Give the employee your full attention. Ask questions to clarify and to check your understanding. Complaints may be symptoms of a deeper problem, so be sure to listen carefully to get to the heart of the matter.
- *Give the best explanation possible.* If you need further information, say so, and then make sure you follow through.
- *Treat the employee and the complaint seriously* and with respect. It has probably taken a great deal of courage for the employee to come to you. If you ignore a complaint or brush it aside, it is likely to blow up into something more serious.
- *Assure the employee that you will look into the matter and take appropriate action.* Then keep your promise. Make sure you deal with it fairly and impartially.

- *If possible, let employees check some things out for themselves.* This will often relieve their anxiety that they are being treated unfairly. Seeing is believing.
- *Be prepared to talk at length.* Something is wrong somewhere when a grievance is expressed, and you need to get to the bottom of it.
- *Gather information before reaching a decision.* Only when you have the facts straight will you be in a position to make a sound decision. 'Decide in haste, repent at leisure' holds true here.
- *Document employee grievances.* Keep full and accurate notes of any conversations that occur and actions taken, as well as their outcomes. You might use a special 'grievances' file, your diary or a daily log book.

Reducing grievances

You may find that complaints revolve around certain things (often rules and regulations, seniority, work assignments or job evaluation). If this is the case, you may be able to take preventive action or at least pay special attention to these areas.

Be sensitive to any situation that might cause a grievance and try to correct it. Keep people informed about what's going on in their department and in the organisation generally and abreast of any impending changes and the reasons for them. Discuss work-related matters and listen to people's opinions.

COUNSELLING POOR PERFORMANCE—IT'S YOUR RESPONSIBILITY

Just as an organisation and its management team have duties towards employees and other stakeholders, employees also have responsibilities to their employer. These revolve around carrying out their duties honestly and to the best of their ability and training.

As we saw in Chapter 8, supervisors should make expectations about the standard of performance clear to each employee. If an employee's performance is unsatisfactory, you have a responsibility to recognise and resolve the problem. If you fail to take corrective action, you're only adding to the problem. You will probably find that you can resolve most work performance problems constructively, to the benefit of everyone concerned, providing you address them promptly. Box 24.4 lists some of the signs of poor performance.

FROM THEORY TO PRACTICE

Most organisations have procedures for dealing with grievances. Know what they are and use them correctly and impartially. Better still, operate a department where conflict is less likely to develop by:
- removing temptations to break the rules;
- setting a good example;
- expecting and maintaining high standards;
- maintaining employees' dignity;
- treating everyone impartially;
- keeping calm and not acting in anger; and
- being a good leader!

SIGNS OF POOR PERFORMANCE

- *Absenteeism*, multiple instances of unauthorised leave, excessive sick leave, a higher absenteeism rate than other employees and frequent unscheduled short-term absences. These can be even more problematic when absences follow a pattern, such as after a day off, at the beginning of shifts or where improbable reasons for absences or tardiness are given.
- *'On-the-job' absenteeism*. This can include long coffee breaks, more absences from work stations than the job requires, frequent trips to the rest area or spasmodic work quality.
- *Reporting-to-work* problems, such as arriving at, or returning to, work in an obviously abnormal condition, arriving late or leaving early.
- *Difficulty in concentration*, e.g. an employee continually forgets instructions, takes too long over jobs or has to make a greater than normal effort to complete a task.
- *Lowered job efficiency*, such as missed deadlines, mistakes due to inattention or poor judgment, wasting materials, lack of care for the customer's or the organisation's equipment, failing to follow safety or standard operating procedures, and falling productivity or quality.
- *Poor relationships* with supervisors, management, colleagues or customers. These may include overreaction to real or imagined criticism, wide mood swings and avoiding colleagues or supervisor.
- *Failure to observe the organisation's regulations, policies and procedures.*

Is it always a work performance problem?

We discussed the **85:15 rule** in Chapter 8. This rule shows us that, 85% of the time, poor performance is outside the employee's control. Often what looks like a work performance problem is not really one at all. As Box 24.5 shows, there are many causes of poor performance and employees often struggle on despite them, trying to do the best they can. Less than 15% of cases of poor performance result from employees having a pressing personal or motivational problem that is sapping their ability or willingness to perform their job in the short term.

So investigate carefully. Before you jump into a performance counselling session, ask yourself these four questions:

1. Is there a clear standard of performance and is the employee aware of it?
2. Is there a clear and measurable or quantifiable deviation from the performance standard?
3. Has the employee been fully trained in the job?
4. Is there anything in the environment, such as poor tools, insufficient information or time, inadequate materials or awkward procedures, that makes good performance difficult?

FIVE KEYS TO GOOD PERFORMANCE

Chapter 8 detailed the five conditions that must be present for people to do their jobs well:

What to   We must know what is expected of us in terms of clear standards and targets to achieve.

Want to   We must be motivated to perform well. This means we must know that the job is worth doing and worth doing well and that this will be worth our effort. We must also believe that we can do the job well (see Chapter 21).

BOX
24.5

POSSIBLE CAUSES OF POOR PERFORMANCE

85% of the time
- poor or insufficient training or experience
- faulty tools, equipment or materials
- cumbersome procedures or systems
- unclear or unspecified performance standard
- performance standard not understood or seen as unimportant
- poor performance is as rewarding as good performance
- lack of information
- lack of time
- poor job placement
- poor teamwork or disharmony in the team

15% of the time
- personal problems
- acts of God
- poor motivation or morale

How to   We must know *how to* do the job. This requires experience to reinforce our training, skills and knowledge.

Chance to The necessary tools, equipment, materials, work systems and other job conditions such as time and information must support us.

Led to   We must also have leadership that inspires us with a compelling vision, coaches us to get the best out of us and sets a good example.

Figure 24.3 illustrates this path to good performance. Who is primarily responsible for putting these five keys in place? You guessed it—the supervisor!

OFFERING FEEDBACK ON PERFORMANCE

Smart supervisors know how to use feedback to make sure productive behaviour continues and to change unproductive behaviour. They know how to provide feedback in a positive way, so that the recipient feels supported, valued and encouraged.

You can give employees three types of feedback: *positive, negative* and *none at all.* Positive and negative feedback can be *general* or *specific*. These are summarised in Box 24.6 while Box 24.7 gives some examples of each type of feedback.

Unless it involves the whole team, offer feedback in private. Make sure you stick to facts, and state them objectively and calmly; don't criticise someone's character or abilities. If you give feedback in a confrontational or impolite way, you are likely to receive a defensive response and create bad feelings. Show how what you're asking will meet the organisation's needs or will help the employee in some way. Describe the effects, too. For example, telling someone it is rude to hold side conversations is likely to draw a less cooperative response than explaining that side conversations distract you from the meeting and make it hard for you to concentrate. Make sure your comments clearly describe the behaviour that concerns you.

Keep your feedback non-coercive. You can't force people to change; you can only bring something to their attention. Offer improvement suggestions rather than criticism; think of it as sharing ideas and information rather than giving orders or advice. Choose your words to show the receiver that you are both on the same side.

'We can't make someone do better by making them feel bad.'

FIGURE 24.3   THE PATH TO GOOD PERFORMANCE

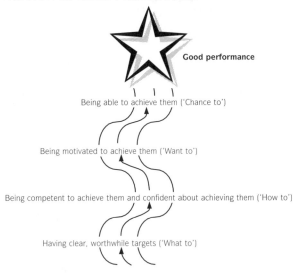

Good performance

Being able to achieve them ('Chance to')

Being motivated to achieve them ('Want to')

Being competent to achieve them and confident about achieving them ('How to')

Having clear, worthwhile targets ('What to')

BOX 24.6   TYPES OF FEEDBACK

	General	*Specific*
Positive feedback	Feedback you give employees just for being themselves. This important supervisory tool helps develop positive working relationships. It makes people feel good and raises their self-confidence and self-esteem. It is excellent for general motivation and morale and for maintaining a positive work climate.	Give this when someone has done something you want, such as meeting a performance target. As a rule, behaviour that gets positive specific reinforcement will be repeated. Use it to ensure that performance standards continue to be met and to increase employees' *task readiness levels* (see Chapter 20).
Negative feedback	Feedback given to people whatever they do, right or wrong, good or bad. It makes people feel unimportant and lowers morale and self-esteem.	Negative reinforcement given for a specific action. The 'hot stove principle' (discussed in Chapter 8) is based on specific negative feedback. It can help reduce or eliminate the behaviour in question. The best specific negative feedback is *constructive feedback*. State precisely what is wrong and offer an improvement suggestion. This strengthens relationships and helps people perform a task better.
No feedback at all	This is dangerous because it gives people the idea that neither they nor their performance matters. The supervisor who ignores an employee or walks by their desk each morning without saying 'Good morning!' is guilty of this. When this happens, performance, motivation and even self-esteem are likely to fall.	

EXAMPLES OF FEEDBACK

Supervisor says	Type of feedback
Beth, it's great to have you on the team.	Positive general
Beth, your productivity met all our targets again this week. I really appreciate the contribution you make to our department.	Positive specific
Beth, you'll need to try harder.	Negative general
Beth, you're doing that wrong.	Negative specific
Beth, do it *this* way.	Constructive
Supervisor walks past the employee's work station and ignores her.	No feedback at all
Supervisor continually ignores targets being met or not being met.	No feedback at all

No matter how constructive, negative feedback can still sting. So be considerate and don't crush the employee's confidence or enthusiasm. Offer it in the most helpful way you can. Criticise actions or work, not people. Make sure you are giving feedback on something the employee can do something about. A person can't help having a high-pitched voice or a nervous giggle and probably can't do much to change it. Choose an appropriate time to offer feedback. Don't wait too long, but make sure the person has the time to listen and will be in the right frame of mind. And don't give too much information all at once; generally, it's better to deal with one issue at a time.

How often should supervisors give feedback?

> 'Feedback is the wheel that moves performance forward.'

Don't wait for a monthly meeting or an annual performance appraisal to tell people they are doing a good job or to suggest areas for improvement. Address both poor and acceptable job performance every chance you get. If you don't have much opportunity, make it! Supervisors who only tell people when they're doing something wrong are less effective than supervisors who also provide recognition and encouragement for work well done.

Receiving feedback

> 'What's good for the goose is good for the gander.'

Supervisors also need to be able to receive feedback. People will soon stop listening to the feedback you offer them if they aren't allowed to offer you any! Feedback is a two-way street. Box 24.8 shows the main points to bear in mind when giving and receiving feedback.

FROM THEORY TO PRACTICE

Avoid saying, 'You did a great job, but ...' People know when they hear 'but' that bad news is about to follow. Instead, say 'and'. 'You did a great job, and one thing you could do to improve it is ...'

FROM THEORY TO PRACTICE

To build or activate new behaviours—with new recruits or transfers or when retraining existing staff, for example—use a lot of positive specific feedback. Gradually reduce it to maintain behaviours once they are established.

BOX
24.8

GIVING AND RECEIVING FEEDBACK

When offering feedback
- Keep it factual and non-personal
- Describe the behaviour and its effects objectively
- Make it non-coercive (don't force!)
- Be considerate
- Make sure it is actionable
- Keep away from hearsay
- Make it timely
- Offer it frequently

When receiving feedback
- Don't argue, just listen
- Check that you have understood
- Don't explain, defend or justify
- Don't 'give as good as you've got'
- Thank the speaker for bringing it to your attention
- Take it on board and think about it
- Make any changes you feel are needed

PERFORMANCE GAPS

Attendance and timekeeping, safety, behaviour towards co-workers, the supervisor or customers, care of tools and equipment, productivity and quality of work are common performance shortfalls that supervisors must address. Before this can happen, they need to be measured. A **performance gap** is a shortfall in the expected performance that can be precisely detailed and measured or quantified in some way.

First, you need a clear **performance measure** or standard against which to measure the employee's current performance. Then you measure the current performance. If there is a clear deviation from the standard, you have a performance gap. You then discuss this with the employee to establish the reasons for the gap so that corrective action can be taken.

> 'There's no point telling people what they're doing "wrong"
> if you don't tell them what "right" looks like.'

This gap is very important because it will form the basis of your performance counselling discussion. It is a mandatory starting point: *performance improvement always begins with establishing the performance gap.*

What should performance gaps cover?

A clear performance gap can be about one of two things. The first is the *behaviour* of the employee—what the employee says or does. This means that you should see it with your eyes or hear it with your ears. For example, you may expect an employee dealing directly with customers to greet them with eye contact and a friendly greeting. Instead of observing this, you may instead see that the employee does not look up from her paperwork and says to the customer 'Yes?' This is a performance gap. The expectations of eye contact and a friendly greeting are not being met.

If the performance gap is not about behaviour, it should be about a *work target* that is not being met. This target should be achievable and measurable. For example, you may expect employees to acknowledge and greet customers within 16 seconds. Taking longer than this, perhaps by leaving the customer waiting while they finish paperwork, is a performance gap.

Ensure that performance gaps are about either behaviour or a work target not being met. This will help you to be both specific and clear in your discussions with the employee. You will be able to give the employee feedback on performance objectively and factually, without personal attacks or criticisms, and in a way that will not produce defensiveness. Then you can work together to solve the problem constructively. Giving performance feedback that is neither soft nor rude, but *clear,* makes for a cooperative approach to performance improvement. Box 24.9 presents examples of performance gaps.

What about attitude?

We often talk about a person's 'attitude' as a shorthand way of describing characteristics that we do or do not like. We may say: 'Jackie has a good attitude … Kit has a bad attitude.' While this may mean something to the speaker, it generally has no value in terms of clear and accurate communication. What 'attitude' means to one person is quite different from what it means to another.

In addition, if we say to an employee: 'You haven't got the right attitude' or 'You've got a bad attitude', they probably won't know what we're talking about. After all, would you set out to go to work with the 'wrong attitude'?

Furthermore, supervisors are interested in what people do. When employees fail to do what they are paid for, action should be taken to correct the situation. What people *think* is their own business, as long as they perform their duties effectively.

THE CYCLE OF PERFORMANCE IMPROVEMENT

Figure 24.4 shows a systematic sequence for improving the work performance of an employee.

BOX 24.9 EXAMPLES OF PERFORMANCE GAPS

Behavioural

- Keeping customers waiting more than five minutes without acknowledging them.
- Speaking abruptly and curtly to customers or colleagues, especially during busy times.
- Going for a smoke instead of helping team mates complete their work.
- Having to be reminded two or three times a day to complete routine work.

Targets not met

- Arriving 10–15 minutes late two to three times a week for the past six weeks.
- Producing the last three reports two days late.
- Not meeting the 95% accuracy target on documents; producing an average of 80% accuracy for the past two weeks.
- Not answering the telephone within four rings and not identifying the department or saying your name.

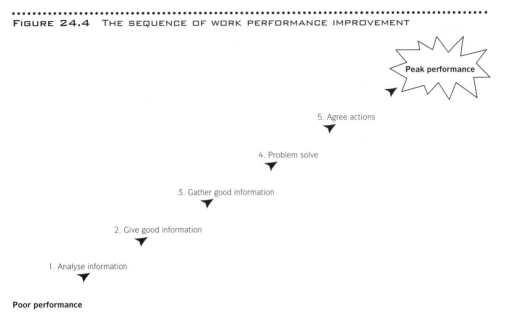

FIGURE 24.4 THE SEQUENCE OF WORK PERFORMANCE IMPROVEMENT

1. *Analyse your information.* Before sitting down and discussing the situation with the employee, you need to do some thinking. You need to know and be able to describe the precise *behaviour* you want people to display or the precise *target* you want them to reach. You then need to be able to describe the employee's precise behaviour or their current performance standard. What is being done well? What is the employee's **task readiness level** and what leadership style does it suggest (see Chapter 20)? Where are the performance gaps? You must be able to document and describe any performance gaps clearly in specific *behavioural* or *measurable* terms. Make sure your description of the problem will be factual and non-arguable, and not based on hearsay. This will ensure that you are being fair, objective and clear in your communications. Gather your facts and prepare for the discussion.
2. *Give good information.* Now it's time to sit down with the employee and discuss the situation. This does not mean starting an argument or walking up to the employee and saying, 'Clean up your act or you're out!' It means sitting down calmly with the employee and discussing the problem.

    Set the scene by beginning your discussion with a **frame**. Present constructive information, describing the performance gap clearly and explaining why it's important that the employee reaches the required standard of behaviour or targets. Provide information in a way that will build the employee's self-esteem and make it clear you are interested only in improving performance, not in seeking to apportion blame or to punish. Use language that shows you are taking a 'we' approach; that is, you will be looking at and trying to sort out the problem together in a cooperative, win–win manner. Then switch gears to listen to what the employee has to say.

What if the employee doesn't accept that a performance gap exists or that it presents a problem? Keep repeating your main message; don't be sidetracked. Stay focused on the performance gap and use supportive messages that make it clear your intention is to help the employee improve performance. Try stating the problem as a goal and focus the discussion on how you can help the employee achieve it.

As with any interview, ensure that you won't be interrupted and that the interview will be free of other distractions. Have any information you need to hand, such as the employee's actual production or quality figures compared with the targets, or the employee's actual timekeeping record.

3. *Gather good information.* Listen to the employee's point of view without interruption. Ask questions. Try to see things as the employee sees them. (Remember, this doesn't mean you have to agree, just see things their way for a while.) People need to feel they've been given a fair hearing.

4. *Problem solve.* Try to find the cause of the poor performance by working through the five keys. What's preventing the employee from reaching the required standard?

5. *Agree actions.* Now focus on the future and a solution to the problem. Decide what steps you will each need to take to improve the employee's performance. You may need to

provide further training or on-the-job coaching of some sort. You may need to restructure the job so that it provides the employee with more challenge, or delegate one or two extra duties to develop the employee further and increase motivation. You might need to examine and rearrange poorly designed work systems or provide more accurate or timely information. Your role here is to help the employee, in any way that is reasonable, to improve their performance so that it reaches the required standard. Since you are aiming at commitment, not mere compliance, it is usually best to allow the employee to come up with the solution. You may or may not need to offer suggestions or ideas and, as with any problem solving, the more solutions you consider, the better the chosen course of action is likely to be.

Agree how you will monitor the performance improvement. Simply holding a performance counselling discussion isn't the end of the story. Monitor the employee's performance to ensure that the agreed improvement is achieved. Beth and her supervisor might agree to meet next week and go over her accuracy figures. John and his supervisor might agree that he will keep a record of what time he arrives for the next week and meet to review it with his supervisor half-way through the week. Or the supervisor might know that John is a dependable employee and decide to allow him some leeway in his arrival times for the next week (only) provided he completes his work; this might mean he will work a bit later at the end of the day or work through part of his breaks if necessary.

When the employee shows improvement, offer specific positive feedback, so they'll know you've noticed. If you don't do this, the employee will think that performance doesn't matter after all, and it may drop off again. Positive support and encouragement, showing that you have noticed and appreciated the improvement, will ensure that it continues. Rome wasn't built in a day and neither is excellent performance.

If the employee has not made the expected improvement, go back to step 4 and look harder for the cause of the poor performance. If this happens several times with the same performance gap, you may consider implementing the dismissal procedure (discussed later in this chapter) or transferring the employee to a job more suited to their skills and abilities.

Summarise what you have both agreed and who will do what. Part on a positive note. Ken Blanchard and Spencer Johnson, in *The One Minute Manager*, advise that you stand up and make fleeting physical contact—squeeze the employee's shoulder or elbow. This does wonders for an employee who is feeling a bit bruised and battered.

Three possible reactions

How might the employee react? Here are three likely reactions.

1. The employee may simply say something like: 'Okay, sorry, I hadn't realised. I'll make sure to do that in future.' This will take you directly to a brief step 5.
2. The problem may be complex and you will need to spend time thoroughly exploring the problem (step 4).
3. The employee may deny or not accept that there is a problem. Keep giving good information (step 2) until they understand. If this fails, switch to the change/time/consequence formula:

'If not this change by this time, then this will be the consequence.'

If you need to do this, the consequence is usually a formal discipline or dismissal process. Say something like: 'Beth, I need to be able to rely on you to produce at 95% accuracy or better. If you continue to miss accuracy targets, I will need to begin a formal dismissal process. I hope that won't be necessary. Let's meet on Friday to review your figures. If they haven't improved, I will have to give you a formal warning. Beth, you could lose your job because of this. If you need some help from me or if there's something I should know, now is the time to say.' Make it clear that the employee has two choices: continued poor performance (and possible loss of employment) or improved work performance.

THE AIMS OF A PERFORMANCE COUNSELLING INTERVIEW

You have two overall goals: to maintain or enhance the employee's self-esteem and to help the employee accept and correct their performance shortfall.

During these discussions, make sure you do the following:
- point out the specific performance gap;
- ensure the employee understands it and agrees that it exists and is a problem;
- explore the possible reasons for the performance gap together; and
- agree what actions need to be taken so that performance expectations will be met in future.

Performance improvement discussions are best held soon after work performance deteriorates. The longer you leave a problem, the more difficult it becomes to rectify. To be successful, performance counselling interviews need to be undertaken skilfully and without hostility or animosity (see Box 24.10). They need to be carried out in a fair and consistent way. The employee must clearly understand:
- what the performance gap is;
- the standard of performance required;
- that you are prepared to help them achieve that standard;
- that nothing less than meeting the performance standard will do;
- that the choice of whether or not they improve their performance is theirs; and
- the consequences of continued poor performance.

FROM THEORY TO PRACTICE

What if the employee is totally uncooperative? Try having her or him write short weekly reports under the headings:
- What I've achieved this week.
- What went right?
- What went wrong?
- Do I need any help?

These reports should take less than 15 minutes to write and five minutes to read.

BOX 24.10   SKILLS NEEDED IN PERFORMANCE COUNSELLING INTERVIEWS

1 Give good information
Skills required
- Assertiveness
- Framing
- 'I' messages
- Non-evaluative behaviour descriptions
- Self-disclosure

2 Gather good information
Skills required
- Empathy
- Acknowledgment listening
- Active listening
- Summarising
- Clarifying

- Broken record
- Fogging
- Negative inquiry
- Asking open questions
- Asking clarifying questions

3 Problem solving
Skills required
- Problem solving
- Coaching
- Creating a spirit of 'win–win'

4 Agreeing actions
- Planning
- Gaining commitment and cooperation

TWO KEY SKILLS

Two key skills in opening a performance counselling session are (1) framing the discussion and (2) providing 'I' messages.

Frames

We often say 'I shouldn't have jumped into that' if we have handled a discussion poorly. This is usually the result of giving too little thought to the 'whats, hows and whys' of a conversation before we begin it. Jumping into conversations can stop us from achieving the outcome we want.

The opposite of 'jumping into' a conversation is to frame it. Just as the frame around a picture defines the limits of the picture and draws our attention to it, a **framing statement** sets the limits for and draws attention to what will be discussed. A framing statement begins a conversation by presenting the 'whats', 'hows', 'whys', 'whens', 'wheres' or expected outcome.

For example, to introduce a performance counselling interview, you might first discuss how to go about talking: 'Before talking about your productivity rate, I suggest we first review the required standards. Then I'd like to move on to the possible reasons why you are not meeting them consistently. How does that sound to you?' Or you might state the positive outcome you're looking for: 'James, I want you to be a top loans officer and I'd like to discuss some ideas that may help you.'

You might *establish what will be focused on and what won't*: 'Today we won't be talking about your overall job performance, which is excellent, but only about the incident with Fred last Tuesday.' Another way to frame a conversation is to *review the key events that have a bearing on it*: 'We have spoken twice over the past month about production targets not being achieved, and yesterday's figures were also below target.'

You can also *present your expectations for the interview and check whether the other person's expectations are similar or different*: 'We've had several conversations to the effect that your level of customer service is generally below expectations; today I want to discuss actions we will both need to take to turn this around. All right?' Or you might say something like: 'Annette, I'd like to explain how I see things. You may see the situation differently and that's fine.' You may decide to present an overview of the different kinds of information you hope to discuss: 'During this meeting, I would like to review your safety record and your timekeeping and formulate an action plan for improving both of them.' Box 24.11 lists some typical topics for framing statements.

Since you are handling 'negative' information such as another person's unsatisfactory performance, it is vital to begin these interviews with a frame. This will ensure you have analysed and organised your thoughts and information, and help you to clarify your purpose and the way you will go about achieving it. It will help you to set the scene for a productive discussion.

'I' messages

'I' messages, and 'I' language in general, can be tremendously helpful in performance improvement interviews. As we learned in Chapter 19, they are assertive, and allow you to state your concerns cleanly and clearly. They make it less likely that employees will 'counterattack' or become defensive and more likely that they will agree to improve their performance or be willing to work cooperatively with you in seeking ways to improve it.

BOX 24.11 TYPICAL TOPICS FOR FRAMING STATEMENTS

History	Review the events in the past which have led up to the current interview and set the context for it.
Problem	State aspects or areas of the problem or performance gap and summarise relevant facts.
Boundaries	State which areas of performance will be discussed and which will not.
Feeling	State how you feel about the employee's behaviour (e.g. disappointed, worried).
Consequences	State the consequences to you or the employee of the performance gap.
Purposes	State the expected outcome of the interview.
Next steps	State what you will do if this attempt to bring about change does not work.
Positive intent	Express the positive outcome you're looking for.
Problem-solving steps	State the steps you want to take with the employee to bring about the required improvement.

FROM THEORY TO PRACTICE

Keep your frames short, to one or two sentences.

To give an 'I' message you need to be able to do three things:

1. clearly describe the unacceptable behaviour or the performance target not being met using non-emotive language;
2. describe your own feelings in response to this behaviour or failure to meet targets; and
3. explain why the performance shortfall matters.

Box 24.12 shows an example of an 'I' message. You will see that it is in three parts. The first part of the statement describes the performance gap in terms that are specific, not fuzzy; for example, 'When you are ten minutes late ...' is specific, while 'When you dawdle ...' is fuzzy and judgmental. Keep the description observable and factual, not a conjecture or guess; for example, 'You left work 15 minutes early' is a factual, observed behaviour, while 'You don't seem to care about your job these days' is speculation.

Your description must also be objective; it should avoid character assassination, absolutes such as 'never', 'always' or 'constantly', profanities and judgmental words (e.g. 'lackadaisical' or 'careless'). Keep the description as brief and concise as possible, directed to your real concerns, not substitutes for them, and directed to the employee, not a second party.

The second part of an 'I' statement deals with *your feelings* in response to the behaviour or failure to meet targets. It discloses the effect the performance shortfall has on you—not what you *think* about it, but how you *feel* about it. For example, if someone continually arrives at work two, three, ten or 15 minutes late, you might feel angry, irritated, annoyed, or worried about the effect it will have on the rest of the team. The third part of the statement deals with *consequences* and *clarifies the effect* of the performance shortfall on you, the work team, the organisation or the employee. It does so specifically, openly and honestly (see Box 24.13).For example, you may say: 'Jo, you're not wearing your safety goggles again. This really upsets me and I'm concerned about the example this could set for the rest of the team. What can we do about this problem?'

For straightforward performance gaps, where the solution is obvious, you could state precisely what you want to happen instead of what is happening, following the rules for

---

BOX 24.12   **EXAMPLE OF AN 'I' MESSAGE** ••

1. What you saw or heard   Behaviour
           or   *or*
   What you think the facts are   Target not met
   - *When you speak before I've finished ...*
           or
   - *My records show that you have been absent for six Mondays out of the last 15.*

2. How you feel about it   Your response
   - *I am/get/feel uncomfortable/annoyed/angry/concerned/irritated ...*

3. Why it matters   Tangible effects
   - *This means ...*
           or
   - *Because ...*

BOX
24.13

SUMMARY OF 'I' MESSAGES

···

1. Description
Non-judgmental descriptions of behaviour
- Specific
- Observable—not inferential
- Objective—not judgmental
- Brief
- Of real issues
- To the right person

2. Feelings
Disclosure of your feelings
- Non-judgmental
- What you feel—not what you think

3. Consequences
- Concrete
- Honest

offering constructive feedback. For example, you could say: 'Jo, you're not wearing your safety goggles again. This really upsets me. I need you to *always* wear them when you come into this area. How about helping me out here?'

Notice that the final question in both examples moves you from giving good information to gathering good information by giving the employee an opportunity to have a say.

DOCUMENTING PERFORMANCE COUNSELLING DISCUSSIONS

Proper documentation is an essential part of **performance counselling**. It provides an authentic record that will avoid the confusion of, for example, trying to evaluate an employee's work performance from memory.

Keep written factual records, or summaries, of all performance counselling discussions. Include the date, time and place, outcome and any other persons present (such as someone from the HR department or a union representative). Also note in a specific, objective and precise way the specific performance gap, how long the problem has existed, where and how often it occurs, and your specific evidence of the performance gap. Make sure the performance gap is work-related. File these in the employee's personal file or your work diary. If the employee's performance does not improve and you must take further action, such as dismissal, this documentation will be vitally important.

You may also want to record any above-average performance. This is useful at performance appraisal and salary review time.

THE HOT STOVE PRINCIPLE

As we saw in Chapter 8, many supervisors have had success with the '**hot stove principle**' of discipline. They know from experience that it isn't always necessary to sit down with an employee and have a lengthy discussion about performance shortfalls, especially when the employee is clearly capable of giving you the performance you require. Three types of employee respond well to the 'hot stove': skilled and experienced employees (those with a high level of **task readiness**), newer employees who inadvertently break a rule and employees who are 'testing' rules to see how far they can go. The hot stove principle is particularly useful for safety and other straightforward infringements of company rules and policies.

The hot stove principle works well because it provides *advance warning*: you can see and feel from a distance that the stove is hot, so you know you will be burned. It is *immediate*:

if you touch the stove, you are burned, right away. It is *consistent*: every time you touch a hot stove you are burned. Finally, it is *impartial*: everyone who touches a hot stove will be burned because a hot stove plays no favourites.

To apply the hot stove principle, follow these four steps:

1. Make sure all employees are aware of the rules and policies they are expected to follow, the behaviours expected of them and targets they must meet.
2. Let them know immediately and specifically if performance is not up to the standards required.
3. Be consistent—every time performance is not up to scratch, address it. Don't let standards slip and don't make exceptions.
4. Set a good example and expect everyone else to follow it.

Make sure you don't use this technique if performance has dropped for reasons outside the employee's control or because of a personal problem. To do so under such circumstances would be seen as harsh, aggressive and unfair.

WHAT CAN GO WRONG?

Performance counselling needs skill, practice and patience. Too often, busy supervisors jump into performance counselling discussions without sufficient preparation or thought. Sometimes they hold them in the heat of the moment, without the benefit of facts: a clear performance target and a measurable or behavioural performance gap.

Inexperienced supervisors can fall into the trap of attacking the person instead of the problem, or conducting the interview in a way that is punitive, malicious and motivated by fear, hurt or anger. Instead of staying objective and factual and dealing with the issue, they become personal, argumentative and demoralising. They allow threats and personal insults to destroy goodwill and cooperation.

If led without skill or a real desire to improve performance, these discussions can leave resentment, anxiety, stress and frustration in their wake. Poor performance counselling interviews generally contribute to poor employee relations and a decline in motivation.

FROM THEORY TO PRACTICE

At one time or another, every supervisor has to deal with someone who used to be an excellent performer but has somehow 'fallen off the rails'. Here's what to do:

■ Acknowledge the change in performance. 'Scott, you've always been one of our top performers. Lately, you seem to have "lost your edge".'
■ Uncover any problems. 'Is anything the matter?'
■ Brainstorm solutions. 'Let's put our heads together and see what we can do.'
■ Show your faith. 'I really need you back up to speed and at your best again.'

A highly skilled employee probably knows what's wrong and what to do about it. They probably just need your support.

TERMINATION OF EMPLOYMENT

People can lose their job for four reasons: their performance is not up to the required standard; they do something seriously wrong (e.g. theft); their job is redundant; or there is insufficient work to keep them employed. Dismissing people is always unpleasant. Box 24.14 lists the grounds on which termination of employment is prohibited. This section deals with dismissing people for the first two reasons. The requirements outlined below apply to full-time and permanent part-time employees; they do not apply to contractors or casual employees of less than 12 months service with the organisation. We deal with continued unsatisfactory work performance first.

If you must dismiss someone for poor performance, it is essential that you adopt the performance counselling procedure described earlier, document it fully and follow the warning procedure set out in your workplace agreement.

First, make every attempt to help the employee improve her or his performance. At all times, your intent should be to bring performance to an acceptable level, thus developing a win–win situation where the employee's self-esteem and sense of job satisfaction are re-established and the organisation benefits from improved performance.

Your workplace agreement will set down clear guidelines to follow if it becomes necessary to dismiss an employee because of continued unsatisfactory work performance. Follow these precisely, taking the advice of your HR department if possible. The guidelines will probably incorporate the three-step procedure detailed below. This procedure dovetails with the performance counselling procedure.

If all your efforts fail and you must dismiss the employee, you should be able to avoid penalties for a harsh, unjust or unreasonable dismissal if you follow your agreed workplace procedure. Although recent legislation removes the strict focus on the procedure followed when dismissing an employee, it still requires the dismissal to be fair and reasonable and comply with the procedure outlined in your workplace agreement.

BOX **24.14**   **TERMINATION OF EMPLOYMENT IS PROHIBITED ON CERTAIN GROUNDS**

- Temporary absence due to illness or injury
- Union membership or participation in union activities during working hours with employer consent or outside working hours
- Non-membership of a union
- Acting or having acted or seeking to act as an employee representative
- Filing a complaint or participating in proceedings against an employer involving an alleged violation of laws or regulations
- Antidiscrimination reasons (race, colour, sex, sexual preference, age, physical or mental disability, marital status, family responsibilities, pregnancy, religion, political opinion, national extraction or social origin)
- Absence from work during maternity or other parental leave
- Refusal to negotiate an Australian Workplace Agreement or refusal to make, sign or vary the terms of, or extend one
- Constructive dismissal or forced resignation (where an employee is forced to resign, e.g. by making conditions intolerable or difficult for them)

Unfair dismissal claims

Employees must lodge any claim against their ex-employer for unfair dismissal within 21 days of that dismissal. If the claim is upheld, it can result in reinstatement and/or a judgment ordering a significant sum of money to be paid to the dismissed employee as compensation.

Such claims are made possible by legislation concerning unfair dismissal. Legislation was necessary because too many employers dismissed employees unfairly, unjustly or with undue harshness. These laws protect employees from unfair dismissal and also benefit organisations by attempting to ensure that unjust dismissals are not made, with resulting damage to employee morale and goodwill. They do not in any way remove or infringe on the responsibilities of supervisors to ensure that employees carry out their duties to agreed performance standards.

Dismissal procedure

Step 1: Verbal warning

Where an employee's work performance is measurably or demonstrably below an acceptable level, the initial warning will take the form of a performance counselling interview as described above. This should be a serious discussion between the supervisor and the employee. The intent of this session is to point out the performance gap, explore the reasons for it and jointly arrive at, and put into effect, a permanent plan of corrective action.

This two-way session will involve a verbal warning specifying the performance gap in behavioural terms or specifying the target not being met. Make sure the employee understands the consequences of continued poor performance—dismissal. Your discussion should result in an agreed plan of corrective action. You should allow a reasonable amount of time for the performance improvement to occur and provide any help (e.g. training) that might be necessary.

Some organisations require this first warning to be in writing. If yours does not, note the details of this discussion in your diary or in the employee's personal file. *Document it fully and carefully* as described above, because these notes could be used as legal evidence should the employee lodge an unfair dismissal complaint.

Step 2: Written warning

If the agreed performance improvement does not occur within the agreed time frame, hold another discussion and issue a second warning. Provide a written warning referring to the date of the previous verbal warning, the performance gap and the performance standard required. Also specify the time by which the improved performance should occur. (In New Zealand, write this letter 24 hours after this performance counselling interview takes place. This allows both parties to think things through.)

This letter should be on your organisation's letterhead or specially designed form. Make a copy of it for your own records and another copy for your HR department if there is one. Give the original to the employee. Ask the employee to sign the copy or copies. Box 24.15 shows a checklist of the information that a warning about poor performance should contain.

<table>
<tr><td>BOX
24.15</td><td>**FORMAT FOR A WRITTEN WARNING ABOUT POOR PERFORMANCE**
....</td></tr>
</table>

- *Letterhead*
- *Memo format*
  Subject: Work performance statement, first/second written warning
  Memo should be to: the employee, described by name and work location
- A copy should be kept for your own files and one given to the next level of management up or the personnel department if relevant.
- *Checklist*

When?	Times, dates, shifts.
How long?	How long has the problem existed? State this clearly and specifically. State dates of previous performance counselling discussions and what was agreed.
What?	Describe the performance gap in a factual, measureable, specific way.
Where?	Clearly and accurately describe locations.
Who? To whom?	Names of any other people involved.
Substantiated?	What material, sources, witnesses, facts, records, etc. are available to substantiate the performance gap?
Work-related?	Make sure it is work-related and does not include aspects that are not work-related.
Date?	Is the date of documentation included?

Caution: Be consistent in your warnings. Mean what you say and say what you mean. Follow through with your warnings. Take disciplinary action when required. Be specific and definite in your details to avoid confusion. Avoid getting into personalities and subjective observation and 'psychoanalysing'. Stick to the facts only.

Step 3: Final written warning

If performance does not improve and a further warning is required, repeat the procedure outlined in Step 2. Double-check the *five keys* to quality performance and productivity to make sure the employee is clear about what the required performance is (*what to*), understands that it is important to meet it (*want to*), has been trained correctly (*how to*), that nothing in the work environment is preventing acceptable performance (*chance to)* and that you are providing appropriate leadership (*led to*) (see also Chapter 8).

If, after the final written warning, the employee's performance remains below the required standard, termination of employment should result. This should be done in a formal interview. (Again, in New Zealand, the written warning and termination of employment should take place 24 hours after the final formal interview.)

If the employee is a member of a trade union, they may request that their union representative attend any or all of these interviews. Agree to this and consider inviting your manager to attend, too, to 'keep the numbers even'.

Because termination of employment is a serious business, many organisations take the precaution of requiring supervisors to talk it over with their manager before beginning the process. Others require the manager's involvement in each step along the way. Organisations with HR departments sometimes require that a senior HR officer or manager become involved at the verbal warning or first written warning stage. These are sensible precautions that safeguard the organisation and the supervisor as well as the employee. Be sure that you know, and follow, your organisation's procedures.

How long does the dismissal process take?

The dismissal process can take a few days or several months, depending on the nature of the performance shortfall. If an employee refuses to wear safety gear, for example, it need only take two or three days to complete the dismissal procedure. If complex remedial training or coaching is needed, the process may take several months to complete. The golden rule is that the length of time allowed for an improvement in performance to take place must be reasonable.

Instant dismissal

Most workplace agreements have agreed provisions for **instant dismissal** (termination without notice or pay in lieu of notice) in certain very specific instances. These often include theft of, or wilful damage to, company or customer property, physical violence against co-workers, supervisors, customers or others on company property or while on duty, substance abuse while on duty or blatantly unsafe conduct that would endanger the employee, others in the area or the public.

Many workplace agreements specify a 'cooling-off period' prior to instant dismissal and legal precedent in Australia requires that you give the employee an opportunity to respond. (A 'cooling-off period' of 24 hours is mandated by legislation in New Zealand.) You might, for example, send the employee off the premises immediately, asking them to return the next day to discuss the matter. After you have both had a chance to think, you may or may not decide to dismiss the employee. If an investigation will take longer than this, suspend the employee on full pay. If you have an HR department, discuss the matter with them; if not, discuss it with your manager and refer to your workplace agreement before taking any action.

FROM THEORY TO PRACTICE

Is instant dismissal appropriate? In most cases, it's better to investigate first. Here's how:

- Speak to any witnesses.
- Discuss it with the employee.
- Give the employee time to think and listen to what he or she has to say.
- Take the employee's comments into account in your deliberations.
- Ask yourself: was the misconduct serious by objective (not subjective) standards?
- Were the employee's actions provoked in any way, e.g. by other employees or by management?
- Are there any mitigating circumstances, e.g. the employee's personal situation?
- Is termination proportionate to the misconduct?

Follow your organisation's policy at all times.

PERFORMANCE COUNSELLING TIPS

- *Don't delay—address performance gaps when they arise.* Waiting and hoping they will go away usually only makes things worse.

- *Make it clear that your primary concern is satisfactory work performance.* Employees who think you're 'out to get them' or 'picking on them' won't be able to improve their performance. Make sure they understand that you are really trying to help them improve their performance. Being constructive is the key.
- *Interview in private.* Airing people's performance shortfalls in public is a sure way to lose cooperation and respect.
- *Clearly specify the performance you require.* Vague statements such as 'I expect more loyalty', 'You have a bad attitude' or 'You are uncooperative' are unlikely to bring about the desired performance. Instead, clearly specify the unacceptable behaviour: 'You failed to check the brake pads on that vehicle'; 'That invoice was difficult to read and not totalled correctly'; 'You did not follow our safety procedure of wearing safety glasses during that operation.'
- *Stick to clear behavioural or measurable facts.* This will help the employee hear what you're saying and safeguard you from showing favouritism, dragging up past mistakes or arguing over opinions.
- *Get agreement that there is a problem.* If the employee doesn't agree that work performance is below acceptable levels, you may not have provided a clear and measurable target or clear evidence of current performance levels. Or the employee may not understand why the performance target is important. Be sure of your facts: unless employees agree that their performance needs improving, they won't improve it.
- *Listen!* Railroading the employee probably won't result in long-term performance improvement. Listen carefully to what the employee has to say. Use active listening techniques to get to the heart of the matter and hear their point of view.
- *Don't attempt to 'psychoanalyse' an employee.* The only causes of poor work performance you need to diagnose are in the five keys, particularly inadequate training and environmental factors such as systems or equipment that hinder good performance.
- *Agree a specific performance target and monitoring schedule.* This will show you are serious about wanting to see an improvement.
- *Get a commitment to improve.* If people have made a verbal commitment, they are more likely to stick to it.
- *Don't make idle disciplinary threats.* If you say you will begin dismissal proceedings, do it. Keep calm and don't get personal.
- *Monitor carefully and follow up.* Acknowledge performance improvements. This will make sure the effort continues and performance goes on moving in the right direction.
- *Ensure the employee is aware that help is available to resolve any personal problems that may be causing the poor work performance.* Not many supervisors get through their careers without having to counsel an employee with a personal problem. And don't be afraid to say: 'This is too much for me. I think you should speak with a professional.'
- *Document performance gaps and performance improvement interviews.* Records can be important and they help to keep things in perspective.

PERSONAL COUNSELLING

Few people go through life without the occasional personal crisis, problem or difficulty. Often these affect their performance at work. At such times, supervisors may identify the need to have a personal chat with the employee, to provide a 'shoulder to cry on', to let the person 'talk it through' or to act as a 'sounding board'. This is **personal counselling**.

No one expects supervisors to be professional counsellors. Employee counselling from a supervisor's standpoint is really a helping and a listening activity.

What are the signs of a personal problem? Any change in a person's usual performance or behaviour is a sign that someone may be having personal difficulties. The most obvious sign is a slip in work performance. Any behaviour change is worthy of note—for example, when a normally cheerful person becomes quiet and glum or when a normally shy and reserved employee becomes unusually boisterous or talkative. There are also some obvious things to look out for if you suspect drug or alcohol abuse. If you take an interest in your team members, you will probably notice if something is wrong.

Personal counselling sessions

A personal counselling session is a talk in private during which you listen carefully to what the employee has to say and keep your own advice and suggestions to a minimum, especially early on in the meeting. Don't argue, criticise or judge. Instead, use your empathy to understand what you are being told from the employee's point of view.

A good counselling session may provide employees with sound advice. More often, talking things through helps them clarify their own thinking. Talking problems through with someone who is prepared to listen but not judge or give endless advice often helps to get things in perspective, whether the problems are personal or work related. Counselling sessions may also allow release of emotional tension.

Begin gently. Don't ask pointed questions, especially about personal issues. Instead, try to say something that will open up the conversation and get the person talking freely.

Counselling sessions take time—you may need to spend 30–40 minutes on it. Often more than one session will be needed.

Phases in personal counselling

Most counselling sessions proceed through three predictable phases: exploration, understanding and action. How quickly you move through these phases will vary with each situation, problem and employee.

1. The *exploration* phase begins when the employee tells you what the difficulty is. Show that you have heard and understood and that you are willing to listen further. Make **active listening** responses and concise, accurate *summaries* of the employee's situation as you understand it. Don't imply in any way that you think the employee is responsible for the difficulties, as this would effectively bring the counselling session to a halt. Other skills for the exploration phase include **acknowledgment listening**, asking **open questions** and **empathy**.

   Your aim in the exploration phase is to allow the employee to talk about the problem and view it from different angles. This exploration would include not just the down-side of the problem, but also the resources available to help.

2. *Understanding*, the second phase of a counselling session, begins when the employee has explored the problem and all its related issues and moves towards a better understanding of it. They can then identify helpful action to deal with it.

3. Often, problems cannot be solved, but only resolved, in that they can be lived with more easily or more effectively. The third phase, *action*, occurs when the employee begins to formulate realistic plans for dealing with the problem.

Should supervisors become involved in personal counselling?

Many personal problems affect work performance and when this happens you need to address it. It is unwise, however, to get too involved in giving advice about problems that are primarily personal. This is a good time to refer the employee to someone more qualified to deal with such problems, such as a professional counsellor.

Generally, it is better to be available as a sounding board, no matter what the problem, than to decide that it is beyond your scope and ignore it. Show that you care, but don't become too involved through advice-giving.

How involved you become is up to you. Some supervisors do not feel able to counsel, or they believe that 'people should leave their problems at home', while others see employee counselling as an important part of their role. Supervisors who view counselling as part of their job have two main reasons for this, both equally valid—they are morale and cost.

First, from a morale point of view, nothing is worse than for a person to be in some sort of trouble and feel that no help is at hand. Employees with problems can do more harm than good if they are not helped; they are difficult to motivate and supervise, and can demoralise other employees. When you show concern about employees' problems, you will be doing them a favour as well as making your own work easier and your department more efficient. Supervisors who can be effective counsellors usually have staff who are motivated to give something back, in whatever form they can, which often means greater loyalty and higher productivity.

Second, there is the cost factor. Anyone with a personal problem is unlikely to be performing optimally. It is easy to imagine a scene where an employee is thinking about a personal problem at the expense of some small but vital detail of their duties; this could be expensive in terms of quality or safety.

And there is certainly a cost attached to losing an employee through resignation. Not only has the organisation lost valuable experience, but there is a significant replacement cost: uniforms, training, time taken for interviewing, induction, job training and the cost of all those little errors that new recruits make while they learn the job. There is also the intangible, but potentially large, reputation cost to an organisation that becomes known for an uncaring attitude towards its employees. This makes it difficult to attract the right sort of employees. And research shows that a company's reputation affects buying behaviour.

What if I get out of my depth?

In counselling sessions your main job is to listen. Let people talk through their problems and how they can deal with them. If, after discussing the matter with the employee, you find that their difficulty is beyond your expertise, or that it will take too much of your time to deal with it no matter how skilled you are, this is the time to refer them to a professional counsellor.

Sometimes, of course, it is difficult to know when you should try to help an employee and when you should suggest that they seek professional counselling. If you are unsure about how to handle a situation, it is better to err on the side of caution and suggest professional help.

Most communities have professional counsellors, social workers and psychologists who can offer help to your employees. If you don't know of any, start by asking the company doctor, the employee's doctor or your own personal doctor for a recommendation.

Styles of personal counselling

The counselling style you choose will depend on the nature and sensitivity of the employee's problem, your own experience and/or knowledge of such problems, and your skills at counselling.

Figure 24.5 shows the counselling styles in a diagrammatic form. (Note the resemblance to the continuum of leadership styles discussed in Chapter 20.)

Counselling can be divided into three main types: directive, cooperative and non-directive. These are summarised in Figure 24.6. The difference between them lies mostly in the use of direction versus support that the counsellor provides.

FIGURE 24.5   CONTINUUM OF COUNSELLING STYLES

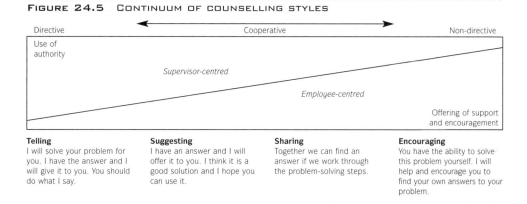

Telling	Suggesting	Sharing	Encouraging
I will solve your problem for you. I have the answer and I will give it to you. You should do what I say.	I have an answer and I will offer it to you. I think it is a good solution and I hope you can use it.	Together we can find an answer if we work through the problem-solving steps.	You have the ability to solve this problem yourself. I will help and encourage you to find your own answers to your problem.

FIGURE 24.6   TYPES OF PERSONAL COUNSELLING

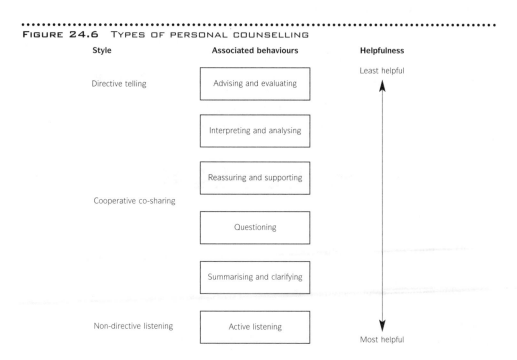

With *directive counselling*, you will be taking on the role of an expert, solving the employee's problem yourself, telling the person what to do and how to do it. This might be appropriate for simple, clear-cut problems and those where you have considerable personal experience, or where the employee has asked specifically for your guidance.

At the other end of the continuum is *non-directive counselling*, where you help employees solve their own problems. You act as a listening post and ask questions to help the employee think through the problem. Complex problems that are very personal or thorny and have many possible solutions are best treated this way.

In between is *co-sharing*, where employee and supervisor 'put their heads together' and between them come up with a plan of action. This is useful if you have direct experience of, or expertise in, the employee's problem that the employee accepts as relevant.

You can also conduct a counselling session by moving back and forth along the continuum as appropriate. Whatever you do, it should be based on a genuine desire to help the employee through a difficult period. One of your main goals is to help employees return to their previously good level of performance.

Common mistakes in personal counselling

Because it is not our problem and we have the advantage of being able to view it objectively, our responses to the employee may sound condescending, placating, patronising, judgmental or manipulative, or they may seem to indicate a lack of respect for the employee.

Many supervisors find it difficult to take off their 'expert hat'. They find they are telling the employee exactly what to do before they have listened well enough to gain a clear understanding of the problem. Or they give advice about a complex, personal problem when they should be listening actively and non-directively.

Some supervisors become caught up in the employee's problem and begin sympathising rather than empathising. Others try to reassure the employee, often with such trite comments as: 'Don't worry, things will get better'; 'Every cloud has a silver lining'; 'Things will look better in the morning'. This belittles the problem and discounts the employee's concerns. Still other supervisors get nervous about treading on a delicate, personal matter and change the subject, simply ignoring the problem.

Some supervisors find that their main problem is a lack of good listening skills: they interrupt, cross-examine, talk too much and so on. Any of these mistakes can bring a counselling session to a rapid halt.

·················· **RAPID REVIEW** ··························

		True	False
1.	Conflict can be defined as verbally and/or non-verbally expressed disagreement between individuals or groups.	☐	☐
2.	The absence of conflict is a positive sign that everything is going well.	☐	☐
3.	Assertiveness and a 'win–win' approach are important ingredients in successfully resolving conflict.	☐	☐
4.	If supervisors handle conflict well, they get exactly what they want.	☐	☐
5.	Ignoring conflict in its early stages can make it go away.	☐	☐

	True	False
6. Supervisors usually need to take into account both their own concerns and the concerns of the other party in order to resolve conflict successfully.	☐	☐
7. Grievances are formally registered complaints.	☐	☐
8. Since performance counselling is difficult and often ends in ill-will and arguments, it is often better to ignore poor performance in the hope that it will right itself.	☐	☐
9. Unsatisfactory performance is often caused by factors outside the employee's control.	☐	☐
10. The aim of a performance counselling interview is to tell the employee straight out that she'd better 'shape up or ship out'.	☐	☐
11. Supervisors can use feedback to build good performance and stop poor performance.	☐	☐
12. A performance counselling interview should seek to identify the cause of poor performance so that it can be rectified.	☐	☐
13. An example of a performance gap is a person's general attitude and willingness being below expectations.	☐	☐
14. A 'frame' opens a conversation and sets the scene for a productive performance counselling session.	☐	☐
15. 'I' messages help you to give clear and factual information.	☐	☐
16. Supervisors need to document a performance counselling session only if they believe termination of employment will be the eventual outcome.	☐	☐
17. The 'hot stove' should not be used with experienced employees or employees who are 'trying it on'.	☐	☐
18. Supervisors should always follow their organisation's termination guidelines scrupulously.	☐	☐
19. People should leave their problems at home and supervisors should not become involved in employees' personal problems.	☐	☐

· ┤ **APPLY YOUR KNOWLEDGE** ├ ·

1. Discuss the steps a supervisor can take to prevent serious conflicts. Is it always possible to avoid conflict?
2. In what ways can conflict be healthy?
3. Explain why assertiveness in managing conflict is important. Contrast an assertive conflict management style with a passive and an aggressive style and discuss the effects of these three approaches to conflict on a supervisor's effectiveness.
4. List the steps for resolving conflict and explain the skills supervisors need.

5. List several signs indicating that a supervisor should hold a performance counselling interview.
6. Explain how feedback can be used to improve employees' performance.
7. What is the path to good performance? Explain what supervisors need to do at each step along the path.
8. Explain the steps in performance counselling.
9. Write an essay outlining and giving examples of the skills required to conduct a successful performance counselling interview.

10. Below are four examples of how a supervisor might begin a performance improvement discussion. Analyse why they are unsatisfactory and suggest an alternative for each.

    (a) 'You've been coming in late. You've got a really bad attitude towards your work and it had better change.'

    (b) 'You made a mess of that last job. You're obviously either not competent or you've lost your drive.'

    (c) 'I was talking. You're rude to interrupt me.'

    (d) 'You're not doing a good enough job. You need to boost up your confidence.'

11. Explain the 'hot stove principle' of performance improvement. When should it be applied?

12. What steps should a supervisor follow when terminating someone's employment? What documentation is necessary?

13. List several signs that could indicate that an employee needs personal counselling.

14. What benefits can a supervisor expect from personal counselling?

15. Explain the styles of personal counselling and the circumstances to which each is best suited.

.... **DEVELOP YOUR SKILLS** ....

Individual activities

1. From your own experience, describe the common causes of conflict outlined in this chapter.

2. Think of a conflict you have experienced with another person or, perhaps, between groups. Analyse it following the stages shown in Figure 24.1.

3. Explain how conflict can occur, using a personal example.

4. How can supervisors use feedback to promote the behaviours and work performance they want?

5. Referring to the vignette on page 724, list Jed's performance gaps.

6. If you have completed Chapter 20 on leadership, how would you assess Jed's readiness level for the tasks referred to in the vignette on page 724? What is your evidence for this? According to Hersey and Blanchard, what leadership style should Susan employ with Jed?

7. Find out your own organisation's procedures (or your college's) for termination of employment and instant dismissal.

8. Draft a first written warning letter to an employee who has been late seven times over the last 12 shifts and who has been unable to provide a satisfactory explanation for the lateness. If you live in New Zealand, state when you should write this letter.

9. Write a frame and an 'I' message a supervisor could use to open a performance counselling session in each of the following situations.

    (a) An employee has been absent the last three Mondays following public holidays occurring on a Friday.

    (b) An employee argues with a colleague in front of the rest of the team at least once a fortnight about non-related work matters.

    (c) An employee fails to wear a hairnet when in the food preparation area unless you remind him. This has been going on since the employee was transferred to your section (from a non-food area) three weeks ago.

(d) An employee's work quality is spasmodic. In the last six weeks, their reject rate has been 30% above average and this is costly in terms of material wastage.

Group activities

1. Interview three or four people who work in manufacturing, service, not-for-profit or public sector organisations. Have they experienced any grievances in their organisations? What were they about? Compare your findings with those of others in your class and produce a list of the major causes of grievances that you have found.

2. Form into groups of three. Using a typical grievance from activity 1, role-play a discussion between employee and supervisor. Begin with the employee bringing the grievance to the attention of the supervisor. The supervisor should follow the advice provided in this chapter. The observer should give feedback to the supervisor on the skills they used successfully, and what further improvements they could make.

3. Referring to the vignette on page 724, discuss the approach Susan should take in her upcoming discussion with Jed. Do you think she has left it too late? How could she have intervened earlier?

4. On your own, write a 'framing' statement suitable for opening the performance counselling interview with Jed. Then form into groups of three and compare your framing statement with those of others. Together, agree on one framing statement that satisfies everyone.

5. Construct an 'I' message to give to Jed, following the procedure in question 4 above.

6. Referring to Case Study 24.2, prepare a frame and an 'I' message that Shauna could say to Fred. Select someone in the class to role-play Fred. Take turns to open the performance counselling interview with Fred, getting feedback from Fred and others in the class on the effectiveness of your opening statements.

7. In small groups, define the terms 'harsh', 'unjust' and 'unreasonable' in relation to termination of employment.

CASE STUDY 24.1

A 'Timid' Supervisor?

Zed was clearly the best suited employee in the Service Centre, in terms of skills, knowledge and experience, to replace Anna as supervisor, who was leaving next month to take up a new position. Yet one thing worried Russell, the Centre's manager, as he contemplated the decision: could Zed handle conflict?

The department had certainly had its fair share of that over the past ten months, due partly to Anna's rather aggressive supervisory style, partly to the recent technological changes and partly to one or two 'bad apples' who loved a good argument, especially when it involved 'riding' the supervisor.

Zed had always struck Russell as rather timid, although that of course by no means meant that he was. Perhaps he could stand up to some of these difficulties as well as anyone; better perhaps. What to do ... a mistake could mean disaster!

Could Zed be trained to resolve conflict, wondered Russell? Or could he perhaps be coached through the first few months until he found his feet? Perhaps he'd better not take the risk. Yet Zed was, in all other respects, by far the best choice for the supervisory role.

Questions

1   What could Russell do to find out whether Zed could handle conflict?
2   Assuming Zed needs training in conflict management, what skills would you suggest he develop?
3   If Russell is correct in his guess that Zed is 'timid', what conflict management style would he be most likely to adopt? What would be the repercussions of this style?

CASE STUDY 24.2

Shauna Kumar Versus Fred Knox

Shauna Kumar was not looking forward to Friday morning. Management had instructed her to formally discipline her most experienced employee, Fred Knox, for unsatisfactory work behaviour.

Shauna had been the supervisor of the data processing section for three months and her appointment was a shock to most of the employees. Everyone had expected the job to go to Fred, who had been with the organisation for 15 years. In fact, he was one of the original staff selected to start up the data processing section when the organisation had been computerised.

Fred had always provided valuable assistance to the previous department supervisor through his knowledge of organisational procedures, his loyalty to the organisation and his devotion to carrying out his responsibilities. In selecting the new supervisor, however, management felt that Fred's lack of tertiary qualifications and his age would restrict his capacity to meet the changing needs of the job.

Fred was not satisfied with this explanation. He suggested to some close associates that it was Shauna's golfing skills that really got her the job. (Shauna had partnered a senior officer in winning a prestige golf tournament.) Being aware of Fred's disappointment at not getting the job, Shauna had shown leniency in her treatment of him since taking up her new position, and made every effort to get him 'on side'. She hoped that time would heal Fred's disappointment and that eventually she would get the same support from Fred that her predecessor had enjoyed.

In the three months, however, things had not happened the way Shauna had hoped. Fred was displaying a 'don't care' attitude to the job and was adversely influencing many of the younger staff members. Several times Shauna found Fred talking to people in other sections while work was piling up on his desk, causing the section to fall behind schedule and miss deadlines. Fred's explanation for these visits was that other people were asking for his help, as he appeared to be the only one in the place who knew what should be done and how to do it.

On two or three occasions Shauna had discovered Fred, accompanied by two or three other staff members, arriving back from lunch up to three-quarters of an hour late and showing obvious signs of drinking, which then affected that afternoon's work output.

Shauna had informally warned Fred on two occasions that his behaviour was a breach of the rules and assumed that this would be enough to settle the matter. Unfortunately, it had no effect.

Shauna's immediate supervisor had recently become aware of the extended lunchtime drinking and discussed it informally with Shauna. When she explained the difficulties she was having with Fred's disregard of her directions, he instructed her to conduct a formal performance counselling interview with Fred before the end of the week and to warn him that, unless there was an immediate change in his attitude, the formal termination of employment procedure would begin.

Time was now up and Shauna was about to call Fred to her office to carry out her manager's instructions. She was wondering whether she could get Fred to change, and what she should do if Fred threatened to resign.

Questions

1   Has Shauna handled Fred's behaviour adequately? How else could she have handled it?
2   Develop an outline that Shauna could follow to conduct the interview, showing the skills she will need to use.
3   What will Shauna need to be careful to avoid doing during the interview?

Answers to Rapid Review questions

1. T   2. F   3. T   4. F   5. F   6. T   7. T   8. F   9. T   10. F   11. T   12. T   13. F
14. T   15. T   16. F   17. F   18. T   19. F

CHAPTER 25

APPRAISING PERFORMANCE

Appraisal time

'Oh, no, here we go again,' thought Mark as he opened up the parcel of papers the human resources department had sent him. It was that time of year—performance appraisal time. Each year he was asked to complete a lengthy performance appraisal on each of his staff and discuss it with them. It was supposed to be good for the staff, but Mark wasn't so sure. Each year, there would be a good few of his people wandering around with hurt and sullen expressions.

The HRM people insisted that the appraisals be completed on time: they seemed to think he had nothing better to do than fill out forms and hold 'appraisal interviews' with his staff. The HRM manager claimed he used the appraisals for predicting staff requirements, formulating training and career development plans and structuring the annual salary review.

'Well, that's fair enough,' Mark thought, 'but how am I supposed to tell Margaret, who thinks she's "tops", that her work is only average? And how can I tell Ken, who has been here for years, that, although his work is fine, his sullen and uncooperative attitude is getting on my nerves? And what about Lena—such a pleasant girl and she tries so hard—if I give her a poor rating, she may get discouraged and stop trying. And Tom—he's already at the top of the pay scale; if I give him the excellent rating he deserves and a pay increase doesn't result, won't he become demotivated? Oh, these performance appraisals—I wish someone would tell me how I'm supposed to manage them!'

. . . . ▮▮▮▮▮▮▮▮▮▮▮ OVERVIEW ▮▮▮▮▮▮▮ . . . .

The thought of conducting performance appraisals fills many supervisors with dread. They fear an unpleasant confrontation; they fear the result will be a demotivated, hurt or angry employee; they fear damaging working relationships. You can learn how to avoid these pitfalls in this chapter and how to plan and conduct effective, motivating and honest performance appraisals with your staff.

■ How can performance appraisals help supervisors and employees work better together and achieve results more easily?

■ What types of performance appraisals are there?

■ What should be discussed at a performance appraisal meeting and what is off limits?

■ What are the three main parts of a performance appraisal interview?

■ Should you conduct informal appraisals?

■ What should you do if you are being appraised?

■ What are the primary uses of performance appraisals?

THE ROLE OF PERFORMANCE APPRAISALS

. . . We evaluate things every day. We form opinions about people, products and ideas. We usually do this unconsciously. How often do you know that you 'like' a product or person without having gone through any conscious, systematic evaluation procedure?

Supervisors also evaluate employees—often unconsciously. They know whether they are 'good workers', reliable and conscientious. Most organisations ask supervisors to make conscious formal evaluations of employees, too. It may be for a transfer, promotion or special assignment, to identify training and development needs, for a pay increase or even for retrenchments. It may be as part of the organisation's normal annual or biannual performance appraisal system, which gives everyone a chance to clarify aims and objectives, build on strengths and plan to strengthen weaknesses.

How should you make these appraisals? By intuition? Hunch? No! It is far better to do it by using some systematic, carefully thought-out process. Otherwise, your assessments may be unsound. A systematic method of performance appraisal will help turn your unsystematic, unconscious appraisals into a useful tool for motivating employees, monitoring individual and departmental progress and planning for future improvements. It will help you replace emotional judgments based on incomplete knowledge with an objective consideration of performance, not personality.

A formalised appraisal system helps you to be fair and consistent. It shows your interest in each employee's job and their potential for training and development. A formal approach guides you through an appraisal interview where you discuss an employee's work behaviour, skills and ambitions, and set goals for the future. This careful assessment of employees' skills and abilities is so important that most major organisations now regularly use some formal system to appraise employee performance.

PERFORMANCE APPRAISALS

. . . A **performance appraisal** consists of a systematic, face-to-face discussion of an employee's work performance, training and development needs, future job goals and job aspirations.

It looks backwards, reviewing the employee's performance during the period under review, and forwards, helping the employee prepare and set goals for the upcoming review period. The forward-looking aspect of appraisals should align individual job-holder goals with the overall goals of the organisation and their department.

The discussion should also review each of the five keys—what to, want to, how to, chance to and led to (see Chapter 8) to make sure they are operating optimally. To be effective, both parties need to have thought in advance about the topics the discussion will cover, and be prepared to be open and honest with each other.

Assessment areas differ from organisation to organisation and from job to job, according to the requirements of the job, the department and the organisation. Some typical areas for assessment include:

- quality/accuracy of work;
- quantity of output;
- ability to make decisions;
- job knowledge;
- technical and job-related skills;
- attendance and punctuality;
- ability to work as a member of a team;
- future potential/ability to work in other areas;
- training and development needs;
- commitment to safety; and
- dependability.

Performance appraisals are usually held annually or every six months or, in the case of some operator and customer service jobs, even more frequently. They are carried out by the employee's immediate supervisor and in many organisations they are reviewed by the supervisor's manager.

The purpose of performance appraisals

The purpose of a performance appraisal is to discuss performance, plan for the future and discuss how the job can be made easier or done more effectively. It is not intended to punish for misdeeds, make someone feel bad or provide a 'short, sharp kick'. Unfortunately, too many performance appraisals end up this way.

Performance appraisals should be two-way discussions. They provide a formal arena for each employee to sit down and discuss their job with their supervisor. In this way, communication channels are opened and working relationships can be strengthened. Each party has a chance to discuss how they see the employee's job and the supervisor's job in relation to it. This ensures that both are 'speaking the same language' and holding the same realistic expectations. It also provides a chance to 'get things out in the open' and discuss any small but nagging doubts, questions or irritations.

The review function of performance appraisals allows the employee and supervisor to sit down and take a serious look at the previous period's job performance. What was done

---

THE BIG PICTURE

Performance appraisals form an important element in the performance management process. Other elements of performance management are feedback, coaching and performance counselling.

particularly well? What needs improving? What skills or behaviours need strengthening? What mistakes were made and what can be learned from them? What problems did the employee run into? Did anything get in the way of doing the job well? This gives supervisors an ideal opportunity to recognise good work, uncover problems and increase an employee's motivation. It also provides an opportunity to clarify any areas of misunderstanding.

Even more importantly, performance appraisals provide a chance to look towards and plan for the future. What training would the employee benefit from? What new goals or targets will be worked towards? What additional or delegated duties would provide increased job development or job satisfaction? What new directions would the employee like to see the job and their career take? What other jobs in the organisation interest them? What can be done to streamline the job and eliminate 'hassles'?

This is your golden opportunity to ensure that the employee is clear about future job performance requirements and is motivated to work towards them. Box 25.1 lists other purposes of performance appraisals. They are not in order of importance—each organisation uses performance appraisals for different purposes.

For performance appraisals to succeed, you need to be able to set clear performance targets and carry out an appraisal interview. These are discussed in detail later in this chapter.

The benefits of performance appraisals

Although they are about as popular as a visit to the dentist, performance appraisals offer many benefits. Some of these benefits are:
- an opportunity to stand back from your daily routine and look clearly and objectively at each employee's level of performance;
- an opportunity to give credit where it is due;

BOX 25.1 SOME REASONS FOR APPRAISING PERFORMANCE

- To set mutually agreed goals for future job performance and development
- To evaluate past performance and improve or correct performance
- To provide regular, comprehensive feedback to all employees on how their supervisor sees their performance

- To identify training and/or development needs
- To identify people suitable for promotions, transfers and further development
- To determine merit-based pay increases
- To monitor the effectiveness of selection or promotion procedures

---

THE BIG PICTURE

The person being appraised can have feelings that range from indifference to eagerness, looking forward to the interview, to nervousness and anxiety, to defensiveness and anger. Do what you can to make the meeting as relaxed, constructive and pleasant as possible. Use it as an opportunity to enhance the employee's self-esteem.

- opening communication channels and encouraging mutual understanding of career aspirations, working relationships, areas of strength and areas needing improvement;
- an opportunity to discuss and agree on job goals, targets, objectives and priorities, and measures for assessing their achievement;
- encouraging supervisors and managers to analyse systematically employees' performance, potential and training and development needs;
- providing a permanent written record of the relative strengths and weaknesses of employees to use for salary and wage changes, promotions, transfers, court evidence, retrenchments and training plans;
- providing a record of, and a sound basis for, decisions regarding promotion, pay, dismissal, etc.;
- helping to prevent employees being poorly placed or misplaced in jobs;
- increasing the likelihood that an individual employee's talents will be recognised and used where they are most needed in the organisation;
- most employees need and want to know how they are getting on; performance appraisals provide the opportunity for this feedback;
- highlighting areas where training or coaching are needed;
- providing an opportunity to work through the five keys to good performance and identify areas where improvements could be made; and
- fitting in with the trend towards open, participative communication with employees.

METHODS OF APPRAISING PERFORMANCE

The job description or competency rating method

The job description method, in its simplest form, provides a list of duties that the job-holder is expected to perform or key result areas and targets the employee is expected to achieve. The supervisor ticks those that are being performed adequately and puts a cross against those requiring improvement. This method is quick and easy and highlights training needs. It is particularly effective for routine jobs such as file clerks or assembly operators. An accurate, up-to-date job description that includes measurable standards of performance, or competencies, is the key to this method of appraisal.

The critical-incident method

The critical-incident method of appraising performance is gaining in popularity, possibly because it helps to ensure fair appraisals. Critical-incident appraisals are based on a record of important incidents, both positive and negative, which have occurred during the appraisal period. The supervisor maintains this record and employees often keep their own records as well. A shortcoming of this method is that people often record only negative incidents, with positive incidents seen as merely normal job performance.

The essay method

With the essay method, the supervisor writes a few paragraphs about each employee, usually according to set guidelines. This method requires a lot of thought and care and can be quite time-consuming. Some people can write more convincingly than others; therefore, employees whose supervisors are not good writers may suffer by comparison with those rated by a supervisor who writes well.

The comparison method

The ranking, or comparison, method compares each employee with all the others in a section against set criteria, ending up with, for example, the most/least productive employees, the highest/lowest quality producers and so on. Because it is difficult to compare every individual with every other one, some ranking methods place employees only into the top third, middle third and lowest third instead of ranking each one individually. An employee might rank in the top third of employees for planning and organising work and in the bottom third for accuracy of work, for example.

The rating-scale method

Using the rating-scale method, a supervisor rates specified job-related skills and abilities of each employee according to a defined scale. This is an easy method to use and allows quick comparison between employees. An example is given in Figure 25.1. The danger here is the tendency of some supervisors to rate all employees similarly, that is, to rate in a 'hard' or 'lenient' way.

Peer review

Some organisations include peer reviews as part of their performance appraisal efforts. Members of work or management teams review each other's performance against key criteria such as the ability to work as a member of and contribute to the team, job knowledge, and ability to innovate, solve problems and recommend actions. This can be effective in high-performing teams where members work well together and value each other's contributions in achieving work-related objectives. If teamworking is not critical or if the members do not work well together, peer reviews offer few benefits.

360 degree feedback

Most often used to appraise supervisors and managers, **360 degree feedback** provides anonymous feedback to a job holder from the other positions that interact with it:

FIGURE 25.1   PART OF AN EMPLOYEE EVALUATION FORM USED IN THE RATING-SCALE METHOD

Employee evaluation

Employee . . . .
Department . . . . Section . . . .
Supervisor . . . . Date . . . .

Please rate the employee on the skills or qualities listed below. Following each skill is a line with points along it to serve as a rating scale. The phrases beneath the line link the number of points that will be awarded to the rating. Rate the employee by marking at any point on the line the position that best describes the employee's ability in each area.

Job knowledge

0	5	10	15	20
Gaps in knowledge of a critical nature	Understands only routine aspects of job	Is well informed on all aspects of job	Has better than average knowledge of all aspects of job	Superior understanding of job; very well informed

Quality of work

0	5	10	15	20
Quality unsatisfactory	Quality not quite up to standard	Quality quite satisfactory	Quality superior	Quality exceptionally high

the supervisors, other managers, any direct reports, peers and, often, external and internal suppliers and customers. Although this feedback requires careful organisation and collation from the HR department, it can provide job-holders with valuable insights into how their behaviour helps or hinders others in their pursuit of the organisation's goals, and form a sound basis on which to plan improvements to their operating style. It can also provide organisations with perhaps more meaningful information than the traditional performance appraisal conducted by only the job-holder's supervisor.

The mixed method

Many organisations, trying to retain the advantages of all these methods, use them in combination. This is called the **mixed method**. Appraisal documents are divided into several sections, each consisting of one or more of the above methods. In striving to retain a wide variety of features and benefits, however, designers of the performance appraisal documents can fall into the trap of creating overly lengthy and cumbersome forms that take too long to complete and may become 'ends in themselves'.

The best method

The best method is one that people understand and use. The best method is one that facilitates open discussion between job-holders and their supervisor. The best method is one that helps job-holders improve their performance and find ways to meet their personal goals. The best method is one that sheds light on organisational difficulties and problems and helps to fix them. The best method is one that builds understanding between job-holders and their supervisor.

PITFALLS IN EMPLOYEE APPRAISALS

In appraising the performance of others, take care to avoid the following hazards.

- Don't succumb to the **halo/horns effect** by allowing the rating you assign to one area of an employee's performance influence how you rate other areas of performance.
- Avoid any tendency to be either *too lenient* or *too strict*. Similarly, avoid *averaging* (ranking everyone as 'average'). Rate each aspect of an employee's performance individually and objectively.
- Personal bias and blind spots can affect judgment, so don't allow your objectivity to be lessened by whether or not you personally like an employee, or how easy or difficult they are to supervise.
- Avoid vague statements and generalisations about the person you are appraising.
- Don't be tempted to psychoanalyse a person during an appraisal. This is extremely dangerous and is usually not only incorrect but also offensive to the person being 'analysed'.
- Criticising negatively sets up barriers of suspicion and resentment and will damage your relationship with the employee. Be constructive. Stick to factual descriptions of behaviour and work performance and be helpful, not hurtful, in your comments. Focus on the future ('From now on …', 'Next time …') and be a coach not a critic.
- Don't use different standards to rate employees doing the same jobs. For example, don't rate a low-performing but highly motivated employee higher than an employee who is performing the job adequately but unenthusiastically. Keep your rating standards fair and consistent.

- If you find yourself using words like 'always' or 'never', be alert to the possibility that you may be exaggerating. Similarly, overemphasising non-typical or most recent incidents, either good or bad, limits the fairness and accuracy of a performance appraisal. Base your appraisal on the performance of the whole job and the whole period under review, not just a small part of it or what has occurred most recently.
- Don't offer a long chain of criticism. This is hard to take and hard to digest. Stick to facts and be careful to distinguish between a fact and your opinion.
- Don't overemphasise uncharacteristic performance. If a person has done something unusually well or unusually poorly, don't let it overshadow their more typical job performance or behaviour.
- To overcome an overreliance on 'hunches' or 'intuition', appraise performance based on previously agreed-upon targets.
- Don't confuse personality traits and attitudes with performance criteria. Always appraise a person's work performance, not their personality.
- No matter how busy you are or how efficient you want to be, don't rush the appraisal interview. This could result in a 'telling' interview rather than a joint exploration of the employee's performance. While this may give you the chance to say what you intended to say, it doesn't give employees a chance to air their opinions or ask questions. Don't jump in and try to get the appraisals over with as quickly as possible. Avoid an 'assembly line' approach (holding one interview after another). These mistakes not only let you down, but let the organisation and the employees down, too. Prepare carefully for each appraisal interview. Remember that each employee has only one—their own—and it is important to them. Take time to listen and discuss.
- Don't forget the power of appraisals to reward and motivate staff.
- Don't feel awkward and embarrassed at having to 'judge' employees or be tempted to gloss over any mistakes or areas needing improvement. Use the opportunity to raise any concerns as well as recognise areas of good performance.
- Don't focus too much on the past and not enough on the future. Make planning for the future your main objective. Use the opportunity to agree on future performance targets and strengthen your working relationship.

To overcome these potential pitfalls in appraisals, you will need to invest time and energy. Fair, objective appraisals start with a clear and agreed-upon statement of an employee's duties and responsibilities (the job description and key result areas) and the performance indicators that will be used to assess performance (targets). A genuine desire to provide constructive feedback to improve an employee's performance and a commitment to holding a two-way discussion complete the picture.

MANAGEMENT BY OBJECTIVES

Management by objectives, or MBO, is a process by which a supervisor and employee or work team jointly establish work goals and targets and agree to time frames for their achievement. Using MBO, a supervisor might, for example, explain to a word processor operator that the departmental goal is to reduce expenses by 3% and increase output by 2% during the next quarter. They would discuss ways in which the operator could reduce expenses and increase output to help to meet this goal. The operator might, for example, suggest a personal target of producing 35 documents a day by the end of the next quarter and to begin at once to use recycled paper to produce all drafts. If the two of them agree that this is reasonable, then this becomes the operator's target. In a similar fashion, targets would be set with all employees in the department, with each employee setting personal targets contributing to reducing expenses and increasing output to reach the department's overall goals.

In the above example, supervisor and employee have together agreed upon a target that is *SMARTT*:

Specific
Measurable
Achievable
Related to the overall departmental goals
Time-framed
Trackable

(See also Chapter 8.)

The future of MBO

MBO works particularly well with clearly defined jobs. However, as organisations build more flexibility into their job designs and as the pace of change quickens and the environment becomes less predictable, many jobs are becoming less clear-cut. In such organisations, MBO may not serve as an effective means of managing employee productivity. It is seen as too 'prescriptive' for complex, broad or ambiguous jobs.

These organisations are adapting MBO by introducing outcome-based performance measures. For example, a work team might be responsible for attaining the outcome of responsive customer service. It might set itself a variety of MBO-type objectives such as greeting customers within 16 seconds, answering the telephone within four rings, responding to customer inquiries within three working days, and delivering on time and to specification within one week of receiving an order. The work team itself would be appraised on its ability to provide responsive customer service and individual team members on their ability to meet the agreed objectives.

Job-holders in matrix organisations may work on several projects and, because of the nature of the projects, their contribution may be difficult to specify in MBO terms. The organisation might instead appraise employees' ability to 'add value' to each project through their expertise, the ideas they help to generate, and the quality and timeliness of their contributions to the teams they are part of.

Another example of modifying MBO to suit complex jobs might be a human resources officer who is responsible for designing and introducing a productivity management system to the organisation. Rather than set specific MBO-type measures to assess their success in this, the HR manager might find it more helpful to appraise the officer on the strategic 'fit' of the system with the organisation's overall aims and objectives, and the degree to which it is accepted and used throughout the organisation.

TARGETS

What gets measured gets the most attention and *targets* identify what gets measured. They should help people focus on what is important and help them do their jobs well.

Targets show us where we're going.

Establishing targets

We learned in Chapter 8 that once **key result areas**, or KRAs, are established, showing us what the important areas in a job are, we then set targets that will direct our efforts and attention towards important indicators of success. In fact, some organisations use the term *measures of success* for targets. Establish targets in the most meaningful areas.

Flexible targets

Targets aren't set in concrete. They need to change to accommodate changes in the market-place and operating environment. This might mean altering targets that have been in effect for a long time if work conditions, processes, materials or other factors demand it. You may also need to change targets to reflect changing priorities or to provide a focus to develop employees' skills and extend and broaden their contributions to the organisation.

Particularly with new projects, it is not unusual for people to be so enthusiastic about possibilities that they agree on overly ambitious targets. Later, when they attempt to put them into practice, they find that resources and specifications are not as generous as they thought they would be or that they run into problems they didn't expect. When this happens, they take another, more realistic look at the job and its targets and set more realistic ones.

Lead and lag targets

In Chapter 5 we learned the difference between **lead** and **lag indicators**. Try to set some targets that are lead indicators so you will know how things are progressing. Lag indicators are merely historical and, therefore, not as useful.

CONDUCTING AN APPRAISAL INTERVIEW

A good performance appraisal interview is not an argument. It is not an attack on a person ('Let me point out to you some of your shortcomings, Mavis ...'). It is not a game of cat and mouse ('You tell me how you think you did and I'll tell you what I think'). A performance appraisal interview should be a free and frank exchange of views. It should be a conversation. The appraiser should do most of the listening and the appraisee most of the talking. Box 25.2 shows the sort of information you will discuss.

Review the employee's progress since the last evaluation and agree on targets for the future period. Discuss areas in which the employee has made real improvement and where they are consistently performing well—don't forget the 'praise' in 'appraise'! In areas where progress has not been shown or where performance is unsatisfactory, you should make constructive suggestions for improvement or, better still, get the employee's ideas on how to improve performance. The agreed actions should be specific and directed at steps the employee can take in order to reach the agreed targets more satisfactorily. (For example, think about what the employee can do to improve work practices, or training courses the employee might undertake.)

> 'Treat people as if they were what they ought to be and you help them become what they are capable of being.'
>
> Johann W. von Goethe (1749–1832)

Your approach should be to compare the agreed targets with actual performance. Consider what might have caused any deficiencies in performance. Can the individual be

SUMMARY OF THE APPRAISAL INTERVIEW

What do you need to know from the appraisee?
- Attitudes, feelings about their job
- Ambitions/aspirations
- Successes
- Expectations of job, work, rewards, etc.
- Views on any job changes
- Self-assessment of performance
- Main problems faced
- How you can be of more help as a supervisor

What does the appraisee need to know from you?
- Clarification of job, targets, responsibilities

- Departmental objectives and how the appraisee contributes
- Objectives, standards, targets for the next review period
- Recognition of good work
- Constructive help with any problem areas

Ideally, what should you agree together?
- Targets for the next review period
- Action plan for future development
- Any training needs
- How you will help, what support you will provide
- An overall assessment of performance

---

held accountable or were there circumstances beyond the employee's control? What organisational barriers or missing ingredients are hampering effective performance? Look for causes you can put right rather than laying blame (see also Chapter 8).

'Never mind who you praise but be very careful who you blame.'
Sir Edmund Gosse (1849–1928)

The steps in a performance appraisal interview

There are three main parts to a performance appraisal interview: preparation for the interview; the interview itself; and after the interview (follow-up).

Step 1: Preparation for the interview

First of all, both you and the appraisee must prepare for the interview. The better prepared you both are, the more beneficial the discussion will be. One to two weeks before the appraisal interview, let the employee know when and where it will be held and how you plan to conduct it. If possible, give the appraisee a copy of the form(s) to be used and ask them to consider the past (any successes, what have been the most and least enjoyable parts of the job, any problems and the causes of them) and the future (aims for performance improvement, any help that will be required, any training that might be useful).

You must prepare thoroughly, too. Gather as many facts as you can: personnel files, record cards, a summary of training both on and off the job, the job description, the agreed targets or goals, the measures of success (or lack of it) in attaining them. Your information should be 'naturally acquired'—that is, not obtained through spying, listening to gossip, encouraging informers or snooping. This helps to ensure it is objective.

Consider where you will hold the interview. Arrange to meet in private, with no interruptions. Put a 'no interruptions' sign on your door if necessary and ask the switchboard to hold any calls. Your office may not be the best place to meet if it is a busy one.

Consider conducting the interview in a 'neutral' area. This can help reduce anxiety and make the interview more constructive. Conference rooms and canteens are often suitable places. An informal atmosphere is often less threatening. For instance, can you sit in chairs by a low coffee table rather than facing each other from opposite sides of a desk? Make sure you have chairs of similar height and arrange the blinds so that light is not shining in anyone's face.

Step 2: The interview itself

Box 25.3 outlines the three stages in an appraisal meeting. In addition to following this outline, bear in mind the main purposes of the appraisal—to review and improve the employee's performance, acknowledge satisfactory performance and plan for the future. It is crucial that you focus on facts. An appraisal is something that is done *with* an employee, not *to* an employee. And remember at all times to appraise performance, not the person, their personality or their attitudes. Centre your attention on things people can change and the five keys to good performance.

In cases of poor performance, it will help to view the appraisal discussion as a problem-solving meeting. Most people want to do a good job and, if you handle the interview carefully, you can jointly explore the causes of poor performance and the steps that each of you can take to improve it (see Chapter 24 for a full discussion on performance counselling).

The meeting should also give the appraisee an opportunity to discuss any job problems and aspirations. Answer questions truthfully and as fully and tactfully as possible.

'A performance appraisal should contain no surprises for the appraisee!'

BOX 25.3 THE PERFORMANCE APPRAISAL INTERVIEW

Stage 1: Create the climate
1. Put at ease:
   - relaxed
   - talking freely.
2. Review the purpose of the interview—a discussion about the employee's performance and contributions, and plans for the future.
3. Outline how the interview will proceed.

Stage 2: The body of the interview
1. Review job performance against targets.
   - What should have happened?
   - What actually happened?
2. Give credit and praise where due.
   - Reinforce what went well.
3. Tackle any problem areas.
   - What went wrong?
   - Specify, in terms of quantity, quality, cost, time and safety, the targets that were not met.
   - Why did it go wrong? Review the five keys to good performance (see Chapter 8).
   - Reserve your judgment. Seek the employee's diagnosis first.
   - Be constructive and focus on the future and lessons learned.
   - What can be done to improve?
4. Give positive guidance/coaching/counselling if necessary.
5. Agree on targets for the next review period.
   Remember to listen—how is it from the appraisee's point of view?

Stage 3: Final summary
1. Make a positive round-up of the discussion:
   - Confirm the main points covered and the action agreed.
   - Review priorities.
   - Write down agreed joint action plan.
2. The appraisee should leave feeling confident that you have appreciated strong points and contributions made to the department.
3. Use genuine praise and constructive criticism—avoid clichés, 'noises' and paternalism.

FROM THEORY TO PRACTICE

Beware: People tend to hear negative information the loudest, even when the majority of comments are positive. If you need to offer a constructive comment, move straight into what you want. Use phrases like 'from now on ...', 'in future' or 'how can we improve this?' This is a way of saying: 'Let's not dwell on the past, it's done; let's get it right from now on.' It is also a way to make an improvement in performance more likely, a key goal in performance appraisals.

Before closing the interview, make sure that the employee understands the rating method and that there are no unanswered questions. Make sure that you have agreed on targets and goals as well as priorities, if appropriate, for the next appraisal period. These may not have changed much from the last period, but it helps to review them nevertheless. Any agreed-upon actions, for either of you, should be written down and each of you should receive a copy.

Four things will help the appraisal interview to go well:

1. thorough preparation, by both yourself and the appraisee;
2. a sound and accurate knowledge of the appraisee's job;
3. being positive and constructive during the interview and accepting the employee as a person, no matter how good or bad their performance may be; and
4. encouraging the appraisee to participate actively in the appraisal discussion.

Step 3: After the interview

Keep any promises or agreements you have made. Show a continuing interest in the employee and their performance and career. Refer to the written action plan you made during the appraisal interview at regular intervals, say monthly, as a reminder of what needs to be done. Keep up the two-way communication with regular informal appraisals, using this plan as the basis. Remember also to continue with formal appraisals regularly, at least once a year.

INFORMAL APPRAISALS

Supervisors who wait until the annual performance appraisal to sit down and have a talk with employees about their work performance are making a big mistake. This approach leaves praise and performance counselling too late—until after the 'horse has bolted'. The time to recognise that something has been done extra well is as soon as it happens. Equally, as soon as a mistake is made or standards slip, corrective action should be taken.

People need regular feedback, by word or action, on how they are going. These informal appraisals help build motivation and morale. They help you show a continuing interest in employees and their job performance and keep the focus on what is important. Good supervisors speak with team members regularly and find opportunities to encourage people to 'keep up the good work'. They make sure standards are maintained at all times and address problems and 'slip-ups' as soon as they occur. This builds good work habits

FROM THEORY TO PRACTICE

Have you conducted an impartial appraisal? You probably have if you can say 'yes' to the following:

❏ I have spent enough time thinking this person's performance through and discussing it with them to be confident I have been fair and objective.

❏ I have specific examples of both strengths and weaknesses.

❏ We identified and discussed factors in the organisation and department that affected job performance.

❏ I have built a good relationship with this person already, which made our discussions open and honest.

❏ I phrased any criticisms in a helpful and constructive way and the person listened and took them on board without becoming defensive.

❏ We both have a clear plan of action.

❏ I asked for and received feedback about my own performance as a supervisor.

and ensures standards of excellence are met. So, while you may hold regular documented formal performance appraisal interviews, you should also regularly appraise performance informally.

TIPS ON EMPLOYEE APPRAISALS

• *Keep good records.* You will need all the information and data you can find, especially if you expect the interview to be a difficult one—and some of them will be! Records of attendance, lateness, job rejects, targets not met and missed deadlines can be useful to ensure that you both stick to the facts. If you are able to say: 'Pat, as you know, your output was down by 8% over the last period and you were late four times this month. This isn't like you and I'm concerned about what is happening', you will have a far more constructive discussion than if you say: 'Pat, your work is slipshod and going to pot. You'll have to improve. And make sure you're in on time in the mornings, too—I can't tolerate lateness!' The first statement opens the door to joint and constructive problem solving, while the second is non-specific and accusing and likely to lead to defensiveness rather than problem solving.

• *Let the appraisee have their say.* Ask open questions, questions that can't be answered with a 'yes' or 'no', such as 'What do you think you can do about this?' or 'What do you see as your main strengths?' or 'What do you think contributes to this problem?'

• *Remember that you are not evaluating the person, but the person's performance.* Make sure the appraisee is aware of this.

• *Establish clear, measurable, attainable performance targets.* People need something to work towards and SMARTT targets give you both something concrete on which to base your performance discussion.

• *Focus your discussion on what the employee can do to improve performance or continue to grow and develop.* Discuss ways in which the employee can learn and apply new skills and concepts.

- *Give the appraisee an opportunity to discuss your performance as a supervisor.* Ideally, performance appraisals should be two-way. You may get a lot of useful tips that will help you improve your own job performance, and the appraisee will probably respect your openness and willingness to listen and learn. A simple question like: 'What can I do to make your job easier?' can start the ball rolling. Encouraging and listening to feedback models the behaviour you expect in your employees.
- *Treat all appraisals as confidential.* They should not be discussed with other employees.
- *Assess a person's skill against job requirements.*
- *Don't rush through an appraisal interview.* Allow time for questions, discussion and sharing ideas.
- *Build on strengths.* Reinforce good performance in order to breed more.
- *Prepare to face problems.* Problems ignored tend to grow worse. Bring them into the open in an impartial, non-threatening way. Criticism is more acceptable if it is supported by facts and directed at behaviour, not at the person.
- *Be honest.* If an employee's work has been poor, say so. Then turn the discussion to where and how it can be improved.
- *Don't confuse length of service with job performance.* Just because an employee has been with the organisation a long time doesn't guarantee excellence in performing a job. Conversely, just because someone is new to a job doesn't automatically mean they are unable to do it very well.

BEING APPRAISED

Supervisors are appraised, too. Both your work team and manager appraise you informally and your manager will probably also appraise you formally. Here are some tips to follow when it is time for your own performance appraisal.

- Be clear about which of your responsibilities are most important. Organising your job into key result areas (KRAs) and targets will show you the main areas to focus on.
- Try to get measurable criteria upon which your performance will be assessed, so that you will have a sound and objective basis for discussion. Make sure you get feedback about these criteria.
- Keep a note of your successes so that, if your manager has a short memory, you can jog it.
- Review the five keys and identify any performance difficulties you experience and their causes so that you can discuss possible remedial action. Ensure that your manager knows you have taken or intend to take positive action.
- Decide what you want to talk about. What problems bother you most? Which, if resolved, could provide a key to solving others? Which, if left alone, will grow worse? Which require most help or support from others? From what training and development opportunities would you benefit?
- Approach the appraisal discussion in a positive frame of mind. Be open to your manager's advice and listen carefully to any suggestions and constructive feedback.

OTHER USES OF PERFORMANCE APPRAISALS

Supervisors frequently make decisions that affect the pay, promotion, transfer, demotion or discharge of their employees. Many organisations offer a component of merit-based pay or pay-for-skills and they need an objective way to calculate what this will be. When vacancies arise, many organisations prefer to look internally first, or at least offer existing employees the opportunity to apply for a position. If it becomes necessary to discharge some employees for business reasons (e.g. lack of work, or restructuring), they need a fair and unbiased way to select who should remain and who should go.

Perhaps you have made an error in judgment in placing an employee in a job and you want to transfer them to a more suitable position. Perhaps you want to move someone laterally to provide continuing job challenge or give greater all-round experience and development. Sometimes, although an employee may be doing well in the current position, the organisation may need them more in another job.

Should these critical personnel actions be based on spur-of-the-moment decisions or on carefully thought-out assessments made in a systematic way? The answer is obvious. Systematic performance appraisals provide a sound basis for supervisors to be fair, equitable and just, and for organisations to protect their employees from arbitrary decisions.

Because you may make many such decisions during your supervisory career, and because these decisions vitally affect employees' jobs and even their lives, the question is not whether you need to evaluate your employees' performance, but how you will do it. The overwhelming vote by most supervisors is for some formalised system incorporating one or more of the methods referred to earlier in this chapter. These methods provide the most accurate and fair estimate of an employee's capacity and value to the organisation. At the same time, they provide employees with protection against a variety of subjective and unfair decisions. By using performance appraisals, therefore, you can move or promote employees from one job to another with greater assurance that the moves are fair and will benefit both the employees and the organisation.

Dismissing employees

Termination of employment is a permanent separation from the organisation. Dismissal is usually a result of poor job performance or a serious offence by the employee.

Because of unfair dismissal laws, people can't be fired at will. Dismissed employees can sue former employers and get their job back, win back pay and even sue for damages for emotional injury if a dismissal was harsh, unjust or unreasonable. Objective performance appraisals can be of tremendous help because they document the employee's performance over a period of time and can show that the dismissal was fair and justified (see also Chapter 24).

Demotion

Economic or business reasons may make demotions, retrenchments or redundancies necessary. Performance appraisals can help supervisors to be equitable and fair when making decisions about who will be demoted, retrenched or made redundant.

A **demotion** is a reassignment to a job of lower rank and pay. This usually results from factors beyond an employee's control. Recessions, changing technology or changes to production or service requirements may cause restructuring and redundancies, with some demotions occurring among the remaining employees. It is unwise to demote a person for disciplinary reasons although some organisations will occasionally demote an employee for continued substandard performance rather than dismiss them.

Redundancy and retrenchment

Redundancies occur when positions are no longer required in an organisation. This may be due to job redesign, or a restructuring of the organisation or department. In such cases, it is the position, not the individual, that is no longer required. **Retrenchments**, or lay-offs, are caused by a lack of sufficient work to keep people fully occupied.

An employer must notify Centrelink in advance if 15 or more redundancies or retrenchments are planned.

Transferring employees

Whenever you consider changing an employee from one job to another, being able to refer to past performance appraisals will be very helpful. They can assist in making decisions on which job to assign to which employee and help to ensure that people are placed in the jobs best suited to their capabilities.

Internal promotions

Promoting an employee to a job of higher rank and pay rather than hiring an outsider to fill the vacancy has many advantages. If promotion is seldom from within, employees will suspect that all the better jobs are reserved for outsiders. Consequently, there is little motivation for them to work harder to develop themselves and improve their job skills. Promoting an employee who has been with an organisation for several years can be a great morale booster and provide strong incentives for other employees to perform better or upgrade their skills.

For the organisation, promotion from within means having an old hand on the payroll who knows the organisation and its ways of operating, instead of a new employee who may or may not work out well. Promotion from within therefore can result in better selection and placement. Internal promotions show that the organisation recognises ability and rewards good performance. Basing promotions on performance appraisals will help to ensure that the most suitable employees are promoted.

There is a danger to promoting from within which should not be overlooked. Organisations that continually promote from within, to total or near total exclusion of outsiders, are in danger of 'inbreeding'. 'New blood', new attitudes, new ideas, new ways of doing things—a fresh approach—are important benefits of recruiting from outside the organisation. Changes in technology, work or production methods, products, services or markets may force the organisation to recruit from outside if it is to have an efficient and effective workforce.

Who should get promoted?

Some employees are not interested in promotion. Others seek job changes and promotions. This would be indicated during their performance appraisal.

Performance appraisals can also help you decide who to recommend for a promotion. As with filling any vacancy, you should start with the job description and personnel specification (see Chapter 15). Begin by looking at the vacancy to be filled and the skills, knowledge and attributes required to fill it well. Then consider candidates' performance appraisals. These, combined with careful observation of employees, will help you to assess a person's suitability for promotion.

.... **RAPID REVIEW** ....

	True	False
1. Since supervisors are always evaluating employees anyway, formal written performance appraisals waste everyone's time.	☐	☐
2. Performance appraisals are an opportunity for supervisors to highlight an employee's faults in a clear and direct way.	☐	☐
3. Performance appraisals allow supervisors to plan productivity improvements and strengthen working relationships.	☐	☐
4. Performance appraisals provide a written record of employee strengths, weaknesses and aspirations and can be useful when considering changes to an employee's status in the organisation.	☐	☐
5. Different types of formal appraisals are suited to different jobs.	☐	☐
6. Supervisors need to be objective, fair and factual when appraising employee performance.	☐	☐
7. Rating each employee as 'average' saves a lot of time and trouble. This should be the supervisor's main aim in appraising employee performance.	☐	☐
8. Management by objectives is a good way for supervisors and employees to agree on work targets.	☐	☐
9. Targets need to be flexible.	☐	☐
10. If an employee's performance is not up to scratch in certain areas, this should be ignored and areas where performance is good should be focused on.	☐	☐
11. Both supervisors and employees need to prepare for performance appraisals.	☐	☐
12. Formal performance appraisals can effectively replace informal appraisals.	☐	☐
13. Performance appraisals evaluate performance, not people.	☐	☐
14. When being appraised, you can sit back and let your supervisor do all the work.	☐	☐
15. Agreeing on job targets, training needs and career paths are some of the uses of performance appraisals.	☐	☐

.... **APPLY YOUR KNOWLEDGE** ....

1. Discuss the benefits that result from well conducted systematic performance appraisals.

2. What methods of performance appraisal are commonly used? Explain the main characteristics of each.

3. List what you believe are the main flaws a supervisor should watch for in assessing employees' performance, and state how each of these can be overcome.

4. What is MBO and how can it be adapted for complex or wide-ranging jobs?

5. List and explain the steps in conducting a performance appraisal interview and describe what should happen before and after the interview.

6. Discuss five practices that supervisors should follow when conducting performance appraisals.

7. Why do employees change jobs within an organisation? How can performance appraisals help in these changes?

Individual activities

1. Interview someone who either conducts or receives performance appraisals. What do they see as the difficulties and benefits involved? How do they try to overcome the difficulties? Compare your findings with others in your class.
2. Do some independent research on management by objectives. Write a short paper describing how it works, its benefits and its shortcomings.
3. Why are informal appraisals important?
4. How should a person go about being appraised?
5. Discuss the main uses of performance appraisals.
6. Relate performance appraisals to the types of feedback discussed in Chapter 24.

Group activities

1. Form into groups of three, with an observer/coach, appraisee and appraiser. The appraisee should take the part of Mark in the vignette on page 778 and the appraiser should take the role of Mark's supervisor. Role-play the part of the appraisal interview that focuses on Mark's ability to conduct performance appraisals. Your aim should be to help Mark understand the benefits of well conducted appraisals and plan specific actions he can take to carry them out effectively. When you have finished, the coach/observers should offer the appraisers feedback on what they did well and how they could improve. Observers should also offer Mark similar feedback on his role as appraisee.
2. In small groups, brainstorm the purposes and benefits of formal performance appraisals.
3. In small groups, brainstorm the mistakes supervisors make in conducting performance appraisals. Agree on the ten biggest mistakes and discuss how supervisors can overcome each of them.

The Perfect Opportunity

Peter reflected on his forthcoming performance appraisal meeting with Samantha. For several months now, he had been concerned about her ability to perform her job to the required standards, both in terms of quality and quantity. If her quality rate met requirements, the quantity of her output fell markedly. If her quantity met requirements, quality suffered. She just couldn't seem to get the balance right, despite thorough on-the-job training. Peter decided the performance appraisal meeting next week would be the perfect opportunity to set termination of employment for unsatisfactory performance in motion.

When he sat down with Samantha and explained that her performance was unsatisfactory and he couldn't afford to keep her on, she seemed to be truly shocked. While she had known that her output was less than some of the others, she clearly hadn't realised how serious the problem was. She said that she was trying as hard as she could and she really enjoyed her job. She also indicated that she felt she had made progress over the last two or three months. With this, she burst into tears, leaving Peter at a loss to know what to do.

Questions

1   Was the performance appraisal meeting the perfect opportunity to begin the termination of employment process? Why, or why not?
2   What mistakes did Peter make with Samantha's appraisal?
3   What should Peter have done before the meeting? What should he do now?

The Evaluation Conference

Harry Chan was the uncontested chief. He was the picture of what a bank manager should be—neat, well groomed, conservative, pleasant and articulate. As you might expect, Harry wanted his staff to fit into the same mould. He wasn't always successful, however, even though he used every opportunity to try to get the message across.

In his annual evaluation conference with Bob Regan, for example, he brought up the subject of how a bank employee should act and look. The conversation went as follows:

Chan: 'Come in, Bob, and let's get this show on the road.'

Regan: 'Sorry I'm late, Mr Chan, but a customer wanted to change an account.'

Chan: 'I'm glad you brought up changes, because I'd like to see you change somewhat. Your looks don't say "You can trust me" to a customer.'

Regan: 'I'm afraid I don't understand, Sir.'

Chan: 'Well, take that stubbly beard you wear. Our customers don't like to deal with employees who wear beards and loud ties. You do both.'

Regan: 'I've never had a complaint and ...'

Chan: 'And another thing, your general demeanour is far too glib for a savings bank and loan institution. You ought to be more subdued in the way you approach people. This isn't a fairground, you know.'

Regan: 'Mr Chan, I've been working in banks for seven years and I've never had a customer refuse to see me. On the contrary, I have a good many who wait for me. In fact, as far as I can tell, my beard and manner have never interfered with services to our customers. I think you're wrong about ...'

Chan: 'This review session is for you to find out what I think, not for me to find out what you think. I think you present the wrong image and I hope you will work on changing it—starting with a shave.'

Regan: 'What about my job performance, Mr Chan? Is my work satisfactory?'

Chan: 'No real complaint in that department, Regan. You ought to know your job by now. Oh, there is one thing. I noticed that you took a loan application last week that was totally outside the criteria we use. You've placed the bank and the customer in an embarrassing situation. You'd better watch that.'

Regan: 'Mr Chan, I remember the case you are referring to. As a matter of fact, I knew it was marginal, but with the emphasis on equal treatment I thought we ought to look at it. In fact, if you consider that the husband's father is willing to co-sign the note, it meets our criteria.'

Chan: 'Hmm. Yes, well, that about wraps up the evaluation for this year. Send Rhonda in, will you? She's next.'

Questions

1 What mistakes did Mr Chan make in this evaluation?
2 If a particular image is desired in a workplace, how should it be promoted?
3 How would you rate this evaluation conference? Why? How would you have handled it?

Answers to Rapid Review questions

1. F   2. F   3. T   4. T   5. T   6. T   7. F   8. T   9. T   10. F   11. T   12. F   13. T   14. F   15. T

GLOSSARY

85:15 rule   Provided people know precisely what is expected of them and are trained to do it well, 85% of the causes of poor performance and low productivity can be found in the work environment (tools, equipment, teamwork, systems and processes, time, information, job design) and are not the direct fault of the worker. The remaining 15% is accounted for by 'acts of God' and personal problems.

360 degree review   A form of performance appraisal where a selection of all people dealing with a job-holder comment on the job-holder's performance. This might include peers, subordinates, a person's supervisor and other managers the person deals with, customers and suppliers (both external and internal). The intention is to build up a full picture of how a person does their job so that they can improve their performance.

accountability   Being held answerable for the work for which you are responsible.

acknowledgment listening   Responding to a speaker with eye contact, nods, 'uh-huhs' and other minimal encouragers.

active listening   Briefly restating your understanding of the speaker's feelings and/or meaning.

affirmative action   Equal employment opportunity measures aimed at removing the past and present effects of discrimination against women in the workforce.

agenda   A list of the topics to be covered during a meeting and the order in which they are to be covered. Modern agendas are often written with verbs to indicate what is to be achieved, or the objective of each discussion (agree X, decide Y, explore N).

aggressive behaviour   Putting your own wants and needs ahead of others, often discounting the wants and needs of others. *See also* assertive behaviour and passive behaviour.

antidiscrimination legislation   Legislation designed to stop specific groups and individual members of those groups from being treated unfairly and to ensure they are treated solely on the basis of their skills and abilities.

assertive behaviour   A learned style of communicating and relating to others based on mutual respect and resulting in clear, open communication; the ability to state your own wants and needs while at the same time respecting the wants and needs of the other person. *See also* aggressive behaviour and passive behaviour.

Australian Workplace Agreements (AWAs)   A system of individual or collective employment contracts agreed through workplace bargaining which become operative once signed by each employee.

authority   The right to decide what is to be done and who will do it; can be formally conferred by the organisation or informally by others such as a work group.

award A collective agreement between unions and employer representatives detailing the minimum conditions of and remuneration for specified jobs.

award restructuring The movement by the Australian federal Labor government and the ACTU in the late 1980s–early 1990s to reduce the number of trade unions and remove unnecessary demarcation between union members in order to increase the competitiveness of Australian industry.

behavioural interviewing A method of interviewing that focuses on what the candidate has done in the past and uses it to predict what they will do in the future, comparing the needs of the job with the abilities of the candidate.

benchmarking Meaningful standard measures of performance either internal to an organisation or across organisations. *See also* best practice benchmarking.

best practice benchmarking Comparing measures of an organisation's performance with those of other organisations in the same or different industries.

board of directors The policy- and strategy-establishing body of a corporation which represents its shareholders and guides the operations of an organisation.

boomerang principle The concept that what we 'send out' to others returns to us; e.g. if we are polite to someone, they will probably be polite to us in return.

brainstorming A technique that helps a group to come up with a large number of ideas for later evaluation.

budget A target expressed in financial terms such as dollar value of sales or expenses.

bullying Continual aggressive, demeaning remarks and behaviour.

bureaucracy An organisation characterised by a formal chain of command, a rigid or semi-rigid hierarchy, specialisation of tasks and strict rules and procedures.

burnout The 'syndrome of just being sick', first identified by Dr Hans Serle, resulting from unalleviated stress.

business ethics The way an organisation conducts its affairs according to the morals and principles accepted by society and to its stated values.

cause-and-effect diagram A pictorial representation that helps to identify problems, isolate the main cause of a problem or specify/clarify a problem by allowing us to view it in its entirety. Also called Ishikawa diagrams and fishbone diagrams.

centralised organisation One in which decision-making authority resides with management.

certified agreement A workplace agreement negotiated either with unions or directly with employees which becomes operative once signed by a majority of employees.

check sheet A method of gathering data based on sample observations that helps detect and isolate patterns of non-conformance and variation.

checkerboard analysis A matrix used to analyse a problem by comparing various elements of the problem with each other.

closed question One that can be answered with a 'yes', 'no', or short statement of fact.

collective bargaining A process whereby employment wages and conditions are agreed centrally, between main groups representing the parties concerned.

competency A skill, knowledge or aptitude needed to carry out a task successfully; discrete, observable behaviours which enable a person to perform an activity to the standard expected in a job context.

competency-based job description   A job description that shows the competencies required by the job-holder.

competency-based training   Training focused on outcomes where trainees are required to demonstrate they have the required skills.

competency statement   Defines what is to be done, to what standards, under what conditions; often includes knowledge (cognitive), manual (psychomotor) and attitudinal (affective) skills.

conciliation and arbitration   A process whereby a neutral third party helps two disagreeing parties (e.g. an employer and an employee) reach agreement (conciliation). If agreement is not reached, the third party, having heard and considered both sides, makes a ruling by which both parties must abide.

consensus   The process by which an issue is explored, analysed and discussed, and agreement reached.

consultation   An approach to management that seeks the opinions of employees before reaching decisions. *See also* industrial democracy.

continuous improvement   Continual incremental improvements to a process, product or service. *See also* kaizen.

control chart   A type of run chart showing the upper and lower acceptable limits of variation in the results of a process on either side of the average; used for quality control purposes.

core process redesign   *See* process re-engineering.

corporate citizenship   An organisation's legal and moral obligations to its community and society, including philanthropy, care for the environment and for future generations.

corporate governance   The way an organisation is governed and controlled, particularly by its board of directors.

corporation   A business that exists independently of its owners and employees; a legal entity in its own right.

cost-driven organisation   One whose primary focus is on reducing the costs of its products or services. *See also* customer-driven organisation and product-driven organisation.

cost of employment   The total cost to an organisation of employing a person, including pay plus contribution to overheads (e.g. infrastructure costs such as cost of office space, equipment and support staff, and other employment costs such as superannuation contributions, workers compensation and other payments).

covert discrimination   Unequal treatment based on characteristics that belong to, or are connected with, some members of a group of people; often subtle and unconscious.

critical control points   The most important aspects of a task or project to monitor.

cross-skilling   Increasing the ability of employees to carry out a wider range of tasks at the same or similar levels of responsibility.

culture   The collection of unwritten rules, codes of behaviour and norms by which people operate; 'how we do things around here'.

customer   The person who benefits from our efforts; can be internal or external to the organisation.

customer-driven organisation   Organisations which place a high priority on identifying and meeting the needs of their external customers. *See also* cost-driven organisation and product-driven organisation.

customer–supplier chain   A systems view of an organisation which sees the internal relationships in the organisation (departments or activities) as one continuous process of supplying and receiving products, services or information.

decentralised organisation   Organisations where decision-making authority is located as close as possible to the area affected by the decision.

decisional roles   *See* roles.

demarcation dispute   Disagreement over boundary lines between unions.

demotion   Reassignment to a job of lower rank and pay.

direct discrimination   Refusal or consistent failure to treat people from disadvantaged groups equally in employment matters. *See also* indirect discrimination.

discrimination   Unequal treatment before, during, or after employment on the grounds of sex, age, national origin, religion, criminal record, sexual preference, trade union activities, political opinion, physical or intellectual disability, marital status, medical record, nationality, parental status or social origin; a distinction, exclusion or preference on the basis of one or more of the above grounds which has the effect of impairing equality or opportunity or treatment in employment or occupation.

distress   Negative stress or pressure that undermines our ability to cope. *See also* eustress.

downsizing   Reducing the number of employees in an organisation in an effort to lower costs, increase profitability and, often, be more responsive in the marketplace by streamlining internal operations.

empathy   The ability to see problems or situations from the other person's point of view.

employment contract   The agreement between an organisation and an employee covering such things as remuneration, hours of work, location of work.

empowerment   Providing training and conditions which enable employees or a work team to increase their range of decision-making authorities and responsibilities.

enterprise bargaining   The process where employers and employees, or their representatives, sit down together to review the performance of the enterprise, decide what measures employees will take to help improve productivity, and what changes will be made to their terms and conditions of work (hours, pay, etc.).

espoused theory   What people say they value, believe or believe in. *See also* theory-in-use.

eustress   Positive stress or pressures that energise and invigorate us. *See also* distress.

exit interview   A discussion, usually held between a 'neutral' party such as a HR Officer and an employee, to discover the reason the employee has resigned. The information is used to improve the organisation's ability to retain valued employees.

external customers   The people or organisations who purchase or use our products and services. *See also* internal customers.

feedback analysis   A technique to analyse and improve your performance. You write down your expected outcome of a decision or important event and, 9–12 months later, compare this with the actual outcome. This highlights where we need to improve skills or acquire new ones.

fight/flight response   An instinctive reaction to a dangerous or unpleasant situation: to stay and fight it, or turn and flee from it.

first-line management   The level of management between the non-management work-force and the rest of management.

fishbone diagram   *See* cause-and-effect diagram.

flow chart   A pictorial representation showing all the steps of a process or activity.

force field analysis   A technique that helps to ensure smooth implementation of a plan or decision by highlighting factors working against us (resisting forces) which we should diminish or remove, and factors in our favour (driving forces) which we can capitalise on to move from the current to the desired situation.

formal leader   The official leader of a group or team.

formal organisation   The official structure depicted in an organisation chart showing the officially recognised lines of authority, communication and responsibility. *See also* informal organisation.

framing statement   A short declaration used to introduce and specify a topic for discussion.

fuzzy logic   A superset of conventional (Boolean) logic that has been extended to handle the concept of partial truth and to generalise any specific theory from go-no go to 'fuzzy', allowing 'shades of grey'. Used in very complex processes when there is not a simple mathematical model, for very non-linear processes and for processing expert knowledge. Used in some computer programs, automobile cruise controls, optimising bus time tables, controlling back light on camcorders, single button control for washing machines, etc.

gainsharing   Passing on some of the benefits of productivity increases to employees through increased earnings.

Gantt chart   A planning and monitoring aid, listing planned activities vertically and time periods horizontally.

gap analysis   An exploration of 'Where are we now?' and 'Where do we want to be?', establishing the actions required to bridge the gap, or move from the current to the desired situation.

goal   An overall aim providing focus and direction for day-to-day activities and a reference point for decision making.

grievance   A complaint that has been formally registered with an employee's super-visor, trade union or management official in accordance with the recognised grievance procedure.

group dynamics   The unique pattern of forces operating in a group that affects particularly the interactions between members and their relationships with each other; the way people operate together and their behaviour towards each other which influences how they go about achieving the task.

group process The way a group of people work together, including communication patterns and style, level of participation, absence or presence of tension, group norms.

groupthink A phenomenon of highly cohesive groups which occurs when group members would rather maintain a group's equanimity than cause friction by challenging ideas, stating an opposing point of view or tabling contrary evidence, thus inhibiting disagreement, constructive criticism, full assessment of alternatives and filtering out contraindications to a decision or chosen course of action.

halo/horns effect *See* self-fulfilling prophecy.

harassment *See* sexual harassment.

hazard Something that is likely to cause an accident or injury.

histogram Bar chart that displays the distribution of measurement data in graph form, showing the frequency with which these events occur; reveals the amount of variation in a process and helps to discover and describe a problem and monitor its solution.

holistic organisation One that is organic and humanistic, honouring employees as individuals.

hotdesking Where employees book desks or offices by the hour, day or week. *See also* hotelling.

hot stove principle Providing advanced warning followed by immediate, consistent and impartial discipline.

hotelling Where employees book an office for a particular day(s) and arrive to find it furnished with their own personal memorabilia—family photos, favourite reference books, etc. *See also* hotdesking.

hygiene factors Factors in the surroundings of the job which, when satisfactory, put people in 'neutral' and, when not satisfactory, can 'demotivate' workers.

'I' language An assertive style of communication which involves taking responsibility for and communicating your own feelings, thoughts and opinions.

'I' message A clear, succinct and blame-free statement of the effect of another's actions on you, and your preferred outcome.

indirect discrimination Occurs when policies and practices appear on the surface to be neutral but which act to disadvantage members of some disadvantaged groups. *See also* direct discrimination.

induction The process of welcoming and introducing new employees to, and familiarising them with, the organisation, their department and their workmates in order to help them fit in smoothly and efficiently.

industrial democracy The move towards increasing the influence of employees in decisions affecting their organisation and their jobs.

influence The informal power a person holds.

informal leader A leader unofficially 'appointed' by the group or team itself.

informal organisation The unofficial power hierarchy and relationships in an organisation.

informational roles *See* roles.

instant dismissal   Termination of employment without notice or pay in lieu of notice for a serious offence such as theft or wilful damage to company or customer property. In New Zealand, there must be a 24 hour 'cooling off' period.

integrated value chain   The entire process an organisation uses to produce value, beginning with and including external suppliers and ending with and including external customers.

interference listening   Verbally or non-verbally signalling to a speaker our own thoughts or feelings about the message they are trying to communicate. This interferes with their thought processes and hinders their ability to communicate fully.

internal customers   People inside our organisation who benefit from our efforts. *See also* external customers.

interpersonal roles   *See* roles.

Ishikawa diagram   *See* cause-and-effect diagram.

job analysis   A study and description of precisely how a job is done and any special safety needs.

job breakdown   An instruction tool which divides a job or task into its stages and key points.

job description   A document which outlines the key objectives, duties, tasks, activities, responsibilities and relationships of a job and any special conditions such as requirements to work overtime or travel away from home. *See also* competency-based job description.

job design   The way a job is structured in terms of its specific duties, responsibilities and tasks. An important source of job satisfaction and an influencer of performance.

job enlargement   Expanding a job horizontally, at the same or similar level of responsibility and authority.

job enrichment   Expanding a job vertically, at a higher level of responsibility and authority.

job purpose   A succinct, motivational statement that expresses the main reason a job exists.

Johari Window   A model for self-awareness developed by Joe Luft and Harry Ingham, based on two dimensions: aspects of ourselves known or not known to ourselves and aspects of ourselves known or not known to others; this gives us four 'windows' or areas of knowledge about ourselves.

just-in-time (JIT)   A method of stock management which aims for raw materials to arrive just when they are required for production to minimise the need for expensive stock holdings and storage.

kaizen   Continuous incremental, or small step, improvements. *See also* continuous improvement.

key performance indicators   Measures of success in reaching targets and goals. *See also* measures of performance.

key result areas (KRAs)   The main areas of responsibility and accountability of a job.

labour costs   A function of labour rates and productivity.

labour rates   How much the organisation pays employees per hour or other unit of time.

lag indicators   Measures of results after the process is completed; historical measures. *See also* lead indicators.

lead indicators   Measures taken during a process; current measures of what is happening as the process occurs.

learning organisation   One where individual employees continually learn and transmit their learning through the organisation, enabling the organisation itself to learn, develop and improve along with its employees; one that is able to learn continually from its experiences, successes and mistakes.

levels of management   The traditional categorisation of management into three levels: senior, middle and first-line or supervisory management.

lifetime customer value   The value of a customer during the time she/he does business with an organisation.

line positions   Those whose activities are directly associated with the production of the goods or services of an organisation. *See also* staff positions.

locus of control   The location of the impulses which guide our behaviour; can be internal or external.

lose–win position   The 'I lose and you win' mind-set that characterises passive behaviour.

maintenance functions   The actions that serve to enable people to achieve the task, such as morale-building, nurturing feelings of belonging and cohesion, time out for a bit of fun or humour, and establishing a friendly and supportive working climate.

management by exception   Asking people to report only important deviations to you. If nothing is reported, this means everything is going according to plan and agreed targets are being reached.

management by objectives (MBO)   A managerial process in which employees and management agree on set specific employee objectives and targets, aligned with corporate targets and goals, to be accomplished within a given period of time.

materials resources planning   Sophisticated computer software program that helps a business to plan, coordinate and control its goods inwards, manufacturing, inventory and dispatch functions.

matrix organisation   *See* structure, matrix.

measures of performance   Also called *measures of success*, these key performance indicators measure important aspects of a job or task to track how well it is being performed.

mechanistic organisation   One with specialised and standardised jobs, authority based on hierarchy and formal channels of communication, making it suited to stable and predictable environments.

mentor   A person (often older, more senior or experienced) who takes an interest in someone's career and provides positive help, support, advice and encouragement.

middle management   The level of management between senior management and supervisory management.

mind-set   *See* paradigm.

minutes   A record of what has been said and agreed during a meeting. They also indicate the time, date and place of the meeting.

mission The overriding or overall strategic goal set by senior managers and directors of an organisation; answers the questions, 'What business are we in?' and 'How will we achieve our vision?'

moments of truth Any contact a customer has with an organisation, e.g. personally or electronically.

motivation factors Factors in the job itself which provide satisfaction and encourage people to perform enthusiastically. *See also* hygiene factors.

multifunctional team A team responsible for delivering the entire product or service including design, marketing, manufacture, after-sales service and delivery.

multiskilling Training across a broad range of skills enabling employees to carry out a wider range of tasks.

netiquette Commonly accepted procedures, or protocol, to follow when composing and sending emails.

networking Building a web of mutually supportive, informal relationships with others inside and outside the organisation in order to share help, advice and support.

nominal group technique A way to ensure that the opinion of everyone in the group is considered; based on a multiple voting system.

non-programmed decisions Decisions for which there are many possible satisfactory solutions and which need to be considered individually. *See also* programmed decisions.

non-verbal communication Communication that takes place through symbols, facial expressions, body language and other non-oral means.

norms Commonly accepted standards of behaviour in a group.

not-for-profit sector Non-government organisations whose purpose is to fulfil a mission other than making a profit.

objective A clear, specific measuring post indicating progress towards achieving a goal. A short-term goal.

online chats Real-time conversations held on screen via the Internet.

open question One that encourages a full response, not just a 'yes', 'no' or short statement of fact.

organic organisation One where jobs are flexible, authority is based on relevant skills and knowledge, and communication is open, making the organisation reasonably flexible and adaptable and therefore suited to volatile environments.

organisation chart A diagram that shows the deployment of people into functions or responsibilities and how these relate to each other; depicting the formal organisation structure or framework, span of management and lines of authority and responsibility.

organisation design The process of creating or developing the most suitable organisation structure.

organisation structure The official framework that links the employees and functions of an enterprise.

overt discrimination Direct, clear discrimination on the grounds of, for example, sex, race or national origin. *See also* covert discrimination.

paradigm Our beliefs about the world and how it operates; often an unconscious and unquestioned mind-set that guides our behaviour. Also called *world view* and *mental models*.

Pareto chart   A vertical bar chart which displays the relative importance of problems or events, showing the data in descending order of quantity.

Pareto principle   The 80:20 rule of Vilfredo Pareto which says that 20% of our efforts gain us 80% of our results and vice versa.

participation   An approach to management where the workforce becomes involved in the operations of an organisation and in its decision-making processes. *See also* industrial democracy.

participative management   *See* participation.

partnership   An enterprise in which two or more people share the ownership of a business and have unlimited liability.

passive behaviour   Putting the wants and needs of others ahead of one's own.

passive listening   Gazing at the speaker without giving any verbal or non-verbal signals that we are hearing or understanding their message.

PDCA cycle   The Plan-Do-Check-Act process for making and maintaining improvements to a system or process.

performance appraisal   A formalised, systematic assessment and discussion of an employee's performance and his or her potential and desire for development and training.

performance counselling   The process of discussing an employee's performance with a view to improving it so that performance expectations are met.

performance gap   The difference between the expected performance and actual performance, preferably measurable, although it can be behavioural (i.e. something you see or hear).

performance measure   A clear, quantifiable standard of performance.

personal counselling   Helping an employee explore, understand and sometimes solve or resolve problems of a personal, non-work-related nature.

personality types   A systematic method of categorising people's key personality traits which can help us deal with them more effectively. Jung's personality types sees introverts and extroverts as two basic ways of relating to the world, and four ways of receiving and dealing with information: thinking, intuiting, feeling and sensing.

personnel specification   A description of the skills, knowledge and abilities, or competencies, required by an ideal job-holder.

pie chart   A circular graph showing percentages of the data being studied displayed like slices of a pie.

power   A person's ability to 'make things happen', arising from their formal position and/or their personal attributes.

private company   The term for a proprietary company in Queensland.

private sector   Corporations, firms and partnerships whose primary goal is to make money for their owners through the provision of goods or services.

process capability chart   A graph used to show whether a process is capable of meeting the specifications and to monitor the performance of a system.

process re-engineering   Using technology and systematic analytic methods to radically redesign processes and operating procedures to achieve dramatic improvements in productivity; radically rethinking an organisation's processes, systems and procedures from top to bottom. Also known as *re-engineering* and *core process redesign*.

product-driven organisation   One whose main priority is producing goods or services and then finding customers who want to buy them. *See also* cost-driven organisation and customer-driven organisation.

programmed decisions   Routine decisions for which one answer consistently applies.

proprietary company   A corporation with limited liability which has up to 50 owners; signified by the abbreviation Pty Ltd after its name.

psychological contract   The unwritten and usually unstated expectations and norms about how we will work with others and our employer.

public company   A corporation with limited liability which has any number of owners and is quoted on the Stock Exchange; signified by the abbreviation Ltd or the word Limited after its name.

public sector   Organisations involved either directly or indirectly in the business of governing the country.

Pygmalion effect   *See* self-fulfilling prophecy.

quality circle   An aspect of the TQM movement which involves employees in problem solving and decision making in areas that directly affect them, particularly ways to improve work processes and methods; quality circles use a range of systematic analytic techniques to identify, analyse and solve problems and improve procedures.

quality system   The internal procedures by which an organisation formally controls its processes and activities to ensure the quality of its products or services.

quango   Quasi-autonomous government organisation.

redundancy   Termination of employment because the position is no longer needed by the organisation, usually due to job redesign or restructuring.

re-engineering   *See* process re-engineering.

remuneration   The total reward package of an employee, also known as compensation, including pay plus fringe benefits such as penalty rates, annual leave, sick leave loading and provision of motor vehicle.

responsibility   The obligation that an employee has to his or her supervisor to do a job that has been assigned.

restructuring   Altering the design of an organisation.

retrenchment   Lay-offs caused by lack of sufficient work to keep people fully occupied.

risk   The degree of likelihood that a hazard will cause an accident or injury.

role clarification   A process to ensure each member of a team is clear about what is expected of them in their job role (task) and behaviours (process).

role conflict   When the various roles a person plays require different and incompatible behaviour, beliefs or attitudes.

role expectations   The expectations that others hold about a certain role.

role model   A person whose behaviour and actions we can copy in order to acquire skills and attributes and use to determine appropriate behaviour.

role perception   Our own idea of what a role demands regarding behaviour, attitudes, dress and so on.

roles   The functions identified by Henry Mintzberg which managers fulfil in various situations: interpersonal roles (figurehead, leader, liaison), informational roles (monitor, disseminator, spokesperson) and decisional roles (entrepreneur, disturbance handler, resource allocator, negotiator). Other life roles include sibling, parent, student, supervisor, colleague, friend and employee.

run chart   A simple way to graph trends in a process.

safety analysis   An examination of a task or job to pinpoint its hazards and safety requirements.

satellite offices   Fully equipped offices run by public or private sector organisations for their own teleworkers, or run by community or private groups for independent workers to lease.

scatter diagram   A way of displaying what happens to one variable when you change another variable, revealing any relationships or correlations between the variables.

self-awareness   The degree to which a person understands their own motivations, feelings, beliefs, values, attitudes and perceptions of the world.

self-esteem   Our feelings of self-respect and self-worth; how we value ourselves.

self-fulfilling prophecy   The process by which our beliefs, paradigms and self-esteem influence the way we perceive the world and others and our behaviour; we tend to perceive what we expect, which reinforces our beliefs.

self-image   How we see ourselves; the view we hold of ourselves that describes us and defines us.

self-talk   The often unconscious messages we give ourselves about ourselves which tend to govern our behaviour.

senior management   The highest level of management in an organisation.

sexual harassment   Unwanted or unwelcome sexual advances, requests for sexual favours or unwelcome conduct of a sexual nature, including verbal as well as non-verbal behaviour and innuendo.

single bargaining unit   The work site which is the focus of a workplace agreement.

SOHO   The small office/home office from which teleworkers and others often operate.

sole trader   A person who is the single owner of a business with unlimited liability.

span of management   The number of people an individual supervises.

special measures   Actions aimed at redressing discrimination that has occurred in the past; helps people from disadvantaged groups to 'catch up' and compete equally for jobs, training and promotion.

staff positions   Those positions whose activities are indirectly associated with the production of goods or services of an organisation (advisory and internal service positions).

stakeholders   An organisation's stakeholders are considered to be: owners, employees, customers/clients, suppliers, the wider society and the closer community.

standard operating procedure (SOP) A document listing the step-by-step method of carrying out a task.

state agreements Individual or collective workplace agreements which override federal awards.

stratification chart A way to graph and analyse data by breaking it down into meaningful categories, helping to isolate a problem.

stress The pressures, demands and constraints we place on ourselves and are placed on us by our environment and by others, resulting in physical or psychological tension; can be positive or negative. *See also* distress and eustress.

stressors Sources of stress.

structural discrimination *See* systemic discrimination.

structure, customer-type An organisation in which relationships and activities are arranged according to the major customer groups.

structure, functional An organisation in which relationships and activities are arranged so that each function works independently.

structure, geographic location An organisation in which relationships and activities are arranged along geographic divisions.

structure, matrix An organisation in which relationships and activities are arranged so that individuals report to different supervisors for different activities.

structure, product An organisation in which relationships and activities are arranged so that product groupings are kept together.

subculture The culture of subgroups which form part of a larger group. *See also* culture.

SWOT analysis A way to identify an organisation's internal strengths and weaknesses and external opportunities and threats.

synergy The ability of the whole team to achieve more than its individual members could achieve singly.

systemic discrimination The result of longstanding direct and indirect discrimination that seems to be the 'natural order of things'.

target A specific, measurable and trackable indicator of performance against objectives and goals.

task functions Actions that move us towards achieving the job at hand. *See also* maintenance functions.

task readiness level An employee's skills and willingness to carry out a particular task; used to determine an appropriate leadership style.

team briefing A systematic process, cascading from the top down, of holding meetings to keep all employees informed about important events and results in the organisation.

team building The process of working with a team to clarify its task and the way team members can work together better (process issues) to achieve it.

team maintenance *See* maintenance functions.

teleconference A meeting between people using simultaneous telephone line connections allowing participants to hear and speak to each other.

teleworkers People who work from home, a satellite office near home, or from a mobile office such as a vehicle.

termination of employment   A permanent separation from the organisation, usually a result of poor job performance or a serious offence by the employee.

theory-in-use   What people actually do, which may or may not be consistent with their espoused theory. *See also* espoused theory.

Theory X   A leadership style based on a belief that employees are lazy and work only for money, evoking leader behaviours of coercion and threats of punishment. *See also* Theory Y.

Theory Y   A leadership style based on a belief that employees want to do their jobs well and will seek responsibility and challenge, evoking leader behaviours of high expectations and coaching.

total quality control (TQC)   *See* total quality management.

total quality management (TQM)   The culture, mind-set and methods that drive quality in an organisation.

trading partnerships   The view that organisations and suppliers operate together to achieve mutually satisfactory outcomes; if one 'loses' so does the other.

training needs analysis   Gathering information to identify gaps between required job performance or competency and what a person or group is able to achieve.

unity of command   A principle which states that each employee should receive instructions from only one person about a task, job or project.

upwards delegation   This occurs when employees pass work tasks or responsibilities 'up' to their supervisor to do for them.

value system   The set of personal values or beliefs that a person holds as important about what is wrong and right, good and bad, important and not important; the system guides our behaviour and the way we live our lives; our 'inner compass'.

values   What a person or an organisation believes is important and worthwhile; operating principles that guide action and behaviour.

variation   The normal ups and downs in a process.

verbal communication   Spoken or oral communication between people or groups.

videoconference   Meeting held between people or groups in different locations with a real-time video link which allows participants to see and hear each other.

virtual organisation   One where people work together but are based in different locations, seldom meeting face-to-face. Communication is primarily electronic and via video- and tele-conferencing.

vision   A statement that describes the culture, operating philosophy and beliefs an organisation aspires to, answering the questions, 'Who are we?' and 'How do we operate?'

win–lose position   I win and you lose; a mind-set that characterises aggressive behaviour.

win–win position   I win and you win too: we can both be satisfied; a mind-set that characterises assertive behaviour.

workplace agreement   *See* Australian Workplace Agreements.

workplace bargaining   *See* enterprise bargaining.

BIBLIOGRAPHY

Journals and periodicals

Company Director, Australian Institute of Company Directors.

Harvard Business Review, Boston, Mass.

Harvard Management Update, Harvard Business School Publishing Corp. newsletter.

HRMonthly, Australian Human Resources Institute, Hardie Grant Magazines, Victoria.

Management Today, Australian Institute of Management, BRW Media.

Management Today, British Institute of Management, Management Publications Ltd, London.

National Occupational Health and Safety Commission: various publications, particularly *Small Business Management Training: Integrating Occupational Health and Safety Competencies, A Guide for Trainers and Educators*.

Professional Manager, Institute of Management, UK.

Training and Development, US Society of Training and Development, November 1999.

Workmatters, newsletter of Workplace Services, Dept for Administrative and Information Services, Canberra.

Miscellaneous publications

Australian Centre for Industrial Relations Research & Training, University of Sydney. *Australia at Work*, Prentice Hall, Melbourne, 1999.

The Australian Mission on Management Skills. Commonwealth of Australia, 1991.

Australian National Training Authority. *Frontline Management Competencies*, Prentice Hall, Sydney, 1998.

Australian National Training Authority. *Generic Management Competency Standards for Frontline Management*, ANTA, June 1996.

Australian Quality Council. *Australian Business Excellence Framework*, 1998.

Compendium of Workers Compensation Statistics, Australia, 1993–1994, Australian Government Publishing Service, Canberra.

Glenn, J. C. & T. J. Gordon (eds). *The Millennium Project*, American Council for the United Nations University, 1996.

Greenleaf, Robert K. Two essays called 'The Servant as Leader' (first published 1970 by R. K. Greenleaf) and 'The Institution as Servant' (first published 1972 by R. K. Greenleaf). Now available through the Robert K. Greenleaf Center for Servant Leadership, Indianapolis, Indiana.

Heart and Soul, a recent report on the impact of values, published by Blessing/White, UK; copies available from *julietd@uk.bwinc.com*

McLean, C. G. *Occupational Fatalities in Victoria 1990–1993,* VIOSH, Ballarat.

The Memory Jogger: A Pocket Guide of Tools for Continuous Improvement, GOAL/QPC, Methuen, Mass., 1988.

Morehead, A. et al. *Changes at Work: The 1995 Australian Workplace Industrial Relations Survey,* Addison-Wesley Longman, Melbourne, 1997.

Report of the Industry Task Force on Leadership and Management Skills: Enterprising Nation— Renewing Australia's Managers to Meet the Challenges of the Asia Pacific Century (known as the *Karpin Report*), Commonwealth of Australia, April 1995.

Books

Adair, John. *Action Centred Leadership,* McGraw-Hill, London, 1973.

Argyris, C. *Reason, Learning, and Action,* Jossey-Bass: San Francisco, 1982.

Argyris, C. *Overcoming Organizational Defenses,* Allyn & Bacon, Boston, 1990.

Bennis, Warren. *On Becoming a Leader,* Hutchinson Business, London, 1989.

Blanchard, Ken & Spencer Johnson. *The One Minute Manager,* Berkley Books, New York, 1983.

Bolman, Lee G. & Terrence E. Deal. *Leading with Soul: An Uncommon Journey of Spirit,* Jossey-Bass, San Francisco, 1995.

Burrus, Daniel with Roger Gittines. *Technotrends,* Bookman Press, Melbourne, 1993.

Carlzon, Jan. *Moments of Truth,* Harper & Row, Sydney, 1987.

Cole, K. *Crystal Clear Communication,* Prentice Hall, Sydney, 1993 (2nd edn 2000).

De Vrye, Catherine. *Good Service is Good Business,* Prentice Hall, Sydney, 1994.

Deming, W. Edwards. *The New Economics for Industry, Government, Education,* MIT CAES, Cambridge, Mass., 1993.

DePree, Max. *Leadership Jazz,* Information Australia, Melbourne, 1991.

Drucker, Peter F. *Post Capitalist Society,* Butterworth-Heinemann, Oxford, 1993.

Drucker, Peter F. *Management Challenges for the 21st Century,* HarperBusiness, New York, 1999.

Etzioni, A. *A Comparative Analysis of Complex Organisations,* The Free Press, New York, 1975.

Gilbert, Roy. *Reglomania,* Prentice Hall, Sydney, 1991.

Gordon, Ian. *Relationship Marketing,* John Wiley & Sons, Etobicoke, Canada, 1998.

Hamel, Gary & C. K. Prahalad. *Competing for the Future,* Harvard Busniess School Press, Boston, 1996.

Hammond, J. S., R. L. Keeney & Howard Raiffa. *Smart Choices: A Practical Guide to Making Better Decisions,* Harvard Business School Press, 1998.

Handy, Charles. *The Age of Unreason,* Arrow Books, London, 1991.

Handy, Charles. *The Empty Raincoat,* Random House, Sydney, 1994.

Herman, Stanley & Michael Korenich. *Authentic Management: A Gestalt Orientation to Organizations and their Development,* Addison-Wesley, Sydney, 1977.

Holbeche, Linda. *Career Development: The Impact of Flatter Structures on Careers*, Butterworth-Heinemann, London, 1997.

Kanter, Rosabeth Moss. *The Change Masters*, Simon & Schuster, New York, 1983.

Kanter, Rosabeth Moss. *When Giants Learn to Dance*, Touchstone Books, New York, 1990.

Kanter, Rosabeth Moss. *World Class: Thriving Locally in the Global Economy*, Touchstone Books, New York, 1995.

Kanter, Rosabeth Moss. *Kanter on the Frontiers of Management*, Harvard Business School Press, Boston, Mass., 1997.

Kipfer, Barbara Ann. *Roget's 21st Century Thesaurus*, Dell Publishing, New York, 1992.

Kolb, David A., Irwin M. Rubin & James M. McIntyre. *Organizational Psychology: A Book of Readings*, Prentice Hall, Englewood Cliffs, NJ, 1974.

Krass, Peter (ed.). *The Book of Business Wisdom: Classic Writings by the Legends of Commerce and Industry*, John Wiley & Sons, 1997.

Kruithof, Johan. *Quality Thinking, Thinking Quality*, The Business Library, Melbourne, 1993.

LeBoeuf, Michael. *How to Win Customers and Keep Them for Life*, Berkley Publishing Group, New York, 1989.

Long, Alan. *The Manager's and Supervisor's Guide to Continuous Improvement*, Statman Publishing, Diamond Creek, Victoria, 1992.

Mackay, Hugh. *Reinventing Australia*, HarperCollins, Sydney, 1993.

Mant, Alistair. *Leaders We Deserve*, Australian Commission for the Future Ltd, Victoria, 1985.

Meister, Jeanne. *Corporate Universities: Lessons in Building a World-Class Work Force*, Irwin Professional Publications, 1998.

Morehead, A. et al. *Changes at Work*, Longman, Melbourne, 1997.

Morita, Akio. *Made in Japan*, Collins, UK, 1987.

Mumford, Alan. *Action Learning at Work*, Gower Publishing, Aldershot, UK, 1997.

Nair, Keshavan. *A Higher Standard of Leadership*, Berrett-Koehler Publishers, San Francisco, 1997.

Naisbitt, John. *Megatrends*, Futura Macdonald & Co, Sydney, 1982.

Popcorn, Faith. *The Popcorn Report*, Random House, Sydney, 1991.

Senge, Ross, B. Smith, C. Roberts et al. *The Fifth Discipline Fieldbook*, Nicholas Brealey Publishing, 1994.

Smith, Stanley E. *The Sacred Rules of Management: How to get Control of your Time and your Work*, VanderWyk & Burnham, 1997.

Stewart, T. A. *Intellectual Capital: The New Wealth of Organizations*, Doubleday, New York, 1997.

Toffler, Alvin. *Future Shock*, Bantam Books, New York, 1991.

Toffler, Alvin. *Powershift: Knowledge, Wealth and Violence at the Edge of the 21st Century*, Bantam Books, New York, 1991.

Trout, Jack. *The New Positioning*, McGraw-Hill, New York, 1995.

Walton, Mary. *The Deming Management Methods*, The Business Library, Melbourne, 1986.

Wheatley, Margaret. *Leadership and the New Science*, Berrett-Koehler Publishers, San Francisco, 1992.

Wheatley, Margaret J. & Myron Kellner-Rogers. *A Simpler Way*, Berrett-Koehler Publishers, San Francisco, 1996.

Whyte, David. *The Heart Aroused: Poetry and Preservation of the Soul in Corporate America*, Bantam Doubleday Dell, New York, 1996.

INDEX